Architecting Modern
Data Platforms
A Guide to Enterprise
Hadoop at Scale

Jan Kunigk, Ian Buss, Paul Wilkinson,
and Lars George

Beijing · Boston · Farnham · Sebastopol · Tokyo

Architecting Modern Data Platforms

by Jan Kunigk, Ian Buss, Paul Wilkinson, and Lars George

Published by O'Reilly Media, Inc., 1005 Gravenstein Highway North, Sebastopol, CA 95472.

O'Reilly books may be purchased for educational, business, or sales promotional use. Online editions are also available for most titles (*http://oreilly.com/safari*). For more information, contact our corporate/institutional sales department: 800-998-9938 or *corporate@oreilly.com*.

Editors: Nicole Tache and Michele Cronin	**Indexer:** Ellen Troutman-Zaig
Production Editors: Nicholas Adams and Kristen Brown	**Interior Designer:** David Futato
	Cover Designer: Karen Montgomery
Copyeditor: Shannon Wright	**Illustrator:** Rebecca Demarest
Proofreader: Rachel Head	

December 2018:   First Edition

Revision History for the First Edition

2018-12-05:   First Release

See *http://oreilly.com/catalog/errata.csp?isbn=9781491969274* for release details.

978-1-491-96927-4

[LSI]

Table of Contents

Foreword

Many of the ideas that underpin the Apache Hadoop project are decades old. Academia and industry have been exploring distributed storage and computation since the 1960s. The entire tech industry grew out of government and business demand for data processing, and at every step along that path, the data seemed big to the people in the moment. Even some of the most advanced and interesting applications go way back: machine learning, a capability that's new to many enterprises, traces its origins to academic research in the 1950s and to practical systems work in the 1960s and 1970s.

But real, practical, useful, massively scalable, and reliable systems simply could not be found—at least not cheaply—until Google confronted the problem of the internet in the late 1990s and early 2000s. Collecting, indexing, and analyzing the entire web was impossible, using commercially available technology of the time.

Google dusted off the decades of research in large-scale systems. Its architects realized that, for the first time ever, the computers and networking they required could be had, at reasonable cost.

Its work—on the Google File System (GFS) for storage and on the MapReduce framework for computation—created the big data industry.

This work led to the creation of the open source Hadoop project in 2005 by Mike Cafarella and Doug Cutting. The fact that the software was easy to get, and could be improved and extended by a global developer community, made it attractive to a wide audience. At first, other consumer internet companies used the software to follow Google's lead. Quickly, though, traditional enterprises noticed that something was happening and looked for ways to get involved.

In the decade-plus since the Hadoop project began, the ecosystem has exploded. Once, the only storage system was the Hadoop Distributed File System (HDFS), based on GFS. Today, HDFS is thriving, but there are plenty of other choices: Amazon S3 or Microsoft Azure Data Lake Store (ADLS) for cloud storage, for example, or Apache Kudu for IoT and analytic data. Similarly, MapReduce was originally the only option for analyzing data. Now, users can choose among MapReduce, Apache Spark for stream processing and machine learning workloads, SQL engines like Apache Impala and Apache Hive, and more.

All of these new projects have adopted the fundamental architecture of Hadoop: large-scale, distributed, shared-nothing systems, connected by a good network, working together to solve the same problem. Hadoop is the open source progenitor, but the big data ecosystem built on it is vastly more powerful—and more useful—than the original Hadoop project.

That explosion of innovation means big data is more valuable than ever before. Enterprises are eager to adopt the technology. They want to predict customer behavior, foresee failure of machines on their factory floors or trucks in their fleets, spot fraud in their transaction flows, and deliver targeted care—and better outcomes—to patients in hospitals.

But that innovation, so valuable, also confounds them. How can they keep up with the pace of improvement, and the flurry of new projects, in the open source ecosystem? How can they deploy and operate these systems in their own datacenters, meeting the reliability and stability expectations of users and the requirements of the business? How can they secure their data and enforce the policies that protect private information from cyberattacks?

Mastering the platform in an enterprise context raises new challenges that run deep in the data. We have been able to store and search a month's worth of data, or a quarter's, for a very long time. Now, we can store and search a decade's worth, or a century's. That large quantitative difference turns into a qualitative difference: what new applications can we build when we can think about a century?

The book before you is your guide to answering those questions as you build your enterprise big data platform.

Jan, Ian, Lars, and Paul—this book's authors—are hands-on practitioners in the field, with many years of experience helping enterprises get real value from big data. They are not only users of Hadoop, Impala, Hive, and Spark, but they are also active participants in the open source community, helping to shape those projects, and their capabilities, for enterprise adoption. They are experts in the analytic, data processing, and machine learning capabilities that the ecosystem offers.

When technology moves quickly, it's important to focus on techniques and ideas that stand the test of time. The advice here works for the software—Hadoop and its many associated services—that exists today. The thinking and design, though, are tied not to specific projects but to the fundamental architecture that made Hadoop successful: large-scale, distributed, shared-nothing software requires a new approach to operations, to security, and to governance.

You will learn those techniques and those ideas here.

— Mike Olson
Founder and Chief Strategy Officer at Cloudera

Preface

If you're reading this book, it will come as no surprise that we are in the middle of a revolution in the way data is stored and processed in the enterprise. As anyone who has been in IT for any length of time knows, the technologies and approaches behind data processing and storage are always evolving. However, in the past 10 to 15 years, the pace of change has been remarkable. We have moved from a world where almost all enterprise data was processed and analyzed using variants of SQL and was contained in some form of relational database to one in which an enterprise's data may be found in a variety of so-called NoSQL storage engines. Each of these engines sacrifices some constraint of the relational model to achieve superior performance and scalability for a certain use case. The modern data landscape includes nonrelational key-value stores, distributed filesystems, distributed columnar databases, log stores, and document stores, in addition to traditional relational databases. The data in these systems is exploited in a multitude of ways and is processed using distributed batch-processing algorithms, stream processing, massively parallel processing query engines, free-text searches, and machine learning pipelines.

There are many drivers for this transformation, but the predominant ones are:

Volume

> The phrase *big data* has been used too much to retain much value, but the sheer volume of data generated by today's enterprises, especially those with a heavy web presence—which is to say all enterprises—is staggering. The explosion of data from edge computing and Internet of Things (IoT) devices will only add to the volume. Although storing data in as granular a form as possible may not seem immediately useful, this will become increasingly important in order to derive new insights. Storage is cheap, and bad decisions that have lasting consequences are costly. Better to store in full fidelity with a modern data platform and have the option to make a new decision later. Traditional architectures based on relational databases and shared file storage are simply unable to store and process data at these scales. This has led directly to the development of new tools

and techniques in which computations are linearly scalable and distributed by default.

Velocity

Gone are the days in which data for analytics would arrive in nice, neat daily batches. Although this still happens for some datasets, increasingly data arrives in a streaming fashion at high rates. The velocity of its generation demands a new way of storing, processing, and serving it up.

Variety

New insights and new models feed off data—the more the better. Hitherto untapped sources of data, perhaps in semi-structured or completely unstructured forms, are increasingly in demand. All aspects of an enterprise's operation are relevant and potentially valuable sources of information to drive new insights and, ultimately, revenue. It's essential to have a single, unified platform with technologies capable of storing and processing all these many and varied forms of data.

Competition

The enterprises that will succeed in the data age are the ones building new business strategies and products and, crucially, making decisions based on the insights gleaned from new data sources. To make the right data-driven decisions, you need a solid data and computation platform. Such a platform needs to be capable of embracing both on-premises and cloud deployments. It also needs to scale to support traditional data analytics and to enable advances in your business from data science, machine learning, and artificial intelligence (AI).

Some Misconceptions

We have only just begun our exploration of Hadoop in the enterprise, but it is worth dispelling some common misconceptions about data platforms and Hadoop early on:

Data in Hadoop is schemaless

Although it is true that many technologies in the Hadoop ecosystem have more flexible notions of schemas and do not impose schemas as strictly as, say, a relational database, it is a mistake to think that data stored in Hadoop clusters does not need a defined schema. Applications using data stored in Hadoop still need to understand the data they are querying, and there is always some sort of underlying data model or structure, either implicit or explicit. What the Hadoop ecosystem does offer is much more flexibility in the way data is structured and queried. Instead of imposing a globally fixed schema on the data as it is ingested and potentially dropping any fields that don't match the schema, the data gets its structure from the frameworks and applications using it. This concept is often referred to as *schema on read*. You can store any type of data in its raw form and then process, transform, and combine it with other sources into the best format and structure for your use case. And if you get it wrong, you can always build a new representation from the raw data.

One copy of the data

This is a very common mistake when thinking about modern data platforms. Different use cases require different access patterns, and this often means storing the same datasets in different ways using different storage engines. This is a logical consequence of the various optimizations each storage engine provides. This data duplication should be considered par for the course and embraced as a fundamental aspect of the freedom of operating in the Hadoop ecosystem. Hadoop platforms are designed to be horizontally scalable and to be orders of magnitude cheaper (if your enterprise IT department has a sensible approach to procurement, that is) than the proprietary alternatives. But the money you save on storage is just one aspect—maybe not even the most important aspect—of moving to a modern data platform. What it also brings you is a multitude of options for processing and querying the data and for extracting new value through scalable analytics and machine learning.

One huge cluster

In the initial excitement of moving to Hadoop, the notion of a single, all-encompassing *data lake* arose, in which all data was stored in and all processing and querying were performed on a single cluster, which consisted of potentially many thousands of machines. Although Hadoop is certainly capable of scaling to that number of servers, the variety of access patterns and modes of processing data don't necessarily mesh well in a single cluster. Colocating use cases that require strict query completion time guarantees with other ad hoc, variable workloads is likely to lead to an unsatisfactory experience. Multitenancy controls do exist, but they can't change the fact that a finite set of resources can't satisfy all requirements all the time. As a result, you should plan for multiple clusters serving different use cases with similar processing patterns or service levels. Don't go too far the other way, though. Lots of small clusters can be just as bad as a "single cluster to rule them all." Clusters can and should be shared, but be prepared to divide and conquer when necessary.

Some General Trends

The trends in industry are clear to see. Many, if not most, enterprises have already embarked on their data-driven journeys and are making serious investments in hardware, software, and services. The big data market is projected to continue growing apace, reaching somewhere in the region of $90 billion of annual revenue by 2025 (*http://bit.ly/2S4ItWS*). Related markets, such as deep learning and artificial intelligence, that are enabled by data platforms are also set to see exponential growth over the next decade.

The move to Hadoop, and to modern data platforms in general, has coincided with a number of secular trends in enterprise IT, a selection of which are discussed here. Some of these trends are directly caused by the focus on big data, but others are a result of a multitude of other factors, such as the desire to reduce software costs, consolidate and simplify IT operations, and dramatically reduce the time to procure new hardware and resources for new use cases.

Horizontal Scaling

This trend is already well established. It is now generally accepted that, for storage and data processing, the right way to scale a platform is to do so horizontally using distributed clusters of commodity (which does not necessarily mean the cheapest) servers rather than vertically with ever more powerful machines. Although some workloads, such as deep learning, are more difficult to distribute and parallelize, they can still benefit from plenty of machines with lots of cores, RAM, and GPUs, and the data to drive such workloads will be ingested, cleaned, and prepared in horizontally scalable environments.

Adoption of Open Source

Although proprietary software will always have its place, enterprises have come to appreciate the benefits of placing open source software at the center of their data strategies, with its attendant advantages of transparency and data freedom. Increasingly, companies—especially public sector agencies—are mandating that new projects are built with open source technologies at their core.

Embracing Cloud Compute

We have reached a tipping point in the use of public cloud services. These services have achieved a level of maturity in capability and security where even regulated industries, such as healthcare and financial services, feel comfortable running a good deal of their workloads in the cloud. Cloud solutions can have considerable advantages over on-premises solutions, in terms of agility, scalability, and performance. The ability to count cloud usage against operational—rather than capital—expenditure, even if the costs can be considerable over the long run, is also a significant factor in its adoption. But while the use of public cloud services is growing and will continue to do so, it is unlikely to become all-encompassing. Some workloads will need to stay in traditional on-premise clusters or private clouds. In the current landscape, data platforms will need to be able to run transparently on-premises, in the public cloud, and in private cloud deployments.

There are many exciting developments being made in cloud-based deployments, particularly around new ways of deploying and running frameworks using containerization, such as can be done with Docker and Kubernetes. Since they are not yet widely adopted within enterprises, and since best practices and deployment patterns are still emerging, we do not cover these technologies in great detail in this book, but we recommend closely following developments in this space.

Decoupled Compute and Storage

The desire to decouple compute from storage is strongly related to the move to cloud computing. In its first few years, when high-throughput networking was relatively rare and many data use cases were limited by disk bandwidth, Hadoop clusters almost exclusively employed direct-attached storage (for good reason, as we'll see in future chapters). However, the migration of many workloads to the public cloud has opened up new ways of interacting with persistent data that take advantage of their highly efficient networked storage systems, to the extent that compute and storage can be scaled independently for many workloads. This means that the data platform of the future will need to be flexible in how and from where it allows data to be accessed, since data in storage clusters will be accessed by both local and remote compute clusters.

What Is This Book About?

As we discussed writing this book, we gave serious thought to the title. If you saw the early drafts, you'll know it originally had a different title: *Hadoop in the Enterprise*. But the truth is, the clusters are about much more than the Hadoop Distributed File System (HDFS), Yet Another Resource Negotiator (YARN), and MapReduce. Even though it is still common to refer to these platforms as *Hadoop clusters*, what we really mean is Hadoop, Hive, Spark, HBase, Solr, and all the rest. The modern data platform consists of a multitude of technologies, and splicing them together can be a daunting task.

You may also be wondering why we need yet another book about Hadoop and the technologies that go around it. Aren't these things already well—even exhaustively—covered in the literature, blogosphere, and conference circuit? The answer is yes, to a point. There is no shortage of material out there covering the inner workings of the technologies themselves and the art of engineering data applications and applying them to new use cases. There is also some material for system administrators about how to operate clusters. There is, however, much less content about successfully integrating Hadoop clusters into an enterprise context.

Our goal in writing this book is to equip you to successfully architect, build, integrate, and run modern enterprise data platforms. Our experience providing professional services for Hadoop and its associated services over the past five or more years has shown that there is a major lack of guidance for both the architect and the practitioner. Undertaking these tasks without a guiding hand can lead to expensive architectural mistakes, disappointing application performance, or a false impression that such platforms are not enterprise-ready. We want to make your journey into big data in general, and Hadoop in particular, as smooth as possible.

Who Should Read This Book?

We cover a lot of ground in this book. Some sections are primarily technical, while other sections discuss practice and architecture at a higher level. The book can be read by anyone who deals with Hadoop as part of their daily job, but we had the following principal audiences in mind when we wrote the book:

IT managers
    Anyone who is responsible for delivering and operating Hadoop clusters in enterprises (Chapters 1, 2, 5, and 14)

Enterprise architects
    Those whose job is making sure all aspects of the Hadoop cluster integrate and gel with the other enterprise systems and who must ensure that the cluster is operated and governed according to enterprise standards (Chapters 1–4, 6–7, and 9–18)

Application architects and data engineers
    Developers and architects designing the next generation of data-driven applications who want to know how best to fit their code into Hadoop and to take advantage of its capabilities (Chapters 1–2, 9–13, and 17–18)

System administrators and database administrators (DBAs)
    Those who are tasked with operating and monitoring clusters and who need to have an in-depth understanding of how the cluster components work together and how they interact with the underlying hardware and external systems (Chapters 1, 3, 4, and 6–18)

We've noted particularly relevant chapters, but readers should not feel limited by that selection. Each chapter contains information of interest to each audience.

The Road Ahead

This book is about all things architecture. We've split it up into three parts. In Part I, we establish a solid foundation for clusters by looking at the underlying infrastructure. In Part II, we look at the platform as a whole and at how to build a rock-solid cluster that integrates smoothly with external systems. Finally, in Part III, we cover the important architectural aspects of running Hadoop in the cloud. We begin with a technical primer for Hadoop and the ecosystem.

Conventions Used in This Book

The following typographical conventions are used in this book:

Italic
> Indicates new terms, URLs, email addresses, filenames, and file extensions.

`Constant width`
> Used for program listings, as well as within paragraphs to refer to program elements such as variable or function names, databases, data types, environment variables, statements, and keywords.

`Constant width bold`
> Shows commands or other text that should be typed literally by the user.

`Constant width italic`
> Shows text that should be replaced with user-supplied values or by values determined by context.

> This element signifies a tip or suggestion.

> This element signifies a general note.

> This element indicates a warning or caution.

O'Reilly Safari

 *Safari* (formerly Safari Books Online) is a membership-based training and reference platform for enterprise, government, educators, and individuals.

Members have access to thousands of books, training videos, Learning Paths, interactive tutorials, and curated playlists from over 250 publishers, including O'Reilly Media, Harvard Business Review, Prentice Hall Professional, Addison-Wesley Professional, Microsoft Press, Sams, Que, Peachpit Press, Adobe, Focal Press, Cisco Press, John Wiley & Sons, Syngress, Morgan Kaufmann, IBM Redbooks, Packt, Adobe Press, FT Press, Apress, Manning, New Riders, McGraw-Hill, Jones & Bartlett, and Course Technology, among others.

For more information, please visit *http://oreilly.com/safari*.

How to Contact Us

Please address comments and questions concerning this book to the publisher:

O'Reilly Media, Inc.
1005 Gravenstein Highway North
Sebastopol, CA 95472
800-998-9938 (in the United States or Canada)
707-829-0515 (international or local)
707-829-0104 (fax)

We have a web page for this book, where we list errata, examples, and any additional information. You can access this page at *http://bit.ly/architectingModernDataPlatforms*.

To comment or ask technical questions about this book, send email to *bookquestions@oreilly.com*.

For more information about our books, courses, conferences, and news, see our website at *http://www.oreilly.com*.

Find us on Facebook: *http://facebook.com/oreilly*

Follow us on Twitter: *http://twitter.com/oreillymedia*

Watch us on YouTube: *http://www.youtube.com/oreillymedia*

Acknowledgments

The main goal of this book is to help our readers succeed in enterprise Hadoop integration. This required us to go beyond technical facts and specifications to give actionable advice, which is, essentially, an account of how big data is done in enterprise IT. This would have been completely impossible without the help of many experienced individuals who have long practiced big data, among them many of our current and former colleagues, clients, and other industry experts. We feel privileged that we could rely on their knowledge and experience when we reached the limit of our own.

Thank you Jörg Grauvogl, Werner Schauer, Dwai Lahiri, and Travis Campbell for providing so much feedback and best practices on networks, private clouds, and datacenter design. We would also like to thank Stefan Letz and Roelf Zomerman for patiently discussing and answering our many questions regarding public clouds. A special shout-out goes to Andrew Wang for helping us extensively on the ins and outs of HDFS erasure coding and its capabilities for zero-copy reads! Further thanks go to Dominik Meyer, Alexis Moundalexis, Tristan Stevens, and Mubashir Kazia.

We also must thank the amazing team at O'Reilly: Marie Beaugureau, Nicole Tache, and Michele Cronin—thank you so much for your relentless push and supervision. Without you, we'd be lost in space. Additional thanks to Kristen Brown, Colleen Cole, Shannon Wright, and Nick Adams.

Our deepest obligation is to our reviewers: David Yahalom, Frank Kane, Ryan Blue, Jesse Anderson, Amandeep Khurana, and Lars Francke. You invested much of your valuable time to read through this work and to provide us with invaluable feedback, regardless of the breadth of subjects.

Now for our individual acknowledgments:

Ian Buss

> For supporting me throughout the entire process with both time and encouragement, I am extremely grateful to my employer, Cloudera, and, in particular, to Hemal Kanani and my colleagues in New York, Jeremy Beard, Ben Spivey, and Jeff Shmain, for conversations and banter. Thanks also to Michael Ernest for providing much advice on "verbal stylings."
>
> As with many things in life, writing a book is always more work than expected, but it has been a rare privilege to be able to work with my fellow authors, Jan, Paul, and Lars. Thanks for the reviews, discussions, and all the hard work you have put in—and for the camaraderie. It's been fun.
>
> Finally—and most importantly—I want to thank my wonderful family, Jenna, Amelia, and Sebastian. Thank you for letting me embark on this project, for your unfailing love, support, and encouragement throughout the long process, and for

never uttering a word of complaint about the lost evenings, weekends, and holidays—not even when you found out that, despite its cover, the book wasn't about birds. This book is for you.

Jan Kunigk

For Dala, Ilai, Katy, and Andre. Thank you for believing in me.

I would also like to express my gratitude to my fellow authors: Ian, Paul, and Lars —we went through thick and thin, we learned a lot about who we are, and we managed to keep our cool. It is an honor for me to work with you.

Paul Wilkinson

To my family, Sarah, Tom, and Evie: thank you. Writing this book has been a rare privilege, but, undoubtedly, the greatest sacrifice to enable it has been yours. For that, for your patience, and for your support, I am truly grateful.

I'm also incredibly grateful to my coauthors, Jan, Ian, and Lars. I have no doubt that this book would be greatly diminished without your contributions—and not just in word count. Your friendship and camaraderie mean a lot to me.

Finally, this is also a rare opportunity to thank the wider supporting cast of thousands. To all of my friends, teachers, lecturers, customers, and colleagues: each of you has played a significant role in my life, shaping my thinking and understanding—even if you're not aware of it. Thank you all!

Lars George

This is for my loving family, Katja, Laura, and Leon. Thank you for sticking with me, even if I missed promises or neglected you in the process—you are the world to me.

Thank you also to my coauthors, Doc Ian, Tenacious Jan, and "Brummie" Paul, who are not just ex-colleagues of mine but also friends for life. You made this happen, and I am grateful to be part of it.

And to everyone at O'Reilly for their patience with us, the reviewers for their unwavering help, and all the people behind Hadoop and big data who built this ecosystem: thank you. We stand tall on your shoulders.

Despite its vast complexity, the Hadoop ecosystem has facilitated a rapid adoption of distributed systems into enterprise IT. We are thrilled to be a part of this journey among the fine people who helped us to convey what we know about this field. Enterprise big data has reached cruising altitude, but, without a doubt, innovation in data processing software frameworks, the amount of data, and its value will continue to soar beyond our imagination today.

This is just the beginning!

## CHAPTER 1

Big Data Technology Primer

Apache Hadoop is a tightly integrated ecosystem of different software products built to provide scalable and reliable distributed storage and distributed processing. The inspiration for much of the Hadoop ecosystem was a sequence of papers published by Google in the 2000s, describing innovations in systems to produce reliable storage (the Google File System), processing (MapReduce, Pregel), and low-latency random-access queries (Bigtable) on hundreds to thousands of potentially unreliable servers. For Google, the primary driver for developing these systems was pure expediency: there simply were no technologies at the time capable of storing and processing the vast datasets it was dealing with. The traditional approach to performing computations on datasets was to invest in a few extremely powerful servers with lots of processors and lots of RAM, slurp the data in from a storage layer (e.g., NAS or SAN), crunch through a computation, and write the results back to storage. As the scale of the data increased, this approach proved both impractical and expensive.

The key innovation, and one which still stands the test of time, was to distribute the datasets across many machines and to split up any computations on that data into many independent, "shared-nothing" chunks, each of which could be run on the same machines storing the data. Although existing technologies could be run on multiple servers, they typically relied heavily on communication between the distributed components, which leads to diminishing returns as the parallelism increases (see Amdahl's law (*http://bit.ly/2QbCBxJ*)). By contrast, in the distributed-by-design approach, the problem of scale is naturally handled because each independent piece of the computation is responsible for just a small chunk of the dataset. Increased storage and compute power can be obtained by simply adding more servers—a so-called *horizontally scalable* architecture. A key design point when computing at such scales is to design with the assumption of component failure in order to build a reliable system from unreliable components. Such designs solve the problem of cost-effective scaling because the storage and computation can be realized on standard commodity servers.

 With advances in commodity networking and the general move to cloud computing and storage, the requirement to run computations locally to the data is becoming less critical. If your network infrastructure is good enough, it is no longer essential to use the same underlying hardware for compute and storage. However, the distributed nature and horizontally scalable approach are still fundamental to the efficient operation of these systems.

Hadoop is an open source implementation of these techniques. At its core, it offers a distributed filesystem (HDFS) and a means of running processes across a cluster of servers (YARN). The original distributed processing application built on Hadoop was MapReduce, but since its inception, a wide range of additional software frameworks and libraries have grown up around Hadoop, each one addressing a different use case. In the following section, we go on a whirlwind tour of the core technologies in the Hadoop project, as well as some of the more popular open source frameworks in the ecosystem that run on Hadoop clusters.

What Is A Cluster?

In the simplest sense, a *cluster* is just a bunch of servers grouped together to provide one or more functions, such as storage or computation. To users of a cluster, it is generally unimportant which individual machine or set of machines within the cluster performs a computation, stores the data, or performs some other service. By contrast, architects and administrators need to understand the cluster in detail. Figure 1-1 illustrates a cluster layout at a high level.

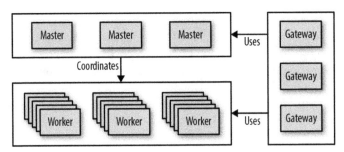

Figure 1-1. Machine roles in a cluster

Usually we divide a cluster up into two classes of machine: *master* and *worker*.[1] Worker machines are where the real work happens—these machines store data, perform computations, offer services like lookups and searches, and more. Master machines are responsible for coordination, maintaining metadata about the data and services running on the worker machines, and ensuring the services keep running in the event of worker failures. Typically, there are two or three master machines for redundancy and a much larger number of workers. A cluster is scaled up by adding more workers and, when the cluster gets large enough, extra masters.

Often, we want to allow access to the cluster by users and other applications, so we provide some machines to act as *gateway* or *edge* servers. These servers often do not run any services at all but just have the correct client configuration files to access cluster services.

We discuss the various machine types and their purpose in more detail in Chapter 3 and introduce the different types of cluster you might need in Chapter 2.

A Tour of the Landscape

When we say "Hadoop," we usually really mean Hadoop *and* all the data engineering projects and frameworks that have been built around it. In this section, we briefly review a few key technologies, categorized by use case. We are not able to cover every framework in detail—in many cases these have their own full book-level treatments —but we try to give a sense of what they do. This section can be safely skipped if you are already familiar with these technologies, or you can use it as a handy quick reference to remind you of the fundamentals.

The zoo of frameworks, and how they relate to and depend on each other, can appear daunting at first, but with some familiarization, the relationships become clearer. You may have seen representations similar to Figure 1-2, which attempt to show how different components build on each other. These diagrams can be a useful aid to understanding, but they don't always make all the dependencies among projects clear. Projects depend on each other in different ways, but we can think about two main types of dependency: data and control. In the *data plane*, a component depends on another component when reading and writing data, while in the *control plane*, a component depends on another component for metadata or coordination. For the graphically inclined, some of these relationships are shown in Figure 1-3. Don't panic; this isn't meant to be scary, and it's not critical at this stage that you understand exactly how the dependencies work between the components. But the graphs demonstrate the importance of developing a basic understanding of the purpose of each element in the stack. The aim of this section is to give you that context.

---

1 In common with most open source projects, we avoid the term *slave* wherever possible.

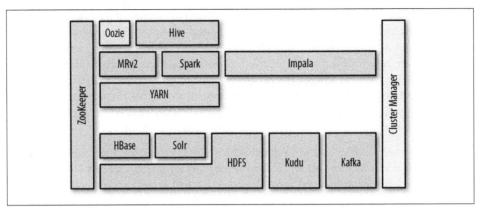

Figure 1-2. Standard representation of technologies and dependencies in the Hadoop stack

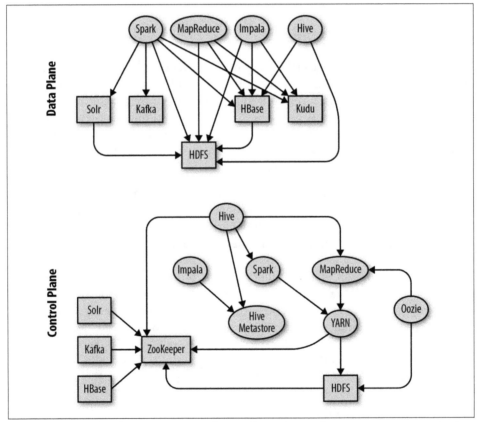

Figure 1-3. Graphical representation of some dependencies between components in the data and control planes

Where there are multiple technologies with a similar design, architecture, and use case, we cover just one but strive to point out the alternatives as much as possible, either, in the text or in "Also consider" sections.

Core Components

The first set of projects are those that form the core of the Hadoop project itself or are key enabling technologies for the rest of the stack: HDFS, YARN, Apache ZooKeeper, and the Apache Hive Metastore. Together, these projects form the foundation on which most other frameworks, projects, and applications running on the cluster depend.

HDFS

The Hadoop Distributed File System (HDFS) is the scalable, fault-tolerant, and distributed filesystem for Hadoop. Based on the original use case of analytics over large-scale datasets, HDFS is optimized to store very large amounts of immutable data with files being typically accessed in long sequential scans. HDFS is *the* critical supporting technology for many of the other components in the stack.

When storing data, HDFS breaks up a file into *blocks* of configurable size, usually something like 128 MiB, and stores a *replica* of each block on multiple servers for resilience and data parallelism. Each worker node in the cluster runs a daemon called a *DataNode* which accepts new blocks and persists them to its local disks. The DataNode is also responsible for serving up data to clients. The DataNode is only aware of blocks and their IDs; it does not have knowledge about the file to which a particular replica belongs. This information is curated by a coordinating process, the *NameNode*, which runs on the master servers and is responsible for maintaining a mapping of files to the blocks, as well as metadata about the files themselves (things like names, permissions, attributes, and replication factor).

Clients wishing to store blocks must first communicate with the NameNode to be given a list of DataNodes on which to write each block. The client writes to the first DataNode, which in turn streams the data to the next DataNode, and so on in a pipeline. When providing a list of DataNodes for the pipeline, the NameNode takes into account a number of things, including available space on the DataNode and the location of the node—its *rack locality*. The NameNode insures against node and rack failures by ensuring that each block is on at least two different racks. In Figure 1-4, a client writes a file consisting of three blocks to HDFS, and the process distributes and replicates the data across DataNodes.

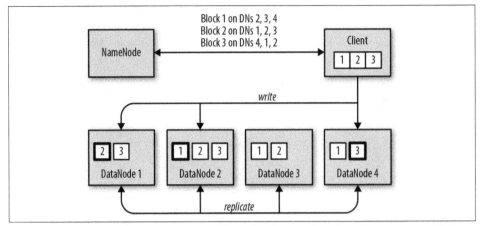

Figure 1-4. The HDFS write process and how blocks are distributed across DataNodes

Likewise, when reading data, the client asks the NameNode for a list of DataNodes containing the blocks for the files it needs. The client then reads the data directly from the DataNodes, preferring replicas that are local or close, in network terms.

The design of HDFS means that it does not allow in-place updates to the files it stores. This can initially seem quite restrictive until you realize that this immutability allows it to achieve the required horizontal scalability and resilience in a relatively simple way.

HDFS is fault-tolerant because the failure of an individual disk, DataNode, or even rack does not imperil the safety of the data. In these situations, the NameNode simply directs one of the DataNodes that is maintaining a surviving replica to copy the block to another DataNode until the required replication factor is reasserted. Clients reading data are directed to one of the remaining replicas. As such, the whole system is self-healing, provided we allow sufficient capacity and redundancy in the cluster itself.

HDFS is scalable, given that we can simply increase the capacity of the filesystem by adding more DataNodes with local storage. This also has the nice side effect of increasing the available read and write throughput available to HDFS as a whole.

It is important to note, however, that HDFS does not achieve this resilience and scaling all on its own. We have to use the right servers and design the layout of our clusters to take advantage of the resilience and scalability features that HDFS offers—and in large part, that is what this book is all about. In Chapter 3, we discuss in detail how HDFS interacts with the servers on which its daemons run and how it uses the locally attached disks in these servers. In Chapter 4, we examine the options when putting a network plan together, and in Chapter 12, we cover how to make HDFS as highly available and fault-tolerant as possible.

One final note before we move on. In this short description of HDFS, we glossed over the fact that Hadoop abstracts much of this detail from the client. The API that a client uses is actually a *Hadoop-compatible filesystem*, of which HDFS is just one implementation. We will come across other commonly used implementations in this book, such as cloud-based object storage offerings like Amazon S3.

YARN

Although it's useful to be able to store data in a scalable and resilient way, what we really want is to be able to derive insights from that data. To do so, we need to be able to compute things from the data, in a way that can scale to the volumes we expect to store in our Hadoop filesystem. What's more, we need to be able to run lots of different computations at the same time, making efficient use of the available resources across the cluster and minimizing the required effort to access the data. Each computation processes different volumes of data and requires different amounts of compute power and memory. To manage these competing demands, we need a centralized cluster manager, which is aware of all the available compute resources and the current competing workload demands.

This is exactly what YARN (Yet Another Resource Negotiator) is designed to be. YARN runs a daemon on each worker node, called a *NodeManager*, which reports in to a master process, called the *ResourceManager*. Each NodeManager tells the ResourceManager how much compute resource (in the form of virtual cores, or *vcores*) and how much memory is available on its node. Resources are parceled out to applications running on the cluster in the form of *containers*, each of which has a defined resource demand—say, 10 containers each with 4 vcores and 8 GB of RAM. The NodeManagers are responsible for starting and monitoring containers on their local nodes and for killing them if they exceed their stated resource allocations.

An application that needs to run computations on the cluster must first ask the ResourceManager for a single container in which to run its own coordination process, called the ApplicationMaster (AM). Despite its name, the AM actually runs on one of the worker machines. ApplicationMasters of different applications will run on different worker machines, thereby ensuring that a failure of a single worker machine will affect only a subset of the applications running on the cluster. Once the AM is running, it requests additional containers from the ResourceManager to run its actual computation. This process is sketched in Figure 1-5: three clients run applications with different resource demands, which are translated into different-sized containers and spread across the NodeManagers for execution.

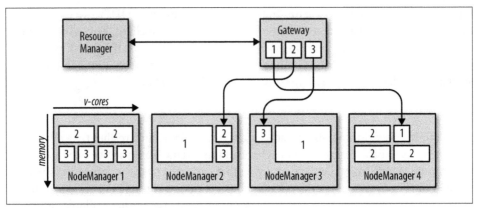

Figure 1-5. YARN application execution.

The ResourceManager runs a special thread, which is responsible for scheduling application requests and ensuring that containers are allocated equitably between applications and users running applications on the cluster. This scheduler strives to allocate cores and memory fairly between tenants. Tenants and workloads are divided into hierarchical *pools*, each of which has a configurable share of the overall cluster resources.

It should be clear from the description that YARN itself does not perform any computation but rather is a framework for launching such applications distributed across a cluster. YARN provides a suite of APIs for creating these applications; we cover two such implementations, MapReduce and Apache Spark, in "Computational Frameworks" on page 10.

You'll learn more about making YARN highly available in Chapter 12.

Apache ZooKeeper

The problem of *consensus* is an important topic in computer science. When an application is distributed across many nodes, a key concern is getting these disparate components to agree on the values of some shared parameters. For example, for frameworks with multiple master processes, agreeing on which process should be the *active* master and which should be in *standby* is critical to their correct operation.

Apache ZooKeeper is the resilient, distributed configuration service for the Hadoop ecosystem. Within ZooKeeper, configuration data is stored and accessed in a filesystem-like tree of nodes, called *znodes*, each of which can hold data and be the parent of zero or more child nodes. Clients open a connection to a single ZooKeeper server to create, read, update and delete the znodes.

For resilience, ZooKeeper instances should be deployed on different servers as an *ensemble*. Since ZooKeeper operates on majority consensus, an odd number of servers is required to form a *quorum*. Although even numbers can be deployed, the extra server provides no extra resilience to the ensemble. Each server is identical in functionality, but one of the ensemble is elected as the *leader* node—all other servers are designated *followers*. ZooKeeper guarantees that data updates are applied by a majority of ZooKeeper servers. As long as a majority of servers are up and running, the ensemble is operational. Clients can open connections to any of the servers to perform reads and writes, but writes are forwarded from follower servers to the leader to ensure consistency. ZooKeeper ensures that all state is consistent by guaranteeing that updates are always applied in the same order.

 In general, a quorum with n members can survive up to floor($(n-1)/2$) failures and still be operational. Thus, a four-member ensemble has the same resiliency properties as an ensemble of three members.

As outlined in Table 1-1, many frameworks in the ecosystem rely on ZooKeeper for maintaining highly available master processes, coordinating tasks, tracking state, and setting general configuration parameters. You'll learn more about how ZooKeeper is used by other components for high availability in Chapter 12.

Table 1-1. ZooKeeper dependencies

Project	Usage of ZooKeeper
HDFS	Coordinating high availability
HBase	Metadata and coordination
Solr	Metadata and coordination
Kafka	Metadata and coordination
YARN	Coordinating high availability
Hive	Table and partition locking and high availability

Apache Hive Metastore

We'll cover the querying functionality of Apache Hive in a subsequent section when we talk about analytical SQL engines, but one component of the project—the Hive Metastore—is such a key supporting technology for other components of the stack that we need to introduce it early on in this survey.

The Hive Metastore curates information about the structured datasets (as opposed to unstructured binary data) that reside in Hadoop and organizes them into a logical hierarchy of databases, tables, and views. Hive tables have defined schemas, which are specified during table creation. These tables support most of the common data types that you know from the relational database world. The underlying data in the storage engine is expected to match this schema, but for HDFS this is checked only at runtime, a concept commonly referred to as *schema on read*. Hive tables can be defined for data in a number of storage engines, including Apache HBase and Apache Kudu, but by far the most common location is HDFS.

In HDFS, Hive tables are nothing more than directories containing files. For large tables, Hive supports partitioning via subdirectories within the table directory, which can in turn contain nested partitions, if necessary. Within a single partition, or in an unpartitioned table, all files should be stored in the same format; for example, comma-delimited text files or a binary format like Parquet or ORC. The metastore allows tables to be defined as either *managed* or *external*. For managed tables, Hive actively controls the data in the storage engine: if a table is created, Hive builds the structures in the storage engine, for example by making directories on HDFS. If a table is dropped, Hive deletes the data from the storage engine. For external tables, Hive makes no modifications to the underlying storage engine in response to meta-data changes, but merely maintains the metadata for the table in its database.

Other projects, such as Apache Impala and Apache Spark, rely on the Hive Metastore as the single source of truth for metadata about structured datasets within the cluster. As such it is a critical component in any deployment.

Going deeper

There are some very good books on the core Hadoop ecosystem, which are well worth reading for a thorough understanding. In particular, see:

- *Hadoop: The Definitive Guide*, 4th Edition, by Tom White (O'Reilly)
- *ZooKeeper*, by Benjamin Reed and Flavio Junqueira (O'Reilly)
- *Programming Hive*, by Dean Wampler, Jason Rutherglen, and Edward Capriolo (O'Reilly)

Computational Frameworks

With the core Hadoop components, we have data stored in HDFS and a means of running distributed applications via YARN. Many frameworks have emerged to allow users to define and compose arbitrary computations and to allow these computations to be broken up into smaller chunks and run in a distributed fashion. Let's look at two of the principal frameworks.

Hadoop MapReduce

MapReduce is the original application for which Hadoop was built and is a Java-based implementation of the blueprint laid out in Google's MapReduce paper (*http://bit.ly/2QbTN6d*). Originally, it was a standalone framework running on the cluster, but it was subsequently ported to YARN as the Hadoop project evolved to support more applications and use cases. Although superseded by newer engines, such as Apache Spark and Apache Flink, it is still worth understanding, given that many higher-level frameworks compile their inputs into MapReduce jobs for execution. These include:

- Apache Hive
- Apache Sqoop
- Apache Oozie
- Apache Pig

 The terms *map* and *reduce* are borrowed from functional programming, where a map applies a transform function to every element in a collection, and a reduce applies an aggregation function to each element of a list, combining them into fewer summary values.

Essentially, MapReduce divides a computation into three sequential stages: map, shuffle, and reduce. In the map phase, the relevant data is read from HDFS and processed in parallel by multiple independent map *tasks*. These tasks should ideally run wherever the data is located—usually we aim for one map task per HDFS block. The user defines a map() function (in code) that processes each record in the file and produces key-value outputs ready for the next phase. In the shuffle phase, the map outputs are fetched by MapReduce and shipped across the network to form input to the reduce tasks. A user-defined reduce() function receives all the values for a key in turn and aggregates or combines them into fewer values which summarize the inputs. The essentials of the process are shown in Figure 1-6. In the example, files are read from HDFS by mappers and shuffled by key according to an ID column. The reducers aggregate the remaining columns and write the results back to HDFS.

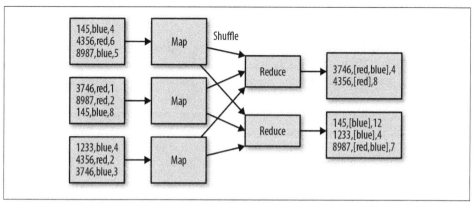

Figure 1-6. Simple aggregation performed in MapReduce

Sequences of these three simple linear stages can be composed and combined into essentially any computation of arbitrary complexity; for example, advanced transformations, joins, aggregations, and more. Sometimes, for simple transforms that do not require aggregations, the reduce phase is not required at all. Usually, the outputs from a MapReduce job are stored back into HDFS, where they may form the inputs to other jobs.

Despite its simplicity, MapReduce is incredibly powerful and extremely robust and scalable. It does have a couple of drawbacks, though. First, it is quite involved from the point of view of a user, who needs to code and compile `map()` and `reduce()` functions in Java, which is too high a bar for many analysts—composing complex processing pipelines in MapReduce can be a daunting task. Second, MapReduce itself is not particularly efficient. It does a lot of disk-based I/O, which can be expensive when combining processing stages together or doing iterative operations. Multistage pipelines are composed from individual MapReduce jobs with an HDFS I/O barrier in between, with no recognition of potential optimizations in the whole processing graph.

Because of these drawbacks, a number of successors to MapReduce have been developed that aim both to simplify development and to make processing pipelines more efficient. Despite this, the conceptual underpinnings of MapReduce—that data processing should be split up into multiple independent tasks running on different machines (maps), the results of which are then shuffled to and grouped and collated together on another set of machines (reduces)—are fundamental to all distributed data processing engines, including SQL-based frameworks. Apache Spark, Apache Flink, and Apache Impala, although all quite different in their specifics, are all essentially different implementations of this concept.

Apache Spark

Apache Spark is a distributed computation framework, with an emphasis on efficiency and usability, which supports both batch and streaming computations. Instead of the user having to express the necessary data manipulations in terms of pure `map()` and `reduce()` functions as in MapReduce, Spark exposes a rich API of common operations, such as filtering, joining, grouping, and aggregations directly on *Datasets*, which comprise rows all adhering to a particular type or schema. As well as using API methods, users can submit operations directly using a SQL-style dialect (hence the general name of this set of features, Spark SQL), removing much of the requirement to compose pipelines programmatically. With its API, Spark makes the job of composing complex processing pipelines much more tractable to the user. As a simple example, in Figure 1-7, three datasets are read in. Two of these unioned together and joined with a third, filtered dataset. The result is grouped according to a column and aggregated and written to an output. The dataset sources and sinks could be batch-driven and use HDFS or Kudu, or could be processed in a stream to and from Kafka.

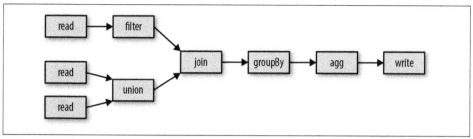

Figure 1-7. A typical simple aggregation performed in Spark

A key feature of operations on datasets is that the processing graphs are run through a standard query optimizer before execution, very similar to those found in relational databases or in massively parallel processing query engines. This optimizer can rearrange, combine, and prune the processing graph to obtain the most efficient execution pipeline. In this way, the execution engine can operate on datasets in a much more efficient way, avoiding much of the intermediate I/O from which MapReduce suffers.

One of the principal design goals for Spark was to take full advantage of the memory on worker nodes, which is available in increasing quantities on commodity servers. The ability to store and retrieve data from main memory at speeds which are orders of magnitude faster than those of spinning disks makes certain workloads radically more efficient. Distributed machine learning workloads in particular, which often operate on the same datasets in an iterative fashion, can see huge benefits in runtimes over the equivalent MapReduce execution. Spark allows datasets to be cached in memory on the executors; if the data does not fit entirely into memory, the partitions that cannot be cached are spilled to disk or transparently recomputed at runtime.

Spark implements stream processing as a series of periodic microbatches of datasets. This approach requires only minor code differences in the transformations and actions applied to the data—essentially, the same or very similar code can be used in both batch and streaming modes. One drawback of the micro-batching approach is that it takes at least the interval between batches for an event to be processed, so it is not suitable for use cases requiring millisecond latencies. However, this potential weakness is also a strength because microbatching allows much greater data throughput than can be achieved when processing events one by one. In general, there are relatively few streaming use cases that genuinely require subsecond response times. However, Spark's *structured streaming* functionality promises to bring many of the advantages of an optimized Spark batch computation graph to a streaming context, as well as a low-latency continuous streaming mode.

Spark ships a number of built-in libraries and APIs for machine learning. Spark MLlib allows the process of creating a machine learning model (data preparation, cleansing, feature extraction, and algorithm execution) to be composed into a distributed pipeline. Not all machine learning algorithms can automatically be run in a distributed way, so Spark ships with a few implementations of common classes of problems, such as clustering, classification and regression, and collaborative filtering.

Spark is an extraordinarily powerful framework for data processing and is often (rightly) the de facto choice when creating new batch processing, machine learning, and streaming use cases. It is not the only game in town, though; application architects should also consider options like Apache Flink (*http://flink.apache.org*) for batch and stream processing, and Apache Impala (see "Apache Impala" on page 16) for interactive SQL.

Going deeper.   Once again, *Hadoop: The Definitive Guide*, by Tom White, is the best resource to learn more about Hadoop MapReduce. For Spark, there are a few good references:

- The Spark project documentation (*https://spark.apache.org/docs/latest/*)
- *Spark: The Definitive Guide*, by Bill Chambers and Matei Zaharia (O'Reilly)
- *High Performance Spark*, by Holden Karau and Rachel Warren (O'Reilly)

Analytical SQL Engines

Although MapReduce and Spark are extremely flexible and powerful frameworks, to use them you do need to be comfortable programming in a language like Java, Scala, or Python and should be happy deploying and running code from the command line. The reality is that, in most enterprises, SQL remains the lingua franca of analytics, and the largest, most accessible skill base lies there. Sometimes you need to get things done without the rigmarole of coding, compiling, deploying, and running a full application. What's more, a large body of decision support and business intelligence tools interact with data stores exclusively over SQL. For these reasons, a lot of time and effort has been spent developing SQL-like interfaces to structured data stored in Hadoop. Many of these use MapReduce or Spark as their underlying computation mechanism, but some are computation engines in their own right. Each engine is focused on querying data that already exists in the storage engine or on inserting new data in bulk into those engines. They are designed for large-scale analytics and not for small-scale transactional processing. Let's look at the principal players.

Apache Hive

Apache Hive is the original data warehousing technology for Hadoop. It was developed at Facebook and was the first to offer a SQL-like language, called HiveQL, to allow analysts to query structured data stored in HDFS without having to first compile and deploy code. Hive supports common SQL query concepts, like table joins, unions, subqueries, and views. At a high level, Hive parses a user query, optimizes it, and compiles it into one or more chained batch computations, which it runs on the cluster. Typically these computations are executed as MapReduce jobs, but Hive can also use Apache Tez and Spark as its backing execution engine. Hive has two main components: a metadata server and a query server. We covered the Hive Metastore earlier, so we focus on the querying functionality in this section.

Users who want to run SQL queries do so via the query server, called HiveServer2 (HS2). Users open *sessions* with the query server and submit queries in the HQL dialect. Hive parses these queries, optimizes them as much as possible, and compiles them into one or more batch jobs. Queries containing subqueries get compiled into multistage jobs, with intermediate data from each stage stored in a temporary location on HDFS. HS2 supports multiple concurrent user sessions and ensures consistency via shared or exclusive locks in ZooKeeper. The query parser and compiler uses a cost-based optimizer to build a query plan and can use table and column statistics (which are also stored in the metastore) to choose the right strategy when joining tables. Hive can read a multitude of file formats through its built-in serialization and deserialization libraries (called *SerDes*) and can also be extended with custom formats.

Figure 1-8 shows a high-level view of Hive operation. A client submits queries to a HiveServer2 instance as part of a user session. HiveServer2 retrieves information for the databases and tables in the queries from the Hive Metastore. The queries are then optimized and compiled into sequences of jobs (J) in MapReduce, Tez, or Spark. After the jobs are complete, the results are returned to the remote client via HiveServer2.

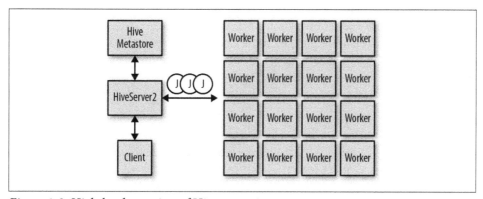

Figure 1-8. High-level overview of Hive operation

Hive is not generally considered to be an interactive query engine (although recently speed improvements have been made via long-lived processes (*http://bit.ly/2S4Dh5c*) which begin to move it into this realm). Many queries result in chains of MapReduce jobs that can take many minutes (or even hours) to complete. Hive is thus ideally suited to offline batch jobs for extract, transform, load (ETL) operations; reporting;

or other bulk data manipulations. Hive-based workflows are a trusted staple of big data clusters and are generally extremely robust. Although Spark SQL is increasingly coming into favor, Hive remains—and will continue to be—an essential tool in the big data toolkit.

We will encounter Hive again when discussing how to deploy it for high availability in Chapter 12.

Going deeper. Much information about Hive is contained in blog posts and other articles spread around the web, but there are some good references:

- The Apache Hive wiki (*http://bit.ly/1ACj9rX*) (contains a lot of useful information, including the HQL language reference)

- *Programming Hive*, by Dean Wampler, Jason Rutherglen, and Edward Capriolo (O'Reilly)

 Although we covered it in "Computational Frameworks" on page 10, Spark is also a key player in the analytical SQL space. The Spark SQL functionality supports a wide range of workloads for both ETL and reporting and can also play a role in interactive query use cases. For new implementations of batch SQL workloads, Spark should probably be considered as the default starting point.

Apache Impala

Apache Impala is a massively parallel processing (MPP) engine designed to support fast, interactive SQL queries on massive datasets in Hadoop or cloud storage. Its key design goal is to enable multiple concurrent, ad hoc, reporting-style queries covering terabytes of data to complete within a few seconds. It is squarely aimed at supporting analysts who wish to execute their own SQL queries, directly or via UI-driven business intelligence (BI) tools.

In contrast to Hive or Spark SQL, Impala does not convert queries into batch jobs to run under YARN. Instead it is a standalone service, implemented in C++, with its own worker processes which run queries, the Impala *daemons*. Unlike with Hive, there is no centralized query server; each Impala daemon can accept user queries and acts as the *coordinator* node for the query. Users can submit queries via JDBC or ODBC, via a UI such as Hue, or via the supplied command-line shell. Submitted queries are compiled into a distributed query plan. This plan is an operator tree divided into *fragments*. Each fragment is a group of plan nodes in the tree which can run together. The daemon sends different *instances* of the plan fragments to daemons in the cluster to execute against their local data, where they are run in one or more threads within the daemon process.

Because of its focus on speed and efficiency, Impala uses a different execution model, in which data is streamed from its source through a tree of distributed *operators*. Rows read by scan nodes are processed by fragment instances and streamed to other instances, which may be responsible for joining, grouping, or aggregation via exchange operators. The final results from distributed fragment instances are streamed back to the coordinator daemon, which executes any final aggregations before informing the user there are results to fetch.

The query process is outlined in Figure 1-9. A client chooses an Impala daemon server to which to submit its query. This coordinator node compiles and optimizes the query into remote execution fragments which are sent to the other daemons in the cluster (query initialization). The daemons execute the operators in the fragments and exchange rows between each other as required (distributed execution). As they become available, they stream the results to the coordinator, which may perform final aggregations and computations before streaming them to the client.

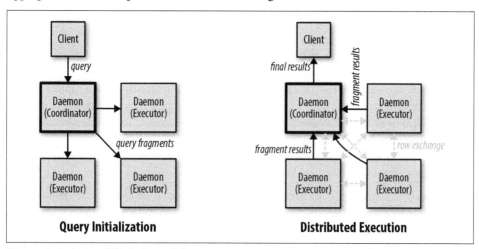

Figure 1-9. A simplified view of the query execution process in Impala

Impala can read data from a wide range of data sources, including text files, HBase tables, and Avro, but its preferred on-disk format is Parquet. Impala can take advantage of the fact that Parquet files store data by columns to limit the data read from disk to only those columns referenced in the query itself. Impala also uses *predicate pushdown* to filter out rows right at the point that they are read. Currently Impala can read data stored in HDFS, Apache HBase, Apache Kudu, Amazon S3, and Microsoft Azure Data Lake Store (ADLS).

Going deeper. For more details on Impala, we recommend the following sources:

- Cloudera's Apache Impala Guide (*http://bit.ly/2zijYyA*)
- *Getting Started with Impala*, by John Russell (O'Reilly)

Also consider. There are many more analytical frameworks out there. Some other SQL-based distributed query engines to certainly bear in mind and consider for your use cases are:

- Presto (*https://prestodb.io*)
- Apache Drill (*https://drill.apache.org*)
- Apache Phoenix (*http://phoenix.apache.org/*) (based on Apache HBase, discussed in the next section)

Storage Engines

The original storage engine in the Hadoop ecosystem is HDFS, which excels at storing large amounts of append-only data to be accessed in sequential scans. But what about other access patterns, such as random record retrieval and updates? What about document search? Many workloads deal with large and varied datasets but are not analytical in nature. To cater to these different use cases, a few projects have been developed or adapted for use with Hadoop.

Apache HBase

The desire by some early web companies to store tens of billions to trillions of records and to allow their efficient retrieval and update led to the development of Apache HBase—a semi-structured, random-access key-value store using HDFS as its persistent store. As with many of the Hadoop projects, the original blueprint for the framework came from a paper published by Google describing its system Bigtable. Essentially, HBase provides a means by which a random-access read/write workload (which is very inefficient for HDFS) is converted to sequential I/O (which HDFS excels at).

HBase is not a relational store. Instead, it stores semi-structured key-value pairs, called *cells*, in a distributed table. HBase subdivides the cell key into a hierarchy of components to allow related cells to be stored and accessed efficiently together. The first portion of the key is called the *row key*, and it defines a logical grouping of cells, called a *row*. Next, the key is further subdivided into *column families*, which again represent a grouping of cells. Column families are stored separately in memory and on disk, and there are usually no more than a handful per table. Column families are the only part of the key schema that need to be defined when the table is created.

Within a column family there is a further subdivision, called a *column qualifier*, of which there can be millions or more per row. Finally, each cell has a timestamp which defines a *version*. Multiple cells with different timestamps but otherwise the same key can be stored as different versions. HBase treats each component of the key (apart from the timestamp) and the value as arrays of bytes. As a result, HBase doesn't impose any restrictions on, or have any knowledge of, types in any part of the cell, making it a semi-structured store.

In HBase, cells are stored in order according to their key components. They are sorted first by their row key and then by column family, column qualifier, and finally by timestamp. HBase employs horizontal partitioning—that is, the cells in a table are divided up into partitions, which are distributed around the cluster. The space of row keys in a table is divided up into partitions called *regions*, each responsible for a non-overlapping range of the sorted row keys. The boundaries between regions are called *region splits*. For example, if you know your rows will have row keys with a random alphabetical prefix, you might create your table initially with 26 regions with splits at b, c, d, . . ., v, w, x, y, z. Any key starting with a will go in the first region, with c the third region and z the last region. New splits can be added manually or can be automatically created by HBase for busy regions. In this way, a table can be easily distributed and scaled.

The learning curve for operational aspects of HBase can be steep, and it is not necessarily for the faint of heart. Getting the right design for the table and the cell keys is absolutely critical for the performance of your given use case and access pattern. Designing the right table layout requires a solid working understanding of how HBase works, or you are liable to end up with pathological behaviors, such as full-table scans, region hotspotting, or compaction storms. HBase excels at servicing random I/O workloads: well-distributed write or read requests for relatively small groups of cells, via either row gets or range scans. It is not as good at supporting much larger scans, such as those that are typical in analytical workloads. These are expensive to execute and return to the client. Such workloads are typically much better performed directly against the HDFS files themselves.

If managed well and used correctly, HBase is one of the most valuable tools in the ecosystem and can deliver blazing fast performance on huge datasets. It should absolutely be used—just be sure you are using it for the right thing and in the right way.

Going deeper.   There are some absolute must-read references if you are serious about using or running HBase:

- *HBase: The Definitive Guide*, 2nd Edition, by Lars George (O'Reilly)
- *Architecting HBase Applications*, by Jean-Marc Spaggiari and Kevin O'Dell (O'Reilly)

- The Apache HBase Reference Guide (*http://hbase.apache.org/book.html*)

Also consider. HBase is not the only semi-structured store based on HDFS. Others include:
- Apache Cassandra (*http://cassandra.apache.org*)
- Apache Accumulo (*http://accumulo.apache.org*)

Apache Kudu

One of the principal pain points of the traditional Hadoop-based architecture is that, in order to support both efficient high-throughput analytics and low-latency random-access reads on the same data, multiple storage engines must be used. This results in relatively complex ingestion and orchestration pipelines. Such use cases require something like HBase or Accumulo to service the random-access queries, along with a combination of HDFS, Parquet and Impala, Spark SQL, or Hive for the analytical workloads.

If the incoming data includes updates to existing rows, the picture becomes even more complicated, as it can require wholesale rewrites of data on HDFS or complex queries based on application of the latest deltas. Recognizing this, the creators of Kudu set out to create a storage and query engine that could satisfy both access patterns (random-access and sequential scans) and efficiently allow updates to existing data. Naturally, to allow this, some performance trade-offs are inevitable, but the aim is to get close to the performance levels of each of the native technologies—that is, to service random-access reads within tens of milliseconds and perform file scans at hundreds of MiB/s.

Kudu is a structured data store which stores rows with typed columns in tables with a predefined schema. A subset of the columns is designated as the primary key for the table and forms an index into the table by which Kudu can perform row lookups. Kudu supports the following write operations: insert, update, upsert (insert if the row doesn't exist, or update if it does), and delete. On the read side, clients can construct a scan with column projections and filter rows by predicates based on column values.

Kudu distributes tables across the cluster through horizontal partitioning. A table is broken up into *tablets* through one of two partitioning mechanisms, or a combination of both. A row can be in only one tablet, and within each tablet, Kudu maintains a sorted index of the primary key columns. The first partitioning mechanism is *range partitioning* and should be familiar to users of HBase and Accumulo. Each tablet has an upper and lower bound within the range, and all rows with partition keys that sort within the range belong to the tablet.

The second partitioning mechanism is *hash partitioning*. Users can specify a fixed number of hash buckets by which the table will be partitioned and can choose one or more columns from the row that will be used to compute the hash for each row. For each row, Kudu computes the hash of the columns modulo the number of buckets and assigns the row to a tablet accordingly.

The two partitioning mechanisms can be combined to provide multiple levels of partitioning, with zero or more hash partitioning levels (each hashing a different set of columns) and a final optional range partition. Multilevel partitioning is extremely useful for certain use cases which would otherwise be subject to write hotspotting. For example, time series always write to the end of a range, which will be just one tablet if only range partitioning is used. By adding a hash partition on a sensible column, the writes can be spread evenly across all tablets in the table and the table can be scaled by dividing each hash bucket up by range.

With all storage and query engines, choosing the right schema and table layout is important for efficient operation. Kudu is no different, and practitioners will need to familiarize themselves with the trade-offs inherent in different row schemas and partitioning strategies in order to choose the optimal combination for the use case at hand. Common use cases for Kudu include:

- Large metric time series, such as those seen in IoT datasets
- Reporting workloads on large-scale mutable datasets, such as OLAP-style analyses against star schema tables

Going deeper.   The best place to start to learn more about Kudu is the official project documentation (*http://bit.ly/2Tv16os*). Other resources well worth reading include:

- "Kudu: Storage for Fast Analytics on Fast Data" (*http://bit.ly/2OUEuKC*), by Todd Lipcon et al. (the original paper outlining the design and operation of Kudu)
- *Getting Started with Kudu*, by Jean-Marc Spaggiari et al. (O'Reilly)

Apache Solr

Sometimes SQL is not enough. Some applications need the ability to perform more flexible searches on unstructured or semi-structured data. Many use cases, such as log search, document vaults, and cybersecurity analysis, can involve retrieving data via free-text search, fuzzy search, faceted search, phoneme matching, synonym matching, geospatial search, and more. For these requirements, often termed *enterprise search*, we need the ability to automatically process, analyze, index, and query billions of documents and hundreds of terabytes of data. There are two primary technologies in the ecosystem at present: Apache Solr and Elasticsearch. We cover only Apache

Solr here, but Elasticsearch is also a great choice for production deployments. Both are worth investigating carefully for your enterprise search use case.

To support its search capabilities, Solr uses *inverted indexes* supplied by Apache Lucene, which are simply maps of *terms* to a list of matching *documents*. Terms can be words, stems, ranges, numbers, coordinates, and more. Documents contain *fields*, which define the type of terms found in them. Fields may be split into individual *tokens* and indexed separately. The fields a document contains are defined in a schema.

The indexing processing and storage structure allows for quick ranked document retrieval, and a number of advanced query parsers can perform exact matching, fuzzy matching, regular expression matching, and more. For a given query, an index searcher retrieves documents that match the query's predicates. The documents are scored and, optionally, sorted according to certain criteria; by default, the documents with the highest score are returned first.

In essence, Solr wraps the Lucene library in a RESTful service, which provides index management and flexible and composable query and indexing pipelines. Through the SolrCloud functionality, a logical index can be distributed across many machines for scalable query processing and indexing. Solr can additionally store its index files on HDFS for resilience and scalable storage.

Solr stores documents in *collections*. Collections can be created with a predefined schema, in which fields and their types are fixed by the user. For use cases that deal with documents with arbitrary names, *dynamic fields* can be used. These specify which type to use for document fields that match a certain naming pattern. Solr collections can also operate in so-called *schemaless* mode. In this mode, Solr guesses the types of the supplied fields and adds new ones as they appear in documents.

SolrCloud allows collections to be partitioned and distributed across Solr servers and thus to store billions of documents and to support high query concurrency. As with all storage and query engines, Solr has its strengths and weaknesses. In general, a well-operated and configured SolrCloud deployment can support distributed collections containing billions of documents, but you must take care to distribute query and indexing load properly. The strengths of Solr lie in its flexible querying syntax and ability to do complex subsecond searches across millions of documents, ultimately returning tens to hundreds of documents to the client. It is generally not suitable for large-scale analytical use cases which return millions of documents at a time. And for those who can't live without it, Solr now supports a SQL dialect for querying collections.

You'll learn more about using Solr in highly available contexts in "Solr" on page 367.

Going deeper. We have only covered the very basics of Solr here. We highly recommend that you consult the official documentation (*http://bit.ly/2zj4jz8*), which has much more detail about schema design and SolrCloud operation. The following are also worth a look:

- *Solr in Action*, 3rd Edition, by Trey Grainger and Timothy Potter (Manning). Although slightly dated, this resource contains an excellent description of the inner workings of Solr.

- Solr 'n Stuff (*http://yonik.com*). Yonik Seeley's blog contains a wealth of background information about various Solr features and an "Unofficial Solr Guide."

Also consider. As we noted earlier, Elasticsearch (*https://www.elastic.co*) is a strong alternative to Solr.

Apache Kafka

One of the primary drivers behind a cluster is to have a single platform that can store and process data from a multitude of sources. The sources of data within an enterprise are many and varied: web logs, machine logs, business events, transactional data, text documents, images, and more. This data arrives via a multitude of modes, including push-based, pull-based, batches, and streams, and in a wide range of protocols: HTTP, SCP/SFTP, JDBC, AMQP, JMS, and more. Within the platform ecosystem, there are multiple sinks for incoming data: HDFS, HBase, Elasticsearch, and Kudu, to name but a few. Managing and orchestrating the ingestion into the platform in all these modes can quickly become a design and operational nightmare.

For streaming data, in particular, the incumbent message broker technologies struggle to scale to the demands of big data. Particular pain points are the demands of supporting hundreds of clients, all wanting to write and read at high bandwidths and all wanting to maintain their own positions in the streams. Guaranteeing delivery in a scalable way using these technologies is challenging, as is dealing with data backlogs induced by high-volume bursts in incoming streams or failed downstream processes. These demands led directly to the development of Apache Kafka at LinkedIn.

Read more about the background and motivations for a log-based, publish/subscribe architecture in "The Log: What every software engineer should know about real-time data's unifying abstraction" (*http://bit.ly/2vjpJv9*).

Apache Kafka is a publish/subscribe system designed to be horizontally scalable in both volume and client read and write bandwidth. Its central idea is to use distributed, sequential logs as the storage mechanism for incoming messages and to allow clients, or groups of clients, to consume data from a given point using simple numerical offsets. Kafka has become a critical glue technology, providing a resilient and highly available ingestion buffer, which integrates multiple upstream sources and downstream sinks. Increasingly, stream processing and stateful querying of streams is supported within the Kafka ecosystem itself, with Kafka operating as the system of record.

The fundamental data structure in Kafka is the *topic*, which is a sequence of *messages* (or *records*) distributed over multiple servers (or *brokers*). Each topic can be created with multiple *partitions*, each of which is backed by an on-disk *log*. For resilience, partitions have multiple replicas residing on different brokers.

Messages in Kafka are key-value pairs, where the key and value are arbitrary byte arrays. Clients publish messages to partitions of Kafka topics via *producers*. Each partition of a topic is an ordered and immutable log. New messages are appended sequentially to the end of the log, which makes the I/O operation very efficient. Within the partition, each message is written together with an *offset*, which is an always-increasing index into the log. Clients can read from topics using *consumers*. For scalability, separate consumers can be combined into a *consumer group*. Consumers can retrieve their last known offset on startup and easily resume where they left off.

Kafka can be used in many ways. Most commonly, it is used as a scalable buffer for data streaming to and from storage engines on Hadoop. It is also frequently used as a data interchange bus in flexible stream processing chains, where systems such as Kafka Connect (*http://bit.ly/2TuEnZy*), Apache Flume (*http://flume.apache.org*), or Spark Streaming consume and process data and write their results out to new topics.

Increasingly, architectures are being built in which Kafka acts as the central system of record and temporary views are built in external serving systems, like databases and key-value stores. It is for this reason that we categorized Kafka as a storage engine rather than as an ingestion technology. However it is used, Kafka is a key integration technology in enterprise big data platforms.

Going deeper.   There is a wealth of information about Kafka's background and usage. Some good places to start include:

- The Apache Kafka documentation (*http://kafka.apache.org/documentation/*)
- *Kafka: The Definitive Guide*, by Gwen Shapira, Neha Narkhede, and Todd Palino (O'Reilly)
- *I Heart Logs*, by Jay Kreps (O'Reilly)

Ingestion

There are a lot of technologies in the ingestion space—too many to cover in this survey. Traditionally, two of the main ingestion technologies have been Apache Flume, which is targeted at scalable ingestion for streams of data, and Apache Sqoop, which is focused on importing and exporting data in relational databases. Many other options have emerged, though, to simplify the process of ingestion pipelines and to remove the need for custom coding.

Two notable open source options are:

- Apache NiFi (*http://nifi.apache.org*)
- StreamSets Data Collector (*https://github.com/streamsets/datacollector*)

Orchestration

Batch ingestion and analytics pipelines often consist of multiple dependent phases, potentially using different technologies in each phase. We need to orchestrate and schedule such pipelines and to be able to express their complex interdependencies.

Apache Oozie

Apache Oozie (*https://oozie.apache.org*) is the job scheduling and execution framework for Hadoop. The basic units of execution within Oozie jobs are *actions*, which represent tasks that run in the Hadoop ecosystem, such as Hive queries or Map-Reduce jobs. Actions are composed into *workflows*, which represent logical sequences or orderings of tasks that need to be run together. Workflows can be run to a schedule via *coordinators*, which in turn can be grouped together into *bundles* for logical grouping of applications. An Oozie job can refer to a workflow, coordinator, or bundle.

Oozie jobs are defined via XML files. Each workflow contains a directed (acyclic) graph of actions, basically akin to a flowchart of processing. Coordinators define an execution schedule for workflows, based on time intervals and input dataset availability. Bundles define groups of related coordinators with an overall kickoff time.

Jobs are submitted to the Oozie server, which validates the supplied XML and takes care of the job life cycle. This means different things for different job types. For workflows, it means starting and keeping track of individual action executions on the Hadoop cluster and proceeding through the graph of actions until the workflow completes successfully or encounters an error. For coordinators, the Oozie server arranges for workflows to be started according to the schedule and checks that all input datasets are available for the particular instance of the workflow execution, potentially holding it back until its input data is ready. The Oozie server runs each of the coordinators defined in a bundle.

Workflow actions come in two flavors: *asynchronous* and *synchronous*. The majority of actions are run asynchronously on YARN via *launchers*. Launchers are map-only jobs which, in turn, may submit a further Hadoop job (e.g., Spark, MapReduce, or Hive). This architecture allows the Oozie server to remain lightweight and, consequently, to easily run hundreds of actions concurrently. It also insulates long-running applications from Oozie server failures; because the job state is persisted in an underlying database, the Oozie server can pick up where it left off after a restart without affecting running actions. Some actions are considered lightweight enough to not need to be run via YARN but instead run synchronously, directly in the Oozie server. These include sending emails and some HDFS commands. Oozie job definitions and all associated files and libraries must be stored in HDFS, typically in a directory per application. Oozie exposes a RESTful HTTP API backed by a multi-threaded web server through which a user submits, monitors, and controls jobs.

We cover Oozie further in relation to high availability in "Oozie" on page 371.

Also consider

Oozie isn't everyone's cup of tea, and a couple of very capable contenders have emerged. They are arguably more flexible and usable and well worth considering for greenfield deployments:

- Apache Airflow (incubating) (*https://airflow.apache.org*)
- Luigi from Spotify (*https://github.com/spotify/luigi*)

Summary

We have covered a fair amount of ground in this primer, beginning with the basic definition of a cluster, which we will cover more in the next chapter. From there, we looked at the core components of Hadoop clusters, computational frameworks, SQL analytics frameworks, storage engines, ingestion technologies, and finally, orchestration systems. Table 1-2 briefly summarizes the components that were covered and outlines their primary intended functionality.

Table 1-2. Component summary

Project	Description	Used for	Depends on
ZooKeeper	Distributed configuration service	Sharing metadata between distributed processes and distributed locking	-
HDFS	Distributed file storage	Scalable bulk storage of immutable data	ZooKeeper

Project	Description	Used for	Depends on
YARN	Distributed resource scheduling and execution framework	Frameworks requiring scalable, distributed compute resources	ZooKeeper, HDFS
MapReduce	Generic distributed computation framework	Batch compute workloads	YARN, HDFS
Spark	Generic distributed computation framework	Batch, analytical SQL, and streaming workloads	Resource scheduler (e.g., YARN or Mesos), data sources (e.g., HDFS, Kudu)
Hive	SQL analytics query framework	Analytical SQL workloads	YARN, data sources (e.g., HDFS, Kudu)
Impala	MPP SQL analytics engine	Analytical, interactive SQL workloads	Data sources (HDFS, Kudu, HBase)
HBase	Distributed, sorted store for hierarchical key-value data	Random, low-latency read/write access to row-based data with structured keys	HDFS, ZooKeeper
Kudu	Distributed store for structured data	Combined random read/write access and analytical workloads	-
Solr	Enterprise search framework	Scalable document indexing and querying on arbitrary fields	HDFS, ZooKeeper
Kafka	Distributed pub/sub messaging framework	Scalable publishing and consumption of streaming data	ZooKeeper
Oozie	Workflow scheduler	Regular and on-demand data processing pipelines	-

With this working knowledge under your belt, the rest of the book should be easier to digest. If you forget some of the details, you can always use this section to refamiliarize yourself with the key technologies.

PART I
Infrastructure

The defining characteristics of big data—volume, variety, and velocity—don't just apply to the information stored within a modern data platform; they also apply to the knowledge required to build and use one effectively.

The topics touched upon are varied and deep, ranging from hardware selection and datacenter management through to statistics and machine learning. Even from just a platform architecture perspective, which is the scope of this book, the body of knowledge required is considerable. With such a wide selection of topics to cover, we have decided to present the material in parts.

In this first part, our intention is to equip the reader with foundational knowledge and understanding relating to infrastructure, both physical and organizational. Some chapters will be a deep dive into subjects such as compute and storage technologies, while others provide a high-level overview of subjects such as datacenter considerations and organizational challenges.

## CHAPTER 2

Clusters

Before we perform a deep dive into modern cluster infrastructure, this chapter will consider clusters from a wider perspective, showing how multiple modern data platforms fit together within the enterprise context.

First, we dispel the myth of the single cluster, describing how and why organizations choose to deploy multiple clusters. We then briefly look at the black art of cluster sizing and cluster growth, and finally at the data replication implications of deploying multiple clusters.

Reasons for Multiple Clusters

The aspiration to have a single large cluster that stores everything and removes data silos is tantalizing to many organizations, but the reality is that multiple clusters are inevitable—particularly within an enterprise setting. As we describe in this section, there are many valid reasons for deploying multiple clusters, and they all have one thing in common: the need for independence.

Multiple Clusters for Resiliency

Architecting a system for resilient operation involves ensuring that elements are highly available, and designing out any single points of failure such as power or cooling, as discussed in Chapters 6 and 12. Ultimately, every cluster sits within a single point of failure simply due to geography—even a cloud deployment built using multiple availability zones (AZs).

Total system resiliency can therefore only be assured by using multiple datacenters in different geographic regions, ensuring that business processes can withstand even catastrophic events, such as earthquakes, floods, or political instability.

Although it can be tempting to consider deploying a single cluster over multiple locations, the bandwidth and latency requirements almost certainly make this unfeasible. However, deploying an independent cluster at each of two sites is an entirely practical and achievable solution, leading to our first reason for deploying multiple clusters: disaster recovery (DR), which is discussed in Chapter 13.

Sizing resilient clusters

In many cases, organizations deploy a second cluster at a remote site with the same storage and processing capabilities as the main cluster, with the intention of migrating production workloads in the event of a disaster. Rather than being inactive, the remote cluster can provide additional business value by performing data exploration or reporting workloads that are more ad hoc in nature.

Alternatively, depending on the requirements, remote clusters can be sized for data archiving than for workload migration—effectively building a backup/archive cluster rather than a secondary active cluster. Obviously, this approach has drawbacks regarding recovery time in comparison to a secondary cluster.

Multiple Clusters for Software Development

Innovation is undoubtedly one of the main benefits of a modern data platform and a significant reason for enterprise adoption. Paradoxically, many organizations find that the high level of change within the platform presents an uncomfortable level of risk.

Any software or configuration change has an element of risk, since it has the potential to cause a performance or functional regression, whether that change is within the OS, data platform, or application. By deploying separate clusters for some (or all) phases of the development process, changes can be staged through these lower environments and validated through testing, mitigating the risk of impacting critical production environments.

Although this practice is common throughout the traditional IT landscape, it is particularly relevant to modern data platforms due to their inherent scale, complexity, and pace of innovation. Examples of this practice include:

- Deploying separate *system integration testing* (SIT) clusters to perform upgrade testing in isolation
- Deploying separate *user acceptance testing* (UAT) clusters to tune platform configuration in isolation

Since the balance between innovation and stability is a common enterprise concern, platform vendors strike a balance by providing guarantees of stable platform interfaces while supplying fixes to critical issues.

Variation in cluster sizing

Because the various phases of the development process often have different storage and processing requirements, it follows that each environment can be sized differently.

In traditional enterprises, it is common for development phases such as implementation (dev), testing (test), and quality assurance (QA) to require smaller clusters, since those phases focus more on functional correctness than on performance and thus don't require large datasets. Phases such as user acceptance and preproduction are often larger, since testing at scale is required to ensure that processes perform and scale correctly when run over production-level data volumes.

However, when using modern data platforms for machine learning workloads, the size balance can be inverted. Experimentation, exploratory data analysis, and model training are often intensive processes, requiring larger platforms than production, which only runs known, verified workloads, such as model scoring.

Multiple Clusters for Workload Isolation

Every workload performed by a cluster uses resources from the underlying hardware —CPU cycles, memory space, memory bandwidth, storage space, storage bandwidth, or network bandwidth—and each has capacity limits. Concurrent workloads often need the same resources at the same time, so it necessarily follows that there is always the possibility of resource contention.

Workloads vary in how they react to contention. Although some degrade gracefully, even under high contention, others are more severely affected, often to the point that it makes more sense to deploy those workloads in isolation to guarantee their performance.

Resource contention can also occur between cluster services. Each service is designed to support a particular use case or access path. For example, HBase is highly optimized for random reads and writes, while HDFS is far better at handling sequential scans. During operation, each service makes very different demands of the underlying hardware resources, which can lead to contention.

The following are some common scenarios in which a dedicated cluster makes sense:

HBase
> HBase is designed to support highly concurrent random read and random write workloads. If predictably low-latency queries are a requirement, as determined by a specific *service level agreement* (SLA), HBase needs predictable disk seek latency for reads as well as high levels of predictable, sequential file I/O for *write-ahead logging* (WAL) and compactions.

If HBase workloads are co-deployed against heavy analytical workloads, such as Spark or MapReduce, query throughput can drop drastically, since the disk usage pattern significantly differs.

Kafka

Kafka is designed to support high-performance messaging by using memory-mapped files to store messages. Effectively, this means that the Linux page cache (rather than Kafka) is responsible for caching the most recently written messages. This approach has several advantages:

- The Linux page cache is already very highly tested and optimized.
- The latest messages are mostly read from memory rather than from disk.
- The disk workload consists mostly of sequential writes.
- The cache remains in place even when restarting Kafka.

The Linux page cache is an opportunistic optimization, since it's better for memory to be used for caching files than to be empty. The corollary is that if memory is in demand, such as when Kafka is codeployed against workloads that use large amounts of physical memory, the page cache is reduced in size and pages relevant to Kafka are evicted. When that occurs, Kafka may need to read messages from disk, causing slower read performance and unpredictable latency. For this reason, Kafka is commonly deployed on a dedicated cluster that doesn't run any other workload.

Sizing multiple clusters for workload isolation

A clear advantage of deploying services such as Kafka and HBase separately is that they can be scaled to match their service-specific workload demands. Furthermore, that advantage extends throughout the lifetime of a service—changes in demand profile over time can be directly reflected in the size of the cluster.

Multiple Clusters for Legal Separation

As every system architect knows, not all architecturally significant decisions can be made on a purely technical basis—legal obligations and company policies are often preeminent.

Many countries have laws that control where data can be stored and processed, particularly when that data relates to health, finance, or other sensitive personal information. Large multinational organizations routinely collect data, both intentionally and incidentally, about their customers and employees around the world. When legal frameworks specify that this data should be kept segregated, it is highly likely that the result is multiple clusters.

Multiple Clusters and Independent Storage and Compute

Computing workloads come in all shapes and sizes. Some workloads, such as bitcoin mining, use huge amounts of CPU but almost no network or disk resources. At the opposite end of the scale, data archiving makes heavy use of disk storage but very little CPU.

As multipurpose environments, modern data platforms need to support a wide range of workloads, often simultaneously. We discuss how clusters can vary in terms of their hardware profiles to support a variety of workloads in Chapter 3.

At the time of Hadoop's inception, network bandwidth was a precious resource. Moving the code rather than the data ensured that the first hop in the analysis chain was almost always performed by reading local disks rather than by requesting huge data volumes over the network.

Decoupled storage and compute has been a design goal of the IT industry for many years. The architectural basis for this is compelling, since it allows system designers to size each resource separately. Fast-forward a few years, though, and the large cloud vendors demonstrated that, with enough network capacity, storage can again be remote.

Object stores such as Microsoft Azure Data Lake Storage (ADLS) and Amazon Simple Storage Service (Amazon S3) allow transient virtual machines (VMs) to store data persistently at low cost. Crucially, these object stores can also be used by multiple clusters simultaneously, thereby enabling transient workload isolation. For example, a department can request that a transient cluster be created and run for a few hours, storing the results in ADLS, while a different department performs similar work patterns, but with a cluster five times the size due to its particular computational demand.

Decoupling storage and compute (while also allowing parallel access) enables modern data platforms to provide novel patterns for workload isolation. However, for the enterprise, sharing data between clusters is necessary but not sufficient. Enterprises need consistent security, governance, and lineage applied across environments in order for data management to scale. Vendors like Cloudera are introducing architectures, such as the Shared Data Experience (SDX), in order to provide that consistent *data context* around shared data.

Multitenancy

Part of the reason that many organizations find the single large cluster so compelling is that it has the potential to realize significant cost savings and reduced complexity. Any time a dataset is required on multiple clusters, the additional copies increase costs due to additional server and network hardware, installation, ongoing cluster management, and data management and governance.

Multitenancy is the practice of sharing a cluster between multiple groups or workloads. Although this can simply mean sharing the physical storage and processing capabilities, a better value proposition is to enable the sharing of stored data. Much of the benefit of a modern platform such as Hadoop is the emergent value that can arise when combining data from disparate parts of an enterprise—in essence, the data can become more valuable than the sum of its bytes. For this kind of benefit to occur, data from multiple sources must necessarily be cohosted.

Multitenancy is a broad term though, and it can be applied to a cluster in different ways. Consider the following examples:

- A cluster shared between multiple departments within an enterprise
- A cluster used for multiple development phases, such as implementation (dev) and user acceptance testing
- An archive cluster used to back up data from multiple remote production clusters

Each of these examples could be described as multitenancy, yet each is dissimilar.

Multitenancy can also be attractive to an enterprise because it fits well with the idea of centralizing cluster management to a specialist team, rather than having a disparate platform administration function within each department. There are certainly advantages and disadvantages to both approaches, which are discussed in more detail in Chapter 5.

Requirements for Multitenancy

In order for multiple workloads to coexist on a cluster, the following areas of compatibility must be considered:

Cluster life cycle
For this discussion, a cluster life cycle is defined as the major events in the lifetime of a cluster, such as installation, starting and stopping of services (whether temporary or permanent), software upgrades, significant configuration changes, and, ultimately, decommissioning.

Any workload hosted on a cluster needs to be compatible with the life cycle changes that cluster imposes. When multiple workloads require mutually incompatible life cycle events to occur, those workloads are in conflict and should not be cohosted.

As an example, consider platform upgrade testing. This activity requires software upgrades, service (re)configuration, and restarts—life cycle changes that are incompatible with a production cluster. Clearly, production workloads are fundamentally incompatible with upgrade testing, and so multiple clusters are a strong requirement.

Resource management

For multitenancy on a cluster to be possible, workloads must be compatible in the resources they intend to share—or at least degrade gracefully when under contention. Perhaps less obviously, multitenancy also requires that workloads agree about which resources should be actively managed and how. This is known as the *resource model*.

Within a single server, resource management is performed by the Linux kernel using *container groups* (cgroups). This enables hierarchical groups of processes to be controlled through prioritization, determining CPU scheduling and access to block I/O and network I/O. In simple terms, processes with higher priorities are given more frequent access to server resources. Beyond processes, filesystems (such as ext4 and XFS) also perform simple resource management in the form of storage quotas.

Platform services such as YARN provide cluster-level resource management that spans multiple servers, allowing distributed applications such as Spark to request CPU resources (allocated in virtual cores) and memory resources (allocated in bytes) from a pool of servers. Other platform services, such as Apache Impala and Apache Kafka, allow query concurrency and message ingestion or consumption rate quotas to be specified—effectively, higher-level forms of resource management.

 Although cgroups in the Linux kernel do provide block I/O prioritization, this only applies to processes that read or write directly to a local filesystem. Writes to HDFS are actually performed as network operations between the client and the DataNode rather than block I/O. The same is true of remote reads.

As network operations, writes and remote reads are not subject to block I/O prioritization (but may be subject to network I/O prioritization in the future). When *short-circuit reads* are enabled in HDFS, local reads are performed through a shared memory segment. As such, local reads are subject to I/O prioritization.

Sizing Clusters

After the number and purpose of clusters is determined, the logical next step is to decide how large each of those clusters should be. We discuss several approaches to sizing in this section, and we consider data storage, ingestion, and processing requirements. In practice and where possible, all three should be considered and combined.

Keep in mind that none of the approaches listed here can be considered an exact science. Always consider including additional overhead capacity as a safety net.

Sizing by Storage

When building out a new cluster to host an existing dataset, the size of the dataset is often known in advance. Sizing the cluster based on how much data it needs to store follows a simple algorithm:

1. Determine how much data needs to be stored.
2. Determine how much storage space is needed in total.
3. Determine how much storage space is provided per server.
4. Divide the storage needed by the storage per server.

Sizing HDFS by storage

The cluster size required to store a given data volume in HDFS depends on how the data will be stored. If using the default replication strategy, simply multiply the dataset size by a factor of four. This allows for 3× replication and 1× additional scratch space for temporary data. If using erasure coding, multiply the data size by 2.5. This allows for the 50% overhead of erasure coding and 1× additional scratch space for temporary data.

If this approach seems surprisingly straightforward to you, you'll be pleased to note that there are several additional complexities to consider:

Data representation
Will the data remain in its original format, or will it be transformed into a more efficient columnar representation, such as Apache Parquet? If transformed, will the data also be compressed? What compression codec will be used, and what compression ratio can we expect? Will data compaction be required to manage the number of files?

Data growth
Is the size of the dataset expected to increase over time? If so, do we size the cluster based on the near-term demand and expect to add capacity, or do we size for the longer term? Do we size based on a conservative growth estimate or include additional contingency?

Data retention

Do we need to keep data over the long term for regulatory purposes? Do we need to keep data in its original supplied format in addition to the transformed/filtered/cleansed version? Do we need to keep all transactions for all time, or will aggregations suffice for older data?

Dataset size accuracy

Is the dataset being used for cluster sizing already stored in a file-based storage format, or are we basing size estimates on what another IT system is using to store the dataset? If the source system is another relational database management system (RDBMS), the reported dataset size is dependent on the data representation of that system.

Helpfully, HDFS has thousands of production-level installations comprising more than 100 servers, with several well-known examples of clusters of up to 3,000 servers, at the time of this writing. The scalability of HDFS is unlikely to be a limitation.

Sizing Kafka by storage

The storage available within Apache Kafka is bounded by the storage capacity of the servers on which it operates. A typical retention policy is to keep messages for seven days, with an optional hard limit on how large a particular topic can become.

If a producer sends an unusually high volume of messages, the effective retention time may be reduced, since Kafka limits the storage space used. If seven-day retention is required for business reasons, it follows that the Kafka cluster needs to be sized large enough to maintain seven days' worth of retention, even during peak ingest periods.

Sizing Kudu by storage

Kudu stores data in a highly optimized columnar format on disk. Since this is necessarily a change in data representation, we highly recommend that you perform an ingestion *proof of concept* (PoC) to fully understand how much space your dataset will require when stored in Kudu.

At the time of this writing, the following deployment recommendations exist:

- The recommended maximum number of tablet servers is 100.
- The recommended maximum number of masters is three.
- The recommended maximum amount of stored data, post-replication and post-compression, per tablet server is 8 TB.
- The recommended maximum number of tablets per tablet server is 2,000, post-replication.

- The maximum number of tablets per table for each tablet server is 60, post-replication, at table-creation time.

Sizing by Ingest Rate

Although the size of a dataset is often readily apparent, the rate at which that size increases is sometimes less understood. Finding out how the rate varies, whether due to time of day, seasonality, or growth patterns, is invaluable when designing high-performance ingestion pipelines.

After the maximum required ingest rate for all datasets is understood, that property can be considered when sizing a cluster. Sizing for ingest rate follows another simple recipe:

1. Determine how fast data will arrive.
2. Determine how fast the data platform can ingest per server.
3. Divide the two to find out how many servers are needed.

Ingest rate requirements are often associated with streaming ingest patterns, but they apply equally to bursty ingest patterns generated by traditional batch-style applications, particularly if the batch process has an SLA to adhere to.

As an example, consider a calculation grid that computes a 1 TB financial risk analysis. The resulting dataset is small enough to fit on a single hard drive, yet writing it to a single drive would take several hours. If the requirement is to write the result in less than 5 minutes, at least 35 drives would be required, assuming each could be pushed to 100 MB/s and the write could be performed in parallel.

In practice, the speed of a single write to HDFS could be as low as 40 MB/s due to the replication pipeline. Writing 1 TB at that rate in less than 5 minutes requires a minimum of 88 parallel writes. As we discuss in Chapter 3, modern servers with 24 physical drives can make even an 88-way parallel write trivial with only a handful of servers.

Determining cluster size from a target ingest rate does have some additional complexities to consider, however:

Peak versus average ingest rate
Ingest rates for many datasets vary over time, but in some scenarios this can be a dramatic shift. Cluster sizing must therefore be derived from the maximum expected ingest rate rather than the average; otherwise, performance problems and system instability could occur.

Ingest bandwidth

Data ingestion necessarily means transferring data via the network, often using existing systems and infrastructure from beyond the cluster boundary. Sufficient data ingest bandwidth between a cluster and source systems is therefore essential. More details on how to design performant networking can be found in Chapter 4.

Write durability

When writing data to a modern data platform, it is often possible to specify how durable that write operation is. For example, in HDFS, a client can specify the level of replication for each file as it is written, and Kafka producers can specify how many brokers should have accepted the message before it is considered reliably written.

This ability allows clients to directly express how critical the data is, choosing the most appropriate option for a given use case. Higher levels of write durability almost always have a performance impact, since ensuring data is correctly replicated takes time and effort.

Sizing by Workload

Sizing a cluster by storage space or ingest rate is straightforward because those properties are fundamentally knowable, even if they aren't known. Sizing by workload is a greater challenge because the performance depends on a huge number of variables, including infrastructure capability and software configuration.

Crucially though, the performance depends on the following questions:

- What processing does the workload perform?
- What the data look like?

Both of these questions are unanswerable by infrastructure teams. The answers may not even be known by the architects until the cluster is in place and operating. Data and processing skew can negatively affect parallelization and are intrinsically linked to data content and processing. This means that the most accurate estimate of how a workload will perform can only be obtained by performing PoC testing.

Cluster Growth

Data has been described as "the new oil"—a largely untapped, hugely valuable resource to be extracted, processed, and refined. The commercial imperative to collect ever more data and use it effectively is clear. Organizations that can become *data-driven* will be more successful, more innovative, and better able to adapt to the world around them, simply because their decisions are based on evidence.

The Drivers of Cluster Growth

Unlike oil, data can be created at will, at close to zero cost. As an example, consider a company selling a product or service: within a single development sprint, a usage metrics feature can be added that publishes psuedonymized data back to the company's datacenters. By understanding historical usage (and correlating that to previous outcomes), companies can more accurately predict customer satisfaction, retention, and ultimately future revenue.

Data growth obviously drives cluster growth in terms of storage, but often also requires additional compute capacity in order to maintain processing SLAs—a form of workload growth. Fortunately, cluster workloads are often linearly scalable. That is, if incoming data grows in size, increasing the cluster size to match can keep the processing time constant, if needed.

After being extracted and stored, data (again unlike oil) can be reprocessed without limit. As new questions arise, analytical processes can be created at will to search for answers. Indeed, the process of *exploratory data analysis* (EDA) is iterative by design, and, as is true of all good research, each answer often gives rise to further questions.

In addition, many organizations have a backlog of potential workloads that are suppressed by the inability of their existing systems to handle them. After a highly flexible and scalable modern platform is introduced, that *latent demand* finds an outlet. After cluster capacity becomes available, new workloads arrive to exploit it. In economic theory, this effect is known as *induced demand*.

Implementing Cluster Growth

Modern data platforms, such as Spark and Hadoop, may have horizontal scalability as a core architectural principle, but adding nodes can still be challenging.

In many enterprises, the procurement and installation of cluster servers requires the effective cooperation of multiple teams, which may include purchasing, datacenter operations, networking, and system administration—before we even consider platform software installation and configuration. Chapter 5 talks about these aspects, and Chapter 17 talks about *automated provisioning*, a critical aspect of cluster management.

Implementing cluster growth by adding single servers is entirely possible with cloud environments, but on-premises clusters are more likely to grow by adding multiple servers at once; it's more cost-effective to amortize the procurement and installation costs by adding a rack at a time.

From a technical perspective, adding servers to services, such as HDFS and Kafka, can be done with minimal difficulty. For HDFS, rebalancing can be helpful to ensure that the new servers share the existing read workload; otherwise they remain underutilized until they accumulate enough data. For Kafka, the partition reassignment tool can be used to perform data migration to new servers. If additional throughput capacity is required on a particular topic, the number of partitions for that topic can also be increased.

Data Replication

Whenever multiple clusters are deployed there is the possibility that data needs to be replicated, but this is particularly true when deploying multiple clusters for geographic resiliency. In that scenario, each cluster requires an identical copy of the data, which is synchronized on a frequent (or even continuous) basis. Since disaster recovery is a frequent concern within many enterprises, replication is discussed in great detail in Chapter 13.

DR is the most common reason for using data replication, but it's far from the only reason. At the start of this chapter, we covered some of the many reasons why multiple clusters might be the right architectural choice. Often, those scenarios call for data replication.

Replication for Software Development

In many forms of software and platform testing, data is required to ensure software correctness and performance. Although some testing can be performed using synthetic data, real data is often preferable, since the underlying complexities of real data are time-consuming and difficult to model with any accuracy.

Testing often takes the form of comparing expectations to reality. For example, in unit testing, developers explicitly code their expectations and then run their code to see where the differences occur. User acceptance testing is similar, but often the comparison is against a baseline (a known good previous result) rather than an explicitly coded set of results.

A key strategy in any testing is to change one thing at a time, in order to accurately understand the source of any variances. Another is for a dataset to remain unchanged to enable repeatable testing. Without this, comparing performance and correctness to a baseline is impossible.

For these reasons, data replication is often a strong requirement when performing testing. When testing is performed on a separate cluster, the replication process takes the form of a distributed copy (DistCp) operation or similar.

Replication and Workload Isolation

When workloads require a common dataset but also need to be isolated enough that multiple clusters are required, replication is inevitable. Conversely, if datasets are already replicated between multiple clusters for resiliency, workload isolation can be achieved by ensuring that both clusters are active.

For example, consider an organization that has a mix of production workloads and ad hoc data exploration jobs. One approach would be to cohost these on a single cluster using multitenancy. However, if there is a DR cluster available, a potential alternative would be to host the ad hoc exploration workload on the DR cluster. This approach is interesting for several reasons:

- The workloads are fully isolated.
- The data exploration workload has access to more resources.
- The DR cluster is active, not passive.

From a commercial viewpoint, the capital and operational expenses of a cluster can be nontrivial. By ensuring both clusters are in active use, the return on investment of both can be maximized.

Recall that workload isolation can also be required when specific technologies are deployed, due to their usage of underlying platform resources. In those scenarios, data replication is also likely to occur.

Summary

This chapter introduced a range of architectural and pragmatic reasons for considering both multitenant and multicluster deployments. These strategies, though sometimes seen as in opposition, are orthogonal. Deploying multiple multitenanted clusters is common practice in many organizations, particularly for software development life cycle (SDLC) management.

Deploying a number of clusters brings with it the requirement for data to exist in multiple places, so data replication is a must. This is a broad topic, but we mention it here in order to raise awareness of the requirement. Further details on the practical aspects and challenges are available in Chapter 13.

Finally, we discussed the topics of cluster sizing and growth, which apply to all clusters, regardless of their intended usage.

## CHAPTER 3

Compute and Storage

Although it is perfectly possible to use a machine without understanding its inner workings, for best results, a practitioner should understand at least a little of how it functions. Only then can the user operate the machine with what Jackie Stewart called "mechanical sympathy" (*http://bit.ly/2OTA2eQ*). This principle is particularly true when the machine is actually composed of many smaller machines acting in concert and each smaller machine is composed of many subcomponents. This is exactly what a Hadoop cluster is: a set of distributed software libraries designed to run on many servers, where each server is made up of an array of components for computation, storage, and communication. In this chapter, we take a brief look at how these smaller machines function.

We begin with important details of computer architecture and the Linux operating system. We then talk about different server sizes, before finally covering how these different server types can be combined into standard cluster configurations.

You probably won't need to memorize all the details in this chapter, but understanding the fundamentals of how Hadoop interacts with the machines on which it runs is invaluable in your mission to build and operate rock-solid use cases on Hadoop clusters. Refer to this chapter when you need to guide decisions on component selection with infrastructure teams, procurement departments, or even your manager.

During the initial years of its enterprise adoption, the recommendation for Hadoop IT infrastructure was simple and unambiguous: Hadoop should be run on dedicated commodity servers, each with locally attached storage.

These requirements are seemingly at odds with the apparent state of the art in compute and storage and with the emergence of cloud environments for Hadoop. From its beginnings as a large-scale backend batch framework for the big Web 2.0 content providers, Hadoop is today evolving into a versatile framework required to operate in heterogeneous IT environments. Although Hadoop's paradigm of colocating compute and storage is still mandatory to achieve the best performance and efficiency, Hadoop distributors in the meantime invest intensively to support Hadoop in cloud environments, either with local or remote storage, as we will see in Part III.

Even while the number of cloud-based Hadoop deployments is rapidly growing, on-premises installations are still the dominant form of deploying Hadoop. Therefore, the concepts in this chapter are developed with on-premises Hadoop infrastructure in mind.

Computer Architecture for Hadoop

We first review fundamental concepts in computer architecture that are required to understand Hadoop's function and performance on the individual worker node. These concepts include commodity server designs and form factors, CPU memory architectures, and a full-stack analysis of the storage stack in a modern computer, running on Linux. Having a working knowledge of these concepts will prove to be quite useful when we talk about cluster-wide functionality in later sections. An understanding of the content here will greatly help when comparing offerings in public and private cloud infrastructure in Part III.

Commodity Servers

It is widely understood that Hadoop, like most commercial computation workloads today, runs on standard x86 servers, which over the last 10 years have become commodity products. A *commodity server* consists of components that are manufactured by a multitude of vendors according to industry standards. The commoditization in the case of x86 servers has gone up to the level of the mainboard and the chassis itself as a result of initiatives such as Open Compute (*http://www.opencompute.org/*) and original design manufacturing (ODM) (*http://bit.ly/2DziLFZ*).

That being said, you should not think that "commodity" implies simplicity or mediocre performance. Modern x86 servers are extremely powerful and complex machines that need to keep up with the ever-increasing demand of computational needs in the enterprise and consumer sectors. The vast majority of servers in a modern datacenter use the 64-bit x86 CPU architecture, and they almost always have multiple cores nowadays. The largest commercial x86 server processors feature 24 cores, but with many cores come many challenges. Writing an application that fully takes advantage of multicore parallelism is far from trivial.

The increase in processing cores in CPUs that started in the mid-2000s and continues today is a technical necessity. Core scaling ensures the continuing growth of computational capability of server processors in the face of the physical limits of scaling the single core clock frequency of processors.

As we will see, the majority of Hadoop clusters are implemented with two processors per system (often referred to as a *two-socket system*), although it is also possible to run Hadoop on servers that feature four or even eight processors per system. Figure 3-1 shows a simplified block diagram of the relevant hardware components in a commodity server. In this example, two CPUs, each of which has three cores, are interconnected via an *inter-processor link*.

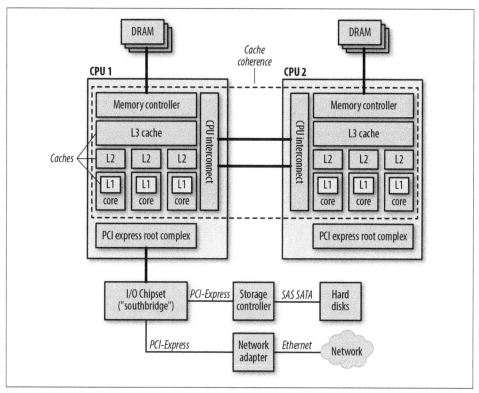

Figure 3-1. A modern computer

Central components that speed up computation on modern CPUs are *caches*, which buffer the most frequently used portions of data in the main memory in very fast storage. The CPU cores on each processor typically have three hierarchies or *levels* of cache, which are called the L1, L2, and L3 caches. The latter of these is typically shared by all cores in a processor. L1 is the fastest cache and the smallest. L3 caches have the largest size but are also significantly slower than L1 or L2 caches. L3 caches are still much faster than the main memory, referred to as *random access memory* (RAM).

All changes to the data in caches must be propagated to all others *coherently*, meaning that any change by any processor core is reflected in the caches of all other processor cores for read accesses that occur after the change, and further changes become visible in the same order they were performed. All caches thereby present a uniform view of the memory; they are coherent (*http://bit.ly/2KiOj4p*).

Cache coherency becomes more difficult when multiple processors are involved. As shown in Figure 3-1, the cache coherence domains of both CPUs become one; i.e., a core on CPU 1 will see the updates of a core on CPU 2 exactly the same way that a core on CPU 1 will see the updates of another core on CPU 1.

Each processor implements a memory controller to attach DDR3/4 DRAM (dynamic RAM) memory. The memory controller takes part in cache coherence, since it also snoops on the bus. If none of the caches is the owner of the address in question, the memory controller is the owner.

I/O operations are implemented via a *PCI Express root complex*, which attaches downstream I/O controllers for SATA, USB, and Ethernet connections, among others. All CPU-internal components—the cores, L3 cache, memory controller, PCI Express root complex, and interconnect unit—are themselves interconnected via an on-die interconnect bus. Commodity servers that feature more than two CPUs will typically be organized in a ring topology via the CPU interconnect, but otherwise adhere to the same general structure as illustrated in Figure 3-1. Although it is always possible to populate a two-socket server with only a single CPU, commodity servers with only a single processor socket are rare today.

Server CPUs and RAM

It goes without saying that the CPU is by far the most complex component in a computer. However, if we look at a CPU in isolation in the context of Hadoop, there are only a few things for architects to consider beyond the CPU's basic specifications. This is because so much commoditization has occurred around the x86-based processor architectures in recent years. Therefore, we can distill the essence of the current state of server CPU technology and its market in rather simple terms.

The role of the x86 architecture

The x86 architecture dominates the market for server CPUs with a market share of more than 90%, according to most sources. Although there have been efforts by various commercial and noncommercial parties to port Hadoop to ARM and the IBM Power Architecture, reliable Hadoop distributor support focuses on x86-based processors and the Linux operating system. The main driver for this focus is the testing effort on behalf of distributors that is required to support additional architectures, when there is a small market demand to run on other architectures.

Although other large open source software projects, such as the Linux operating system, can be versatile assets in the server, mobile, embedded, and desktop markets, Hadoop is really just focused on scalable infrastructure in the datacenter. Other drivers for the focus on x86 include technical issues around certain native Java libraries and third-party dependencies, such as the Java NIO libraries and Google's protocol buffers, but also JDK/JRE distribution and availability on other architectures. More novel components, like Apache Impala and Apache Kudu, are implemented in C++, and so far there are no efforts to port these to other architectures.

Many Hadoop components today make use of x86-specific instruction set extensions, such as the AES New Instructions (AES-NI) (*http://bit.ly/2Dzj8jR*), which are supported by most AMD and Intel-based server processors. Intel has also led several software initiatives around Hadoop security, and for a brief period marketed its own Hadoop distribution. Intel continues to invest in this area by aligning its processor features closely to open source library implementations, such as the Apache Commons Crypto library (*http://bit.ly/2Q9A4El*), which is optimized to support AES-NI. Another example of x86-specific optimizations for Hadoop is the Intel Intelligent Storage Acceleration Library (ISA-L); it uses Advanced Vector Extensions (*http://bit.ly/2S4RvmK*), which play a significant role in speeding up HDFS erasure coding, as we discuss in "Erasure Coding Versus Replication" on page 71.

Within the x86 realm, according to most sources, Intel holds a consistent market share of more than 70%, and the remainder is deployments on AMD processors.

Threads and cores in Hadoop

Whether you are a Hadoop engineer and you manage the resources of your cluster or you are a Hadoop developer and need to fit a computational problem into the cluster's resource footprint, you'll be continuously involved with *cores.*

Cores in Hadoop, whether in the context of Spark, YARN, or MapReduce, always map to a processor's *thread*, which is distinct from the processor's core. These terms are often confused, especially when someone is drawing comparisons among multiple clusters. In this section, we provide the information you need when talking about threads and cores in hardware.

Everyone who works in IT has heard the term *hyper-threading*, which is the Intel brand name for a technology known as *simultaneous multithreading* (SMT).

SMT means that multiple computation threads simultaneously execute the same CPU core, and these threads appear as completely separate processes to the operating system. The rationale behind SMT is to better utilize the existing hardware on a single core by adding just a small amount of additional core logic. SMT works by sharing certain components, such as the L2 cache and instruction units and their pipelines, while each thread maintains its own state with its own set of instruction registers, stack pointer, and program counter.

By no means does an additional thread give you twice the performance, though vendors claim an improvement of up to 30% versus running an equivalent core without

SMT. Hyper-threading is useful when threads wait for I/O frequently and the shared resources can be used by the partner thread, for example when accessing disks or even just the main memory. For very compute-heavy workloads, it is often recommended to switch off hyper-threading since it may pose an overhead. Hadoop is typically all about data and I/O, which includes in-memory computation by services such as Spark. Thus, hyper-threading is in general deemed very beneficial for big data workloads.

Conversely to SMT, an additional core really means a complete replication of on-die logic and typically results in double the performance (always assuming that your workload can be linearly scaled). However, all cores typically share the L3 cache. When a processor features multiple cores and/or when multiple processors are present in the same system the term *symmetric multiprocessing* (SMP) is used.

To summarize, a core in YARN or Spark is a processor thread as in hyper-threading, as in SMT.

Nonuniform Memory Access

A crucial element of the discussion around SMP and SMT is an understanding of the concept of *nonuniform memory access* (NUMA) that they incur.

When multiple processors share the memory in a system, the mechanism by which it is made accessible becomes an important factor in the overall system design. In some early multiprocessor designs, all memory was exposed to the processors equally on a common bus or via a crossbar switch, but this approach is not practical anymore. Today, CPUs need to accommodate DRAM with bus speeds beyond 2 GHz, and since CPUs are considered modular pluggable entities, each processor implements an interface to the DRAM. The result is that any program that is running on a given CPU that also needs to access memory from another CPU must first traverse the inter-processor link, as shown in Figure 3-1.

Although this link can serve billions of transfers per second and individual requests complete very quickly, running from another processor's memory introduces a significant overhead when compared to running on the processor's local memory. This distinction between local and distant memory is what we mean when we talk about NUMA. A common example could be a process of a Hadoop service that is allowed to be very large and may actually be allocated in a memory range that physically must span both processors. In this scenario, multiple threads could be running on both physical CPUs, each trying to access a location of memory that is distant for some of these threads and local to others.

To improve the speed of repeated access, some of this remote memory will naturally reside in the local processor's L3, L2, or L1 caches, but this comes at the cost of additional overhead in the coherency protocol, which now also spans the inter-processor connect.

Linux provides tools and interfaces through which users and programs can influence NUMA behavior directly. Crucially, this allows for requesting an optimal *mapping* for applications on a given processor, which in NUMA terminology is called a *NUMA node* (not to be confused with a core or a thread within a processor).

Showing NUMA Topology

NUMA information for a process in Linux can be obtained and influenced via the `numactl` command. Assume that we have a system with two processors, as indicated in Figure 3-1. Each of the processors is responsible for 128 GB of memory. Let's start with displaying the available NUMA nodes (i.e., processors) on the system:

```
# numactl --hardware
available: 2 nodes (0-1)
node 0 cpus: 0 1 2 3 4 5 6 7 8 9 10 11 24 25 26 27 28 29 30 31 [...]
node 0 size: 130946 MB
node 0 free: 111703 MB
node 1 cpus: 12 13 14 15 16 17 18 19 20 21 22 23 36 37 38 39 40 41 [...]
node 1 size: 131072 MB
node 1 free: 119840 MB
node distances:
node   0   1
  0:  10  21
  1:  21  10
```

In the first row of the output, we see the number of available NUMA nodes. Next, the amount of attached and free memory is shown per node, after which the output ultimately lists a table of NUMA distances. Linux assigns a score of 10 for access to the local processor and 21 for an adjacent processor. Higher costs may be associated with topologies where there is no direct connection between the originating processor and the target processor, in which case access would occur by traversing through an adjacent processor in order to reach the processor that manages the target memory range. In this example, we see that most memory on this machine is not allocated (free) and that the existing allocations are fairly evenly distributed.

There are certain problems related to NUMA that you will encounter with system performance, especially when you dedicate large amounts of memory to single Hadoop services, such as Hive, Impala, or HBase.

As a programmer for these systems, you should be aware of NUMA. If you know that your query will need more memory than is available on a single NUMA node, you should make a conscious decision about the NUMA policy with which it runs.

NUMA Example

You can access detailed NUMA information for a process via the proc filesystem, as shown in the following simplistic example. Here we see how a YARN NodeManager maps the gcc runtime library:

```
cat /proc/<process-id>/numa_maps|grep libgcc
7f527fa8e000 prefer:1 file=/[...]libgcc[...]so.1 mapped=3 N0=3
7f527faa3000 prefer:1 file=/[...]libgcc[...]so.1
7f527fca2000 prefer:1 file=/[...]libgcc[...]so.1 anon=1 dirty=1 active=0 N0=1
7f527fca3000 prefer:1 file=/[...]libgcc[...]so.1 anon=1 dirty=1 active=0 N0=1
```

The output fields are:[1]

<address>
The starting address in the virtual memory address space of the region mapped.

 Mapping memory is a common term used in operating systems related to virtual memory. Software and the operating system look at physical memory and even I/O devices for the PCI Express bus via a large virtual memory address space. This address space is so large that the operating system can conveniently give all running applications their own subset address space and manage permissions to actual memory and I/O devices by mapping those virtual addresses to physical addresses. As you'll see later in this chapter, such mapping can even be established directly for a file via the mmap() system call. Access to unmapped addresses does not succeed and raises the infamous "segmentation fault" under Linux.

`prefer:1`
The NUMA placement policy in effect for the memory range. It is always best practice to prefer a specific NUMA node, such that reads to distant memory are minimized. For processes that consume lots of memory, there is a point where the preference cannot be fulfilled anymore. This can easily happen for certain processes on Hadoop worker nodes, such as Impala daemons.

`file=<file>`
The file that backs mapping. Often multiple disjoint mappings are created for a file, and frequently only part of the file is mapped.

---

1 For full documentation of the output fields, see the "numactl(8) Linux man page" (*https://linux.die.net/man/8/numactl*), die.net.

N*<node>=<number of mapped pages>*
> The number of pages mapped by a certain node. This is what you should look out for. It may pose a problem with performance when you see many node entries (for instance, `N0=50000 N1=50000`).

`anon=`
> The number of pages that are anonymously mapped. These correspond to stack and runtime program data which is not backed by a file.

`dirty=`
> The number of dirty pages—that is, pages that have not been flushed to storage.

`active=`
> Shown only if there are also inactive pages in the mapping. This tells you whether pages from this range may be about to be evicted due to infrequent use.

In the previous example, node 1 is preferred, while all pages are actually mapped to node 0.

Linux allows you to control the NUMA characteristics when a process is launched via the `numactl` command, which we just looked at. Most importantly, `numactl` provides options to control the NUMA node on which a process is launched:

```
$ numactl --preferred=0 <process>
```

This launches *<process>* and allocates its memory on node 0. If memory allocation is not possible there, it launches the process on another node. When you launch a process in this way, all of its children inherit the same NUMA policy. In the preceding sidebar, which shows actual NUMA mappings, all entries have inherited their preference from the original command, which started the NodeManager.

Most Hadoop distributions today leverage some amount of optimization for NUMA configuration for the processes that are launched by their management tools, such as Cloudera Manager or Apache Ambari. However, those optimizations are currently limited, for the most part, to Java garbage collection.

Why is NUMA important for big data?

You should take away the following points on NUMA:

- People may be unaware of NUMA, but it significantly affects system performance.

- When applications access memory from another NUMA node, this can drastically impact performance. Hadoop job completion times can be affected by up to 15%, as recent research[2] shows.

- Since Hadoop very frequently launches JVMs (e.g., as part of executor launches and more) and since non-JVM processes occupy large portions of memory (e.g., the Impala daemon), nonuniform memory access is quite likely without proper optimizations.

- NUMA optimizations (*https://issues.apache.org/jira/browse/YARN-5764*) for YARN are gradually being added to the Hadoop software stack, and at the time of this writing, modern JVMs are getting them. For Impala, there are now some optimizations[3] that avoid migrations of memory buffers, for example during memory recycling to a distant NUMA node.

- If job completion times show significant and otherwise inexplicable variations, you should certainly investigate NUMA as a possible root cause. The commands in our example give you an initial starting point to conduct these investigations.

In addition to NUMA, the access to I/O hardware also occurs in a nonuniform fashion, as illustrated in Figure 3-1. Each processor implements its I/O fabric via PCI Express, which is a high-speed, point-to-point communications protocol and the de facto standard for I/O interconnects in modern servers. This implies that the I/O chip, which connects further downstream bus systems like SATA, SAS, and Ethernet, can only connect to a single upstream PCI Express root complex. For obvious reasons, only a single I/O chipset is actually connected to any I/O device, such that all but one of the processors are required to communicate via the inter-processor link before they can reach I/O devices. Even though I/O completion time may increase by up to 130% as a result of the additional hop, this overhead must be accepted since all processors need to communicate with the outside world via a single I/O hub.

CPU Specifications

Software frameworks in the Hadoop ecosystem are specifically designed to take advantage of many servers and many cores, and they often spend time on I/O waits. Thus, with Hadoop, you do not rely on high single-thread performance, and when you choose a CPU for Hadoop, your main objective should be to maximize cores.

The greatest number of physical cores in x86 processors today is 24, though a core count this high is mostly intended for large-scale 4U SMP systems (see "Server Form

---

2 Ahsan Javed Awan et al., "Architectural Impact on Performance of In-memory Data Analytics: Apache Spark Case Study" (*https://arxiv.org/pdf/1604.08484.pdf*), April 2016.

3 See, e.g., IMPALA-4835 (*https://issues.apache.org/jira/browse/IMPALA-4835*) and IMPALA-3200 (*https://issues.apache.org/jira/browse/IMPALA-3200*), Apache Software Foundation.

Factors" on page 91). In today's Hadoop deployments, a core count between 12 and 18 per CPU is most common. Apart from core count and core frequency, you may consider the L3 cache size, which typically increases with the core count and may go as high as 60 MB. More cores usually make it necessary to operate with a slightly reduced clock speed. However, all modern x86 processors are able to dynamically overlock by as much as 150% if other cores are idle. The practical limitations to buying the beefiest CPUs are typically rack power consumption and cost. Server vendors typically have a set of preferred models which they offer at lower rates, since they in turn can procure them at lower rates from the chip manufacturers.

Finally, it is important to be mindful that the processor lines are distinguished by how many inter-processor links are supported. Most server processors support two-socket configurations, and four-socket support adds significant cost. A few of the available Intel chips even support eight-socket configurations.

RAM

As described in the previous sections, the main memory interconnect is implemented by the CPU itself. Your only worry about main memory should be that you have enough per node, since there is now a clear focus in all Hadoop-based software frameworks (which include Apache Spark and Apache Impala) on leveraging memory as well as possible. Earlier frameworks, such as MapReduce, were really tailored for batch workloads, and they frequently used the disks to persist data in between individual processing stages. But for the most part, everything to which the ecosystem has since evolved, such as Apache HBase, Apache Impala, Apache Spark, and Hive on Spark, easily leverages dozens of gigabytes of memory, making it possible to run large-scale SQL or Spark join operations without having to spill to disk.

Recent worker node configurations typically have a minimum of 128 GB of RAM, but more and more deployments go beyond this, up to 256 GB or more. DDR4 RAM is specified to operate at between 1.6 and 2.4 gigatransfers per second, but as we described, the focus is on avoiding using the disk and fitting into RAM rather than on the ability to access RAM quickly.

Commoditized Storage Meets the Enterprise

In this book, we often stress that Hadoop means a paradigm change. That change manifests itself most clearly in the storage realm. Although CPU and memory are indeed the most commoditized components of modern servers, a frequent area of optimization in Hadoop deployments is the storage subsystem. So, before we dive into the nitty gritty of storage in big data clusters, let us look at the drivers and some typical friction points that emerge during strategic decision making around big data:

From terabytes to petabytes

We have worked with web-native companies as well as with players from the industrial and financial sectors that already manage petabytes of data with Hadoop storage systems. If your organization is not there yet, it is highly likely that it will be in less than a few years. Enterprises increasingly comprehend data as an asset, transitioning from necessity to opportunity, while legally required retention periods of data are increasing in most industries.

The global data lake, hub, and store

Everyone aspires to have one place where all data is stored, which represents a single version of truth. Data silos are costly and unmanageable, but it is likely that every enterprise has had at least one unsuccessful project to consolidate the silos. In our view, the technology for enterprise data lakes was not ready for fully fledged, large-scale enterprise adoption until recently. But now it is, and it requires organizations to think differently about storage. We are at a defining point, even more so than with the adoption of data warehouses or CRM systems about 15 years ago. Leveraging data at scale can impact the business models of companies as a whole.

Terabytes need bandwidth

Running through dozens, hundreds, or thousands of terabytes requires investment. There is no big data for small money. You can and should use commodity hardware to process big data, and it reduces cost. Nevertheless, advanced data analytics at unprecedented scale require organizations to invest.

It is clear to most organizations that the sheer volume, novel access patterns, and unprecedented throughput requirements require new answers, beyond the prevalent model of storage area network– and network attached storage–centric datacenter storage design. This is not to say that SAN and NAS storage technologies are not relevant for Hadoop. As we will see in Chapter 14, in addition to all its existing merits in enterprise IT, a SAN is also a very convenient way to implement small virtual Hadoop clusters. SAN-based Hadoop mainly has to do with the public cloud, and we rarely see it support clusters of greater than 30 nodes, which would already be cost-prohibitive as an on-premises solution to most enterprise IT organizations.

The storage systems included in Hadoop distributions help organizations to solve many of these challenges already, but technical and organizational friction often remain. Some of this friction is an inevitable part of the aforementioned paradigm change, and some of it simply needs to be clarified.

Let us step through the following possible challenges to make informed choices about them.

Modularity of Compute and Storage

This concerns the fact that in its default form, Hadoop uses servers with local storage. Point taken. However, Hadoop distributors have reached out to embrace modularizing compute and storage, which they didn't do early on. Yet the laws of physics still apply, and you can't have it all. You need to colocate—or at least tightly couple compute and storage—or spend millions on your storage network infrastructure and operations, which typically only makes sense in the hyperscale context of public clouds.

Everything Is Java

Well, first of all, it's not. Storage systems in the big data open source ecosystem today include Apache Kafka as well as Apache Kudu, which were introduced in Chapter 1. They are implemented in alternative languages, such as C/C++ or even Scala. HDFS is written in Java, but is that really a problem? In some organizations, there seems to be reluctance to run on an enterprise storage system that is implemented in Java. But consider that some of the world's largest operational datasets are run on HDFS:

- Facebook (*http://bit.ly/2JrzmMH*) is known to run many dozens-of-petabyte volumes in production on HDFS.
- Years ago, Twitter (*http://bit.ly/2R0lxI4*) publicly referred to more than 300 PB of HDFS-based storage.
- Yahoo! (*http://bit.ly/2A7KZEA*) has presented about its massive use of HDFS several times.

Just like others, these three companies cannot afford to lose data, particularly since data is the basis of their business model. Many commercial users of HDFS are running very successfully in the petascale range, mainly via the help of Hadoop distributors. Today, HDFS is a commercial enterprise storage system that also happens to be an open source project.

Replication or Erasure Coding?

Time and time again, we have witnessed strategic discussions that fundamentally questioned the usage of Hadoop for its storage efficiency. Many IT departments are plainly disappointed by the prospect of replicating data when SAN appliances have featured RAID and parity schemes for years.

Indeed, many modern storage appliances today use erasure coding or advanced RAID technology, but with a few exceptions, those are single- or dual-rack enclosures and not distributed systems. Modern big data platforms, however, are distributed and run on commodity servers, which makes the implementation of erasure coding much more challenging than in an appliance context.

At around the time of this book's release, though, Hadoop 3.0 will become generally available in Hadoop distributions, and it introduces erasure coding (*http://bit.ly/2A6q4Sj*) as one of its most important features.

So that solves everything then, right? Not quite.

Depending on the context, either erasure coding or replication may be appropriate for your use case. We cover both in detail in "Erasure Coding Versus Replication" on page 71.

Alternatives

The overwhelming number of successful data lake projects that we currently see in an enterprise context rely on HDFS, but there are alternatives for scale-out storage on commodity hardware that are slowly establishing themselves in the enterprise context. We briefly discuss those approaches in Chapters 14 and 16.

Hadoop and the Linux Storage Stack

In this section, we review the fundamental concepts of the Linux storage subsystem on a single Hadoop worker node.

Figure 3-2 provides an overview of the layers that make up the storage operations of a Hadoop worker node. Storage in modern computing includes two key concepts: a *persistence layer* and *caching*. Persistence is achieved via physical media such as hard disk drives or solid state disks. Caching is achieved on multiple levels in a modern server. The discussion in the following sections focuses on how caching goes hand in hand with the actual persistence layer, which means that you, as an engineer or a programmer, need to assert influence over both.

The design and function of HDFS itself are described in much more detail in existing literature, such as *Hadoop: The Definitive Guide*, by Tom White. Our discussion of the Hadoop storage stack focuses on how HDFS and related storage frameworks interact with the facilities of the Linux storage subsystem and the underlying hardware.

User Space

We begin our discussion at the top level, which in our case is the Linux user space (*http://bit.ly/2PHRE2P*). This is where all the Hadoop storage services, such as HDFS or Kafka, run. Figure 3-2 illustrates various Hadoop storage systems that may be used alternatively or concurrently.

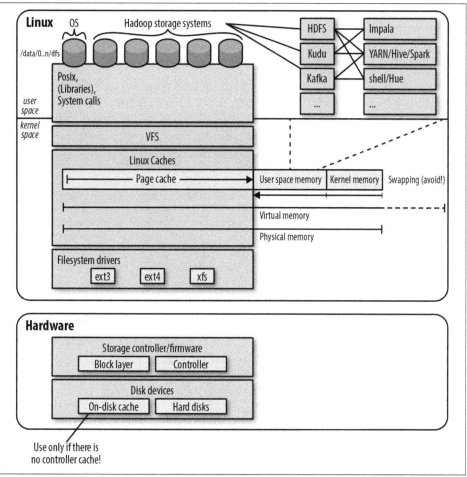

Figure 3-2. Simplified overview of the Linux storage stack

Whether to run multiple storage services on a single node, like Kafka and HDFS, is a typical and often fiercely debated question in Hadoop projects. For example, Hadoop engineers often prefer to run Kafka and HDFS on separate nodes, to ensure that enough memory and dedicated throughput are available to each service. Project managers may be unable to spare budget for this and see a synergy in colocating both services. Hadoop distributors are typically supportive of each case but prefer separated services on dedicated nodes. We strongly recommend against sharing disks between services, since the colocation would be detrimental to the throughput gains of sequential access (which each service benefits from individually).

Hadoop distributions support HDFS as the main storage system, and some also include support for Kafka, which provides an alternative for use cases focusing on data in flight. Kudu provides an alternative persistence layer for optimizing random access. We briefly introduced both in Chapter 1.

To achieve high aggregate throughput and to support large storage capacity per node, it is common to equip a worker node with 12 to 24 physical disks, where either a single or a pair of mirrored disks are typically reserved for use by the operating system. Although the raw device cannot be accessed from user programs directly, it becomes accessible by *mounting* it via a filesystem implementation to a user-chosen location in the directory tree, which is referred to as the *mount point*.

> Linux and the underlying storage controller can also apply intermediate mechanisms, which combine multiple disks into a single logical disk. Examples for this are Linux's Logical Volume Manager/device mapper (*http://bit.ly/2R475PD*) or RAID (*http://bit.ly/2A852CK*). We strongly discourage use of those technologies for worker node disks, and this is mostly unsupported by distributors. For a detailed discussion of this subject, see "RAID?" on page 82.

When Hadoop storage systems interact with the mount points of disks, they rely on a Linux filesystem implementation such as ext4 or XFS, to handle each disk's block-level interface, as indicated in Figure 3-2. Filesystems are accessed via a standard *system call* interface and certain additional user space libraries. Linux models its system call interface according to Portable Operating System Interface (POSIX) standards (*http://bit.ly/2A6qesT*). All system call interaction in Linux is abstracted via a common generic layer, called the *virtual filesystem* (VFS), before the filesystem itself is invoked. As a Hadoop admin, you will not interfere with the VFS, but it is important to understand that it provides abstractions before actual filesystem implementations are invoked in the Linux kernel. The VFS is also the layer that gives Linux the ability to mount multiple filesystems into the same root-level directory tree, and it provides uniform and automated access for filesystem I/O to various Linux caches (most importantly the page cache, which we cover in "The Linux Page Cache" on page 62).

When a user space daemon on the Hadoop worker node, for example an HDFS Data-Node, has successfully retrieved blocks from the Linux storage subsystem to fulfill a client's read request, the default is to transfer them to the client via TCP/IP. Correspondingly, for the write case, the default is that the daemons receive blocks from clients via TCP/IP. This network transfer can be avoided to speed up the overall transfer, as we discuss in "Short-Circuit and Zero-Copy Reads" on page 65.

Important System Calls

As just mentioned, system calls are the fundamental means for user space applications to interact with storage. Let us review the most relevant system calls used by Hadoop storage systems in that standard and put them in perspective of common usage patterns by client Hadoop services. In the following descriptions, you may come across some terms you have not heard before. You will find explanations in the following sections:

read(), write(), open(), seek()
> These are regular POSIX system calls for reading a range of blocks from a file. The HDFS DataNodes use them to service block read or append requests from clients. The classes BlockSender and BlockReceiver in HDFS DataNode implementations use the FileInputStream and FileOutputStream classes, which in turn use these system calls via the Java RandomAccessFile class.

fsync()
> This important POSIX system call synchronizes all pending data for the file out to the disk and blocks until the synchronization completes. This flushes relevant portions of the Linux page cache and, depending on the underlying filesystem, on-disk caches. When fsync() completes, you can be sure that everything is stored persistently on disk. A common example where this behavior is crucial is a database checkpoint. Depending on how much of the file is cached, this can take a long time, so only use fsync() if it is really required. In HDFS, it is exposed to clients via the hsync() API call. If you want to dig deeper, you can study the FileChannelImpl class, which calls fsync() via FileDispatcherImpl.force(). The force() method invokes the native implementation of the Java file I/O subsystem, the NIO library (libnio.so on Linux). fsync()s are, for example, a crucial operation for the function of the HDFS JournalNodes, as we will see further on.

fflush()
> This system call is very similar to fsync() except that it does not block. This means that the operating system will begin to force data to disk, just like with fsync(), but fflush() returns without waiting for hardware to confirm that the persistence operations concluded. The advantage is that your program can continue immediately. HDFS offers similar, but not equal, semantics via the hflush() API call. If invoked, this call blocks until the full replica pipeline to all DataNodes has completed but does not wait until that data is persistently stored on disk on any of the DataNodes. For example, if a file has three replicas on DataNode 0 to DataNode 2 (DN0–2), the successful completion of hflush() means that DN2 has sent back acknowledgments for all packets in the file to DN1, which in turn has sent back acknowledgments for those packets to DN0,

which has sent back acknowledgments to the client. hflush() also invokes the flush() method on the Java OutPutStream on each replica, but this merely ensures that the JVM's internal buffers are flushed to the operating system's underlying file descriptor and does not imply a POSIX fflush(). After hflush(), you are safe from single disk or DataNode failures, but if multiple DataNodes fail at the same time, you could lose data. If your application requires a guarantee for data durability at a critical point, use hsync().

mmap()

> This POSIX system call maps a portion of the Linux page cache into the user space memory of the calling process. This allows users to access the pages which are backing the file on disk directly, without the need to copy the user space application buffers into kernel space, as with write(). It is used by HDFS to implement caching and zero-copy reads, which we explain shortly.

mlock()

> This locks a mapped memory region and prevents it from being swapped out to disk. *Paging* (see the next section) may occur to make room for more frequently used file content. mlock() prevents this from happening. HDFS uses this system call to implement caches. MappableBlock uses calls into the Hadoop native I/O libraries, which implement the mlock() Java method as a wrapper around the mlock_native() method in NativeIO.java which, in turn, invokes the Linux mmap() method in NativeIO.c.

Figure 3-3 (in the next section) illustrates various ways by which Hadoop services can interface with the storage subsystem.

 The actual pattern of system calls for reading a file is abstracted by the JVM's InputStream implementation, which runs the DataNode daemon. It will actually include more system calls, such as open(), seek(), and so on, to traverse the requested file. In Linux distributions of JVMs, this function is implemented in the libnio.sh library.

The Linux Page Cache

Linux uses any physical memory not used by user space processes or the Linux kernel as a RAM-based cache for filesystems, called the *page cache*. All memory in Linux is managed in multiples of 4 KB, called memory *pages*. The page size typically also lines up with the hard disk *block size*, which defines the minimum unit of transfer between disks and the host system. Linux filesystem implementations use blocks as a common layer of abstraction, and all of them use the page cache as a buffer for frequently accessed blocks.

The size of the page cache is continuously adapted by Linux during runtime. When applications request more file content than can be contained in the page cache at its current size, Linux identifies the least recently used pages and persists them to backing storage media in favor of newer, more frequently used file content. Its current size is shown as Cached in */proc/meminfo*.

Since program code and libraries also have a filesystem-backed source, they are cached in the page cache too. As such, every process, including all of the Hadoop daemons, automatically benefits from the page cache. It is arguably the most important means for Linux to safeguard adequate performance of the storage subsystem for applications. The process of automatically reading newer pages into the page cache and of evicting infrequently used pages is generally referred to as *paging*.

In addition to the page cache, all Linux distributions use a feature called *swapping* to buffer infrequently used anonymous memory assigned to applications on a dedicated partition on a physical disk, which is called *swap space*.

 The term "swapping" originates from a much older mechanism to implement virtual memory, before paging existed.

The memory regions that are subject to swapping are called *anonymous*, since they represent application data and program stack space, which is not backed by file content. In "NUMA Example" on page 52, we saw that some pages were flagged as anon. You can also see the swap space as anonymous user space memory in Figure 3-3.

The impact of swapping can be quite disruptive for query systems like Impala or HBase, which is why swapping should be avoided in all circumstances. Linux can be explicitly instructed to not swap or to limit swapping via a sysctl command. However, in newer releases and/or distributions of Linux, completely disabling swapping may lead to out-of-memory exceptions, which may force Linux to kill processes of Hadoop services. This often necessitates permitting a minimum amount of swapping, e.g., by setting vm.swappiness to 1.

In certain situations it is necessary to instruct the operating system to persist data to disk immediately, which can be achieved on the HDFS level via the hsync() API call, as discussed in the previous section.

In yet other situations, you may want to avoid the page cache altogether. When assessing the performance of the storage stack with certain microbenchmarks, you may want to target the raw disks without using a Hadoop storage system and without using operating system caches. As illustrated in Figure 3-3, you can instruct Linux to minimize caching by supplying the O_DIRECT flag during the system call when opening a file. See Chapter 8 for an overview of such microbenchmarks.

Although fsync() makes sure that pages are written to disk, and although O_DIRECT will not use the cache for writing data, this does not ensure that blocks of the given file are not resident in the page cache from previous operations. If you want to be certain that file data is not contained in the cache, you can instruct Linux to persist the complete page cache to disk:

```
$ echo 3 > /proc/sys/vm/drop_caches
```

The page cache is a facility from which all of the Hadoop daemons greatly benefit. When planning Hadoop deployments, it is important to factor in a certain percentage of the overall RAM capacity to always be available for the page cache. If not enough memory is available for the page cache, the likelihood of frequent paging increases, and this will negatively impact overall system performance. On the other hand, if not enough memory is reserved for mission-critical queries, such as large in-memory join operations, they may have trouble performing adequately. The exact ratio of page cache versus application memory will likely depend on the specifics of your use case. As a general recommendation, you should reserve 20–30% of the overall system memory on a worker node for the operating system.

Figure 3-3 illustrates various examples of how Hadoop clients access storage through the layers of Linux on an HDFS DataNode. For simplicity, we focus mainly on the read path. The HDFS DataNode identifies the files on its local filesystems that make up the requested HDFS blocks and queries the operating system via the read() system call. The size of these files aligns with the HDFS block size, which is typically 128 MB. As shown in the image, the requested data is copied from the Linux page cache. If the data is not present in the page cache, the Linux kernel copies the requested pages from the disk storage subsystem. The read() system call concludes by copying the data from the page cache to a user space buffer in the DataNode. Linux performs this copy via a special-purpose internal call, copy_to_user().

As we have mentioned before, the DataNode—or equally the daemons of other storage systems, such as Kudu—then delivers the blocks to the requesting clients. There are two basic cases that we distinguish here, and they greatly differ in overall access performance:

- Reads where the client is local to the DataNode process (i.e., executes on the same host). In this case, we can apply the optimizations detailed in the next section.
- Reads where the client is remote. The copied data is then forwarded to the HDFS client (not as a whole) via a TCP connection as a continuous stream of data.

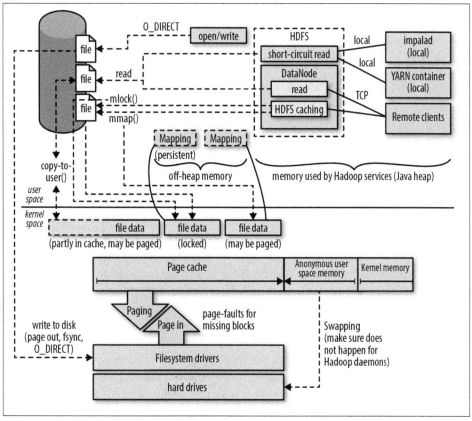

Figure 3-3. How Hadoop uses the Linux storage stack via HDFS

Short-Circuit and Zero-Copy Reads

More often than not, HDFS clients reside side by side with the DataNode on the same worker node; for example, a YARN NodeManager and an Impala daemon are almost always local clients of a DataNode. In that case, it is unnecessary overhead to transfer data from the DataNode buffer to the client via TCP, which would incur another copy of the data and would be slow due to the nature of the socket connection. As an optimization, it is possible to configure clients to take advantage of a feature called *short-circuit reading* (SCR) in HDFS, which allows clients to access the file data directly. In Figure 3-3 you can see that Impala takes advantage of this feature, but YARN containers can also be configured to take advantage of short-circuit reads. HDFS exposes an API that allows for local short-circuit reads via the `DFSInput` `Stream` class by overloading the HDFS `read()` API call:

```
public synchronized ByteBuffer read(ByteBufferPool bufferPool,
    int maxLength, EnumSet<ReadOption> opts)
```

For short-circuit reads to succeed, the following conditions must be met:

- The client is local to the DataNode.
- The client requests short-circuit reads in the opts object of the read() call.
- The client and the DataNode are using the native Hadoop I/O libraries (libha doop.so (*http://bit.ly/2DOyzFF*)).
- The client is using the dfs.client.read.shortcircuit configuration flag in *hdfs-site.xml.*
- The client is using the short-circuit read API just shown.

In addition to short-circuit reading, HDFS provides the ability to avoid the copy_to_user() call shown in Figure 3-3. Linux achieves this via the mmap() system call.

As introduced in "Important System Calls" on page 61, mmap() creates a mapping in the user's logical memory space which points to a range in the page cache that holds the file data that a client wants to access. User space applications can then directly read from and write to this mapped memory range. If the blocks that pertain to the mmap()ed file are already in the page cache, the application is accessing the page cache memory directly—i.e., without the need to copy them to user space. If the blocks that pertain to the mmap()ed file are not yet in the page cache, reading them will create page faults and will result in first paging in the required blocks from disk before they can be read in the same direct fashion. Linux can also *lock* mmap()ed pages via the mlock() system call, such that it will not page them back to disk when it tries to make room for new pages.

The combination of short-circuit reads with mmap() and mlock() is referred to as *zero-copy reading* (ZCR) in HDFS, since all unnecessary copies are avoided in this access pattern.[4]

For zero-copy reading to kick in all conditions required for short-circuit reads need to be fulfilled, as well as the following additional condition:

- Data being read is mlock()ed by the DataNode, or the client explicitly asks that checksums for the read are not used.

You're probably wondering when and why blocks are mlock()ed by the DataNode. HDFS provides a feature known as *HDFS caching.* HDFS administrators can create a cached region for an HDFS path via the hdfs cacheadmin -addPool command. The Hadoop project website has a list of all cache administration commands (*http://bit.ly/*

---

4 See HDFS-4949 (*http://bit.ly/2QZdviC*) and HDFS-4953 (*http://bit.ly/2KlDVZB*).

2Q7sNF8). When a cache is created, the NameNode identifies a DataNode that holds a replica for the blocks. The DataNode is requested to mmap() and mlock() the blocks in its main memory. As shown in Figure 3-3, local and remote clients can access cached data on a DataNode that holds data in its page cache. When creating a block list for clients that request a cached file, the NameNode will prefer DataNodes that are known to hold the file in their cache.

Optionally, a number of replicas can be specified for the cached region—i.e., multiple DataNodes may be instructed to mmap() and mlock(). From an API perspective, clients use the same short-circuit read API in the HDFS client library introduced earlier to perform ZCR reads.

If no cache directive exists for the data being read, the client library falls back to an SCR read or, if the request was not performed locally, regular reads. If a cache directive exists for the data being read, the HDFS client library performs its own mmap() on the same HDFS blocks a second time. This second mmap() is necessary to give the client an address range in its own memory space.

If you are curious about the source code, the MappableBlock class in the DataNode invokes mmap() via the FileChannel.map() method. For local zero-copy and short-circuit reads, BlockReaderLocal creates a mapping via the ShortCircuitReplica class, which also relies on FileChannel.map(). The FileChannel.map() method is implemented in libnio.so on Linux.

The reason that ZCR is only available via a caching directive is a deliberate caution by the developers of HDFS. The cache directive ensures that mmap()ed data has been checksummed by the DataNode and does not have to be checksummed again during the life cycle of the cache directive, since it is mlock()ed. A client can, however, circumvent this restriction by explicitly opting out of DataNode checksumming via the dfs.client.read.shortcircuit.skip.checksum configuration option in *hdfs-site.xml* or by directly specifying SKIP_CHECKSUM in the read() call's ReadOptions. In this case, we recommend that the client implement its own checksumming, for example via the file format.

SCR and ZCR: What Is the Benefit?

Performance data on SCR stems from the open source development community process and is by no means exhaustive for deriving a scientific analysis. Related experiments[5] indicate a speedup of up to 30% for SCR. Zero-copy reads allow throughput improvements even up to 100%, but the benefits greatly depend on the access pattern:

---

5 See Colin McCabe, "How Improved Short-Circuit Local Reads Bring Better Performance and Security to Hadoop" (*http://bit.ly/2zldoGv*), Cloudera Engineering Blog, August 16, 2013.

- Accessing data hotspots via `mmap()` is arguably the best-case scenario.
- Really, with Hadoop's distributed nature, a hotspot could cover terabytes of data in a given dataset.
- In addition, large-scale scans, where data sizes outweigh the available RAM, are ultimately bound by the transfer speed of the disk.

But beyond the debate of sheer numbers, SCR and ZCR are a best practice for all HDFS clients:

- Apache Impala always uses short-circuit reads when an Impala daemon is local to a DataNode. Impala automatically performs zero-copy reads when you cache a table. Cached tables can help resolve problems with reference tables that are used in joins with many other large tables. Such a reference table should have three characteristics: it should be small, it should be always required, and there should be an indication that it is getting evicted from the page cache often (e.g., when the cluster is very busy). If this is the case, the replication count can be increased to the number of DataNodes, and each replica is pinned into memory via an HDFS cache directive.
- Impala actually supports checksumming in its scanner Parquet data pages (*http://bit.ly/2Q94g2b*), and future optimizations might include the ability to enable completely `mmap()`ed tables.
- The YARN NodeManager also can leverage this feature, which is a great help to Spark applications (*http://bit.ly/2qVeqFz*).
- HBase benefits even more from SCR and ZCR due to much more frequent requests for small data items. Since HBase performs its own checksumming on the HFile level, it is an excellent candidate to invoke the ZCR API with the `SKIP_CHECKSUM` flag.

Unless checksumming is explictly skipped, ZCR can only be used in conjunction with HDFS caching, which `mlock()`s regions into memory once the data is initially checksummed by the DataNode. Thus it makes finite space available, since naturally only a small fraction of the HDFS data can be pinned in RAM.

As mentioned earlier, any user space application can deactivate DataNode checksumming at its own peril. You could also argue that checksumming for disk I/O already happens at lower levels in the kernel, since modern hard drives perform cyclic redundancy check (CRC) and error correction code (ECC) checking on a per-sector level. There is, however, good reason to perform integrity checks at the application level as well.

Filesystems

The choice of block-level filesystem usually does not play a decisive role in the architecture of a Hadoop cluster, but it can have an important impact on operational procedures.

The available choices of block-level filesystems, given today's market of Linux and Hadoop distributions, boil down to these three:

ext3

This has been the traditional choice for years in most Linux distributions. It is likely to have the most coverage in conjunction with HDFS. ext3 was among the first filesystems in Linux to introduce journaling capabilities—for every update of data written to disk, ext3 also updates a journal to track the changes. As per the default setting in most Linux distributions, ext3 starts to persist changes on data immediately and then triggers journal updates. A change in the journal only gets committed after data changes have been persisted to disk. This makes ext3 very robust compared to some other filesystems, as it guarantees consistency in the internal structure of the filesystem. Compared to more modern filesystems, this robustness comes at the cost of performance.

ext4

This is the successor to ext3 and introduced a range of new features, most of them targeted toward better performance. A prominent feature is delayed allocation, which allows ext4 to defer the physical allocation of disk blocks until they are ultimately flushed to disk, enabling more efficient I/O. ext4 also relaxes the rigidity of journal commits. Although there is nothing inherently wrong with that (you can always use `fsync()`—see "Important System Calls" on page 61), this initially resulted in an outcry among some users. The behavior, which trades performance for the operational risk of losing filesystem consistency, however, can be directly configured by two `sysctl` variables in the Linux kernel.[6] ext4's developers have since gone to lengths to include additional heuristics to control when files are required to be immediately flushed.

XFS

XFS is a longtime contender in the filesystem space, supporting large-scale and high-performance use cases. Like ext4, it uses delayed allocation. Unlike ext4, it uses a B+-tree for filesystem allocation, which yields significant performance advantages during file and filesystem creation, as well as consistency checks. Some Linux distributions are now using XFS as their default.

---

6 See Jonathan Corbet's article "ext4 and data loss" (*https://lwn.net/Articles/322823/*), LWN.net, March 11, 2009.

In addition to these general points, when choosing a filesystem from the list you should consider the following points:

- ext3 will easily become fragmented and is notoriously slow when performing filesystem consistency checks via `fsck`. ext4 performs these checks up to 10 times faster, and XFS is faster than ext4 by a factor of 2 to 4, depending on filesystem size and file count. From an operational standpoint, this can play a role in your Hadoop cluster. Consider scheduled maintenance, requiring a worker node to reboot. If your Linux operations team requires that periodic filesystem checks are enabled on your worker node, which happens to have very large disks (say, 6 TB or larger), an `fsck` on all of that node's disks may be forced due to the `fsck` schedule. This can take up to 30 minutes (*http://bit.ly/2TxeV5A*) for an inode (file-object) count of about 5 million, assuming there is no contention on the CPU side. In the case of HDFS, the grace period for that node's blocks to be unavailable could be exceeded, causing it to start re-replicating all the missing blocks on that node—and there may be a lot. Though re-replication is slow in comparison and a node coming back would stop the process, it could lead to unnecessary operational overhead. Although Hadoop storage systems mostly create rather large files, you might not host this many blocks on your disks. However, file-object count ultimately depends on the behavior of the user base.

- XFS can create very large filesystems significantly faster than its ext counterparts, which may also play into operational processes, depending on your organizational setup.

- When considering performance over consistency, bear in mind the many layers of caching as discussed in the previous sections. The loss of filesystem-level consistency in the event of a node crash is only one aspect to consider with regard to the overall consistency of the Hadoop storage system. Hadoop is able to recover node failures and quickly remedy the situation due to the plurality of other filesystem instances in your cluster. In practice, you may choose to relax rigid journal updates in favor of better storage performance.

Also note the following points that apply to all of these choices:

- Linux normally tracks file access times in filesystems. Since Hadoop storage systems implement their own metadata layer and the actual content on the block layer filesystem is meaningless without the higher-level metadata, it is generally recommended to supply `noatime` as a mount flag. This flag will direct Linux to stop recording the access times for both files and directories.

- With regard to explicit consistency, an `fsync()` will trigger a SCSI SYNCHRONIZE CACHE command or its SATA equivalent FLUSH CACHE EXT for ext3, ext4, and XFS. This is important in terms of durability. We talk about this more in "Disk Layer" on page 84, when we cover disk caches.

- All of the discussed filesystems reserve some space that is available only to privileged processes. This amount can typically be reduced on large disk drives, since for example 5% would equate to 500 GB on a 10 TB drive. The percentage of this area can be changed via the `tune2fs` command. For example, `tune2fs -m 1 /dev/sdX` sets the area to 1% for ext filesystems. With all desire to optimize, there are still good reasons to keep some extra space around:

  — ext3 runs into problems with fragmentation and becomes very slow when the disk is filled up more than a certain amount, depending on disk size. The merit of an extra few percent of space is drastically limited if the other fraction does not perform adequately. Changing the amount of reserved space to a few gigabytes rather than hundreds allows defragmentation operations to continue, while increasing the footprint of available space for Hadoop.

  — ext4 and XFS are are better at avoiding defragmentation, but they also need a very small amount of reserved blocks during initial file-allocation operations (for example, during a mount operation).

  — For XFS, you could use the `xfs_io` utility to reduce reserved space, but this is strongly discouraged by Linux distributors since it could actually result in `ENOSPC` errors during mount.

Which Filesystem Is Best?

All of the Linux filesystems we list here can get the job done. ext3 nowadays is a legacy choice, but it might be necessary. Operational experience of the support staff is key when dealing with filesystems. As far as ext4 and XFS go, that experience still widely differs, just like experience with the user space utilities (such as `resize2fs`, `tune2fs`, `xfs_repair`, and `xfs_admin`) themselves. First and foremost, determine whether any of the options pose added operational risk in your case.

Erasure Coding Versus Replication

As we mentioned in "Commoditized Storage Meets the Enterprise" on page 55, HDFS erasure coding (*http://bit.ly/2A6q4Sj*) is a novel feature that is becoming available in commercial Hadoop distributions.

Erasure coding is a well established and very effective error recovery technique, which turns a chunk of data into a longer, coded chunk. When part of the data is lost, it can be reconstructed from the remaining parts. The size of the data chunk that is added and the size that can be lost and reconstructed depend on the implementation. Although we do not provide details of the theory of erasure coding (*http://bit.ly/2ziCuGO*) here, it is very well covered in existing sources.

Crucially, replication and erasure coding in HDFS can be run in parallel on the same HDFS instance on a per-directory basis.

The community around HDFS has chosen a specific implementation of erasure coding based on Reed–Solomon codes. Although multiple policies are supported, the default uses six data cells and three parity cells, which means that data can still be reconstructed when up to three out of the total nine resulting cells (including parity cells) are lost.

Erasure coding has been used in a variety of distributed storage systems for quite some time. For example, Facebook has been using an implementation of erasure coding for cold data and archival use cases, which is referred to as HDFS RAID, since 2014.

Now that we have covered context, let us focus on how erasure coding will be available to enterprises, beginning with Hadoop 3.0.

In Figure 3-4, we provide an overview of how erasure coding works in HDFS, as compared to the well-known replication approach. In the example, we chose a small HDFS cluster with nine DataNodes, which is the minimum number of nodes, as we will see. In our example, those DataNodes are installed across two racks, which is also crucial for understanding the differences between erasure coding and replication.

To highlight the differences, the same file is stored in HDFS in an erasure-coded directory (1) and a directory using triple replication (2). Initially, the file is logically split into blocks of 128 MB. The illustration shows how the first four blocks of the file are processed by either method.

128 MB is currently the default block size in HDFS. The block size is configurable on a per-file basis. We could have chosen any other value for the sake of the example.

With standard replication, as indicated under (2), the 128 MB block directly corresponds to the storage layout on the DataNode. For each 128 MB block in the original file, HDFS creates three copies, called *replicas*, which we denominate with n, n', and n'' for the first, second, and third replica, respectively.

With erasure coding, as shown in (1), the storage layout vastly differs, but the Name-Node still manages the file content in units of the block size on a logical level, which is why the 128 MB block in erasure coding is referred to as a *logical block*.

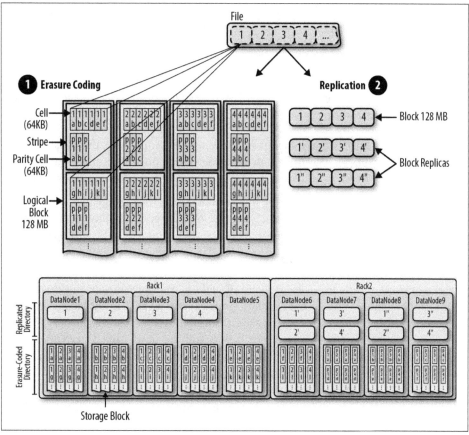

Figure 3-4. Erasure coding and replication at a glance

In (1), note that erasure coding splits the file into small chunks of 1 MB of data, called *cells*. For each six cells that are read from the file, HDFS computes three parity cells, which together form a *stripe*. The next stripe is then generated from the next six cells in the original file. This process happens for all logical 128 MB blocks.

The first 128 MB in the file, i.e., logical block 1, thus consists of a contiguous range of stripes. The first stripe is made up of cells 1a–1f with parity cells p1a–p1c, the second stripe includes cells 1g–1l with parity cells p1d–p1f, and so on, until all 128 MB are completely striped. Likewise, logical block 2 consists of a range of stripes, the first of which contains cells 2a–2f with parity cells p2a–p2c; the second stripe of cells 2g–2l with parity cells p2d–p2f, and so on until logical block 2 is completely striped. The illustration goes on to indicate the same process for logical blocks 3 and 4.

The nomenclature around *logical blocks*, *stripes*, and *storage blocks* is HDFS-specific, and even within the HDFS community alternative terms are used for these concepts.

Before we look at how the logical layout is physically distributed, let us note the following intuitive observations:

- The erasure-coded storage layout is much more complicated than just copying blocks into replicas. We must calculate the parity information for each stripe. The encoding of parity information in Reed–Solomon is compute-intensive.

- On the other hand, for any stripe in erasure coding, the storage overhead is only 50%: six blocks, for example 1a–1f, require only three parity blocks, for example p1a–p1c. Hence, the total overhead of all stripes in a block is also just 50%.

- Replication requires an overhead of 200%: block 1 is replicated to 1' and 1''.

The erasure-coded cells in each stripe are placed on all DataNodes in the cluster in a *round-robin* fashion. In fact, this distribution is exactly what striping means and why the group of nine cells is called a stripe. Our example is the most simplistic: there are nine cells in a stripe (including parity cells), and we have nine DataNodes. This means that each DataNode will hold exactly one cell of each stripe, as shown in the illustration. Cells 1a, 1g, 2a, 2g, and so on reside on DataNode1. Cells 1b, 1h, 2b, 2h, and so on reside on DataNode2. The last cell in all stripes is always placed on Data-Node6. The parity blocks of all stripes are placed on DataNodes 7–9, accordingly. It should be apparent that nine is therefore also the minimum number for DataNodes to tolerate three DataNode failures, as the 6,3 erasure coding scheme advertises.

While the cells in a logical block are striped across DataNodes, many of them naturally end up on the same DataNode. These cells are stored together and form a contiguous *storage block*. In our example, there is a storage block for logical block 1 on DataNode1, starting with cells 1a and 1g and a storage block for logical block 2 on DataNode3, which starts with cells 2c and 2i. With the changes introduced around erasure coding in Hadoop 3.0, the storage block is used as an index in the Name-Node's block map and points the client to the DataNode on which the required cell is stored.

With replication, the blocks are, in turn, placed on the set of available DataNodes as a whole. The standard block placement policy in HDFS places a block on a DataNode, identifies a DataNode in a different rack for the second replica, and uses another randomly chosen DataNode in the second rack for the third replica.

How Are Blocks Distributed Again?

The placement of blocks when using replication is determined entirely by the Name-Node. When a client writes a file into HDFS, it queries the NameNode for the block locations it should use. However, if the client resides on a DataNode, the NameNode, in an attempt to optimize for locality, chooses that DataNode as the location of the first replica of each block written.

You can test this by running the following simple commands on either a DataNode or a gateway host:

```
dd if=/dev/zero of=./640MB bs=1M count=640
hdfs dfs -put 640MB
hdfs fsck /user/<your user>/640MB -files -blocks -locations
```

When executing these commands on the DataNode, the first replica of all five blocks will reside on the same node and the second and the third replicas of all five blocks will reside on two additional hosts.

When executing these commands on a host that is not a DataNode, all five blocks and their replicas will be distributed across the set of DataNodes in round-robin fashion or in available space, depending which block placement policy is configured.

A few more observations:

- HDFS can direct applications to run their work directly on DataNodes that hold the blocks of the file in question. This well-known feature is called *block locality*. With erasure coding, this feature is lost, since the logical blocks are striped across DataNodes.

- As you can see with cell 1f, cells from a given stripe can be distributed across racks. This means that even reading a single logical block from a file has a high likelihood to entail cross-rack traffic, if your cluster is implemented across racks.

 With two racks, a single failure of a whole rack means data loss. To tolerate as many rack fails as can be compensated in a Reed–Solomon stripe, you would actually have to run on nine racks, which is not feasible for initial adopters with small to medium clusters. However, in "Rack Awareness and Rack Failures" on page 165, we discuss how to minimize the likelihood of rack failure by using standard mechanisms available to most enterprise IT organizations.

- When a client is reading an erasure-coded block of an HDFS file, many DataNodes at once participate in sending data to the client. Several DataNodes sending data to a single client at once can yield a significant speedup for reads. In contrast, when a client reads a replicated block, only a single thread on a single DataNode delivers its content to the client.

We now know the most important concepts regarding how erasure coding functions in the cluster, but we have not looked at the motivation behind some of the design decisions. The Cloudera blog post "Introduction to HDFS Erasure Coding in Apache Hadoop" (*http://bit.ly/2S2QHyM*) offers more background on the implementation details and the reasoning behind them.

Here, we move on to discuss the ramifications of erasure coding for your uses cases and cluster planning.

Discussion

HDFS erasure coding is useful for a range of use cases, but others are better served by replication. This also holds true for any other large-scale enterprise storage systems outside of the HDFS context.

This may sound like a typical "it depends" answer, but it actually does depend, and we give you the specifics in the following sections.

Network performance

This is the most relevant criterion when contemplating erasure coding in HDFS. Due to the cross-rack distribution of cells we just noted, cross-rack network bandwidth for reads becomes a key design factor for erasure-coded areas in HDFS. Typically, cross-rack transfers take longer than those of the rack-local cells.

You can compensate for this simply with faster cross-rack connections. To put it concisely, 10 Gbps of intra-rack bandwidth can be seen as a practical minimum requirement for erasure coding. If you aim to maintain the performance characteristics of replication, 20 Gbps via port trunking is recommended, and likewise cross-rack bandwidth oversubscription should be as small as possible, ideally not greater than 1:1.5.

 As you have undoubtedly noticed, the discussion around erasure coding requires a fair amount of knowledge of how Hadoop uses the network, and especially about network *oversubscription*, all of which we introduce in Chapter 4.

On large clusters, this could be cost-prohibitive and may quickly negate the savings that are generated by the reduction of disk space.

On the other hand, the release of HDFS erasure coding roughly coincides in timing with the first waves of 40 Gb Ethernet adoption in many enterprise datacenters. For some organizations that are already firm adopters of Hadoop, this may be a good opportunity to rethink scale-out enterprise storage.

Write performance

The next key factor to consider is write performance. Creating parity information with Reed–Solomon requires a significant amount of compute power. This can make the CPU a bottleneck in the write path, which negatively impacts write performance compared to replication.

 From a networking perspective, erasure coding actually relaxes the write path. Replication always writes 200% of all data to remote racks, but erasure coding only transfers, at most, 150% of net data to remote racks.

The key influence on local write performance in erasure coding is the software library that is used for generating the parity information, which is referred to as the *coder*. Currently, two coders exist in the context of HDFS erasure coding:

Java coder

   The standard Java encoder is quite demanding, in terms of CPU consumption. For most scenarios the CPU will become a bottleneck when using this coder, and thus, despite parallel communication, with many DataNodes up to 15% performance degradation has been observed[7] in tests with this coder, compared to replication. Its main purpose now is actually testing.

ISA-L coder

   This coder uses the Intel ISA library (*https://github.com/01org/isa-l/*), which provides assembly-level code optimization for a variety of storage and encryption-related functions. With the ISA-L SIMD optimizations[8] for the required matrix operations, the CPU of the client is not a bottleneck when stripes are encoded and it can fully benefit from the performance gains that are yielded when writing to multiple DataNodes in parallel. This makes it possible to achieve up to an 80% performance increase[9] compared to replication with this coder. Because of the round-robin striping, write performance may still be degraded compared to

---

7 Rui Li et al., "Progress Report: Bringing Erasure Coding to Apache Hadoop," (*http://bit.ly/2BogKej*) Cloudera Engineering Blog, February 3, 2016.

8 Greg Tucker, "Storage Acceleration with ISA-L," (*http://bit.ly/2QXwEBJ*) Intel, 2017.

9 Rui Li et al., "Progress Report: Bringing Erasure Coding to Apache Hadoop" (*http://bit.ly/2BogKej*).

replication, if the network turns out to be a bottleneck. The ISA-L coder is the default coder in relevant Hadoop distributions.

Locality optimization

Since block locality is not available, some workloads may suffer performance impacts. This, of course, depends on the aforementioned factor of network performance, but also on the profile of the cluster's workload in general:

- There are certain workloads that rely strongly on locality, such as certain Hive and Impala queries. For these types of workloads, erasure coding may actually impose a performance penalty.

- Because of the striped block layout, some functions in the HDFS API, such as append() or hflush(), become very difficult to implement, which is why they are not available in the initial release of HDFS erasure coding. The work to improve this is documented under HDFS-11348 (*http://bit.ly/2Fy4VX9*).

Some Hadoop query systems depend on append() and hflush(). For example, the HBase write-ahead log uses hflush(). Thus, it is currently not possible to run HBase on top of erasure coding.

There is an effort in the open source community to compensate for the missing locality features of erasure coding, which is also documented as a JIRA under HDFS-8030 (*http://bit.ly/2KmyY2t*).

Read performance

Unlike with write performance, the coder is less relevant in this scenario, since the data merely needs to be reassembled and no actual decoding work is required. Only when cells are missing in a stripe during read requests does the client depend on the coder to perform online recovery. In both cases, the client loads cells in a stripe from many disks on many DataNodes in parallel, which can increase read performance by several hundred percent compared to replication. But this only works when the aggregate bandwidth of the disks in question is not already fully saturated and, as we covered, requires that network performance is not a bottleneck.

Recovery can happen online, i.e., when the client discovers missing cells during read, or offline, i.e., when the DataNodes discover bad cells outside of serving read operations.

Also bear in mind that, with erasure coding, there is only one real copy of the data to read from. When dealing with datasets that are read by many clients at once, replication helps to avoid hotspotting.

However, rebuilding lost cells is more complicated and more CPU-intensive than re-replicating a lost block, which may affect read performance significantly compared to replication.

Guidance

Erasure coding makes HDFS a much more versatile option for large-scale distributed storage in the enterprise context. Organizations that have previously been cautious about HDFS replication as a strategy for enterprise storage can look to it as a path toward more efficiency. As with any scale-out storage system, though, there is a price tag attached to it, in the form of added performance requirements in the network.

Table 3-1 attempts a comparison between replication and erasure coding.

Table 3-1. Erasure coding and replication

	Erasure coding (RS-6-3)	Replication (3n)
Write performance	• Depending on network topology, significant performance increase compared to replication when using ISA-L coder. • Performance degradation with standard Java coder.	Full speed of current replica (typically disk-bound).
Read performance	Depending on network topology, significant increase in read throughput.	Full speed of current replica (typically disk-bound).
Storage requirement	1.5n	3n
Locality optimization	Currently none. Performance of certain queries is degraded compared to replication.	Locality can be fully leveraged by execution frameworks.
Durability	Tolerates failure of up to three DataNodes/disks.	Tolerates failure of up to two DataNodes/disks.
Recovery impact on throughput (two DataNodes failing)	• 25% degradation of read throughput with ISA-L coder. • 60% (or more) throughput degradation with Java coder.	No impact.

Champions of Hadoop can take erasure coding as a quick win for storage efficiency for a variety of use cases. Erasure coding is often recommended for archival use cases due to the missing block locality and the overhead in the write path, but it is important to differentiate and to note that the challenges with erasure coding in distributed systems—especially those around network bandwidth—are universal. Some appliances, such as EMC Isilon, deal with this challenge by incorporating a dedicated backbone network for the distribution of data. Other challenges around compute requirements for the write and rebuild functions are met by enterprise storage appliances via an optimized combination of software and hardware.

With HDFS erasure coding, it is up to you, the Hadoop architect or Hadoop engineer, to create the right infrastructure for it—and this, again, depends on your use cases. It is hard to get definitive decision criteria, but we when we decided to write a book around Hadoop in enterprise IT, we pledged to be as descriptive as possible in our guidance. Thus, you can use the flowchart in Figure 3-5 as a decision methodology around the current state of erasure coding and replication in HDFS. The thresholds in this flowchart are debatable and don't appropriately address each and every use case or datacenter infrastructure setting, but you may use it as a checklist to help define your decision making.

It is good practice to test the same workload in both modes, and that is easy since it only involves a simple temporary copy of the data from a replicated directory to an erasure-coded directory and vice versa.

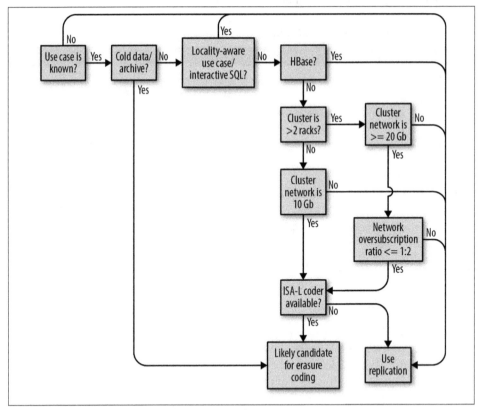

Figure 3-5. Deciding when to use erasure coding

As you can see, the main criterion is the use case itself. Archived and cold data—i.e., any datasets where higher retrieval latencies are tolerable—are almost always a good fit for erasure coding. Some use cases that depend heavily on locality[10] should most likely remain in replicated areas of HDFS.

For everything else, take into account your infrastructure as indicated by the flow-chart. Do you have the budget and organizational backing to implement a fast, non-blocking cluster network? This obviously depends on the size of your cluster. It is relatively easy to provide very fast networking across one or two racks, simply by using a single large switch. The adoption of 40 Gb Ethernet and the time when your network team intends to support it as a production standard both play an obvious role here, as well. 40 Gb Ethernet and low cross-rack oversubscription ratios may bring you into the efficiency zone, even for a complete multirack cluster.

Finally, make sure you take advantage of hardware optimizations via the ISA-L library, if at all possible.

Erasure coding is generally very good news for the Hadoop practitioner, since it is not mutually exclusive with replication and you can run both in parallel on a per–use case basis. We strongly recommend testing both alternatives for a given use case on the same cluster before moving it to production.

Even though erasure coding sounds intriguing as an advanced technology, in many cases you may simply be better off with replication. Taking all things into account, the additional storage requirements of replication often are quite tolerable, especially since HDD and flash memory prices continue to decline. Replication is also undoubt-edly less CPU-intensive for the write path and for rebuild operations.

Low-Level Storage

Hadoop storage does not end at the operating system level or when deciding on era-sure coding versus replication. In order to build performant distributed storage, you also need to be quite knowledgeable about the hardware layers below Linux. These include the storage controller and the various options for disk storage.

Storage Controllers

Much mystery has surrounded the choice of storage controllers for Hadoop DataNodes ever since the Hadoop platform hit enterprise computing. Hadoop is designed to tolerate component failure and hence does not require any additional logic on behalf of the storage controller. It is merely required for the storage control-ler to present the individual devices to the operating system, which is commonly

---

10 See Rui Li et al., "Progress Report: Bringing Erasure Coding to Apache Hadoop" (*http://bit.ly/2BogKej*).

known as a *just a bunch of disks* (JBOD) array. However, as enterprises mostly procure their hardware assets from established server vendors, many server vendors actually had to deliberately unlock the JBOD feature in their storage controllers to fulfill this requirement. In many cases, where JBOD was not available, Hadoop clusters have been deployed on a range of single-disk *redundant array of independent disks* (RAID) 0 volumes.

RAID?

Indeed, the use of RAID (*http://bit.ly/2A852CK*), in most cases, is highly inefficient for Hadoop. It may appear that there is no merit to a discussion of RAID versus raw disk setups, but it provides us with several interesting observations about HDFS's capabilities when handling errors versus the error handling in storage arrays, which we use when we discuss private cloud environments.

All Hadoop storage systems are capable of managing the failure of disk drives. The required resilience level can be managed centrally and can be overridden for each storage artifact, such as a directory or a file in HDFS or a topic in Kafka.

Let us compare standard HDFS replication to a RAID scenario in a cluster. By default, all blocks are replicated three times. This guarantees that data is available, as long as no more than two disks in the cluster suffer failure at the same instant:

- In this scenario, if one or two disks fail on a worker node, the missing blocks are immediately reconstructed from other replicas in the cluster. This process occurs swiftly and does not even have to involve the node on which the disk failure occurred (it may be down). Due to the block distribution, there is a high chance that many other worker nodes contribute to it.

- If more than two disks fail at the same instant, blocks may be lost. The probability of this is influenced by the total number of blocks and the number of disks in the cluster. Even then, the node can still service blocks that it stores on the non-faulty disks.

- During and after a successful rebuild of replicas, the worker nodes can continue with their normal operation, even if several of their disks fail at once. And when the worker nodes no longer hold a certain block locally, they may still be chosen to contribute their compute capacity for tasks in the Hadoop cluster and process block content, which they read remotely from other worker nodes.

Conversely, when considering large arrays of between 12 and 24 disks configured as a RAID-6 array:

- If one or two disks fail on a worker node, the missing blocks can get reconstructed only if a sufficient amount of hot-spare disks are present in the array or after the faulty disks are replaced. The rebuild can only happen locally on the same node. If the node is unavailable (it may be down), the rebuild must wait until the node becomes available again. The rebuild itself will take a lot of time, since it happens locally on the node.

- If more than two disks fail in the RAID-6 scenario, data is definitely lost and the node can no longer service any blocks.

- The amount of traffic that is incurred by the rebuild will make it unlikely to perform adequately in HDFS. If push comes to shove and the rebuild is done offline, the NameNode may decide to replicate the missing blocks on other locations.

Controller cache

When server infrastructure is purchased for Hadoop, a frequent question is whether hardware caches on enterprise-grade RAID controllers are required. Although not required, their usage can, in fact, prove to be of significant benefit for overall storage performance.

Read-ahead caching.   Many storage controllers and disk devices alike use an adaptive read-ahead algorithm, which detects sequential disk accesses. In addition, certain storage controllers are able to detect this even if the overall workload stems from different operating system threads. The rationale of these firmware-based algorithms is that, when there are sequential accesses, there will be more sequential accesses at successive addresses. The controller thus lifts that data in anticipation of the following read requests into its cache. This significantly reduces request latency, since the OS's I/O request can now be fulfilled in microseconds rather than in milliseconds. Because many workloads in Hadoop, such as database scans or text search, feature fairly sequential access patterns, hardware read caching typically proves to be very beneficial.

Write-back caching.   When write requests arrive at the controller, without write-back caching it needs to locate the target device and wait until the device confirms that the data has been written before it returns the call to the operating system.

Conversely, if the controller uses write-back caching, the overall performance will improve:

- Write requests from the operating system will be posted to the cache memory, which is significantly faster than spinning media. The posted request will return to the operating system immediately, which minimizes I/O latency in the user program.

- Typically, the cache quickly fills up with written data. The controller continuously analyzes the contents for adjacent addresses on-disk and waits until it can rearrange the order of requests (i.e., merge requests that write into adjacent logical disk blocks) so that the head movement of the underlying disk devices is reduced.

- Read requests to hotspots (i.e., areas of storage that are accessed often) benefit from the resident data in the cache, since it will be returned almost immediately from high-speed cache memory.

Guidelines

In general, the read cache on storage controllers should be enabled. It is important to understand, though, that the contents of the cache are lost in the case of a server-level failure or loss of power. Anything that has not been committed to disk at this point will be lost, which is why most enterprise-level controllers feature a battery that will refresh the cache's DRAM for an extended period of time (typically more than 24 hours). Apart from the discussion on hardware caches, you will recall from our discussion on filesystems and the page cache that OS-level caches are equally volatile. Although it is possible to explicitly instruct the OS to write the cache contents to the physical disk via `fsync()` and `fflush()`, the controller may not pass on the corresponding SCSI synchronization commands to the disks, which is why the on-disk write cache should always be disabled when the disks are operated behind a battery-backed cache. If the controller does not support pure JBOD, each individual disk should be configured as a one-disk RAID-0 array. In the case when a multitude of RAID-0 arrays must be configured, it is advisable to experiment with the arrays' stripe size to optimize throughput. Also make sure to review the various storage options covered in Chapter 14.

Disk Layer

Even though most workloads in Hadoop prove to be compute-bound, the choice of physical storage media can have a significant impact on the Hadoop cluster's performance. Typically, as an architect or engineer, you may not be consulted about disks at all when a new service is implemented, but if you are involved in the component selection process, you have a chance to change the cluster's performance for the better by making intelligent choices about the disks.

For most Hadoop clusters, sheer throughput is imperative (also see "Workload Profiles" on page 96). And you will probably want to design your worker nodes to contain more disks before you optimize the individual device. For an individual device, higher rotational speed, which results in shorter seek times, is the more decisive factor than theoretical throughput, though.

A common question we get from customers is, "Can a single disk really deliver 200 MB/s?" Yes, it can, but these values are based on a completely idealistic access pattern, often found in disk microbenchmarks. The values serve to establish a baseline for throughput capabilities. A clean baseline of best-case performance is important before you consider advanced tests and disk access patterns (though disk access patterns are more sequential in Hadoop than in most other enterprise workloads). You can find more details about testing your Hadoop cluster in Chapter 8.

Table 3-2 shows a few key characteristics of various drive types. The values are averages based on the specification across multiple vendors.

Table 3-2. Characteristics of different hard disk drive types

Drive type (rotational speed, interface)	Sustained max. throughput rate (MB/s)	Access time (ms)	Capacity range
3.5 in, 7200 RPM, SAS	140–250	10.6–16.4	1–10 TB
3.5 in, 7200 RPM, SATA	140–250	10.6–16.4	1–10 TB
2.5 in, 10K RPM, SAS	224–247	6.6–6.8	300 GB–1.8 TB
2.5 in, 15K RPM, SAS	233–271	4.8–5	300 GB–600 GB
2.5 in, 7,2K RPM, SAS/SATA	136	10,6–16,4	1 TB–2 TB

SAS, Nearline SAS, or SATA (or SSDs)?

Until recently, the realm of enterprise versus consumer disks was neatly separated via SAS versus SATA drives. SAS is traditionally the more enterprise-targeted option— more durable and also more costly—and SATA is traditionally targeted for consumer devices.

For a number of reasons, most disk vendors today also include SATA drives in their enterprise lines. There are many features that hard disk vendors can employ to make a disk more resilient to failure. Some of those depend on the choice of SAS versus SATA, but most don't.[11] Here are a few examples:[12]

- Hard disks can be designed with a higher maximum operating temperature. Entry-level drives usually cannot exceed operating conditions of more than 40°C, whereas enterprise-grade drives can operate at up to 60°C.

- Command queue depths can significantly differ. SAS allows for up to 216 commands to be queued and reordered, and SATA allows up to 32 commands.

- There are many options in internal mechanical design, such as vibration compensation, dual or single anchoring of the disk spindle, actuator magnet sizing, and more, that influence performance, error rates, and durability. None of these are tied to the storage interface.

---

11 See Unix & Linux Stack Exchange, "In what sense does SATA "talk" SCSI?" (*http://bit.ly/2qTNs18*).

12 See "Comparing SAS and SATA, Enterprise and Desktop Hard Drives for Server RAID Systems" (*https://intel.ly/2PI566W*), Intel Support.

- SAS allows for dual connectors, such that a single drive can fail over to another controller if the initial controller becomes unavailable.

- Disk quality is further distinguished by the amount of electronics, e.g., to control actuators and the data path via separate processors, and the amount of internal integrity checks that are performed. This is not related to the storage interface.

- The spindle motor may or may not allow for high RPMs (i.e., beyond 7,200). Typically, these speeds are only available for SAS drives.

Instead of the traditional segmentation into consumer and enterprise disks, hard disk vendors have changed their portfolios to address use cases, such as high-performance/low-latency database workloads versus big-data/volume versus hot-archive for the enterprise segment of the market, and backup use cases or high performance in the consumer-centric sector. All of the itemized points are considered when hard disk vendors target either segment of their market. In simple terms, this signifies low cost versus high value, and now SATA is also present in the enterprise segment to address volume-centric use cases. Often the term *Nearline SAS* (NL-SAS) emerges in this discussion. Though not necessarily dominant in the nomenclature of all disk vendors, NL-SAS denotes a disk drive that implements the full SAS command set, but which mechanically consists mostly of components that would only be used in standard SATA drives.

SAS also still generally coincides with higher cost, typically by a factor of 1.5–2x, as outlined earlier.

Ultimately, the choice of hard drive depends on your use case and total cost of ownership, which would also include service time for disks. That said, in the section "RAID?" on page 82, we noted that Hadoop is quite resilient to losing disks. In HDFS, you can configure the number of disks that are allowed to fail per DataNode before the entire DataNode is taken out of service. Even if that happens, HDFS will still automatically recreate the lost block replicas. Thus, you may deliberately decide to opt for less-resilient disks (though it is best practice to leave enough headroom in HDFS to cover for lost capacity when blocks are re-replicated after failures via HDFS quotas).

Solid-State Drives (SSDs)?

Occasionally, architects or engineers ask why they shouldn't use SSDs for Hadoop. SSDs can be several categories faster than spinning disks, but not significantly so for sequential access, and Hadoop applications and storage systems access storage in a fairly sequential way. This is due to the applications themselves, as well as to the large block sizes of storage systems such as HDFS.

Furthermore, when you want to storage large volumes of data, SSDs become cost-prohibitive. There are some models that exceed 3 TB in size, but they also exceed the price of a 3 TB HDD by a factor of more than 15, so it is generally safe to say that scaling Hadoop storage with SSDs is still cost-prohibitive today. Large SSD drives also have decreased durability—although a 400 GB SSD drive can sustain up to 25 daily full writes per device (DWPDs), the top-capacity models can only sustain up to 3 DWPDs.

Disk sizes

With available disk sizes of 10 TB (at the time of this writing), you may wonder whether there is too much capacity on a disk. This is a plausible question for two reasons:

- Disk capacity for newer disk generations increases more quickly than possible throughput. For search or scan-heavy use cases, the amount of data that needs to be accessed will, therefore, grow more while single disk performance stays more or less constant, which ultimately results in reduced scan performance.

- Disk failures take longer to recover. As covered in "RAID?" on page 82, we know that HDFS is very efficient at restoring lost block replicas, but you should consider best- and worst-case scenarios for the loss of a disk drive, which is influenced by the number of DataNodes/disks, available network bandwidth, and overall cluster load. For example, a very small cluster with five DataNodes with twelve 6 TB drives each, which is connected via 1 Gb Ethernet, may actually struggle to keep up with acceptable recovery objectives.

Disk cache

Just like storage controllers feature a cache, all modern hard disk drives have a hardware cache, typically between 32 MB and 256 MB in size. Considering the amount that can be cached on a disk device and the amount of storage in the higher-level caches in the storage controller or the OS, there will typically be only very few direct cache hits on the disk cache's read path. The disk cache is still tremendously helpful in opportunistically prefetching data from the disk, though, and typically does so without adding cost in time to other pending storage requests. Due to these benefits and since there are no concerns about data durability, the read cache is always enabled on modern disk drives.

When the disk's write-back cache is enabled, the disk device is able to post a request to the cache and return to the calling entity immediately, which reduces latency. When the write portion of the disk's cache is filled up, the disk drive will *destage* cache content—i.e., write it to physical media. The disk's I/O scheduler can typically operate very efficiently when destaging writes from the disk cache, since the scheduler can choose from many more options when sorting and rearranging I/O requests into a more ideal, more sequential order. Further information on the principles of hard disk operation can be found in Bruce Jacob et al.'s book *Memory Systems: Cache, DRAM, Disk* (Morgan Kaufmann).

Despite its benefits, there is some conventional wisdom in the IT industry that says to not use the on-disk cache for buffering write operations, especially for database workloads. Due to Hadoop's distributed nature, you can generally rely on the following:

- Running write pipelines for HDFS file data begin shipping data to replica locations immediately, regardless of explicit consistency operations. However, you do not have a guarantee that they are finished without explicitly using consistency operations.

- When consistency operations are used, they will return only if the data has been fully replicated. In the case of hsync(), this ensures that all data actually resides on all disks of the identified replicas (assuming proper filesystem behavior). In the case of hflush(), it is ensured that all data has at least been transferred to the identified replica nodes' RAM.

- When one or more DataNodes fail during a consistency operation, the operation will fail on the client, enabling the client to appropriately handle the error.

Data loss or inconsistency occurs only if all of the corresponding replica disks/ DataNodes suffer a catastrophic error. To summarize the discussion on hardware caches in the I/O subsystem, let us take a brief look at how they affect performance. We omit latency and input/output operations per second (IOPS) and focus on throughput.

The listings that follow show a simple, idealistic experiment for testing throughput under Linux, running with the hard disk cache enabled and disabled. Note that the impact on throughput is significant. The traffic pattern inflicted by using the dd tool, as follows, is by no means realistic in that it is purely sequential, but it serves to establish a baseline for most Hadoop workloads and access patterns (which are largely sequential):

```
root@linux:~# hdparm -W1 /dev/sdb1
 /dev/sdb1:
  setting drive write-caching to 1 (on)
  write-caching   1 (on)
root@linux:~# dd if=/dev/zero of=/mnt/dd-run bs=1024K /
                count=1024 oflag=direct conv=fdatasync
1024+0 records in
1024+0 records out
1073741824 bytes (1.1 GB, 1.0 GiB) copied, 9.58533 s, 112 MB/s

root@linux:~# hdparm -W0 /dev/sdb1
 /dev/sdb1:
  setting drive write-caching to 0 (off)
```

```
write-caching    0 (off)
root@linux:~# dd if=/dev/zero of=/mnt/dd-run bs=1024K /
                count=1024 oflag=direct conv=fdatasync
1024+0 records in
1024+0 records out
1073741824 bytes (1.1 GB, 1.0 GiB) copied, 18.1312 s, 59.2 MB/s
```

We now extend these measurements to include the cache of the storage controller, which sits in front of 12 SATA drives. Figures 3-6 and 3-7 show various measurements based on concurrent runs of dd on each disk. The measurements vary in cache settings and total transfer size to show how increasing transfer sizes impact the benefit of the cache.

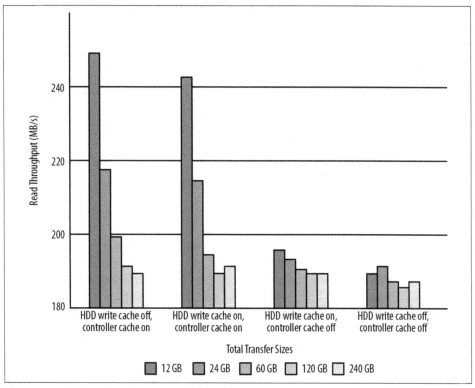

Figure 3-6. Effect of caches on read throughput

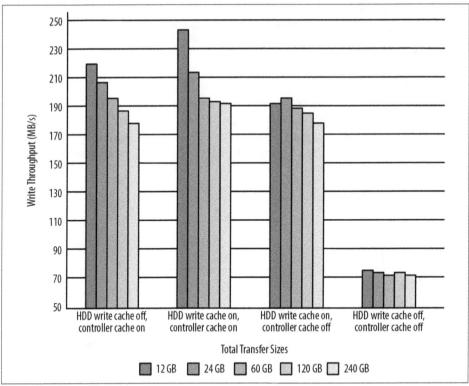

Figure 3-7. Effect of caches on write throughput

We can see that running with both the controller and hard disk write caches enabled, read throughput is actually slightly less than when using the controller's cache only. This can be attributed to the strictly sequential access pattern and the twofold prefetching and the additional hop that the data takes through both caches. Writes benefit most with both caches enabled, since it allows them to be posted. Running only with the disk write cache yields slightly worse performance than the two options involving the controller cache for both reads and writes. When not using any write caching, write throughput drops to less than half.

> Running with the disk write cache and the controller cache enabled poses a risk to data durability, since many hardware RAID implementations do not pass the SCSI SYNCHRONIZE CACHE command down to the disks, which can effectively break the semantics of the fsync() system call.

In summary, we highly advise that you try to leverage hardware caches at some point in the I/O subsystem. If you trust consistency operations, such as hflush() and hsync(), in your applications, you can rely on disk caches to gain additional performance, as long as you do not enable both controller and disk caches in conjunction. If you cannot rely just on those consistency operations, you should not use disk caches, since they are not battery-backed. You should invest in the controller having a significant amount of battery-backed cache.

Server Form Factors

Now that we know how the individual layers of hardware and software in a Hadoop server work together, we review which server form factors are available to implement Hadoop clusters. We focus on standard 19-inch rack-mount (*http://bit.ly/2qZJdkK*) architectures, which is the predominant form factor in most datacenters today. Other standards such as Open Compute (*http://opencompute.org/*), which are motivated by large Web 2.0 content providers (especially Facebook), propose alternatives but are typically not relevant to enterprise IT.

A central part of this discussion is the *rack unit* (*http://bit.ly/2PLSoEh*), which is a measure of the server enclosure's *height*. A 19-inch rack is between 40 and 42 rack units high and the server form factors simply differ in how many rack units they use; width and depth are common among all enclosure types. Rack units are abbreviated with the letter *U*.

We evaluate several rack-mount form factors based on the following characteristics:

CPU density
> Expressed via the normalization (CPU cores x (GHz/core)) / rack unit, similar to Amazon's ECU metric (*https://amzn.to/2PJRVSE*)

Memory density
> The amount of GB per rack unit for RAM

Storage density
> The capability of raw storage in TiB/U

Storage I/O density
> The capability of local storage I/O throughput per rack unit in MB/s (max)

Network I/O density
> The capability of I/O throughput per rack unit

Software license efficiency
> The amount of software licenses per CPU (lower values are better, obviously)

1U servers can provide high compute density by making two CPU sockets available per rack unit. If you have a sufficient amount of network ports in a single rack and if power and cooling budgets allow, it is possible to build very dense and performant medium-sized Hadoop environments within a single rack with the 1U form factor. As depicted in Figure 3-8, a 1U server can package up to 10 front-accessible 2.5" HDDs, allowing for a good balance between compute and storage bandwidth. The HDD front section is followed by a series of fan packs, behind which the processor and RAM are located, allowing up to 12 memory modules per processor with most vendors.

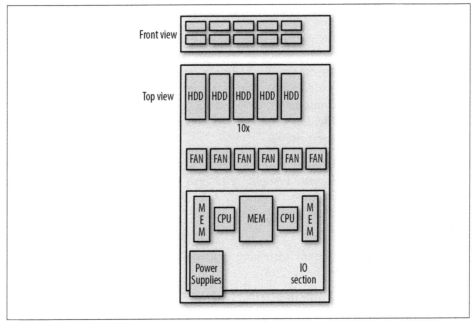

Figure 3-8. 1U form factor

2U servers have evolved into the most widely used form factor for enterprise Hadoop deployments. As shown in Figure 3-9, most models can accommodate 12 3.5" hard disks and thereby combine high storage density and bandwidth with adequate memory and compute density for most applications. 2U servers are typically shipped with two CPU sockets and allow for 12 memory modules per CPU, like 1U servers. A few models exist that are able to fit four CPUs and double the amount of memory into a single 2U enclosure while maintaining the same I/O density and storage density. However, like with dense 1U systems, such density may not be easily scalable due to power and cooling budgets in your datacenter.

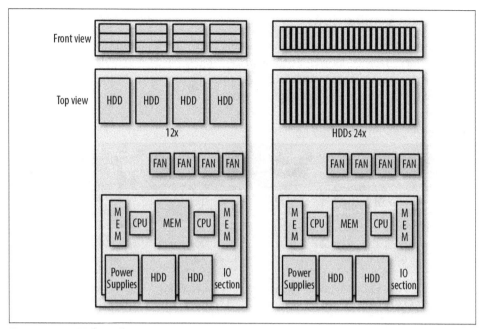

Figure 3-9. 2U form factor

4U servers are typically used for large SMP systems. They typically hold four CPU sockets, but they provide only relatively small amounts of storage capacity and throughput. Since the CPUs in 4U servers are typically the most powerful in the chip vendor's portfolio, the fan packs used for cooling often use up a lot of server front space, which reduces the available space for front-accessible disk drives. Certain implementations allow an HDD capacity of up to 24 in this form factor, but they are quite rare.

In certain applications of Hadoop, storage density and high storage I/O are not required. If that is the case, the 4U form factor might be used to provide better efficiency of software licensing, since most Hadoop distributions are licensed per node. A downside of 4U servers in the case of Hadoop is often network connectivity. A 2U system is typically connected via a dual-port 10 Gb Ethernet adapter, yielding one 10 GbE port for one CPU. To achieve the same ratio on a 4U system, you will likely be required to purchase additional network adapters but may potentially deviate from the production standards of your network department when using four instead of two ports per system.

In addition, it must be considered that CPUs that support four-socket SMP setups are significantly more expensive than two-socket alternatives.

Form Factor Comparison

This section compares a number of applicable hardware configurations amongst the discussed form factors, as well as their price ranges, based on publicly available list prices across various server vendors. Server form factors are differentiated mostly by density of CPU, memory, and storage, as shown in Table 3-3.

Table 3-3. Standard rack-mount form factors

Form factor	CPU density	Memory density	Storage density (raw TB/U)	Storage I/O density (disks/U)	Network I/O density	License efficiency[a]
1U	Up to 2 x 22 cores © x (2.2 GHz/C) / 1U (**96.8**)	1,536 GB / 1U	Up to 20 TB / 1U	Up to approximately 2,700 MB/s / 1U	Up to 20 Gbps / 1U (practical limit)	0.5
2U	Up to 2 x 22C x 2.2 GHz/C / 2U (**48.4**)	1,536 GB / 1U	Up to 60 TB / 1U	Up to approximately 3,200 MB/s / 1U	up to 10 Gbps / 1U (practical limit)	0.5
4U	up to 4 x 24C x 2.2 GHz/C / 4U (**52.8**)	1,536 GB / 1U	Up to 12 TB / 1U	Up to approximately 1,600 MB/s / 1U	Up to 5 Gbps / 1U (practical limit)	0.25

[a] Lower values are better.

Some additional notes on this data:

- Storage I/O density is based on 2.5" HDDs (not SSDs).
- Storage density values on 2U servers are based on 3.5" HDDs.
- Some 2U servers are available as 4-CPU systems: for example, the HPE ProLiant DL560. The 2U row does not include those models.

Let us next look at some representative example configurations and their pricing. For this, we compiled samples from different hardware vendors for worker node configurations in 1U, 2U, and 4U form factors. For each form factor, a minimal configuration and a real-life configuration are presented in Table 3-4.

The minimal configuration reflects the low end of what can be configured for a given form factor—basically the chassis and the smallest set of compute and storage resources. As implied by its name, the real-life configuration reflects a useful configuration for a Hadoop worker node in that form factor. Note that, in some cases, it is not possible to find exactly the same configuration for a given form factor among multiple vendors.

Table 3-4. Configurations used for price sampling

Configuration	Specifications
1U minimal	1 x 4 core @ 1.8 GHz, 10 MB cache, 8 GB RAM, 1 x 1 TB 2.5" HDD
2U minimal	1 x 4 core @ 1.8 GHz, 10 MB cache, 8 GB RAM, 1 x 1 TB 2.5" HDD
4U minimal	1 x 8 core @ 2 GHz, 20 MB cache, 8 GB RAM, 1 x 1 TB 2.5" HDD
1U real-life	2 x 18 core @ 2.1–2.3 GHz, 45 MB cache, 256 GB RAM, 8 x 1 TB 2.5" HDD
2U real-life	2 x 18 core @ 2.1–2.3 GHz, 45 MB cache, 256 GB RAM, 12 x 8 TB 3.5" HDD
4U real-life	4 x 18 core @ 2.2 GHz, 45 MB cache, 512 GB RAM, 8x–24x 1 TB 2.5" HDD

Figure 3-10 shows the price spans for each configuration, indicating the median of the samples. The image also displays the price differences between the median of the minimal and real-life configurations for each form factor. This price difference reflects approximately how much you invest into pure compute and storage capabilities on top of the pure chassis in a given form factor.

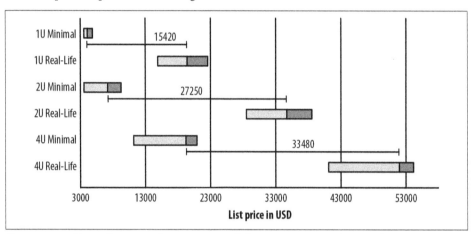

Figure 3-10. Form factor configurations and their price ranges (in USD)

Naturally, the capabilities that are thereby added to the resulting worker node differ depending on the form factor. For example, the 2U servers in Table 3-4, while also upgraded with additional CPU and RAM, would most importantly be enriched with lots of disks to get to the real-life configuration. On the other hand, the 4U form factor would add significantly more compute and RAM and only very few disks for a real-life configuration.

Guidance

If you need a balance of compute and storage, you most likely should choose 2U servers, due to their ability to hold a large amount of 3.5" disks. If you know for certain that the focus in your cluster is on computational capabilities, you may consider

1U or 4U form factors. Since most Hadoop distributors charge licenses on a per-server basis, we have sometimes seen organizations consider 4U servers to achieve advantages on software license efficiency. For example, as shown in Table 3-3, on a 4U server a license can serve four CPUs, but a 2U server typically only serves two CPUs.

Figure 3-10 shows, however, that the investment in a 4U chassis is disproportionately higher than that of a 2U chassis, and we can also see that the cost of adding roughly the same compute and storage capabilities results in a similar increase of cost in both form factors. Whether there really is an advantage to using a 4U chassis in terms of software licensing is therefore likely to be a close call that depends on the actual license price you pay.

The presented data should not be considered reference data, since list prices are short-lived and do not include any discounts. However, the data serves to offer a rough idea of how the cost between form factors varies.

Workload Profiles

Now that you know all about servers and their available form factors, you need to decide which server configuration is best for the use cases that will run on your Hadoop cluster. In this section, we introduce how certain use cases and Hadoop workloads are typically more compute-bound or more I/O-bound. If you know beforehand the workloads your cluster will predominantly run, you can choose your worker nodes more wisely, equipped with the learnings from the previous sections in this book.

Most clusters, especially during initial Hadoop adoption, aim to keep compute and I/O capabilities balanced. Beyond initial adoption, many users run a mixture of use cases that require that this balance be maintained, even though certain use cases are clearly bound by I/O or compute. Other users determine over time that they typically run short of either CPU and/or RAM or I/O for the vast majority of their jobs. This is typically determined via continuous profiling of cluster resources in a third-party hardware monitoring tool, such as Ganglia, Cloudera Manager, or Ambari.

Even though the actual usage pattern is very individual to your specific mix of applications, most can be roughly categorized by their use of the worker node's resources. In Figure 3-11, we plot a range of application categories by their usage of I/O resources, i.e., disk and network, on the x-axis, and compute resources, i.e., CPU and RAM, on the y-axis. Of course, none of the actual metrics on the axes are thought to be precise. However, the plot can give you a head start in understanding how an application will or won't use the resources on your cluster. For example, if you already know that your cluster is hopelessly strained on compute capabilities, adding a heavyweight classification app will certainly add to that strain, but adding a sorting application may not add conflict.

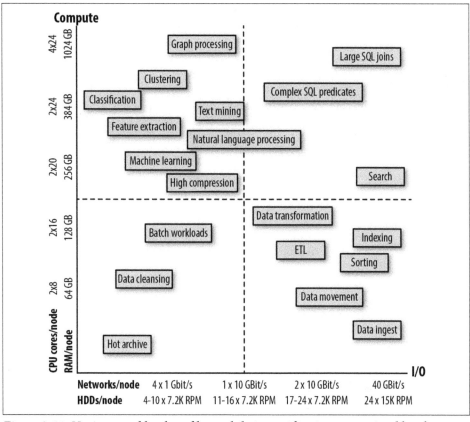

Figure 3-11. Various workload profiles and their ramifications on optimal hardware selection

Cluster Configurations and Node Types

Up to now, we have focused on worker nodes. In this section, we present sample configurations for all the nodes required to build fully fledged Hadoop clusters. We look at configurations for small, medium, and large clusters, all of which are based on the server form factors introduced in the previous section. These configurations will build on a set of *master nodes* that combine various *master roles* of the services, as well as a larger set of *worker nodes* that combine the *worker roles* of services. For example, the HDFS NameNode and the YARN ResourceManager are master roles that run together on the same set of master nodes, while an HBase RegionServer and an HDFS DataNode are worker roles that run together on the same set of worker nodes.

If you are not familiar with the individual roles of these services, refer back to Chapter 1, where we introduce them briefly and provide further pointers.

The cluster configurations will show redundant roles throughout to provide for high availability, a concept which we introduce by example here and cover in much more depth in Chapter 12.

Master Nodes

Master nodes run the roles that control the various Hadoop services, such as:

- HDFS NameNode
- HDFS JournalNode
- HDFS Failover Controller
- YARN ResourceManager
- YARN History Server
- Spark History Server
- HBase Master
- Kudu Master
- Impala StateStore Server
- Sentry server
- ZooKeeper server

In Table 3-5, we recommend using two 450 GB hard disks for the operating system. In Table 3-6, we show the recommended layout for those disks.

Table 3-5. Recommended configuration for master nodes

	Small cluster	Medium cluster	Large cluster
Form factor	1U		
CPU	2x10 core	2x 16 core	
RAM	128 GB	256 GB	384 GB
OS disks	2 x 450 GB		
Data disks	2 x 300 GB		

Table 3-6. Recommended disk layout for OS disks on master nodes

OS disks	Disk 1	Disk 2
Option 1: 450 GB RAID-1/2+	Operating system NameNode metadata Hadoop service data OS log files and Hadoop log files (*/var/log*)	Option 2: 2 x 450 GB, separate disks

It is typical for master nodes to have the operating system installed on a RAID-1 array. If that is not the case, we recommend that you configure the NameNode to store replicas of its metadata on an additional disk drive, which can be conveniently configured in the NameNode's service configuration via the dfs.name.dir setting. Optionally, in that case, we recommend mounting the log directory to the additional disk.

Regarding the layout for data disks, we strongly recommend Option 1 in Table 3-7; i.e., that you store ZooKeeper and HDFS JournalNode data on separate disks. Both of these services are very latency-sensitive, due to the quorum and locking functionality they implement. If you have a strict requirement to leverage RAID to avoid disk-related outages, ensure that the presence of RAID on your controller does not in any way negatively influence latency characteristics.

Table 3-7. Recommended disk layout for data disks on master nodes

Data disks	Disk 1	Disk2
Option 1: 2 x 300 GB, separate disks	ZooKeeper data	JournalNode data
Option 2: 2 x 300 GB, RAID-1	ZooKeeper data JournalNode data	

In an enterprise context, it is typically advisable to procure master nodes with dual power supplies and redundant fan pack configurations.

Worker Nodes

Worker nodes perform the actual heavy lifting in the cluster. They typically implement the following roles:

- HDFS DataNode
- YARN NodeManager
- HBase RegionServer
- Impala daemon
- Solr server
- Kudu Tablet Server
- Kafka broker

The worker node form factor and configuration depend on your use case, as described in "Server Form Factors" on page 91 and "Workload Profiles" on page 96.

Although it is perfectly fine to colocate roles from multiple query or compute systems (e.g., Spark and Impala) on a single worker node, we recommend, as noted in "User Space" on page 58, that you run only one data service (DataNode, Kudu Tablet Server, or Kafka broker) per worker node.

An additional design decision on the worker nodes includes whether to provision the OS disk as RAID-1 to provide additional redundancy, in addition to redundancy of power supplies and fan packs.

Utility Nodes

Utility nodes run the roles that control the various Hadoop services, such as:

- Vendor/distributor-specific management and monitoring tools, such as Cloudera Manager or Apache Ambari
- (Optional) Service databases, MySQL, or PostgreSQL, needed by various Hadoop services to keep internal state and metadata (see also "Service Databases" on page 194 for more details on setting up your service databases)
- (Optional) Kerberos Key Distribution Center (KDC) and Kerberos admin server, if Kerberos is enabled in your cluster
- Hive Metastore server
- Impala Catalog Server
- Oozie server
- Flume agent

In Table 3-8, we recommend providing 1–4 TB of hard disk space, depending on cluster size, optionally protected by RAID-1. The reason for the increased hard disk space is the extensive amount of logging data that the vendor-specific Hadoop management tools typically accumulate.

Table 3-8. Hardware specifications for utility nodes

	Small cluster	Medium cluster	Large cluster
Form factor		1U	
CPU	2 x 8 core	2 x 12 core	2 x 18 core
RAM	128 GB	256 GB	384 GB
OS disks	1-2x 1 TB	1-2 x 4 TB	

Edge Nodes

Edge nodes implement the contact points of the outside world with the cluster and therefore typically run the following roles:

- Hadoop clients, to expose necessary command-line utilities, (typically to power users)
- Hue, to provide a web UI for many common tasks around SQL and HBase queries, Spark applications, HDFS interaction, and more
- HiveServer2, to implement a SQL interface into the cluster
- Custom or third-party software for data ingestion
- A Flume agent, to receive continuous ingest events

Also, edge nodes may be used as a landing zone for data, which is why they might offer additional local storage capacity.

Depending on the size of the cluster, there may be several edge nodes to keep up with the large amounts of incoming data. Thus, the actual hardware configuration of edge nodes widely varies. We recommend a typical configuration range, as shown in Table 3-9.

Table 3-9. Hardware specifications for edge nodes

	Small cluster	Medium cluster	Large cluster
Form factor		1U	
CPU		1 x 8 core – 2 x 16 core	
RAM		64 GB – 196 GB	
OS disks		1–2 x 300 GB	
Data disks		Use case–dependent	

In small cluster configurations, the roles of an edge node may be run on a master node. Alternatively, edge nodes are often colocated with utility nodes.

Small Cluster Configurations

We define a small cluster as not exceeding 20 worker nodes. Small clusters are typically implemented on a single rack, but if Hadoop services are deployed redundantly, it is perfectly feasible to distribute even small clusters on multiple racks. (See Chapter 12 for an in-depth discussion of Hadoop high availability.) Figure 3-12 shows a single-rack cluster. In this example there are three management nodes, of which one also colocates utility and edge cluster roles.

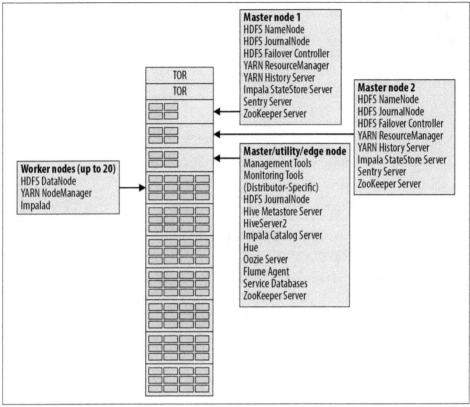

Figure 3-12. Example of a small cluster configuration

Medium Cluster Configurations

Medium cluster sizes do not exceed 200 nodes. Figure 3-13 shows an entry-level, medium-size cluster with two racks. All master nodes are now exclusively dedicated to master roles, and two utility nodes are dedicated to utility roles. Two edge nodes are dedicated to expose the cluster to the outside world. When the amount of worker nodes scales beyond the second rack, you should distribute your third master role to the third rack to optimize redundancy.

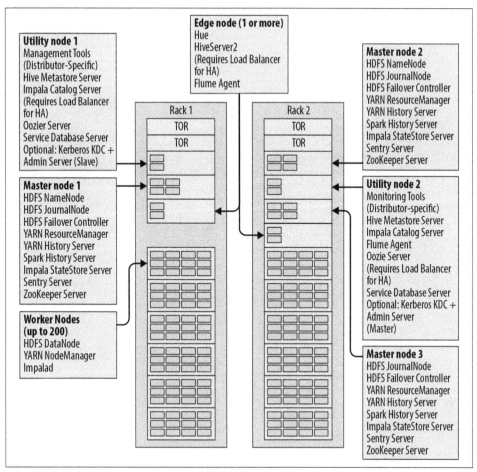

Utility node 1
Management Tools
(Distributor-Specific)
Hive Metastore Server
Impala Catalog Server
(Requires Load Balancer
for HA)
Oozier Server
Service Database Server
Optional: Kerberos KDC +
Admin Server (Slave)

Master node 1
HDFS NameNode
HDFS JournalNode
HDFS Failover Controller
YARN ResourceManager
YARN History Server
Spark History Server
Impala StateStore Server
Sentry Server
ZooKeeper Server

**Worker Nodes
(up to 200)**
HDFS DataNode
YARN NodeManager
Impalad

Edge node (1 or more)
Hue
HiveServer2
(Requires Load Balancer
for HA)
Flume Agent

Rack 1
TOR
TOR

Rack 2
TOR
TOR

Master node 2
HDFS NameNode
HDFS JournalNode
HDFS Failover Controller
YARN ResourceManager
YARN History Server
Spark History Server
Impala StateStore Server
Sentry Server
ZooKeeper Server

Utility node 2
Monitoring Tools
(Distributor-specific)
Hive Metastore Server
Impala Catalog Server
Flume Agent
Oozie Server
(Requires Load Balancer
for HA)
Service Database Server
Optional: Kerberos KDC +
Admin Server
(Master)

Master node 3
HDFS JournalNode
HDFS Failover Controller
YARN ResourceManager
YARN History Server
Spark History Server
Impala StateStore Server
Sentry Server
ZooKeeper Server

Figure 3-13. Example of a medium cluster configuration

Large Cluster Configurations

Large Hadoop clusters can scale up to very high node counts. However, within the scope of enterprise computing today, one rarely encounters node counts beyond 500. Hadoop distribution vendors usually keep a practical limit of scalability in their management technology if higher node counts are attempted. In Figure 3-14, there are five master nodes, each of which runs NameNode, ResourceManager, JournalNode, ZooKeeper Server, and other roles. We recommend that you not exceed a practical limit of five NameNodes so as not to overburden the system with the overhead of HDFS metadata management. Quorum services, such as ZooKeeper or HDFS JournalNodes, should only be deployed in odd numbers, such as three or five, to maintain quorum capability.

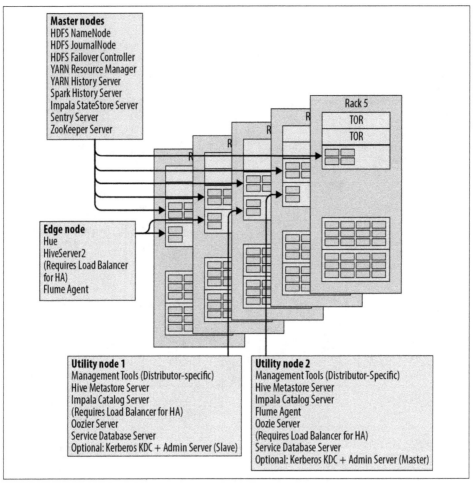

Master nodes
HDFS NameNode
HDFS JournalNode
HDFS Failover Controller
YARN Resource Manager
YARN History Server
Spark History Server
Impala StateStore Server
Sentry Server
ZooKeeper Server

Rack 5
TOR
TOR

Edge node
Hue
HiveServer2
(Requires Load Balancer
for HA)
Flume Agent

Utility node 1
Management Tools (Distributor-specific)
Hive Metastore Server
Impala Catalog Server
(Requires Load Balancer for HA)
Oozier Server
Service Database Server
Optional: Kerberos KDC + Admin Server (Slave)

Utility node 2
Management Tools (Distributor-Specific)
Hive Metastore Server
Impala Catalog Server
Flume Agent
Oozie Server
(Requires Load Balancer for HA)
Service Database Server
Optional: Kerberos KDC + Admin Server (Master)

Figure 3-14. Example of a large cluster configuration

Summary

In this chapter we reviewed everything you need to know about commodity servers and their building blocks for your big data platform. We covered the basics of computer architecture and modern design points for symmetric multiprocessing and the resulting NUMA characteristics. We then explored the storage path in Hadoop systems, especially that of HDFS, covering the user space as well as Linux internals and the page cache. And we looked at how Hadoop optimizations around short-circuit and zero-copy reads enhance overall performance.

We compared standard replication in HDFS to erasure coding and learned that erasure coding does not simply supersede replication, but that they can be run side by side. In terms of which storage path is more beneficial, we discovered that it depends on use cases.

We continued our discussion of storage by moving into the hardware layer, which can prove crucial in the performance of the overall system. We covered various relevant server form factors and their advantages and disadvantages for given requirements, before we put it all together into various blueprints for small, medium, and large cluster configurations.

The concepts we've discussed are important foundational knowledge for the planning and architecture cycle of on-premises Hadoop solutions. Even for public cloud infrastructure, where most low-level specifications are conveniently hidden from the user, the size of virtual machine instances and their storage capabilities are based on the underlying physical machines, which influence performance and cost.

The role of the Linux storage stack, the relationship between compute and I/O, the performance of individual components, and their contribution to cost equally apply to cloud infrastructure, as we will learn in Part III.

As such, this chapter should serve as your baseline when comparing any Hadoop infrastructure choices.

## CHAPTER 4

Networking

This chapter looks at how cluster services such as Spark and Hadoop use the network and how that usage affects network architecture and integration. We also cover implementation details relevant to network architects and cluster builders.

Services such as Hadoop are *distributed*, which means that networking is a fundamental, critical part of their overall system architecture. Rather than just affecting how a cluster is accessed externally, networking directly affects the performance, scalability, security, and availability of a cluster and the services it provides.

How Services Use a Network

A modern data platform comprises of a range of networked services that are selectively combined to solve business problems. Each service provides a unique capability, but fundamentally, they are each built using a common set of network use cases.

Remote Procedure Calls (RPCs)

One of the most common network use cases is when clients request that a remote service perform an action. Known as *remote procedure calls* (RPCs), these mechanisms are a fundamental unit of work on a network, enabling many higher-level use cases such as monitoring, consensus, and data transfers.

All platform services are distributed, so by definition, they all provide RPC capabilities in some form or other. As would be expected, the variety of available remote calls reflects the variety of the services themselves—RPCs to some services last only milliseconds and affect only a single record, but calls to other services instantiate complex, multiserver jobs that move and process petabytes of information.

Implementations and architectures

The definition of an RPC is broad, applying to many different languages and libraries —even a plain HTTP transfer can be considered to be an RPC.

Data platform services are a loosely affiliated collection of open source projects, written by different authors. This means there is very little standardization between them, including the choice of RPC technology. Some services use industry-standard approaches, such as REST, and others use open source frameworks, such as Apache Thrift. Others, including Apache Kudu, provide their own custom RPC frameworks, in order to better control the entire application from end to end.

Services also differ widely in terms of their underlying architectures. For example, Apache Oozie provides a simple client-server model for submitting and monitoring workflows—Oozie then interacts with other services on your behalf. By contrast, Apache Impala combines client-server interactions over JDBC with highly concurrent server-server interactions, reading data from HDFS and Kudu and sending tuple data between Impala daemons to execute a distributed query.

Platform services and their RPCs

Table 4-1 shows examples of RPCs across the various services.

Table 4-1. Services and how they use RPCs

Service	Client-server interactions	Server-server interactions
ZooKeeper	Znode creation, modification, and deletion	Leader election, state replication
HDFS	File and directory creation, modification, and deletion	Liveness reporting, block management, and replication
YARN	Application submission and monitoring, resource allocation requests	Container status reporting
Hive	Changes to metastore metadata, query submission via JDBC	Interactions with YARN and backing RDBMS
Impala	Query submission via JDBC	Tuple data exchange
Kudu	Row creation, modification, and deletion; predicate-based scan queries	Consensus-based data replication
HBase	Cell creation, modification, and deletion; scans and cell retrieval	Liveness reporting
Kafka	Message publishing and retrieval, offset retrieval and commits	Data replication
Oozie	Workflow submission and control	Interactions with other services, such as HDFS or YARN, as well as backing RDBMS

Process control

Some services provide RPC capabilities that allow for starting and stopping remote processes. In the case of YARN, user-submitted applications are instantiated to perform diverse workloads, such as machine learning, stream processing, or batch ETL, with each submitted application spawning dedicated processes.

Management software, such as Cloudera Manager or Apache Ambari, also uses RPCs to install, configure, and manage Hadoop services, including starting and stopping them as required.

Latency

Every call to a remote procedure undergoes the same lengthy process: the call creates a packet, which is converted into a frame, buffered, sent to a remote switch, buffered again within the switch, transferred to the destination host, buffered yet again within the host, converted into a packet, and finally handed to the destination application.

The time it takes for an RPC to make it to its destination can be significant, often taking around a millisecond. Remote calls often require that a response be sent back to the client, further delaying the completion of the interaction. If a switch is heavily loaded and its internal buffers are full, it may need to drop some frames entirely, causing a retransmission. If that happens, a call could take significantly longer than usual.

Latency and cluster services. Cluster services vary in the extent to which they can tolerate latency. For example, although HDFS can tolerate high latency when sending blocks to clients, the interactions between the NameNode and the JournalNodes (which reliably store changes to HDFS in a quorum-based, write-ahead log) are more sensitive. HDFS metadata operation performance is limited by how fast the JournalNodes can store edits.

ZooKeeper is particularly sensitive to network latency. It tracks which clients are active by listening to *heartbeats*—regular RPC calls. If those calls are delayed or lost, ZooKeeper assumes that the client has failed and takes appropriate action, such as expiring sessions. Increasing timeouts can make applications more resilient to occasional spikes, but the downside is that the time taken to detect a failed client is increased.

Although ZooKeeper client latency can be caused by a number of factors, such as garbage collection or a slow disk subsystem, a poorly performing network can still result in session expirations, leading to unreliability and poor performance.

Data Transfers

Data transfers are a fundamental operation in any data management platform, but the distributed nature of services like Hadoop means that almost every transfer involves the network, whether intended for storage or processing operations.

As a cluster expands, the network bandwidth required grows at the same rate—easily to hundreds of gigabytes per second and beyond. Much of that bandwidth is used within the cluster, byserver nodes communicating between themselves, rather than communicating to external systems and clients—the so-called *east-west traffic pattern*.

Data transfers are most commonly associated with a few use cases: ingest and query, data replication, and data shuffling.

Replication

Replication is a common strategy for enhancing availability and reliability in distributed systems—if one server fails, others are available to service the request. For systems in which all replicas are available for reading, replication can also increase performance through clients choosing to read the closest replica. If many workloads require a given data item simultaneously, having the ability for multiple replicas to be read can increase parallelism.

Let's take a look at how replication is handled in HDFS, Kafka, and Kudu:

HDFS
HDFS replicates data by splitting files at 128 MB boundaries and replicating the resulting blocks, rather than replicating files. One benefit of this is that it enables large files to be read in parallel in some circumstances, such as when re-replicating data. When configured for rack awareness, HDFS ensures that blocks are distributed over multiple racks, maintaining data availability even if an entire rack or switch fails.

Blocks are replicated during the initial file write, as well as during ongoing cluster operations. HDFS maintains data integrity by replicating any corrupted or missing blocks. Blocks are also replicated during rebalancing, allowing servers added into an existing HDFS cluster to immediately participate in data management by taking responsibility for a share of the existing data holdings.

During initial file writes, the client only sends one copy. The DataNodes form a pipeline, sending the newly created block along the chain until successfully written.

Although the replication demands of a single file are modest, the aggregate workload placed on HDFS by a distributed application can be immense. Applications such as Spark and MapReduce can easily run thousands of concurrent tasks, each of which may be simultaneously reading from or writing to HDFS. Although those application frameworks attempt to minimize remote HDFS reads where possible, writes are almost always required to be replicated.

Kafka

The replication path taken by messages in Kafka is relatively static, unlike in HDFS where the path is different for every block. Data flows from producers to leaders, but from there it is read by all followers independently—a fan-out architecture rather than a pipeline. Kafka topics have a fixed replication factor that is defined when the topic is created, unlike in HDFS where each file can have a different replication factor. As would be expected, Kafka replicates messages on ingest.

Writes to Kafka can also vary in terms of their durability. Producers can send messages asynchronously using fire-and-forget, or they can choose to write synchronously and wait for an acknowledgment, trading performance for durability. The producer can also choose whether the acknowledgment represents successful receipt on just the leader or on all replicas currently in sync.

Replication also takes place when bootstrapping a new broker or when an existing broker comes back online and catches up with the latest messages. Unlike with HDFS, if a broker goes offline its partition is not automatically re-replicated to another broker, but this can be performed manually.

Kudu

A Kudu cluster stores relational-style tables that will be familiar to any database developer. Using primary keys, it allows low-latency millisecond-scale access to individual rows, while at the same time storing records in a columnar storage format, thus making deep analytical scans efficient.

Rather than replicating data directly, Kudu replicates data modification operations, such as inserts and deletes. It uses the Raft consensus algorithm to ensure that data operations are reliably stored on at least two servers in write-ahead logs before returning a response to the client.

Shuffles

Data analysis depends on comparisons. Whether comparing this year's financial results with the previous year's or measuring a newborn's health vitals against expected norms, comparisons are everywhere. Data processing operations, such as aggregations and joins, also use comparisons to find matching records.

In order to compare records, they first need to be colocated within the memory of a single process. This means using the network to perform data transfers as the first step of a processing pipeline. Frameworks such as Spark and MapReduce pre-integrate these large-scale data exchange phases, known as *shuffles*, enabling users to write applications that sort, group, and join terabytes of information in a massively parallel manner.

During a shuffle, every participating server transfers data to every other simultaneously, making shuffles the most bandwidth-intensive network activity by far. In most deployments, it's the potential bandwidth demand from shuffles that determines the suitability of a network architecture.

Shuffles and the Network

During large workloads, shuffles can cause data transfers to occur between every pair of servers in a cluster. Since physically interconnecting all servers in a full mesh is clearly impractical, network switches are deployed as intermediaries between servers, considerably reducing the number of physical connections.

In a sense, the physical network *modulates* the ideal shuffle transfer flows by imposing connectivity and bandwidth constraints. This idea is shown in Figures 4-1 and 4-2, where we can see the logical flows that exist directly between servers being physically constrained by the available connectivity.

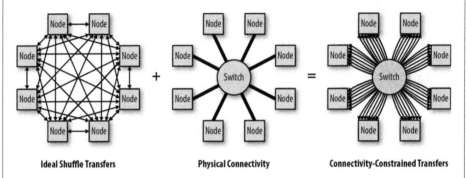

Figure 4-1. *Logical and physical shuffle flows*

It follows that when the same logical cluster is deployed over a different network architecture, different physical flows will result. Figure 4-2 shows the effect of naively adding a second switch to our previous example.

Although this architecture contains more switches, it actually performs significantly worse than the single-switch architecture. On average, 50% of the total network traffic would need to transit between the switches, causing congestion on the inter-switch link.

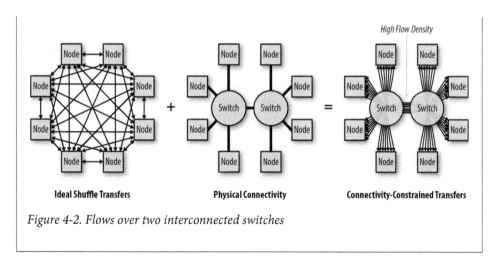

Figure 4-2. Flows over two interconnected switches

Monitoring

Enterprise-grade systems require use cases such as enforcing security through auditing and activity monitoring, ensuring system availability and performance through proactive health checks and metrics, and enabling remote diagnostics via logging and phone-home capabilities.

All of these use cases fall under the umbrella of monitoring, and all require the network. There is also overlap between them. For example, activity monitoring logs can be used for both ensuring security through auditing and historical analysis of job performance—each is just a different perspective on the same data. Monitoring information in a Hadoop cluster takes the form of audit events, metrics, logs, and alerts.

Backup

Part of ensuring overall system resiliency in an enterprise-grade system is making sure that, in the event of a catastrophic failure, systems can be brought back online and restored. As can be seen in Chapter 13, these traditional enterprise concerns are still highly relevant to modern data architectures. In the majority of IT environments, backup activities are performed via the network since this is easier and more efficient than physically visiting remote locations.

For a modern cluster architecture comprising hundreds of servers, this use of the network for backups is essential. The resulting network traffic can be considerable, but not all servers need backing up in their entirety. Stored data is often already replicated, and build automation can frequently reinstall the required system software. In any event, take care to ensure that backup processes don't interfere with cluster operations, at the network level or otherwise.

Consensus

Consider a client that performs an RPC but receives no response. Without further information, it's impossible to know whether that request was successfully received. If the request was significant enough to somehow change the state of the target system, we are now unsure as to whether the system is actually changed.

Unfortunately, this isn't just an academic problem. The reality is that no network or system can ever be fully reliable. Packets get lost, power supplies fail, disk heads crash. Engineering a system to cope with these failures means understanding that failures are not exceptional events and, consequently, writing software to account for —and reconcile—those failures.

One way to achieve reliability in the face of failures is to use multiple processes, replacing any *single points of failure* (SPOFs). However, this requires that the processes collaborate, exchanging information about their own state in order to come to an agreement about the state of the system as a whole. When a majority of the processes agree on that state, they are said to *hold quorum*, controlling the future evolution of the system's state.

Consensus is used in many cluster services in order to achieve correctness:

- HDFS uses a quorum-based majority voting system to reliably store filesystem edits on three different JournalNodes, ideally deployed across multiple racks in independent failure domains.
- ZooKeeper uses a quorum-based consensus system to provide functions such as leader election, distributed locking, and queuing to other cluster services and processes, including HDFS, Hive, and HBase.
- Kafka uses consensus when tracking which messages should be visible to a consumer. If a leader accepts writes but the requisite number of replicas are not yet in sync, those messages are held back from consumers until sufficiently replicated.
- Kudu uses the Raft consensus algorithm for replication, ensuring that inserts, updates, and deletes are persisted on at least two nodes before responding to the client.

Network Architectures

Networking dictates some of the most architecturally significant qualities of a distributed system,including reliability, performance, and security. In this section we describe a range of network designs suitable for everything from single-rack deployments to thousand-server behemoths.

Small Cluster Architectures

The first cluster network architecture to consider is that of a single switch.

Single switch

Although almost too simple to be considered an architecture, the approach is nevertheless appropriate in many use cases. Figure 4-3 illustrates the architecture.

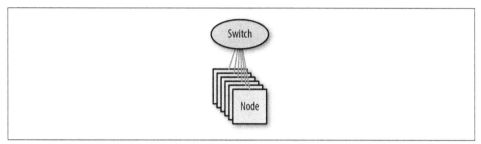

Figure 4-3. A single-switch architecture

From a performance perspective, this design presents very few challenges. Almost all modern switches are non-blocking (meaning that all ports can be utilized simultaneously at full load), so internal traffic from shuffles and replication should be handled effortlessly.

However, although simple and performant, this network architecture suffers from an inherent lack of scalability—once a switch runs out of ports, a cluster can't grow further. Since switch ports are often used for upstream connectivity as well as local servers, small clusters with high ingest requirements may have their growth restricted further.

Another downside of this architecture is that the switch is a SPOF—if it fails, the cluster will fail right along with it. Not all clusters need to be always available, but for those that do, the only resolution is to build a resilient network using multiple switches.

Making Cluster Networks Resilient

Multiple physical connections can be bonded together into a single logical link using the *Link Aggregation Control Protocol* (LACP), but this only increases the resiliency of a link. If the switch itself fails, a resilient link won't help.

To become truly resilient, a server needs to connect to two switches simultaneously. If either switch fails, the other switch continues to supply all connected devices. However, rather than connecting to multiple independent networks, what's required is a way for a single logical connection to span multiple switches.

Multi-Chassis Link Aggregation (MC-LAG) can be used to design a resilient network by replacing the top-of-rack switch with a pair of switches, which function as a single logical switch. Network devices connect to both switches using LACP and behave as if they're connected to a single device.

Scalability, however, remains limited to the size of a single switch, and any upstream links also need to be made resilient in the same manner. Oherwise, the external link could become yet another single point of failure. Figure 4-4 shows the resulting architecture.

Figure 4-4. A resilient switch pair cluster

A range of proprietary technologies, including those discussed in "Network Fabrics" on page 127, provide the same functionality and are widely used in enterprises. MC-LAG and most of these alternatives can be deployed in either an active-passive or active-active configuration. Although both improve resiliency, active-active also increases the available bandwidth (and thus increases cluster performance).

In practice, most organizations deploy LACP using failover (active-passive) mode rather than using round-robin or balance (active-active) configurations, since the aggregation groups typically need to be built on each switch pair individually, which is a considerable administrative effort. It also makes sense from a resource management perspective because a simple failover does not result in a reduction of the available bandwidth to a server.

Implementation. With a single-switch architecture, because of the inherent simplicity of the design, there is very little choice in the implementation. The switch will host a single Layer 2 broadcast domain within a physical LAN or a single virtual LAN (VLAN), and all hosts will be in the same Layer 3 subnet.

Medium Cluster Architectures

When building clusters that will span multiple racks, we highly recommend the architectures described in "Large Cluster Architectures" on page 124, since they provide the highest levels of scalability and performance. However, since not all clusters need such high capabilities, more modest clusters may be able to use one of the alternative architectures described in this section.

Network Oversubscription

Whenever a cluster network is built using multiple switches there is the possibility of encountering *oversubscription*—a performance bottleneck imposed by the physical network design. The term originates in telephony, in which a old-fashioned telephone exchange has more local subscribers than *long-distance* lines available, resulting in long distance service being temporarily unavailable at busy times.

Network switches that connect a high number of local devices with a small number of remote switches can become similarly oversubscribed if the uplink bandwidth capacity is insufficient. In essence, there is more bandwidth demand than capacity, leading to contention that results in slower data transfers.

The degree of oversubscription present is simply the ratio between the bandwidth demand and capacity. For example, a switch with 24 x 1 Gb/s ports could potentially demand 24 Gb/s in total. If that demand was entirely for remote systems via an uplink of 4 Gb/s, there would be an oversubscription of 24:4, or 6:1.

Stacked networks

Some network vendors provide switches that can be stacked—connected together with high-bandwidth, proprietary cables, making them function as a single switch. This provides an inexpensive, low-complexity option for expanding beyond a single switch. Figure 4-5 shows an example of a stacked network.

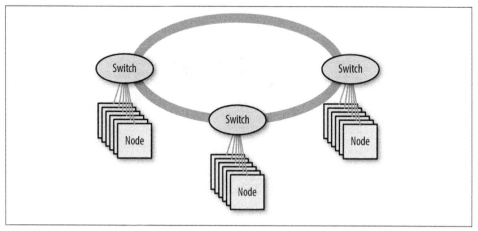

Figure 4-5. A stacked network of three switches

Although stacking switches may sound similar to using a highly available switch pair (which can also function as a single logical switch), they are in fact quite different. Stackable switches use their proprietary interconnects to carry high volumes of user data, whereas a high-availability (HA) switch pair only uses the interconnect for managing the switch state. Stacking isn't limited to a pair of switches, either; many implementations can interconnect up to seven switches in a single ring (though as we'll see, this has a large impact on oversubscription, severely affecting network performance).

Resiliency. Stackable switches connect using a bidirectional ring topology. Therefore, each participant always has two connections: clockwise and counterclockwise. This gives the design resiliency against ring link failure—if the clockwise link fails, traffic can flow instead via the counterclockwise link, though the overall network bandwidth might be reduced.

In the event of a switch failure in the ring, the other switches will continue to function, taking over leadership of the ring if needed (since one participant is the master). Any devices connected only to a single ring switch will lose network service.

Some stackable switches support Multi-Chassis Link Aggregation (see "Making Cluster Networks Resilient" on page 115). This allows devices to continue to receive network service even if one of the switches in the ring fails, as long as the devices connect to a pair of the switches in the stack. This configuration enables *resilient stacked networks* to be created (see Figure 4-6 for an example).

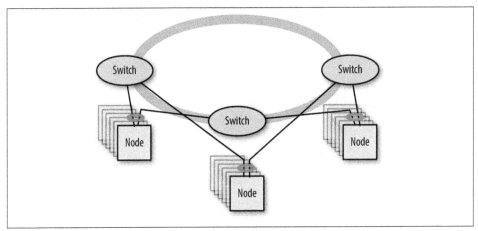

Figure 4-6. A resilient stacked network of three switches

In normal operations, the bidirectional nature of the ring connections means there are two independent rings. During link or switch failure, the remaining switches detect the failure and cap the ends, resulting in a horseshoe-shaped, unidirectional loop.

Performance. The stacking interconnects provide very high bandwidth between the switches, but each link still provides less bandwidth than the sum of the ports, necessarily resulting in network oversubscription.

With only two switches in a ring, there are two possible routes to a target switch—clockwise and counterclockwise. In each direction, the target switch is directly connected. With three switches in a ring, the topology means that there are still only two possible directions, but now a target switch will only be directly connected in one direction. In the other direction, an intermediate switch is between the source and the target.

The need for traffic to traverse intermediate switches means that oversubscription increases as we add switches to the ring. Under normal circumstances, every switch in the ring has a choice of sending traffic clockwise or counterclockwise, and this can also affect network performance.

Determining oversubscription in stacked networks. Within a stacked network, there are now two potential paths between a source and destination device, which makes oversubscription more complex to determine, but conceptually the process is unchanged.

In this first scenario, we look at oversubscription between a pair of stacked switches, each of which has 48 10 GbE ports and bidirectional stacking links operating at 120 Gb/s (the flow diagram can be seen in Figure 4-7). Each switch is directly connected to the other by two paths, giving a total outbound flow capacity of 240 Gb/s. Since there is a potential 480 Gb/s inbound from the ports, we see an oversubscription ratio of 480:240, or 2:1.

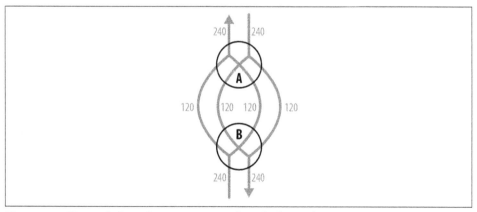

Figure 4-7. Network flows between a pair of stacked switches

With three switches in the ring, each switch is still directly connected to every other, but the 240 Gb/s outbound bandwidth is now shared between the two neighbors. Figure 4-8 shows the network flows that occur if we assume that traffic is perfectly balanced and the switches make perfect decisions about path selection (ensuring no traffic gets sent via an intermediate switch). In that scenario, each neighbor gets sent 120 Gb/s and the total outbound is 240 Gb/s, making the oversubscription ratio 2:1.

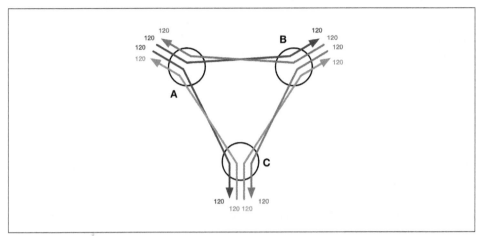

Figure 4-8. Best-case network flows between three stacked switches

If somehow the stacked switches were to make the worst possible path selections (sending all traffic via the longer path, as shown in Figure 4-9), the effective bandwidth would be reduced because each outbound link would now carry two flows instead of one. This increased contention would reduce the bandwidth available per flow to only 60 Gb/s, making the oversubscription ratio 480:120, or 4:1.

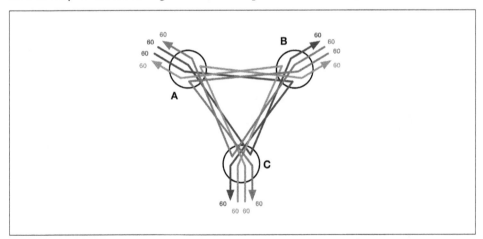

Figure 4-9. Worst-case network flows between three stacked switches

While this is a pathological example, it nevertheless demonstrates clearly the idea of a load-dependent oversubscription ratio. A real-world three-switch stack would almost certainly perform far closer to the best case than the worst, and in any case, even a 4:1 oversubscription ratio is still a reasonable proposition for a Hadoop cluster.

With only two switches in the stack, the traffic on the interconnection links was always direct. With three switches, the traffic is still mostly direct, with the possibility of some indirect traffic under high load.

When the ring has four switches or more, indirect traffic becomes completely unavoidable, even under perfect conditions. As switches are added to a stack, indirect traffic starts to dominate the workload, making oversubscription too problematic. Alternative architectures become more appropriate.

Stacked network cabling considerations. The proprietary stacking cables used to make the ring are very short—typically only a meter or so—and are designed for stacking switches in a literal, physical sense. It is possible for stacking switches to be placed in adjacent racks, but it's generally best to avoid this, since not all racks allow cabling to pass between them.

One way around the ring cabling length restriction is to place the switch stack entirely in a single rack and use longer cables between the switches and servers. This has the disadvantage, though, of connecting all of the switches to a single *power distribution unit* (PDU), and is therefore subject to a single point of failure. If you need to place racks in different aisles due to space constraints, stacking isn't for you.

Implementation. With a stacked-switch architecture, there are two implementation options to consider—deploying a subnet per switch or deploying a single subnet across the entire ring.

Deploying a subnet per switch is most appropriate for when servers connect to a single switch only. This keeps broadcast traffic local to each switch in the ring. In scenarios where servers connect to multiple stack switches using MC-LAG, deploying a single subnet across the entire ring is more appropriate.

In either scenario, a physical LAN or single VLAN per subnet is appropriate.

Fat-tree networks

Networks such as the *fat-tree network* are built by connecting multiple switches in a hierarchical structure. A single-core switch connects through layers of aggregation switches to access switches, which connect to servers.

The architecture is known as a fat tree because the links nearest the core switch are higher bandwidth, and thus the tree gets "fatter" as you get closer to the root. Figure 4-10 shows an example of a fat-tree network.

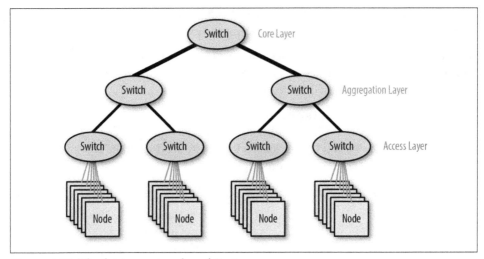

Figure 4-10. The fat-tree network architecture

Since many small clusters start by using a single switch, a fat-tree network can be seen as a natural upgrade path when considering network expansion. Simply duplicate the original single-switch design, add a core switch, and connect everything up.

Scalability. The performance of a fat-tree network can be determined by looking at the degree of network oversubscription. Consider the example in Figure 4-11.

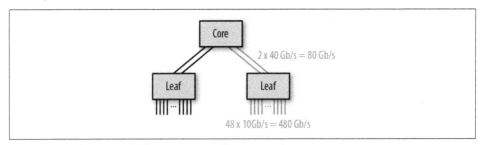

Figure 4-11. An example fat-tree network

The access switches each have 48 10 GbE ports connected to servers and 2 40 GbE ports connecting to the core switch, giving an oversubscription ratio of 480:80, or 6:1, which is considerably higher than recommended for Hadoop workloads. This can be improved by either reducing the number of servers per access switch or increasing the bandwidth between the access switches and the core switch using link aggregation.

This architecture scales out by adding access switches—each additional switch increases the total number of ports by 48. This can be repeated until the core switch port capacity is reached, at which point greater scale can only be achieved by using a larger core switch or a different architecture.

Oversubscription as a Worst Case

Figure 4-11 shows an access switch with 480 Gb/s inbound and 80 Gb/s outbound, making the oversubscription ratio 6:1. In other words, if all servers decided to send traffic over the uplink to nonlocal destinations, each could only send about 1/6 of its capacity—around 1.7 Gb/s.

Oversubscription only applies to traffic leaving the switch via uplinks, not to traffic routed locally. During a shuffle, every server transfers data to every other, but that includes servers that are local. With two access switches a server sends, on average, around 50% to local and 50% to nonlocal servers, assuming that the shuffle itself is evenly distributed across servers. That lowers the effective oversubscription since, of the 480 Gb/s potential demand, only 240 Gb/s requires the uplink. When 240 Gb/s is constrained down to 80 Gb/s, that makes an effective oversubscription ratio of 240:80, or 3:1.

As the number of access switches increases, the percentage of servers that are remote goes up with it, increasing the impact of the oversubscription. With four access switches, 75% of the servers are remote, resulting in an effective oversubscription ratio of 4.5:1. With eight access switches, 87.5% of the servers are remote, raising the effective ratio to 5.25:1. At the limit, when 100% of the traffic is destined for nonlocal destinations, the oversubscription ratio would be 6:1, as originally calculated.

The oversubscription ratio calculated at the access switch therefore represents the worst possible case, which assumes all traffic requires upstream bandwidth.

Resiliency.   When implemented without redundant switches, the reliability of this architecture is limited due to the many SPOFs. The loss of an access switch would affect a significant portion of the cluster, and the loss of the core switch would be catastrophic.

Removing the SPOFs by replacing single switches with switch pairs greatly improves the resiliency. Figure 4-12 shows a fat-tree network built with multichassis link aggregation.

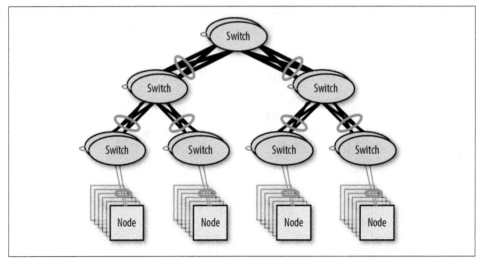

Figure 4-12. A resilient fat-tree network

Implementation. A hierarchical network can either be built using a single subnet across the entire tree or using a subnet per switch. The first option is easiest to implement, but it means that broadcast traffic will traverse links beyond the access layer. The second option scales better but is more complex to implement, requiring network administrators to manage routing—a process that can be error-prone.

Large Cluster Architectures

All of the architectures discussed so far have been limited in terms of either scale or scalability: single switches quickly run out of ports, stacked networks are limited to a few switches per stack at most, and fat-tree networks can only scale out while the core switch has enough ports.

This section discusses network designs that can support larger and/or more scalable clusters.

Modular switches

In general, there are only two ways to scale a network: scaling up using larger switches or scaling out using more switches. Both the fat-tree and the stacked network architectures scale out by adding switches. Prior to modular switches, scaling a switch vertically simply meant replacing it with a larger variant with a higher port capacity—a disruptive and costly option.

Modular switches introduced the idea of an expandable chassis that can be populated with multiple switch modules. Since a modular switch can function when only partially populated with modules, network capacity can be added by installing additional modules, so long as the chassis has space.

In many ways, a modular switch can be thought of as a scaled-up version of a single switch; thus it can be used in a variety of architectures. For example, a modular switch is well suited for use as the core switch of a fat tree or as the central switch in a single-switch architecture. The latter case is known as an *end-of-row architecture*, since the modular switch is literally deployed at the physical end of a datacenter row, connected to servers from the many racks in the row.

Modular switches, such as Cisco 7000, are often deployed in pairs in order to ensure resiliency in the architecture they are used in.

Spine-leaf networks

For true cluster-level scalability, a network architecture that can grow beyond the confines of any single switch—even a monstrous modular behemoth—is essential.

When we looked at the architecture of a fat-tree network, we saw that the scalability was ultimately limited by the capacity of the core switch at the root of the tree. As long as the oversubscription at the leaf and intermediate switches is maintained at a reasonable level, we can keep scaling out the fat tree by adding additional switches until the core switch has no capacity left.

This limit can be raised by scaling up the core switch to a larger model (or adding a module to a modular switch), but Figure 4-13 shows an interesting alternative approach, which is to just add another root switch.

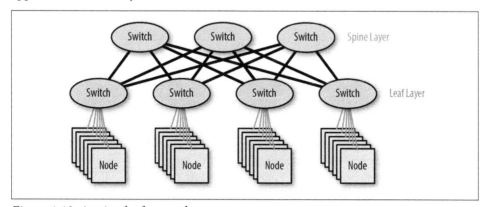

Figure 4-13. A spine-leaf network

Since there isn't a single root switch, this isn't a hierarchical network. In topology terms, the design is known as a *partial mesh*—partial since leaf switches only connect to core switches and core switches only connect to leaf switches.

The core switches function as the backbone of the network and are termed *spine switches*, giving us the name *spine leaf*.

Scalability. The most important benefit of the spine-leaf architecture is linear scalability: if more capacity is required, we can grow the network by adding spine and leaf switches, scaling out rather than scaling up. This finally allows the network to scale horizontally, just like the cluster software it supports.

Since every spine switch connects to every leaf switch, the scalability limit is determined by the number of ports available at a single spine switch. If a spine switch has 32 ports, each at 40 Gb/s, and each leaf switch needs 160 Gb/s in order to maintain a reasonable oversubscription ratio, we can have at most 8 leaf switches.

North-South vs. East-West Traffic Patterns

The network scalability provided by the spine-leaf architecture is particularly suitable for handling the bandwidth requirements of modern data platforms because the dominant traffic pattern observed is *server-server*. This within-network traffic between cluster servers (often generated by shuffles or replication) is also known as *East-West* traffic since the flows are mostly between pairs of servers at the same *height* within the network hierarchy.

In contrast, traditional *client-server* traffic is carried via external networks and travels in via a core network, transiting down through the spine and leaf layers. This type of flow is often known as *North-South* traffic. Keep in mind that for a platform such as HDFS, client-server traffic is more likely to be East-West than North-South due to the highly parallel activity generated on-cluster by platforms such as Spark.

Resilient spine-leaf networks. When making networks resilient, the primary technique has been to use redundant switches and MC-LAG. Until now, this has been required for all switches in an architecture, since any switch without a redundant partner would become a SPOF.

With the spine-leaf architecture, this is no longer the case. By definition, a spine-leaf network already has multiple spine switches, so the spine layer is already resilient by design. The leaf layer can be made resilient by replacing each leaf switch with a switch pair, as shown in Figure 4-14. Both of these switches then connect to the spine layer for data, as well as each other for state management.

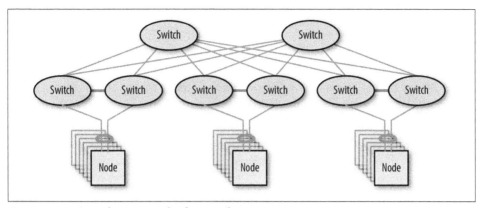

Figure 4-14. A resilient spine-leaf network

Implementation. Since a spine-leaf architecture contains loops, the implementation option of putting all devices into the same broadcast domain is no longer valid. Broadcast frames would simply flow around the loops, creating a broadcast storm, at least until the Spanning Tree Protocol (STP) disabled some links.

The option to have a subnet (broadcast domain) per leaf switch remains, and is a scalable solution since broadcast traffic would then be constrained to the leaf switches. This implementation option again requires network administrators to manage routing, however, which can be error-prone.

An interesting alternative implementation option is to deploy a spine-leaf network using a network fabric rather than using routing at the IP layer.

Network Fabrics

Layer 2 offers compelling features, such as zero configuration and high switching performance, but the lack of frame routing impacts scalability and the lack of time-to-live leads to broadcast storms. Layer 3 mitigates these by adding routing and time-to-live at the IP packet level, but this still means that larger networks can only be built out of multiple interconnected Layer 2 networks.

Network vendors and standards bodies have been developing hybrid Layer 2/3 architectures for some time, resulting in two main competing standards: *Transparent Interconnection of Lots of Links* (TRILL) and *Shortest Path Bridging* (SPB). Both of these technologies (and their proprietary variants, such as Cisco FabricPath) combine the benefits of Layers 2 and 3.

TRILL works by providing a completely new Layer 2 protocol that encapsulates regular Layer 2 Ethernet traffic. TRILL frames include a time-to-live field as well as source and destination switch identifiers. Switch addresses are automatically assigned and the switch routing tables are automatically maintained, enabling frames to be routed with zero switch configuration.

Servers still use standard Ethernet frames when sending data, but these are then transformed into TRILL frames by the fabric switches when entering the TRILL network. The frames are transmitted along an optimal path to the destination switch and converted back to a standard Ethernet frame, before finally being passed to the destination device. The use of TRILL is entirely transparent.

Although Hadoop doesn't directly benefit from a flat Layer 2 network, the operational simplicity of the approach can be compelling for many organizations.

Network Integration

A cluster is a significant investment that requires extensive networking, so it makes sense to consider the architecture of a cluster network in isolation. However, once the network architecture of the cluster is settled, the next task is to define how that cluster will connect to the world.

There are a number of possibilities for integrating a cluster into a wider network. This section describes the options available and outlines their pros and cons.

Reusing an Existing Network

The first approach—only really possible for small clusters—is to add the cluster to a preexisting subnet. This is the simplest approach, since it requires the least change to existing infrastructure. Figure 4-15 shows how, at a logical level, this integration path is trivial, since we're only adding new cluster servers.

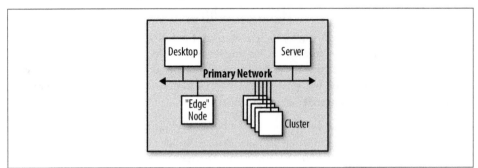

Figure 4-15. Logical view of an integration with an existing network

From a physical perspective, this could be implemented by reusing existing switches, but unless all nodes would be located on the same switch, this could easily lead to oversubscription issues. Many networks are designed more for access than throughput.

A better implementation plan is to introduce additional switches that are dedicated to the cluster, as shown in Figure 4-16. This is better in terms of isolation and performance, since internal cluster traffic can remain on the switch rather than transiting via an existing network.

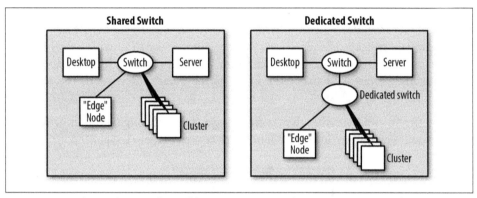

Figure 4-16. Physical view of possible integrations with an existing network

Creating an Additional Network

The alternative approach is to create additional subnets to host the new cluster. This requires that existing network infrastructure be modified, in terms of both physical connectivity and configuration. Figure 4-17 shows how, from a logical perspective, the architecture is still straightforward—we add the cluster subnet and connect to the main network.

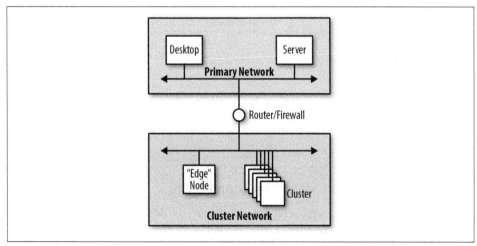

Figure 4-17. Logical view of integration using an additional network

From a security perspective, this approach is preferable since the additional isolation keeps broadcast traffic away from the main network. By replacing the router with a firewall, we can entirely segregate the cluster network and tightly control which servers and services are visible from the main network.

Edge-connected networks

Edge nodes are typically cluster servers that are put in place to provide access to cluster services, offering SSH access, hosting web UIs, or providing JDBC endpoints to upstream middleware systems. They form the boundary, or *edge*, of the software services provided by a cluster.

Figure 4-18 shows how, rather than connecting a cluster through a router or firewall, the edge nodes could provide external network connectivity to the cluster.

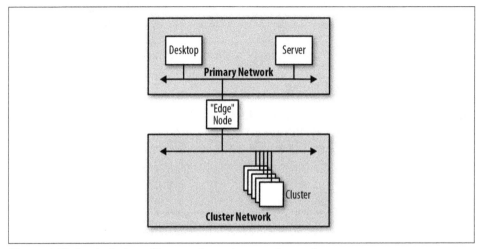

Figure 4-18. Logical view of integration using an edge node

When connected in this manner, the edge nodes literally form the physical edges of the cluster, acting as the gateway through which all communication is performed. The downside of this approach is that the edge nodes are multihomed, which, in general, isn't recommended.

Upstream Connectivity

The need for performance and resiliency are significant drivers of network architecture within a cluster, but the same is true (though to a lesser extent) of upstream connectivity. In many clusters, the bandwidth requirements for ingest and reporting are modest in comparison to internal traffic, except in one circumstance—replication to another cluster.

Although almost all cluster services are designed for high availability, there is always the possibility that an entire datacenter could suffer a catastrophic failure. Multiple racks and power distribution units can help mitigate some SPOFs, but the fact remains that a single datacenter will always exist in a single location—mitigation that requires the use of multiple sites, which means replicating data between them.

Cluster services often provide software tools to accomplish data replication between geographic sites. In the case of Hadoop, a tool called *distributed copy* (DistCp) can be used to copy data between HDFS instances. Since HDFS can store an immense amount of data, DistCp was designed to copy data in parallel. As a result, it can drive significant network load. Apache HBase and Apache Kafka offer similar tooling to replicate data to alternative installations.

Network Design Considerations

This section outlines network design recommendations and considerations based on reference architectures, known best practices, and the experiences of the authors. The intent is to provide some implementation guidelines to help ensure a successful deployment.

Layer 1 Recommendations

The following recommendations concern aspects of Layer 1, known as the *physical layer*. This is where the rubber meets the road, bridging the gap between the logical world of software and the physical world of electronics and transmission systems.

Use dedicated switches

Although it may be possible to use existing network infrastructure for a new cluster, we recommend deploying dedicated switches and uplinks for Hadoop where possible. This has several benefits, including isolation and security, cluster growth capacity, and stronger guarantees that traffic from Hadoop and Spark won't saturate existing network links.

Consider a cluster as an appliance

This is related to the previous point, but it is helpful to think of a cluster as a whole, rather than as a collection of servers to be added to your network.

When organizations purchase a cluster as an appliance, installation becomes a relatively straightforward matter of supplying space, network connectivity, cooling, and power—the internal connectivity usually isn't a concern. Architecting and building your own cluster means you necessarily need to be concerned with internal details, but the appliance mindset—thinking of the cluster as a single thing—is still appropriate.

Manage oversubscription

The performance of any cluster network is entirely driven by the level of over-subscription at the switches. Cluster software, such as Hadoop and Spark, can drive a network to capacity, so the network should be designed to minimize oversubscription. Cluster software performs best when oversubscription is kept to around 3:1 or better.

Consider InfiniBand carefully

Hadoop clusters can be deployed using InfiniBand (IB) as the Layer 1 technology, but this is uncommon outside of Hadoop appliances.

At the time of this writing, InfiniBand isn't supported natively by services such as Hadoop and Spark. Features such as *remote direct memory access* (RDMA) are thus left unused, making the use of IP over InfiniBand (IPoIB) essential. As a consequence, the performance of InfiniBand is significantly reduced, making the higher speeds of InfiniBand less relevant.

InfiniBand also introduces a secondary network interface to cluster servers, making them multihomed. As discussed in "Layer 3 Recommendations" on page 135, this should be avoided. Finally, the relative scarcity of InfiniBand skills in the market and the cost in comparison to Ethernet make the technology more difficult to adopt and maintain.

Use high-speed cables

Clusters are commonly cabled using copper cables. These are available in a number of standards, known as *categories*, which specify the maximum cable length and maximum speed at which a cable can be used.

Since the cost increase between cable types is negligible when compared to servers and switches, it makes sense to choose the highest-rated cable possible. At the time of this writing, the recommendation is to use Category 7a cable, which offers speeds of up to 40 Gb/s with a maximum distance of 100 meters (for solid core cables; 55 meters for stranded).

Fiber optic cables offer superior performance in terms of bandwidth and distance compared to copper, but at increased cost. They can be used to cable servers, but they are more often used for the longer-distance links that connect switches in different racks. At this time, the recommendation is to use OM3 optical cabling or better, which allows speeds up to 100 Gb/s.

Use high-speed networking

The days of connecting cluster servers at 1 Gb/s are long gone. Nowadays, almost all clusters should connect servers using 10 Gb/s or better. For larger clusters that use multiple switches, 40 Gb/s should be considered the minimum speed for the links that interconnect switches. Even with 40 Gb/s speeds, link aggregation is likely to be required to maintain an acceptable degree of oversubscription.

Consider hardware placement

We recommend racking servers in predictable locations, such as always placing master nodes at the top of the rack or racking servers in ascending name/IP order. This strategy can help to reduce the likelihood that a server is misidentified during cluster maintenance activities. Better yet, use labels and keep documentation up to date.

Ensure that racks are colocated when considering stacked networks, since the stacking cables are short. Remember that server network cables may need to be routed between racks in this case.

Ensure that racks are located no more than 100 meters apart when deploying optical cabling.

Don't connect clusters to the internet

Use cases that require a cluster to be directly addressable on the public internet are rare. Since they often contain valuable, sensitive information, most clusters should be deployed on secured internal networks, away from prying eyes. Good information security policy says to minimize the attack surface of any system, and clusters such as Hadoop are no exception.

When absolutely required, internet-facing clusters should be deployed using firewalls and secured using Kerberos, Transport Layer Security (TLS), and encryption.

Layer 2 Recommendations

The following recommendations concern aspects of Layer 2, known as the *data link layer*, which is responsible for sending and receiving frames between devices on a local network. Each frame includes the physical hardware addresses of the source and destination, along with a few other fields.

Avoid oversized layer 2 networks

Although IP addresses are entirely determined by the network configuration, MAC addresses are effectively random (except for the vendor prefix). In order to determine the MAC address associated with an IP address, the Address Resolution Protocol (ARP) is used, performing address discovery by broadcasting an address request to all servers in the same broadcast domain.

Using broadcasts for address discovery means that Layer 2 networks have a scalability limitation. A practical general rule is that a single broadcast domain shouldn't host more than approximately 500 servers.

Minimize VLAN usage

Virtual LANs were originally designed to make the link deactivation performed by the Spanning Tree Protocol less expensive, by allowing switches and links to simultaneously carry multiple independent LANs, each of which has a unique spanning tree. The intention was to reduce the impact of link deactivation by allowing a physical link to be deactivated in one VLAN while still remaining active in others.

In practice, VLANs are almost never used solely to limit the impact of STP; the isolating nature of VLANs is often much more useful in managing service visibility, increasing security by restricting broadcast scope.

VLANs are not required for cluster networks—physical LANs are perfectly sufficient, since in most cases a cluster has dedicated switches anyway. If VLANs are deployed, their use should be minimized to, at most, a single VLAN per cluster or a single VLAN per rack for clusters built using Layer 3 routing. Use of multiple VLANs per server is multihoming, which is generally not recommended.

Consider jumbo frames

Networks can be configured to send larger frames (known as *jumbo frames*) by increasing the maximum transmission unit (MTU) from 1,500 to 9,000 bytes. This increases the efficiency of large transfers, since far fewer frames are needed to send the same data. Cluster workloads such as Hadoop and Spark are heavily dependent on large transfers, so the efficiencies offered by jumbo frames make them an obvious design choice where they are supported.

In practice, jumbo frames can be problematic because they need to be supported by all participating switches and servers (including external services, such as Active Directory). Otherwise, fragmentation can cause reliability issues.

Consider network resiliency

As mentioned previously, one approach to making a network resilient against failure is to use Multi-Chassis Link Aggregation. This builds on the capabilities of *link aggregation* (LAG) by allowing servers to connect to a pair of switches at the same time, using only a single logical connection. That way, if one of the links or switches were to fail, the network would continue to function.

In addition to their upstream connections, the redundant switches in the pair need to be directly connected to each other. These links are proprietary (using vendor-specific naming and implementations), meaning that switches from different vendors (even different models from the same vendor) are incompatible. The proprietary links vary as to whether they carry cluster traffic in addition to the required switch control data.

Enterprise-class deployments will almost always have managed switches capable of using LACP, so it makes good sense to use this capability wherever possible. LACP automatically negotiates the aggregation settings between the server and a switch, making this the recommended approach for most deployments.

Layer 3 Recommendations

The following recommendations concern aspects of Layer 3, known as the *network layer*. This layer interconnects multiple Layer 2 networks together by adding logical addressing and routing capabilities.

Use dedicated subnets

We recommend isolating network traffic to at least a dedicated subnet (and hence broadcast domain) per cluster. This is useful for managing broadcast traffic propagation and can also assist with cluster security (through network segmentation and use of firewalls). A subnet range of size /22 is generally sufficient for this purpose since it provides 1,024 addresses—most clusters are smaller than this.

For larger clusters not using fabric-based switching, a dedicated subnet per rack will allow the switches to route traffic at Layer 3 instead of just switching frames. This means that the cluster switches can be interconnected with multiple links without the risk of issues caused by STP. A subnet range of size /26 is sufficient, since it provides 64 addresses per rack—most racks will have fewer servers than this.

Each cluster should be assigned a unique subnet within your overall network allocation. This ensures that all pairs of servers can communicate, in the event that data needs to be copied between clusters.

Allocate IP addresses statically

We strongly recommend allocating IP addresses statically to cluster servers during the OS build and configuration phase, rather than dynamically using DHCP on every boot. Most cluster services expect IP addresses to remain static over time. Additionally, services such as Spark and Hadoop are written in Java, where the default behavior (*http://bit.ly/2R2p7l6*) is to cache DNS entries forever when a security manager is installed.

If DHCP is used, ensure that the IP address allocation is stable over time by using a fixed mapping from MAC addresses to IP addresses—that way, whenever the server boots, it always receives the same IP address, making the address effectively static.

Use private IP address ranges

In most cases, internal networks within an organization should be configured to use IP addresses from the private IP address ranges. These ranges are specially designated for use by internal networks—switches on the internet will drop any packets to or from private addresses.

The multiple private IP ranges available can be divided into subnets. Table 4-2 shows the ranges.

Table 4-2. Private IP address ranges

IP address range	Number of IP addresses	Description
10.0.0.0–10.255.255.255	16,777,216	Single Class A network
172.16.0.0–172.31.255.255	1,048,576	16 contiguous Class B networks
192.168.0.0–192.168.255.255	65,536	256 contiguous Class C networks

For clusters like Hadoop, we strongly recommend use of a private network. When deploying a cluster, however, take care to ensure that a private network range is only used once within an organization—two clusters that clash in terms of IP addresses won't be able to communicate.

Prefer DNS over /etc/hosts

Cluster servers are almost always accessed via hostnames rather than IP addresses. Apart from being easier to remember, hostnames are specifically required when using security technologies such as TLS and Kerberos. Resolving a hostname into an IP address is done via either the Domain Name System (DNS) or the local configuration file */etc/hosts*.

The local configuration file (which allows for entries to be statically defined) does have some advantages over DNS:

Precedence

Local entries take precedence over DNS, allowing administrators to override specific entries.

Availability

As a network service, DNS is subject to service and network outages, but */etc/hosts* is always available.

Performance

DNS lookups require a minimum of a network round trip, but lookups via the the local file are instantaneous.

Even with these advantages, we still strongly recommend using DNS. Changes made in DNS are made once and are immediately available. Since */etc/hosts* is a local file that exists on all devices, any changes need to be made to all copies. At the very least, this will require deployment automation to ensure correctness, but if the cluster uses Kerberos changes will even need to be made on clients. At that point, DNS becomes a far better option.

The availability and performance concerns of DNS lookups can be mitigated by using services such as the Name Service Caching Daemon (NSCD).

Finally, regardless of any other considerations, all clusters will interact with external systems. DNS is therefore essential, both for inbound and outbound traffic.

Provide forward and reverse DNS entries

In addition to using DNS for forward lookups that transform a hostname into an IP address, reverse DNS entries that allow lookups to transform an IP address into a hostname are also required.

In particular, reverse DNS entries are essential for Kerberos, which uses them to verify the identity of the server to which a client is connecting.

Never resolve a hostname to 127.0.0.1

It is essential to ensure that every cluster server resolves its own hostname to a routable IP address and never to the localhost IP address 127.0.0.1—a common misconfiguration of the local */etc/hosts* file.

This is an issue because many cluster services pass their IP address to remote systems as part of normal RPC interactions. If the localhost address is passed, the remote system will then incorrectly attempt to connect to itself later on.

Avoid IPv6

There are two types of IP address in use today: IPv4 and IPv6. IPv4 was designed back in the 1970s, with addresses taking up 4 bytes. At that time, 4,294,967,296 addresses was considered to be enough for the foreseeable future, but rapid growth of the internet throughout the 1990s led to the development of IPv6, which increased the size of addresses to 16 bytes.

Adoption of IPv6 is still low—a report from 2014 indicates that only 3% of Google users use the site via IPv6. This is partly due to the amount of infrastructural change required and the fact that workarounds, such as Network Address Translation (NAT) and proxies, work well enough in many cases.

At the time of this writing, the authors have yet to see any customer network—cluster or otherwise—running IPv6. The private network ranges provide well over 16 million addresses, so IPv6 solves a problem that doesn't exist within the enterprise space.

If IPv6 becomes more widely adopted in the consumer internet, there may be a drive to standardize enterprise networking to use the same stack. When that happens, data platforms will take more notice of IPv6 and will be tested more regularly against it. For now, it makes more sense to avoid IPv6 entirely.

Avoid multihoming

Multihoming is the practice of connecting a server to multiple networks, generally with the intention of making some or all network services accessible from multiple subnets.

When multihoming is implemented using a *hostname-per-interface* approach, a single DNS server can be used to store the multiple hostname entries in a single place. However, this approach doesn't work well with Hadoop when secured using Kerberos, since services can only be configured to use a single *service principal name* (SPN), and an SPN includes the fully qualified hostname of a service.

When multihoming is implemented using the hostname-per-server approach, a single DNS server is no longer sufficient. The IP address required by a client now depends on which network the client is located on. Solving this problem adds significant complexity to network configuration, usually involving a combination of both DNS and */etc/hosts*. This approach also adds complexity when it comes to Kerberos security, since it is essential that forward and reverse DNS lookups match exactly in all access scenarios.

Multihoming is most frequently seen in edge nodes, as described in "Edge-connected networks" on page 130, where edge services listen on multiple interfaces for incoming requests. Multihomed cluster nodes should be avoided where possible, for the following reasons:

- At the time of this writing, not all cluster services support multihoming.
- Multihoming isn't widely deployed in the user community, so issues aren't found as quickly.
- Open source developers don't often develop and test against multihomed configurations.

Summary

In this chapter we discussed how cluster services such as Spark and HDFS use networking, how they demand the highest levels of performance and availability, and ultimately how those requirements drive the network architecture and integration patterns needed.

Equipped with this knowledge, network and system architects should be in a good position to ensure that the network design is robust enough to support a cluster today, and flexible enough to continue to do so as a cluster grows.

## CHAPTER 5

Organizational Challenges

In this chapter, we cover organizational aspects of successful Hadoop integration. It is written for decision makers who build the teams that will deal with big data use cases and operations, or for people who influence these decisions. That said, this chapter may also be of interest to a wider audience, including HR professionals. We will highlight how Hadoop's architecture results in organizational challenges when building teams that run and use it, and we will give you guidelines on what you require from your larger organization to overcome those challenges and ensure the success of Hadoop.

Although it is mostly apparent to technical staff that shifting an organization to be data-driven means a big paradigm change, Hadoop projects often end up being just another piece of software to onboard, and human factors are omitted. Especially in the case of Hadoop, that can be a mistake. Just sticking to the traditional concepts of IT operations may not result in negative effects when deploying Hadoop at small scale and the PoC level, but as you scale and take your clusters to production, problems are almost guaranteed.

To address these appropriately, you should plan for a new team, one that is dedicated to Hadoop operations. This team will not only combine many of the existing skills in your organization but will also include disciplines that are not yet common in corporate IT.

For this discussion we assume classic on-premises IT operations. As with any other workload, your mileage will vary if you decide to run in the cloud. Where appropriate, we will call out the differences of running in the cloud.

Who Runs It?

A very common challenge with adopting Hadoop is the way that its operation technologically surpasses the classic disciplines in the IT organization. You end up with two choices:

- Place the responsibility for big data on an existing operations department.
- Create a new team for big data.

We aim to show that the first option is not sustainable in the long term, given the way that big data systems and Hadoop are structured.

The second option, that of building a big data team, should not imply that this team will manage clusters and Hadoop technologies in complete autonomy, but rather that it must assume end-to-end responsibility for them. This team will control certain layers in the enterprise IT stack that were previously covered by other teams, such as storage. It will also be responsible for new layers, like YARN or Spark or HBase operations, in their entirety. On the other hand, it will need to rely on other teams, either via a split operations model, as is mostly the case with Linux, or by change requests, as is often the case with networks.

It is important to understand the reasoning behind this: Hadoop is a distributed software framework by design, and distributed systems cannot be sliced across clear boundaries. The preexisting roles in IT are not easily applied in separation anymore —for example, each node in a cluster provides both compute and storage resources. Operations teams have to think about the individual nodes' impact on the network in the event of a large join or shuffle operations and have to take into account the physical placement and partitioning of database tables. Data scientists and developers need to seriously consider how Spark applications are distributed on these tables and partitioned datasets in order to write efficient distributed applications that stay within SLAs. All participants should know how the query systems (such as Spark, HBase, and Impala) function to a fair degree, and you should also have some experts who can debug these systems and their interaction with the Linux operating system. Equally, everyone should be familiar with the various file formats, such as Avro and Parquet, that are important to achieve superior results.

Is It Infrastructure, Middleware, or an Application?

Hadoop cannot be categorized in the classic sense—it's infrastructure, middleware, *and* application. We could say it is a middleware software framework that provides a distributed infrastructure layer for compute and storage, exceeding the scalability of state-of-the-art infrastructure.

Hadoop shifts a fair amount of infrastructure-level features into the middleware and application domains and, in many aspects, requires application designers to pay attention to the mechanisms on the infrastructure level to unleash its full feature set and potential. Take, as a prime example, data replication in HDFS, which lifts the durability guarantees from hardware failsafes into a Java-based software framework.

Another key aspect is that, despite being distributed systems, big data clusters are monolithic. Hadoop services, for example, scale horizontally across many servers but vertically integrate hardware, system-level software, and middleware infrastructure across all these servers into a single system. This requires an understanding of the cluster as a whole, rather than focusing on individual components.

Case Study: A Typical Business Intelligence Project

The type of organizational change that Hadoop drives is best described by an example. In the following, we compare the team setup of a business intelligence (BI) application on top of state-of-the-art data warehouse infrastructure against the proposed team setup when implementing the same solution on Hadoop.

The comparison and technical description will be very high level so that we can focus on the organizational factors. Typically, BI and data science organizations have naturally evolved on top of original use cases.

The Traditional Approach

Let us start with an overview of the traditional solution approach, as shown in Figure 5-1. The data stored in data warehouses mostly originates from the core business use cases, which are sophisticated applications—in our example a web frontend and business logic implemented in a middleware application server. The use cases that run on the application server are each implemented by a team of developers. This could be a webshop, a hotel booking system, or a message board, for example.

The BI solution is typically implemented by a separate development team. Conducting analytical queries on the transactional system would likely impact overall system performance. The query response times of the transactional database are therefore typically optimized by regularly deleting finalized and expired transactions that are no longer needed for the actual use case. The expired or completed transactions are *extracted* and *loaded* into the data warehouse system. Optionally, *transformations* are applied while the data transitions into the data warehouse, as indicated by the ETL arrow.

As shown in Figure 5-1, the data warehouse is accessed via a server running a BI solution, which implements web-based dashboards to graphically present aggregate results of analytical queries. Some solutions also require separate client software to interface with the server. To provide scalability, it is common, although not necessary, that several servers host the data warehouse implementation.

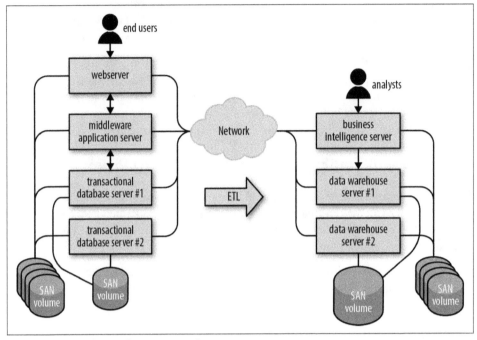

Figure 5-1. Traditional reporting solution

 Scaling state-of-the-art data warehouses has practical limits. Installations with more than three or four servers are typically implemented as appliances, but solutions rarely scale beyond the double-digit terabyte range. This is partly for technological reasons and partly for economic reasons and is one of the drivers for organizations to consider Hadoop.

To drive up utilization of IT infrastructure, the majority of organizations use compute and storage virtualization. The BI server will most likely run in a virtual machine (VM) that connects to a remote storage volume implemented on a *storage area network* (SAN). This is frequently also true of data warehouse servers; however, many warehouse solutions are built as bare-metal appliances to provide the performance advantages of local storage, just like storage systems in the Hadoop realm do.

Typical Team Setup

Next, we break down the typical IT job roles shown in the traditional setup in Figure 5-1. Although all of these roles are well known to the reader, we review them here to set the stage for our revised team setup in the next section.

We require the following roles:

- Architect
- Analyst
- Software developer
- Systems engineer
- Administrator

The horizontal axis of Figure 5-2 shows how these individual job roles cover the spectrum of required skills. The vertical axis provides a rough gauge of the required depth of skill for a given role. As the figure indicates, there is a fair amount of overlap among the roles. In the following sections, we look at each role individually and how they relate to each other.

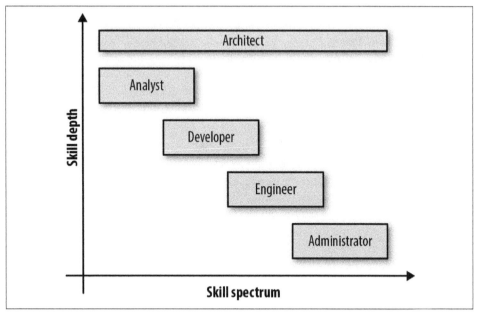

Figure 5-2. Skill sets and overlap among typical roles in a business intelligence stack

Architect

The IT or enterprise architect is found in almost every corporation. Architects have a very wide range of skills across all technologies involved in a given solution. They take on technical coordination among the other roles involved, provide a blueprint for the solution, and oversee the technical implementation. They also work closely with project management, line management, and all other stakeholders as the technical representatives of particular projects. Architects typically grow into their role from an expert role in one of the other disciplines.

Analyst

The analyst usually has a sophisticated background in statistics or mathematics. Analysts understand and apply the models centered around descriptive and predictive analytics.

> Although there are also business analysts, when we mention analysts in this text, we are referring to *data analysts*.

Most analysts are able to process and explore data in statistical or scientific programming languages such as R or Python. For scalable productive BI reports, the analyst uses a range of algorithms on multidimensional views on the data in tabular form (also known as *cubes*) based on star or snowflake database schemas in the data warehouse. This achieves a high degree of abstraction for the analyst, who focuses on the data algorithms that often have been optimized for cubes in the BI solution.

Software developer

Software developers not only write, build, and maintain code, but also are involved with the continuous integration and operation of the underlying infrastructure. In our example, a software developer would likely be involved in providing the presentation layer of the overall solution, producing dashboards according to the requirements of the analyst team.

> So as to avoid confusion with the term *systems engineer* (introduced in the text that follows), we do not use the term *software engineer*.

This may either be done via a custom-built solution or by leveraging BI software. Depending on the organization, the same or an additional team of developers will design the data model of the data warehouse.

Administrator

Administrators, also called *operators* in some organizations, are responsible for the day-to-day process of keeping the infrastructure up and running, including updates, incident resolution, and monitoring of the infrastructure and the applications created by the developers and engineers. Administrators typically use configuration management and monitoring frameworks and often develop and maintain scripts or code to support these systems and to increase the degree of automation.

Some solutions are implemented on top of appliances—in our case, a data warehouse appliance. In this case, there is no need for Linux, storage, or virtualization administrators; however, a highly specialized administrator would have to tend to the operation of the appliance itself. The need for a virtualization administrator naturally depends on whether virtualization is used.

Systems engineer

In addition to software engineering, the title *engineer* refers to job roles concerned with defining operational standards and procedures for the various IT infrastructure domains. These people may be called *systems engineers*, but even more often the specific domains of infrastructure are used in the name of the role. For example, *network engineers* design the address layout of a Layer 2 domain and its failover strategy for a certain use case. *Storage engineers* define the type of storage and high-availability and performance characteristics, as well as quotas for the given use case. *Virtualization engineers* focus on VM provisioning and on meeting required SLAs on the compute layer.

The systems engineer often has some software development skills, along with those of an administrator. As such, in our example, multiple engineering and administration roles would be involved in the full BI stack:

- Database engineer/administrator
- Linux engineer/administrator
- Server engineer/administrator
- Storage engineer/administrator
- Virtualization engineer/administrator
- Network engineer/administrator

In many organizations engineering and operations are not separate disciplines, and the operational standards and design for a given solution are defined by the architect at a high level, after which the administrator designs and implements the low-level details. When an organization chooses to employ engineers, it is typically due to heavy reliance on operational standards and procedures, such as within hosting or outsourcing companies. Also, the use of offshore operations teams and the resulting need to define the operational standards at a single place in the corporation—for example, a center of competence—are strong drivers to employ systems engineers.

 If you run in the cloud, basically there are no server, storage, or virtualization engineers or administrators, since that part of engineering is mostly automated by the cloud platform. You are likely to still have a team of Linux and database engineers and administrators.

Compartmentalization of IT

We went through the previous exercise to introduce the typical roles and to remind ourselves of the strict separation of duties that many corporate IT environments have adopted in the past, to make the delivery of complex IT stacks a true service for their corporations.

The large number of roles and responsibilities involved can be challenging. The reason behind *compartmentalization* is that administrators and engineers are all responsible for a large number of different systems and can easily scale their work by the operational standards and interfaces in the organization. This often results in the organizational structure depicted in Figure 5-3.

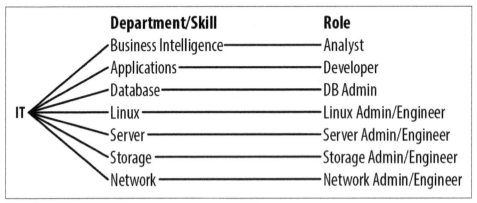

Figure 5-3. Classic enterprise IT team organization

The end user or customer in this scenario is the analyst. Any changes required at any layer are usually requested by one of the layers above it via a ticketing system. For example, a request by the analysts to add more tables to the data warehouse would be brought to the database administrators, who may in turn request a new storage partition from the Linux team, which then needs to ask the storage team to resize a SAN volume.

As you can see in Figure 5-4, in order to run the data warehouse systems, server administrators and engineers, Linux and virtualization professionals, and database administrators must interact with each single system, creating a complex stack of duties and responsibilities.

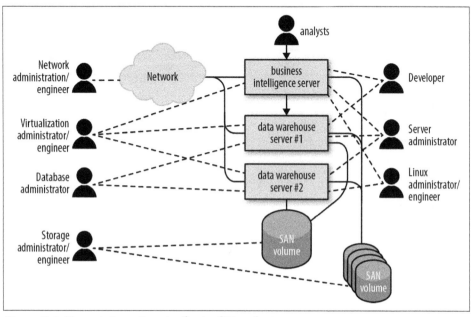

Figure 5-4. Team interactions in the traditional setup

Revised Team Setup for Hadoop in the Enterprise

Similarly, analyzing data at the scale provided by Hadoop requires the analyst to understand how Hadoop, as a distributed system, works. Often, the only way to bring the data into the format required to run an algorithm at scale is to craft an ETL pipeline directly as a Spark job. Equally often, scaling algorithms and developing machine learning applications require going beyond the capabilities of business intelligence solutions and hand-tailoring big data applications in code. Coming full circle on these additional capabilities, while maintaining the analyst's solid understanding of statistical methods, is what best characterizes the transition to the *data scientist* role.

On the operational side, we show that Hadoop requires knowledge of several engineering disciplines that we mentioned earlier, such as Linux and storage, in a single role. The complexity and the velocity of evolution in the Hadoop ecosystem require a tight coupling of the definition of operational procedures and actual operation. Therefore, in most enterprise Hadoop deployments we have come across, the staff operating the platform always work at the level of an engineer, as well. We refer to the corresponding role as the *big data engineer*.

Big data architect

Let us now turn to how Hadoop technology changes requirements for successful teaming within the organization. Figure 5-5 provides an overview of a revised setup of roles, which we describe in detail in the following sections.

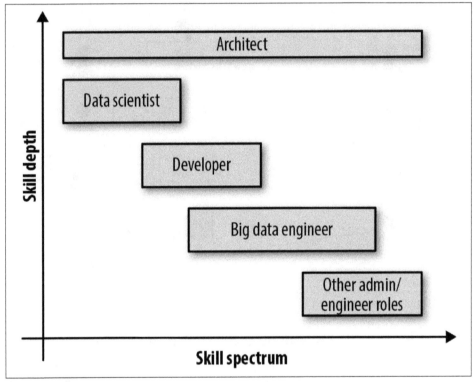

Figure 5-5. Skill sets and overlap in the example Hadoop team setup

Much like the architect in our original solution, the *big data architect* oversees the overall solution on a technical level and performs stakeholder management. However, the big data architect ideally also shows an extensive set of prior experience on the Hadoop platform.

It is well worth mentioning that, since technical architects largely work as the mediators between the technical teams and management, architects for Hadoop also represent the paradigm change in IT organizations that we are describing in this chapter.

Since the big data architect role overlooks the complete skill spectrum of Hadoop, it is certain that internal and external teams will turn to the architect with questions on how to best build big data solutions and how to interface with the Hadoop team.

The architect is responsible for technical coordination and should have extensive experience working with big data and Hadoop.

Data scientist

Although the term "data scientist" has been around for some time, the current surge in its use in corporate IT reflects how much big data changes the complexity of data management in IT. It also reflects a shift in academia, where data science has evolved to become a fully qualified discipline at many renowned universities.[1]

Sometimes we see organizations that are largely indifferent to data science per se, or that simply try to rebrand all existing analyst staff as data scientists. The data scientist, however, actually does more:

Statistics and classic BI
> The data scientist depends on classic tools to present and productize the result of his work, but before these tools can be used, a lot of exploration, cleansing, and modeling is likely to be required on the Hadoop layer.
>
> This is due to the massive increases of volume and variety of the data in the Hadoop realm, It is also due to the fact that the data scientist gains an enormous set of capabilities, via tools such as Spark, to evaluate the data at scale before it transitions into its final form, for example, a denormalized relational model, which previously was not an option.
>
> Many BI vendors have made large technology investments to supply an equal degree of abstraction for Hadoop datasets as for data cubes in relational warehouses, but their ability to efficiently scale varies from use case to use case. Another common challenge when transitioning analytics problems to the Hadoop realm is that analysts need to master the various data formats that are used in Hadoop, since, for example, the previously dominant model of cubing data is almost never used in Hadoop. Data scientists typically also need extensive experience with SQL as a tool to drill down into the datasets that they require to build statistical models, via SparkSQL, Hive, or Impala.

Machine learning and deep learning
> Simply speaking, *machine learning* is where the rubber of big data analytics hits the road. While certainly a hyped term, machine learning goes beyond classic statistics, with more advanced algorithms that predict an outcome by learning

---

1 See, for example, Berkeley's Master of Information and Data Science program (*http://bit.ly/2OW8HZy*).

from the data—often without explicitly being programmed. The most advanced methods in machine learning, referred to as *deep learning*, are able to automatically discover the relevant data features for learning, which essentially enables use cases like computer vision, natural language processing, or fraud detection for any corporation. Many machine learning algorithms (even fairly simple ones) benefit from big data in an unproportional, even unreasonable way, an effect which was described as early as 2001.[2] As big data becomes readily available in more and more organizations, machine learning becomes a defining movement in the overall IT industry to take advantage of this effect. Competitors are setting themselves apart by how well they embrace this advanced part of data-driven decision-making.

Although we do not go into the details of machine learning in this book, its techniques are becoming essential for enterprises. Machine learning typically requires a solid background in mathematics/statistics and algorithms. Computationally, instead of the prepackaged, cube-based algorithms of statistical software packages, data scientists rely on programming languages such as Python, Scala, or R to implement and run machine learning models. Frameworks like TensorFlow, PyTorch, or DeepLearning4J enable support the data scientist to abstract and build machine learning models or neural networks, regardless of the execution environment. At scale, however, this requires in-depth knowledge of parallel computational frameworks, such as Spark. Keras and TensorFlow, in turn, support running on Spark but also leverage GPUs, for example, which are becoming an increasingly important topic for Spark itself.

Coding

Whereas the typical analyst or statistician understands methods and models mathematically, a good data scientist also has a solid background in parallel algorithms to build large-scale distributed applications around such models. As we already mentioned, the data scientist is well versed in coding in third-generation and functional programming languages, such as Scala, Java, and Python, in addition to the domain-specific languages of the classic analytics world. In this function, the data scientist collaborates with development departments to build fully fledged distributed applications that can be productively deployed to Hadoop. The work split could be that the development organization builds the ingest and business logic of the application and maintains the build-and-deployment process, while the data scientist owns and tests the modules and routines that perform the actual learning and modeling algorithms at scale.

---

2 Michele Banko and Eric Brill, "Scaling to Very Very Large Corpora for Natural Language Disambiguation" (*http://www.aclweb.org/anthology/P01-1005*), Microsoft Research.

In order to apply state-of-the-art analytics methods to big data, organizations should ensure that their analyst staff extend their skill sets into these domains and evolve into what we refer to as data scientists. This requires some leeway for experimentation but is certainly also a clear-cut directive to embrace distributed systems.

Many organizations that have gone through the initial Hadoop adoption cycle have developed a firm conviction that their data is among their most important assets. The data scientist is an extremely skilled role that unlocks this asset and is, in turn, one of the most difficult roles to staff in an organization. Data scientists are also likely to be among the most expensive roles to staff from the open market. When hiring for this role we recommend extra scrutiny because of the current inflationary use, throughout the industry, of the term data scientist.

Big data engineer

Because Hadoop is a disruptive technology, operations teams will spend a fair amount of time defining standards for it. The standards for Hadoop will constantly evolve and grow as new projects and services are onboarded. Thus, administrators will often face engineering work, and conversely, engineers will often find standardizing and adopting Hadoop technology into fully industrialized procedures so short-lived that they tend to also operate the platform. As a result, for Hadoop, we have frequently seen operations and engineering merge into one role. Therefore, if possible, you should make the corresponding role of the big data engineer official.

As far as the skill profile goes, you probably already know that there is simply nobody within an enterprise IT storage team who can, for example, run and maintain an HDFS instance or oversee a multitenant YARN scheduling environment without profound knowledge of the Hadoop platform itself. To do so, the big data engineer requires a versatile set of skills and needs to evolve it into the specifics of Hadoop. The best way to demonstrate this is to break down these skills by the classic disciplines, which we do in the following list. We also try to give a range of examples to demonstrate why a particular area of skill is required:

Linux
> The big data engineer needs to be able to assume full control over the servers, their operating system, and their storage subsystem. Big data engineers regularly perform low-level analysis on Linux. Tools such as `strace` or access to the */sys* and */proc* filesystems may be required to debug problems with the various Hadoop daemons. Other examples of the big data engineer's Linux skills include debugging with secondary services, such as DNS, the Network Time Protocol (NTP), or the System Security Services Daemon (SSSD), which are essential for Hadoop's function (as we learned in Chapter 7 and will see again in Chapter 10).

> These activities create a common point of friction: in most cases, it does not make sense to have the Hadoop team assume full responsibility for Linux admin-

istration. Most Hadoop experts will neither display the interest nor have the time to pursue all the challenging tasks required to keep Linux up and running according to a corporation's operational and security standards. Yet, as illustrated earlier, it is imperative that big data engineers have root-level access to each Linux instance in the cluster. There is a plethora of additional administrative tasks, from basic restart of Hadoop service roles across upgrades to storage management and problem debugging, which require administrator-level access. Working these tasks via Linux tickets would simply paralyze your Hadoop team. This results in a *split administrator model* for Linux, as shown in Figure 5-7. This needs to be negotiated with Linux operations.

Storage

With Hadoop, storage management, storage resilience, and durability logic that used to be implemented in hardware moves into the software and middleware layer. Physically, storage is implemented on local disks across many commodity servers, which run on Linux. This requires that the big data engineer's skill set not only include storage and distributed applications but also an understanding of the characteristics of the storage subsystem and server hardware, such as RAID controllers and hard disks in the Hadoop nodes, as well as the network layer that affects HDFS performance, as covered in Chapter 3.

Resource management

A significant part of the work performed by the big data engineer is concerned with managing and separating the cluster's resources among tenants and with imposing a cluster-wide information architecture and security model. This includes but is not limited to management of:

- Static and dynamic resource allocations such as Linux cgroups and YARN queues
- Permissions and access control lists in HDFS, Kafka, or Apache Kudu
- Role-based access control via tools such as Apache Sentry or Apache Ranger
- Integration points with identity management and external security systems, such as LDAP, Microsoft Active Directory, or Kerberos

Although every big data engineer should be knowledgeable about these areas, not all of them will be focused on resource management and storage. They may also be experts in higher-level query systems, databases, and application services of big data and Hadoop systems. This may mark a natural boundary and an opportunity for specialization in your team.

Applications

To fully unlock the huge throughput and performance advantages of massively scalable clusters, the work of the big data engineer transcends into query and application design itself, supporting software development teams. Today, "applications" mostly refers to Spark applications, whether they are Spark batch jobs,

Spark SQL, Spark Streaming, or Structured Streaming applications. Big data engineers have expertise in Spark mechanisms for parallelization—i.e., transformations such as `map()` or `join()`—and their ramifications for the partitioning pattern of the data, as well as Spark's internal resource management, to just name a few examples. Additionally, big data engineers frequently install third-party software packages, such as certain Python distributions, manually on cluster hosts to support specific use cases.

SQL-based systems and databases

The big data engineer needs to understand how to design databases, tables, and partitioning schemas in the various Hadoop database implementations that may support their use cases. For SQL query systems such as Hive or Impala, best practices recommend staffing the big data engineering team with database administrators. For many organizations, it is therefore tempting to assign the entire responsibility for Hadoop databases to existing database administration teams. This often helps to partly fill a required skill gap for SQL-based systems but typically does not help for systems such as HBase, Solr, or Kafka. It also neglects the high degree to which Hadoop-based query systems are intertwined with the platform itself. For example, to be able to properly design large tables for complex queries in Impala or SparkSQL, detailed knowledge about HDFS and the Parquet file format are required to optimize performance via proper partitioning and choice of split size in HDFS. Another example would be the choice of compression type and ratio and Hadoop file formats to achieve best throughput on predicate evaluation in SQL queries.

Other query systems

Maybe not initially, but eventually (and based on use cases in the business), big data engineers also typically command at least one Hadoop service, such as Solr, HBase, or Kafka, in addition to the base services. Nowadays it is also common to find HBase, Kafka, or Solr talent on the open market.

Networks

Even though networking is not included in the big data engineer's direct responsibilities, big data engineers often trace network communication via the *Wireshark* tool to analyze problems with the various RPC communication threads we discussed in Chapter 4. Even a simple call to the `netstat` command to identify a blocked port on the firewall requires knowledge of the Linux network stack and root-level privileges. As a follow-up, it is often necessary to engage directly with the network team on the design of the network itself. Many times, Hadoop requires changes to the production standard on the leaf level of the datacenter network. The network department is the only one that can make sure that any of those adaptions integrate well with the remainder of the datacenter network. The big data engineer should seek a close liaison with the network engineering team, working toward an optimized infrastructure, as introduced in Chapter 4.

Apart from the open market, sources for staffing big data engineers may, for example, be database administrator teams or Linux operators with an affinity for software development, or developers with an advanced knowledge of Linux. These professionals initially operate the base platform layer, but also eventually assist other business units with application design. Additionally, software developers are often recruited into big data engineering and then are predestined to support the business units in application design and in maintaining and operating the application layer in the cluster.

Solution Overview with Hadoop

Now that we have changed the roles and skill profiles to wield cluster technology, we attempt a new solution design based on a Hadoop cluster.

Figure 5-6 shows how the proposed roles interact with the technical solution built on top of Hadoop. As you can see, the number of roles that are involved in the solution is now reduced from eight to six.

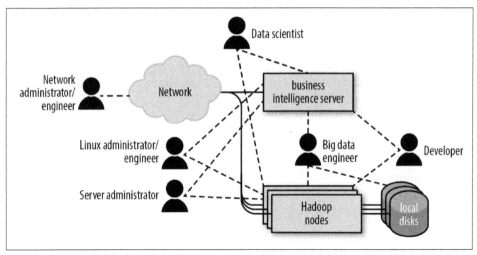

Figure 5-6. Solution overview with Hadoop

The data warehouse is now likely implemented with Impala or Hive, or potentially with Spark SQL. In almost all cases, an existing BI solution would remain in place and would be integrated with Hadoop via JDBC/ODBC. In some cases, BI solutions also launch Spark queries themselves.

The Linux and server administrators conduct minimum system maintenance, such as patch management, firmware upgrades, parts replacement, etc., and the big data engineer handles all necessary system customization to run Hadoop on the nodes. In our target solution, a storage and virtualization engineer is not required. As depicted, the big data engineer drives storage engineering and administration by taking over responsibility for HDFS. The big data engineer also takes over the responsibility of database administration on top of Hadoop and fulfills the classic role of database administrator.

Data scientists design and use the BI solution but also spend much of their time interfacing with the Hadoop cluster, to explore and curate the data and to develop applications directly on Hadoop.

Just like in the original solution, a team of developers writes and maintains applications on the BI server. The same team of developers (or, alternatively, a second team) is responsible for implementing applications on top of the Hadoop cluster.

New Team Setup

How does this affect the typical IT organizational structure we reviewed in "The Traditional Approach" on page 141? We are perfectly aware that staff reorganization does not happen overnight and that one size does not fit all. But the best way to provide prescriptive guidance is to use an example, so this section can be used as the blueprint for a *big data team*.

In Figure 5-7, we illustrate that a new department for big data includes Hadoop developers as well as big data engineers. Data scientists would likely remain in the BI department but would closely collaborate on big data application development with the big data department, as indicated via the dotted line. The big data engineering team assumes full responsibility for Hadoop cluster management—especially for all Hadoop query systems, such as Hive, Impala, HBase, or Solr—and for the underlying storage layer. As outlined earlier, the big data engineers share responsibility for the underlying servers with the Linux and server operations departments.

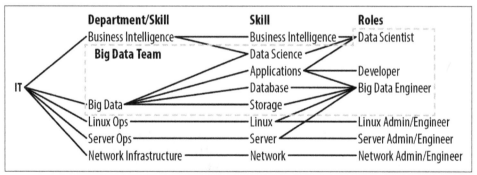

Figure 5-7. How big data typically impacts enterprise IT organizations

Split Responsibilities

As we discussed, the changes we describe at certain points require a split in responsibility for certain technology components among the big data engineering and other operations and engineering teams.

A common example is Linux administration. The the big data engineer might require a specific version of a Java Development Kit (JDK), which is normally fixed as part of the Linux team's standardized rollout. You need to establish whether such a change can be unilaterally performed by big data engineering or whether this needs to be requested via service tickets. If you figure in many nodes from larger clusters and a multitude of these integration points, this may well result in a large number of service tickets, which may not always complete successfully. It's imperative to establish the right balance between self-sufficiency and standardization at exactly these points.

Another example is hardware component replacement, The server operations team owns most of the process for replacing defective parts or entire servers. Although many software services in Hadoop instantly kick off a process of self-healing after a server or disk is impaired, the big data engineer depends on the server team to recover full capacity. As opposed to virtualized environments, where virtual machines may be automatically migrated to other hosts, you need to determine the process, for example, for the replacement of a complete server. Does the server team maintain a small stockpile of spare systems, or do they rely on service by the manufacturer? If the model is that of external service, what is the service level in terms of response time? After a server is replaced, who does the basic configuration, such as storage-controller configuration, and how long will it take to deploy the server with Linux?

 When you run in the public cloud, as you will see in Chapter 16, you can also choose PaaS/SaaS solutions, which reduce the footprint of roles (as well as your flexibility and control over infrastructure components).

Do I Need DevOps?

In a sense, the rise of the term *DevOps* mirrors the rise of corporate distributed computing. In some definitions DevOps signals a merging of the developer and operator roles into one, often skipping any compartmentalization as described earlier. Others simply define it as operators who automate as much as possible in code, which is certainly beneficial in the world of distributed systems.

To a degree, the big data engineer falls into both definitions, and in a closely organized group, even the data scientist may take the initiative on certain tasks around deployment automation and platform performance optimization.

For the most part, however, our experience is that a full implementation of DevOps only occurs in companies whose entire business is centered around a few large-scale, web-based services; classic enterprise IT as a service to the core business is too diversified to give up compartmentalization.

Hadoop does indeed encourage heavy consolidation and building the equivalent of a large-scale internal service for data, also often referred to as the *data lake*.

To summarize, in our experience, it is best to start with a dedicated big data engineering role that consolidates engineering and operations for Hadoop and maintains a close liaison with development teams.

Do I Need a Center of Excellence/Competence?

Many organizations have a center of excellence (or center of competence) to establish new technology internally and to enable quick movement on related projects. For Hadoop, we have come across this setup often, and for the most part it is helpful. Often, the center of excellence directly inherits the responsibility to operate Hadoop environments. Alternatively, the center of excellence may be the bridgehead to offshore Hadoop operation teams. You should think about how much such a center of excellence would depend on existing processes and compartmentalization. If the new team cannot act autonomously as described here, the excellence might be on paper only. If you can, aim to staff a center of excellence with big data engineers, developers, and optionally, data scientists.

Summary

Hadoop moves the policies for storage durability, high availability, multitenancy, and many other infrastructural aspects into software, while the basic mechanisms it relies on are implemented in commodity infrastructure. This requires Hadoop staff to operate, maintain, patch, and debug many infrastructure layers at once.

In this chapter we introduced the role of the data scientist, implemented in many organizations today. The data scientist represents the natural evolution of BI analytics toward more sophisticated methods, such as machine learning and large, scalable data curation and complex event processing.

We further introduced the role of the big data engineer, who is required to display a very versatile skill set, in addition to expertise in several layers of hardware infrastructure and Hadoop software. The big data engineer partly consolidates responsibilities of other IT departments into a single role, gaining necessary autonomy over distributed technology, which is operated monolithically. In practice, big data engineers depend on other functions, such as Linux and server operations, to perform their work.

Effectively, as you probably realize, the main audience for this book is big data engineers and big data architects. You may wonder whether the big data engineer's responsibility is not simply too much specialization for a typical IT job role, and you would be right. Big data engineering is not yet a typical job role, and it is hard to staff and to grow into.

As we pointed out, though, this does not mean that an organization will get away with treating Hadoop as just another middleware application or database.

Today, there is no clear, de facto model that is the right way to run. What can be said for certain is that Hadoop disrupts strict compartmentalization and requires engineers with a broad range of sophisticated skills.

## CHAPTER 6

Datacenter Considerations

Hadoop architects and engineers are not primarily concerned with the datacenter, which offers rather mechanical and commoditized layers of enterprise IT. However, some key features of Hadoop only work as advertised if they are met by the correct layout of datacenter technology. You need to be aware of these effects when placing Hadoop into an existing enterprise IT environment, which has typically been optimized for virtualized host environments and remote storage solutions over the course of the last 10 years.

The content in this chapter, although not an exhaustive discussion on datacenters, may well be of crucial importance for certain key architectural decisions related to reliability and disaster tolerance.

We initially focus on some basic datacenter infrastructure concepts before we revisit some of the ways in which Hadoop differs from other commodity infrastructure setups. We provide a section that addresses common issues with data ingest in the context of datacenters, and finally we highlight common pitfalls that emerge around topics like multidatacenter disaster tolerance.

If you run Hadoop on a public cloud service, much of this chapter is not relevant to your situation, but "Quorum spanning with three datacenters" on page 179 specifically covers an important subject around cluster spanning that you should observe.

Why Does It Matter ?

Intuition tells us that the distributed nature of Hadoop is likely to have ramifications for the datacenter. But how exactly is Hadoop different from other workloads on this level? Two topics come to mind:

Failure tolerance

For classical applications that rely on SAN storage, there often is the assumption that they can be restarted on spare infrastructure in the case of error—either in another zone of the same datacenter or in a different datacenter altogether. As a result of the inertia of the vast amounts of data that it manages, Hadoop does not offer the same flexibility. Fundamental assumptions in your organization about failure tolerance may not hold in the case of Hadoop, and this needs to be reflected in operational concepts for disaster recovery, maintenance, and datacenter-level fire drills.

Performance and scalability

Anything upwards from a medium-sized Hadoop deployment will not fit in a single rack, while most other applications in the datacenter run on a single server. Hadoop allows for configuration of additional failover capabilities and performance optimizations when deployed across multiple racks. However, as we will see, the actual rack boundary may be different than the physical boundary, in terms of power distribution, cooling, and networking. For networking performance, it is equally important to understand the actual rack boundaries.

Basic Datacenter Concepts

Datacenter design is not widely regarded as an academic discipline. Although much research and many publications exist around distributed systems and high-performance computing, there is very little literature around the subject of the datacenter itself, and it is mostly excluded from academic research.

Strikingly, it is at the center of many research efforts of large-scale web content providers such as Google[1] and Facebook.[2] These companies have an existential need to deliver their services on huge distributed platforms. They are thus driven by a strong incentive to treat a whole warehouse full of servers as a monolithic computing layer, on which they strive to consolidate services and end users as much as technically possible. (See, for example, the initial paper by Google on GFS.[3])

This obviously differs a lot from the compartmentalized IT solutions found in many enterprises. Physically, a Hadoop cluster is a collection of commodity servers. But as we mentioned in Chapter 5, a Hadoop cluster should be regarded as a *monolithic*

---

1 See Luiz André Barroso, Jimmy Cildaras, and Urs Hölzle, *The Datacenter as a Computer: An Introduction to the Design of Warehouse-Scale Machines*, 2nd Edition (*http://bit.ly/2PFLcJE*) (Morgan & Claypool Publishers, 2013).

2 Nathan Farrington and Alexey Andreyev, "Facebook's Data Center Network Architecture," (*http://bit.ly/2S8j8LP*) and Arjun Roy et al., "Inside the Social Network's (Datacenter) Network." (*http://bit.ly/2PNiBSU*)

3 Sanjay Ghemawat, Howard Gobioff, and Shun-Tak Leung, "The Google File System" (*http://bit.ly/2rYbrNs*).

appliance since, despite its distributed nature, its components work in tightly coupled concert. This is especially relevant for datacenter planning.

Apart from server housing and racking, the architecture of the datacenter affects Hadoop through the following infrastructure layers:

- Networking
- Power distribution
- Cooling

Figure 6-1 shows an example layout for datacenter facilities that accommodates a Hadoop cluster across multiple racks. We focus on the servers in Rack 1 and Rack 2. The servers are built into standard 19-inch racks. For the sake of simplicity, the figure only shows the top portion of the racks and the wiring of a single server on each rack; i.e., servers R1Server1 and R2Server1.

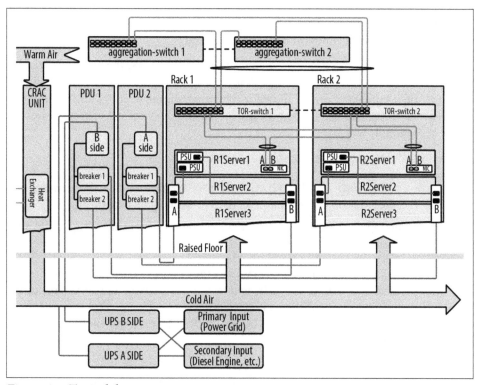

Figure 6-1. Typical datacenter setup

As is common in most enterprise IT datacenters, the power and cooling infrastructure is built redundantly along with the network layer. We investigate this infrastructure in detail in the following sections.

Your datacenter layout may look different, but the example serves to establish the important concept of *failure domains* in each of the infrastructure layers. In "Rack Awareness and Rack Failures" on page 165 we show why it is important to understand all failure domains in your cluster, especially when the cluster only runs on a small number of racks.

Cooling

Cooling in our example is conducted via an air circuit underneath a *raised floor*, as is conventional for many datacenters. The raised floor is indicated via the strong gray line beneath the rack component. The required airflow is delivered via so-called *Computer Room Air Conditioning units* (CRAC units), which are located on top of the raised floor. They absorb warm airflow, which is emitted by the servers. Each unit typically connects to a secondary cooling cycle via a heat exchanger, which removes the heat from the primary cycle. Then the CRAC unit delivers cold air to the datacenter floor under a slight amount of pressure, which causes it to emerge from the floor on the cool side of the server racks. In this configuration, the plurality of CRAC units contributes to the overall amount of cooling required.

Although one CRAC unit is closer to a given rack than others, there is no particular local binding of a given unit to a rack. Rather, the overall budget of cooling should allow for sufficient headroom to allow for downtime of one or more CRAC units for maintenance or failure. Thus, in our example, cooling does not affect rack awareness in any configurable way.

Alternative cooling infrastructure solutions exist:

- In-row cooling (*http://bit.ly/2S2vaGk*) devices are placed directly between two racks and provide cooling for the racks in their immediate proximity.
- In-rack cooling (*http://bit.ly/2zjCir6*) devices cool the heat that dissipates from a single rack only.

Both alternatives provide more efficiency than raised-floor cooling, especially when they are operated as a closed *hot aisle*, where the hot sides of the server racks are pushed against each other and the gap on the top is typically closed. Some designs— for example, Google's Hot Huts (*http://bit.ly/2DPJfUK*)—turn the entire ceiling of a hot aisle into a cooling device.

Because of the large amount of heat dissipation, these solutions often require a cooling medium. Bringing the coolant close to the rack drives a significant cost increase in plumbing and is deemed a potential hazard by some datacenter architects.

The key takeaway from this discussion is that, depending on the technology that you use, you bind the capacity of a cooling device to a set of racks. This set of racks becomes your *failure domain for cooling*. Needless to say, all failure domains ought to be cooled redundantly.

 Do you know which cooling technology is used in your datacenter and what the operational experiences of the datacenter operators are? A conversation about this may reveal important information about the role that cooling should play in your failure domain planning.

With raised-floor cooling, the device that yields cooling capacity is a CRAC unit. The failure domain in this case is hard to pinpoint—it is surely not all racks but also surely not a single rack. Redundancy is achieved by the plurality of all CRAC units.

Conversely, if you use in-row cooling, the failure domain is likely limited to just two racks and redundancy for these two racks is achieved by just a pair of devices.

Power

In our example, each server is equipped with dual modular power supply units (PSUs) to provide for redundancy. These are offered by all major server manufacturers. Each rack provides two power strips, an A side and a B side, and one PSU is connected to each.

The power strips redundantly run into the raised floor, where they in turn connect to a *power distribution unit* (PDU). As implied by the name, the PDU distributes a large power feed to a multitude of smaller circuits. Each circuit is protected by its own breaker switch, so that any problems—for example, a short in a server or a power supply—are contained within the circuit. In Figure 6-1, each breaker protects exactly one rack, but in other cases several racks might be connected.

Since a PDU may fail as a whole, it should be implemented in redundant pairs, each feeding the A and B side of a rack, as we show in Figure 6-1. Some PDU models, however, directly group the A and B side redundantly into a single enclosure.

To provide uninterrupted service in the event of a loss in primary power distribution, datacenters always use *uninterruptible power supplies* (UPSs), which are essentially large collections of batteries that bridge the gap in power until secondary power distribution sources, typically diesel engines, take over. The PDUs connect to the UPS, which is usually also laid out redundantly into two independent systems for the A side and the B side.

Depending on the datacenter's architecture, the A side and the B side are independent power feeds from the regional power grid, in which case the substations and the primary switchgear that performs voltage conversions from high to medium voltages are also implemented redundantly.

Because of the distinct breakers for Rack 1 and Rack 2 in Figure 6-1, it makes sense from a high-availability and Hadoop rack-awareness standpoint to consider both racks as separate, but bear in mind that a failure of the entire PDU would affect both racks.

 The ideal case, from a redundancy standpoint, is that Rack 2 would be connected to a separate pair of PDUs, which often cannot be guaranteed. However, it may be possible for someone from the datacenter team to put your master nodes on different PDU pairs.

Power distribution designs may differ in the usage of alternating or direct current between the UPS layer and the PSU to optimize conversion loss and sometimes to reduce the number of components in the final solution. Some designs (*http://bit.ly/ 2S6egXs*), also actively developed by Google, even integrate the UPS directly at the PSU level. However, these sorts of optimizations are rarely found in enterprise IT, where company colocation is common and standardization is thus important.

It should be noted that redundant power supplies are not strictly necessary for Hadoop, if you can deal with rack failures. Some of the large-scale Web 2.0 content providers reduce redundancy on the hardware layer, since most of the services we have covered—especially HDFS—by design allow the loss of replicas. If you can fully recover a failed rack, running with a single PSU can be an option, but read "Rack Awareness and Rack Failures" on page 165 to fully understand the ramifications of reducing server-level and rack-level redundancy.

Network

In our example, we show a fully redundant network layer—no matter which of the components fails, all servers can still communicate with each other. Figure 6-1 shows each server redundantly connected to a pair of top-of-rack (TOR) switches, one each in Rack 1 and Rack 2, which implement the *access layer*, as introduced in "Resiliency" on page 123. In our example, each server uses link aggregation technology, such as LACP, to be able to compensate for a failure of one network connection. To also be able to compensate for the loss of one of the switches each such aggregated link is split across TOR-switch 1 and TOR-switch 2, which would both be in the same MC-LAG group. Both TOR switches in our example directly feed into an *aggregation layer* of the datacenter via two uplinks, to provide for the same level of redundancy as between the servers and the TOR switches.

Although the process of cross-cabling racks, as shown in our example, is relatively complex and error-prone, it is still pursued in many cases since it allows for the consolidation of more ports on fewer switches. A redundant alternative is to have a pair of TOR switches in each rack to compensate for switch failures.

The goal of many network departments is to implement a single Layer 2 domain across all switches and revert to Layer 3 routing only if really necessary. This is possible via an Ethernet fabric, which we describe in more detail in "Network Fabrics" on page 127. The access layer in our example uses MC-LAG for the hop of the servers to the TOR switches, but often networking teams run a standard that requires the fabric protocol to be on the access layer.

If you choose a link aggregation mode that round-robins packets on server ports A and B, network traffic for Rack 1 and Rack 2 will actually be shared by all switches equally and Hadoop rack awareness should group all servers in Rack 1 and Rack 2 into a single logical rack, which also becomes your failure domain.

In many cases, ports A and B are set up in a pure failover configuration, which is easier in operations but also omits half of the maximum possible bandwidth. Considering Hadoop's dependence on swift east-west communication performance, it is best to implement a round-robin policy, which can be achieved by using MC-LAGs for each rack.

Rack Awareness and Rack Failures

Now that we know about failure domains for each layer, we can investigate how they work together best with Hadoop rack awareness. Hadoop is aware of racks for two reasons: performance and increased data durability.

Our discussion here focuses on the durability aspect. Rack failure is a severe event, especially on small to medium-sized clusters. Hadoop has a range of built-in mechanisms that alleviate the failure of a whole rack in software, but they work best in big environments with many racks and they sometimes do not work in small environments. The obvious example of this is a single-rack cluster, but the guidelines pertain to small multirack clusters as well.

For example, if you run on two racks and then lose one, your data is still available (assuming correct distribution of cluster roles, as discussed in "Cluster Configurations and Node Types" on page 97), but degradation of the overall service is likely to be so severe that many of your jobs will fail. As we learned in "Erasure Coding Versus Replication" on page 71, without redundancy in power, cooling, and network, erasure coding requires a minimum of nine racks to effectively protect against rack loss. However, enterprises often begin their journey with just a single rack and then grow to multiple racks within the first year, depending on the overall adoption process. If there is a single point of failure in your datacenter infrastructure—the power, cooling, or networking layer—a problem in one of those layers will very likely impact multiple racks at once. Luckily, as we have just learned, the various redundancy mechanisms that should be built into your infrastructure make it much less likely that entire racks go down, and thus it's also very unlikely that a single rack fails in isolation.

Let us look at a few possible scenarios. We have grouped them by the three infrastructure layers and different cases (see Table 6-1):

The good case
> Where highly available infrastructure conveniently covers failures, even for small clusters

The single point of failure (SPOF) case
> Where high availability of the infrastructure is decreased and the cluster is too small to properly compensate for the infrastructure error by software mechanisms

The case of bad luck
> Where, despite highly available infrastructure, you suffer service disruption

Table 6-1. Good and bad failure scenarios

	Good case	SPOF	Bad luck
Cooling	One of your CRAC units fails, but the other CRAC units, which ran at slightly reduced capacity before, compensate for the missing peer by increasing their airflow output.	Too many servers were put on the raised floor, and you have no headroom in the output of the remaining CRAC units left to cover a failing unit. Several racks, among them both racks in your two-node cluster, eventually exceed target operating temperatures and their servers shut down.	The coolant supply to your redundant in-row cooling experiences a leak on both feeds. Several racks cannot be cooled without the cooling medium and eventually exceed operating temperature. (Regular inspections of plumbing infrastructure helps to avoid this.)
Power	All component layers in power distribution from the main feeds to the PSU are laid out redundantly. The A-side PDU that feeds several racks in your cluster fails. The B-side power distribution continues to supply the affected racks all the way to the redundant PSUs in the affected server.	You operate a three-rack cluster with a single power supply per server, effectively not connecting one side of your power distribution. One power supply suffers an electrical short, which triggers the breaker switch on the PDU and brings down all the servers on that circuit. Two of those servers were HDFS JournalNodes.	Your cluster consists of two racks. Both racks are connected to the same pair of PDUs, each on its own breaker circuit. The A-side PDU fails and the power strip on the B side of Rack 1 experiences a short. Rack 1 is down and unfortunately held two JournalNode instances, which puts HDFS into read-only mode.

	Good case	SPOF	Bad luck
Network	The switches in your cluster need an urgent firmware upgrade. The network team can safely reboot one switch after another for maintenance, since the entire cluster network is built redundantly by bonding network connections into the access layer.	All hosts in your two-rack cluster use bonded network connections to increase throughput but connect to a single TOR switch. One TOR switch fails and leaves half of the nodes unavailable. The heavily reduced compute capacity results in failing Spark jobs and missed SLAs.	A cluster like the one shown in Figure 6-1 experiences many frame errors, and the network team sets out to replace aggregation switch 1. Instead of disconnecting the uplink of TOR 1 to aggregation switch 1 after shutting it down, its uplink to aggregation switch 2 is accidentally disconnected. This disconnects Rack 1 and Rack 2 from each other.

The key takeaway for most enterprise adopters of Hadoop should be that hardware redundancy mechanisms for power, cooling, and networking make up failure domains that typically span multiple racks, which makes an isolated rack failure still possible, but quite improbable in practice.

If you run without said redundancy mechanisms, the failure domain is the rack for some failures, such as a single top-of rack switch, but you may be susceptible to much more drastic failures spanning across multiple racks, such as a failing multi-rack PDU.

That being said, it is always possible to simply be struck by bad luck or user error. It is also noteworthy to point out a somewhat dated but still relevant research effort by Google (*http://bit.ly/2zi5AGw*) which suggests that failures of multiple servers within the same rack are more highly correlated than simultaneous failures of the same number of servers across different racks. The root cause of this observation is hard to pinpoint but may well be related to manufacturing batches, especially if you purchase servers and components in bulk, like the big web content providers.

To summarize, your goal should be to minimize the chances of rack failure by using redundancy in cooling, network, and power distribution. If you intend to leverage Hadoop rack awareness to increase the availability of your cluster, you should understand the failure domains for power distribution, networking, and cooling. As we learned in "Erasure Coding Versus Replication" on page 71, rack failures become even more severe events for HDFS durability with erasure coding, and you should make every effort to avoid them.

Failure Domain Alignment

In addition to the failure domains and the ramifications of failures in the layers we've discussed, the way that the failure domains of each layer align with other layers is also important.

Figure 6-2 shows an example of failure domains that are not aligned. Racks 1 and 2 form a failure domain on the network level, while Rack 3 belongs to a different network failure domain. However, for power distribution, Rack 1 (and most likely other racks not shown) is in a different failure domain than Rack 2, which shares its power failure domain with Rack 3. When you assign a rack to R2Server1, for example, there is no clear way to do this: from a networking perspective, you should set the rack of R2Server1 to Network Failure Domain 1, like all servers in Rack 1. From a power distribution perspective, however, you should set the rack to Power Failure Domain 2, like all servers in Rack 3.

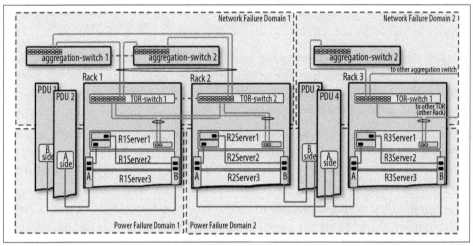

Figure 6-2. Failure domains in the datacenter

In order for Hadoop to take the best corrective measures as part of its rack-awareness features, failure domains for all infrastructure layers should always align. If they do not, typically the network failure domains are used as the leading parameter to configure rack awareness, since their maintenance usually incurs more complexity than power equipment and rack awareness also serves to improve network performance. However, your situation may be different. If your PDUs happen to be non-redundant internally, a PDU failure would catastrophically affect a large portion of the cluster. It would be wiser to align rack awareness with power failure domains.

In summary, racks are the mechanical packaging of servers but can also be thought of as groups of servers in a group of congruent failure domains. But in some cases, the failure domains are not congruent, nor do they necessary align with rack boundaries.

Understanding your datacenter failure domains gives you a notion of how highly available your Hadoop clusters really are.

Space and Racking Constraints

Often, during initial planning, one assumes that a rack in the datacenter can be completely populated with servers. Due to constraints in available airflow or power budget on PDUs, it may only be possible to fill fractions of whole racks, and this may make it necessary to cross the rack boundary sooner than anticipated. The same may apply to available network switch ports. In both cases, we recommend that you carefully consider your options. You should not compromise by connecting into an oversubscribed fabric or spreading Hadoop nodes across multiple network segments. Instead, revisit options to build a Hadoop-specific network and/or rack segment in your datacenter.

Ingest and Intercluster Connectivity

A common question regarding Hadoop and datacenters is, "How fast do I get stuff into or out of my cluster?" This could be either from systems within the corporate network or over WAN connections.

The demand to know this is often driven by use cases that depend on large-scale geo-dispersed data collections, but naturally it also informs the sizing of the recovery point objective (RPO) and recovery time objective (RTO) parameters when building cluster-to-cluster replication pipelines (see "Policies and Objectives" on page 378).

The answer is, "It depends—on a lot of factors." In this section, we present the specifics and propose how to deal with them.

Software

One group of factors that affect ingest and extraction speed are related to software:

Compression support
> Regardless of whether your ingest is batch-oriented, as it is with DistCp or Cloudera Backup and Disaster Recovery, or message-based, as with Flume or Kafka, when transferring large amounts of data over long-distance links, use high compression ratios wherever possible. Usually, when comparing the time and cost used for compression and decompression compared to bandwidth and the cost of increasing it accordingly, compression over WAN connections wins. There may be an argument about the compression codec. Among the commonly supported formats in Hadoop are Snappy, LZO, GZIP, and BZip2. BZip2 requires the most CPU resources but achieves the highest compression ratios. GZIP achieves compression similar to BZip2 and is supported by Kafka compression (*http://bit.ly/2A9EMYK*), as are Snappy and LZ4. In the case of Kafka, the compression codec will not become transparent in the downstream systems since it only pertains to internal communication between consumers, producers, and brokers. Snappy, LZO, and BZip2 are all splittable formats, enabling direct consumption by parallel computation in Hadoop after ingesting. GZIP content, on the other hand, is not splittable and first has to be converted. Splittability is not relevant when your ingest path is message-based; e.g., when using Kafka as

an ingest mechanism. Often, the choice of compression codec is mandated by the originating systems, such as ETL tools, Change Data Capture (CDC) systems, or autonomous devices.

 Surprisingly for many, DistCp does not offer built-in compression support. There is an argument about whether compression only for transfers makes sense, given that Hadoop administrators/software developers could always precompress the data. A global configuration flag may entail double compression due to inadvertently compressing twice. Work by the HDFS community to include compression support into DistCp (*http://bit.ly/2S3INoQ*) is not yet conclusive.

Parallelism

After ensuring you have sufficient bandwidth available in your hardware infrastructure and leveraging compression, you should try to optimize for transfer parallelism. In some scenarios, single-stream TCP performance may not be sufficient to deal with the amount of data flowing into the cluster at high network latency times—e.g., when data comes in via many-hop WAN connections. When transferring between Hadoop clusters, you can take full advantage of parallelism by distributing many instances of the software transferring and receiving data.

Configuration

Although we want to transfer data as quickly as possible, distributed systems like Hadoop may easily consume all available bandwidth and negatively impact other workloads. Hence, in many situations, the transfer rate must be throttled to a known limit. DistCp supports this via the -bandwidth flag on a per-mapper basis. At the time of this writing, Kafka does not support any form of throttling or quota mechanism, although it is actively pursued (*http://bit.ly/2QVjcOG*) by the Kafka community. As a general rule, the scarcer bandwidth is, the more you should consider designing a filtering mechanism into the application logic to avoid ingesting data or fields known to be irrelevant. This is often a trivial change.

Hardware

Hardware factors such as the following also play a role:

Firewalls and load balancers

Some very common bottlenecks for big data applications are firewall and load balancer appliances. This equipment is typically very expensive, and therefore required resources are carefully calculated. It may actually be cost-prohibitive to match required bandwidth. Although applications on small- to medium-cluster implementations may not be impacted, their demands on the firewall and load-balancing configurations may impact other solutions in the datacenter. Ultimately, these physical appliances cannot keep up with the traffic incurred by large-cluster configurations. Even scaling these solutions to the largest configurations may impose a limitation on certain use cases. Depending on the exact throughput requirements of external data sources, you may enable a separate dedicated route at the WAN boundary for your Hadoop cluster, which is filtered by a different and less costly solution. Filtering may not be required at all in the case of backup/disaster recovery replication use cases.

Network equipment

Due to oversubscription, the network itself almost always imposes bandwidth limitations between the cluster and the rest of the corporate network, as discussed in Chapter 4. To ensure bandwidth requirements for high-intensity ingest use cases and cluster replication scenarios are met, there may be merit in—or even the necessity of—routing this portion of Hadoop traffic to dedicated equipment instead of a highly oversubscribed fabric core layer. A typical planning oversight is to assume the best case without chatty neighbors who use the same core or access layers, which can result in significant impacts during bursts. Also, if the ingest path requires a very large number of connections, take care to ensure that access-layer switches do not trigger mitigation mechanisms for distributed denial-of-service (DDos) attacks.

Replacements and Repair

Server replacements and repair are normally not at all the concern of the workload owner, since they mostly are conveniently abstracted in a virtualized infrastructure layer. For Hadoop, though, you should at least consider the following points:

Component replacement policy

The components in your cluster are expected to fail while the software itself performs recovery and continues in a degraded state. Since many servers run in parallel, this may actually happen again before the original server has been recovered, which is a rather uncommon situation for most enterprise IT organizations. Therefore, be sure you know whether your organization keeps a small stockpile of disks for quick replacements or whether someone has to call the hardware manufacturer. In the latter case, who places the call to the manufacturer, and what is the agreed-upon service time? Ideally, you test the mean time to recovery for a given component (failed disk, failed fan pack, or failed server) to assess how these procedures affect SLAs on the Hadoop platform level.

Hardware life cycle

You may eventually have to scale your cluster. Are the same servers still available in your company's procurement basket, in the event that you have to scale a cluster before the end of its depreciation period? If at all possible, you should try to order nodes of the same configuration and to avoid heterogeneous node types.

Operational Procedures

Often, end-to-end operational procedures for disaster recovery in the datacenter are based on virtualized storage and compute infrastructure. An example of this is the complete loss of a datacenter site. In virtualized environments, mission-critical virtual machines are commonly live-migrated and rebooted from SANs in the alternative sites, since their storage is synchronously replicated. This is also true of certain maintenance tasks and even datacenter-wide fire drills.

For Hadoop, this is not possible. We cover this in more detail in "Cluster Spanning" on page 173.

Typical Pitfalls

Now that you are familiar with the technical concepts at work in the datacenter and how they affect Hadoop, let us review some typical pitfalls that you may encounter when you fit into your existing datacenter.

Networking

Network infrastructure contains a few very common pitfalls:

Firewalls between cluster hosts
We have seen this attempted many times, and each time brought its own world of pain. There is no other way to describe the amount of organizational strain, the increase of operational risk, and the day-to-day inefficiencies that ensue when traffic between Hadoop worker nodes is filtered. Considering that most organizations run firewall changes through a ticketing system (sometimes requiring review by a board), the lack of automation to scale or replace nodes in the firewall rule matrix, and the number of ports (sometimes transient port ranges) that the individual services require, firewalling can be simply prohibitive for the project as a whole. It is more common, however, to place an edge node in another network zone and to filter the communication of the edge node with the rest of the cluster, as introduced in Chapter 3. The monolith analogy really applies to firewalling in the context of Hadoop—you would normally not restrict all interprocess communication on a single server.

We should also note that intranode communication can indeed be filtered via systems such as SELinux. Some organizations require it, and it works for well-defined application stacks where Linux distribution–specific policy files exist in abundance. For Hadoop, however, none of this has been standardized, nor has it seen full-fledged support by any of the Hadoop distributors. This is due to the manifold and ever-changing communication paths in the set of distributed services at work in the cluster.

Network oversubscription

Oversubscription of the network is not a bad thing per se, and is actually inevitable in most multirack designs. Often, however, the existing production standard imposes oversubscription even for intra-rack traffic, since the assumption for the majority of workloads, such as web services, is that most traffic is directly directed at user sessions. Hadoop, however, introduces significant intra-rack traffic, which is why we recommend always using true Layer 2 switches without any oversubscription within the rack or the access-layer aggregation domain. See Chapter 4 for concrete recommendations on oversubscription ratios.

Lack of network isolation

Hadoop-internal traffic is best run on its own Layer 2 network. Otherwise, other workloads may be unnecessarily impaired. The monolith rule helps again here; consider the Hadoop-internal network as the backplane of an appliance. A final point to consider is that debugging problems related to Hadoop internode communication sometimes involves tracing network traffic, which is much harder when Hadoop shares the network with other workloads.

Placing racks/nodes far apart

This relates closely to the previous point on network isolation. Often, to optimize an existing datacenter footprint, or because of a shortage of rack space, Hadoop nodes end up on separate and distant racks. This results in a heavy mixing of network traffic with other workloads and causes communication bottlenecks between cluster nodes due to the oversubscription ratios between the network layers that must be crossed. Hadoop nodes should be kept in one place, whenever possible—again, resembling a monolith.

Cluster Spanning

Cluster spanning is a specific pitfall that we have come to realize should be mentioned in the context of datacenters. It means placing part of the Hadoop cluster in one datacenter and another part of the cluster in another datacenter, in an effort to achieve *disaster tolerance*. We strongly discourage this practice, but we frequently run into organizations that attempt this setup.

As noted, the driver behind cluster spanning is a desire to achieve true disaster tolerance, as opposed to settling for more realistic *disaster recovery* objectives. Disaster tolerance means that the operation of the cluster continues, despite the failure of a datacenter, as if nothing happened.

There are ways to achieve this setup safely, but there are very specific conditions that must be met. Operational experience is very rare in this environment.

To understand the technical issues with this practice, let us first break it down into two fundamental cases:

Spanning across two datacenters
    This is the most common but least feasible case, as we see in "Quorum spanning with two datacenters" on page 175.

Spanning across three datacenters
    This is covered in "Quorum spanning with three datacenters" on page 179. It is possible if all datacenter interconnects are extremely capable and reliable by modern standards.

Before we cover those two cases, however, we turn to a few obvious and general observations about spanning clusters.

Nonstandard use of rack awareness

If a Hadoop cluster is deployed across several datacenters, Hadoop itself does not really have any awareness of it. This means that data replicas may all be placed into a single datacenter, not yielding the intended benefit for disaster tolerance. In order to create awareness for the different sites in HDFS, each datacenter is set up as its own rack. The obvious drawback here is that you don't have actual rack awareness anymore. This may not be harmful in small clusters, but it means the loss of a key feature for larger environments.

Bandwidth impairment

The misuse of rack awareness leads to the next problem: the network link between both datacenters.

The obvious drawback here is that the link between both datacenters is a bottleneck for Hadoop. If the interconnect is run over WAN connections, it ranges between 10 Gbit/s for small datacenters and 100 Gbit/s for very large facilities. Bandwidth sizings beyond this exist but are mostly cost-prohibitive.

Spanning a Hadoop cluster naturally also requires spanning the cluster network across said WAN link.

For traditional applications, communication between both datacenters is ideally kept at a minimum by placing groups of workloads that need to communicate internally into one single datacenter.

To allow for easy virtual machine migrations, organizations often span Layer 2 networks over the datacenters via a fabric, which we introduced in Chapter 4.

Conversely, assuming Hadoop is eligible to consume a certain fraction of this interconnect, it will do so permanently with replication and shuffle traffic. For anything beyond a small cluster, it is unlikely that the WAN connection, which now effectively becomes the rack-interconnection, meets the common recommendations for inter-rack oversubscription that we covered in Chapter 4.

Hadoop will therefore likely put both the actual fabric technology and the configured interconnect bandwidth to a massive test and, when the cluster grows beyond a certain point, will be unable to function properly unless the interconnect is scaled. This, in turn, is often not possible, which renders you unable to deliver on the fundamental promise of scalability that Hadoop features.

Quorum spanning with two datacenters

If you can disregard arguments on bandwidth and scalability, we concede you have at your command an impressive network infrastructure (or are a true daredevil—or maybe both).

You must also be thinking about quorum services, which we introduced earlier and discuss in more detail in "Quorums" on page 332. Quorum services in Hadoop are needed to establish unambiguous coordination among the individual instances of services such as HDFS, Solr, and HBase.

In this section, we demonstrate the challenges in spanning Hadoop quorum services across two datacenters—problems that, in essence, make the whole concept of spanning Hadoop clusters impractical.

Since quorum services always operate with an uneven number of participants, the loss of one datacenter site may entail the loss of quorum—i.e., the larger number of instances from a quorum service. In the two-datacenter case, organizations sometimes try to deal with this by placing one instance of quorum services (e.g., HDFS JournalNodes) on a virtual machine. The quorum VM uses a datacenter/datacenter-replicated SAN volume to materialize all disk writes across both datacenter sites.

The intent of the quorum VM is that, in a event of catastrophic failure in one datacenter, the VM is either located in or can be quickly rebooted in the surviving datacenter, thereby maintaining quorum capabilities.

Figure 6-3 shows this process in a setup where a cluster spans across two datacenters.

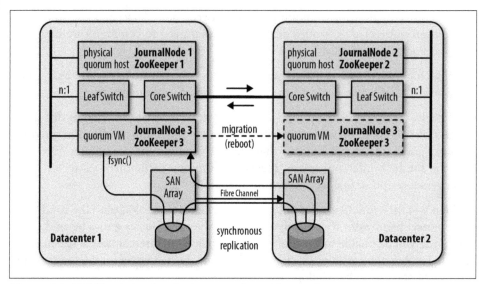

Figure 6-3. Pitfall: attempting cluster spanning with two datacenters

The intended migration of the quorum VM is indicated by a dotted line between the quorum VM in its current location and a future location. Third-party virtualization software offers automated reboots in case of disaster, but as we will see, this may lead to the split-brain problem.

 Rebooting the machine in case of disaster, either manually or auto‐matically, is not necessarily a safe bet: you need to reserve enough headroom in both CPU and RAM resources in the recovery data‐center. Even if this is done, the emergency reboot of your specific VM may not be included as part of a datacenter-wide fire drill. If the reboot eventually succeeds, it may be too late. This could result in hundreds or thousands of block requests in HDFS being turned down while quorum was temporarily lost, resulting in application failures.

The most important criterion is obviously that, when the reboot does happen, the content of the storage volume in the surviving datacenter equals that of the original storage volume in the failed datacenter.

In the world of SANs, this feature is referred to as *synchronous replication*. In terms of the filesystem consistency operations we introduced in "Important System Calls" on page 61, this means that any consistency operation, such as an `fsync()`, must not return before the corresponding blocks are persisted on the local SAN volume as well as on the distant SAN volume.

Quorum services, such as ZooKeeper and JournalNodes, permanently perform fsync() operations to persist successful transactions to disk. The long curved arrow in Figure 6-3, which originates on the quorum VM and traverses both datacenters, depicts the path of I/O that each successful change of HDFS data, such as an HDFS block write, will trigger in the JournalNode quorum VM.

Naturally, synchronous replication introduces additional latency. Since quorum services, especially ZooKeeper and JournalNodes, are very latency-sensitive (values beyond 20 ms are known to be an operational risk), there are practical limits in terms of how far apart datacenters can be in this approach. This problem of synchronicity is massively compounded by the bottleneck in available bandwidth.

But even if we omit latency, three difficult problems arise when synchronous replication is used in conjunction with the JournalNode quorum:

Failed synchronous writes
What happens when Datacenter 2 fails during a large burst of changes to HDFS, as shown in Figure 6-4? Just like JournalNode 1, the quorum VM (JournalNode 3) will try to invoke the fsync() call on all incoming requests by the NameNode Quorum Journal Manager (QJM). To maintain a consistent state in both datacenters, these fsync() requests must not complete until also acknowledged by Datacenter 2. This cannot happen, since Datacenter 2 is down. fsync() keeps blocking until finally JournalNode 3 fails the outstanding requests and declares itself as *outOfSync*. At this time, the cluster's quorum is lost.

Blocked consistency operations for synchronous replication are actually a typical challenge outside of the big data context, for example, with relational databases (*http://bit.ly/2qXxFy8*).

In addition to lost quorum, you must now recover quorum from the remaining JournalNodes, one of which is out of sync. Although theoretically you can declare one of the remaining JournalNodes as the source of truth and replace the other's edit log on the file level, either survivor may theoretically be behind some of the other's committed transactions. The process for successful recovery in this instance is not defined, and you may simply have lost blocks.

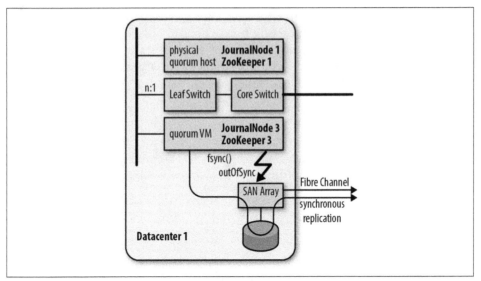

Figure 6-4. Loss of quorum: a synchronous journal edit is blocked when the backup site does not respond

Hit by the CAP theorem

When synchronous writes fail, can you loosen the requirement of `fsync()` to wait for the failed datacenter and continue operation in Datacenter 1, where you still have quorum? Let us assume that you can be absolutely certain that Datacenter 2 has suffered an unrecoverable disaster and none of the Hadoop service instances in this datacenter survived—and that, if you automatically detect this programmatically, you might somehow be able to disable the synchronization of `fsync()` to the other datacenter. Even then, you may still be much too late to prevent JournalNode 3 from going into an *outOfSync* state. And really, there is no good way to reliably detect that the other site is down. You could naively determine Datacenter 2 to have failed if JournalNode 2 is no longer available on the network. But what if you're just dealing with a temporary glitch in network connectivity, and in reality, Datacenter 2 is still operating? This glitch could occur shortly before Datacenter 1 actually fatally fails and before the transactions you allowed to only be stored in Datacenter 1 were replicated to Datacenter 2. In this event, the rebooted quorum VM (JournalNode 3) is again out of sync. Here, you will have effectively traded the availability of JournalNode 3 and the ability to lose a network partition (Datacenter 2) for the consistency of JournalNode 3's state.

When we operate the full quorum in a single datacenter, we do not regard the network to be partitioned. It is safe to assume that the Layer 2 network that the JournalNodes run in will either fail in its entirety or be available for all. Note that loss of network communication here is explicitly distinct from the crash of a JournalNode. When rack awareness is used and JournalNodes are placed in different racks, we may regard those racks as network partitions. However, we would not expect operation to continue if the majority of partitions fail. This is the key to the cluster spanning discussion: spanning your cluster across datacenters is as good or bad as spanning your cluster across racks, as far as failure tolerance goes.

Split-brain scenarios

Now let us consider the case where Datacenter 1 fails, while it hosts the quorum VM. In order to continue operation, the quorum VM must be rebooted in Datacenter 2, but who will do this quickly enough, in the middle of the night, to prevent important jobs from failing? Again, you would ideally use a nifty mechanism that does this automatically, when you are certain that the other datacenter has failed entirely. But again, you are unlikely to find a hard criterion to establish this fact programmatically. If you automatically reboot the quorum VM in Datacenter 2 while Datacenter 1 is merely disconnected (rather than stopped), you are effectively spawning a fourth instance of the JournalNode. In this fourth instance, the standby NameNode, which we assume to reside in Datacenter 2, becomes active. This will effectively constitute a second instance of HDFS, which will now begin to accept requests. If the mechanism used to declare Datacenter 1 as faulty does so based only on the cessation of communications, there is a chance that the HDFS instance in Datacenter 1 is also still operating. Both instances may now deviate, and this could yield catastrophic consequences from a data governance consistency perspective.

Quorum spanning with three datacenters

By now you have probably guessed that, if you cannot span a cluster across two datacenters, you can simply use a third datacenter to run the third quorum machine, as we illustrate in Figure 6-5.

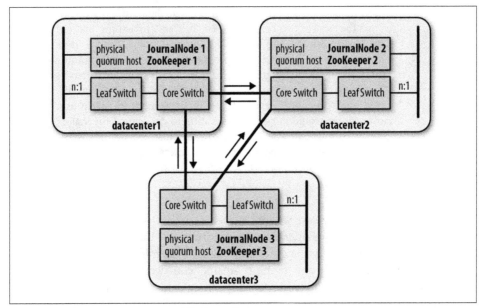

Figure 6-5. Quorum spanning with three datacenters

This architecture relieves us of blocked consistency operations, problems with network partitions, and split-brain scenarios. But as we covered in "Bandwidth impairment" on page 174, the success of this setup depends on low-latency communication between all datacenter sites. The setup almost always becomes bandwidth-prohibitive for large clusters.

We just covered that the interconnects between datacenter sites in on-premises enterprise IT are typically unfit to sustain stable operations, even in the three-datacenter scenario. Also, after you chose this architecture you are mostly bound to it, due to the inertia of big data, and it may be unable to scale beyond a given point. Would you limit your growth capabilities in this way for any other IT system?

That said, we do not want to generalize lightly. You may well be the proud operator of an infrastructure capable of spanning even a large Hadoop cluster. The one piece of advice we offer here is a strong recommendation to test rigorously. You must be certain that the latencies between your quorum services are not detrimental to HDFS performance under stress scenarios.

Finally, quorum spanning with three datacenters is a very relevant case in hyperscale public cloud services. As you'll see in Chapter 16, public cloud providers offer extremely capable network infrastructure between distinct datacenters in a given service region, also known as *availability zones*. Cloudera has recently updated its reference architecture for AWS (*http://bit.ly/2TlYLfg*) to explicitly cover best practices for spanning a cluster across three availability zones.

Alternative solutions

Despite the imponderables of disaster tolerance via cluster spanning, there are alternatives. These center around disaster recovery, which allows recovery to normal operation within a defined amount of time (the recovery time objective) to a defined past state of the data (the recovery point objective). Relevant alternatives range from third-party solutions to proprietary augmentation of tools in the Hadoop software ecosystem by distributors of user-built custom solutions. We discuss these options in detail in Chapter 13.

Summary

In this chapter, we looked at how big data clusters align with datacenter operations.

We determined that the concept of rack awareness in Hadoop requires a certain level of scale to truly improve availability and to increase durability. This led us to high availability of datacenter infrastructure, where we covered cooling, power, and networks and their failure domains. We reconciled those failure domains with best practices for rack awareness and moved on to more advice around space, ingest, and intercluster connectivity.

We also explored some common concerns around operational procedures for repairs, before we turned to typical pitfalls for big data clusters in datacenters. Most crucially, we covered the pitfall of cluster spanning, where a cluster is installed across two or more datacenters. Although we looked in detail at the reasons why a two-datacenter deployment for cluster spanning is unfeasible, we also looked at the case of spanning across three datacenters, which may become a feasible practice in on-premises situations in the future and is slowly beginning to see adoption in the public cloud across availability zones.

## PART II

Platform

In Part I, we covered the essentials of putting together an efficient and resilient physical and organizational infrastructure for your clusters. Upon this solid foundation, we can now build comprehensive distributed software platforms that can cope with the rigors of large-scale data storage and processing inherent to the requirements and use cases of large enterprises.

In the following chapters, we explore the architectural aspects of modern data platforms, ranging from the basic operating system and supporting software to the provisioning of Hadoop and other distributed systems. Organizations require that these platforms fit into a preexisting ecosystem of users and applications, and enterprise standards demand that the deployments meet certain standards of security, availability, and disaster recovery. We cover these concerns in detail.

By the end of this section, our hope is that the reader—be they an architect, application developer, or cluster operator—will feel confident in how and, crucially, why clusters are put together. This understanding will be of immense value in building and operating new clusters and in designing and running applications that work in sympathy with distributed enterprise data platforms.

## CHAPTER 7

Provisioning Clusters

This chapter discusses the provisioning and configuration of Hadoop cluster nodes. If you are using a cloud environment, then Part III is the more suitable section to read, as far as provisioning is concerned. In any event, the vast majority of Hadoop nodes run on Linux, so the operating system (OS)–related topics in this chapter still apply.

Operating Systems

The first task after acquiring physical hardware in the form of rack-mountable servers (for example, a 19" rack server or blades) is to provision the OS. There are many options, some dating back decades, which allow you to automate that process considerably. Separate technologies are often used for each step of the process:

Server bootstrap
> The initial phase of a machine provisioning process is to automatically assign it an IP address and install the OS bootstrap executable. The most common technology used for this is called *Preboot Execution Environment* (PXE), which was introduced as part of the larger open industry standard *Wired for Management* (WfM). The latter also included the familiar *Wake-on-LAN* (WoL) standard. WfM was replaced by the *Intelligent Platform Management Interface* (IMPI) (*http://bit.ly/2DPEDhi*) in 1998.

The PXE Boot Process

The flow is as follows: when a machine starts, the PXE-enabled network interface card (NIC) of the server sends out a DHCP request. The local DHCP server answers that request, returning an IP address, subnet mask, gateway, and more. In addition, and assuming the DHCP server is PXE-aware, it includes the location of the Trivial FTP (TFTP) server that hosts the boot image (called `pxelinux.0`). The server receives this information, downloads the boot image from the TFTP server, and executes the image.

After the boot loader is running, it downloads a machine-specific configuration file from the *pxelinux.cfg* directory on the TFTP server, trying to match the MAC address or the IP address of the server with a provided configuration file. The address is first checked in full; if there is no match, it is then partially matched by broadening the address scope. The matching process makes it possible to provide configuration files for a larger group of nodes; for example, all nodes that have an IP address starting with "192.168.10.".

Finally, after the configuration is loaded, the machine fetches an OS-specific installation binary (often a minimal OS setup executed in memory only) and subsequently executes it.

OS setup

> After bootstrapping, the minimal installer does the rest of the work, contacting the OS-specific configuration service. For Red Hat Linux, a common tool for this task is Kickstart, which defines all of the parameters that should apply to the installation of the OS on a particular machine. In other words, Kickstart is a template that mimics an interactive user entering the desired details while configuring the OS during the setup process. All of the choices are recorded in files and handed to the installer, which automatically executes the installation.

OS configuration

> Lastly, after the OS is operational, the node has to be configured for the specific task to which it was assigned. Common choices of tools in this category include Ansible, Chef, and Puppet. These *software configuration management* (SCM) tools enable not only node configuration at provisioning time but also configuration during its full life cycle. This includes reconfiguring the OS for other tasks or handling changes due to new application releases. "OS Configuration for Hadoop" on page 188 provides an example of an Ansible playbook that configures a cluster node for Hadoop services.

Note that there are tools available that further combine these three distinct provisioning steps into one, including Red Hat Satellite (which is, in part, based on the open source project Foreman). With these technologies and tools, you can fully automate the rollout of new server hardware, allowing you to build out a cluster as fast as you can install and wire machines into racks.

Handling Failures

For all of the automation to work, you require a server machine that supports the aforementioned IPMI standard. Included in that is support for remote *keyboard, video, and mouse* (KVM) connections, allowing an admin to connect to the server as if they were in the same physical location. Example implementations of IPMI are HP's Integrated Lights-Out (iLO) and the Dell Remote Access Controller (DRAC); both support KVM access.

Should an automated installation and an automated repair fail, the automation system of choice should raise an alarm to an operator, who can then investigate the problem using the KVM connection. It is also common for IPMI implementations to support the mounting of remote media, such as CD-ROMs and USB drives, which in rare cases might be needed to supply hardware drivers or firmware updates. In practice, the remote access and media features should fix most automated deployment problems.

OS Choices

When it comes to Hadoop, the OS choices are limited to what is supported out of the box by the distributions, unless you want to build your own. (See "Hadoop Deployment" on page 202 for a discussion of this topic.) Broadly speaking, most distributions support a mix of common Linux distributions, including Red Hat Enterprise Linux (RHEL) and CentOS, Oracle Linux, SUSE Linux Enterprise Server (SLES), Debian, and Ubuntu. Each vendor has a website that lists the supported OS types and versions. Of note is the absence of Microsoft Windows and any Unix variant. This is mainly due to what customers are requesting.

The vast majority of Hadoop clusters are set up on top of Linux distributions. Deviating from that standard greatly reduces the availability of support. There are scripts available in Hadoop (*http://bit.ly/2TxBNSI*) that allow for it to run on Windows machines, but there is minimal commercial support for Hadoop on Windows, which is another reason not to pursue that path.

For Linux, all of the components of the OS are hosted by the vendors in online repositories. You typically install the OS kernel first, plus a list of initially selected packages (containing applications and tools such as SSH or Java), after which you can boot into the new system. Over time, you can add, update, or remove any part of the OS, as required, again making use of the vendor's repositories. The location where these repositories are hosted is a configuration setting, often defaulting to a load-balancer server that routes the request to the nearest repository mirror. In essence, repositories are simple, web-based services, which are backed by a web server process and which host the packages with metadata files in a particular, well-defined layout. The client on the OS is able to talk to any conforming service and to verify its authenticity using cryptographic signatures so that the service cannot be used to provide malware or other compromised executables.

The choice you have, at this point, is to use a repository that is available on the internet or only in your local environment:

Online repository
> If all the nodes in the cluster have sufficient internet connectivity, you usually have little to prepare because all packages are downloaded from the vendor's online repository (or from one of the official signed mirrors).

Offline repository
> In practice, though, especially in enterprise environments and highly regulated industries (like banking or telecommunications), it is common for the Hadoop infrastructure to be behind a firewall with limited or no internet access at all. In that case, you first have to download all the packages and create a private mirror. This entails setting up a web server on an accessible machine and making the packages available through it.
>
> In addition, you often have to tweak the metadata of the mirror to reflect the local nature, for example by disabling security checks or by updating the repository with the necessary signatures yourself. Afterward, you can configure the installation scripts to use the local mirror repository and install as if you had direct internet access.

After you have decided which repository to use—whether online or local—the installation is performed manually, or automated, as discussed earlier (using, for example, Kickstart for Red Hat–based systems). After the installation is complete, you can move on to configure the more dynamic OS settings, as explained in the next section.

OS Configuration for Hadoop

Running the Hadoop processes requires some configuration of the OS itself. For example, it is known that the Hadoop DataNodes are dealing with file-level I/O, reading and writing Hadoop Distributed File System (HDFS) blocks. And YARN, through the ResourceManager and the per–worker node NodeManagers, is spawning Java tasks that count against the number of processes an application is allowed to start. These limits are usually set to a conservative default, which may apply to a good range of Linux use cases—but for Hadoop, these limits are too restrictive beyond a small test setup. This section highlights the common process limit and network settings to adjust, and why.

 The following settings are commonly provided by Hadoop distribution vendors as part of a *prerequisite checklist*. Ask your vendor of choice to provide the checklist. In addition, many of the vendor-provided management tools have a built-in *host inspection process*, which warns the administrator if an important low-level setting is missing.

The recommended OS configuration steps are:

Adjust filesystem settings

Hadoop stores its data blocks using binary files, directly in the configured Linux filesystem for the data volumes. Refer to "Filesystems" on page 69 for details, but suffice it to say that the default volume settings are not perfect and should be adjusted to gain more from your hardware. This includes disabling the access time handling (HDFS does not use it) and reducing the reserved disk space for administrative purposes. The former speeds up file operations, whereas the latter increases the yield of available storage per physical disk.

Disabling the access time for a volume requires adding the `noatime` option to the */etc/fstab* configuration file for Linux. This includes setting `nodirtime` implicitly, since it is also not needed. For example, here is how you can configure this for a specific volume:

```
# Edit "/etc/fstab" and add "noatime" to
# disk mounts, e.g:
# ...
# /dev/sdb /data01 ext3 defaults,noatime 0
# ...

# Remount at runtime, required for each volume
$ mount --o remount /data01
```

You need to add the `noatime` option to all lines that represent volumes used as Hadoop data drives.

Reducing the reserved disk space for the same drives containing only Hadoop data is accomplished using the Linux-provided command-line tools:

```
# Set space during file system creation
$ mkfs.ext3 -m 0 /dev/sdb

# Or tune the filesystem afterwards
$ tune2fs -m 0 /dev/sdb
```

Setting the value to 0 means no space for administrative tasks is kept at all. This is all right for pure data disks that do not contain any *root*-owned files. Do *not* do this for the drive that contains the OS files.

Increase process limits

The default numbers of allowed file handles and processes per application are quite low and need to be increased to avoid having HDFS or YARN (and other subsystems) run out of those low-level resources. In worst-case scenarios, running out of these resources renders the cluster inoperable, or severely impacts its performance.

Setting the limits is done per (technical) user account and must be persisted across system restarts:

```
# Set file handles higher (default is 1024)
$ echo hdfs - nofile 32768 >> /etc/security/limits.conf
$ echo mapred - nofile 32768 >> /etc/security/limits.conf
$ echo hbase - nofile 32768 >> /etc/security/limits.conf

# Set process limits higher
$ echo hdfs - nproc 32768 >> /etc/security/limits.conf
$ echo mapred - nproc 32768 >> /etc/security/limits.conf
$ echo hbase - nproc 32768 >> /etc/security/limits.conf
```

Reduce swappiness

Since main memory is a finite resource in servers, the OS moves inactive memory pages to disk as needed. This *swapping* of pages causes processes to seemingly slow down at random during their life cycle. This is not what is desired for many Hadoop-related services, such as HDFS or HBase. The eagerness to swap, referred to as *swappiness*, can be tuned to avoid it as much as possible. For example, from the OS command line:

```
# Ad hoc setting, works temporarily
$ echo 1 > /proc/sys/vm/swappiness

# Persist setting across restarts
$ echo "vm.swappiness = 1" >> /etc/sysctl.conf
```

See "The Linux Page Cache" on page 62 for more details on this topic.[1]

Enable time synchronization

Writing data to storage in a distributed system requires some form of synchronization, and time is a common choice for that task. After a server is started, its time may drift apart from other servers, based on the accuracy of the built-in

---

1 See also Ovais Tariq's Percona blog post (*http://bit.ly/2zjDef6*) for a discussion of its value, depending on the Linux kernel version.

clock. As discussed in "Essentials" on page 344, you have to install a time maintenance service, such as ntp or chrony, on each cluster node, which at configured
intervals updates the local time to that of an external, shared time service.

The commands to install and start the NTP service daemon for a Red Hat–based
system are:

```
$ yum install ntpd
$ systemctl enable ntpd
$ systemctl start ntpd
```

Enable advanced network settings

The very nature of Hadoop, being a big data platform, implies that you should
adjust the network I/O settings to gain the most performance. It is common to
enable *jumbo frames* (see "Measuring throughput" on page 223), which can
improve the network throughput by reducing intrinsic overhead.

On the command line, run the following command:

```
$ ip link set eth0 mtu 9000
```

This sets the frame size to the allowed maximum of 9,000 bytes. You should add
this to a bash script and use an automated system service (such as a *systemd* service unit (*http://bit.ly/2A6WCvk*)) to have it run at system restarts.

We also advise that you disable IPv6 on Hadoop cluster machines. Generally
speaking, Hadoop nodes are in a separate VLAN inside a corporate network, and
in that environment, the number of available IP addresses is plentiful. There is
no need to enable IPv6, because package routing is handled on the LAN level,
and the overhead that comes with dual address handling can be avoided
altogether.

Here is an example of how to add the necessary setting to the system-wide
systctl.conf file:

```
$ echo "net.ipv6.conf.all.disable_ipv6 = 1" >> /etc/systctl.conf
$ echo "net.ipv6.conf.default.disable_ipv6 = 1" >> /etc/systctl.conf
```

Enable name service caching

Considering that Hadoop is an inherently distributed system that can span thousands of nodes, it may not come as a surprise that intracluster communication
requires some scaffolding that is responsible for establishing the network connection. Part of that process is resolving the IP addresses of other nodes using
their domain names; for example, *node-0122.internal.foobar.com*. Because
Hadoop's batch framework, YARN, is scheduling tasks across many machines in
parallel, making domain name lookups a bursty operation (one that can overload
an underprovisioned DNS server—or at least cause noticeable latency spikes), we

recommend that you install the *Name Service Cache Daemon* (NSCD) to alleviate the problem.

For a Red Hat–, *systemd*-based Linux distribution, you can install and start the caching daemon using the command line:

```
$ yum install nscd
$ systemctl enable nscd
$ systemctl start nscd
```

 Take special care when combining NSCD with the *System Security Services Daemon* (SSSD). Please refer to the official Red Hat documentation (*https://red.ht/2DNbpQh*).

Disable OS-level optimizations

We recommend that you disable Transparent Huge Pages (THP). This is an OS-level feature that interferes with how Hadoop works. Disabling it helps to reduce high CPU loads.

The following commands should be added to a system startup script such as */etc/rc.local*:

```
# Edit "/etc/rc.local" to contain these lines
echo never > /sys/kernel/mm/redhat_transparent_hugepage/defrag
echo never > /sys/kernel/mm/redhat_transparent_hugepage/enabled
```

In addition to the general OS settings for processes, network, and file systems, there are also some system security adjustments that you should make:

Disable Security-Enhanced Linux (SELinux)

This and the next option can be safely disabled for the same reason: because IPv6 is not needed. All of the traffic is firewalled (which means that only allowed network nodes and ports are accessible) on a higher level, usually by means of unroutable VLANs or firewall appliances on the LAN itself. This allows for simplification of per-host security, which includes disabling SELinux. Although Hadoop is known to run under SELinux, it requires an incredibly high level of expertise and configuration prowess. Therefore, vendors often recommend avoiding any hassles that enabling this feature might entail.

Disable local firewalling

Dropping the host-level firewall goes hand in hand with the previous option. Vendors recommend that you not set any *iptables-* or *firewalld*-related rule, and prefer that you disable these services completely.

Explore other hardening options

There are more options you should look into when architecting the environment for a Hadoop cluster, including the cluster node settings. One of those is mounting the local */tmp* directory as a separate partition and with the noexec flag set. This improves the resilience of a node against malware that uses the world-writable temporary directory to create a script or binary and execute it.

Another option is to issue OS-level user IDs outside of the privileged range, which is commonly all IDs below 1000. Hadoop, and in particular YARN, has a matching setting that allows the admin to specify a minimum user ID (*http://bit.ly/2KpAAZk*) for submitted processing jobs:

```
# Comma-separated list of users who cannot run applications
banned.users=
# Comma-separated list of allowed system users
allowed.system.users=
# Prevent other super users
min.user.id=1000
```

Setting min.user.id to a number just at or below the range of IDs assigned to the interactive users and Hadoop technical accounts causes YARN to reject any job that is below the specified number. This prevents system accounts from being able to execute jobs and, for example, from abusing the spawned Java task process to issue malicious commands. The configuration properties shown also include the additional settings to ban certain users from submitting jobs or to allow specific system users to submit them.

Automated Configuration Example

All of these options can be provisioned using the mentioned configuration management approach. Here is an example of how this is done using an Ansible playbook (*http://bit.ly/2Ku8r3H*), which has built-in modules for most of the tasks. For some configuration files, the necessary entries are simply added line by line:

```
...
# Disable host-level security features
- name: Create SELinux config file if it does not exist
  file: path=/etc/selinux/config state=touch owner=root group=root
- name: Disable SE Linux
  selinux: state=disabled

- name: Stop firewalld
  service: name={{ item }} state=stopped enabled=no
  with_items:
    - firewalld

# Set process-level limits
- name: Set file limits
```

```
        lineinfile: dest=/etc/security/limits.conf line="{{ item }}" \
        state=present
        with_items:
          - '* - nofile 32768'
          - '* - nproc 65535'
          - '* - memlock unlimited'

    # Adjust OS-level settings
    - name: Adjust values in sysctl.conf
      sysctl: name={{ item.name }} value={{ item.value }} \
      state={{ item.state }}
      with_items:
        - { name: 'vm.swappiness', value: '1', state: 'present' }
        - { name: 'net.ipv6.conf.all.disable_ipv6', value: '1', \
            state: 'present' }
        - { name: 'net.ipv6.conf.default.disable_ipv6', value: '1', \
            state: 'present' }
    - name: Disable transparent huge page defragmentation
      command: echo never > /sys/kernel/mm/transparent_hugepage/defrag

    # Set network-level details
    - name: Set hostname
      hostname: name={{ inventory_hostname }}.{{ CLUSTER_DOMAIN }}

    # Add shared environment details
    - name: Add variables to /etc/environment
      lineinfile: dest=/etc/environment line="{{ item }}" state=present
      with_items:
        - 'JAVA_HOME={{ JAVA_HOME }}'
        - 'JAVA_LIBRARY_PATH=/usr/local/lib'
        - 'HADOOP_HOME={{ HADOOP_HOME }}'
        - 'HADOOP_CONF_DIR={{ HADOOP_CONFIG }}'
    ...
```

Service Databases

You might wonder why we are discussing databases, and, more specifically, relational
database management systems (RDBMSs). After all, this book is about Hadoop and
its associated set of open source projects, which are commonly bundled together in
the form of a Hadoop distribution (see "Hadoop Deployment" on page 202). The
Apache Hadoop project itself is a platform that offers affordable and scalable storage
in the form of a distributed filesystem, and is combined with a resource management
and scheduling framework that is subsequently used to analyze the stored data. All
other tasks, such as facilitating data ingest, running data pipelines that are built by
connecting many separate processing jobs, or implementing the processing logic in
some higher-level abstraction or domain-specific language (like SQL or Apache
Spark) run on top of that platform and services.

Looking at the many different projects that make up a Hadoop distribution, you can imagine that there is a need to store settings, metadata, or state to ensure some level of fault tolerance. After all, the aforementioned core Hadoop components are built to sustain, for example, node failures and to be able to recover gracefully, so complementary services should also be reliable.

In addition, the system has to collect vital machine and other operational data so that later, you can report the workloads executed by varied users and groups and can possibly provide a chargeback option. If you are using the management components offered by the distributions, you also need to enable their provided machine metric collection and rendering services, in the form of dashboards and ad hoc graphing. That data, to some degree, needs to be stored as well, and should be made available to internal and external consumers.

Many of the aforementioned sources of operational data need transactional features, which are provided by the underlying data stores. For example, Apache Hive includes a component called the Hive Metastore (HMS),[2] which is responsible for storing and maintaining all the SQL schemas defined by users and applications using the Hive Query Language (HiveQL). Since modifying Hive schemas while running queries need to access them is nontrivial, it is crucial to atomically and consistently update schemas in an isolated and durable manner—which is exactly what the atomicity, consistency, isolation, and durability (ACID) properties of database transactions stand for.

You might ask yourself why you cannot use one of the storage systems that are already included in your Hadoop distribution. There are (among others) two that offer transactional qualities for random access clients: ZooKeeper and HBase. The former is the central *registry* for many of the distributed frameworks, such as HDFS and HBase. It is useful for smaller data, like the state of distributed processes, the membership of nodes in a cluster, or leader elections, but it is not made for general-purpose use akin to an RDBMS. In addition, ZooKeeper does not claim to be a database, nor does it have a native API that would lend itself to providing the more general transactional requirements of the various tools discussed.

HBase, on the other hand, is suited to handling many of the transactional requirements, given that it has random access and per-row ACID property compliancy. On the other hand, it is not a trivial system to set up and does require significant resources to reliably operate. Although HBase can scale to thousands of machines and petabytes of data, it is less optimized to run in a small environment, making the overall barrier to entry considerable.

---

2 As of this writing, there is a proposal (*http://bit.ly/2zmkRWS*) to split out the Hive Metastore into its own project. That has no bearing on this chapter, because it just moves the need to persist data into another component.

And, quite often, the IT department is already hosting an array of database systems that are ready to be used by clients and applications—especially assuming that earlier heavy data processing workloads have already been moved to Hadoop, freeing up resources in the process. The requirements for the Hadoop tools that need transactional storage are often manageable, and using JDBC (or REST, among others) is an easy option for connecting applications to the relational database services.

Required Databases

Here are the Hadoop projects that require a database to operate a cluster, along with a classification of how large these databases can become:

Hive Metastore

All of the user schemas created using the available Data Definition Language (DDL) commands are stored in a relational database (including database names and field types, among others) so that these can be accessed when clients run SQL queries. Other information written concerns user permissions, table partitioning, table statistics, locks and compaction details, and more.

Sizing: Every table, column, and partition recorded for a user table requires storage, and this increases with the number of tables you manage in a cluster. In large installations, there can be thousands of tables with hundreds or thousands of partitions for each, driving the database requirements into the multiple-gigabyte range.

Apache Oozie

The submitted workflow, coordinator, and bundle details are persisted in a relational database. Also, the current state of a workflow is persisted so that the Oozie server can be restarted, without losing track of pipelines that are running.

Sizing: The more jobs you execute through Oozie, the more storage you need to allocate for the backing database. It also holds the history of jobs that were executed, and an administrator can extend or shorten the number of days being kept in the database. Overall, in practice, the Oozie database is usually smaller in size compared to the Hive database, but it still may need multiple gigabytes to hold all of the information.

 Even if you use another scheduler, for example Apache Airflow (*https://airflow.apache.org/*),[3] a database is almost certainly required to store its state. The requirements should be about the same as what is described here.

---

3 Incubating, at the time of this writing.

Hue

This Apache-licensed project offers a user interface into Hadoop that can give access to files in HDFS and data in HBase tables, and it can help create and execute SQL queries. Like many user interfaces, Hue manages user accounts (to control who is allowed to access which features) and requires a relational database to directly store local accounts. Optionally, it can also synchronize the user and group names from a central directory, such as an LDAP server.

Sizing: Since only small amounts of data are recorded in the required database system, the requirements for Hue are very moderate, and should be in the megabyte range.

Apache Ranger/Apache Sentry

There are two competing projects in the Hadoop ecosystem that handle tag- or role-based user authentication and audit logging. Both store their users, groups, and associated rules and permissions in a database. All access to data and other protected resources is recorded for posterity, such as audits performed by security personnel or automated processes (like security information and event management [SIEM] tools).

Sizing: The user, group, and permission information is often comparatively small and rather static in nature. The larger part is the audit log, which can be configured to hold only a certain number of entries. Also, that data can be exported to, for instance, a central log collection framework, keeping the amount of data stored in the transactional database system under control. The amount of data is similar to what Oozie creates, ranging in the multiple gigabytes.

Apache Ambari/Cloudera Manager

These are both examples of cluster management tools that can be used to conveniently operate one or more Hadoop clusters, with thousands of nodes per cluster. They use one or more databases, called *service databases*, to record operational data, such as user accounts, job execution details, system alerts and health check results, usage reports, node metrics, and more.

Sizing: Both examples defer the most taxing data collection, which is of the node metrics, to a more suitable storage system, like a LevelDB instance in Cloudera Manager or, for Ambari (which uses Grafana as its dashboarding tool), InfluxDB or HBase. The remaining data is again comparable to the previously mentioned databases, for example Oozie, and ranges in the multiple gigabytes in practice.

Database Integration Options

There are several options for integrating the databases with the tools that need them, including:

Test setup

First, a warning: this mode is *only for testing* and should never be used in a proper environment, including the ones explained in Chapter 2. Figure 7-1 shows a possible cluster configuration, where many of the Hadoop tools are using separate embedded databases, such as SQLite or Derby.

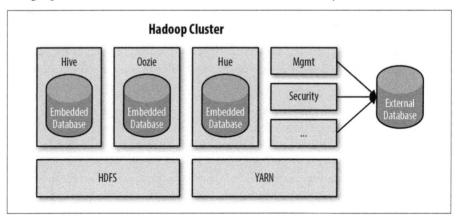

Figure 7-1. Test mode setup

Using embedded databases for a test setup frees the user from any additional dependencies and makes bootstrapping an environment faster. But those are about the only benefits of using embedded databases. They typically do not scale at all, have no special availability features, and cannot be shared across multiple applications or users.

Production setup

For all proper cluster installations that are meant to stay around longer or that should more closely mirror the setup found in the production environment, we recommend setting up a database service that is shared by all of the applications. Figure 7-2 shows this, with an external RDBMS acting as the transactional data store for all Hadoop components.

No matter how the database service is implemented, the advantage is that all metadata stored can be shared by many users. The drawback is that the setup is more complex because it involves more resources.

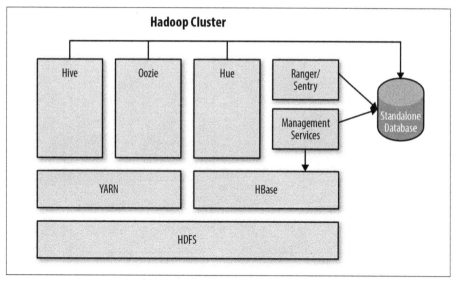

Figure 7-2. Production setup

When it comes to setting up production-like environments, there are additional choices to be made. Figure 7-3 shows some of the possible scenarios described here:

Shared database mode

This is depicted in both Scenario 1 and Scenario 2 in the diagram. You can have all Hadoop-related services share the same database, which would be either part of the Hadoop cluster itself and managed by the Hadoop team, or be provided by the existing IT department. The latter requires a close relationship with the IT DBAs because they are responsible for many other database-related infrastructure components and services, placing a burden on the IT department and its resources. Without the access to the shared RDBMS, many Hadoop services stop working immediately (or within a very short amount of time). In other words, should the shared database fail, it must be repaired as soon as possible to keep the impact to a minimum.

Separate database mode

A similar model is shown in Scenario 3, where each service in the Hadoop stack is connected to its own RDBMS instance. The probability (assuming that the database systems are not colocated on the same host) of more than one database being inoperable at any given time is much lower than when using a single RDBMS. Not shown here is that this mode can also be deployed as part of a Hadoop cluster and can be managed by its team directly.

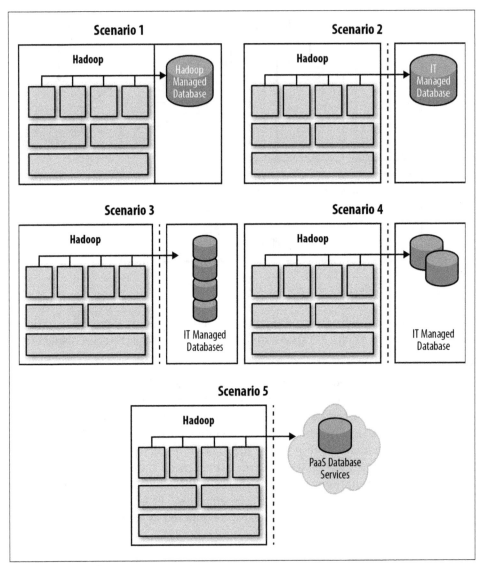

Figure 7-3. Database setup scenarios

High-availability database mode

This leads us to Scenario 4, where the database is configured in *high-availability* (HA) mode. This requires multiple RDBMS instances to replicate data between them and to use a kind of load-balancing technique to make database failover seamless. Not shown here is that this can be done with a shared or separate RDBMSs and can be managed by the Hadoop team, in case the HA RDBMS instances are deployed outside of the IT-managed resources.

Deploying the service databases on an HA-enabled RDBMS is the recommended way to keep any impact on resource availability to an absolute minimum. In practice, the setup mode is the most prevalent one, and it mitigates the need for having separate database systems, considerably reducing the operational overhead.

See "Database HA" on page 341 for an in-depth discussion on the HA setup for service databases.

Hosted database mode

If your Hadoop installation is hosted—that is, deployed in a private or public cloud infrastructure, providing *infrastructure as a service* (IaaS) and, optionally, *platform as a service* (PaaS)–you might be able to defer all of the complexities to the service provider. For example, Amazon Relational Database Service (Amazon RDS) provides hosted RDBMSs that can be configured to run in a replicated, HA-enabled mode. Following the same principles as with non-hosted setups, you have the choice of not owning the infrastructure but paying for what you need on a per-usage basis. See "Data availability" on page 494 for more information.

In summary, the recommended setup for any of your Hadoop environments is a dedicated RDBMS instance (one per environment), which is managed by either the Hadoop or the IT team. And, at the very least for the production environment, you should use a setup that is HA-enabled. If possible, you should choose an HA setup for all environments that cannot handle a database outage that exceeds the defined recovery time objective (see "Policies and Objectives" on page 378 for details).

Database Considerations

Next, we need to discuss the question of which database system to use. There is a long list of commercial and open source RDBMSs at your disposal, and many of them may be available to you inside your infrastructure. The first filter to narrow down the choices is what the Hadoop subsystems support out of the box, which often is a recent version of Oracle, PostgreSQL, and/or MySQL.

Which vendor you choose, and whether you host the databases yourself or have them hosted by an IaaS or PaaS provider, is not as important as ensuring that you secure the setup with regard to access and reliability. We have seen various clusters with any of the previously mentioned databases run for years without any problems—given that the RDBMS was professionally configured and managed. Because some projects may not support all of these databases, we also see setups where more than one of the supported database types is in use. This spreads the load across multiple RDBMS instances, while keeping the complexity lower than when setting up a separate database system for each Hadoop service (as previously discussed).

An interesting challenge is the maintenance of the databases themselves. For example, newer versions of Hive or Hue may need to update their internal database schemas. Since the recommended way of dealing with Hadoop is having multiple environments (see Chapter 2), you can stage the service database-related schema updates first and then roll them out, as supported by each Hadoop subsystem. For example, Oozie can be shut down briefly to update the software and database schemas, without interrupting data pipelines that are in flight.

Instead of manually dealing with these maintenance tasks, the Hadoop management systems support the automated upgrade of components and their internal database schemas. Therefore, you can simply press a button, wait, and see all of the systems return to operational again.

Hadoop Deployment

This section discusses the details of installing Hadoop as part of a larger system deployment. As discussed in Chapter 2, an organization often has multiple Hadoop environments that need to be provisioned and subsequently maintained. It is a common practice to set up all of these environments in the same, or a very similar, manner. In other words, what we discuss here applies to all Hadoop environments within the same organization.

Hadoop Distributions

Similar to the development in other open source spaces, like the operating system Linux, Hadoop went from providing just the raw, low-level bits and pieces for each ecosystem project separately, to being supported by commercial companies that package the components into coherent and tested distributions that can be much more easily installed and maintained. Today, anyone who wants to set up a Hadoop cluster has the following options:

Vanilla Apache
> From the beginning, Hadoop, like many other open source projects, has come as a set of source code repositories that contain the core components—that is, the filesystem (HDFS) and resource management framework (YARN). But those two components are often not enough to build fully functional data pipelines. You also need a job scheduler and tools for ingress and egress, in addition to processing engines that offer abstractions, such as SQL or a programming language–based domain-specific language (DSL). Each of these additional components typically comes as a source code repository. Instead of having to deal directly with the source code, you can download archives of releases of each subproject and assemble them as needed. We discuss this in the next section.

Using Vanilla Apache project resources gives you the most freedom, in terms of defining what Hadoop is for your enterprise. This is akin to downloading the Linux kernel sources (*https://www.kernel.org/*) and building your custom OS yourself—which, in practice, not many companies do. Rather, they use one of the prepackaged solutions, known as *distributions*, leading us to the next item on the list.

Vendor Hadoop distribution

Using a prepackaged, shrinkwrapped software bundle has many advantages: you can rely on the selected components included to match, and you get free quality assurance (QA) time. Any serious software vendor ensures that what they are offering works on the supported platforms, which entail a range of hardware- or OS-level choices. Conversely, this is also one of the limiting factors, since using anything that is not supported leaves you without much help apart from internet searches. Also, the list of included components is often rather fixed, which means that you might not be able to get the latest processing engine as a supported tool, nor might you be able to upgrade those tools to the newest releases without forfeiting the mentioned support.

Common examples of Hadoop distribution vendors are Cloudera, Hortonworks, and MapR.[4] Apart from the core Hadoop components of HDFS and YARN, these distributions also include things like:

- Apache HBase
- Apache Hive
- Apache Kafka
- Apache Oozie
- Apache Pig
- Apache Spark
- Apache Sqoop
- Apache ZooKeeper

But even if two distributions include the same Hadoop ecosystem projects, they might be at different version levels or might be packaged with varying numbers of features. And selecting a distribution is not without long-term consequences, because switching from one to another is a considerable task, both on a technical and an organizational level.

---

4 There used to be a larger number of vendors, including Intel, IBM, and Pivotal, but a consolidation has taken place, in which Intel merged with Cloudera, and IBM and Pivotal with Hortonworks.

Supported or Support

When referring to *supported platforms*, we are talking about the infrastructure with which a packaged Hadoop distribution was tested; for example, RHEL or CentOS, Ubuntu, SUSE, and others for the OS. This reassures you that installation on such platforms was tested and should work. And, because those choices greatly overlap for not only Hadoop distributions but also other related software systems, such as RDBMSs, you can find much supporting information about them online. There are community-driven sites with a lot of free information available—if you know how to find them.

This leads us to the other part, which is *vendor support*. Commonly with a commercial offering, a paid subscription gives you access to automated knowledge bases and human support services. You can open a ticket, upload cluster details—which is supported by the vendor's cluster-management tooling—and expect an answer within a reasonable amount of time. Since Hadoop is made available under the Apache Software License, all vendors offer their packaged Hadoop and related projects as free software, as well.

One crucial difference is how much you get with the free version of the distribution versus the licensed one. Is it just the vendor support services, or is it more features for tools that are otherwise missing or restricted? No matter your choice, you can self-support if you want or pay a fee for remote support, but you always have access to the distributions beforehand to try them out. However, when you pay for a vendor distribution, any deviation from the provided packages is most likely no longer going to be supported.

PaaS Hadoop

This option is also considered a Hadoop distribution, since hosted versions of Hadoop often have their own name and release versioning. The difference is that you cannot install the available distributions on your own hardware. Instead, they are provisioned as part of a larger IaaS offering. This means that the cloud services provider will not only provision the Hadoop software components, but also the underlying OS, the virtual machines, networking, storage, and more. (See Part III for an in-depth discussion.)

The advantages of a hosted distribution include the level of automation, the available infrastructure services (such as Hadoop service database systems, monitoring, alerting, elasticity, and reporting), and not having to own any of these pieces. Obviously, though, like renting an apartment or leasing a car, you must pay a premium for this service.

Installation Choices

Before we look into the steps required to install a distribution, let's extend what we have previously discussed and explore the choices you have from which to install:

Sources

Use of the vanilla Hadoop source code to compile your own distribution is not for the faint of heart. Although compiling alone is challenging, combining the various ecosystem projects is even more so, because you cannot assume that the newest version of each project will work with the others. Rather, you need to find the best denominator of versions that work, and/or apply patches (which have updates to the code base) from newer versions of a project to older ones to get access to required features (referred to as *backporting*).

Another option is to compile the provided sources of a vendor-backed Hadoop distribution. The sources for each release, including all patches that are applied on top of it, are available online and can be used as a basis to compile your own release.

What you end up with is a set of compiled binaries (usually in the form of *tarball* archives, which are the compiled bits, like JARs in an optionally compressed *.tar* file), but not much more. You still need to deploy and manage the binaries on your Hadoop infrastructure. In practice, this variant of installing Hadoop is rare.

Binary releases

Continuing the previous discussion, you could also download the binaries directly from the projects that offer them for each release. This makes applying patches nearly impossible and leaves you in the same predicament—that is, you still need to deploy everything and manage it all.

This applies to vendor-provided distributions, too, because they offer binary archives for each of their releases, and you can deploy them within your clusters manually—with the same caveats.

Dependent on your choice, you have the following options for rolling out the software:

Software configuration management tool

The next step in automating the installation of the Hadoop binaries is often the use of an SCM system, like Ansible, Puppet, or Chef. These allow the definition of a target state for any managed machine in a cluster, in addition to the use of SSH or agents to reach that state. This includes the installation of the binaries, setting up the configuration for each, handling related services (for example, creating the service databases), and more.

Although this sounds like a great addition to managing your own Hadoop distribution, it still leaves you without any commercial support or free QA time.

Instead, it builds what could be described as *technical debt*—there is no one but you to take care of updates and additions to the platform. This binds resources and becomes a considerable cost factor over time.

Hadoop distribution installer
Here, you make use of what is provided by the vendors to guide you in installing the Hadoop cluster. There are wizard-style helpers that check all of the dependencies and prerequisites on all cluster nodes and then push out the binary packages during the deployment process.

Containerization

Although it is a hot topic in many areas of IT, using container frameworks, such as Docker, is not without its challenges with regard to Hadoop. The common design for applications inside a container is to have a rather small footprint, when it comes to resources such as disk space. With HDFS, especially, you need access to the low-level hard drives that hold the HDFS data blocks, and usually there are plenty of those drives inside each node. Docker, for example, has the concept of *volumes*, which allow you to mount storage space from the host filesystem into the container, but that is not without its own challenges: there have been reports in the past in which these mounted volumes were not as fast as native access.

Having said that, there are plenty of open source projects to help you to package Hadoop into containers. None of the commercial distributions—which are the vast majority of installations—have built-in native container support. In other words, you can leave the beaten path if you want to. Just be aware that you will find little to no support for your setup.

Using a well-rounded distribution makes the most sense, in practice. Going forward, we are only going to talk about distributions for the reasons just discussed. The next sections look more closely into how Hadoop distributions work and what the installation process looks like.

Distribution Architecture

Distributions are more than just installers that move the binaries into place. As mentioned, distributions also add tooling that helps to manage and maintain the cluster after it is up and running. There is commonly a management application that handles the state of the cluster, like node status and membership. Some distributions use a closed-source management layer, whereas others rely on open source tools such as Apache Ambari.

Standardization Efforts

In 2015, a group of vendors, including Hortonworks and IBM, collaborated to create the *Open Data Platform initiative (ODPi)* (*https://www.odpi.org/*) for Hadoop. The goal of the Linux Foundation Projects–hosted group is to define what is included in a Hadoop distribution and how it is tested to prove compliance. The ODPi specifications define what a core Hadoop platform includes, along with the version of Hadoop it supports, which components it must include (that is, HDFS, YARN, and MapReduce), and more.

The *operations* specification further details that an ODPi-compliant distribution must provide a Hadoop management tool, and it goes on to define features of that tool which map to Apache Ambari. Although not explicitly stated, the close tie to Ambari makes it difficult (or even impossible) for those distributions that use a closed-source, proprietary tool for cluster management to comply with the ODPi rules.

The specs also define what a *runtime environment* must include to be compliant, including the environment variables that must be set and the minimum version of Java that is used. There is also a section that defines more optional features—those that should be provided to be compatible with the ODPi specification. This helps to make applications more agnostic when running against an ODPi-conforming platform.

The ODPi released version 1.0 of its specification in 2016 and is working on a version 2.0, which adds Apache Hive as a prerequisite for all compliant distributions. It is of note that neither Cloudera nor MapR uses Ambari for cluster management, and neither is part of the ODPi.

The general architecture of Hadoop distributions with management tooling is shown in Figure 7-4. The main components are the management tool itself, often installed on one of the management nodes in a cluster or on an edge node for setups where direct access to the Hadoop cluster nodes is not allowed, and the *agent* process on each cluster node. The latter is used by the management tool to detect the state of the node and the processes running on it.

The agents have a varying degree of built-in features. For example, some include process management, which can restart local applications and services as needed. Others only report metrics about the host to the management tool or might help with installing Hadoop-related binaries on each machine. Whichever features the agent provides, it is necessary for the management tool to do its job and must be installed before everything else. The next section discusses how this fits into an overall installation process.

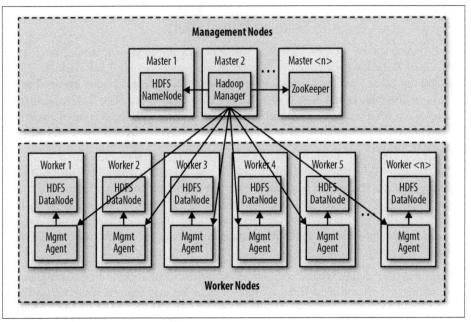

Figure 7-4. Common Hadoop cluster management architecture

Installation Process

After provisioning the cluster nodes and the operating system as described in "Operating Systems" on page 185, you can install the Hadoop platform itself. We refrain
from reiterating this process in detail and refer you to the installation guides that
come with each vendor-provided Hadoop distribution. These guides are usually
comprehensive and thorough, discussing various approaches for installing the platform. The first choice is how you want to access the Hadoop distribution binaries
and packages. You have the same online and offline choices as explained in "OS
Choices" on page 187).

Package Management Options

Depending on your selected distribution, you may have an interesting choice to make
here: how you want to install the binaries. Although some offer only the package
management tool that comes with the OS—for example, yum for Red Hat–based OSs
(using *.rpm* extensions), or apt for Debian-based ones (using *.deb* extensions)—there
are other distributions that have additional options. For example, Cloudera has its
own package format, called *parcels*, aside from the OS-native ones.

This begs the question, which option is better? Cloudera makes the case that the
native package management is too strict when it comes to managing Hadoop versions. Keep in mind that, with the native package manager, you can only have one

version of the software installed at any time. This makes upgrading the Hadoop plat-form more error-prone because all packages need to comply with the rules enforced on the OS level, including dependencies.

On the other hand, parcels are separate from the OS and handled by Cloudera Man-ager, the management tool provided by Cloudera, without any interference from other processes, packages, or rulesets. In fact, Cloudera Manager can install multiple versions of Hadoop on the same machine and manages to switch between them locally with little effort.

Whichever Hadoop distribution you choose, check what package formats it offers and weigh the pros and cons of each.

The next major decision to make is how you want to install the management tool and its agents on each machine of the cluster. Your choices include:

Manual installation

In this scenario, an administrator needs to set up the management tool on one or more of the management nodes and set up its agent on all worker nodes. This can be done in a couple of ways. You can use a terminal and command-line interface (like bash), or you can use an SCM tool to deploy and configure the necessary binaries.

Fully automated installation

The other option is to set up the management tool manually (or using an SCM tool) but to then let the Hadoop management tool install the agents on all machines in an automated manner. Some distributions offer a small install script that downloads the management tool and installs it, making the initial step as frictionless as possible.

After you have the main management software running, you need for the tool to remotely access the nodes and to issue the necessary commands locally on each machine. This is done through SSH, with either *root* or passwordless *sudo* cre-dentials.

The entire process is outlined in Figure 7-5.

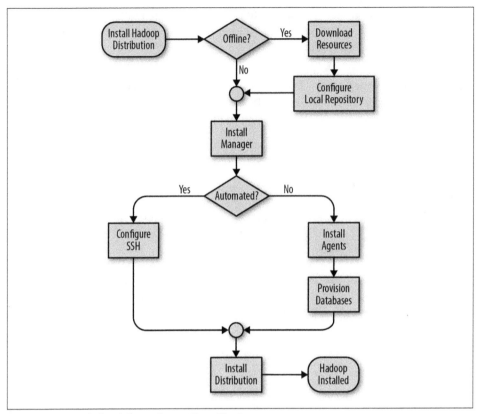

Figure 7-5. High-level flow of installing Hadoop

Summary

This chapter walked through the provisioning and configuration of Hadoop cluster nodes, beginning with the operating system and data stores. We then discussed the details of installing Hadoop itself, weighing the various distribution and installation options.

After the cluster with all the Hadoop platform pieces is up and running, you can move on to Chapter 8, which helps you to determine whether the setup is fully functional.

Platform Validation

After your hardware has been racked and the software installed, it's time to validate the installation. You want to ensure that the cluster works within a reasonable, expected range of performance and that all the components work well with each other. Validation may include a variety of practices, such as:

Smoke testing

To detect bad hardware and platform misconfigurations. Any setup can have disks that are dead on arrival, memory sticks that aren't seated right, network adapters that work intermittently, and more. Storage disks, in particular, tend to fail according to the *bathtub curve (http://bit.ly/2FAR2Y6)*.[1] You can use burn-in tests to "smoke" these components out and replace them before demand on the system comes into play.

Baseline testing

To demonstrate or prove degraded performance. For this you need evidence, not expectations. If you exercise your system at regular intervals while you configure the hardware, the operating system, and the Hadoop components, you can correlate recent changes to a change in system efficiency. You can identify regressions (or progressions!) caused by new hardware or software upgrades simply by running regular, repeatable tests for performance.

Stress testing

To ensure that your monitoring, alerting, day-to-day operations, and other triage operations work as you expect. Rehearsing your recovery procedures and playbooks before the system goes into service—without the pressure of production

---

1 See Bianca Schroeder and Garth A. Gibson, "Disk Failures in the Real World" (*http://bit.ly/2OXTOpE*).

demand or the clamor of angry tenants—is the best time to establish your response practice.

 It is important that the first validation occurs *before* you add users and applications. Once you run your applications and open them to users, you have what amounts to, from a validation perspective, a system in constant flux. With users, in particular, you introduce not only more activity but also competing perspectives on what constitutes good performance.

As an operator, you want to hand the platform over to users knowing that it is able to perform correctly in its native state. You want confidence in your ability to help separate platform, application, and user errors—and your processes—to deal with platform issues and failures.

Performance is often a rather nebulous and subjective thing. It depends on the particular cluster hardware, network topology, the planned use cases, user demand, and, of course, the code. The key here is agreement. If the cluster operators and users share one view of its expected services and performance goals, it's much easier to avoid changes that answer more to politics than consensus.

We approach validation in a bottom-up fashion. We start with disk and network tests to confirm that each component operates within a reasonable range of performance. Then we look at OS configuration to ensure that it is suitable for Hadoop—namely, HDFS and YARN—and the other services in the ecosystem that we intend to use, such as Impala, HBase, and Solr.

Testing Methodology

For their results to be taken seriously, our tests need to demonstrate some degree of rigor. For us this means:

- Run each test at least three times, accepting the median value as valid.
- Ensure that every test is repeatable, and record all the testing parameters and the results they generate.
- Use the same tools (compilation options, bit-orientation, software version, etc.) on every machine.

Take care when comparing between clusters that are not made up of the same network topology, hardware, operating environments, and tools. Benchmarks on different clusters can sometimes be useful for comparisons, for example after a hardware upgrade or environmental change, but beware of spurious comparisons between unrelated setups.

Useful Tools

You'll find a few specific tools invaluable when conducting platform validation tests. A listing by category follows:

Configuration management software
> You'll need to run some of your tests across all the nodes in the cluster and to coordinate them to handle distributed processing tasks. Tools such as Ansible, Puppet, and Chef will make this work simpler and faster to execute. You should also seek out a parallel command execution tool, such as Puppet MCollective or Python Fabric, to address many nodes at once.

Monitoring software
> You'll also need a centralized monitoring solution to collect measurements on diagnostic data on each node. A cluster manager, such as Cloudera Manager or Apache Ambari, has this capability built in. You can also use more general-purpose monitoring and visualization tools, such as InfluxDB and Grafana.

Hardware Validation

Hardware validation includes verifying the performance of the CPUs, disks, and network.

CPU

Problems with a CPU are rare, thankfully. It's equally rare that any direct tuning is necessary. That said, running CPU-intensive tasks on new hardware will ensure that you're getting the performance you've paid for, and these tests can expose some hardware misconfigurations. As an example, we've used a CPU-intensive task to trace the cause of a two-times performance difference—with otherwise identical machines—to the power-saving mode setting in the BIOS.

Validation approaches

You have several options for benchmarking CPUs, but to start, here's a simple but surprisingly effective method. Make the CPU generate many random numbers, compress the result, and dump it:

```
$ dd if=/dev/urandom bs=1M count=1000 | gzip - >/dev/null
1000+0 records in
1000+0 records out
1048576000 bytes transferred in 108.590273 secs (9656261 bytes/sec)
```

Here we generated a thousand 1 MB blocks of random numbers and used gzip (which is computationally expensive) on the output. Dropping the results in the bit bucket limits our I/O costs to the bare minimum. The throughput comes to 9.65 million bytes/sec, which we can take as acceptable for a casual, single-threaded test on the machine at hand.

Now let's test our capability at scale using several threads. If you have installed Hadoop and Spark, you can run the following test to calculate *pi* using a thread count that is appropriate to the worker node CPUs you have. We use eight threads in this example:

```
$ spark-submit --master local[8] \
  --class org.apache.spark.examples.SparkPi \
  /opt/cloudera/parcels/CDH/lib/spark/lib/spark-examples.jar 10000
...
16/11/16 18:06:23 INFO Executor: Finished task 0.0 in stage 0.0 (TID 0)...
16/11/16 18:06:23 INFO TaskSetManager: Starting task 1.0 in stage 0.0 (...
16/11/16 18:06:23 INFO Executor: Running task 1.0 in stage 0.0 (TID 1)
16/11/16 18:06:23 INFO TaskSetManager: Finished task 0.0 in stage 0.0 (...
16/11/16 18:06:23 INFO Executor: Finished task 1.0 in stage 0.0 (TID 1)...
16/11/16 18:06:23 INFO TaskSetManager: Starting task 2.0 in stage 0.0 (...
16/11/16 18:06:23 INFO Executor: Running task 2.0 in stage 0.0 (TID 2)
16/11/16 18:06:23 INFO TaskSetManager: Finished task 1.0 in stage 0.0 (...
16/11/16 18:06:23 INFO Executor: Finished task 2.0 in stage 0.0 (TID 2)...
16/11/16 18:06:23 INFO TaskSetManager: Starting task 3.0 in stage 0.0 (...
16/11/16 18:06:23 INFO Executor: Running task 3.0 in stage 0.0 (TID 3)
16/11/16 18:06:23 INFO TaskSetManager: Finished task 2.0 in stage 0.0 (...
16/11/16 18:06:23 INFO Executor: Finished task 3.0 in stage 0.0 (TID 3)...
16/11/16 18:06:23 INFO TaskSetManager: Starting task 4.0 in stage 0.0 (...
...more...
```

The parameter given the SparkPi program (10000) specifies how many iterations we'd like to approximate *pi*. A higher number calls for more computations and results in an approximation with greater precision.

If you're going all-out, consider a multipurpose benchmarking tool such as sysbench (*https://github.com/akopytov/sysbench*). We use sysbench primarily to profile database servers, but it also contains tests for CPU performance that are general enough for validation testing.

An example invocation of the tool using a test that calculates prime numbers using multiple threads follows. The resulting runtimes for this test system are plotted in Figure 8-1:

```
for n in 1 2 3; do
  for t in 1 2 4 8; do
```

```
        echo $n $t
        sysbench --num-threads=$t \
            --test=cpu \
            --cpu-max-prime=10000 run > sysbench_cpu_${t}_${n}.out
    done
done
```

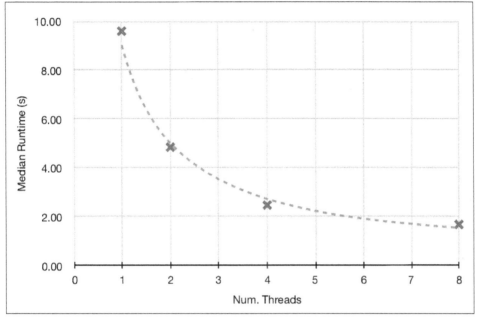

Figure 8-1. Runtimes for the sysbench CPU test—notice the diminishing returns of extra threads as the system becomes saturated

You may not find sysbench in the standard repositories of your Linux distribution, but it is a useful tool and worth your time to find and install. Table 8-1 lists some sources.

Table 8-1. Obtaining sysbench

Distribution	Repository
Red Hat Enterprise Linux 6	EPEL (`yum install sysbench`)
Red Hat Enterprise Linux 7	EPEL (`yum install sysbench`)
Debian/Ubuntu	Core (`apt-get install sysbench`)
SLES	openSUSE sysbench (*http://bit.ly/2PHBITs*)
Source code	*https://github.com/akopytov/sysbench*

Disks

Recall from Chapter 3 that worker node disks are mounted individually, as we want each device to read and write independently of the others. All disk I/O is directed to a storage controller that supports disk connections through multiple physical channels. We expect a transfer rate of at least 6 Gb/s, or 600 MiB/s, from each channel.[2]

Each disk model will cite some maximum data transfer rate for reading and writing data. In practice, you should expect 100–150 MiB/s for sequential reads and writes with spinning disks. For Hadoop, the usual aim is for the predominant disk access pattern to be large sequential reads and writes, although the access pattern and mix of reads to writes is largely dependent on the workload.

We will validate our platform accordingly, first establishing that every disk is healthy and performs well for large sequential I/O. We also want to show that the controllers have the bandwidth to support the disks operating at maximum rate. Once we're satisfied this is so, we can then test different workloads to assess their read/write ratios and how efficient they are. Finally, we can test application performance using Hadoop components to find our peak performance. We also want to know how many tasks we may run at one time without bogging the disks down and degrading performance.

Sequential I/O performance

The dd tool we used earlier can also help us verify our top sequential transfer rates. dd can copy raw bytes from one device to another, whether it is virtual (e.g., */dev/null*), logical (a filesystem), or physical (the disk volume itself), meaning you can test at any layer. In this example, we write 1 GiB of zero-filled blocks to a file:

```
$ dd if=/dev/zero bs=1M count=1000 of=/data/01/ddtest conv=fdatasync
1000+0 records in
1000+0 records out
1048576000 bytes (1.0 GB) copied, 8.0458 s, 130 MB/s
```

In this instance, we see a transfer rate of 130 MiB/s, about the middle of our expected range.

 Be careful! If you name a physical device, dd will happily overwrite whatever it holds. You can corrupt an entire filesystem by writing to the device underneath it, possibly rendering all the files unusable.

---

2 With disk controllers, a general guideline of 10 bits to the byte is often used to account for the controller overhead.

To read data from disk, we reverse the input and output devices:

```
$ dd if=/data/01/ddtest bs=1M of=/dev/null
1000+0 records in
1000+0 records out
1048576000 bytes (1.0 GB) copied, 7.39555 s, 142 MB/s
```

We expect disk reads to be faster than writes, as seen here, but there's a catch. By default, dd operations on filesystems will use the standard OS page caching mechanism provided by the Linux kernel. If the data you read has been cached in memory, the observed transfer rates will be well beyond what disks can do. This boost is great for applications, of course, but it can complicate your attempt to verify device performance.

Your system will tend to cache pages of frequently used data, so it's not always the case that all or even some of your test data will be available in memory. Fortunately, dd supports settings (*http://bit.ly/2PNm7wA*) to bypass the cache so we can know we're observing actual disk transfer rates. These flags are:

oflag=direct
> Instructs the kernel to bypass I/O management, including the page cache, by invoking the system O_DIRECT flag.

oflag=dsync
> Waits on the physical write (i.e., fdatasync()) of each write system call. This setting invokes the O_DSYNC flag.

conv=fdatasync
> Uses kernel I/O management, but forces a physical write to disk at the end of the process by issuing a single final fdatasync() call.

The oflag=dsync setting is the most expensive since it calls fdatasync() for each block of data.[3] We don't need to simulate synchronous I/O behavior for any workload we care about, so we can ignore this option. To observe disk health and performance under heavy I/O load, use conv=fdatasync or oflag=direct.

Building Blocks

There is significant, and unfortunate, overloading of the term *block* in the data engineering space. At the lowest level, a Linux filesystem reads and writes data to disk in blocks of (usually) 4 KiB (equal to the Linux memory page size).

---

[3] See "Synchronized I/O" and "Direct I/O" in Chapter 2 of *Linux System Programming*, 2nd Edition, by Robert Love (O'Reilly).

In the dd utility, blocks refer to the user-space buffer used for each write. There are count calls made to the write() system call with a given *block size* (bs).

In Hadoop, a block refers to the unit of storage for HDFS. Files are composed of one or more blocks, each of which is replicated between nodes. An HDFS block has a *maximum* size of dfs.blocksize, often 128 MiB. The effective minimum size of an HDFS block is the smallest amount of data that can be stored to a disk device, which is equivalent to the Linux filesystem block size of 4 KiB.

Parquet files are divided up into groups of rows, occasionally called blocks. In Spark, resilient distributed dataset (RDD) partitions are stored as blocks for replication and storage. In HBase a block refers to the portion of an HFile that can be read and cached in memory. And there's more...

When using the term "block," be sure to be clear which meaning is implied.

When reading data, we have two options to ensure we are reading from disk:

- Use the iflag=direct setting, which tells dd that it should instruct the kernel to bypass (as much as possible) the OS's I/O management, including the page cache, and read directly from the device (the O_DIRECT flag again).

- Empty the page cache by calling echo 1 >/proc/sys/vm/drop_caches. This ensures that there are no blocks from the file about to be read in memory; the data must be physically read from the disk device.

In the spirit of not artificially bypassing the kernel's I/O management and for simulating a *cache miss*, the latter should be preferred when doing performance testing, although realistically, there should be very little difference between the two.

The other consideration is parallel sequential I/O to different devices. In the Hadoop case, multiple processes will be reading and writing from and to disks, and we want to ensure that our disk controller can support parallel access to all disks, ideally at the maximum possible transfer rates.

To simulate parallel I/O, we can launch multiple simultaneous background dd processes, one for each disk. For example, if there are 12 disks mounted at /data/ 01, /data/02, we can do parallel writes as follows:

```
$ for n in $(seq 1 12); do
>   num=$(printf "%02d" $n)
>   of="/data/${num}/ddtest"
>   dd if=/dev/zero bs=1M count=1000 of=${of} conv=fdatasync 2>${of}.out &
>   WAITPIDS="$WAITPIDS ${!}"
> done
$ wait $WAITPIDS
$ grep copied /data/??/ddtest.out
/data/01/ddtest.out:1048576000 bytes (1.0 GB) copied, 7.05083 s, 149 MB/s
```

```
/data/02/ddtest.out:1048576000 bytes (1.0 GB) copied, 7.04237 s, 149 MB/s
/data/03/ddtest.out:1048576000 bytes (1.0 GB) copied, 7.01174 s, 150 MB/s
...truncated...
/data/11/ddtest.out:1048576000 bytes (1.0 GB) copied, 7.15214 s, 147 MB/s
/data/12/ddtest.out:1048576000 bytes (1.0 GB) copied, 6.9216 s, 151 MB/s
```

Using the data written in the previous step, we can then clear the cache and read in parallel:

```
$ echo 1 >/proc/sys/vm/drop_caches
$ for n in $(seq 1 12); do
>    num=$(printf "%02d" $n)
>    if="/data/${num}/ddtest"
>    dd of=/dev/null bs=1M if=${if} 2>${if}.in & WAITPIDS="${WAITPIDS} ${!}"
> done
$ wait $WAITPIDS
$ grep copied /data/??/ddtest.in
/data/01/ddtest.in:1048576000 bytes (1.0 GB) copied, 8.43961 s, 124 MB/s
/data/02/ddtest.in:1048576000 bytes (1.0 GB) copied, 8.54024 s, 123 MB/s
/data/03/ddtest.in:1048576000 bytes (1.0 GB) copied, 8.35292 s, 126 MB/s
...truncated...
/data/11/ddtest.in:1048576000 bytes (1.0 GB) copied, 8.67109 s, 121 MB/s
/data/12/ddtest.in:1048576000 bytes (1.0 GB) copied, 8.6997 s, 121 MB/s
```

Repeated at least three times on each node, these tests should highlight any immediate issues with individual disk transfer speeds and controller bandwidth.

To test more complex workloads, we can use a tool called fio (*https://github.com/ axboe/fio*). With fio, we can simulate a mixed workload of sequential and random reads and writes. We do not have space to cover too many scenarios in this book, but here is an example configuration file for a test that performs a 50:50 sequential read/ write workload across 12 disks:

```
$ vim seq-rw.fio
[global]
rw=readwrite
size=1g
bs=1m
direct=1

[d1]
filename=/data/01/fiow

[d2]
filename=/data/02/fiow

[d3]
filename=/data/03/fiow

...etc...
```

```
[d12]
filename=/data/12/fiow
```

The test is launched as follows (output truncated for clarity):

```
$ fio seq-rw.fio | grep "runt="
read : io=544768KB, bw=48184KB/s, iops=47 , runt= 11306msec
write: io=503808KB, bw=44561KB/s, iops=43 , runt= 11306msec
read : io=520192KB, bw=47926KB/s, iops=46 , runt= 10854msec
write: io=528384KB, bw=48681KB/s, iops=47 , runt= 10854msec
read : io=535552KB, bw=49328KB/s, iops=48 , runt= 10857msec
write: io=513024KB, bw=47253KB/s, iops=46 , runt= 10857msec
read : io=527360KB, bw=49240KB/s, iops=48 , runt= 10710msec
write: io=521216KB, bw=48666KB/s, iops=47 , runt= 10710msec
read : io=515072KB, bw=47393KB/s, iops=46 , runt= 10868msec
write: io=533504KB, bw=49089KB/s, iops=47 , runt= 10868msec
read : io=524288KB, bw=48255KB/s, iops=47 , runt= 10865msec
write: io=524288KB, bw=48255KB/s, iops=47 , runt= 10865msec
read : io=548864KB, bw=48888KB/s, iops=47 , runt= 11227msec
write: io=499712KB, bw=44510KB/s, iops=43 , runt= 11227msec
read : io=519168KB, bw=47530KB/s, iops=46 , runt= 10923msec
write: io=529408KB, bw=48467KB/s, iops=47 , runt= 10923msec
read : io=537600KB, bw=50498KB/s, iops=49 , runt= 10646msec
write: io=510976KB, bw=47997KB/s, iops=46 , runt= 10646msec
read : io=513024KB, bw=48108KB/s, iops=46 , runt= 10664msec
write: io=535552KB, bw=50221KB/s, iops=49 , runt= 10664msec
read : io=535552KB, bw=49501KB/s, iops=48 , runt= 10819msec
write: io=513024KB, bw=47419KB/s, iops=46 , runt= 10819msec
read : io=546816KB, bw=51071KB/s, iops=49 , runt= 10707msec
write: io=501760KB, bw=46863KB/s, iops=45 , runt= 10707msec
```

There are a few interesting observations from this. First, for rotational disks, we should expect a best case of around 100 IOPS per device, and we get pretty close to that here (read + write). Second, we can see that an aggregate of 100 MiB/s I/O bandwidth (50 MiB/s each for read and write) per device is about the right ballpark. If our tests deviate too far from this, it is cause for further investigation. Note that, based on your understanding of your projected workload, you can configure fio as appropriate, potentially including random access elements.

Disk health

Modern disks include a self-reporting mechanism, called SMART (*http://bit.ly/2PcbePE*), which can report on some errors and provide indications of imminent disk failures. Disk health can be reported via:

```
# smartctl -H /dev/sda
smartctl 5.43 2012-06-30 r3573 [x86_64-linux-2.6.32-431.5.1.el6.x86_64] \
  (local build)
Copyright (C) 2002-12 by Bruce Allen, http://smartmontools.sourceforge.net

SMART Health Status: OK
```

Note that while an OK output is not a guaranteed indication of continued disk health, problems highlighted by the tool should not be ignored. Increased errors reported by the SMART monitoring tools have been shown to have some degree of correlation with impending disk failures.[4] Disks failing this health test should usually be immediately replaced.

Network

Virtually all useful workloads on Hadoop clusters involve communication between machines, whether it be shuffling data between operators during distributed queries, routine heartbeats from a coordinator process to its children, the use of network-based services such as DNS or Kerberos, data replication for resilience, or any number of other operations. Networks, naturally, are at the heart of distributed systems. A properly configured network is therefore essential to the smooth running of a Hadoop cluster. Chapter 4 covered networking concepts in detail, including the range of topologies available for connecting machines and switches together.

In order to validate the performance of your chosen topology, you need to test two things: network latency and available network bandwidth. You need to benchmark and validate these metrics, both between individual pairs of machines in the same rack (i.e., connected to the same switch) and between pairs of machines in different racks. Moreover, the throughput tests should be repeated with many pairs of machines participating in the tests concurrently to get an idea of the performance of the network under load.

Latency Versus Throughput

The *latency* of a network is the typical time taken to perform a single operation between two machines on the network. Usually measured in milliseconds, *network latency* typically refers to the time taken for a packet to traverse the network from machine A to machine B and back again. It does not include the time taken to perform the operation on the destination machine (e.g., the time taken from the issuing of a query to the result being returned, which includes both network latency and the time spent in the application itself). There are a number of factors that affect network latency, primarily:

- The network distance or number of intervening network *hops* between machine A and machine B
- The amount of traffic on the network

---

4 Eduardo Pinheiro et al., "Failure Trends in a Large Disk Drive Population," (*http://bit.ly/2zyKZfx*) *Proceedings of the 5th USENIX Conference on File and Storage Technologies* (FAST'07), February 2007.

Each intervening network device between two machines will naturally add some small amount of latency (routing and switching is not free). Likewise, the physical distance will also dictate the minimum possible latency between two machines.

While the latency indicates the time taken for an individual packet to make the trip between two points, the *throughput* measures how much data can be sent or received by each device on the network in a given slice of time.

Just like latency, network throughput can be affected by the bandwidth available to each device traversed and by how busy the network is at a given time.

It should be noted that there are a wide variety of configurable parameters at every point in the network (e.g., TCP/IP kernel parameters, switch configuration, etc.), and it is beyond the scope of this book to go into detail on network tuning. However, these tests can demonstrate whether the network is performing within expectations under load.

Measuring latency

Latency between two points is most easily measured using the humble ping. This simple program uses the ICMP protocol to send sequential *echo request* packets to a remote IP address and measures the time it takes to receive a reply for each packet, along with summary statistics. Running pings between pairs of machines connected to the same network switch should result in latencies in the single-digit milliseconds or lower. Pings between machines in different racks should be in the tens of milliseconds or lower. Latencies longer than this should be investigated. Whatever the absolute values, the key thing is that for comparable network distances (i.e., number of network hops), the latencies should be roughly the same for all machines in the cluster and deviations may indicate a problem; for example, if pings to machines in one rack consistently have longer latencies when compared to different pairs of machines in other racks.

ping is a very well-known program. An example invocation for four pings is as follows:

```
$ ping -c 4 futura.local
PING futura.local (172.31.55.130) 56(84) bytes of data.
64 bytes from futura.local (172.31.55.130): icmp_seq=1 ttl=64 time=0.186 ms
64 bytes from futura.local (172.31.55.130): icmp_seq=2 ttl=64 time=0.207 ms
64 bytes from futura.local (172.31.55.130): icmp_seq=3 ttl=64 time=0.212 ms
64 bytes from futura.local (172.31.55.130): icmp_seq=4 ttl=64 time=0.212 ms

--- futura.local ping statistics ---
4 packets transmitted, 4 received, 0% packet loss, time 3002ms
rtt min/avg/max/mdev = 0.186/0.204/0.212/0.014 ms
```

Latency under load

Measuring the "quiescent" latency is important, but another characteristic that's useful to know in a cluster is how latency increases (or not) under heavy network loads —in particular, latency to the master nodes from other nodes in the cluster. Several services in the Hadoop ecosystem rely on low-latency communications with master processes for efficient operation, notably when interacting with the HDFS Name-Node and ZooKeeper services. When performing some of the more intensive load tests outlined later in the chapter, a concurrent ping test from a gateway node (or any node not participating in the load test) to the master node can reveal how much, if any, latency suffers due to network load. As a general guideline, if the latency increases into the seconds range, this indicates a problem that needs to be addressed.

Measuring throughput

Network throughput is measured in denominations of bits per second, with the most common being megabits per second (Mbps) and gigabits per second (Gbps). Commonly, in cluster-grade servers, an Ethernet network interface card (NIC) can communicate at either 1 Gbps or 10 Gbps, although speeds of 40 or even 100 Gbps are possible. Hadoop services are designed to minimize "global" network communication as much as possible by using memory, disk, and network locality, so usually NICs with speeds greater than 10 Gbps cannot be justified. As a general guideline, when translating bits per second (bps) into bytes per second (B/s) we often allow 10 bits per byte to account for the various network overheads and for ease of calculation. Under this rule, a 1 Gbps NIC can send and receive at a maximum rate of approximately 100 MiB/s and a 10 Gbps NIC at approximately 1,000 MiB/s. The theoretical maximum rates are approximately 119 MiB/s and 1192 MiB/s. It is rare for a NIC to achieve these rates consistently in real scenarios, but we should be able to get close in testing.

NICs can communicate in either half-duplex (either send or receive) or full-duplex (send and receive concurrently) mode. Full duplex is by far the most common. A useful tool to check and modify NIC configuration is `ethtool`:

```
# ethtool eth0

Settings for eth0:
  Supported ports: [ ]
  Supported link modes:    10000baseT/Full
  Supported pause frame use: No
  Supports auto-negotiation: No
  Advertised link modes:  Not reported
  Advertised pause frame use: No
  Advertised auto-negotiation: No
  Speed: 10000Mb/s
  Duplex: Full
  Port: Other
```

```
PHYAD: 0
Transceiver: Unknown!
Auto-negotiation: off
Current message level: 0x00000007 (7)
        drv probe link
Link detected: yes
```

> ## Jumbo Frames
>
> In TCP communication, each packet sent must be acknowledged by the sender, so it
> follows that if we can pack our data into fewer, larger lumps, we can transfer that data
> more efficiently. The Ethernet protocol defines a maximum size for any single unit of
> communication (a *frame*), the *maximum transmission unit* (MTU), which is typically
> 1,500 bytes. In cluster networks with dedicated switches and machines where we are
> free (or at least it is possible) to change network configurations, we can make use of
> so-called *jumbo frames* with an MTU of 9,000. For large streaming transfers, as are
> common in Hadoop workloads, this can improve network performance by a signifi-
> cant margin.
>
> A word of warning, though: each network device must be configured with the same
> frame size, or mysterious dropped packets and hard-to-diagnose issues may result.

A very useful tool in measuring network throughput between machines is iperf3
(*http://iperf.fr*), which is available as a package in most Linux distributions. iperf3
has a lot of functionality and can test speeds across a number of protocols, but we will
be using it to simply test the speed of TCP communication between two machines.
We will then expand this pair-wise approach to include more and more machines to
create a mesh test of the network. iperf3 operates in a client-server model. To set up
a test, we start an instance listening on the target machine:

```
$ iperf3 -s -p 13000
------------------------------------------------------------
Server listening on 13000
------------------------------------------------------------
```

Then, on the source machine, we start the client and configure it to run a 10-second
speed test:

```
$ iperf3 -c futura.local -p 13000 -t 10
Connecting to host futura.local, port 13000
[  4] local 172.31.61.61 port 43780 connected to 172.31.55.130 port 13000
[ ID] Interval           Transfer     Bandwidth       Retr  Cwnd
[  4]   0.00-1.00   sec   240 MBytes  2.01 Gbits/sec    5   1.17 MBytes
[  4]   1.00-2.00   sec   119 MBytes   996 Mbits/sec    0   1.56 MBytes
[  4]   2.00-3.00   sec   119 MBytes   996 Mbits/sec    0   1.88 MBytes
...more output...
[  4]   8.00-9.00   sec   119 MBytes   996 Mbits/sec    1   1.70 MBytes
[  4]   9.00-10.00  sec   118 MBytes   986 Mbits/sec    0   1.98 MBytes
```

```
- - - - - - - - - - - - - - - - - - - - - - - - - -
[ ID] Interval           Transfer     Bandwidth       Retr
[  4]   0.00-10.00  sec  1.28 GBytes  1.10 Gbits/sec   8             sender
[  4]   0.00-10.00  sec  1.27 GBytes  1.09 Gbits/sec                 receiver

iperf Done.
```

The tool reports the interval throughput (bandwidth) for each second in the test and then reports the overall throughput for the entire test. Note that, although the server also reports statistics about bandwidths and transfers, the iperf3 documentation advises that only the client's numbers are to be trusted (*http://bit.ly/2A9P3nM*). Most useful for our purposes is an option to send a defined amount of data. Here we transfer 100 MiB:

```
$ iperf3 -c futura.local -p 13000 -n 104857600
```

Between any two machines, either intra-rack or inter-rack, in the absence of other network loads it should be possible to achieve transfers at close to the maximum possible rate for the NIC. Running repeated tests to establish this fact is an important part of platform validation.

Testing all possible combinations of racks without some form of automation becomes unwieldy for large clusters with many racks. For example, to test all unique pairs of a 10-rack cluster requires 45 pairwise tests.[5] Therefore, we recommend that you use your source code configuration management system to install iperf3 and create a task to start a server process in daemonized mode on all nodes in the cluster, as follows:

```
$ iperf3 -s -p 13000 -D -I /var/run/iperf3.pid
```

Further tests then only need to start off client processes to begin a test.

Throughput under load

The next round of tests is to perform transfers simultaneously to simulate network load:

Intra-rack throughput

Beginning with all N nodes within a rack, we can set up some number P connections between pairs, increasing P to add to the simulated load up to a maximum of $2N$ connections, with each machine being both the source and target of a connection pair. As the load increases, we test the ability of the switch to support increasing traffic from all machines. Top-of-rack switches should be capable of supporting all nodes sending and receiving within the rack at maximum line rate

---

5 Mathematically, 10 choose 2.

(hence our maximum of 2N). If this is not what is observed, it is time to investigate.

 To account for the different startup times for the tests, we can make use of the -O s parameter to the client side of iperf3 to ignore the first s seconds when calculating bandwidths.

Inter-rack throughput

Much as we did for intra-rack throughput testing, we can run tests of cross-rack traffic by running simultaneous iperf3 speed tests for pairs of machines, but this time where the pairs are in different racks. For R racks, in the first round, we set up R pairs and measure the bandwidth achieved for simultaneous connections; then for the next round we set up 2R pairs, and so on. An example testing plan for five racks is shown in Figure 8-2. Here, in the first round, five connections are made to the neighboring rack; in the next round another five connections are made between Rack 1 and Rack 3, Rack 2 and Rack 4, and so on. Finally, in the fourth round, each rack has both an inbound connection and an outbound connection to each other rack in the topology.[6] We can simply repeat these rounds, adding more and more connections, to test how the bandwidths hold up under increasing traffic. Each new pair should be between previously unused nodes, such that each machine only has a maximum of one inbound and one outbound connection. This ensures, as far as possible, that we are measuring the maximum bandwidth of the switches rather than that of the NIC.

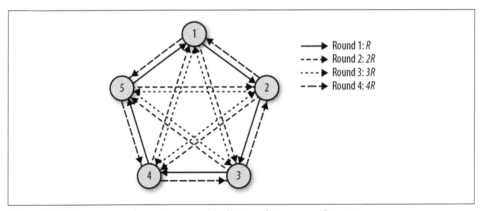

Figure 8-2. Four example testing rounds for iperf3 inter-rack testing

---

6 For graph theory fans, it is now a complete directed graph.

As we increase the number of connections, we should expect initially to see the band-width of individual connections be maintained at some plateau level, and then, as we begin to saturate the cross-rack connections, the bandwidths should begin to decrease. If all the average bandwidths from each test are summed together, we should see a maximum level for cross-rack traffic where the links are saturated. This is illustrated in Figure 8-3, where the dotted lines show the idealized saturation inflection point. In reality, the effects will not be so tidy, but we should expect perfor-mance to drop off roughly at the point where the total bandwidth exceeds the over-subscription ratio we have designed for the network topology. Because Hadoop services try to minimize cross-rack traffic, it is usual to allow some degree of oversub-scription. For example, with an oversubscription ratio of 4:1, in a cluster with 5 racks and 20 machines per rack, we would expect the inflection point to occur where we have 50 concurrent cross-rack connections (i.e., 25 connections in each direction, 5 per rack).

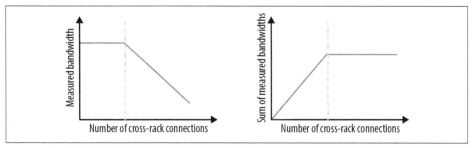

Figure 8-3. Idealized profiles for individual connection bandwidth and summed con-nection bandwidths, as number of concurrent cross-rack connections increases

By comparing the results of the tests with our understanding of the network topology and what it should support in theory, we can validate that the network is performing as expected, and if not, we can provide information for further investigation.

Hadoop Validation

Once the underlying platform is validated, we can validate the services installed on the cluster, beginning with HDFS and YARN/MapReduce.

> It can be useful to perform these platform benchmarks first without security enabled. Kerberos, on-disk encryption, and SSL can add layers of complexity that may mask or confuse investiga-tions into poor performance. Knowing the performance before and after enabling security can also help you understand its perfor-mance impact.

HDFS Validation

HDFS is the basis for most other components in the Hadoop ecosystem, so it is important to establish a baseline for its performance.

Single writes and reads

The first test is simply to act as a single client to HDFS to write and read data. This is an important check because it can reveal misconfigurations such as the use of an inefficient data transfer encryption algorithm. To perform this simple test, write a 1 GiB file from a gateway node, as follows:

```
$ dd if=/dev/urandom bs=1M count=1000 | hdfs dfs -put - /tmp/hdfstest.out
```

HDFS should be able to write data at a rate of *at least* 35 MiB/s for this simple case. The same file can be read back to time read performance:

```
$ time hdfs dfs -cat /tmp/hdfstest.out >/dev/null
```

We should be looking for read speeds of at least 70 MiB/s. Note that we eliminate any I/O to local disks on the gateway node by using the special devices /dev/urandom and /dev/null as input and output devices.

Distributed writes and reads

Although the individual read and write speeds for HDFS are less than we can achieve with direct local disk accesses, HDFS is designed to support vast amounts of distributed concurrent I/O. Hadoop ships with a built-in test for performing a distributed HDFS I/O test, called TestDFSIO. This tool uses MapReduce as a convenient way to spawn many concurrent I/O tasks and can read, write, or append a configurable number of files of a specified size, optionally with compression (see Chapter 1 for a MapReduce refresher). The tool proceeds by writing a control file for each file with the filename and the file size. A mapper is created for each control file input, and the requested I/O is performed from the mapper process. A single reducer collects the statistics from each mapper and produces aggregate statistics at the end.

Here is an example invocation on Cloudera Distribution Hadoop (CDH) for writing six 512 MiB files on a small test environment:

```
$ MRLIB=/opt/cloudera/parcels/CDH/lib/hadoop-mapreduce
$ yarn jar ${MRLIB}/hadoop-mapreduce/hadoop-mapreduce-client-jobclient.jar \
  TestDFSIO \
  -D test.build.data=/user/ian/benchmark \
  -write \
  -resFile w18_128 \
  -nrFiles 6 \
  -size 512MB
17/01/03 19:51:22 INFO fs.TestDFSIO: TestDFSIO.1.7
17/01/03 19:51:22 INFO fs.TestDFSIO: nrFiles = 6
```

```
17/01/03 19:51:22 INFO fs.TestDFSIO: nrBytes (MB) = 512.0
17/01/03 19:51:22 INFO fs.TestDFSIO: bufferSize = 1000000
17/01/03 19:51:22 INFO fs.TestDFSIO: baseDir = /user/ian/benchmark
17/01/03 19:51:23 INFO fs.TestDFSIO: creating control file: \
    536870912 bytes, 6 files
17/01/03 19:51:23 INFO fs.TestDFSIO: created control files for: 6 files
...more output...
17/01/03 19:51:49 INFO fs.TestDFSIO: ----- TestDFSIO ----- : write
17/01/03 19:51:49 INFO fs.TestDFSIO:           Date & time: \
    Tue Jan 03 19:51:49 EST 2017
17/01/03 19:51:49 INFO fs.TestDFSIO:       Number of files: 6
17/01/03 19:51:49 INFO fs.TestDFSIO: Total MBytes processed: 3072.0
17/01/03 19:51:49 INFO fs.TestDFSIO:      Throughput mb/sec: \
    54.656086538803685
17/01/03 19:51:49 INFO fs.TestDFSIO: Average IO rate mb/sec: \
    54.66523742675781
17/01/03 19:51:49 INFO fs.TestDFSIO:   IO rate std deviation: \
    0.7159597238650328
17/01/03 19:51:49 INFO fs.TestDFSIO:      Test exec time sec: 26.296
17/01/03 19:51:49 INFO fs.TestDFSIO:
```

Note that, at the end of the run, the tool presents us with some statistics: throughput, average, and standard deviation, all expressed in MiB/s. The throughput is the total amount of data written by all mappers divided by the total time taken for all mappers, whereas the average is the total of the rates reported by each mapper divided by the number of mappers. Note that these are actually slightly different measures. When combined with the standard deviation, the average is probably more useful in practice. The standard deviation is calculated for the rates reported by the individual mappers and tells us how much variation there was between tasks.

There are some things to note about TestDFSIO. First, because it uses MapReduce as a means to distribute HDFS reads and writes, we are somewhat at the mercy of the YARN scheduler as to how tasks are distributed across the cluster. During a write test, this might mean that some nodes have a disproportionate write load, due to running more mappers.[7] To account for this, we can size the mapper container memory to try and spread tasks across the cluster as evenly as possible. However, during a read test, since TestDFSIO uses the control file as the input split and the actual input file to read is specified in the control file, the mapper may not be reading the data locally.

Before running the test, we need to think about how many files to read or write and what size they should be. As with the networking tests, we can start small and steadily increase the number of files to see how the I/O rate holds up under increasing load. Although there are fewer files than the number of disks in the cluster, we should

---

7 This might especially be the case if yarn.scheduler.fair.assignmultiple is enabled in the YARN configuration.

expect to see I/O rates in excess of 50 MiB/s and small standard deviations, but as we increase the number of tasks past the number of physical disks in the cluster, we will start to see lower rates and potentially increased deviation as the tasks compete for disk I/O.

 As with the raw disk tests from before, be sure to drop the OS page caches before running the read tests.

General Validation

One of the most useful tools in our platform validation toolbox is the TeraSort benchmark. The primary purpose of TeraSort is to benchmark distributed systems by sorting large amounts of data (archetypally 1 TiB) in as short a time as possible. The Hadoop implementation has been used to win the Sort Benchmark (*http://sortbench mark.org/*) a number of times in the past. The Hadoop TeraSort suite consists of three phases:

TeraGen
This phase creates the input for the sort phase, consisting of a specified number of 100-byte records with 10-byte keys and random values. It runs as a map-only job, and each mapper writes a chunk of the records.

TeraSort
The data from the TeraGen phase is read from HDFS, globally sorted, and written back to HDFS.

TeraValidate
Each sorted output is read back, and the keys are checked to ensure that they are in sorted order.

In terms of platform validation, the first two are the most useful and can be used as proxies to test the performance and configuration of the cluster. We look at how in the next couple of sections.

TeraGen

TeraGen can be a very useful platform validation tool, and it allows us to test both disk and network performance. Before using it to test disk I/O we need to understand a little of how this works in practice.

We know that each mapper in a TeraGen job independently writes a slice of the data to HDFS. If we run the job with enough mappers, the YARN ResourceManager distributes these tasks approximately evenly across all available NodeManagers, as they heartbeat in looking for work.[8]

We also know that an HDFS DataNode process, by default, uses a round-robin policy when allocating a disk to a block write request. This means that, if we ensure that the number of write threads is less than or equal to the number of disks in the cluster, we *should* get close to one write thread per disk.

Of course, in practice, things aren't always so neat. We may end up with some Node-Managers running slightly more tasks than others, and a small number of disks will end up with more than one writer thread and some with none. But, over a few runs, these effects should even out.

Disk-only tests. For the first test, we want to test pure disk performance, so we set the HDFS block replication to 1 such that mappers are writing to local disk only. This allows us to eliminate network effects. The general form of a TeraGen invocation is:

```
$ yarn jar \
  /path/to/lib/hadoop-mapreduce/hadoop-mapreduce-examples.jar \
  teragen -Ddfs.replication=<REP> -Ddfs.blocksize=<BLOCKSIZE> \
  -Dmapreduce.job.maps=<MAPS> <ROWS> <HDFS_OUTPUT_DIR>
```

The following is an example invocation on CDH to write 1 TiB on a cluster with 50 nodes, each with 12 disks (for a total of 600 mappers):

```
$ yarn jar \
  /opt/cloudera/parcels/CDH/lib/hadoop-mapreduce/hadoop-*-examples.jar \
  teragen -Ddfs.replication=1 -Ddfs.blocksize=536870912 \
  -Dmapreduce.job.maps=600 11000000000 /user/ian/benchmarks/terasort-input
```

It's worth noting that YARN needs enough resources to run all 600 mappers at once —in this case, an allocation of at least 12 vcores per NodeManager. We also need to allow headroom of at least one vcore for the ApplicationMaster container.

After the job is complete, we can analyze the results and check the performance. If we configure the job such that the number of rows modulo the number of mappers is zero, each mapper will write exactly the same amount of data. By analyzing both the individual runtime for each mapper and the statistical spread of all mapper runtimes, we can identify both slow disk write speeds and potential problem nodes. This is illustrated in Figure 8-4. Note the peak around 65–70 MiB/s. A smaller peak at around 35 MiB/s may indicate one or more bad disks. If the same node repeatedly displays slow tasks, it should be further investigated.

---

[8] For the mappers to be spread most evenly, YARN's `yarn.scheduler.fair.assignmultiple` configuration parameter should be set to `false`.

Combined with platform monitoring showing disk I/O statistics, this is a nice way of verifying disk write performance and identifying bad disks. You should hope to see at least 70 MiB/s from each task. If you have time on your side, you can extend this test by increasing the number of mappers to have two or three write tasks per disk to see at what point the underlying disks saturate.

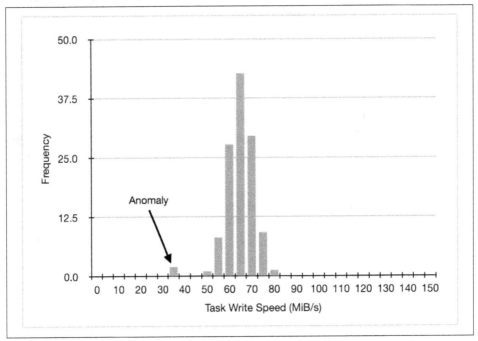

Figure 8-4. An example distribution of task write speeds with replication at 1

Disk and network tests.   To test the effect the network has, and where it starts to become a bottleneck, we can reduce the number of map tasks to one-third of the number of disks in the cluster. We do this to account for three times replication and maintain one writer thread per disk. Repeating the tests first with replication at 1 (for a baseline) and then with the default replication of 3, allows us to see the effect of the replication traffic on the network. It will always be slower when replication is involved, but this initial test should not show *too* much degradation.

Due to the way HDFS places block replicas, approximately half of the induced network traffic will be cross-rack. Again, we can use the job statistics to analyze the individual map times and the standard deviation between all mappers to identify outliers and potential problems.

To explore the limits of the network, increase the number of mappers and plot a distribution of the resultant mapper write speeds. As the network and disk contention effects come into play, we should see the mean write speed decrease and the standard deviation increase, as the contention introduces more variation in the resources allocated to each task.

We can use these tests to validate the oversubscription ratio for cross-rack traffic. As an example, if we assume a 10 Gbps NIC, an oversubscription ratio of 2.5:1, 10 nodes per rack, 12 data disks per node, and an average write speed of 80 MiB/s, we should start to see network contention with more than 5 tasks per node.[9]

TeraSort

The primary utility of terasort in platform validation is not to achieve the lowest runtime to sort 1 TiB (although this can be fun to do), but instead to lay down a marker for cluster performance for a known workload which pushes the CPU, disks, and network. You can rerun TeraSort on a regular basis to ensure that cluster performance is holding up and to rebenchmark the cluster when it is expanded. An example TeraGen/Sort invocation follows:

```
$ yarn jar \
/opt/cloudera/parcels/CDH/lib/hadoop-mapreduce/hadoop-*-examples.jar \
terasort -Dyarn.app.mapreduce.am.resource.mb=4096 \
-Dyarn.app.mapreduce.am.command-opts=-Xmx4294967296 \
-Dmapreduce.job.reduces=2500 /user/ian/benchmarks/terasort-input \
/user/ian/benchmarks/terasort-output
```

We will not go into too much more detail here on running TeraSort benchmarks, because they don't really reflect a real-life workload. But here are a couple of general pointers:

- Increase the default HDFS block size during TeraGen to 256 MiB or 512 MiB to avoid too many map tasks in the TeraSort phase.

- Try to align the size of files written by TeraGen to the block size, to ensure full files for mappers to read, by setting the number of rows accordingly. For example, if you are using 400 mappers with a block size of 256 MiB, you could specify $(400 \times 256 \times 1024 \times 1024)/100 = 1073741824$ rows, which would generate 100 GiB (remember that each row is 100 bytes).

- Set the number of reducers large enough to provide good parallelism for the final sorting phase but small enough so they can all run at once.

- Do not waste time optimizing for TeraSort, because it does not represent a real-life workload.

---

9 Maximum cross-rack traffic is $10 \times 1000 / 2.5 = 4000$ MB/s. Number of tasks is $4000 / 10 / 80 = 5$ tasks.

- Take care to delete the files produced by TeraGen and TeraSort, both to free up space and to avoid sysadmin panics when blocks with a replication factor of one go missing.

Validating Other Components

Other frameworks in the Hadoop ecosystem ship with their own benchmarking tools, a few of which we will outline in this section. In addition, there are a few general performance evaluation tools or benchmarking suites for assessing data storage engines. There is not enough space here to cover each in detail, but we provide some pointers to what is available. To start with, a couple of general tools:

YCSB

Yahoo! Cloud Serving Benchmark (YCSB) (*http://bit.ly/2FwAZL2*) is a benchmarking suite designed to test the performance of various random access (as opposed to analytical warehouse) NoSQL data stores. It can apply a series of different core workloads comprising different mixes of reads, writes, updates, deletes, and access patterns, such as random access and range scans, and can be extended with custom workload definitions. Currently, plug-ins exist for many serving systems, but most interesting for our purposes are the plug-ins for HBase, Solr, and Kudu. For full details on YCSB and its operation, refer to the documentation (*http://bit.ly/2Q9uYYF*).[10]

TPC-DS

The Transactions Processing Council (TPC) produces a number of benchmarks for evaluating various relational database engines. The benchmarks cover a wide range of functionality, and they are divided into a number of domains. Each benchmark has a defined set of queries, and performance is assessed by their runtimes. TPC-DS (*http://bit.ly/2zl6CBD*) is a benchmark covering decision support workloads and is focused on benchmarking analytical queries—workloads that process a large volume of data in support of business decisions. Modified versions of TPC-DS are regularly used to test query engines such as Impala, Hive, and Spark SQL.

Load Testing

In some cases, a custom load-testing tool is appropriate—for example, applying a known query workload to Impala. There are a few open source tools around to achieve this, but perhaps the most popular is Apache JMeter (*http://jmeter.apache.org/*). Out of the box, it has the ability to run load tests via HTTP,

---

10 Note that YCSB is also available as a parcel for Cloudera (*http://bit.ly/2S4quQf*).

JDBC, JMS, and more and also can run arbitrary shell scripts. Among the most commonly used example use cases are:

- Submitting a set of queries from a real workload concurrently to Impala via JDBC
- Stress testing a SolrCloud deployment via HTTP requests
- Load testing APIs providing interfaces to Hadoop services, such as the HBase REST server or a custom abstraction layer

Specific benchmarking tools also exist for HBase and Impala:

HBase
In addition to using YCSB, HBase ships with two tools that can be used for running benchmark tests: `LoadTestingTool` and `PerformanceEvaluation`. For details and usage, see the "Performance Tuning" chapter of the upcoming *HBase: The Definitive Guide*, by Lars George (O'Reilly).

Impala
As already mentioned, a version of the TPC-DS benchmark suite has been written for benchmarking Impala. The queries are slightly modified from the published benchmark suite, but as a means of laying down a marker for cluster performance, it can prove useful.

The underlying data for TPC-DS is a data warehouse-style schema oriented around a retail use case with a large fact table and supporting dimensional tables. The actual volume of data is defined by a scale factor, which can be used to increase the scale of the benchmark.

Operations Validation

Although the focus of this chapter has been on performance, we should not leave the subject of platform validation without briefly talking about operational tests. An essential part of validating an installation is confirming that all nodes can be rebooted successfully and that their essential configuration parameters (such as swappiness) persist across reboots. It's also a great time to test out procedures for disk replacement in both master and worker nodes.

At the software level, ensure that database backups are being taken (and can be restored) and that all layers of the software stack, including Hadoop and the surrounding services, can be restarted without issue. If you are integrating with enterprise monitoring solutions, you should ensure that the alerting is functioning correctly.

Summary

In this chapter, we outlined the tools and techniques that you can employ when validating a Hadoop installation and its underlying hardware. We began by looking at
how to check that the cluster hardware is fit for purpose and how to flush out failing
components. We then examined the various tools for assessing the performance of
services within the Hadoop ecosystem and gave some pointers toward their usage.

As emphasized throughout, in addition to flushing out bad hardware and configurations, the real utility for these techniques is the ability to lay down a marker for performance of a particular cluster which can be used to assess ongoing performance.

## CHAPTER 9

Security

No cluster is an island—users and applications need to access APIs and services, and data needs to flow in and out. In an enterprise context, it is essential that data is stored, processed, and accessed securely. The aspects of security are usually broken into four domains: authentication, authorization, auditing, and confidentiality. In this chapter, we discuss how these four domains intersect with services running in the cluster. Confidentiality controls are often important in protecting the network exchanges of authentication and authorization mechanisms, so we start by looking at in-flight encryption. We then cover authentication and authorization and finish with a discussion of the available options for at-rest encryption.

There is plenty in the Hadoop documentation and general literature about Hadoop and security, but, in the spirit of keeping this book as self-contained as possible, we cover the essentials here. If you are already well versed in the area, feel free to skip to the next chapter, in which we examine how to integrate the available security mechanisms into the wider enterprise context.

For more detailed coverage of all the concepts discussed in this chapter, we strongly recommend that you read *Hadoop Security* by Joey Echeverria and Ben Spivey (O'Reilly).

In-Flight Encryption

Hadoop clusters are big users of the network (see "How Services Use a Network" on page 107), with both data and metadata regularly being transferred between distributed components. In addition to ensuring that data cannot be snooped on while it is in transit, we need to protect client-server interactions, such as RPC calls that might contain sensitive information (e.g., authentication credentials). In a truly secure cluster, we need to protect all these exchanges using *in-flight encryption*.

Cluster services most commonly encrypt transfers by using Transport Layer Security (TLS). Some services also support other mechanisms such as encryption provided via the Quality-of-Protection (QoP) functionality in the Simple Authentication and Security Layer (SASL) framework. Before summarizing how each cluster service makes use of in-flight encryption, we look at both TLS and SASL.

TLS Encryption

The TLS protocol establishes the backbone of secure web communications by providing a framework for encrypting data transfers. Despite its official deprecation, this in-flight encryption is still often referred to as Secure Sockets Layer (SSL) communication. Before a secure data communication is initiated, the TLS protocol allows clients to guarantee the identity of a remote server and to agree on a mutual symmetric encryption key through the use of *public key cryptography*.

In public key cryptography, each party in the communication has a key pair consisting of a *public key* (called a *certificate*) and a *private key*. As part of the initial handshake (*http://bit.ly/2zl4F87*), server and client exchange messages securely by encrypting messages using each other's public keys. These messages can only be decrypted by the corresponding private key. Because this form of asymmetric encryption is generally quite slow, it is used only in the initial exchanges to agree on a mutually supported symmetric encryption cipher and key.

With TLS, the client can ensure it is talking to the right server (and not to an imposter masquerading as the server) by ensuring that the server's public certificate (which contains the server's public key) has been signed by a mutually trusted certificate authority (CA). Servers can likewise optionally check the identity of a client by requiring it to present its own certificate, also signed by a mutually trusted CA.

To make use of TLS encryption, applications must therefore be supplied with both a private key, which must be kept secret, and a public certificate, which can be widely published. Most enterprises have their certificates signed by a public CA or run their own internal public key infrastructure (PKI) deployment. We cover some of the options for integrating Hadoop services with corporate TLS certificate management tools in "Certificate Management" on page 304.

TLS and Java

Connecting Java clients to TLS-protected services requires the configuration of a *trust store*. A trust store is a Java KeyStore (JKS) containing the certificates of one or more CAs, which have signed the server certificates used by services. The built-in

Java networking functionality requires that a full chain of trust be in place when setting up communication with TLS sockets.

 In the absence of a common CA, the trust store can also contain the public certificates of each service being accessed. We highly recommend that you use intermediate or root CA certificates wherever possible because this reduces the number of certificates to manage in each trust store. We strongly discourage self-signed certificates.

By default, the Java virtual machine will use a trust store found in the *jre/lib/security/cacerts* file, relative to the Java installation location. If your certificates are signed by a public CA, you probably do not need to take any further action because these certificates are usually included in the default trust store. However, if you are using an internal CA, you need to add the certificate to this file or override the location where Java looks for the default trust store via system properties. For example, to use a trust store at *opt/pki/jks/truststore* the JVM would be invoked with:

```
java -Djavax.net.ssl.trustStore=/opt/pki/jks/truststore ...
```

Note that because a trust store should contain only public certificates, having a publicly known password should not be an issue, although the public certificates are readable from a JKS file without one. However, to prevent tampering and to avoid installation of bogus certificates, ensure that the trust store JKS file is only writable by *root* or trusted users.

For server processes, private keys and server certificates can also be stored in an encrypted JKS file. In contrast to trust stores, this file should be readable only by the server process for which it is intended. Its location and protected passphrase can be provided to the process at startup using the `javax.net.ssl.keyStore` and `javax.net.ssl.keyStorePassword` system parameters.

Java provides a `keytool` utility for importing certificates and keys from various formats, which we cover in "Converting Certificates" on page 307.

TLS and non-Java processes

The specification of public and private keys varies from service to service, but non-Java processes generally use either the base64-encoded Privacy-Enhanced Mail (PEM) (*http://bit.ly/2A8kZJ6*) or binary PKCS #12 (*http://bit.ly/2DCv0lh*) key file formats.

User programs such as `curl` or Python scripts generally pick up CA *bundles* (the equivalent of trust stores) from the system's default location for certificates, which can vary for each flavor of Linux or can be directly configured with certificate locations. Common locations for public certificate bundles are */etc/ssl/certs*, */etc/pki/tls*, and */etc/pki/ca-trust*, but can vary by Linux distribution.

X.509

Certificates are most often structured according to a common format called X.509. The format defines (*https://tools.ietf.org/html/rfc5280*) many standard fields, but for our purposes, the most important are:

Subject name
> This is the certificate owner's identity. Usually, for server processes, this is the fully qualified domain name (FQDN) of the server.

Issuer name
> This is the unique identity of the CA that has signed and issued the certificate.

Validity
> This defines the valid-from and valid-to dates of the certificate.

Subject alternative name
> This is an X.509 extension field and is a list of alternative names by which the certificate owner might be identified (for example, any DNS aliases). This field is most useful when the certificate is being used as a wildcard certificate (DNS patterns are allowed here) or where the service is located behind a load balancer. If a SAN is specified, the subject name is ignored, so the SAN should include the FQDN as well as any other aliases.

Certificates can also be issued by CAs with specific purposes, or *key usages*. For TLS, the server certificate key usage field needs to enable `keyEncipherment` and, if the extended key usage field is present, needs to denote a TLS web server with `id-kp-serverAuth`. This allows the certificate to be used to establish an encrypted key exchange between client and server.

There are many more fields, but these are the important ones to understand when creating certificates for services running on a Hadoop cluster.

SASL Quality of Protection

SASL is an abstraction API to allow networked protocols to use a generic security API to transparently handle multiple authentication and data protection mechanisms. It supports many authentication mechanisms, including Kerberos. SASL is widely used by RPC protocols across the Hadoop ecosystem, including for data transfer protection in HDFS and in the Thrift-based protocols in Hive and Impala.

Relevant to this section, SASL allows applications to define data protection in addition to authentication. There are three QoP levels: *auth* (authentication only), *auth-int* (authentication and integrity), and *auth-conf* (authentication, integrity, and confidentiality). Although supported by Kerberos, SASL QoP is not supported by all SASL authentication mechanisms. For this reason, it is recommended to use SASL for authentication (auth) but to provide confidentiality between client and server via TLS where it is supported by the service. For some services though, protection of RPC interactions is provided only by SASL.

Enabling in-Flight Encryption

The options for configuring in-flight encryption for data and RPC calls are summarized in Table 9-1. This summary table provides information on the specific parameters for each service, but the project documentation should be consulted for additional information on how to specify keys and certificates.

Table 9-1. Summary table of in-flight encryption options for services

Service	Encrypted traffic	Notes
HDFS	Data transfer encryption to/from DataNodes	SASL-based encryption for data transferred between clients and between DataNodes. Pluggable encryption ciphers via `dfs.encrypt.data.transfer.algorithm`, but AES/CTR/NoPadding is strongly recommended.
KMS	TLS for KMS clients	Configure `hadoop.security.key.provider.path` to use an `https` URL.
Core Hadoop	RPC encryption	SASL-based QoP for RPC calls to Hadoop daemons, such as HDFS NameNode and YARN ResourceManager, from clients. Choose `privacy` for `hadoop.rpc.protection` in *core-site.xml*.
HBase	RPC protection	SASL-based QoP for RPC calls to HBase daemons. Choose `privacy` for `hbase.rpc.protection`.
Kafka	TLS for Kafka broker	TLS protection for producer/consumer connections via `SSL://host:port` or `SASL_SSL://host:port` entries in the `listeners` parameter. Inter-broker protection via `security.inter.broker.protocol=SSL`.
Hive	TLS for HiveServer2 API	TLS protection for query sessions via `hive.server2.use.SSL`.
Impala	Impala daemon client connections and inter-daemon traffic	TLS protection for query sessions via `ssl_server_certificate`.
Solr	HTTPS for Solr servers	Various `SOLR_SSL*` environment variables and `urlScheme=https` in ZooKeeper configuration.
Spark	Encryption for RPC and block transfer service	Controlled via `spark.authenticate=true` and `spark.network.crypto.enabled=true` or `spark.authenticate.enableSaslEncryption=true` in job configuration.
MapReduce	Encrypted shuffle	Controlled via `mapreduce.shuffle.ssl.enabled` in job configuration or *mapred-site.xml*.
Kudu	RPC encryption	Encryption for data and RPC calls for external and internal Kudu communication enabled via the `--rpc-encryption=required` startup flag.

Service	Encrypted traffic	Notes
Oozie	HTTPS for Oozie servers	Configure the Tomcat server to use HTTPS via `oozie-setup.sh prepare-war -secure` (vendor distributions do this automatically).
ZooKeeper	TLS encryption for client connections	For ZooKeeper 3.5.0+, SSL can be configured for a secure port via `zookeeper.serverCnxnFactory="org.apache.zookeeper.server.NettyServerCnxnFactory"` and `secureClientPort=2281`.
Hue	HTTPS for Hue	Enabled by specifying `ssl_certificate` and `ssl_private_key` in *hue.ini*.

Authentication

The various storage, processing, metadata, and management services running on a cluster use a variety of authentication mechanisms. The most widely used is Kerberos, but some components also support Lightweight Directory Access Protocol-based (LDAP) authentication or single sign-on (SSO) technologies via Security Assertion Markup Language–compliant (SAML) providers. We cover the essentials of Kerberos and LDAP authentication in the following sections. Because it is the most common—and often least understood—we spend the most time on Kerberos.

Kerberos

In Hadoop, processes within frameworks such as HDFS need a way to authenticate their own internal traffic and connections from remote clients, and most use Kerberos for this purpose. Kerberos is a network authentication protocol designed to address the challenge of strong and secure mutual authentication in distributed systems, and to do so in an efficient and scalable way. The central idea behind the protocol is that users and services authenticate themselves to a central authority and receive a special time-limited *ticket*, which can be used to obtain further tickets for specific services. These *service tickets* help to establish identity and trust between a client and server.

Kerberos isn't just used by Hadoop. Many other systems make use of it to secure network interactions between users and services. One notable example is Microsoft Active Directory (AD).

Principals

In the Kerberos protocol, users and services are each assigned a *principal*, which is a unique identifier within a given *realm* with its own password, or *key*. A realm is a grouping of principals within the same security environment and is overseen by a single authentication authority. (If you are familiar with LDAP—see "LDAP Authentication" on page 247—you can think of a realm as akin to an LDAP *domain*.)

Principal names are text identifiers with a standard structure consisting of three components: `primary/instance@REALM`. In the Hadoop world, the `primary` component is sometimes also called the *short name* of the principal and usually identifies the particular user who owns the principal.

The optional `instance` component in the principal denotes the role the principal owner is going to adopt in any Kerberos exchanges. For example, a user `ian` who is acting as an administrator might have one principal, `ian/admin@EXAMPLE.COM`, which is used for administrative tasks, and another principal, `ian@EXAMPLE.COM`, for other types of exchange. Each of these examples is a different entity within Kerberos with its own key.

Although each unique principal has a separate key, related principals can be logically grouped together under a common primary, a concept that is used often in Hadoop services. Principals representing real users do not often have an instance component, but as we will see, most services will remove the instance component anyway when processing the principal name.

A special kind of principal, called a *service principal*, places a fully qualified domain name in the instance component to denote a particular instance of a role of a process running on a specific host. For example, the principal `hdfs/master1.sabon.com@SABON.COM` might refer to a specific process of an HDFS role running on `master1.sabon.com`. Another principal, `hdfs/worker42.sabon.com@SABON.COM`, represents another HDFS process running on `worker42.sabon.com`. In this example, all HDFS principals running on different hosts are logically grouped under the `hdfs` primary, while each maintains its own unique identity and key.

The `REALM` component of the principal is mandatory but is generally assumed to be the configured default realm if left off. Table 9-2 gives a few more examples.

Table 9-2. Kerberos principal types

Type	General format	Example
User	`primary@REALM`	`ian@SABON.COM`
User	`primary/instance@REALM`	`ian/admin@SABON.COM`
Service	`primary/fqdn@REALM`	`yarn/master2.didot.com@SABON.COM`

Although principals can be used on any host, service principals are designed to be used by services running on a particular server. A client of the service can ensure that it is operating from the instance location advertised in its principal through DNS canonicalization and reverse hostname resolution. A service principal can also be used as the client in a Kerberos interaction; for example, when one HDFS DataNode talks to a DataNode on a different host.

In Hadoop, a principal is created for each unique service user-host pair on which the service runs. If the service runs multiple roles on the same host—for example, an HDFS NameNode and JournalNode—these roles can share the same principal. Each user wishing to access those services needs to have a user principal.

Accessing services

Let's look at how Kerberos authentication works, by way of an example. In Figure 9-1, we show a user (Alice) who is logged on to an edge node and who wishes to run an HDFS directory listing. To do this, she needs to communicate with the HDFS NameNode process running on a cluster node. To prove her identity to the NameNode process, Alice first needs to obtain a valid service ticket via Kerberos. There are two types of ticket in the Kerberos system. The first type is called a *ticket-granting ticket* (TGT) and is obtained by a user for a particular principal in the realm from a central service called the *authentication server* (AS). A user requests a TGT from the AS, which returns it in a wrapper encrypted with the principal's key, which is known only to the AS and the user. The user decrypts the response using the key and then checks the integrity of the payload. Only those with knowledge of the key can decrypt the response and use the ticket inside for further interactions.

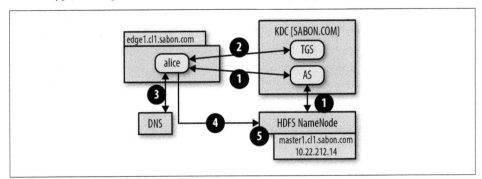

Figure 9-1. Kerberos authentication and service ticket retrieval process

In the example, both Alice and the HDFS NameNode process acquire TGTs for their principals (1). Alice requests a TGT for `alice@SABON.COM` via the `kinit` command-line program, which retrieves the ticket and prompts Alice for her key (password). It uses this to decrypt the response locally on the client and then stores it in a secure cache. The NameNode process obtains a TGT for `hdfs/master1.cl1.sabon.com@SABON.COM` via Java's Kerberos module.

With a valid TGT, a user can then obtain service tickets, which are tickets for a particular service running on a specific node. These are obtained from a separate centralized service called the *ticket-granting server* (TGS). In our example, Alice requests a service ticket for `hdfs/master1.cl1.sabon.com@SABON.COM` (2). The TGS encrypts the responses in such as way that only the client can decrypt them. As part of the process, Alice confirms that she is talking with the right NameNode instance through forward and reverse DNS lookups (3).

Included in the responses from the TGS is a payload encrypted with the service principal's key. The client never decrypts this but instead presents it to the service as part of its initial authentication request (4). The service—here, the HDFS NameNode—decrypts the ticket using its own key and thereby verifies both that it is a valid ticket and that the client is who they say they are (5). This is guaranteed because only an authenticated client can have obtained a valid service ticket from the TGS. One particular advantage of the protocol is that the service does not need to consult the TGS at all to validate the service ticket presented by the user.

The Kerberos AS and TGS services together form a Kerberos Key Distribution Center (KDC) and run on the same server. We cover the KDC integration patterns with Hadoop in "Kerberos Integration" on page 296.

Both TGTs and service tickets are time-limited. Common lifetimes are 10 or 24 hours, but you can configure this. TGTs can be requested with a `renewable` flag, to allow them to be renewed a maximum number of times before they ultimately expire. The ticket lifetime and maximum renewable lifetime are defined by the KDC.

> Responses from KDC servers can be encrypted using a range of ciphers and integrity algorithms. We strongly recommend avoiding the use of ciphers that are known to be weak. See the documentation (*http://bit.ly/2DQPdEW*) for details.

Keytabs

For long-running processes that need to maintain a TGT beyond the maximum ticket renewal lifetime, the key for a principal can be placed into a file called a *keytab*. Keytabs can contain keys for multiple principals, and each principal can have multiple entries with different encryption types. Keytabs are primarily used by services running on cluster nodes, but they can also be used by long-running client applications, such as web services or distributed applications where delegation tokens are not supported (see "Delegation Tokens" on page 248). Note that the possession of a keytab file allows the bearer to obtain TGTs for any of the principals within the file, so they should be strongly protected and their usage kept to a minimum.

Guard your keytab files carefully, using restrictive file permissions. Anyone with access to the file can adopt the identity of the principals it contains.

Kerberos over HTTP

Web-based services can also authenticate users with Kerberos via the HTTP Negotiate authentication scheme (see the next sidebar, "SPNEGO"). To use Kerberos-protected web interfaces, users must present a valid ticket for the service. For Windows users, this can work out of the box for services within the same login domain as the user, since Microsoft Active Directory automatically obtains a TGT on login, which can be used to obtain a service ticket. Microsoft Internet Explorer and Google Chrome can use this ticket automatically and Mozilla Firefox can be easily configured to do the same.

For Windows users who are not in a realm trusted by the cluster KDC, MIT Kerberos provides an installable utility (MIT Kerberos for Windows) that allows users to obtain new tickets alongside their default tickets for the cluster realm.

By convention, Kerberos-protected web interfaces identify themselves using principals with HTTP as the primary (user) and a fully qualified hostname as the instance; for example, HTTP/master3.didot.hadoop.com@HADOOP.COM. The hostname used in the principal depends on where the interface is running and whether it is running behind a load balancer. We discuss this detail further in "Load Balancing" on page 318.

SPNEGO

Under the hood, Kerberos authentication via the HTTP Negotiate scheme uses the Generic Security Service API (GSSAPI) (*https://tools.ietf.org/html/rfc2743*) and the Simple and Protected GSSAPI Negotiation Mechanism (SPNEGO) (*https://tools.ietf.org/html/rfc4178*) frameworks.

The GSS API was designed to allow networked applications and protocols to make use of different authentication mechanisms using a unified interface. In Hadoop, the framework is used primarily to provide Kerberos authentication for web interfaces through its built-in SPNEGO mechanism, as implemented by Java's Java Authentication and Authorization Service (JAAS) and Java Generic Security Service (JGSS) libraries.

SPNEGO enables the negotiation of a mutually supported authentication mechanism between client and server. It is used in the Negotiate scheme to allow Kerberos authentication via HTTP.

Cross-realm trusts

Very often, an enterprise has multiple realms and domains, either because of a desire for separation of business functions or administrative responsibility, or even because of company acquisitions. This can mean that a Hadoop cluster and its services have principals in one realm, while principals for users wishing to access those services are in another. Many times, different Hadoop clusters are in different realms. In these cases, a *trust* must be established between the KDCs of the two clusters. This can be either a *one-way* or a *two-way* trust. In a one-way trust, one cluster's KDC trusts users from the other realm, but not the other way around. In a two-way trust, both KDCs trust users from each other's realms. As part of the trust relationship, the KDC will validate a TGT it receives with the KDC in the originating realm.

In Hadoop, in addition to setting up the trust between KDCs, we explicitly specify a list of rules in the core configuration specifying how to interpret incoming principals (see "Principals and Case Sensitivity" on page 254).

In Active Directory, a Kerberos realm maps to a *domain* (AD provides KDC and LDAP services for the domain) and trust relationships can be set up between domains. At a higher level, related domains are grouped into *forests*, which can also have mutual trusts.

LDAP Authentication

LDAP defines a standard for interacting with directory servers. LDAP-compliant directories are the enterprise standard for centralized administration of users, groups, computers, and other networked resources. LDAP is a critical technology to under-stand when setting up enterprise Hadoop clusters, and we cover it in much more depth in "LDAP Integration" on page 287. For now, we simply need to know that it can be used by components to provide authentication.

Although LDAP supports a number of user authentication protocols (including Ker-beros via SASL), when we talk about LDAP authentication, we are usually referring to authentication of users via username and password (*simple bind*). The process is illustrated in Figure 9-2. A user wishing to use a service initiates a connection and sends them credentials in the form of a username and password (1). The service then forwards the supplied credentials to an LDAP server, which validates them against a matching user in its directory (2). If the credentials are validated, the service consid-ers the user authenticated. To avoid having to repeat the process for each network interaction, services such as web interfaces usually have the concept of a user *session* and can optionally generate a separate secure authentication token (for example, a cookie) and provide this to the user, who can use it in further interactions as proof of identity (3).

When services use LDAP for user authentication, they can choose to use either *direct bind* or *search bind*. With direct bind, the application takes the credentials as supplied by the user and attempts to authenticate (or *bind*, in LDAP terminology) to the LDAP server directly as the user. If the attempt is successful, the user is authenticated.

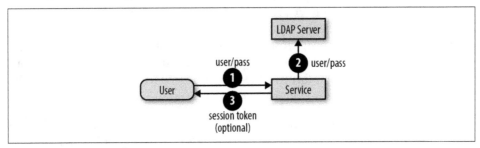

Figure 9-2. LDAP authentication process

By contrast, with search bind, the application typically has its own LDAP user with which it queries LDAP for the user attempting to log in. If found, the application attempts to subsequently bind using the retrieved user's distinguished name (DN) and supplied password. Search bind is useful when the user's unique LDAP bind name cannot be immediately inferred from the username they entered at login. The application can search LDAP for a different attribute of the user object and retrieve the unique bind name.

Unlike Kerberos, LDAP authentication requires that the user supply their password directly to the server. Since the credentials are sent over the network, steps must be taken to protect the transport using in-flight encryption; for example, via TLS (more on this in the next chapter). Note that this applies to both the connection between the user and the service and the connection between the service and the LDAP server.

LDAP authentication is supported across a number of components in the Hadoop ecosystem and is a good option for scenarios in which obtaining Kerberos tickets is problematic or awkward; for example, for Windows users in a different realm or for a business intelligence tool with little or no Kerberos functionality. LDAP authentication is most commonly seen with user-facing services, such as Hue, Hive, and Impala, as well as with notebooks like Cloudera Data Science Workbench and cluster management tools like Apache Ambari and Cloudera Manager.

Delegation Tokens

When a distributed process—for example, a Spark job running on YARN—must access data protected by Kerberos, we need a way for the remote components of the process to authenticate themselves as if they are the user who submitted the job. One way would be to ship the user's credentials along with the job fragments, in the form of a keytab or other credentials file—but obviously this should be avoided. If a malicious actor were to obtain a keytab, they could masquerade as that user up until the point that the breach is detected, which may not be for some time.

Another disadvantage is that each remote process on each node would have to authenticate with the authentication service using the supplied credentials. In the case of Kerberos, the processes would talk to the KDC to obtain a TGT, relevant service tickets, and so on. This might be all right if there were a small number of processes in each but when you start factoring in hundreds of jobs, each of them with potentially tens to hundreds of remote processes, the load on the authentication service becomes nontrivial.

Delegation tokens are a sensible compromise between security and practicality. Services that support delegation tokens allow authenticated users to request a time-bound token, which the bearer can use to access data and services as if they were the user to whom the token was issued. The tokens are issued by the service itself, and each token is requested with an initial lifetime for which it is valid (typically 24 hours), after which it expires. If the requesting user would like the token to be renewed, they can nominate another user (for example, the YARN user) who is authorized to renew the token on their behalf. Tokens have an absolute maximum lifetime (often seven days) defined by the service, beyond which they cannot be renewed.

Jobs that require continued access after the maximum lifetime of a token must request a new one from the service. This can only be done using Kerberos TGT or another primary authentication mechanism—you can't use a token to get a new token. Thus, any malicious actor who gains access to the token has a finite exploitation window and is limited to a single service.

Unlike a service ticket, delegation tokens are not usually limited to particular instance of a service on a specific host, which means that a user can obtain a single token and distribute components of their job to each of the remote hosts. While they may not be limited to a particular host, however, tokens are often limited to a particular purpose.

Tokens are used widely across the Hadoop stack and are supported by the majority of services in the ecosystem. Most commonly, tokens are obtained automatically by MapReduce or Spark jobs accessing HDFS, HBase, Solr, and Kafka, among others.

Impersonation

Core Hadoop provides a mechanism called *impersonation*, which lets a particular user or service, authenticated with its own Kerberos TGT, act on behalf of another user. This is also referred to as *proxying* (and sometimes, somewhat confusingly, as *delegation*), and the user doing the impersonating is the *proxy user*.

At first, impersonation might seem similar to delegation tokens, but there are some important differences. The first is that there are no special service tokens involved in impersonation. The underlying authentication mechanism between the client (the proxy), which is usually itself a daemon process or service, and the server remains Kerberos. In fact, impersonation can be used to obtain delegation tokens on behalf of another user.

Also, the privileges granted to a proxy user are not limited in time or function. Impersonation of other users can be limited by lists of groups, and hosts. This means that we can say that the proxy user is allowed to perform impersonation of another user if—and only if—the proxied user is contained in a specified list or is a member of one of the configured groups. In the same way, impersonation can be limited to a specific set of hosts. Both of these criteria are assessed at the remote end of the interaction. So long as these conditions are met, a proxy user can impersonate a user at any time and can perform any action the user is authorized to do. As such, the ability to perform impersonation should be granted sparingly and only to trusted services. The proxy user should, for all intents and purposes, be considered a superuser.

Impersonation allows a user-facing interface to push down the responsibility for authorizing a user's actions and data access to the underlying services, without having to expose those services directly to the user. It's also useful for cases where Kerberos authentication is not possible or for services that do not support delegation tokens.

Among other services, Hue, Hive, and Oozie all use impersonation when interacting with other services on behalf of a logged-in user. Services supporting impersonated connections include HDFS, YARN, HBase, Oozie, Hive, and Impala.

 If you're examining Hadoop logs, delegation token authentication is denoted as TOKEN and the authentication mechanism is DIGEST-MD5. Impersonation is indicated in the logs by PROXY.

Authorization

After a user is successfully authenticated, the service needs to check whether that user is authorized to perform the action or access the data specified in the request. Although each service in the Hadoop ecosystem has its own way of authorizing operations and data, many have been integrated with a centralized authorization management and enforcement system such as Apache Sentry or Apache Ranger.

In Hadoop, we can apply authorization at the following scopes:

Service level
> Is the user allowed to access the service at all, even if they are authenticated? Is the user a special privileged user? Is the user allowed to access a particular endpoint or use this protocol or method?

Object level
> Is the user allowed to perform the operation on a particular *object* (things like databases, files, tables, topics, and columns) within the service?

Authorization can also be hierarchical, with permissions on higher-level objects, such as databases, conferring the same permissions on objects lower in the hierarchy, such as tables and views. Depending on the point in the hierarchy where it is being applied, authorization can be considered *coarse-grained* or *fine-grained*. There isn't a well-defined boundary between the two, but an example of coarse-grained access would be at the database level, whereas fine-grained access control would be at the table or column level.

At all levels, user authorization is usually expressed in terms of *permissions*. A permission defines what is allowed on the object in question; for example, write access to a file or consumer access to a topic. Permissions can either be applied directly to users (user-based access control [UBAC]) or to *roles* (role-based access control [RBAC]), to which users can be assigned. A third option is to decide what users are allowed to do and see via *attributes* on the objects (attribute-based access control [ABAC]); for example, by tagging a cell as SECRET or PUBLIC.

All three paradigms exist in services running in Hadoop clusters. Most common, though, are UBAC and RBAC. For RBAC, we need a way of determining to which roles a user belongs. Although a list of roles can be maintained for each user, the typical way to map users to roles is through group membership. So, as a prerequisite to making an authorization decision, a common pattern is for a service to check an authenticated user's group memberships.

Because managing access through groups is so common, as a preamble to examining how authorization is managed in some common services we will first look at the process of group resolution. We then move on to look at some concepts that are shared between services, such as superusers and centralized access control, before drilling down into details about how each service manages authorization.

Group Resolution

Users and groups can exist as entities in numerous locations within an enterprise, including as local definitions on a Linux server or in centralized locations, such as an LDAP directory server. Generally, users and groups should be resolved and administered from a central location because this provides superior control, uniformity of identity, and simpler administration. In enterprises, this invariably means using

LDAP, very often as provided by Active Directory. We look at LDAP and how to integrate it with Hadoop in more detail in "LDAP Integration" on page 287.

Hadoop provides a pluggable mechanism via the `GroupMappingServiceProvider` interface for performing group lookups for an authenticated user identity. Apart from core Hadoop, this API is used by many other projects in the wider ecosystem, such as Sentry and HBase. Hadoop ships with the following options for mapping groups:

Operating system lookup

The `ShellBasedUnixGroupsMapping` and `JniBasedUnixGroupsMapping{With Fallback}` implementations delegate the process of performing group lookups for a user to the OS, which in turn may retrieve information from a remote source, like LDAP. For this to work properly, the OS needs to know about all the possible identities of users (end users and service users), either defined locally or in LDAP. Likewise, when referring to groups, the service needs to use the group name as it appears to the OS, which isn't necessarily always the same as the name used in the remote directory. We cover the options in detail in "Linux Integration" on page 292.

 User and group resolution needs to be configured on every node in the cluster, so, for simplicity, consistency, and performance, we usually recommend delegating this task to the OS.

LDAP lookups

The `LdapGroupsMapping` implementation retrieves groups for a user identity directly from an LDAP server. In contrast to the OS delegation techniques, this approach relies on the in-process caching that Hadoop performs. Since this method performs direct lookups, you can use the exact group names as they appear in LDAP when defining authorization controls.

Multiple sources

The `CompositeGroupsMapping` implementation allows a combination of these mapping implementations to be used. It is commonly used to resolve end users from multiple domains within the same cluster.

Static definitions

Hadoop allows groups to be defined statically for named users in the *core-site.xml* configuration file. This can be useful in the rare cases where you wish to override the group memberships for users as they are resolved by the OS or remote LDAP directory.

You can use the `hadoop groups` command from any edge server to determine of which groups Hadoop considers a user to be a member.

Superusers and Supergroups

For most services, there are certain users that are considered *superusers* and for whom the normal authorization controls do not apply. These users are typically identified by the primary (or short name) of the Kerberos service principals used by the service itself. For example, for HDFS, the default superuser is *hdfs*, and HDFS daemons usually use service principals like `hdfs/h2.prod1.example.org@EXAM PLE.ORG`. By default, when extracting a username from a principal, Hadoop strips off the instance and realm components, so a client using this example principal will be resolved to the username *hdfs* and will therefore be conferred superuser rights.

Restricting superusers

Within a cluster, this is fine because the principals for the daemons are well protected in keytabs on the filesystem. However, we need to consider services that are running on hosts outside of the cluster but within the same Kerberos realm and that might be managed by a different team or be running at a different security level. For example, without additional controls, anyone with access to a keytab in a user acceptance testing (UAT) cluster could use these to act as an HDFS superuser in the production cluster.

With default configurations, superuser privileges can be shared across clusters in the same Kerberos realm. Be sure to limit superuser usage via one of the methods outlined in this section.

To guard against leaking superuser privileges in this way, we have the following options:

Network firewall
    We can use perimeter security to prevent network access from outside of the cluster. For production clusters, perimeter firewalls should be strongly considered in any case, but they add complexity for administrators and do not prevent someone using a compromised keytab from a legitimate edge node of the cluster.

Distinct Kerberos realms

Each cluster can have its own Kerberos realm, with cross-realm trusts established only between those clusters managed by the same team and at the same security level. We cover the options and trade-offs in "KDC Integration" on page 298.

Principal mapping rules

This approach employs the `auth_to_local` rules (see "Principals and Case Sensitivity" on page 254) to map any service account not originating from the local cluster to a benign user such as *nobody*.

This is easiest when the fully qualified hostnames of the cluster make the origin obvious, such as *h34.uat2.example.org* versus *h2.pr1.example.org*. For example, the following rules ensure that only service principals from the `prod1` cluster are mapped to a privileged short name. The order of the rules is important:

```
RULE:[2:$1/$2]([a-z]+/[a-z0-9]+\.pr1\.example\.org)s/([a-z0-9]+)\/.*/$1/g
RULE:[2:$1/$2](.*)s/.*/nobody/g
DEFAULT
```

If there is no such pattern, regular expressions can be constructed that match only the hosts in the cluster, but this is unlikely to perform well for large clusters and requires that services be restarted when nodes are added to and removed from the cluster.

Principals for service accounts without an instance, such as `kafka@EXAMPLE.ORG`, should also be restricted. We usually recommend that the Linux accounts used for services be defined locally rather than in centralized systems such as Active Directory, but in the rare cases where they are defined globally, we need to take care to protect our clusters from rogue access. The following rule, which matches principals without an instance component, can be used for this purpose (expand the rule to include other services):

```
RULE:[1:$1]((hdfs|yarn|hbase))s/.*/nobody/g
```

Principals and Case Sensitivity

In Hadoop, Kerberos principals are case sensitive, so `http/a.b.c.d` is not the same as `HTTP/a.b.c.d`. As a result, YARN expects to find a */user/N123456* directory on HDFS if an `N123456` principal is used to submit a job, and Hadoop will use `N123456` to perform group membership lookups for authorization. This can be in conflict with LDAP directories, which generally provide case-insensitive lookups. Often, technologies that map LDAP users and groups to Linux users and groups are also case insensitive and always return results in lowercase. This can cause issues for Hadoop, which checks the ownership of files during shuffles and log aggregation. It considers files owned in Linux by `n123456` to not belong to principal `N123456`.

A common way to overcome these difficulties is to make use of a feature called `auth_to_local` mappings. These are rules that translate two- or three-part Kerberos principals into a local identity (or short name) to be used by Hadoop services for authorization. For example, for Hadoop, the following rule in *core-site.xml* translates all incoming user principals to their lowercase counterparts:

```
RULE:[1:$1](.*)s/(.*)/$1/L
```

For this to take effect across the whole stack you may also need to modify */etc/krb5.conf* with an equivalent rule, but be aware that the rule syntax is slightly different for each file. The equivalent MIT *krb5.conf* rule looks like this (truncated to fit on the page):

```
RULE:[1:$1](.*)s/A/a/g s/B/b/g s/C/c/g ...snip... s/X/x/g s/Y/y/g s/Z/z/g
```

Finally, in services that might not use Kerberos for authentication, there may be configuration parameters to enforce lowercase user and group names. For example, Hue has a `force_username_lowercase` property for several of its authentication backends.

Note that when adding principals using AES encryption types to a keytab, the principal name must *exactly* match the case of the principal in the directory because the case-sensitive principal name is used as a salt in the authentication exchange with the KDC.

Custom principal names

Most services allow the short name that a service uses to be customized via configuration, so instead of the default `hbase` and `sentry`, we might use `hbaseprd1` and `sentryprd1`. Because we can customize this per cluster, we have no risk of leaking superusers across environments. Although this is a fairly elegant solution, there are drawbacks. In the first instance, it requires a lot of additional configuration and extra understanding by the users of the cluster, who now need to ensure that the code is configured to connect to services using non-default principals. Second, not every service supports this customization, so it may be an incomplete solution. Furthermore, some utilities and scripts may make assumptions about the principal names—in the worst case, hardcoding them to the expected defaults. All of these things can be surmounted, but you should be prepared for a slightly bumpier road when using this solution.

Supergroups

Some services, such as HDFS, also allow special groups (so-called *supergroups*) to be set up to give members superuser access. Although it might be convenient to use the service accounts directly to perform administrative activities, administrators should use the superuser approach to perform privileged actions as themselves, wherever possible.

Superuser tasks should always be performed as a user who has been granted superuser access via roles or supergroup membership. Avoid using the service principal directly for this because it is much more difficult to audit. This is analogous to preferring *sudo* to *root* access in Linux.

Some key superuser or supergroup configuration parameters for administrators are listed in Table 9-3. For groups, these are all resolved by the mechanisms configured in `hadoop.security.group.mapping` (see "Group Resolution" on page 251). Unless stated, access control lists (ACLs) are configured as outlined in "Hadoop Access Control Lists" on page 256.

Table 9-3. Superuser and supergroup configuration parameters for some key services

Service	Parameter	Description
HDFS	`dfs.permissions.superusergroup`	Group of superusers who can access all of HDFS.
YARN	`yarn.admin.acl`	ACL of YARN administrators who can perform any action in YARN.
HBase	`hbase.superuser`	ACL of users and groups who are granted full privileges. Instead of the Hadoop syntax for ACLs, this is a single comma-separated list in which group names are prefixed with the @ symbol; e.g., `user1,@group1,@group2,user2`.
Sentry	`sentry.service.admin.group`	List of users who can administer Sentry roles and permissions.
Hive	`sentry.metastore.service.users`	List of users allowed to bypass Sentry authorization in the Hive Metastore.
Hue	`is_superuser` column in database	User-level configuration setting within Hue's database.
Kudu	`--superuser-acl` startup flag	Comma-separated list of superusers.
Kafka	`super.users`	Comma-separated list of superusers.
ZooKeeper	`-Dzookeeper.DigestAuthenticationProvider.superDigest`	Encrypted password with which a user can become a superuser.

Hadoop Access Control Lists

For the uninitiated, the syntax for specifying ACLs in Hadoop configuration parameters can be a bit confusing. Basically, the syntax is a comma-separated list of users and a comma-separated list of groups which are separated by a space (shown here as ⌴):

    user1,user2,user3⌴group1,group2

If you don't need to give ACL access to any groups, you can just specify the list of users with no space after it. But if you just want to specify groups, you *must* prefix the list with a space character. For example, to permission the admins and auditors groups, you would specify the ACL as:

```
 admins,auditors
```

To allow all users, the ACL can be specified as *.

Hadoop Service Level Authorization

Service Level Authorization is an authorization feature available in the core Hadoop libraries and used in HDFS, YARN, and MapReduce. The feature essentially allows us to restrict access to services as a whole or to limit access to specific service functionality. It is an excellent way of limiting end user usage of supported services to just the intended groups of users. Access is controlled through user and group ACLs, the originating host, or both.

We can limit end user access to HDFS and YARN client protocols by configuring the corresponding setting in the *hadoop-policy.xml* file for the service.[1] The parameters to configure are outlined in Table 9-4.

Table 9-4. Service Level Authorization settings for clients

Service	Parameter in hadoop-policy.xml
HDFS	security.client.protocol.acl
HDFS	security.client.datanode.protocol.acl
MapReduce	security.mrhs.client.protocol.acl
YARN	security.applicationclient.protocol.acl
YARN	security.job.client.protocol.acl

For example, to restrict access to HDFS to the saturn_users group, we would configure the following in *hadoop-policy.xml*:

```
<property>
  <name>security.client.protocol.acl</name>
  <value> saturn_users</value>
</property>
<property>
  <name>security.client.datanode.protocol.acl</name>
  <value> saturn_users</value>
</property>
```

---

1 See the "Service Level Authorization Guide" (*http://bit.ly/2BnXg9s*) for further details.

To limit administrative controls on services, such as the ability to perform manual HA failovers or dynamically refresh security policies, we can configure the settings in Table 9-5.

Table 9-5. Service Level Authorization settings for administrators

Service	Parameter in hadoop-policy.xml
HDFS	`security.refresh.policy.protocol.acl`
HDFS	`security.ha.service.protocol.acl`
MapReduce	`security.mrhs.client.protocol.acl`
YARN	`security.refresh.policy.protocol.acl`
YARN	`security.ha.service.protocol.acl`
YARN	`security.resourcemanager-administration.protocol.acl`

Continuing our example, if we want to restrict administration tasks to the `saturn_admins` group, we can specify:

```
<property>
  <name>security.refresh.policy.protocol.acl</name>
  <value> saturn_admins</value>
</property>
<property>
  <name>security.ha.service.protocol.acl</name>
  <value> saturn_admins</value>
</property>
```

By replacing the `acl` with `hosts` in the parameter names, a list of valid IP addresses and hostnames from which the service can be accessed can also be supplied.

Having toured the higher-level authorization controls provided by superusers, supergroups, and Service Level Authorization, we now move on to examine user access control to objects within the services.

Centralized Security Management

Having various security models for each service in the cluster, each with a slightly different way of managing access control, can rapidly become unwieldy and repetitive, not to mention confusing. The need for centralized security management led directly to the creation of Apache Sentry and Apache Ranger.

Both projects use a plug-in architecture to provide authorization controls in each service, as illustrated in Figure 9-3, although the implementations and administration modes are quite different.

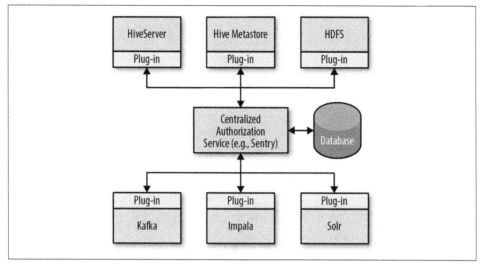

Figure 9-3. Centralized authorization architecture

A key advantage of a centralized role-based authorization system is that membership of a single role can confer rights in many different services, each of which uses its own model of authorization behind the scenes.

As an example, consider an application that loads data into some Hive tables on HDFS and inserts documents into a Solr collection. A single Sentry role, say `app_ro`, can be granted permissions to read the Hive tables, view the underlying files on HDFS, and query the Solr collection. One or more groups can be assigned the role, and any user who is a member of these groups will be able to run Hive, Impala, and Solr queries against the defined objects. Similarly, roles with write or administrator access to objects in different systems can be controlled centrally.

In the following sections, we point out where Sentry and Ranger offer integration with the service and offer examples where appropriate for Sentry.

For further details on Ranger and Sentry and how they integrate with Hadoop clusters and the ecosystem, we recommend the following project and vendor documentation sources:

- Apache Sentry project page (*http://sentry.apache.org/*)
- Cloudera documentation (*http://bit.ly/2A8BFAj*) on Apache Sentry
- Apache Ranger project page (*http://ranger.apache.org/*)
- Hortonworks documentation (*http://bit.ly/2KqbM3m*) on Apache Ranger

HDFS

As you would expect for a filesystem, HDFS implements the standard Unix approach for setting permissions on files and directories according to the read (r), write (w) and execute (x) model for user (owner), group, and other classes.[2] The username used by HDFS is the Kerberos short name of the connecting user.

Sometimes, though, there is not enough control in the traditional Unix model. For example, in many cases, we need to grant access to a directory and its contents to multiple groups, each with differing permissions. Linux extended the filesystem permission model with ACLs for such scenarios, and this approach has been mirrored in HDFS. With ACLs, we can specify permissions on a file or directory for any number of individual users and groups. This functionality is particularly important for protecting Hive tables, where we want the permissions on the files themselves to match the access roles specified in Sentry or Ranger.

With ACLs, we can also specify default permissions for new files and directories created under a directory. For example, to allow rwx rights to the app_admins group on the */data/app_logs* directory and its descendants, including new files and directories, we can use the following command:

```
hdfs dfs -setfacl -R \
  -m group:app_admins:rwx,default:group:app_admins:rwx \
  /data/app_logs
```

 When using default ACL specifications, you need to be mindful of the default filesystem *umask*, which defines the traditional Unix permissions to be used for new files and directories. The umask specifies which rights should be *removed* for users, groups, and others. In Hadoop 2.x, this setting takes precedence over default ACLs and can therefore effectively mask the desired permissions. By default, fs.permissions.umask-mode in *core-site.xml* is set to 022, which means the write permission is removed from all new files and directories for groups and others, even if the default ACL allows write access for named groups. Setting dfs.name node.posix.acl.inheritance.enabled to true in *hdfs-site.xml* corrects this behavior and is the default in Hadoop 3. Because it maintains a constant overlay asserting permissions on relevant directories, automatic HDFS permissions synchronization in Sentry does not suffer from this issue.

---

2 If you're unfamiliar with the Unix filesystem model, see "File system permissions: Traditional Unix permissions" on Wikipedia (*http://bit.ly/2DAUmje*).

If enabled, Sentry will automatically and dynamically apply the correct HDFS ACLs on a directory hierarchy, based on the current roles and permissions in effect for Hive tables. ACLs can also be administered from the Hue security app.

Ranger provides an HDFS plug-in in which HDFS ACLs can be controlled via policy, including by both grant and deny rules.

YARN

Users interact with YARN by submitting and killing jobs; viewing the web interfaces for the ResourceManager, Scheduler, and ApplicationMaster; and retrieving the application logs after the jobs have completed. Most of these activities are authorized through permissions on the resource queue in which the job runs. However, there are some higher-level controls for the service as a whole.

In YARN, containers are run on worker nodes using the ID of the user who submitted the job. The containers are run via the LinuxContainerExecutor, which provides three parameters to give administrators control over which users can run containers. The main aim of these parameters is to prevent privileged Linux and Hadoop users from running jobs on the cluster where they might be able to do accidental or malicious damage. In the *container-executor.cfg* configuration file for the LinuxCon tainerExecutor on each worker node, we can set the following parameters:

min.user.id
: In Linux, users with low numeric IDs (e.g., below 1000) are usually considered special and those accounts are used to run essential system services. In particular, the *root* user has an ID of 0. This parameter ensures that jobs are run by nonprivileged Linux users.

allowed.system.users
: Sometimes, accounts with IDs below the specified minimum should be allowed. This parameter provides a comma-separated list of such users. Common in this list are hive and hbase.

banned.users
: As an extra control, in case their system accounts have numeric IDs greater than min.user.id, you may explicitly want to prevent some service user IDs from running jobs. An example value here is hdfs,yarn,mapred,bin.

Although they are different implementations, the Fair Scheduler and Capacity Scheduler have similar concepts for user authorization. Each resource queue has two ACLs, one to control job submission and one to control queue administration. Any user or group member in the submission ACL can submit jobs and control the life cycle of jobs they've submitted. By contrast, members of the administration ACL for the queue can manage any of the jobs in the queue. ACLs are applied hierarchically, so, if you can submit to or administer a parent queue, you can do the same on its children. Since the default root queue ACLs are *, you want to modify these in a secure cluster.

If authentication for web interfaces is enabled, YARN also applies user authorization for certain content. All authenticated users can view the ResourceManager and Scheduler UIs and see what jobs are running, but job details and ApplicationMaster UIs are limited to authorized users only. YARN applies the following rules when deciding whether a user can access the job information and logs:

- Is the user requesting access the job owner (submitter)?
- Is the user in the ACL defining view access, called VIEW_ACL (app type–specific; e.g., MapReduce, Spark)?
- Is the user a YARN ACL admin?
- Is the user in the admin ACL for the YARN pool to which the job was submitted?

For MapReduce, VIEW_ACL access can be conferred to a user via the mapreduce.job.acl-view-job configuration parameter on the job. For Spark jobs, use spark.ui.view.acls.

After the job is finished, and if log aggregation is enabled, the job logs are stored on HDFS. At this stage, the logs can only be retrieved by the submitter (who owns the files) and members of the relevant history group (by default, mapred for the Map-Reduce Job History Server and spark for the Spark History Server).

Ranger also provides centralized management of YARN queue access controls via configurable policies.

ZooKeeper

The authorization scheme in ZooKeeper is based on ACLs applied to users who are authenticated by various *schemes*. Permissions are granted on znodes to create child nodes (c), read node content (r), write node content (w), delete the node (d), and administer the permissions of the node (a). The schemes denote the authentication mechanism for users. The important ones are world (basically anyone using Zoo-Keeper), digest (an MD5 hash of a username and password), and sasl (Kerberos authentication). Authorization by group is not supported by any of the included mechanisms.

HBase, Solr, and Kafka can be configured to lock down the znodes they use, to prevent accidental or malicious modification by other ZooKeeper users.

Hive

Although Hive includes some rudimentary built-in authorization mechanisms, for enterprise use cases the authorization should be provided by a plug-in providing integration with Sentry or Ranger. Sentry can protect all aspects of user interaction with Hive itself as well as the underlying data on HDFS (see "Centralized Security Management" on page 258). We describe the Sentry functionality in the rest of this section. For more information about the Ranger integration, consult the relevant documentation (*http://bit.ly/2OY1N66*).

In the Sentry permissions model for Hive, users belong to *groups*, which are assigned *roles*, which are granted *privileges* on named *objects*. The objects and the possible permissions are outlined in Table 9-6. Permissions on parent objects confer the same permission to child objects.

Table 9-6. Hive objects and permissions

Object	Permissions	Parent object	Description
SERVER	SELECT, INSERT, ALL	None	The SERVER object contains all objects. ALL permissions grants the role the ability to do all operations.
DB	SELECT, INSERT, ALL	SERVER	Permissions for the database and all objects it contains.
TABLE	SELECT, INSERT, ALL	DB	Permissions for tables. Implies full access to columns.
VIEW	SELECT	DB	Read permission on a view. Does not confer access to the underlying tables.
COLUMN	SELECT	TABLE	Read permission on a column in a table.
URI	ALL	SERVER	Permission to interact with the location on the filesystem as part of queries. Required for external tables, nondefault table locations, and LOAD DATA operations.

For example, consider a user, *alice,* who is a member of an `analysts` group which has been assigned the `sales_ro` role. If the `sales_ro` role is granted the SELECT permission on the `sales` database, *alice* will be able to query every table defined in the database.

As part of the query life cycle, the Sentry plug-in running in HiveServer2 queries the Sentry server to ensure that the user has appropriate access to the objects referenced in the query. Group membership—and therefore role assignments—for the user issuing queries is determined using the Hadoop groups mapping implementation on the Sentry server.

The Hive Metastore (HMS) also has a Sentry plug-in, which ensures that DDL modifications are authorized by one or more Sentry role privileges. This protects the HMS from modifications made outside of HiveServer2 but does not restrict read access for metadata. Read access can be restricted to the HMS by limiting the users it is allowed to proxy, but this can hinder legitimate usage by Spark SQL jobs, which need access to the HMS to read and update Hive table metadata, so this approach needs to be applied with care.

When using Sentry, the impersonation feature of HiveServer2 is disabled and each query runs in the cluster as the configured Hive principal. Thus, each HDFS location associated with a Hive table should be readable and writable by the Hive user or group.

If you are using the HDFS ACL synchronization feature, the required HDFS permissions (r-x for SELECT, -wx for INSERT, and rwx for ALL) on files are enforced automatically and maintained dynamically in response to changes in privilege grants on databases and tables. In our example, the *alice* user would be given r-x permission to files in tables in the sales database. Note that a grant on a URI object does not result in corresponding permissions on the location in HDFS.

Impala

When it comes to user authorization, Impala has much the same model as Hive. The Sentry integration within each Impala daemon caches roles and privileges such that the Impala daemons can authorize queries very quickly without remote lookups. The caches are refreshed on a regular basis to keep the privileges fresh.

 Certain services, such as Impala and Kafka, cache Sentry privileges for performance. Thus, it might take a little time for privilege changes to take effect. In most cases, the privileges should be updated within a few seconds.

HBase

HBase uses ACLs to authorize user operations at different *scopes*. The highest scope is *superuser*, which we described earlier. Next, we have *global*, which allows the defined access to all tables running in all namespaces. The scopes continue to narrow as we move from *namespace*, to *table*, to *column family*. Finally, within memstores and store files, individual cells can be further protected at the cell level, a feature which makes use of cell tags. Authorization is enforced by a special coprocessor which runs in each RegionServer.

At each scope, the following permissions can be granted: read (R), write (W), execute (X: allow users to invoke coprocessor endpoints), create (C: allow creation and dropping of tables at the given scope), and admin (A: perform administration actions, like splitting and merging regions).

Permissions can be administered using `grant` and `revoke` commands within the HBase shell or via the `AccessControlClient` API endpoint. Permissions can be granted to users and to groups. (HBase uses the configured Hadoop group mapping implementation.) As we saw for superuser control, groups can be specified by prefixing the name with `@`. To control permissions at a given scope, a user must themselves have admin (A) permissions at the same scope or higher. As an example, the following commands set up permissions for a group of global admins, a group of application admins in a specific namespace, and the service account that runs the application:

```
> grant '@global_admins', 'RWXCA'
> grant '@app_admins', 'RWXCA', '@appns'
> grant 'appuser1', 'RW', '@appns'
```

So far, we have looked at RBAC controls in HBase. However, HBase does include a seldom-used feature called *visibility labels* that provides a mix of RBAC and ABAC control on cells. In this mode, cells are tagged with Boolean expressions of labels, like `!developer` or `(pii|auditor) & europe`. Users or groups are associated with labels, and these are supplied and evaluated at scan time to determine whether the cell should be returned with the results.

At the time of this writing, Sentry does not provide an HBase plug-in, but Ranger includes an integration that allows HBase permissions to be managed centrally via policies.

Solr

As well as its own rule-based plug-in, Solr integrates with both Sentry and Ranger to provide centralized user authorization for documents stored in collections. Common to all implementations is the ability to regulate read access and write access for a collection, and protect administration and configuration operations.

With Sentry, administrative actions on collections and configurations are protected through QUERY (read), UPDATE (write), and * (both read and write) permissions on a special `admin` collection. The same permissions can be applied to user collections. In a similar way to Hive and Impala, Sentry allows a security administrator to apply these privileges to members of a role, as conferred through group membership.

Sentry also allows for document-level access control in Solr through the use of authorization tokens stored alongside each document. These tokens denote which roles should have access to the document.

The rule-based authorization plug-in in Solr 5.3 and above provides authorization controls on a wide range of API-based accesses, including the security, schema, configuration, core admin, and collection APIs. In this model, roles, permissions, and user-role mappings are defined in a *security.json* file, and roles are assigned directly to users rather than groups. For further detail, see the Solr project documentation (*http://bit.ly/2DNgQi9*).

Apache Ranger also provides a plug-in to authorize user requests to Solr servers.

Kudu

At the time of this writing, Kudu does not natively provide fine-grained user access control to tables and rows. Instead, users are granted or denied access at the service level through a startup flag (`--user-acl`). However, for users who use Kudu primarily through Impala's SQL interface, the Sentry integration provided by Impala can provide fine-grained protection for reading and writing to individual Kudu tables. A common configuration is to limit direct connection to Kudu to the Impala user and to application service accounts and batch or ETL users who run Spark jobs. End users must interact with Kudu through application interfaces, which can impose their own authorization controls, or through Impala, which is protected by Sentry.

Oozie

Oozie implements a basic authorization model that applies the following rules:

- Users have read access to all jobs.
- Users have write access to their own jobs.
- Users have write access to jobs based on an ACL (list of users and groups).
- Users have read access to admin operations.
- Admin users have write access to all jobs.
- Admin users have write access to admin operations.

In addition, when submitting a workflow job, the configuration may contain the `oozie.job.acl` property. If authorization is enabled, this property is treated as the ACL for the job, and it can contain user and group IDs separated by commas. To configure administrator groups, you can add to *oozie-site.xml* the setting `oozie.ser vice.AuthorizationService.admin.groups`.

It's important to remember that interaction with other Hadoop components in Oozie actions is done using impersonation, such that each service applies authorization for the user who submitted the Oozie workflow.

Hue

Hue maintains information about all users in its database. In a default installation, all users are local and are added manually via a Hue administrator, also known as a superuser. The superuser is a normal Hue user who is flagged as being a superuser in

Hue's database. Using the default authentication, backend users are authenticated using encrypted passwords stored in Hue's database.

However, Hue also supports other, more enterprise-friendly authentication mechanisms, including LDAP and SSO via SPNEGO or SAML. Hue can be configured to automatically add new users to its local database and to create an HDFS user directory when a user logs in via one of these other methods. A key point to note is that, regardless of which authentication mechanism is chosen, Hue creates an entry for each user in its local database and, if configured with details of an LDAP server, can synchronize information about these users (such as their email address and group memberships) from LDAP. To ease management of multiple users, Hue can import users in bulk from an LDAP server for a given LDAP group.

For authorization purposes, Hue uses groups, which can be assigned one or more permissions indicating which Hue functionality group members can access. For the most part, these permissions simply define whether a given group has privileges to launch one of Hue's *apps*, for example the File Browser or the Impala Query Editor. In some cases, permissions are more granular and can restrict particular functionality within an app.

Superuser status cannot be conferred through group membership. Individual users must be marked as superusers by an existing superuser. The first user to log in to a new Hue installation is automatically made a superuser.

Just like users, groups are defined locally in Hue's database but can also be imported by name from an LDAP directory. When importing from LDAP, Hue creates a local group with a matching name in its own database and optionally synchronizes the LDAP group members, creating new Hue users where necessary. To prevent its user information from going out of date, Hue can automatically refresh a user's group memberships each time they log in when using the LDAP authentication backend. Alternatively, a superuser can trigger a manual resynchronization.

Hue is only able to automatically synchronize group information for users logging in using the LDAP backend. This is a useful feature, but be aware that it imposes a performance penalty at each login because Hue has to do an additional round trip to the LDAP server.

By default, all users are added to the `default` group when they are created. Therefore, if you want to expose only a subset of Hue functionality, we generally recommend reducing the permissions in the default group to the bare minimum, if you are automatically creating users when they first log in. Additional access can then be conferred and managed directly through LDAP group memberships, which are synchronized by Hue.

Let's take a concrete example. Imagine we have two groups of users defined in LDAP:

business_analysts
These are analysts who just need to issue ad hoc queries via Impala and Hive.

data_engineers
These are engineers who need to access HDFS and who compose and execute Oozie workflows.

The first step is to remove all permissions from the `default` group. A Hue superuser can then synchronize the two LDAP groups to Hue using the *Add/Sync LDAP Group functionality* from the user administration page. This queries LDAP for the given group and, if requested, imports all the group members as users into Hue. After Hue is aware of the groups, we can set up the following permissions:

- *business_analysts*: `beeswax.access`, `impala.access`
- *data_engineers*: `beeswax.access`, `filebrowser.access`, `impala.access`, `job browser.access`, `oozie.access`

Assuming automatic user creation is enabled for the LDAP backend, any user can log in to Hue, but no functionality is available to them unless they are either a superuser or a member of one of the two synchronized groups.

The login process for LDAP authentication and automatic user creation is illustrated in Figure 9-4.

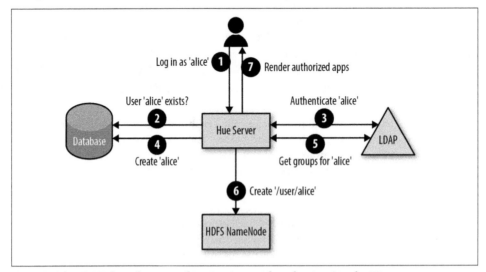

Figure 9-4. LDAP-based user authentication and authorization for Hue

Even if you are not using LDAP for authentication, user and group information can still be retrieved from LDAP on demand. For this to work, the usernames used in login requests need to match those retrieved from LDAP, so you may need to tweak the attributes used by Hue for user and group lookups.

 For more information about configuring Hue for authentication, authorization, and confidentiality, see *Hadoop Security* by Joey Echeverria and Ben Spivey (O'Reilly).

Kafka

The final service we consider for user authorization is Kafka, which provides a plug-gable authorization model.[3] Kafka's underlying ACL model allows permissions on a *resource* to be granted to users and groups who are accessing brokers from given hosts. The resources and privileges are outlined in Table 9-7.[4]

Table 9-7. Kafka's privilege model

Resource	Permission	Description
Cluster	DESCRIBE	List all topics.
Cluster	CLUSTER_ACTION	Perform advanced cluster tasks, such as controlled shutdowns and stopping replicas.
Topic	READ	Fetch messages from a topic from a consumer.
Topic	WRITE	Send messages to a topic from a producer.
Topic	DELETE	Delete a topic via the broker API.
Topic	ALTER	Alter topic configurations via the broker API.
Topic	DESCRIBE	Get various topic-level information, such as offset and consumer metadata.
Consumergroup	READ	Do operations on consumer groups, such as offset requests, heartbeats, and offset commits.

When writing, producers must have WRITE and DESCRIBE permissions on the topic to which they are writing. If dynamic topic creation is enabled, the CREATE permission can also be granted. When reading, consumers must have READ and DESCRIBE permissions on the topic and READ permission on the consumer group to join.

---

3 As an example of providing a custom authorization mechanism, see "Active Directory Group Based Authorization for Apache Kafka" (*http://bit.ly/2PL0Vao*) by Sönke Liebau.

4 For full details, see KIP-11 - Authorization Interface (*http://bit.ly/2Tvkx0l*).

Spark uses a special modified consumer group name for Kafka consumers reading from executors. Administrators therefore need to grant READ access to the *spark-executor-<groupId>* consumer group in addition to *groupId*.

Out of the box, Kafka supports user authorization on read and write access to the topics themselves, as well as their configuration, using ACLs stored in ZooKeeper. Each broker keeps track of the configuration in ZooKeeper and authorizes incoming user requests that have been validated by one of the supported authentication mechanisms.

Centralized authorization control is also provided for Kafka by Sentry and by Ranger —both projects implement the pluggable Authorizer interface. Both implementations store the grants in a central database. Sentry provides a command-line tool, kafka-sentry, that you can use to grant and revoke privileges to and from roles.

Apache Ranger also provides a plug-in to authorize user requests to Kafka.

Sentry

Naturally, you also need to ensure that only a limited set of users are authorized to connect to and modify permissions and roles within Sentry itself.

Sentry restricts the users who can connect using the sentry.service.allow.connect property in *sentry-site.xml*. This should be limited to service users, like *hdfs*, *hive*, and *solr*, who only connect using their built-in Sentry plug-ins.

After it is connected, Sentry authorizes write access to permissions and roles to the set of groups listed in the sentry.service.admin.group property in *sentry-site.xml*. Plug-ins can connect on behalf of end users using impersonation. In this way, privileged groups for Sentry administration can be set up for end users.

At-Rest Encryption

The final topic we cover in this chapter concerns the other half of confidentiality: *at-rest encryption*. Two primary reasons for encrypting data on disk are:

- To prevent accidental or malicious exposure to administrators or staff with direct access to the servers or disks; for example, improperly disposed of or stolen disks
- To provide additional protections to prevent unauthorized or accidental access to data by users and applications through otherwise legitimate means, such as HDFS APIs

There are different types of data you might wish to encrypt, including:

- Data in storage engines, such as HDFS, HBase, or Kudu
- Temporary outputs from transient processes, such as YARN container scratch space or Impala disk spills
- Configurations and metadata, such as database login credentials
- Logs and audit records

Encryption isn't free. There is always a performance overhead to protecting data, so you should carefully assess which, if any, of the encryption mechanisms you actually need. Don't forget that these are extra protections above and beyond those already provided by authentication and authorization controls.

Depending on the type of data, where it is stored, and how it is accessed, you can choose between two encryption mechanisms: *application encryption* and *volume encryption*. With application encryption, the application itself stores the data in the underlying storage mechanism in an encrypted form and performs the decryption when the data is accessed. With this control, the application can apply encryption to data selectively and can use different encryption keys for different clients.

Volume encryption applies encryption to data at a much lower level in the stack—typically within the Linux I/O subsystem itself through a kernel module. Entire mounted volumes are encrypted as a whole and are usually protected by a single key, although more keys can sometimes be used. Processes with access to the volume can access all of its data.

Generally, application-level encryption is preferable since it gives much more control over which data is actually encrypted and with what key. Multitenancy is easily supported since each tenant can be granted access to data protected by different sets of encryption keys. Application-level encryption is mostly used to protect user data in storage engines. We discuss HDFS TDE, the main provider of application-level encryption in the Hadoop ecosystem in more detail in "HDFS Transparent Data Encryption" on page 274.

Volume encryption products usually make use of mechanisms within the Linux kernel, such as *dm-crypt* (*http://bit.ly/2Q8hhJD*), to provide file and volume encryption and to build key management and storage around the technology. Some disk manufacturers also sell self-encrypting drives that do the encryption right at the hardware layer. These drives are generally only useful to protect against unauthorized direct physical access to disks. Volume encryption can be used to provide coarse-grained protection for data in storage engines as well as encryption for logs and configuration files. We discuss one provider of volume encryption in the next section.

The options for encrypting each type of data at rest in a Hadoop cluster are shown in Table 9-8. The generally recommended option is in bold. Note that all data can be protected through volume encryption, but the service-specific options are recommended where possible. Note also that users of services are always free to preencrypt the data stored in storage engines using their own mechanisms, but this might make efficient querying and filtering more difficult.

 It is essential that you or your enterprise assess the options and choose the approach that makes the most sense for your given set of circumstances and that is best supported by your vendor. We cannot make universally applicable recommendations here.

Table 9-8. At-rest encryption options for Hadoop services and data

Data type	Possible providers
HDFS data	**TDE**, volume encryption
HBase data	**TDE**, HBase encryption
Kudu data	**Volume encryption**
Solr data	**TDE**
Kafka data	**Volume encryption**
Service logs	**Volume encryption**
Configurations	**Volume encryption**
Audits	**Volume encryption**
Supporting database data	**Volume encryption**
Flume channel data	**Volume encryption**
Hive local scratch space	**Volume encryption** or disable
MapReduce spills and shuffle data	**Service-specific configurations**, volume encryption
Spark spills and shuffle data	**Service-specific configurations**, volume encryption
Impala spills	**Service-specific configurations**, volume encryption

Application and volume encryption alike both need a secure location to store encryption keys. Within the Hadoop arena, two such providers are Cloudera Navigator Key Trustee Server (KTS) and Apache Ranger Key Management Server (KMS). The first is a general key storage solution and supports any client implementing the standard key server (HTTP Keyserver Protocol [HKP]) (*http://bit.ly/2KnEIcl*) API. KTS thus supports both volume encryption and HDFS TDE. We briefly cover the integration of Cloudera KTS with Navigator Encrypt in the following section, and we look at both Cloudera KTS and Ranger KMS in relation to TDE.

An extra layer of key protection can be provided by *hardware security modules* (HSMs), which are physical devices dedicated to the storage and protection of sensitive key material. Because they provide even more stringent physical access protection, some enterprises mandate the use of HSMs to provide a root of trust for the most sensitive keys. Both Cloudera KTS and Ranger KMS provide integrations with the most common HSM providers.

HSMs are implemented as appliances within hardened enclosures that provide stringent security and enable additional enterprise features. For example, all HSM types provide a way to cluster multiple enclosures as a single appliance for high availability. Key material stored on the HSM (encryption zone keys, in the case of Hadoop) typically never leaves the device in unencrypted form, but rather encrypted secrets are sent to the HSM to encrypt or decrypt them on board the appliance. HSMs also guarantee the production of high-quality key material and are often used with envelope encryption, where the actual data keys are themselves encrypted on the HSM with HSM-resident keys.

Volume Encryption with Cloudera Navigator Encrypt and Key Trustee Server

As an example of full volume encryption, we look briefly at one implementation, Cloudera Navigator Encrypt (NE) (*http://bit.ly/2qTWf38*). On each node where it is installed, NE runs as a kernel module and protects entire volumes (physical block devices, logical volume management [LVM] devices, and loop devices) with encryption keys using *dm-crypt*.[5] Volume data is encrypted and decrypted using efficient symmetric-key block encryption.

On initial installation, NE registers itself with the central key storage server, KTS. For each volume under its control, various encryption keys are created and themselves encrypted using a unique key for each node and persisted to the KTS—the server itself retrieves and decrypts these keys at startup. After the volumes are mounted, no further interaction with the KTS is required until a system restart.

The NE kernel module mounts volumes for which it is responsible, and it mediates all system calls to read and write blocks to the volumes. The module authorizes access to encrypted data using process ACLs, which include the exact binary signature and command-line invocation of the accessing process. Data access is transparent to an authorized process, and volumes are accessed through normal mount points which look and feel like a standard Linux filesystem.

Communication between NE and KTS occurs over the standard HKP (*http://bit.ly/2Bo07zt*) and should be protected via TLS signed certificates. Encryption key material sent to the KTS is persisted in a managed PostgreSQL database. The KTS can be configured to provide high-availability serving of keys through an active-passive archi-

---

5 Navigator Encrypt also supports individual file encryption using eCryptfs, but Red Hat removed support for this encryption mechanism in Red Hat Enterprise Linux 7 (RHEL 7) so it is not recommended.

tecture in which keys and configuration data are automatically replicated from the master to the passive instance.

In case of failure of the master KTS instance, KTS clients (in this case, NE) automatically fail over to the passive instance. In this case, operation can mostly continue, but further deposits—for example, the creation of new encryption keys—are not allowed until the master instance is restored. In practice though, after a cluster has been installed, new key deposits are rare because they occur only for new volumes (disks) in NE or new encryption zones in TDE (discussed in the next section).

Volume encryption is most useful for protecting data that is not otherwise covered by HDFS TDE or the temporary encryption capabilities within a service, such as logs, supporting databases, or underlying Kudu files. Although it is theoretically possible to run volume encryption and TDE together, you pay the price for double-encrypting the data. Unless you have special security circumstances that call for double encryption, avoid it where possible.

HDFS Transparent Data Encryption

In this section, we look briefly at HDFS TDE and how it can be combined with cryptographically strong key management and persistence solutions. The original design document (*http://bit.ly/1KZMeph*) is an excellent source for more detailed information on how TDE works. For in-depth coverage, we recommend that you review Chapter 9 of *Hadoop Security*.

Encrypting and decrypting files in encryption zones

In TDE, files to be protected are placed in *encryption zones*, which are nothing more than HDFS directory hierarchies that have been assigned an encryption key. All blocks of a file within the zone are protected by a *data encryption key* (DEK), which itself is encrypted with the *encryption zone key* (EZK). The result is an *encrypted data encryption key* (EDEK), which is stored in the NameNode's file metadata. Because it is encrypted, the EDEK is not readable by the NameNode or anyone querying the metadata. The concept of storing the EDEKs with the file data (in this case, the metadata) is more generally referred to as *envelope encryption*.

The EZK and the EDEK form a *hierarchy* of keys, where the higher-ranking key is needed to use all lower-ranking keys. Key hierarchies make it possible to create many keys and store them even in unsecure places as long as they are themselves encrypted with a higher ranking. The highest level in the hierarchy is referred to as the *master key*. In contrast to low-ranking keys, it is common for master keys to be stored on HSMs. If a higher-ranking key is lost or deliberately revoked, it is no longer possible to access any data encrypted with lower-ranking keys.

EZKs are only ever accessed by the key management server (KMS) and never distributed to the NameNode or to HDFS clients. Figure 9-5 illustrates the process for a file read.

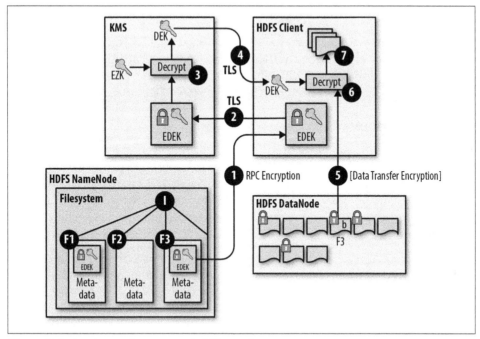

Figure 9-5. Anatomy of an encrypted file read

When a client (for example, an end user, query, or YARN container process) needs to read an encrypted file, it requests the EDEK from the NameNode (1) and sends it to the KMS (2), which, after verifying that the operation is authorized, decrypts it with its EZK (3) and returns the plain DEK to the client (4). Naturally, the communication with the KMS must be performed over a channel secured by TLS, to protect the contents of the DEK. The KMS caches the EZK for a short time, to optimize repeated requests for files within the same encryption zone. The client then requests the file blocks from the DataNodes (5), decrypts them locally (6), and performs the required processing on the file (7).

When writing a new file, the NameNode requests a new EDEK for the zone and attaches it to the file metadata. The client then uses the same procedure to obtain the DEK as for the read path and uses it to encrypt the data. It's important to re-emphasize that the actual encryption and decryption of the data in the file is performed in-process by the client—neither the NameNode nor the DataNode ever sees the unencrypted DEK or file data. When the client is reading data from HDFS, the DataNode transmits the raw data in its encrypted form. Likewise, when it writes data to a DataNode, the data is sent by the client in an encrypted stream.

If in-flight data transfer encryption has been configured for HDFS, this encrypts the already-encrypted stream to and from DataNodes, but it's still worth having to protect files that are not in an encryption zone.

Clients interact with the KMS over HTTP (protected by TLS) via a REST protocol, with endpoints for creating and retrieving keys and for generating and retrieving EDEKs, among other tasks. Within the KMS, retrieval and persistence of keys is abstracted via Hadoop's `KeyProvider` API (*http://bit.ly/2DO7GBZ*).

Authorizing key operations

The KMS protocol provides a set of APIs for authorizing users and groups to perform various key operations on encryption zone keys and data encryption keys through a set of fine-grained ACLs (*http://bit.ly/2AbC70E*). These ACLs are defined in the *kms-acls.xml* configuration file for the KMS. For the sake of brevity, we don't go over all the possible key operations and operation categories but outline the general authorization process.

Access is controlled at two levels. At the first level, controls are applied on operations at the KMS service, without reference to the particular key involved. A user, which can be an end user or a service user like HDFS, must be allowed to perform the requested key operation (such as create key, generate encrypted key, or decrypt encrypted key) and must not be in the corresponding blacklist ACL for the same operation. User requests must be admitted by the ACLs at this level before they are passed to the next level.

One of the main uses of the blacklist ACLs is to prevent HDFS superuser access to encryption keys and thereby to properly restrict access to sensitive data to just the encryption keys. Of course, for this to be effective, there needs to be proper separation of duties between the KMS administrators and the cluster administrators, which can be difficult to achieve in practice.

The next level assesses whether the user should be allowed to perform the category of operation on the specific key in question. The whole process is somewhat involved, including blacklists and whitelists (terms used by the project itself) and default ACLs. Essentially, if the user is in the key operation whitelist ACLs, they are authorized to perform the operation. If not, the user is checked against the ACLs for the specific key name, if they exist. If they do not exist, the user is checked against the default ACLs for key operations.

Ultimately, the official documentation is the canonical resource, but as an aid to understanding, the authorization flow is shown in Figure 9-6.

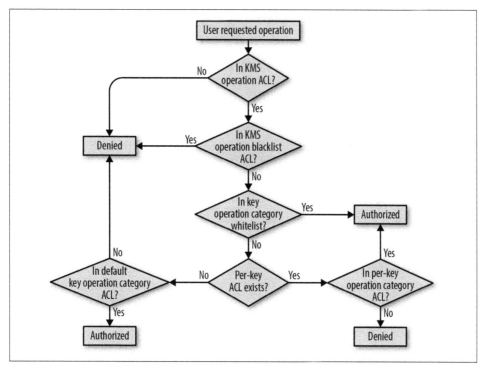

Figure 9-6. Flowchart for KMS key operation authorization

Consult the official documentation (*http://bit.ly/2AbC70E*) to validate your ACL specifications.

KMS implementations

Hadoop ships a default KMS implementation with a file-based Java KeyStore as the key provider. However, a JKS typically does not meet the required standard for high-quality key material and is not deemed secure enough to guarantee confidentiality. It also does not provide high availability. Thus, vendors support additional KeyProvider implementations that either meet the required standards for key material creation and persistence directly, or facilitate the integration of certified appliances such as HSMs.

Let's briefly look at two vendor configurations for KMS and KeyProviders:

Cloudera Navigator Key Trustee Server

As we saw earlier with Navigator Encrypt, Cloudera provides a highly available and hardened key storage implementation, KTS, that can also be used in conjunction with HDFS transparent encryption. Cloudera provides a custom implementation of the Hadoop KMS, called Navigator Key Trustee KMS, with a KeyProvider implementation that uses KTS to securely persist key material. The Key Trustee KMS communicates with KTS over HTTPS.

Instances of Key Trustee KMS are stateless, so multiple instances can be deployed to different nodes. Clients of KMS simply round-robin through the list of KMS instances until a successful connection is made. Each individual instance communicates with KTS using the same client credentials as the other KMS instances, so has access to the same set of keys stored in KTS. Naturally, the Key Trustee KMS supports communicating with a highly available active-passive KTS pair.

KTS supports a variety of HSMs (*http://bit.ly/2S2Ccen*) in highly available configurations via an additional layer of software called Key HSM (*http://bit.ly/2Acm0Qx*). Key HSM calls the HSM to encrypt KTS's own key entries. If Key HSM is used, the key material in KTS can only be used when the HSM decrypts it, allowing additional security and a central revocation point. Key HSM also supports secure connectivity via TLS or Network Trust Link (NTL) connections.

Hortonworks Ranger KMS

Similar to KTS, Ranger KMS provides an alternative to the plain JKS used in Hadoop KMS. Unlike Cloudera's solution, Ranger KMS relies on a third-party external database to persist keys. It combines an alternative Hadoop KMS implementation based on the original Hadoop KMS with a second component that handles communication with the database. Ranger KMS uses a master key to encrypt all other key deposits, and the master key is itself persisted in the database in encrypted form. The connection to the database can be secured by SSL. Hortonworks provides an example of this (*http://bit.ly/2A8CMzZ*) on its website.

Ranger KMS supports high availability by deploying multiple instances, but you need to ensure that the backing database (*http://bit.ly/2FwXQpH*) is also highly available.

Ranger KMS also supports SafeNet Luna HSMs, which leverage a specific type of JKS implementation by SafeNet, that locally interacts with the standard SafeNet Luna client libraries. This also enables the use of multiple HSMs in a highly available fashion, by configuring those client libraries (*http://bit.ly/2zjDElo*) accordingly. If HSMs are used, the master key is persisted on the HSM, but it still needs to be materialized to the KMS hosts to decrypt keys locally. Ranger KMS supports NTL and SSL connections to Luna HSM via the SafeNet client libraries.

Encrypting Temporary Files

Applications running in YARN make use of scratch space on each worker node to store temporary data. For example, both MapReduce and Spark store shuffle data on local disk. Spark also allows datasets to be cached to a local disk for the lifetime of the application. Likewise, Impala automatically spills large join operations to disk under memory pressure.

Each of these types of data may contain sensitive information that we would prefer to have encrypted. One approach would be to apply full volume encryption to the local disks on which the temporary files are stored. However, these disks are typically also used for HDFS data storage, with encryption already covered by HDFS TDE—and, as previously mentioned, we don't want to pay the encryption overhead twice (once for TDE and once for volume encryption).

However, most services offer solutions to encrypt their temporary outputs and the options for each are shown in Table 9-9.

Table 9-9. Data encryption options for services that write temporary scratch data

Service	Description
Impala	`-disk_spill_encryption` startup flag.
Spark	`spark.io.encryption.enabled` job configuration parameter.
MapReduce	`mapreduce.job.encrypted-intermediate-data` job configuration parameter.
Hive	Volume encryption of the disk on HiveServer2 configured for `hive.exec.local.scratchdir`, or turn off local work. Note that disabling local work on HiveServer2 can have performance implications because it can prevent autoconversion of map joins.

Summary

Security can be a complex topic, and doubtless you have many additional questions about the material covered in this chapter. By necessity, the information presented here is a condensed summary of the various security mechanisms employed by projects that may be running on the cluster, but you should now feel confident about how the various aspects of security are used in Hadoop and how they fit together.

It is essential that operators, architects, and developers have a solid grounding in what security mechanisms are available in each component of the cluster. You should not only study each of these sections closely to see how best to manage the security controls in your deployments, but also refer ultimately to the vendor documentation and the individual projects.

Armed with the necessary security background, we can now explore how to integrate these security mechanisms with identity management providers.

Integration with
Identity Management Providers

In Chapter 9, we covered how cluster services provide authentication, authorization, and confidentiality. These security mechanisms rely heavily on a common understanding between clients, services, and operating systems of which users and groups exist. Cluster architects need to be familiar with how cluster services use identity services for authentication and authorization and what providers are available, in order to decide how best to configure the clusters within the enterprise context. In this chapter, we examine these interactions and outline some common integration architectures.

Integration Areas

We need identity management providers in the following areas:

Kerberos
   As we have seen, integration with a KDC is essential to secure authentication in most Hadoop services. Every user wishing to use the cluster must have a principal in one of the trusted realms, and ideally this principal maps to an existing enterprise user account with the same password. Each server in the cluster must be configured to allow users and servers to authenticate to a KDC.

User accounts and groups
   Cluster services will use users and groups when making authentication and authorization decisions and for execution. For example, YARN requires that users exist on every node, to ensure security isolation between running jobs. We therefore need a way of resolving enterprise user accounts on each cluster node, and furthermore these need to correspond to the Kerberos principal name of the

user who submitted the job. Authorization decisions are commonly made by checking a user's group memberships, and the username used is the one supplied through authentication.

Certificate management

For in-flight encryption, we require some sort of TLS certificate management. In an enterprise, this is usually managed by a central CA as part of a PKI deployment. We need to ensure that our cluster service certificates are signed and renewed by the CA. Using the enterprise CA makes for a smoother experience in the browser because users do not have to click past dire warnings about connecting to sites with untrusted certificates.

In each of these areas, we need to set up integration at the application and at the OS level.

Integration Scenarios

We covered the available authentication and authorization mechanisms in Chapter 9, but it is helpful here to consider some example user interaction scenarios, to remind ourselves why we need these different integrations in secure clusters. In particular, notice how a single user identity is used at multiple stages in the process. For each step in the scenarios, we highlight what areas of integration are needed. Note that, in each scenario, we present a slightly simplified version of the interaction.

Scenario 1: Writing a File to HDFS

User Suresh writes a file to HDFS from a cluster edge node:

1. Suresh obtains a Kerberos TGT for his own principal, `suresh@SABON.COM`, from the KDC, using `kinit suresh` (Kerberos integration in the OS).

2. Suresh uses the HDFS CLI to write a file on the local filesystem (*/tmp/foo*) to a location on HDFS (*/data/app/bar*), using `hdfs dfs -put /tmp/foo /data/app/bar`.

3. When executing the command, the HDFS CLI first talks to the HDFS Name-Node to find out which DataNodes to write the data to. To do this, the library obtains a service ticket for the HDFS NameNode, using the Kerberos configuration on the edge node (Kerberos integration in the application).

4. The NameNode checks the service ticket presented by the client, using its own Kerberos TGT (Kerberos integration in the application).

5. The NameNode retrieves the group memberships of the user *suresh*. Depending on the group's mapping provider (see "Group Resolution" on page 251), these lookups will need to be performed either within the NameNode process or, as is

normally recommended, at the OS level (user accounts and groups integration in the application and/or OS).

6. The NameNode verifies whether Suresh is allowed to use HDFS, by checking the username *suresh* and the resolved groups from step 5 against the service policy ACLs (see "Hadoop Service Level Authorization" on page 257).

7. The NameNode checks and whether Suresh has write access to the */data/app* directory, using the username *suresh* and the resolved groups from step 5.

8. If authorized, the NameNode responds to the client with details of a DataNode write pipeline and the necessary access tokens.

We can see that, even in this relatively simple operation, we need Kerberos integration in both the OS and the application and resolution of users and groups by at least the OS.

Scenario 2: Submitting a Hive Query

In this interaction, Sebastian submits a query to a Sentry-protected Hive instance from Hue. Let's examine the interaction and highlight the required integrations:

1. Sebastian uses his browser to access the Hue application, which is protected by TLS encryption. The browser checks that the Hue server's TLS server certificate has been signed by an enterprise CA using its certificate trust chain (certificate management).

2. Sebastian logs in to Hue using his LDAP username, *seb12*, and password (user accounts and groups integration in the application).

3. Sebastian submits a Hive query in the Hue Query Editor. Hue uses Kerberos authentication and impersonation to submit the query to HiveServer2 as itself (hue/server2.sabon.com) on behalf of *seb12*. HiveServer2 also uses TLS encryption, so Hue checks the HiveServer2 server certificate against its own certificate trust chain (Kerberos integration in the application, certificate management).

4. Before HiveServer2 runs the query, it checks that *seb12* is allowed access to the objects in the query using its Sentry authorization plug-in. The plug-in contacts the Sentry server, using Kerberos authentication to retrieve the list of roles for *seb12* (Kerberos integration in the application).

5. The Sentry server retrieves the group memberships of the user *seb12* and returns the roles to the plug-in on HiveServer2. Depending on the group's chosen mapping provider (see "Group Resolution" on page 251), LDAP lookups will need to be performed either within the Sentry process or, as is normally recommended, at the OS level (user accounts and groups integration in the application and OS).

6. HiveServer2 makes an authorization decision based on which roles *seb12* is a member of. If authorized, the query is run via YARN.

This scenario requires Kerberos, user, and group resolution and certificate management integration.

Scenario 3: Running a Spark Job

By now, the integration points should be becoming clear, but, as one final example, we look at application user *appusr4* kicking off a Spark job as part of an ETL task:

1. As part of its operation, the application maintains a Kerberos TGT via a regular login from a keytab within the application (Kerberos integration in the application or OS).

2. The application submits a Spark job to the YARN ResourceManager using a Kerberos service ticket, asks to run the job in the `appusr` queue, and specifies that members of the *appadmins* group can view the job logs and UI via the VIEW_ACL access control list (see "YARN" on page 261) (Kerberos integration in the application).

3. The YARN ResourceManager retrieves the group memberships of the user *appusr4* and checks to see whether it is authorized to run jobs in the *appusr* queue using the configured queue ACLs (user accounts and groups integration in the application and OS).

4. If authorized, the YARN ResourceManager allocates resources on YARN Node-Managers and notifies the application user where it can run the Spark containers.

5. YARN NodeManagers start container processes for the Spark driver and executors, which run on the worker nodes as the *appusr4* OS user (user accounts and groups integration in the application and OS).

6. An administrator, Amelia, checks the progress of the job via the ResourceManager Web UI, which in our scenario requires Kerberos authentication and uses TLS security. Her browser uses her Kerberos TGT from her Windows login session to authenticate as *amelia11* to the UI. It also checks the server TLS certificate against its trust store (application/OS Kerberos integration, certificate management).

7. The ResourceManager retrieves the group memberships of user *amelia11* and checks to see whether she is authorized to view the job UI using the queue and application view ACLs (user accounts and groups integration in the application and OS).

This scenario is another example of requiring integration with the Kerberos KDC, user and group resolution, and certificate management. Hopefully, these examples have shown why we need integration on multiple levels and on every node in the cluster.

Integration Providers

Each integration area has a number of possible providers, and the job of the cluster architect is to choose the providers that fit best within the given enterprise context.

 Although we make general recommendations here, each enterprise is different and we recognize there are valid reasons for not following the recommendations in a specific context. However, in our experience, you will be much more successful if you adhere to these common architectures.

Some commonly used providers for each integration area are:

Kerberos
- MIT Kerberos (*https://web.mit.edu/kerberos/*)
- Heimdal Kerberos (*https://www.h5l.org/*)
- Microsoft Active Directory (*http://bit.ly/2S0rlSa*)
- Red Hat Identity Management (IdM) (*https://red.ht/2qYY6U9*) or its open source equivalent, FreeIPA (*http://bit.ly/2Bo52Ad*)

Users and groups
- Local Linux users and groups
- LDAP-compliant directories:
    - OpenLDAP (*https://www.openldap.org/*)
    - AD
    - IdM/FreeIPA

Certificate management
- Local and self-signed certificates using OpenSSL (*https://www.openssl.org/*)
- AD
- IdM/FreeIPA

A summary of providers and their capabilities is in Table 10-1.

Table 10-1. Common centralized identity management providers and capabilities

Provider	KDC	LDAP	Certificate management
AD	Yes	Yes	Yes
RedHat IdM	Yes	Yes	Yes
OpenLDAP	No	Yes	No
MIT Kerberos	Yes	No	No
OpenSSL	No	No	Yes

For convenience, we usually want users and applications to be able to use existing enterprise-wide user accounts. In addition to lowering the bar for users who want to use the cluster, it makes the task of authorization and audit easier and makes the whole experience of using and administering the cluster smoother.

AD and IdM are examples of *centralized identity management* systems, in which users and groups are defined once and exposed through various interfaces and protocols, such as Kerberos and LDAP. Your enterprise almost certainly uses one of these systems (probably AD), and we *strongly* encourage you to integrate with it.

 There are alternatives to LDAP for centralized user and group administration, but they are not particularly common in enterprises. One approach is to use configuration management software, like Puppet, to declaratively define users and groups, which are then materialized by the software on each server on a regular or on-demand basis.

There are two common ways to use the providers we just listed. In the first configuration, AD or IdM provides a KDC implementation, as well as user and group lookup via LDAP. In the second setup, MIT or Heimdal Kerberos provides the KDC, and OpenLDAP provides the user and groups integration. With the second configuration, user accounts must be synchronized between the KDC and OpenLDAP servers.[1] This is handled automatically by both AD and IdM. The options are illustrated in Figure 10-1. In the first configuration (a), a centralized system provides both KDC and LDAP services and uses a unified model for users and groups. In option (b), KDC and LDAP are provided by different services and the users are synced between them, or manually created in both. There are also combinations of each approach, which we cover in the following sections.

---

1 MIT Kerberos can be configured to use an OpenLDAP backend, although the setup is somewhat complex.

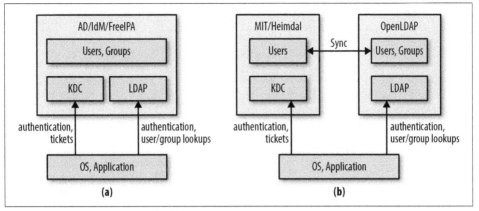

Figure 10-1. Integration with identity management providers

We recommend integrating with a centralized identity management system, such as AD, which can provide Kerberos, LDAP, and certificate management. Even if integrating with an enterprise AD or IdM instance is not possible, we encourage you to set up a centralized system for managing your own clusters, as a best practice.

Having covered the integration at a high level, we now look at each of the three integration areas in greater detail, starting with LDAP, followed by Kerberos and TLS certificate management.

LDAP Integration

We have just seen how we need to integrate with LDAP directories at both the application and the OS level. In this section, we introduce some important background and features of LDAP directories and look at integrating them both within applications and in Linux.

Background

LDAP (*http://bit.ly/2r00Lx6*) is actually a common protocol definition for serving information from a *directory information service* (*http://bit.ly/2r08ICm*). The protocol itself doesn't specify what kind of data should be in a directory or how it should be laid out—it just allows a common way to query objects in the directory. In an LDAP directory, each object has a *distinguished name* (DN), which is a unique identifier in the directory. Objects can also have additional attributes, which provide extra information. For example, if it is a user account, attributes often include full names, email addresses, and a user password (stored in a protected way). Queries and responses from the LDAP server are exchanged using the LDAP Data Interchange Format (LDIF).

In terms of integration with Hadoop clusters, relevant directory objects include:

An organization (or, in AD, a domain)
> An organization has a DN that is a sequence of *domain components* (DCs); for example dc=examplebank,dc=com. Users and groups are created within a domain or organization.

A user
> Users are represented differently in each directory but often have attributes, like *common name* (cn) and POSIX user ID (uidNumber). The attributes used to create the DNs for users vary between schemas. In addition to representing end users, application accounts, and computers, user objects are also used for technical accounts for specific instances of services running on nodes in the cluster. AD defines some special attributes for users:
>
> - sAMAccountName: This is the user login name used in older versions of Windows.
> - userPrincipalName: The UPN is a unique username often of the form *user@domain* for end users, *service/fqdn@REALM* for technical accounts, or *host/fqdn@REALM* for computer accounts.
> - servicePrincipalName: SPNs are principal names with which instances of a service running on a computer can be identified. Multiple SPNs can be assigned to a user object.

A group
> User objects and other groups can be combined into groups. Common attributes are cn and POSIX group ID (gidNumber). In Hadoop, groups are most often used in conjunction with authorization to confer operational or data access rights to users. Groups can have multiple member attributes, each of which specifies the DN of a user in the group.

An organizational unit (OU)
> This is a collection of related objects, like users, groups, and computers. An example DN would be ou=risk,dc=examplebank,dc=com. OUs are often used as containers for the technical accounts associated with instances of services running on cluster nodes.

LDAP servers can be responsible for one or more domains or organizations. In AD, the server responsible for a domain is called a *domain controller*. A trust relationship can be set up between servers responsible for different but related domains. AD has the notion of a *forest*, which is a grouping of related domains that trust each other.

When looking up an object in a particular domain, you usually need to query the LDAP server or servers responsible for that domain.

 AD has a special LDAP endpoint, called the *global catalog*, which allows user and group searches across domains within a forest, without redirecting the client with a referral to the domain controller responsible for the domain. This is recommended for scenarios where users need to be resolved from multiple domains within a single cluster. The default global catalog port is 3268 for unencrypted connections and 3269 for connections protected through LDAP over SSL (LDAPS).

Searching LDAP

You can easily query the contents of an LDAP directory using the `ldapsearch` command-line tool, which is part of the OpenLDAP client utilities. Some directories are set up to allow anonymous searches, but others require some sort of user authentication before issuing queries. The LDAPv3 protocol supports both simple (username and password) and SASL authentication mechanisms, including Kerberos. For Hadoop cluster admins, it's well worth getting acquainted with `ldapsearch` because it's a valuable debugging tool in enterprise deployments. For example, the following command finds all instances of user accounts for the HDFS service in a given domain in AD:

```
$ kinit ian@examplebank.com
$ ldapsearch -H ldaps://gblad.examplebank.com:3269 \
  -b dc=risk,dc=examplebank,dc=com \
  "(userPrincipalName=hdfs/*)"
```

For efficiency, and to reduce the load on the LDAP server, it's best to limit the search space when doing user and group lookups. In this example, the base DN (the `-b` parameter) specifies where to start the search. The smaller the subtree the query has to search, the quicker the response will be. Specifying the right base DN is important when integrating with LDAP at any layer of the stack.

LDAP Security

One thing to be acutely aware of when using LDAP is the security of the connection. By default, information is sent over the network in the clear, when using the plain LDAP protocol. This is especially important to avoid when using simple authentication in services (see "LDAP Authentication" on page 247). There are two mechanisms to keep the connection confidential, both of which establish a TLS-encrypted session.

The first mechanism uses a special operation—STARTTLS—within the standard LDAP protocol to apply encryption to a session running on the standard port (389, by default) before sensitive data is exchanged. The second mechanism—LDAPS—creates a TLS-encrypted connection to the server on a different port (636 by default) before any LDAP protocol messages are exchanged. These connections are denoted through an explicit ldaps protocol. By default, both mechanisms require that the server present a valid TLS certificate signed by a CA which can be verified using a certificate trust store available to the client. AD only supports LDAPS connections.

Load Balancing

Very often, especially in corporate directory setups, a global load balancer is configured in front of directory servers to balance load and provide high availability. Ordinarily, this is a good thing, but it is worth bearing in mind when using and configuring distributed systems. When creating new users and groups, it might take some minutes for them to propagate to all the servers behind the load balancer, so not all nodes in the cluster will be able to resolve the new objects at exactly the same time.

Application Integration

Many applications in a Hadoop cluster can query LDAP directly. In addition to serving as a group mapping provider for the core Hadoop services, like HDFS and YARN, LDAP servers can be used to authenticate end users who supply username and password credentials over JDBC or ODBC connections. Similarly, other tools, such as Hue and Cloudera Manager, also provide LDAP integration and use LDAP group membership as part of the authorization process for logged-in users.

Since users are required to enter a username and password, it is essential that both the client connection to the service and the connection from the service to the LDAP server are encrypted, as shown in Figure 10-2. Most often, this is achieved using TLS encryption, but other mechanisms, such as SASL QoP, are possible. Since these user credentials are then sent over the network to the LDAP server for verification, either STARTTLS or LDAPS must be used between the application and the LDAP server. In the figure, we use a triangle to denote directory information services in line with convention. The padlocks on the interactions indicate where in-flight encryption should be used.

As a best practice, for encrypted connections, you should ensure that the LDAP server is legitimate by validating the server's TLS certificate. In Java applications this is mandatory, since for SSL/TLS connections Java requires the server's public certificate or the certificate of a CA to be in its configured trust store (see "TLS and Java" on page 238).

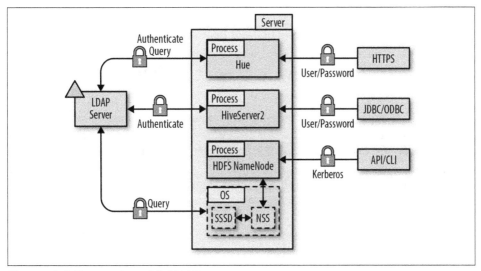

Figure 10-2. Integration with LDAP

For applications using the OpenLDAP client libraries (which can be used to query any LDAP-compliant directory), such as Python or C++ applications, the server certificate verification behavior is often controlled by the `TLS_REQCERT` configuration parameter in */etc/openldap/ldap.conf*. This can be set to:

`never`
> Don't request or validate the server certificate.

`allow`
> Request and try to validate the certificate, but allow the connection if it is invalid.

`try`
> Request the certificate and end the session immediately if it is invalid.

As we have seen, a common pattern with application integration is to authenticate the user and then determine which groups it is in for authorization purposes. Unless the directory supports anonymous searches, any application performing group lookups needs to be configured with user credentials to bind (authenticate) to the LDAP server and issue search requests.

Different applications have various syntaxes for specifying user and group lookup patterns. When using AD, it is often enough to specify that the LDAP server conforms to the AD schema, and the application can usually infer how to do the rest. In other cases—for example, when querying an OpenLDAP server—where the schema might differ from deployment to deployment, sometimes you must specify a replacement pattern to use. For example, with Impala, a user DN pattern can be constructed using the #UID placeholder in the `ldap_bind_pattern` parameter:

```
uid=#UID,ou=users,dc=examplebank,dc=com
```

If using LDAP authentication with Hive and requiring that a user have certain group memberships, you can specify the group lookup pattern using the %s placeholder in the following parameter, hive.server2.authentication.ldap.groupDNPattern:

```
cn=%s,ou=groups,dc=examplebank,dc=com
```

As another example, the following snippet defines how you might configure two LDAP login domains for Hue—one for corporate users in AD and one for administrators in FreeIPA. Notice how, for the first server, the user or group attributes are not supplied, whereas for the IPA installation this is required. Note also how the base DN is specified to reduce the search space:

```
[desktop]
 [[auth]]
 backend=desktop.auth.backend.LdapBackend
 [[ldap]]
  ldap_cert=/etc/hue/conf/cacerts.pem
  create_users_on_login=true
  [[[ldap_servers]]]
  [[[[CORP.EXAMPLEBANK.COM]]]]
  # AD server
  ldap_url=ldaps://gblad.examplebank.com:3269
  # AD does not need search bind - users are always user@nt_domain
  search_bind_authentication=false
  nt_domain=corp.examplebank.com
  # Bind details for user/group LDAP search/sync (not authentication)
  base_dn="ou=corp,dc=examplebank,dc=com"
  bind_dn="huesearch"
  bind_password="AwesomePassw0rd"

  [[[[HADOOP.ADMIN.EXAMPLEBANK.COM]]]]
  ldap_url=ldaps://ipa.hadoop.admin.examplebank.com:636
  search_bind_authentication=true
  base_dn="cn=accounts,dc=hadoop,dc=admin,dc=examplebank,dc=com"
  bind_dn="uid=huesearch,cn=users,cn=accounts,dc=...bank,dc=com"
  bind_password="AnotherGr8Password"
   [[[[[users]]]]]
   user_name_attr="uid"
   [[[[[groups]]]]]
   group_member_attr="member"
```

Refer to the documentation for each component to get full details of how to specify lookup patterns and attribute names.

Linux Integration

We need a way to map users and groups from the corporate directories into users and groups in Linux so that Hadoop services can make use of them to run processes and to make authorization decisions. We don't have the space to cover all the possible integration options for Linux, but there are plenty. The most popular open source integrations are Winbind and the System Security Services Daemon (SSSD), but proprietary offerings, such as Centrify, also exist and may be the preferred option for enterprise environments. Let's take a quick look at SSSD.

SSSD

Despite its name, SSSD is actually a group of daemons and libraries that manage access to remote authentication services and other networked resources. It fits into the Linux stack by providing interfaces into the Name Service Switch (NSS) and Pluggable Authentication Modules (PAM) libraries, as a means of resolving users and groups and providing authentication.

NSS maintains a few useful databases that the kernel consults when it needs information. For our purposes, the most interesting ones are the user database `passwd` and the group database `group`. When you run commands like `getent passwd ian`, `id paul`, or `getent group risk_users`, the program is issuing calls to the NSS API, which in turn consults all the registered providers for the database. You can configure SSSD in */etc/nsswitch.conf* as a provider for these databases.

 SSSD can conflict with the Name Service Caching Daemon (NSCD), if that is also running. NSCD's primary responsibility is to cache the results of DNS lookups, but it can also cache the `passwd` and `group` databases, among others. It's fine to have both running as long as they don't overlap in functionality, so disable `passwd`, `group`, `network`, and `services` caching in */etc/nscd.conf*.

From the operating system point of view, users and groups that SSSD retrieves from remote directories look like and behave like local users. SSSD caches objects to prevent regular round trips to the remote directory and keeps the cache regularly updated.

As an example integration, we demonstrate how to integrate an RHEL or CentOS 7 box with an AD server using the `realmd` library (*https://www.freedesktop.org/soft ware/realmd/*). First, we install the package prerequisites:

```
$ sudo yum -y install adcli authconfig sssd krb5-workstation \
  openldap-clients oddjob-mkhomedir
```

The simplest way to integrate a Linux server with AD is to *join* the server to the domain, which means to register the server with the AD server and create a computer account, if required. Using the `adcli` utility included with the `realmd` library, we can run something like the following, which joins the server to the AD server at `adgbl.corp.example.com`:

```
$ sudo adcli join -S adgbl.corp.example.com -N $(hostname -s) \
  --stdin-password -D corp.example.com -R CORP.EXAMPLE.COM \
  -v <<< ThisIsMyAdminPassword
...snip...
  * Authenticated as user: Administrator@CORP.EXAMPLE.COM
  * Looked up short domain name: CORP
  * Using fully qualified name: ip-172-31-100-163.ec2.internal
  * Using domain name: corp.example.com
  * Using computer account name: ip-172-31-100-163
  * Using domain realm: corp.example.com
  * Enrolling computer name: ip-172-31-100-163
  * Generated 120 character computer password
  * Using keytab: FILE:/etc/krb5.keytab
  * Computer account for ip-172-31-100-163$ does not exist
  * Found well known computer container at: CN=Computers,...,DC=com
  * Calculated computer account: CN=ip-172-31-100-163,CN=...,DC=com
  * Created computer account: CN=ip-172-31-100-163,CN=...,DC=com
...snip...
```

Here we are implicitly using the default OU in AD for computer accounts for the domain, but a custom OU can be specified if required.

 To register a new computer account, we need an administrative user for the OU. In the example command, we supply the administrator's password directly, but it's also possible—and highly recommended—to precreate all the expected computer accounts ahead of time as an administrator and to set up one-time passwords for each host that can be used in the join command. This is the recommended approach when using automated host provisioning with something like Ansible because it means that you do not need to place the administrator's password in configuration files.

After the machine has joined the domain, we can configure SSSD to resolve information from AD. To do this, we populate */etc/sssd/sssd.conf* with something like the following:

```
[sssd]
services = nss, pam
config_file_version = 2
domains = CORP.EXAMPLE.COM

[nss]
override_homedir = /home/%u
default_shell = /bin/bash

[domain/CORP.EXAMPLE.COM]
id_provider = ad
chpass_provider = ad
auth_provider = ad
access_provider = simple
```

```
ad_server = adgbl.corp.example.com
ad_domain = corp.example.com
# Defaults for AD provider but worth noting
ldap_id_mapping = true
case_sensitive = false
enumerate = false
ignore_group_members = true
```

There are some important things to note here. The `ad_server` parameter can be a comma-separated list of servers to provide automatic failover. Often, though, AD administrators set up a global load balancer in front of AD servers anyway. Another key parameter is `enumerate`, which specifies whether all objects should be obtained and cached from the server in the background. We strongly recommend keeping this to the default of `false` because it can significantly harm performance. We also recommend keeping `ignore_group_members` as the default. This limits the scope of group lookups to their existence, rather than also returning their full list of members.

By default, AD accounts do not include POSIX attributes such as numeric user or group identifiers (UIDs or GIDs), so SSSD derives these automatically from the AD account security identifier (`objectSID`). You can control this behavior using the `ldap_id_mapping` parameter. If AD contains the POSIX attributes, you set this parameter to `false`.

If you know that your users and groups will be limited to a specific subsection of the directory, you can limit lookups using the `ldap_group_search_base` parameter. This can give significant speedups for large directories.

We also need to configure the Kerberos client information so that the host can resolve Kerberos principals from AD (more on this subject in "Kerberos Clients" on page 296).

Finally, we need to configure NSS and PAM to use SSSD and to enable the SSSD service:

```
$ sudo authconfig --enablesssd --enablesssdauth --enablemkhomedir --update
$ sudo systemctl enable sssd
$ sudo systemctl enable oddjobd
$ sudo systemctl start sssd
$ sudo systemctl start oddjobd
```

Now, when users log in or a process performs a user or group lookup (for example, the Hadoop group mapping providers) SSSD queries one of the configured remote directory servers for information and caches the results locally.

There is a lot more that can be done with SSSD. It has built-in support for transparently querying AD forests and can support resolving objects from multiple domains. And in addition to AD, SSSD can resolve users from other LDAP providers. For example, you may have users being resolved from corporate AD and sysadmins from a local OpenLDAP deployment. For further information, see the SSSD documentation (*https://red.ht/2DBe8v5*).

Kerberos Integration

We covered Kerberos authentication in detail in "Kerberos" on page 242. Here we explore the integration options for clients and some common KDC architectures. Referring back to our providers, the KDC can be provided by a central identity provider, like AD or IdM, or by standalone KDC implementations like MIT or Heimdal Kerberos. Often, we want to set up trust relationships between KDCs to allow users from other realms to use our clusters. Here we cover some of the common setups.

Kerberos Clients

Most often, Kerberos integration in Linux is provided by the open source MIT Kerberos client libraries. These allow users to run kinit to obtain a TGT for a given realm and subsequently to retrieve service tickets. In Oracle Java, Kerberos integration is provided by classes in the sun.security.krb5 package. For non-Java processes, numerous libraries provide integration, but commonly the Cyrus SASL package is used.

Kerberos can store tickets in a variety of cache types. Some of the more recent versions of the Kerberos utilities default to using the KEYRING type, which uses a secure memory location provided by the OS. However, the Java Kerberos libraries, and thus Hadoop, can only use the FILE cache type.

Each integration refers to a configuration file in a common format, which details such things as the supported encryption types, ticket renewal settings, the available realms and where their KDCs are located, and how to map domain names to realms.

By default, you can find this file at */etc/krb5.conf*, but within a shell the actual file used can be overridden using the KRB5_CONFIG environment variable. To locate the *krb5.conf* file Java first looks at the value of the java.security.krb5.conf system property, if set. It then checks for *<java-home>/jre/lib/security/krb5.conf*, and finally for */etc/krb5.conf*.

In addition, the realm and KDC locations can be overridden with values that supersede those found in the configuration file with the java.security.krb5.realm and java.security.krb5.kdc system properties.

Isolating Ticket Caches

As a systems administration and development best practice, always ensure that you and your applications operate within an isolated Kerberos security context. This is especially important when using shared technical accounts. In scripts, before issuing a kinit, set the KRB5CCNAME environment variable to a private location with a unique name; for example, ~/mycache.GO3HuUh. (You can generate temporary unique file locations using the mktemp command.) This credentials cache will be exclusive to the process and won't be affected by anyone else issuing new kinit or kdestroy commands. Always issue kdestroy when finished, to clean up the credentials cache.

Another option is to use the k5start wrapper program (*http://bit.ly/2QWMuMV*), which can provide isolation and keep the ticket fresh.

Continuing the simple case from the previous section on LDAP integration, the relevant sections of the */etc/krb5.conf* file might look like the following:

```
[libdefaults]
default_realm = CORP.EXAMPLE.COM
default_tgs_enctypes = aes256-cts-hmac-sha1-96... arcfour-hmac-md5
default_tkt_enctypes = aes256-cts-hmac-sha1-96... arcfour-hmac-md5
permitted_enctypes = aes256-cts-hmac-sha1-96... arcfour-hmac-md5
ticket_lifetime = 24h
renew_lifetime = 7d
forwardable = true
udp_preference_limit = 1

[realms]
CORP.EXAMPLE.COM = {
  kdc = adgbl.corp.example.com
  admin_server = adgbl.corp.example.com
}
OTHER.EXAMPLE.COM = {
  kdc = anotherkdc1.other.example.com
  kdc = anotherkdc2.other.example.com
}

[domain_realm]
  .corp.example.com = CORP.EXAMPLE.COM
  corp.example.com = CORP.EXAMPLE.COM
  .other.example.com = OTHER.EXAMPLE.COM
  other.example.com = OTHER.EXAMPLE.COM
```

Note that the encryption types should be restricted to remove the weaker types. To get the most up-to-date list of secure encryption types, refer to the MIT documentation (*http://bit.ly/2OTB8HF*). Your Java installation might need the Unlimited Strength Java Cryptography Extensions policy files, which allow the usage of 256-bit encryption types, although this is no longer required for versions above 8u162 or for version 9.[2]

In an enterprise context, the Kerberos configuration file is often much more complex, with several realms and domain mappings specified.

KDC Integration

When building secure clusters, you need to decide whether to build a standalone KDC infrastructure or to connect your clusters to an existing setup, as provided by AD/IdM. If you are building your own KDCs you will likely need to think about establishing trusts between realms (see "Cross-realm trusts" on page 247). We review and discuss the KDC integration architectures in the next few sections, after looking at how to initiate cross-realm trusts.

 We don't have space here to discuss how to install and configure your own KDCs. If you are starting from scratch, see these links for installation instructions:

- MIT Kerberos (*http://bit.ly/2PGFs2d*)
- AD (*https://bit.ly/2zYIc0l*)

Setting up cross-realm trusts

A great source of information for setting up trusts between realms is the documentation of data platform vendors (*http://bit.ly/2PIewPG*), although you should also consult the documentation of the KDC implementations when setting up trusts to ensure that the right encryption types are used and that all the steps are current.

One-way trust between MIT KDC and AD.   In the following, we show how to set up a one-way trust between an MIT KDC and an AD domain. Remember that a one-way trust means that the (local) MIT KDC trusts users with principals in the (remote) AD realm, but not the other way around.

On the AD server (here with the realm CORP.EXAMPLE.COM), have your AD admins issue the following commands in cmd.exe or PowerShell to create the one-way trust to the MIT KDC realm (SATURN.EXAMPLE.COM):

```
netdom trust SATURN.EXAMPLE.COM /Domain:CORP.EXAMPLE.COM
     /add /realm /passwordt:S3ns!t!vePass
```

---

2 See JDK-8170157 (*http://bit.ly/2Bn5n6b*).

Next, configure the encryption types trust attribute for the trusting domain on the AD server using compatible types between the AD and MIT KDC:

```
ksetup /SetEncTypeAttr SATURN.EXAMPLE.COM <space-separated encryption types>
```

If you are not sure which encryption types are supported by your AD, run `ksetup /?`.

On the MIT KDC and cluster hosts, ensure that the cluster realm is the default realm in both */var/kerberos/krb5kdc/kdc.conf* and */etc/krb5.conf* on the KDC host. In addition, */etc/krb5.conf* on every cluster host needs to include information about the AD realm (see "Kerberos Clients" on page 296).

Run the following to create the trust principal on the KDC host using the same password as that used to create the trust in AD:

```
$ kadmin.local
$ kadmin:  addprinc -e <keysalt> krbtgt/SATURN.EXAMPLE.COM@CORP.EXAMPLE.COM
```

The encryption-salt (*keysalt*) list types should match the encryption types with which AD issues tickets. The possible encryption and salt types can be found in the KDC documentation (*http://bit.ly/2OV5mdu*).

Finally, you need to ensure Hadoop has knowledge of the AD realm and can convert its principal names into short names. Add the following to the `auth_to_local` rules in *core-site.xml* on all hosts:

```
<property>
  <name>hadoop.security.auth_to_local</name>
  <value>
    RULE:[1:$1@$0](^.*@CORP\.EXAMPLE\.COM$)s/^(.*)@CORP\.EXAMPLE\.COM$/$1/g
    RULE:[2:$1@$0](^.*@CORP\.EXAMPLE\.COM$)s/^(.*)@CORP\.EXAMPLE\.COM$/$1/g
    DEFAULT
  </value>
</property>
```

Cluster management software, such as Cloudera Manager, does this last stage automatically if supplied with a list of trusted realms.

One-way trusts between MIT KDCs. The process of setting up a one-way cross-realm trust between MIT KDCs is much simpler. In this case, you just need to create matching trust principals in each KDC, with the general form `krbtgt/TRUSTING_REALM@TRUSTED_REALM`. In the following, it is assumed the KDCs are configured for the same encryption types.

On the local KDC and cluster hosts, ensure that the cluster realm is the default realm in both */var/kerberos/krb5kdc/kdc.conf* and */etc/krb5.conf* on the KDC host. In addition, */etc/krb5.conf* on every cluster host needs to include information about the remote KDC realm and its servers (see "Kerberos Clients" on page 296).

On the local KDC host (SATURN.EXAMPLE.COM), run the following to create a trust principal to the remote KDC (NEPTUNE.EXAMPLE.COM):

```
$ kadmin.local
$ addprinc krbtgt/SATURN.EXAMPLE.COM@NEPTUNE.EXAMPLE.COM
```

Run the exact same command on the remote KDC, using the same password. Just like in the previous example, you need to configure Hadoop to include the realm NEPTUNE.EXAMPLE.COM in the auth_to_local rules.

To set up a two-way trust, simply repeat the process in the reverse direction.

Let's now review some KDC integration scenarios.

Local cluster KDC

In this architecture, each cluster has its own exclusive KDC setup. All principals, plus the user and service, are created in the local KDC. A variation of the architecture shares a KDC between clusters at the same security level; for example, PROD and DR clusters.

Figure 10-3 shows a two-way cross-realm trust to the KDCs of another cluster (NEPTUNE.EXAMPLE.COM). The two-way trust is denoted with a double line. High availability of KDC instances is shown by the double box for each realm. In the figure, we see that services running in cluster nodes obtain their Kerberos TGTs from the dedicated KDCs (1). Users from either realm wishing to use cluster services use the local KDC to obtain service tickets (2), which they then present to the services (3).

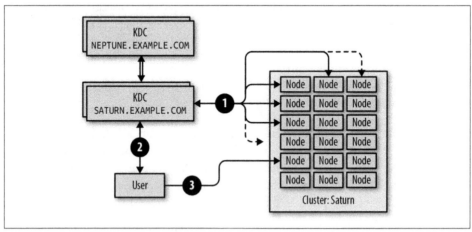

Figure 10-3. Local KDC setup per cluster

Although this model gives maximum control to the cluster administrators, integration with the wider enterprise is more difficult. All user administration must be managed by the cluster admins. This is easiest if you are using a local AD or IdM instance, which provides the local KDC and LDAP services. As mentioned previously, if using standalone MIT KDC, user principals (and their passwords) must be synchronized with a directory service and materialized on Linux using SSSD or similar. In the worst case, users and groups are created locally on each server. Although such integrations are possible, they are nontrivial and error-prone.

 Although creating local user accounts for end users is inefficient, using local users and groups for the service accounts is common practice and recommended. The set of service accounts and their group memberships are static.

Integration with other clusters (for data transfer, for example) may involve the setup of a complex web of one- and two-way trusts between local cluster realms. This setup requires the administrators to populate *krb5.conf* with the correct realm and domain information for all the realms in the trust network and to create the trust between the KDCs themselves.

 Note that Hadoop requires that its service principals be created in the default Kerberos realm.

From an availability standpoint, cluster administrators must ensure that more than one KDC instance is available for each cluster (the double boxes in Figure 10-3) and that multiple endpoints are referenced in the client configuration (see "Identity management providers" on page 344).

This option is best for isolated clusters and use cases that do not require wider integration with the enterprise, or where such integration is impossible for technical or security reasons.

Local cluster KDC and corporate user KDC

To avoid the drawbacks of user and group management, a hybrid architecture uses a local KDC for cluster service principals and a centralized corporate KDC, such as AD or IdM, for users.

As shown in Figure 10-4, services authenticate to their local KDC (1), whereas users authenticate to the corporate KDC (2). Using their corporate TGT, the users obtain service tickets from the cluster KDC (3) and use these to access cluster services (4).

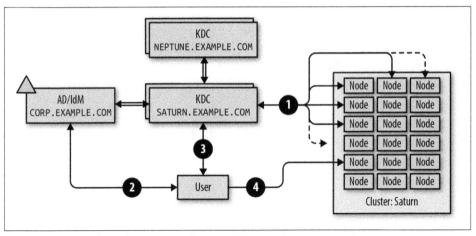

Figure 10-4. Local KDC setup per cluster with users in corporate directory

One advantage of this architecture is that user management can all be delegated to the central directory. But there can still be challenges with user accounts. Principal name collisions between realms need to be dealt with, and there is always the risk that a cluster administrator could create a principal in the local KDC with the same short name as a principal in the corporate KDC and thus be able to masquerade as that user within the cluster. You can mitigate this with careful use of `auth_to_local` rules, which limit the principal patterns that can be in the local KDC realm.

The architecture also requires that at least a one-way trust relationship is set up between the local KDC and the corporate KDC. Although the risk to the corporate KDC is small, getting agreement for such a trust is not always trivial.

This architecture shares many of the downsides of the first option. In addition to the trust to the corporate KDC, trusts between realms of interacting clusters must also be maintained.

Corporate KDC

The final option is to make direct use of a corporate KDC realm for service and for user principals. The provider of centralized KDC functionality is invariably a unified identity management product, like AD or IdM.

In Figure 10-5, services authenticate to the local realm in the forest (here, `EMEA.EXAMPLE.COM`), which should be the default (1). In this example, a domain forest or cross-domain trust exists between different regional directories. Users can be authenticated by any of the realms in the forest but get their service tickets from the local realm (2), which they present to cluster services (3).

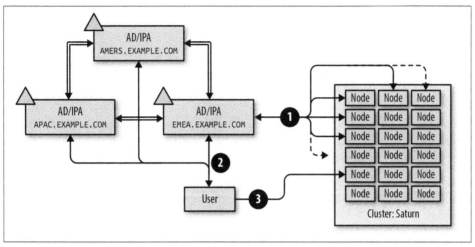

Figure 10-5. Cluster service and user principals are created directly in corporate directories

In this model, a separate user account is created in the directory for each required unique instance of a service principal. In the ideal case—since there can be tens to hundreds of such users within a cluster—the directory administrators allow the cluster management software to create and manage these accounts automatically.

The best approach is to create a dedicated OU within the directory where these accounts can be created (see "LDAP Integration" on page 287). This OU can either be per cluster or for all clusters under management.

 Use per-cluster OUs, because they provide superior isolation. With this model, it is very clear which accounts belong to which clusters, and this helps to avoid accidental deletion or other administration errors. It also allows for effective security isolation between cluster accounts, because the account that the cluster management server uses can be restricted to managing only its own accounts.

A very common practice, even in the most restricted and regulated environments, is for directory administrators to permit the cluster management software to administer accounts—but only in the relevant OUs. The cluster management software, for example Cloudera Manager, will create the user accounts as required, as new services are added or modified.

In cases where this is not possible, the next-best option is to script the creation of user accounts within the directory, with the required service principal names. From Linux, `ldapmodify` can be used to create accounts in the remote directory over a secure LDAP connection. For AD, PowerShell can also be used on the Windows server itself.

Note that this approach imposes an extra burden on the directory administrator, who must be in the loop every time user accounts need to be added, deleted, or updated. These events are more regular than you might initially imagine—remember that each individual instance of a service needs its own user account. A cluster of 100 worker nodes running HDFS, YARN, and HBase needs at least 400 user accounts (*HTTP/ fqdn*, *hdfs/fqdn*, *yarn/fqdn*, and *hbase/fqdn* on each node), plus those required for edge and master processes. Avoid manual account management, wherever possible.

 Do not use manual account creation and maintenance for service principals. Automation is essential.

Potential drawbacks of this KDC architecture are a loss of control over accounts and principals and, consequently, a lack of flexibility and agility in operations. We have also seen latency and performance issues for Kerberos or LDAP interactions to distant (in terms of network) or misconfigured directory servers.

However, the advantages in maintenance are significant, since you do not need to install and look after your own KDC infrastructure. Most importantly, users and groups from the wider enterprise can be easily integrated with the cluster. Of the three presented, this is usually the most recommended integration approach.

Certificate Management

In order to provide proper protection for in-flight data, in a secure cluster TLS encryption should be configured in each service that supports it. Although it is possible to generate and use your own certificates—so-called *self-signed certificates*—we strongly recommend making use of the enterprise PKI infrastructure (if there is one) and having certificates properly signed by a central CA. There are two main advantages to using a centralized corporate CA:

Improved trust
> Usually, central CAs are well protected and form the root of trust within an enterprise, so users of your cluster can feel assured that they are using a legitimate service.

Easier management

If using self-signed certificates, you need to add each and every instance of a public certificate to all trust stores within the cluster. This can rapidly become unwieldy and difficult to manage, especially when renewing or revoking existing certificates.

If you cannot use a central CA, consider creating your own CA root certificate, which can be used to sign server certificates, or purchasing an intermediate CA certificate. Consolidated identity management services, such as AD or IdM, come with built-in certificate-signing CA services. Although the advantage of enterprise-wide trust does not exist, the ease of management should be compelling.

Self-signed certificates can be used for noncritical development or proof-of-concept environments, but production environments should have certificates signed by a trusted authority. Use signed certificates in every circumstance, if possible.

In the following subsections, we look at the process of generating and having certificates signed. We also see how to convert them into useful formats for Hadoop. We present the commands in some detail because it is not always obvious how to do this, and example commands can be extremely helpful. However, make sure that the commands are right for what you want to do and that they fit into your corporate security policies.

Do not just copy and paste the examples here. Ensure that they are valid for your situation, and consult the relevant documentation for the correct commands. Be sure that sensitive files are properly protected.

Signing Certificates

TLS certificates are composed of a private and a public key. In the ideal case, the private key should never leave the server it is intended for (although enterprises often have centralized issuing services). The certificate signing process allows for this through *certificate signing requests* (CSRs) and is illustrated in Figure 10-6. Here's an example of creating a private key:

```
$ openssl genrsa -out server.key 1024
Generating RSA private key, 1024 bit long modulus
...............................++++++
..++++++
e is 65537 (0x10001)
```

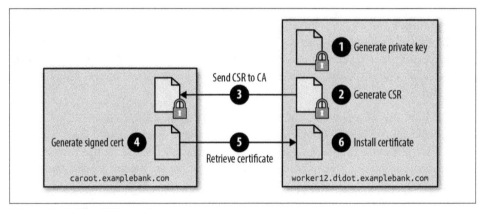

Figure 10-6. The CSR signing process

Next, we create a CSR from the private key. In the CSR, we enter the information that we want included in the public certificate. The most important attribute is the common name, which should be the fully qualified hostname, but we can also add X.509 extensions, like subject alternative names. In this example, we are generating a CSR for an Impala daemon operating behind a load balancer, ensuring that a SHA-2 certificate is requested:

```
$ SAN="[SAN]\nsubjectAltName="
$ SAN="${SAN}DNS:impala.prd1.examplebank.com"
$ SAN="${SAN},DNS:w12.prd1.examplebank.com"
$ openssl req -new -sha256 \
    -key server.key \
    -subj "/C=US/O=Example Bank/CN=w12.prd1.examplebank.com" \
    -extensions SAN
    -reqexts SAN \
    -config <(cat /etc/pki/tls/openssl.cnf <(printf ${SAN})) \
    -out server.csr
```

To keep the CSR secure, you can set an optional challenge password, known only to you and the CA. This CSR is then sent to the CA for signing, and the CA returns a public certificate. Theoretically, you can automate this entire process, including the signing and issuing of certificates.

For multiple services running on the same cluster node, it's usually acceptable for all of them to share a server certificate containing a private-public key pair. The exception to this is when a service is operating behind a load balancer, for which the use of subject alternative names might be required (see "Security considerations" on page 339).

After the certificate has been signed and has been returned (here, as *server.pem*), you can verify that it is valid by using a command like the following:

```
$ openssl verify -CAfile /path/to/cacert.pem server.pem
```

Converting Certificates

Depending on their implementation, cluster services require private and public TLS certificates in different forms. Python and C++ applications most often use the X.509 format, usually encoded as base64 text in Privacy-Enhanced Mail (PEM) (*http:// bit.ly/2A8kZJ6*) files, while Java applications most often use the JKS format. Another common format is PKCS #12 (*http://bit.ly/2DCv0lh*), especially when CAs generate server certificates directly, rather than as a response to CSRs. By contrast, CSRs are usually returned as PEM files. In this case, the signed certificate needs to be combined with the certificate of the intermediate CA that signed it, together with any other intermediate CA certificates, and then converted to JKS.

Finding the right tools and invocations to convert between these formats isn't always easy and usually involves some combination of the openssl and Java keytool utilities. We do not have space to consider every scenario here, but as an example, let's assume that each server has been issued a certificate in PKCS #12 format, with the fully qualified hostname as the certificate common name. We need to convert this into PEM and JKS formats and place it in a central location accessible to all services. First, let's create and protect the central location:

```
$ sudo mkdir -p /opt/hadoop/security/private/{p12,x509,jks}
$ sudo chmod -R 751 /opt/hadoop/security/private
$ sudo cp /path/to/server.p12 /opt/hadoop/security/private/p12/server.p12
$ sudo chmod 400 /opt/hadoop/security/private/p12/*
```

 Be sure that the directory and file permissions are such that the private keys are only readable to the intended processes.

Next, let's convert to PEM format with three output variations. Check the *PASS PHRASE ARGUMENTS* section in man openssl for the different options to supply the password:

```
# Make sure passwords typed in the clear are not recorded for the session
$ set +o history
# Both private and public keys in one output file
$ sudo openssl pkcs12 -in /opt/hadoop/security/private/p12/server.p12 -clcerts \
  -nodes -passin [PASSWORD] -out /opt/hadoop/security/private/x509/cert.pem

# Public key output only
$ sudo openssl pkcs12 -in /opt/hadoop/security/private/p12/server.p12 -clcerts \
  -nodes -nokeys -passin [PASSWORD] \
  -out /opt/hadoop/security/private/x509/cert.crt

# Private key output only
$ sudo openssl pkcs12 -in /opt/hadoop/security/private/p12/server.p12 -clcerts \
```

```
      -nodes -nocerts -passin [PASSWORD] \
      -out /opt/hadoop/security/private/x509/cert.key

$ sudo chmod 400 /opt/hadoop/security/private/x509/*
```

In those commands, we removed the password with -nodes, but if you need to, you can retain it. Next, let's generate a JKS from the P12 certificate:

```
# Make sure passwords typed in the clear are not recorded for the session
$ set +o history
# Import the certificate
$ sudo keytool -importkeystore \
      -srckeystore /opt/hadoop/security/private/p12/server.p12 \
      -srcstoretype PKCS12 \
      -destkeystore /opt/hadoop/security/private/jks/server.jks \
      -srcstorepass [PASSWORD] -deststorepass [PASSWORD]

# Optionally change the password of the key in the keystore to match the store
$ sudo keytool -keypasswd -alias $(hostname -f) \
      -keystore /opt/hadoop/security/private/jks/server.jks -new [PASSWORD] \
      -storepass [PASSWORD] -keypass [PASSWORD]
```

Finally, let's provide access to the files to a select set of users using Linux ACLs:

```
$ cat <<EOF > acls
> user:hdfs:r--
> user:yarn:r--
> user:mapred:r--
...more cluster users...
> EOF
$ setfacl -M acls /opt/hadoop/security/private/{jks,x509}/*
```

For clients to verify server certificates, world-readable trust stores must contain the public certificate of the signing authority on every node in the cluster, including gateways. In this sense, a client is any process accessing a TLS-protected endpoint, so it might be an end user process (like the hdfs CLI tool) or a long-lived process (like an Impala daemon communicating with another Impala daemon). Again, these need to be supplied in both PEM and JKS formats to ensure that all cluster processes can use them.

Although there are some standard locations to find or place CA certificates, it's usually easier to place a single file containing all required certificates in a well-defined location—for example, */etc/hadoop/security/public/ca.pem*—for clients and cluster processes to use. Be sure to put it in a different location than your private keys and to protect the file from write access to prevent the insertion of bogus certificates.

Wildcard Certificates

For very large clusters, it can sometimes be impractical to obtain signed certificates for each and every host. Furthermore, as you add hosts or add load balancers, you

---

need to issue new certificates. If your enterprise does not support automated signing of CSRs, this can be difficult.

If all your hosts are located within a dedicated cluster domain, such as cluster1.example.com, one option can be to use *wildcard certificates (http://bit.ly/2A9REhw)*, which are issued to a domain name pattern, such as *.cluster1.example.com. One certificate can be used by all servers and services in the cluster. After it's signed, the key and public certificate need to be copied to every node in a secure way.

 If you are using wildcard certificates, be sure to protect the private key and ensure that it is not leaked outside of the cluster nodes.

Automation

When generating certificates for hundreds of nodes and services, we highly recommend automation.

This is obviously easiest when you control the full process, from key generation to certificate signing. If you do not control the signing process, it is still worth automating the process of generating CSRs and distributing the public certificates, after they have been signed by the CA. Also, don't forget that certificates expire and you need a process to replace them. Certificate lifetimes of a year or less are common in enterprises.

Some automation tools have been already been written for this that may fit your use case. For example, Cloudera has an Auto-TLS mode for clusters deployed via Cloudera Director.

Summary

Hopefully, this chapter has equipped you with much of the necessary understanding to build solid clusters that can slot neatly into your enterprise. Hadoop clusters often represent a sea change in the way that IT is deployed and managed within enterprises, and consequently some new approaches to integration might be required. It's critical that the teams responsible for building, operating, and governing Hadoop clusters and the wider enterprise IT teams remain flexible to new approaches and requirements.

In this chapter, we covered the various ways of integrating enterprise systems into the security controls of the cluster. We found that we need to integrate identity management at several layers of the stack at the OS and application levels, because it provides authentication, authorization through groups, and certificate management for in-flight encryption. Because it is so important to the efficient operation of a cluster, you should bring your enterprise identity management teams into the conversation as early as possible. Initially, they might feel uneasy, but the information in this chapter should help to relieve any fears about directly integrating clusters with identity management systems.

## CHAPTER 11

Accessing and Interacting with Clusters

It is our job as architects to ensure that users can take full advantage of the data and services hosted in the cluster. To do this, we need to guarantee that users (both humans and applications) can access the cluster services in a safe and secure way. In this chapter, we explore typical architectures for providing users access to cluster services and data while applying the authentication and authorization controls we encountered in Chapter 9.

First we look at the different ways in which a user might interact with the cluster, and then we explore how we can enable these through our cluster architecture and supporting technologies, like proxies and load balancers. After we have established the architecture, we take a look at user workbenches, such as Hue and Cloudera Data Science Workbench (CDSW). Finally, we look at the options for transferring files into and out of the cluster.

Access Mechanisms

Each component in the cluster provides one or more access mechanisms through which users can interact with it. These come in a few different varieties and should be pretty familiar to most practitioners. Table 11-1, at the end of this section, summarizes the access mechanisms supported by commonly used services.

Programmatic Access

Programmatic access mechanisms include the following:

APIs

Many of the components in a Hadoop cluster provide application programming interface (API) libraries to be used by user code, which abstract away much of the mechanics of using RPCs (see "Remote Procedure Calls (RPCs)" on page

107), security negotiation, and data serialization. Most services are implemented using Java, but some projects also provide API implementations in other languages or use RPC protocol libraries that support multiple language bindings.

 Some of the most common sources of error when deploying user code to clusters are API versioning and dependency conflicts. Be sure users compile applications using dependencies that match the versions found on the target cluster. If the code has to run on different versions, use a build tool to define different build profiles for the different targets.

REST

Representational State Transfer (REST) APIs (*http://bit.ly/1a1kVX5*) are a special kind of API in which the interaction with a service is conducted through stateless calls to HTTP endpoints. Unlike with JDBC, there is no persistent connection or server-side state; each call to an endpoint should provide enough context to be operated on independently. We mention them here because certain Hadoop services offer REST APIs, which can be convenient when combined with perimeter security or load balancing. Projects with commonly used REST interfaces include HDFS, Oozie, and Solr.

JDBC or ODBC

All the main SQL-on-Hadoop engines (Hive, Impala, and Presto) provide JDBC or ODBC driver implementations, which allow them to be accessed in a standards-compliant way from user code, SQL clients, and business intelligence tools. Note that some features of the JDBC or ODBC specification may not be implemented by all drivers. They should generally be treated as providing read-only functionality. Although users may associate JDBC with transactions and updates, we should remember that the SQL engines are firmly geared toward analytic queries and ETL.

Command-Line Access

For convenience, many projects provide *command-line interfaces* (CLIs), which wrap their published APIs. These are useful for ad hoc tasks and lightweight scripting. Although some of the tools ship with Windows batch scripts, all the projects with CLIs support execution via a Linux shell, and consequently, the most common way to use them is to log in to a cluster edge node via SSH.

Web UIs

Most services run at least one web interface for administrators or end users. End users commonly access the web interfaces of the YARN ResourceManager, MapReduce Job History Server, and Spark History Server. In addition, the Hue project offers a comprehensive user interface for many components in the stack, including HDFS, Hive, Impala, Oozie, and Solr. Additional user-oriented or specialized web UIs are also available, such as Jupyter Notebook (*http://jupyter.org*), Apache Zeppelin (*https://zeppelin.apache.org*), or Cloudera Data Science Workbench (*http://bit.ly/ 2Q9Bkat*) for data scientists, as shown in Table 11-1.

Table 11-1. A summary of access mechanisms

Project	Programmatic	Command line	Web UI
HDFS	Java, REST (WebHDFS/HttpFS)	`hdfs`	NameNode and DataNode
YARN	Java, REST (RM)	`yarn`	ResourceManager and NodeManager
ZooKeeper	Java/C++	`zookeeper-client`	-
HBase	Java, HBase REST/Thrift server[a]	`hbase shell`	Master and RegionServer
Hive	Thrift, JDBC, ODBC	`beeline`	HiveServer2
Oozie	Java, REST	`oozie`	Server via extension
Spark	Java/Scala/Python, JDBC (via Thrift server)	`spark-shell`, `spark-submit`, `pyspark`	History Server
Impala	JDBC, ODBC	`impala-shell`	Statestore, catalog server, daemon
Solr	Java, REST	`solrctl`	Server
Kudu	Java/C++/Python	`kudu admin utility`	Master and tablet server
Hue	Python SDK	-	Hue Server

[a] Apache Phoenix provides a JDBC interface to Apache HBase.

Access Topologies

Now that you understand a little about how you can access cluster services, let's look at where to place user-facing services and where users should access services from. For a cluster architect, there are multiple and often competing considerations at play when laying out the service endpoints on the cluster nodes—ease of use, security, isolation, performance, high availability, and flexibility.

Recall from "Cluster Configurations and Node Types" on page 97 that there are several types of nodes in a typical cluster, which run different types of service roles: master, worker, and edge. A general cluster design principal is to limit user interaction with master and worker nodes and to prefer access to services with endpoints running on edge nodes. With secure clusters, this is often enforced with network firewalls which only allow access to specific ports on edge nodes. Dual-homed edge nodes that connect isolated cluster networks to the wider corporate network are also common.

Interaction Patterns

Different users and applications need to access services on each of these node types, depending on how the service works. We can broadly define two patterns of interaction, which are illustrated in Figure 11-1:

Fan-out

In this pattern, a typical interaction would see a user application first communicate with a master or coordinator role to retrieve some sort of metadata and then communicate directly with potentially many worker roles to retrieve or modify data. For many services, such as HDFS or HBase, this interaction pattern is a central tenet of their design, providing performance, resilience, and scalability. The point is, with this pattern, the user needs access to potentially all the nodes in the cluster. In addition, the correct client configuration files for the services being accessed should be present on the node.

Single endpoint

A user interaction with the service is limited to connecting to a single physical or logical service endpoint. This endpoint may then interact with other cluster nodes on the user's behalf. For example, both Oozie and Hive use this pattern. To avoid SPOFs, this role is sometimes duplicated across different physical hosts and load-balanced. In addition, some distributed services offer *proxy* roles to act as a single type of endpoint and to avoid direct access to worker nodes (for example, HttpFS for HDFS).

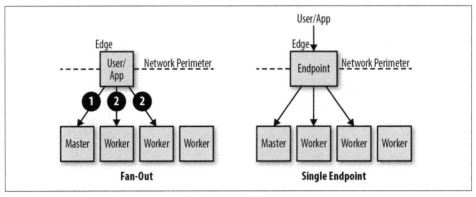

Figure 11-1. Interaction patterns for users and cluster services

In response to the two different interaction patterns, we often see two types of edge nodes being deployed in the cluster:

Configuration-only edge nodes

These edge nodes (also called *gateways*) have no cluster services running on them, but are primed by the cluster manager with the client configuration files

---

necessary for users to use the services. Since the resource demands for configuration-only edge nodes are usually light, they are often implemented as virtual machines. Users can log in to configuration-only nodes and run applications and CLI tools that use the fan-out (accessing cluster nodes) and single-endpoint patterns.

 Applications or tools running on machines outside of the cluster but with the required network access (so-called *unmanaged edge nodes*) will need to keep their configuration up to date manually.

In many cases, edge nodes host service roles with user-facing network endpoints. Examples of such services include query endpoints such as HiveServer2, orchestration services such as Oozie or Apache Airflow, user workbench tools like Hue or Apache Zeppelin, and proxy roles such as the HBase REST and Thrift gateway servers, and HttpFS. Edge nodes are also often used to run custom enterprise applications which abstract away the details of interacting with the cluster behind custom user-facing interfaces.

See Figure 11-2 for some edge node examples.

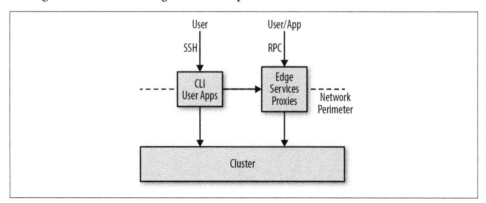

Figure 11-2. The two different edge nodes types support different usage patterns

It is often frowned upon to let users log in to edge nodes that are also hosting important edge services, such as Hive or Oozie, because this increases the risk of service outages as a result of users doing silly or malicious things. There are also security implications (see the following sections). If you can afford it, it's usually safer to confine user logins to configuration-only edge nodes.

Of course, in real clusters, different node types might be combined with other node types or might be entirely absent, for reasons of economy or efficiency. For example, in small clusters, where their resource demands are light, edge services may be colocated on master and utility nodes. User application servers often double up as configuration-only edge nodes.

Proxy Access

For security reasons, we usually don't want to expose direct network access to cluster nodes, but we still want to allow users to access certain limited functionality on those nodes. For example, users and developers often need to access the YARN Resource-Manager Web UI to monitor jobs and to access their ApplicationMaster UIs.

One option is simply to open the relevant service ports on the affected hosts within the firewall configuration. Another option is to mediate access via *proxy servers*. There are a few different types of proxy servers.

HTTP proxies

As we saw in "Access Mechanisms" on page 311, most services provide web UIs for users and administrators. There are a few commonly used proxy implementations, which either operate as *forward* or *reverse* proxies. With forward proxies, the client makes requests to remote hosts via the proxy, but is fully aware of the target host-name and port. With reverse proxies, the client accesses services using the hostname of the proxy itself and has no knowledge of how the proxy fulfills the request or where it forwards traffic to. Although reverse proxies provide the most insulation from clients, they also require a lot of work to rewrite requests and response content and therefore tend to be quite brittle.

Since the desire is usually not to hide the topology of the cluster from the client, but merely to prevent direct access, a forward proxy is usually sufficient. In addition, forward proxies can simplify the management of TLS connections because the client can verify the server certificate of the target machine. Access to the proxy can be restricted by requiring authentication credentials.

Some popular web proxy implementations are Squid, Apache HTTP Server (often just called Apache), HAProxy, and NGINX. HTTP proxies are typically placed on an edge service node in the cluster. One challenge when using web proxies in an enterprise environment is determining which proxy to use for a given URL. Usually selecting the right proxy is determined automatically via a Proxy Auto-Configuration (PAC) file; consequently, you may need to have your proxy servers added to your enterprise PAC file distribution.

SOCKS proxies

Not all traffic is HTTP—we also might wish to proxy other application-layer protocols, such as RPC exchanges. To support these use cases, we can use a SOCKS proxy (*https://en.wikipedia.org/wiki/SOCKS*). SOCKS proxies act as forward proxies but operate at a lower level than application protocols (such as HTTP) and can support both TCP and UDP connectivity.

Those clients who are authorized to log in to an edge node via SSH can set up their own SOCKS proxies via SSH tunneling. For example, using the following command sets up a SOCKS5-compliant server running on port 4567 on the user's local machine:

```
$ ssh -ND 4567 user@edge1.cluster.example.com
```

This can be annoying, though, because the SSH connection must be maintained all the while the proxy access is required. As an alternative, dedicated proxy server software can be deployed to a cluster edge node.

Service proxies

In contrast to web or SOCKS proxies, *service proxies* are more aware of the types of interaction that take place between client and server and proxy-specific service functionality. Usually, proxies like these are used when the cluster architect wants to limit user access only to the single-endpoint pattern or to provide connectivity for non-Java clients or web-based business applications. The HBase REST server and HttpFS server are examples of service proxies in so much as they expose specific APIs and act as proxies to the underlying services, without requiring the user to talk to DataNodes or RegionServers. A coordinator-only Impala daemon running on an edge node is also an example of a service proxy.

Often, multiple instances of a proxy role are run on different edge nodes for redundancy and scaling purposes. On their own, these edge services can act as a bottleneck to what, underneath, is a naturally distributed interaction pattern. Although more convenient for limiting external access, it's important to factor in the load that these endpoints are expected to support and to scale horizontally across many edge nodes, as appropriate. For example, Hue supports a wide range of interactions with cluster services via its web interface but is usually limited to about 50–100 users logged in and using it in earnest. Luckily, most proxy services are either completely stateless or store their state centrally and so can be scaled very easily. For more information about this, see Chapter 12.

Apache Knox (*https://knox.apache.org/*) is a more general-purpose service proxy for Hadoop and provides programmatic proxying for many of the Hadoop components, which themselves expose REST APIs. Knox acts as a unified REST application endpoint to these other services and provides other services, such as user mapping and security services. Applications wishing to use services proxied by Knox need to conform to the Knox APIs, but such a setup can be a nice way to expose many cluster services to business applications and can remove many of the headaches around deploying multiple endpoints that each have differing security requirements and capabilities.

The different proxy types are shown in Figure 11-3. HTTP and SOCKS proxies (left) provide access to Web UIs running on cluster nodes via edge nodes. Service proxies (right) provide a single endpoint for users and applications and implement a fan-out pattern to service roles in the cluster. You can usually load-balance them.

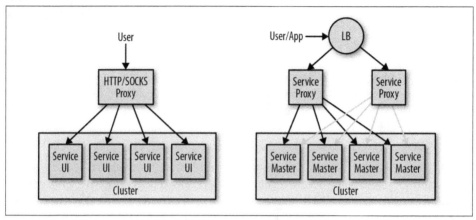

Figure 11-3. Proxy types and user-cluster interactions

Load Balancing

Load balancing is an important component in user cluster access and is closely related to the concept of proxying that we discussed in the previous section. However, load balancing generally performs a function distinct from proxying, and in fact, proxies and load balancers are commonly used together. Depending on the implementation, load balancing allows users and applications to do the following:

- Access a service via a single logical endpoint.
- Ultimately connect to an instance that is running and healthy.
- Transparently open and maintain sessions with the service.
- Connect to a node that is not overwhelmed with users.
- Automatically switch between backend service providers in the event of failure.

Because it is most often used to provide resilience, we cover load balancing in much more detail in the context of high availability in "Dedicated load balancers" on page 336. From the point of view of a user accessing a service, the presence of a load balancer should be largely transparent.

Edge Node Interactions

With an understanding of the various components that make up an access topology, we can define how they are employed by the various user-facing service components.

HDFS

Command-line tools

Users must log in to an edge node with the correct client configuration. The tools use a fan-out pattern to talk to both NameNode and DataNodes.

APIs

Applications requiring API access need to run on an edge node with access to both the NameNode and DataNodes.

Web UIs

The NameNode and DataNodes run web interfaces with details about their current state. These are rarely exposed to end users, being mostly used for administrative activities. If you have administrators who need to access these UIs from outside a network perimeter, you can run an HTTP or SOCKS proxy on an edge node.

Application proxies

HttpFS is a proxy service implementing the WebHDFS protocol, providing single-endpoint access to an HDFS cluster for users running on noncluster nodes. It typically runs on edge nodes to provide access to HDFS for users outside of the cluster.

Load balancing

HttpFS is a stateless REST service, so it can easily be scaled and made resilient using multiple instances and combined with a load balancer to retain a single logical endpoint. Note that HTTP authentication tokens resulting from SPNEGO exchanges stored in cookies by clients may mean that HttpFS instances are not entirely stateless across connections.

YARN

Command-line tools

Users must log in to an edge node with the correct client configuration. The YARN tools use a fan-out pattern to upload job resources to HDFS and a logical single-endpoint pattern to submit jobs to the YARN ResourceManager.

APIs

Applications requiring API access need to run on an edge node with access to the ResourceManager. The ResourceManager also hosts a REST API for gathering information about the cluster state.

Web UIs

The ResourceManager runs a web interface which displays details about the currently running jobs on the cluster and the state of the scheduler, and it acts as a proxy to the UIs of ApplicationMasters running on NodeManagers. Although other tools can display information about a user's jobs, it is extremely useful to have this UI exposed to end users, especially developers and operators. You can run an HTTP or SOCKS proxy on an edge node if you're using a firewall to protect cluster nodes.

MapReduce

Command-line tools

Users need to log in to an edge node which has the MapReduce client configuration and access to HDFS and the YARN ResourceManager.

Web UIs

The MapReduce History Server runs a web interface that shows historical details about MapReduce jobs that have run on the cluster. This should be accessible to users and to operators, so it should either run on an edge node or be exposed via an HTTP or SOCKS proxy on an edge node, if using a firewall. The History Server also hosts a REST API to allow programmatic retrieval of past job status.

Spark

Command-line tools

Users need to log in to an edge node which has the Spark client configuration and access to HDFS and the YARN ResourceManager.

Web UIs

The Spark History Server runs a web interface that shows historical details about Spark jobs that have run on the cluster. Job information is also accessible programmatically via REST. The History Server should be accessible to users and to operators, so should either run on an edge node or be exposed via an HTTP or SOCKS proxy on an edge node, if using a firewall to protect cluster nodes.

Hive

Command-line tools

Users can connect to HiveServer2 using `beeline`, which does not require any client configuration. The tool can run on any node with network access to HiveServer2.

APIs

JDBC and ODBC can be used from any node with network access to HiveServer2.

Web UIs

HiveServer2 hosts a web interface with details of sessions and queries. Typically, this would not be exposed to users, but it can be valuable to administrators and operators.

Application proxies

HiveServer2 acts a single endpoint to the Hive service and should run on one or more edge nodes.

Load balancing

Although it is not stateless, multiple instances of HiveServer2 can be run on different nodes and used with a load balancer (see "Hive" on page 359).

Impala

Command-line tools

The Impala shell tool can run on an edge node with access to the Impala daemons. If a load balancer or coordinator-only daemons are used, only access to these hosts is required.

APIs

JDBC and ODBC can be used from any node with network access to the Impala daemons or a load balancer or coordinator nodes.

Web UIs

Each Impala daemon, as well as the statestore and catalog server, hosts a web interface with details of sessions and queries. Typically, these would not be exposed to users, but they are valuable to administrators and operators, so a proxy may be required.

Application proxies

Impala allows certain daemons to operate in coordinator-only mode and act as proxies to the wider cluster. These can run on edge service nodes with sufficient available resources.

Load balancing

Impala can employ load balancers to provide a single logical endpoint to users outside of the cluster (see "Impala" on page 362).

HBase

Command-line tools

The HBase shell tool uses a fan-out pattern and needs to run on an edge node with client configuration and access to all cluster nodes.

APIs

Programmatic access to HBase also uses a fan-out pattern and must be performed from a node with the correct client configuration and access to cluster nodes.

Web UIs

The Master and RegionServers each run web interfaces which are of most value to administrators and operators. Developers can also sometimes require access, so setting up an edge-node proxy can be useful.

Application proxies

HBase provides two single-endpoint proxies—the REST and Thrift servers—which should run on edge nodes.

Load balancing

The REST and Thrift servers are stateless, so they can be scaled and placed behind a load balancer for resilience and scaling. Note that HTTP authentication tokens resulting from SPNEGO exchanges stored in cookies by clients may mean that REST instances are not entirely stateless across connections.

Solr

Command-line tools

The Solr control utility uses a fan-out pattern and needs to run on an edge node with client configuration and access to all cluster nodes.

APIs

Solr uses a REST API and can query any server in the SolrCloud deployment. Applications, therefore, need to run on edge nodes with cluster access.

Web UIs

The Solr servers each run a web interface, which is of most value to administrators and operators. Developers can also sometimes require access, so setting up an edge-node proxy can be useful.

Load balancing

Solr servers can be placed behind a load balancer to provide a single logical query endpoint to users outside of the cluster.

Oozie

Command-line tools

The Oozie CLI does not require client configuration and can be run from any node with network access to an Oozie server. Because Oozie job definitions must be on HDFS, typically HDFS access is also required.

APIs

Oozie servers expose a REST API. Similar to the CLI (which itself uses the REST API), network access to an Oozie server is the only requirement. Oozie is typically used by developers who can log in to an edge node, so it's not an absolute requirement to run it on service edge nodes, although that is common.

Load balancing

Oozie servers are stateless, storing persistent information in a database, so they can naturally be placed behind a load balancer, after which users only require access to the load-balancer host. For more details, see "Oozie" on page 371.

Kudu

Command-line tools

Although Kudu ships with a command-line tool, it is generally only of use to administrators.

APIs

Kudu interactions use the fan-out pattern, so programmatic access needs to be from an edge node with access to both masters and tablet servers.

Access Security

We covered the various possible authentication mechanisms, such as Kerberos, LDAP, and impersonation, in "Authentication" on page 242, along with confidentiality and privacy controls, such as SASL and TLS, in "In-Flight Encryption" on page 237. As a reference, the security options for some typical edge services are listed in Table 11-2.

Table 11-2. Authentication and confidentiality configuration for edge-node services and typical proxied web UIs

Project	Edge component	Authentication	Impersonation	Confidentiality
HDFS	HttpFS	Kerberos via SPNEGO, short-lived signed cookies	Yes	TLS
HDFS	Web UIs	Kerberos via SPNEGO	No	TLS
YARN	Web UIs	Kerberos via SPNEGO	No	TLS
MapReduce	Web UI	Kerberos via SPNEGO	No	TLS
Spark	Web UI	Configurable via `javax.servlet` filters	No	TLS
Impala	Web UI	Username/password access	No	TLS
Hive	HiveServer2	Kerberos (GSSAPI), LDAP, delegation tokens	Configurable	SASL QoP, TLS
HBase	REST server, Thrift gateway	Kerberos (SPNEGO and GSSAPI)	Yes	TLS
HBase	Web UIs	Kerberos via SPNEGO	No	TLS
Solr	Web UIs	Kerberos via SPNEGO	No	TLS
Kudu	Web UIs	None	No	TLS
Oozie	Oozie server	Kerberos (SPNEGO), signed token	Yes	TLS
Hue	Hue server	Kerberos (SPNEGO), LDAP, SAML, internal DB, signed cookies	Yes	TLS

SSH access to nodes running edge services should be heavily restricted to prevent accidental or malicious interference with the service daemons running on the nodes. In addition, if an edge service is designated as an authorized proxy service, able to perform impersonation, it is critical that its keytab file is protected from outside access because it potentially unlocks a lot of functionality.

If HTTP proxies are used, these can be secured independently via HTTP security mechanisms.

Administration Gateways

Depending on how you decide to architect the network and security layers for your clusters and which auditing policies are in place, you may need one or more edge nodes to act as *administration gateways*. These nodes are typically used to mediate SSH access to nodes within the cluster; administrators who want to log in to internal cluster nodes must first pass through one of those hosts.

Admin gateways are sometimes implemented as *jump servers* (*http://bit.ly/2OT7AKp*) or *bastion hosts* (*http://bit.ly/2S2FH4v*), which are hardened boxes allowed to run only a restricted set of services. Jump servers typically enable SSH forwarding to allow administrators to log in to cluster nodes from their own machines. Bastion hosts might restrict access even further by forcing the administrator to use special software that audits and records all privileged access to cluster nodes.

Such setups are usually reserved only for the most secure of cluster deployments—much of the time, an on-premises enterprise network is considered a trusted zone, and policies dictate that hosts and services implement their own adequate security arrangements for authentication, authorization, and network confidentiality. In many enterprises, administrative login to the boxes is very often protected by centralized privileged account management (PAM) software.

Workbenches

This section explores a few of the workbench tools that are available to facilitate user interaction with cluster services.

Hue

Hue is a popular web-based UI for general Hadoop users. Among other things, it allows users to interact with HDFS through its file browser, execute interactive SQL queries against Impala and Hive, construct and execute Oozie workflows, and build search dashboards over Solr indexes. Hue is often the sole interface that users have for interacting with services and data on the cluster, so it's important we ensure the experience is a good one. Users log in to the Hue web interface using one of the supported authentication mechanisms and then interact with cluster services using Hue's UI applications.

Figure 11-4 shows how, in a secure cluster, Hue servers use impersonation when interacting with cluster services. The Hue server itself maintains a Kerberos ticket cache as a principal that has been granted proxy user privileges in each of the target services. When a user logs in and is authenticated, Hue interacts with other services on behalf of that user, using impersonation as described in "Impersonation" on page 249. After verifying that Hue's principal is authorized to impersonate the user from the Hue server host, the services then apply their own authorization processes to determine whether the user is authorized to perform the requested operation.

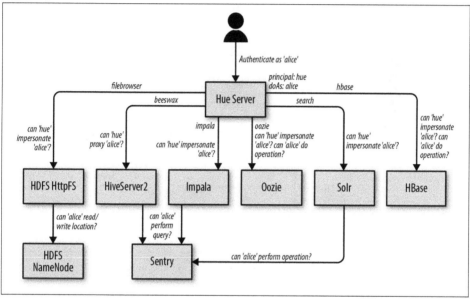

Figure 11-4. Hue's use of impersonation with Hadoop services

For resilience and performance, Hue servers can be run on multiple edge nodes with a load balancer.

Notebooks

Hadoop clusters are increasingly used by data scientists for exploratory analysis and model generation. These users typically want the ability to do such things as launching Spark jobs and retrieving data from the cluster and operating on it in a local Python or R context. Web-based applications such as JupyterHub, Apache Zeppelin, and CDSW aim to support such users by providing a development environment in a notebook suitable for programmatic interaction with the cluster.

The applications typically live on dedicated edge nodes. In order to provide sufficient computational resources for each user and to ensure security isolation, the best practice is to run each user's session in an isolated container. For example, CDSW uses Docker containers and Kubernetes to spin up sessions on one or more dedicated edge nodes. To support many users, multiple edge nodes can be added to the Kubernetes cluster (see Figure 11-5). Master and worker nodes can run isolated containers within a Kubernetes cluster. Each container runs with its own Kerberos security context, and users can run different engines to interact with cluster services and launch computations.

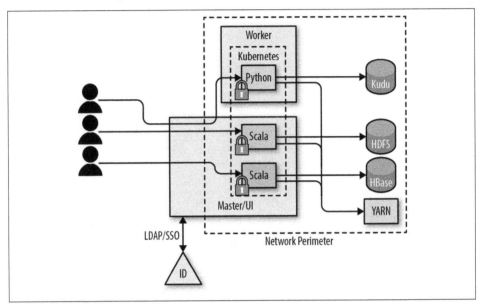

Figure 11-5. Example of CDSW access topology

Notebook applications typically support one or more enterprise authentication methods for their users such as LDAP or SAML. Once authenticated to the notebook application, users start a session (for example, a Jupyter kernel or a CDSW engine) and then must somehow authenticate themselves to the cluster. In CDSW, each container has its own strictly controlled Kerberos security context, ensuring strict isolation between users. A ticket-granting ticket (TGT) is automatically obtained and maintained for the container, using user-supplied credentials or a keytab.

Landing Zones

The term *landing zone* describes storage space, accessible from edge nodes, which exists to exchange data between HDFS and other systems. Very often, enterprise integration systems move batch data around via secure FTP, and because HDFS has no native Secure FTP (SFTP) server interface, the data needs to be placed in an intermediate location before being uploaded to HDFS. Landing zones can reside on local disks on the edge nodes, on shared network filesystems (NFSs), or on storage area networks (SANs).

After the data is in the landing zone, there are several options for loading it into HDFS or other services:

CLI

The simplest method is simply to use the `hdfs` command-line tool to upload the file into HDFS. This is best suited for ad hoc data transfers. General users can also use the File Browser app in Hue to upload files to HDFS.

NFS gateway

The HDFS NFS gateway presents a POSIX-like filesystem interface which can be mounted in Linux. Files in the landing zone can be written to and read from HDFS by copying them to the NFS gateway mount point. One drawback of the NFS gateway is that it does not enforce Kerberos security on the Linux side, effectively opening up HDFS to general access. This can make it unsuitable for use in many secure clusters, unless the access to the edge nodes with NFS gateway roles is restricted. In addition, it is not suitable for large-scale concurrent transfers. As a result, it's best to avoid this option.

WebHDFS

HDFS implements a REST API for reading and writing data. Clients interact with the HDFS NameNode or the HttpFS server, each of which implement the same WebHDFS API. The NameNode redirects the client to the WebHDFS interface on a DataNode to perform actual data transfer. WebHDFS can be used to transfer files from any remote location, provided the client has Kerberos authentication. Using HttpFS as the provider of WebHDFS functionality is preferred because it can run at the edge of the cluster.

Flume

For record-oriented data, a Flume agent running on the edge node can watch a given directory using the *spooling directory source*. This reads the source file record by record and transfers the records to a Flume sink. Because it has to parse the file record by record, this approach is usually much slower than a direct transfer, but it has the advantage that small files can be eliminated by Flume's HDFS sink.

 Although not accessed directly by end users, it should be noted that streaming ingestion services, such as Flume and Kafka, are also typically hosted on dedicated nodes that are often edge nodes of the cluster.

With landing zones, one challenge is to detect new files that have arrived to be uploaded and to subsequently transfer them to HDFS in a reliable way. We touched on one option when we mentioned Flume's spooling directory source, which very carefully tracks the state of files to be ingested. Another approach within the Hadoop ecosystem is to use a periodic Oozie workflow with a remote SSH action that logs into the edge node and uses one of the previously mentioned methods to transfer the files. We don't really recommend this, because it requires storing SSH login credentials within the workflow.

In practice, it's much better to use one of the dedicated ingestion frameworks, such as Apache NiFi or StreamSets, which have a number of built-in operators to transfer the data to the cluster in a reliable way.

We strongly recommend using an integration framework such as Apache NiFi or StreamSets, because they support a wide range of reliable ingestion and enterprise integration patterns.

Summary

Understanding the options for granting users and applications access to the cluster is a critical piece in putting together a solid cluster architecture that will satisfy those users' demands and requirements. In this chapter, we covered the many ways in which a user or application may interact with the cluster, and we outlined the choices you have as an architect for technologies that support each type of interaction.

A general rule is that end users should never get direct access to cluster services but should instead be granted mediated access through external tools, proxies, or user interfaces, such as Hue. For application developers (or power users) who need a distributed access pattern for performance, wider access can and should be granted, but with restrictions on where the application can run and who has access to the machines on which it is running.

In the pursuit of protecting your critical services on production clusters, we generally recommend, if you can afford it, preventing end users from logging in to the same machines as running cluster edge services. In smaller clusters, the master nodes can often double up as edge nodes. Often, configuration-only nodes are implemented as smaller virtual machines.

We finished off the chapter by looking at user-facing interfaces, such as Hue and data science notebooks, and how they interact with the rest of the cluster. Finally, we looked at how users can get files into and out of the cluster and briefly explored the options for landing zones. The best results for these scenarios are likely to come from the use of a dedicated tool for automated file ingest.

## CHAPTER 12

High Availability

A key part of the enterprise architecture of critical services is planning for failure at all levels of the stack. The assumption of this chapter is that users and operators both want services to be as available as possible. But how do we achieve that? What happens if a server hosting some critical service goes down? What if an entire rack with several cluster machines loses power? What about a power distribution unit serving several racks? What if there are transient problems that degrade node performance? Having a plan to handle such scenarios—and regularly testing that plan—is of paramount importance.

The good news is that most of the components in a Hadoop cluster are built from the ground up with failure in mind and have built-in mechanisms for dealing with failure of individual components. In fact, the central design principle behind Hadoop is to build a reliable system from individually unreliable components.

If architected correctly, a single Hadoop cluster will prove incredibly resilient to failure. In this chapter, we cover how core Hadoop services and other projects in the ecosystem can be set up for high availability (HA) within a single cluster. We focus only on the higher-level concepts in this chapter; some of the lower-level aspects related to physical infrastructure, such as dual-power supplies and redundant cabling, are covered in "Basic Datacenter Concepts" on page 160. In Chapter 13 we discuss some of the aspects of backup and replication between clusters running in different datacenters.

We begin this chapter with some definitions of HA concepts and then follow them with some of the critical building blocks of an HA architecture. With these in place, we then move on to discussing how to configure individual services for HA.

High Availability Defined

The phrase *high availability* is hugely overloaded and represents a very broad topic. Indeed, entire textbooks have been written on the subject. For the most part, when we talk about HA, we are seeking to avoid single points of failure (SPOFs) in our architectures. In large part, SPOFs have been eliminated in Hadoop deployments. But before we look at how the various projects have achieved this, let's enumerate some of the dimensions of HA that we should consider when designing our architectures.

Lateral/Service HA

The most obvious aspect we think of when considering HA is that when taken individually, the services themselves need to be configured and deployed across multiple nodes to be resilient to failure of their individual components. We need to understand how to achieve that for each service we deploy and—if that turns out to be impossible—how to minimize impact and downtime for the service.

Some services—for example, stateless web services—can support HA by simply adding more instances. Others, which need to provide strong write consistency and ordering guarantees, use an *active-passive* architecture in which only a single server accepts writes. In the latter case, when the active server fails, we need to initiate a *failover* and promote the passive server to active status. Many services provide a way to do this, and the failover can happen in a matter of seconds. Other services, however, require manual intervention. For manual intervention, the outage is more likely measured in minutes.

Vertical/Systemic HA

When thinking about HA, we need to recognize that it is required at all levels of our architectures. It is no good to make use of a highly available and resilient storage layer, such as HDFS, if we host our critical business application on a single server. Likewise, we have not achieved full HA if we deploy some of our services in HA mode but do not, in turn, configure services they depend on to be resilient and available. The most obvious example of a service dependency is a relational database.

With HA, we need to consider the whole platform, top to bottom, and we must ensure that each and every layer in the cluster is architected and configured to be resistant to individual component failure. Although we only cover the cluster services in this chapter, it is also important to deploy your applications that use these services for HA.

Measuring Availability

When designing our HA architectures, we need a way of expressing how available our service needs to be and measuring how available it is in reality. A *service-level agreement* (SLA) is an agreement between a service provider and a client about the delivery of a service and defines one or more *service-level objectives* (SLOs). SLOs are measurable objectives and can be expressed in a number of ways.

Percentages

The simplest way of defining an availability requirement is to express it as a percentage value. Over a given time period, the percentage defines the maximum allowed downtime for a service. A common way of expressing this is to state it as a number of nines, which translates into a percentage availability requirement. For example, one nine would mean 90% availability, three nines 99.9%, and five nines 99.999%. Over the course of a 30-day month, these three examples represent a maximum downtime of 259,200 seconds (3 days), 2,592 seconds (43 minutes, 12 seconds), and 25.92 seconds, respectively. The more nines there are in the requirement, the more available a service needs to be.

Percentiles

Although a percentage defines in absolute terms the availability of the service, it is abstracted away from the delivery of a useful service to the client and from the experience the client has of the service. A service might technically be up but could be responding very slowly. Thus, another common way to define an SLO is as the proportion of operations that are completed within a certain time.

For example, we could define that we want 95% of HBase lookups to complete within 50 milliseconds. This is known as a *percentile measure*. Percentile metrics can also be used as a measure of overall service health; for example, measuring the time the 99th percentile of YARN containers spend in the *NEW* state.

Operating for HA

Apart from getting the architecture right in the first place, which we cover in detail in this chapter, there are two other essential components to achieving high availability in practice.

Monitoring

Although most services can be configured to survive individual component failures, there is always a risk of total system failure. Any production Hadoop cluster should be closely monitored for health and performance. Organizations running production infrastructure usually have enterprise monitoring and alerting solutions, and Hadoop services should be integrated with these.

Enterprise-grade cluster managers, such as Cloudera Manager, provide monitoring and alerting features and can also integrate with other solutions through standard mechanisms, such as email and Simple Network Management Protocol (SNMP) traps.

Playbooks and Postmortems

Monitoring and alerting is all well and good, but knowing what to do in the event of failure is essential. Thorough familiarity with the services, how they are managed, and how to diagnose the causes of failure is something all production Hadoop operators need.

Each organization should define detailed playbooks for support personnel to follow in the event of failure, and failure scenarios should be regularly simulated and tested, ideally in real production environments. These playbooks should be clear and detailed enough to be followed by support personnel, even at 1 a.m.

In addition to preparing beforehand, you should conduct in-depth, no-blame post-mortems after each significant failure event to identify how to prevent similar situations in the future, how the architecture could be improved, and how to more quickly solve the problem.

A great way to find holes in your HA architecture or operations procedures is to start introducing failures on purpose.[1]

HA Building Blocks

Some foundational building blocks come up over and over again when building HA architectures out of distributed systems, and it is worth spending a little time to explore these. In the following sections, we cover quorums, load balancing, and database HA.

Quorums

During our excursion through HA, we often encounter the concept of a *quorum*. When dealing with distributed systems, a common problem is how to ensure that processes running on different machines agree on the value of something—and the

---

1 Netflix's Chaos Monkey is a notable example; see "The Netflix Simian Army" on their Technology Blog (*http://bit.ly/2yukZU8*), medium.com.

order of value changes—in the presence of faults and failures. This is the problem of *distributed consensus.*

For example, in HDFS, many hundreds of processes may want to add, move, delete, and change the permissions of filesystem objects essentially simultaneously. We need the ordering of these changes, which are often being applied to the same objects, to be well defined. As we will see, when configured for HA, HDFS uses a quorum to ensure that, once accepted, the ordering of filesystem changes remains fixed, even when a NameNode fails.

A lot has been written about how this can be achieved—you may have heard of algorithms such as Paxos (*http://bit.ly/1X2NFew*), Raft (*https://raft.github.io/*), and Zoo-Keeper's very own Zab (*http://bit.ly/2KoLoHg*). We do not go into detail about how these algorithms work, but the enterprise architect should be familiar with the basic concept.

 If you are interested in this topic, we highly recommend Chapter 9, "Consistency and Consensus", from Martin Kleppmann's *Designing Data-Intensive Applications* (O'Reilly).

In brief, to achieve consensus in distributed systems, we need a majority of machines in a quorum to agree on a value for a parameter before it becomes persistent. To be *consistent*, the majority need to agree on a strict sequence of value updates and to serve up the values to readers in the order in which they are written. Each change in the parameter sequence may result from many overlapping requests by distinct clients running from different machines—the quorum has to make sense of this, using one of the aforementioned consensus algorithms. Some machines outside of the majority may be eventually consistent but still apply the changes in the agreed order, even if they serve stale values for a short time.

The concept of a *quorum majority* is common to all these algorithms. What this boils down to, in practice, is that a quorum should consist of an odd number of machines and that the maximum number of node failures in a quorum of *n* nodes for it to remain operational is floor((n - 1) / 2). Although quorums can have even numbers, this does not increase the resiliency. For example, quorums of five and six nodes can both tolerate only two node failures while maintaining a majority (three out of five, or four out of six).

In Hadoop, achieving consensus between master services is key to enabling consistent writes and reads of metadata. Quorums are critical to services such as Zoo-Keeper, HDFS, and Kudu, and by extension, HBase and Solr. As we will see, other services also count on ZooKeeper and its reliable consensus for distributed locking and configuration storage.

Load Balancing

A key requirement in any HA setup is the ability to seamlessly and automatically switch between instances of a service running on different nodes. This is especially important for services which have no built-in mechanism for providing HA or automatic failover. For the purposes of HA, we employ load balancing to:

- Connect to an instance that is running and healthy.
- Connect to a node that is not overwhelmed with users.
- Automatically switch between backend service providers in the event of failure.

Load-balancing implementations act as a proxy in front of a service and—depending on the implementation and usage—address one or more of the noted requirements. In the following sections, we cover three implementations of load balancing: DNS round robin, virtual IPs, and dedicated load balancers.

DNS round robin

The easiest form of load balancing to achieve is DNS round robin. When clients connect to a network service, they first look up the IP address from the DNS server using the service hostname. DNS servers can be configured to cycle through or return a random entry from a list of configured IP addresses. The process is illustrated in Figure 12-1, where clients query the DNS server for a service alias (`svc-lb.example.com`) (1), the server responsds with one of the list of configured IPs (2), and the client contacts the supplied IP (3). Each instance of the service also has its own canonical hostname in DNS apart from the alias.

Although it is simple to configure, DNS round robin has a number of drawbacks. First, the servers listed for a hostname are not typically monitored for health status (though some implementations can detect so-called *lame* servers). DNS lookups are usually cached for some amount of time on the client side and, if the instance at the resolved IP has crashed, the client will continue to fail to connect until the cache expires and a new address is returned. Caching can also occur in other peer DNS servers. DNS round robin also does not actively take into account the current load on a particular host in the list.

Because a secure client attempts to verify network identity through both forward and reverse DNS lookups, Kerberos authentication can be problematic when the canonical reverse lookup does not resolve to the alias name, as is typical for round-robin aliases (see "Kerberos" on page 242). As a result, for production-grade HA solutions, DNS round robin is not usually recommended.

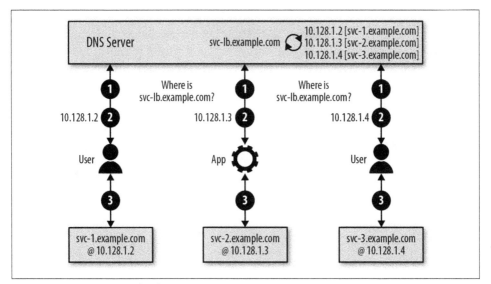

Figure 12-1. DNS round robin

 A closely related concept is DNS aliasing using Canonical Name (CNAME) records. Instead of referring to a list of IPs, a CNAME record refers to another DNS hostname entry. Updating the alias can be used to effect manual failover, but beware of caching of the old entry in clients and on peer DNS servers.

Virtual IP

A *virtual IP* (VIP) or *floating IP* is an IP address that is shared by two or more servers. In the sharing group, only one claims the IP at a time; thus, the servers operate in a sort of active-passive mode. If the live server fails, one of the other servers claims the IP.

In order for this to work properly, there needs to be way of ensuring that only one server uses the IP at any given time and a way to decide which server that should be. To do this, we require a quorum decision. For floating IPs, this is most commonly provided by Linux *clustering* software. Clustering allows two or more servers to constantly monitor each other's health and to enact automatic service migration under failure. Common software packages that work together to provide this functionality in Linux systems include Keepalived (*http://www.keepalived.org/*), Heartbeat (*http://www.linux-ha.org/wiki/Heartbeat*), Pacemaker (*http://clusterlabs.org/pacemaker/*), and Corosync (*http://corosync.github.io/corosync/*).

Figure 12-2 shows a basic setup. A DNS entry for a single hostname points to an individual IP, the virtual IP. Clustering software using a separate network interface constantly monitors the health of the nodes in the cluster. Initially, the clustering software has decided that *S1* should listen with the floating IP. When that node (or the service on the node) fails, the cluster migrates the IP, and thus client traffic, to another node (*S2*).

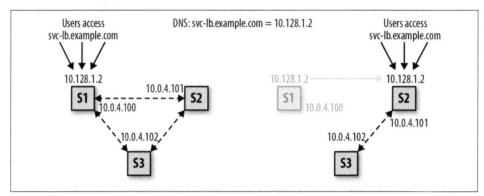

Figure 12-2. A Linux cluster using virtual IPs

A virtual IP provided by clustering technology is a commonly used mechanism for providing failover. It has the disadvantage that it is yet another complex piece of software to configure, manage, and monitor, and it can be tough to master for an operator not already familiar with the technology. Virtual IPs can be combined with software load balancing, as described in the following section.

Dedicated load balancers

A dedicated load balancer is software or hardware that acts as a proxy, accepts incoming network requests on a port, and forwards them to one of a configured *pool* of endpoints for that port.

A software load balancer implements this functionality in—unsurprisingly—software and runs on a standard server. Commonly used projects for software load balancing are HAProxy (*http://www.haproxy.org/*), NGINX (*https://www.nginx.com/*), and Apache httpd (*https://httpd.apache.org/*).

A hardware load balancer is a dedicated network device that can typically support many more concurrent sessions than a software load balancer. It also usually provides much more functionality than a software load balancer, including security and access enforcement and traffic control. Examples of hardware load balancers are BIG-IP (*https://f5.com/products/big-ip*) from F5 and Citrix ADC (*http://bit.ly/2SkrMXI*) (formerly NetScaler). Load balancers tend to be managed by network administrators rather than system administrators.

Unlike DNS round robin, load balancers route traffic in an intelligent way. They routinely monitor the health of the members of the pool and exclude those that are not responding. Typical methods of monitoring include TCP open or HTTP requests. They can also actively attempt to balance the traffic across the pool and typically provide the ability to monitor flows (TCP sessions and HTTP sessions).

You have probably noticed that by employing a single load balancer, we have simply pushed the SPOF to a higher level. To avoid this, multiple load balancers are often deployed and clustered together with a single floating IP. For software load balancers, you have to implement this yourself using one of the Linux clustering techniques we mentioned. But for hardware load balancers, this is usually one of the supported deployments and managed by the network team.

A single load balancer on its own is not enough to avoid a SPOF—you must ensure that the load balancer is also highly available.

Session persistence.   In certain scenarios, it is important for a user to be directed to the same backend server for repeated connections. As an example, for performance, each Hue server maintains a local Thrift connection pool for Impala and Hive. Hue may use a different connection from the pool each time it makes an RPC call to Impala or Hive; for example, for query submission, tracking query progress, and fetching query results. For this to work, Hue must communicate with the same Impala server each time. Other services, such as HiveServer2, also maintain local sessions that can span TCP connections. Redirecting a client to the same backend server across different connections is referred to as *session persistence*.

For HTTP traffic, load balancers are often able to inspect packets for session cookies, which can be used to route the client to the same server for the same login session.

For protocols that the balancer is not aware of (for example, a HiveServer2 Thrift session), the balancer can fall back to establishing session persistence at the transport layer (TCP) by inspecting the source IP of packets and routing the same client to the same server. This is known as *source-IP session persistence*.

Obviously, in either case, if the preferred backend server is unhealthy, the balancer routes to an alternative endpoint and opens a new persistent session.

This ability to always connect a client with the same server is sometimes called *sticky sessions*, or alternatively *simple persistence*. We use the term *session persistence* because that is more common.

The three options for persistence are shown in Figure 12-3. In each scenario, three different clients connect to a service S with three backend servers in the pool (S_1–S_3).

Clients *a* and *b* are connecting from the same server, while *c* connects from a different server. Clients *b* and *c* both make a single connection to *S*, and client *a* makes two separate connections.

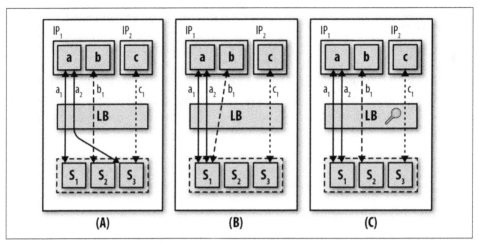

Figure 12-3. Persistent or sticky sessions

In Scenario A, the load balancer is not configured for any session persistence. Each new TCP session is routed to any one of the configured endpoints using the standard balancing algorithm, taking into account server health and current load.

In Scenario B, the balancer applies source IP session persistence at the TCP layer, setting up persistence between the source IP and destination server. Different TCP connections from the same IP (here, a_1, a_2, and b_1 from IP_1) will be directed to the same destination server.

In Scenario C, we imagine *S* is an HTTP server and the balancer is configured to persist sessions based on HTTP session identifiers and to look inside the packets for a cookie pattern. Upon first connection, where no cookie is set, the connection is routed to any of the destination servers. The load balancer checks the response for a cookie, and a session is persisted. Subsequent connections with the cookie set are routed to the same destination server. In this example, two separate services on IP_1 are directed persistently, but this time to two different destination servers.

Obviously, session persistence can result in suboptimal balancing of actual load in some scenarios. Consider the case in which you have a single application server that is used by hundreds of users and that accesses cluster services through a load balancer with source IP persistence. All connections from the application server will be directed to the same backend server, switching only if that server fails. For those applications that must use persistent load balancers (for example, Hue when it uses Hive and

Impala), multiple application servers (each with a different source IP) are recommended to spread the load on the backend service.

Hardware versus software. Your choice of hardware or software load balancers depends on your environment and desire for control. Since hardware load balancers are administered by network administrators, there is typically a greater turnaround time for changes, and so you may feel that you have more control over software-based solutions. Moreover, the devices are not guaranteed to have network locality to the Hadoop cluster and services. One thing to watch out for is *tromboning* of requests —a request for a local cluster service might be made from a cluster or edge node and then disappear off into the core network to the load balancer, potentially several hops away, only to be routed back to the cluster.

On the other hand, deploying a software balancer requires you to architect it for HA with clustering and to ensure proper performance. It is yet another system to worry about in an already complicated stack. A hardware load balancer will (or at least should) be properly configured and monitored by network experts.

> Your enterprise probably already has standards for using hardware or software load balancers. Use these services, if they're available.

Security considerations

When using cluster services configured for Kerberos security and on-wire SSL encryption, there are some things to be aware of around load balancing:

Kerberos

Suppose that we have a Kerberos-protected service svc in the EXAMPLE.COM realm that has instances running on the following nodes: svc-1.example.com and svc-2.example.com (see "Kerberos" on page 242 for a reminder about Kerberos). We want to balance across both instances of svc, so we set up a load balancer behind an IP that resolves to the fully qualified domain name svc-lb.example.com. We ensure that each instance has an entry for the load balancer in its keytab. For svc-2.example.com, this is:

```
svc/svc-2.example.com@EXAMPLE.COM
svc/svc-lb.example.com@EXAMPLE.COM
```

A client accessing the svc service first obtains a service ticket for svc/svc-lb.example.com@EXAMPLE.COM. The Kerberos client library double-checks that the hostname-IP pairs agree when doing forward and reverse DNS lookups against svc-lb.example.com. It then initiates a connection with the svc service via svc-lb.example.com and presents the service ticket as part of the request. The load balancer passes the request through to one of the servers, say svc-2.example.com, unchanged (including the service ticket). The server on svc-2.example.com then validates the service ticket using the svc/svc-lb.example.com@EXAMPLE.COM ticket it obtained using the principal in its keytab file.

To take a more concrete example, when configured for HA, an Oozie server running on gateway-svc-1.example.com with a load balancer at oozie-lb.example.com would need entries for the following principals in its keytab:

```
HTTP/gateway-svc-1.example.com@EXAMPLE.COM
HTTP/oozie-lb.example.com@EXAMPLE.COM
oozie/gateway-svc-1.example.com@EXAMPLE.COM
```

Because the server can still be accessed directly, it needs an entry for each hostname. A client accessing the Oozie server obtains a service ticket for HTTP/oozie-lb.example.com@EXAMPLE.COM and is transparently routed through the load balancer to gateway-svc-1.example.com. The Oozie server is able to validate the service ticket because it has an entry for HTTP/oozie-lb.example.com@EXAMPLE.COM in its keytab.

TLS

A similar concept holds for TLS certificates. Clients performing certificate validation check whether the hostname they are using is in the server TLS certificate (see "TLS Encryption" on page 238). If the load balancer passes TCP connections through unmodified, we should ensure that both the hostname of the server running the service and the hostname of the load balancer are also included in the subject alternative name (SAN) field.

In our Oozie example, this means having both gateway-svc-1.example.com and oozie-lb.example.com in the SAN field.

Some load balancers are TLS-aware and can run in TLS *passthrough* or TLS *termination* modes. In the passthrough mode, the load balancer simply passes on the packet to the server unchanged. With termination, the load balancer acts as the TLS endpoint for the client, decrypts the data, and transparently opens up a new TCP connection (again protected by TLS) to the destination server, relaying the original packet contents.

With Hadoop it is more common to use passthrough mode, since this emulates connections without a load balancer most closely, but this does require the addition of SAN entries to all server certificates being used by services behind the balancer.

TLS termination is a nice option because the alternative name need only be in the balancer's certificate. However, hardware load balancers are usually administered by a different team within the enterprise, which can sometimes make organizing proper TLS termination more difficult.

Database HA

A number of services in the Hadoop ecosystem rely on relational database storage for configuration and metadata (i.e., the Hive Metastore, Oozie, Hue, and more). As described in "Vertical/Systemic HA" on page 330, no setup is truly HA unless all the components on which the service is dependent are also HA, including relational databases. This is important to note, since some of the ecosystem components will default to using local databases, such as SQLite or Derby. All services should be configured to use an enterprise-grade database.

Achieving HA for databases is a broad and detailed topic, covering aspects such as shared storage versus shared-nothing architectures, index sharding, and distributed transactions, and we cannot do it justice in a short section here. Highly available database architectures tend to be different for each vendor. For more in-depth coverage, see texts such as *MySQL High Availability* by Charles Bell, Mats Kindahl, and Lars Thalmann (O'Reilly); *Oracle Essentials* by Rick Greenwald, Robert Stackowiak, and Jonathan Stern (O'Reilly); and the PostgreSQL documentation (*http://bit.ly/2FBaDY4*).

The next few sections give a high-level overview of some of the concepts involved in database HA.

Clustering

Clustering software provides management and configuration for HA and distributed database deployments. Databases are organized into *clusters*, in which each database node is aware of the others and atomicity, consistency, isolation, and durability (ACID) compliance is maintained for reads and writes either via single master/hot standby or multimaster operation via sharding or distributed transactions. Examples of clustered databases are Oracle RAC (*http://bit.ly/2Bo8dYU*), MySQL Cluster (*http://bit.ly/2OV7GBh*), and Galera Cluster (*http://galeracluster.com/*).

We recommend using production-grade clustering software since it manages all the aspects of HA natively and is one fewer headache for the operator of the Hadoop cluster, but be sure it is supported by your Hadoop platform vendor.

 Although their use is recommended in principle, some features of clustered databases may not be supported by some services. You should verify compatibility with both the cluster management software and the components you plan to deploy.

Replication

With replication, a single active instance accepts transactions from clients and ships these to passive instances, which apply them asynchronously. Typically, this is achieved via either statement replication or log shipping/streaming. Statement replication simply applies the same logical SQL statement on all nodes, whereas log shipping is more granular.

Databases maintain a write-ahead log of transactions on disk—any operation is durably written to disk before the actual data structures and indexes are modified. A single master database accepts transactions from clients, writes them to the log, and then applies them to its data structures. Simultaneously, log entries can be shipped to peer servers. The logs can either be shipped row by row (log streaming), or in larger segments or chunks (log shipping). For keeping the passive instances in sync, the recommended approach is to use log streaming.

Passive instances can be configured for *hot* or *warm* standby. In hot standby mode, the passive databases can be configured to serve reads and are continuously applying the logs. These reads should be considered potentially out of date, or stale. If the active server dies, then some sort of trigger is used to bring one of the passive instances to active status and it immediately starts serving writes.

In warm standby, the passive servers do not serve read requests and, when told to become active, must apply any transactions in the shipped logs that have not yet been applied. Only then can they serve writes.

Standby setups can often be used with load balancers, so that clients talk to a single endpoint. The load balancer should be set up to always direct connections to the active server. Upon active server failure, the standby is brought up and the load balancer endpoint is switched across.

Such a setup is illustrated in Figure 12-4. On the left, we have the initial state: connections from database clients are routed via load balancing to the active server, which replicates the log to the standby node. When the active server fails, the standby is promoted to active status and the load balancing is switched across. Finally, when the failed node is brought back online, the replication is established in reverse to restore an active-standby setup.

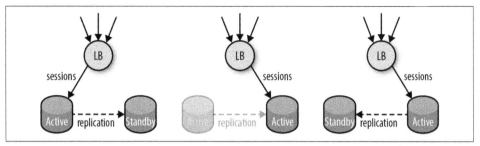

Figure 12-4. Active-standby database replication and failover

 For this to work smoothly, the operational instructions need to be very tightly defined and the failure scenarios should be gamed out and well documented. Even then, it is likely that cluster services using the database will need to be restarted after the switch.

Supported databases

Setting up databases for HA is usually undertaken by enterprise DBAs, and if possible, we recommend that you make use of them for production Hadoop clusters. There are some caveats, though. First, services in the Hadoop ecosystem generally only support one or more versions of MySQL/MariaDB, PostgreSQL, and Oracle. Of these options, MySQL and PostgreSQL are the most widely deployed.

Also note that most Hadoop services have not been designed to cope well with load-balanced master–master databases in which queries might be directed to more than one backend database transparently. Almost all services will automatically reconnect to a backup database in the event of a connection loss, though, so it is usually sufficient to have the database load balancer or DNS entry flip only in the event of primary database server failure.

 It is essential that you test your database HA architecture for failure and failover scenarios to establish how each dependent service reacts to your setup.

Ancillary Services

The following services are typically provided by the IT organization in an enterprise setting, but it is worth knowing about them and how to configure a server to use them in a reliable way.

Essentials

There are some essential services that are required for a Hadoop cluster to function properly. The most basic of these are the Network Time Protocol (*http://bit.ly/2QBUFh2*) and Domain Name System (*http://bit.ly/2OWG9PR*):

NTP
> From an HA perspective, each server should be configured with at least two possible NTP synchronization sources. Often, network switches can act as NTP servers. In such cases, it is common to specify the TOR switch pair as NTP sources, which, in turn, synchronize to their aggregation switches, and so on.

DNS
> For reliable lookups, each server's DNS resolver (usually configured in */etc/resolv.conf*) should be configured with multiple servers. DNS can also be used to facilitate discovery of other network services, such as LDAP servers, through the use of service (SRV) records, which in some cases, can be used as a substitute for absolute hostnames in configuration files.

Identity management providers

These services are covered in much greater detail in Chapter 10, but there are a few points to make with regard to HA:

LDAP
> Although users and groups can be defined locally to a server, we highly recommend that user and group identities representing actual humans be defined in a central repository and that Linux be configured to perform remote lookups. For HA, either multiple LDAP servers should be listed in the client configuration files or a load balancer should be used to direct traffic to available servers.

Kerberos
> Multiple KDC servers can be defined in the client configuration (users and services are clients of Kerberos) for failover. If you are managing your own Kerberos deployment, with MIT Kerberos, for example, ensure that multiple KDCs are deployed. MIT Kerberos comes with a daemon process, kpropd, for synchronizing principals between peer KDCs, but note that you will need to manually configure KDC master failover. The Kerberos client configuration allows multiple KDC servers to be listed for each realm, but a load balancer can also be used.

If your enterprise uses centralized identity services such as Active Directory, we recommend making use of them since they are usually already configured for HA.

General Considerations

When you are architecting a highly available Hadoop cluster for an enterprise system, there are a number of general principles to observe. The following sections should be reviewed in conjunction with the recommendations outlined in "Cluster Configurations and Node Types" on page 97.

Separation of Master and Worker Processes

Except in a noncritical development cluster (and even then, there are strong arguments for observing this principle), worker and master/coordinator roles should not be colocated on the same physical machine. For example, an HDFS NameNode role should not be colocated with an HDFS DataNode process. Master roles require guaranteed resources—CPU, I/O, network—to function correctly and can be severely degraded by hungry worker processes. Master processes are critical to the operation of the cluster and need to be responsive at all times to prevent them from becoming a bottleneck.

Master processes often need to use disks exclusively (HDFS JournalNodes and Zoo-Keeper servers) for low-latency durable storage, meaning these disks would have to be made unavailable for worker processes. Besides removing capacity, this also adds unnecessary complexity to the cluster configuration. We should aim for homogeneous service configurations for worker nodes.

It is worth noting that master servers, in all but the largest clusters, do not need the large CPU, memory, and disk capacity that are required for worker nodes. These roles simply need dedicated and guaranteed system resources.

Although it might feel like a reasonable cost-saving measure to colocate some roles, it is usually a false economy and can result in major performance issues in busy clusters. It is, however, generally reasonable in small to mid-sized clusters (fewer than 50 nodes) to colocate master services with cluster monitoring and management services, such as Cloudera Manager or Apache Ambari, running on utility nodes.

Separation of Identical Service Roles

Although it may seem obvious, the same role type for the same service should not be placed on the same physical machine. For example, two Apache HBase Master processes should not be colocated on the same node. In practice, enterprise cluster management tools, such as Cloudera Manager, do not allow such a configuration.

This principle is easily achievable in bare-metal installations in which we know where all the physical hardware is, but in deployments in virtual environments, we need to take care. As introduced in "Compute Virtualization" on page 412 and "High Availability" on page 488, in these cases, the anti-affinity rules of the hypervisor must be used to ensure that master VMs are not placed on the same physical machines, thereby avoiding coupling the failure modes of two related processes.

Master Servers in Separate Failure Domains

In the ideal case, each master machine should be in a rack separate from other master servers and served by redundant TOR switches. In large enough installations, the machines can also be served by different power distribution units and spine network switches. This reduces as much as possible the risk of coupled failure modes of master roles and ensures the maximum chance of maintaining quorums for highly available services. For more on this, refer to "Rack Awareness and Rack Failures" on page 165.

Balanced Master Configurations

As much for your own sanity as for anything else, attempt to have a uniform configuration for master nodes; that is, as far as possible, run the same roles and services on each master node. This simplifies things from both an operational and a deployment standpoint. However, some services are not set up for more than two master instances in HA configurations. For the rest, attempt to balance out the roles between the masters such that each master has roughly the same expected load. Of course, with automatic failover active roles from different services may end up running on the same machine. In most cases, with monitoring and manual failover an administrator can move the active role of one or more of the services if it becomes problematic.

Optimized Server Configurations

Before HA was generally available for the core Hadoop services, it was the received wisdom to treat master nodes with great love and attention and to make them as robust to failure as possible because they hosted the SPOFs in the cluster. Even with HA support in most services, we would do well to maintain this approach. Critical services have automatic failover, but this can take anywhere from a few seconds to tens of seconds to occur, so we prefer to avoid it in the first place.

In contrast to worker nodes, where we require a JBOD (just a bunch of disks) presentation of data disks, for master roles we want to do as much as we can to keep a process alive. For those processes that write data to disk (for example, HDFS NameNodes or ZooKeeper JournalNodes), one option is to make use of RAID 1 mirror pairs for each dedicated volume to allow these processes to survive a disk failure.

Because master metadata is replicated to other machines in HA configurations, we are not mitigating against data loss here. We are merely increasing resilience. Note, though, that performance of the RAID array may be adversely affected in the event of a rebuild following a disk failure. This can take a few hours (depending on disk size), so be sure to plan to replace the drive during a slow period, if possible. Also, RAID 1 writes are only as fast as the slowest disk in the pair, so monitoring of disk latencies is key to identify degrading disks as soon as possible.

 Other RAID configurations are not recommended for master disks. Be sure to consider the trade-offs when using RAID 1 for master disks.

For more on recommended master and worker server configurations, see "Master Nodes" on page 98.

For similar reasons, employ NIC bonding in at least the master nodes to keep the network connection to and from the rest of the cluster up and running (see "Network Architectures" on page 114).

High Availability of Cluster Services

We now explore how to architect HA for services running in the cluster. For a refresher of the technologies involved, see Chapter 1.

ZooKeeper

For resilience, multiple ZooKeeper instances can and should be deployed on different master machines in an ensemble. Because it operates on majority consensus (see "Quorums" on page 332), an odd number of servers is required.

Each server is identical in functionality, but one of the ensemble servers is elected as the leader node and all other servers become followers. Clients can open connections to any of the servers to perform reads and writes, but writes are forwarded from follower servers to the leader to ensure a consistent order.

Each ZooKeeper server stores periodic snapshots of its in-memory state on disk and maintains a transaction write-ahead log to ensure that the state can be rebuilt in the event of failures and restarts.

ZooKeeper Ephemeral Nodes

ZooKeeper offers an extremely useful primitive that is used by many other services when implementing automatic failover for HA. An *ephemeral node* is a znode (without children), that is tied to the session of its creator. The ephemeral node is removed when it is explicitly deleted by its creator or when the creator's session ends, either deliberately or through a crash and time-out.

Because ZooKeeper guarantees ordering of writes, ephemeral nodes can be used as a distributed locking mechanism for master election. All nodes eligible to take on a

---

master role race to create the ephemeral node, with the winner becoming the master. Nonmaster nodes can use a watcher to automatically poll the presence of the znode. As soon as it disappears, the nonmaster nodes receive a notification of the change and race once again to create the ephemeral node and elect a new leader.

Many use cases can be supported with ephemeral nodes. The interested reader is referred to the documentation for some sample recipes (*http://bit.ly/2OTLvLC*). Additionally, Apache Curator (*http://bit.ly/2PEN1GC*) builds on ZooKeeper to provide higher-level abstractions for performing many useful operations.

Failover

Other than deploying an odd number of servers on different nodes, there are no special steps to make ZooKeeper itself HA—it is already so by design. The ZooKeeper client API library ensures that sessions are automatically and transparently reestablished or moved to new servers after network issues or server failure. For this to work properly, though, the client should be configured with the full ensemble of ZooKeeper servers when the session is constructed.

Deployment considerations

When deploying ZooKeeper, keep the following points in mind:

Deploy an odd number of servers
    As described in "Quorums" on page 332, the maximum number of servers that can be lost is floor ((*n* - 1) / 2).

Use enough servers
    Use 3 servers for smaller clusters (up to 100 nodes) and 5 for larger clusters (100+) that are running HBase and/or Solr, since the read load will be high. More servers come at the cost of increased write latency, as the majority size is larger, so do not make the quorum larger than required for your anticipated read load.

Dedicated disks
    Although not strictly related to the overall HA of ZooKeeper, ensure that at least the transaction log directory is on a dedicated disk, or RAID 1 array, with no other processes writing to it. This ensures minimal latency for ZooKeeper writes and avoids *fsync storms*, when multiple processes issue synchronous writes in quick succession. ZooKeeper is a critical supporting service for HDFS, YARN, Hive, HBase, Kafka, Solr, and more, so its efficient operation is paramount.

HDFS

HDFS is architected to ensure data resilience and availability. File blocks are replicated to multiple DataNodes, and when rack locations are known, HDFS ensures at least one copy of a block is in a different rack from the other copies. So, apart from locating them appropriately and configuring rack awareness, we do not need to consider DataNodes further for the purposes of HA.

In this section, we instead concentrate on configuring the master NameNode processes for HA. It is the NameNode's responsibility to maintain the filesystem metadata and the mapping between the raw block IDs and the file to which each belongs. Any process that needs to read data from, write data to, or make metadata requests of HDFS must communicate with the NameNode. As such, it is essential to all cluster operations.

For performance, the NameNode maintains the current state of the filesystem metadata in memory, with all modifications to the metadata (transactions) being written to a durable write-ahead log (called the *edit log*) on disk. Edit logs are rolled after a certain number of transactions, and periodically the in-memory representation is serialized to disk as a new filesystem image *(fsimage)* file. At this point, edit logs with their entire contents in a serialized fsimage can be discarded. Naturally, in order to prevent data corruption in the event of node failure, it is essential that both the fsimage and edit logs reside on resilient storage or are otherwise made resilient through distributed replication.

HA for HDFS allows two NameNode daemons to run on two separate hosts, one in active mode and one hot standby. Both NameNodes constantly apply filesystem modifications in memory, although only one NameNode accepts reads and writes from clients.

DataNodes send periodic updates, called *block reports*, about all the blocks they are serving to both NameNodes so that each has an up-to-date picture of files to block ID to block replica location mappings. This is particularly important because in large deployments the block reporting process can be lengthy, and it would hinder rapid failover from standby to active mode if the NameNode had to build this mapping from scratch.

In HA mode, instead of addressing the NameNode by hostname and port directly, clients use a logical *name service* alias. The default HDFS client will try first one NameNode and then the other in the logical pair. If the first NameNode does not respond, or is in standby state, the client library transparently tries the other NameNode. If the client was performing an operation at the time of the failure, the client will automatically retry it. When writing data, file leases are requested by the client library and durably logged in the edit log by the NameNode so a client can continue to write to a file, even after a failover.

It is important to stress that the client does not require a load balancer to fail over between NameNodes—it is all handled automatically by the HDFS client libraries.

HA configurations

There are two possible deployment configurations for HDFS HA. The first (*Conventional Shared Storage* mode) uses shared network-attached storage for the edits directory, whereas the second (the *Quorum Journal Manager*, or QJM) uses a quorum of distributed JournalNode processes to maintain consensus on the edits log. Both modes allow two NameNode processes to be deployed—one active, one standby.[2]

Although both are reasonable configurations, we highly recommend using the QJM configuration for HDFS HA. The key reasons for this are:

- The QJM does not require NFS or SAN storage. If your organization does not already have it off the shelf, setting up and maintaining a NAS or SAN system can be painful—especially because it, too, must be made performant and, of course, highly available. Fewer moving parts and external dependencies are a good thing.

- The conventional shared storage mode requires the use of fencing methods to ensure that only one NameNode is active and able to write to the shared edits directory at a time. If both processes considered themselves the active NameNode, concurrent writes to the edit log would corrupt the filesystem, ultimately resulting in data loss. Although fencing is also useful for QJM deployments to prevent stale reads, edit logs are protected from corruption from split-brain scenarios by the quorum-based architecture.

For further information on the conventional storage mode, refer to the official Hadoop documentation (*http://bit.ly/2Qeivmq*).

Manual failover

For maintenance, and in the event of active NameNode failure (if automatic failover has not been configured), an administrative command (`hdfs haadmin -failover`) can promote the standby NameNode to an active state—a so-called *graceful failover*. The failover process includes a step where one or more fencing procedures are executed to ensure that the formerly active NameNode is inactive or disabled. Although the QJM configuration will not allow edit log corruption, the formerly active NameNode may still serve stale reads. To complete the failover, the target NameNode applies any edits it has not yet processed, and it requests that the JournalNodes use a quorum decision to confirm it as the current active server.

---

2 Work is in progress to allow more than two NameNodes for resilience: see HDFS-6440 (*http://bit.ly/ 2R1o9pk*).

Automatic failover

The HDFS HA mechanisms described thus far do not require automatic failover to operate correctly, but for HA we require failover to occur as quickly as possible. A monitoring daemon called the ZooKeeper Failover Controller (ZKFC) runs colocated with each NameNode, monitoring its health. The daemon keeps a session open in ZooKeeper and races the other ZKFC instance to obtain an ephemeral znode.

The NameNode with the local ZKFC process that has the lock becomes the active NameNode. If the node or process holding the lock fails, the ephemeral znode expires and the ZKFC on the other node obtains the lock. At this point, it executes a failover to make its local NameNode the active node. Thus, a failover can be effected in just a few seconds in the event of failure.

Quorum Journal Manager mode

Figure 12-5 illustrates the HDFS HA architecture using the QJM mode and automatic failover. Three dedicated master nodes host a number of HDFS roles: NameNodes, JournalNodes, and ZKFCs. ZooKeeper server roles are also located on these nodes, although colocation is not an absolute requirement.

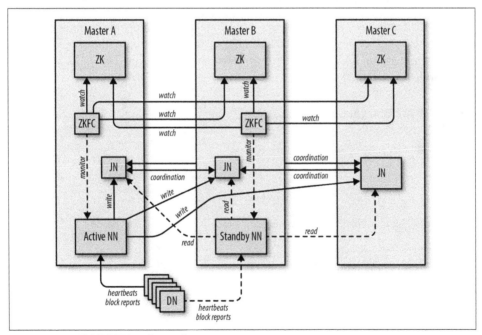

Figure 12-5. HDFS HA roles and interactions

As already described, the NameNode (NN) role maintains the filesystem metadata and the mapping of files to their block replica locations on DataNodes. A NameNode can run in two states—standby and active. The active NameNode writes edit logs to the JournalNodes (JNs). In addition, the standby NameNode is responsible for producing periodic fsimage snapshots and uploading the new version to the active NameNode.

Because blocks are unreadable without the fsimage, the snapshotting by the standby NameNode is not a substitute for a regular, off-cluster backup of the fsimage.

The JournalNodes are responsible for writing filesystem modifications (transactions) received from the current active NameNode to the edit log on durable storage.

Consensus on edit log transactions is achieved by the QJM on the active NameNode writing a transaction to all JournalNodes and awaiting a success response from a majority of nodes. In a typical deployment, at least three JournalNodes on different hosts are required, and this is the recommended number. Just like with ZooKeeper, larger quorum sizes are supported for extra resilience (five, seven, and so on), but at the cost of slower performance of edit log writes.

The ZKFCs maintain constant contact with their local NameNode process and initiate an automatic failover of NameNodes if they determine that either the local process or the remote process has failed. ZKFC processes must be colocated with NameNode processes.

QJM mode is fully described in the associated design document (*https://issues.apache.org/jira/browse/HDFS-3077*).

Security

Security concerns include the following:

Kerberos
> Since both NameNode hosts are listed individually (albeit indirectly) in the client configuration files, there is no need to merge multiple hostnames into keytab files. Clients always talk directly to NameNodes after resolving the hostnames from the logical name service.

Delegation tokens
> Delegation tokens allow a user to provide distributed processes temporary access to the NameNode, as if they were the user. Each delegation token is issued by the NameNode with a specified validity period (by default, 24 hours). In order to

ensure that both NameNodes know about the delegation tokens, the active NameNodes write the token as a transaction to the edit log. When the standby NameNode becomes active, it consumes the edit log transactions that it has not yet applied, including issued delegation tokens. Processes using existing delegation tokens can thus continue to use them transparently.

Deployment recommendations

Some recommendations for deploying and configuring HDFS HA include:

Three master nodes
> The HDFS NameNodes and ZKFC daemons should be on two master nodes, with the JournalNodes on all three masters. Avoid colocating processes with worker nodes.

Unique HDFS name service names
> Ensure that each NameNode pair has a unique name service name for this cluster. in addition to promoting clarity for clients, this is especially important if you wish to communicate with more than one cluster, e.g., for backup using DistCp.

Consider RAID 1 for metadata
> If you can afford to dedicate a pair of disks to each JournalNode, consider setting up a RAID 1 mirror pair for the write-ahead log for increased resiliency, but be aware of the trade-offs around performance when disks fail.

Dedicated disks for JournalNodes
> Each JournalNode process should write to a dedicated physical disk. The edit logs are append-only write-ahead logs and are most performant when the disk is not serving competing reads, writes, and fsync() requests. Although not a strict requirement for HA, keeping the JournalNodes performant prevents them from becoming a bottleneck.

YARN

As introduced in Chapter 1, YARN is the distributed process execution framework in Hadoop. In terms of HA for the YARN service, we only need to consider the master ResourceManager (RM) processes. A failure of an individual NodeManager is handled gracefully by design, and containers running on failed nodes are restarted automatically elsewhere in the cluster.

When YARN is not configured for master HA, the RM holds all information about live NodeManagers, running containers, ApplicationMasters, and scheduling state entirely in memory. Thus, the entire state is lost if the RM crashes or is restarted. Upon RM restart, the NodeManagers automatically report their status via heartbeats, but the containers that were queued or running at the time of the crash are killed.

To provide resilience to restarts, the RM can be configured to persist its state to durable storage. With this in place, running applications can survive a ResourceManager restart without having to be resubmitted.

For full HA, much as with HDFS, in YARN we can deploy multiple RMs. These run in active or standby mode, and the RM state is maintained in a shared storage area. Unlike in HDFS, it is possible to deploy more than one standby RM, although deployment of two is typical.

The recommended configuration is to use ZooKeeper for persistent state storage, since it allows for automatic failover. Using filesystem storage (including HDFS) and local LevelDB storage are also options, but they do not allow for automatic failover or fencing.

When using ZooKeeper as the state store, the RM stores information about running applications in a znode hierarchy, including information about current applications and their execution attempts, delegation tokens, and shared secrets between ApplicationMasters and the RM.

In an HA setup, clients interact with the active RM via a logical ID rather than talking to the host directly. The underlying YARN client library goes about the task of translating a particular logical ID into a hostname and then attempts to contact each RM in turn until the active RM is found. Upon failover, this process repeats until the new active RM is found and is managed transparently by the client library.

The setup is illustrated in Figure 12-6. ResourceManager roles run on master nodes— one in active mode, the other in standby. NodeManagers heartbeat into the active node, report container status, and accept new container requests. ApplicationMasters running on the NodeManagers also provide status updates to the active node and make resource requests. The active node stores state in ZooKeeper, while the standby watches and reads. On failover the standby takes over; NodeManagers and ApplicationMasters fail over via the retry proxy implementation, and they begin sending heartbeats to the new active node.

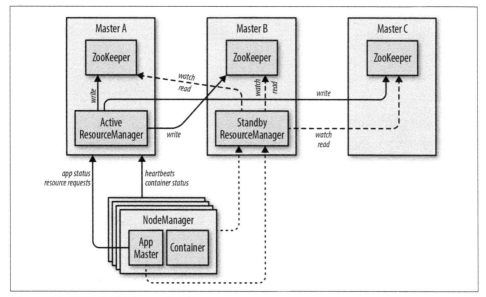

Figure 12-6. YARN high availability

Manual failover

Failover can be configured to be manual or automatic. In manual mode, an operator uses the yarn rmadmin utility to first demote the currently active RM to standby and then promote the standby RM to active. There is no danger of state corruption here when using ZooKeeper for state storage because only one node can hold the ephemeral znode as a lock.

 You might be asking yourself why YARN uses only ZooKeeper for HA, whereas HDFS maintains its own set of JournalNodes (ignoring the ZKFC). The answer is that ZooKeeper is designed for sharing small volume configuration and metadata among distributed processes, whereas HDFS edit logs can become quite large between filesystem checkpoints and can extend essentially without bound, when a standby NameNode is not up and running to perform snapshot creation.

Automatic failover

When configured for automatic failover, an embedded failover controller thread in the RMs monitors the ephemeral znode in ZooKeeper. If the active RM crashes or otherwise fails to keep its lock, the standby RMs race to acquire the fencing lock and become the new active node.

Deployment recommendations

Some recommendations for deploying YARN for HA include:

Use the ZKRMStateStore for storing state
> This both guards against split-brain corruption of state and enables automatic failover.

Enable automatic failover
> Automatic failover provides fast RM switching in the event of failure.

Unique service names
> Choose a unique name for the logical ID for the ResourceManagers and ensure that clients use the logical ID when submitting applications.

HBase

HBase consists of two daemon processes: the worker RegionServer and coordinator HMaster. RegionServers are responsible for reading and writing the data stored in the regions of tables. A region is hosted by a single RegionServer, which can host tens to hundreds of regions from all tables. Clients directly access RegionServers when reading or updating data from regions.

The master service is responsible for the housekeeping of an HBase cluster. It tracks the health of the RegionServers and performs operations to keep the regions and tables balanced, through managing region assignments to RegionServers. It also facilitates the splitting of a region when a RegionServer detects that it is getting too large. In addition, the HMaster coordinates administrative metadata operations from clients, such as table creation, table configuration, and region merging and splitting.

The HMaster is not directly involved in reading or writing data. Instead, clients look up the locations of table regions in ZooKeeper and, using that information, go directly to the RegionServers on which they are hosted. An HBase cluster can still serve data without a running HMaster, but no metadata operations will be possible. Without active monitoring of RegionServer health, regions will eventually become unbalanced and will not be assigned to other RegionServers in the event of a server crash. The HMaster role is therefore essential to the running of a healthy cluster.

HMaster HA

HBase supports HA out of the box simply through the deployment of multiple HMaster instances on different master nodes—no extra configuration is required. The HMasters operate in an active-standby configuration, and ZooKeeper is used to manage the election of the active instance. Although running two HMaster instances is typical, HBase supports deploying more, if required.

Clients automatically discover the currently active master from ZooKeeper when they wish to perform metadata operations, so there is no need for external load balancing or round-robin requests between masters. There are no required changes in client code to support HMaster HA; the underlying client library can automatically, and transparently, retry RPC calls.

Region replication

In the event of a RegionServer crash, the HMaster arranges for other RegionServers to host the regions that the downed server was hosting. This reassignment process can take tens of seconds to complete. Both read and write request to the region will fail in the period the region is offline, and as a result, request latencies can increase dramatically.

To mitigate this and to provide scaling for reads, *region replicas* allow for an administrator to specify that additional read-only (so-called *secondary*) copies of a region be hosted by one or more RegionServers in addition to the original *primary* replica. As currently implemented, region replicas provide HA for reads only. Writes to primary replicas will still suffer a short delay while the region is reassigned away from a crashed RegionServer.

Region replication is not transparent to clients. Clients have to make a conscious decision to make use of stale replicas when reading and to accept the possibility of reading from potentially out-of-date replicas. Users must consider the trade-offs of using region replicas, but the feature can dramatically reduce the instance of high tail latencies in read requests, with a design goal of allowing 99.99% of get requests to be serviced in less than 10 ms.

For more details on HMaster HA and region replication see *HBase: The Definitive Guide* by Lars George (O'Reilly) and the HBase documentation (*http://hbase.apache.org/book.html*).

Deployment considerations

HBase does not have many constraints when deploying in HA mode:

- RegionServers should always be deployed on worker nodes (colocated with HDFS DataNodes), as a best practice.
- HMasters should be deployed on the master or utility nodes in the cluster and not placed on worker nodes. At least two HMasters need to be deployed, and for simplicity of configuration, you could consider placing an HMaster on all master nodes. The process is light on resources, so it is acceptable to colocate with other master processes.

KMS

We met the concept of the key management server (KMS) in "HDFS Transparent Data Encryption" on page 274. Its primary purpose in the Hadoop ecosystem is to support HDFS transparent encryption, but it is designed to support any service wishing to use encryption keys. Its operation in HA mode is essential to the smooth operation of processes accessing encrypted data.

KMS implementations are required to provide a stateless REST API over HTTP. Clearly, in order to support HA, we need to deploy multiple KMS instances. The first approach here is simply to place load balancing in front of two or more instances. Since interactions are stateless, any of the load-balancing methods will work.

A second supported approach is to deploy multiple instances and to specify each hostname in the configuration used by clients. The KMS client libraries can be configured with a list of hostnames of the form:

```
kms://https@host1.example.com;host2.example.com:16000/kms
```

The client library will transparently and automatically try each configured server in turn until it finds a functioning KMS server. Since this approach does not require a load balancer, it is simpler and can be managed entirely by the cluster administrator; it is therefore generally preferred. One drawback, though, is that client load is not spread between instances. A sort of manual balancing can be achieved by varying the order of the services in the client configuration files.

Deployment considerations

There are some things to bear in mind when deploying multiple KMS instances:

- The backing keystore implementation must also be highly available and capable of accepting requests for the same key material from multiple locations. This rules out the Java KeyStore implementation, which is not recommended for production in any case. The principal Hadoop platform vendors provide production-grade keystore implementations.

- KMS instances should be deployed on master or utility nodes not accessible to end users. The KMS caches key material in memory for a short time so as to avoid exposure to malicious processes.

- KMS supports delegation tokens; it should be configured to use the ZooKeeper-based delegation token store so that each instance is aware of the issued tokens.

- If using a load balancer, the KMS Kerberos keytabs and TLS certificates need to be configured with both the load-balancing hostname and the actual hostname where the KMS is running (see "Security considerations" on page 339).

Hive

We introduced Hive in "Apache Hive" on page 14. When configuring HA for Hive, we must consider both the Hive Metastore (HMS) and HiveServer2 (HS2) processes.

Metastore

Except for its support for delegation tokens, the HMS is entirely stateless; all metadata is persisted in its underlying relational database. This makes configuring it for HA relatively straightforward—there is no requirement to elect an active master or to provide for failover between HMS instances.

To set up HA for the HMS, we can deploy multiple instances running on different servers. With multiple instances, we must ensure that the underlying database is configured for HA (see "Database HA" on page 341) and that it can support concurrent remote connections. To ensure that delegation tokens issued by one HMS server are valid on other instances, knowledge of their existence should be persisted in a shared location. This location can either be ZooKeeper (`ZooKeeperTokenStore`) or the database already used by the metastore (`DBTokenStore`).

Clients, including HS2 servers, should be configured with a list of Metastore URIs. Connection attempts are made to each listed URI in turn, until a successful connection is made. Therefore, there is no need to use a VIP or other load-balancing mechanism when setting up Metastore HA.

HiveServer2

Unlike the HMS, HS2 instances are stateful. Clients open sessions with a specific HS2 instance and submit queries, each of which may potentially spawn long-running YARN jobs. HS2 maintains state in memory about which sessions are currently open and which queries are running for which session.

It is important to note that HS2 HA is quite limited. If an HS2 instance crashes, the results of running queries will be lost and subsequent jobs in multistage queries will not be run. If a query stage was running as a job in YARN the job will likely continue, but any further stages will not be executed and any results will not be returned to the client.

Broadly, we have three options if we want to provide HA for HS2. The first, simplest, and most commonly used approach is to deploy multiple HS2 instances and to provide the client with knowledge of the available servers. Implementing connection and failover logic is left up to the client in this option.

The next approach is to employ a load balancer as a proxy in front of multiple HS2 instances. Although clients will need to reconnect in the event of instance failure, they can use a single logical endpoint.

A final option is to make use of *dynamic service discovery* (*http://bit.ly/2DyxQHT*) of HS2 servers. This provides a way for clients to automatically discover a live HS2 server through ZooKeeper lookups. This is a nice option, but for it to work, the Zoo-Keeper ensemble must be accessible to the client, which may be operating outside of the cluster nodes.[3] Some operators may therefore prefer direct client access or a load balancer in order to limit the exposure to critical services from outside the cluster.

HA architecture

Figure 12-7 illustrates the configuration options for Hive HA. An HA relational database setup provides the backend persistent storage for two HMS instances (deploying more than two is possible). Both HMS servers are in the configuration of clients that require direct access. HS2 instances A and B list HMS A first, whereas HS2 instances C and D and the SparkSQL process place HMS B first. Notice that SparkSQL (and other services, such as HCatalog) communicates directly with the HMS.

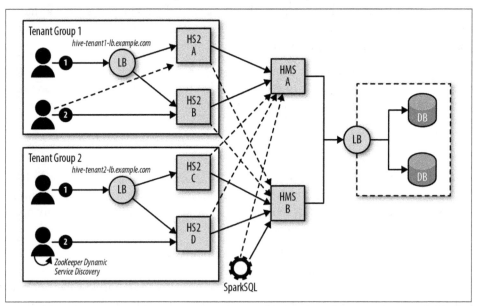

Figure 12-7. Hive HA configuration for HMS and HS2; dotted lines indicate a fallback configuration for clients

The image shows four HS2 instances, two each for two distinct tenant groups. The three options for HS2 HA are shown. In both tenant groups, users can connect to an

---

3 The same argument could apply to clients of HBase and Solr, but these clients are typically applications running on gateway or defined nodes. Hive clients may include applications, BI tools, and SQL workbenches connecting from many nodes in the wider network, so they are more difficult to control.

HS2 instance via a dedicated load balancer (1). A client with knowledge of both instances is also shown (2). The HS2 instances for tenant group 2 are configured to register themselves in ZooKeeper, and users can connect directly using ZooKeeper dynamic service discovery (3).

HS2 supports delegation tokens to allow processes to issue queries on behalf of another user. Despite sessions being tied to a particular server, HS2 employs the same delegation token store as the HMS. Thus, a delegation token issued to a user by one HS2 instance will be honored by another, despite being issued as part of another session. This is a key enabler for tools such as Oozie, which rely on using delegation tokens for successful interaction with HS2.

Deployment considerations

When deploying Hive for HA in production, here are some guidelines to remember:

Understand the Hive Metastore as a master process
HMS instances should be deployed on master nodes not accessible to end users. For HA, two or more should be deployed in production environments. In smaller clusters (fewer than 50 nodes), they can be colocated with other master daemons. For larger clusters, it might be necessary to host the HMS instances on additional master nodes.

Use an HA database
To support Hive HA, the underlying database must itself be robust, be highly available, and support concurrent queries.

Use a persistent token store
In order for delegation tokens to work seamlessly with HA configurations, tokens should be accessible from each HMS or HS2 instance. Either the DBToken Store or the ZooKeeperTokenStore should be used.

Configure keytabs and certificates for load balancing
If a load balancer is used, the HS2 keytab and TLS certificates should include both the hostname of the HS2 instance and that of the load balancer.

Provide a load balancer with session persistence
Depending on how your users intend to interact with HS2, they might or might not need source IP session persistence, given that query sessions are tied to a specific instance of HS2. If users are using Hive within individual JDBC/ODBC connections, session persistence is probably not required. However, a load balancer with source IP session persistence is mandatory for connections from Hue. A best practice is to provide one load-balancer configuration on one port, which enables session persistence for clients who require it (e.g., 10001), and another on a different port (e.g., 10000) that does not implement session persistence. Both load balancers would direct to a pool of HS2 instances listening on port 10000.

Provide separate HA setups for different tenants

Individual HiveServer2 instances have an upper limit on the number of sup-ported concurrent sessions and running queries that can be handled. Vendors have developed empirical guidelines defining the limits. See, for example, the Cloudera documentation (*http://bit.ly/2R1UufN*).

Likewise, HMS instances can only realistically support into the tens of thousands of partitions for tables before query planning performance becomes poor. Addi-tionally, it can sometimes be advantageous to configure different default Hive query parameters for different tenants—for example, to separate and apply quo-tas to the scratch directories for Hive. A common pattern to overcome this is to provide separate groups of HS2 instances for each tenant, with each setup in an HA configuration.

Impala

As we saw in Chapter 1, Impala is a massively parallel processing engine designed for efficiently processing SQL queries on structured data stored in distributed storage engines. To explain how to set Impala up to be as available as possible, we need to briefly describe the different server processes in an Impala cluster.

Impala daemons

The *daemon* processes are the workhorses of an Impala deployment and should be colocated with HDFS DataNode processes. These are the processes that execute query fragments and that read and write data from and to the distributed filesystem. Cru-cially for our understanding, by default, any Impala daemon can act as a *coordinator* —that is, accept client connections, parse a query, generate a distributed query plan, act as the coordinating node for the plan, and finally return results to the client. Dae-mons, again by default, also act as *executors* and run fragments that are part of dis-tributed queries. Originally, each daemon served both coordinator and executor roles, but subsequent releases have allowed a separation of these roles. Daemons can now operate in three modes:

- Executor + coordinator (the default)
- Executor only
- Coordinator only

Each daemon that operates in a coordinator role maintains a cache of metadata, called the *catalog*, detailing what databases, tables, and views exist; it also contains information about where files and blocks are located in HDFS and which other dae-mons are available to execute fragments. The daemon uses this metadata to build dis-tributed query plans, optimizing for data locality when reading from HDFS.

The Impala cluster as a whole is resilient to daemon failure, and the failed daemon will be removed from the set of available executors automatically within a few tens of seconds. However, there can be an impact on running queries and client sessions. Client sessions are tied to the TCP connection to the daemon—if the daemon crashes or fails in some other way, or the connection is lost, the session and any running queries are also lost. In addition, for a daemon failure, any queries from other coordinators that had fragments running on the daemon at the time of failure will also fail. Most queries are short-lived, so the impact of daemon failure should be limited, but as a best practice any application needs to bake in some retry logic to address such situations.

Catalog server

The *catalog server* acts as the intermediary from Impala coordinator daemons to the HMS. It fetches all metadata from the HMS and passes on requests to the HMS from daemons running DDL queries. It also publishes updates to the catalog to all coordinator daemons via the statestore.

The catalog server is not strictly critical to the continued functioning of the cluster. If it fails, Impala daemons will continue to be able to serve read-only queries and certain write queries, but DDL queries that add or remove Hive metadata—for example, adding new tables or partitions to an existing table—will fail. As a result, we highly recommend keeping it operational at all times. Although there is no built-in HA for the catalog server, it is a soft-state process, so if the node on which it is deployed becomes unavailable, it is safe to redeploy it on another node and restart the Impala daemons as soon as possible.

Statestore

The sole purpose of the *statestore* process is to distribute information to registered subscribers.Each Impala daemon heartbeats to the statestore and pulls updated information from subscribed topics. This information includes the catalog from the catalog server as well as the active health status of other Impala daemons, which is used for planning and distributing query fragments. If the statestore fails, the daemons use the last version of the published data until it becomes available again. However, this information will become stale over time, so to maintain service reliability and maintainability, the statestore should be restarted or redeployed as soon as possible.

> Without the statestore or catalog server running, the Impala cluster becomes unstable over time, with stale metadata and out-of-date information about daemon status. These services should be returned to operation as soon as possible after a failure. Cloudera Manager can be configured to automatically restart these services if they crash.

Architecting for HA

Because of the lack of HA for both the statestore and the catalog server, a solid opera-tions playbook for bringing Impala back online in the event of their failure is recom-mended. If these services have to be migrated to another node, the entire cluster needs to be restarted.

We highly recommend employing a load balancer in front of the coordinator dae-mons to balance query coordination load and to allow clients to connect to a live coordinator using a single logical endpoint. Often, without a load balancer in place, a client will always connect to a single daemon, which can result in imbalance in query coordination load.

Impala daemons support two client protocols, and they listen on separate ports. The Beeswax protocol (by default on port 21000) is used by the Impala shell CLI, while the HiveServer2 protocol (by default on port 21050) is used by JDBC and ODBC con-nections (including Hue). Session persistence, although not mandatory for standard clients, is required for connections from Hue, as just described. For this reason, it's typical to have the load balancer expose three ports: one each for Beeswax (21000) and HiveServer2 (21050) connections *without* session persistence, and one for Hive-Server2 connections (say, 21051) *with* persistence for Hue (and any other application that uses connection pooling within a session). Both HiveServer2 load balancers for-ward to port 21050 using the same pool of backend daemons.

> Clients connecting through a load balancer should send regular TCP *keepalive* packets to ensure that the session remains open dur-ing longer queries. If running on Linux, this can be configured in the kernel (*http://bit.ly/2KnHq1y*). Alternatively, or in addition, the load balancer should be configured with an extended connection timeout.

In secure clusters configured with a load balancer, the Impala coordinators accept only client connections using the load balancer's hostname in the service principal.

Synchronous DDL

There is another caveat to be aware of when using a load balancer without session persistence. In most cases, a coordinator's catalog cache is populated by data propa-gated by the catalog server via the statestore. However, for efficiency, when a client issues a DDL query (e.g., `CREATE TABLE`), the catalog server will directly push the metadata back to the original requesting coordinator. If a client closes a connection after issuing the DDL connection and immediately reopens a new connection, the load balancer may direct it to a coordinator that is yet to be updated with the new metadata by the statestore. Queries expecting the new metadata to be in place will

---

therefore fail. To avoid this, there is a session parameter, SYNC_DDL, which synchro-nously waits for full metadata propagation to all live daemons, but it comes at the cost of performance.

A best practice architecture for availability and performance in large Impala deploy-ments is to limit the number of coordinator nodes to a small proportion of the overall cluster. This can dramatically reduce the burden on the statestore when pushing out metadata updates in large clusters, where catalogs can grow to multiple gigabytes. In addition, if you have nodes available, coordinator-only roles can be placed on edge service nodes, leaving the work of fragment execution almost entirely to executor-only nodes.

Coordinators plan queries and still do results aggregation and final computations, so you should provide the same amount of memory on coordinator-only nodes as for a standard Impala daemon and expect heavy CPU usage on these nodes.

These options are illustrated in Figures 12-8 and 12-9. In option A, a subset of dae-mons play the role of both coordinator and executor. A load balancer distributes cli-ent sessions among the coordinators, and query fragments are run on all daemons, including executors. In option B, load-balanced coordinator-only nodes are deployed on edge nodes and query fragments are run only on executor-only daemons running on worker nodes. In both options, the catalog is distributed to only coordinators.

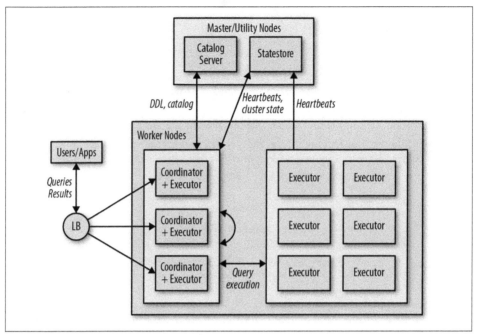

Figure 12-8. Impala coordinators deployed on a subset of worker nodes (A)

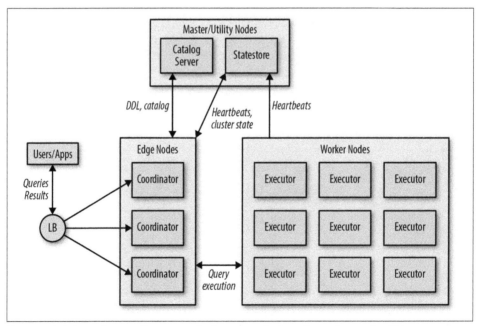

Figure 12-9. Impala coordinator-only daemons deployed on edge nodes (B)

Deployment considerations

Consider the following recommendations when deploying Impala for HA:

Use master nodes for supporting services
> The catalog server and the statestore should be placed on master or utility nodes so that they are not starved of resources by worker processes. In larger clusters, they should be placed on dedicated master nodes.

Limit coordinator roles
> To reduce the burden of metadata propagation, limit the proportion of daemons with a coordinator role, leaving the majority to be executors only. The number of coordinators depends largely on the anticipated query load, but each coordinator can be expected to handle multiple tens of concurrent queries. Consider also deploying coordinator-only daemons to edge service nodes. These daemons are able to support many more concurrent queries, because their only role is coordination.

Employ a load balancer
> Use a load balancer across the coordinator daemons—one that is configured to forward connections for both supported client protocols. Provide an additional balancer for Hue with session persistence. Ensure that, for each balancer configuration, the load balancer connection timeout is longer than both Impala's idle session and idle query timeouts.

Configure certificates for load balancing
> If TLS is used for client connections, the TLS certificates should include both the hostname of the coordinator daemon and that of the load balancer in the SAN field.

Have an operations plan
> Since the catalog server and the statestore do not yet directly support HA, we highly recommend having a planned operations procedure in the event of their failure. Though they are not essential to the immediate operation of Impala, without them, a cluster's stability and metadata currency will gradually degrade over time. If their hosts are unavailable and they must be redeployed to new nodes, note that the Impala daemons will need to be restarted and users should be made aware of the outage.

Solr

Solr is a scalable indexing, analysis, and querying framework built on Apache Lucene (*https://lucene.apache.org/*). We introduced Solr in Chapter 1, and here we cover what you need to know to architect a Solr deployment for HA. In this section, we are strictly referring to SolrCloud but, for simplicity, use the name Solr.

The distributed Solr architecture is built from the ground up to support HA. Solr uses ZooKeeper for metadata and coordination and does not have a dedicated master role. When a Solr server fails, the remaining servers coordinate via ZooKeeper to bring up a new leader for each replica (if required) and to ensure that the requisite number of replicas are available. The new leader replica starts off in recovery mode and replays any missing transactions from the log. New follower replicas can do the same or, if the lag is too great, request a full index replication from a more current replica.

 Note that each replica stores log and index data on HDFS separately, so you might consider reducing the default block replication factor used by Solr if all collections are replicated. With threefold HDFS block replication and two shard replicas, each block is being stored six times in HDFS. Be careful when reducing HDFS replication to one, though. In this case, you need to ensure that shard replicas reside on different racks, for resilience. With HDFS replication, this is handled automatically for you.

Each replica in the collection is a full-featured Solr *core* and can accept both queries and updates. Nonleader replicas automatically forward updates to the leader, which in turn handles each update and propagates it out to all replicas.

Any server in the SolrCloud can handle queries for any known collection and provides native load balancing of reads over the replicas. Despite this, we highly recommend using the provided client `CloudSolrServer` class in the SolrJ library, if possible. This can automatically discover the right endpoints for collections from ZooKeeper, determine the list of shard leaders to which to direct updates, and provide built-in load balancing of reads by randomly selecting a replica for queries. It is thus more efficient than an HTTP load balancer, which has no built-in intelligence for Solr when selecting endpoints to which to connect. If you are using a load balancer, it is better to use the `HttpSolrServer` client.

Deployment considerations

Other than deploying multiple servers, minimal special configuration is required for HA operation. Nonetheless, some recommendations hold:

Use multiple replicas
> To provide read and write HA, configure each shard in a collection to have at least two replicas. When creating a collection, ensure that the number of shards, the number of replicas, and the maximum number of shards per node are configured to allow at least one server to fail and still have all replicas be live. For example, with 10 servers, a collection might be configured to have 8 shards, each with 2 replicas and a maximum of 2 shards per server. The total capacity of the cluster

at 2 shards per node is 20 replicas. Our example collection requires 16 replicas, which allows for two server failures while keeping the collection fully operational.

Place replicas on different racks

In addition to specifying the maximum number of replicas per node, Solr can also apply sophisticated rules (*http://bit.ly/2TrVISW*) when placing shard replicas. These can be used to ensure that replicas are distributed across the racks of your cluster. Of course, Solr servers must also be intentionally deployed on different racks to enable this.

Use the `CloudSolrServer` *client*

Prefer the built-in SolrCloud client over an independent load balancer. Although the latter can be made to work, the provided client interacts with Solr in a more intelligent way when multiple shard replicas are configured. It also avoids the need to specify multiple hostnames in the Kerberos keytabs. If security constraints prevent direct access to worker nodes, consider using proxy applications on edge nodes to query data from Solr.

Kafka

Kafka is architected for HA out of the box and thankfully—apart from deploying multiple broker instances—requires very little in the way of extra configuration for HA. Kafka uses ZooKeeper to provide highly available metadata and coordination services. Each broker server hosts multiple partitions for different topics, which are deliberately distributed across brokers when they are created. Topic partitions have multiple replicas for resilience and availability—three is typical.

For each partition, one replica is elected as the *leader* and exclusively serves reads and writes for the partition to and from clients. The other replicas for the partition run on other brokers and follow the updates to the log by subscribing to the leader.

One broker in the cluster acts as the *controller* and is responsible for detecting broker failure and reassigning the replica leadership if a leader replica has gone offline. The brokers use ZooKeeper to elect a controller among themselves. Thus, if the controller itself crashes, one of the other brokers automatically takes over its duties.

If a broker fails, it is important to know that its partition replicas are not automatically assigned to the other brokers. An administrator must manually run a *partition reassignment* process to bootstrap replicas on other brokers. Usually, this would only be required if the broker is likely to be offline for a long period.

Clients should specify multiple broker endpoints when connecting to Kafka, but the rest is handled automatically and transparently. Consumers and producers are automatically directed to the right brokers for the topics and partitions they are interested in and are automatically rebalanced in the event of broker failure. There is thus no requirement for a load balancer for clients.

Deployment considerations

The following factors should be considered when deploying Kafka for maximum availability:

Deploy at least three brokers
> A typical recommended resilience setting for topics in Kafka is to replicate each partition three times and to ensure that at least two of these replicas acknowledge writes. To support this configuration, we need at least three brokers.

Deploy across multiple racks
> For full resilience, consider deploying Kafka brokers across multiple server racks. From Kafka 0.10 and beyond, Kafka has the ability to specify a rack ID for a broker, and partition replicas can be distributed to ensure that replicas are not all in a single rack. In a cloud deployment, this can map to availability zones.

Assess storage configuration for broker data disks
> Although Kafka has tolerated broker disk failures since version 1.0, it might still be worth considering the use of RAID 10 for broker data disks. RAID 10 can help with distributing data more evenly across the disks through the RAID 0 striping and therefore avoids the requirement to manually move partitions to achieve a better balance. The nested RAID 1 level means that replicas are still available, even after a disk failure. However, it results in the reduction of usable storage space by half, which may be too costly when combined with threefold replication. In addition, although the data is still available, rebuilding a RAID 1 array can be costly, which might hurt performance. Kafka fully supports JBOD configurations, so it is a reasonable choice for new clusters. In the end, it is a trade-off among cost, performance, and risk.

Ensure dependencies are HA
> Kafka relies on ZooKeeper for coordination purposes, so it is critical that it is deployed on multiple nodes and is responsive. We often recommend using a dedicated ZooKeeper ensemble. In small clusters, these can be colocated with three or more of the Kafka broker nodes, but for larger deployments (tens of brokers) they should be deployed on their own nodes.
>
> In addition, where Sentry is used for Kafka authorization, it should also be configured for HA. Brokers cache permissions for a short while but require regular connectivity with Sentry to keep their caches up to date.

Oozie

Oozie servers provide a REST API and store all state (apart from job logs) in an underlying database. Oozie therefore does not require the maintenance of client sessions—each interaction with an Oozie server is a self-contained operation. When running an asynchronous action via a MapReduce job on YARN, Oozie maintains the state of the action in the database. On completion, the action issues a callback to the Oozie server. In addition, each Oozie server runs a monitoring service to check the status of actions and to respond appropriately if an action is found to be complete.

Similarly, although they are executed on the server itself, Oozie maintains the state of synchronous actions in the database. An in-memory locking service ensures that only one thread at a time can update a workflow.

All of this makes the Oozie HA architecture relatively straightforward. The HA architecture allows for two or more Oozie servers to operate in parallel with coordination via ZooKeeper. ZooKeeper is used to coordinate locks on workflow actions and to arrange for the exchange of workflow logs, which are stored locally to each Oozie server. Upon an Oozie server failure, the other servers automatically take up the slack and ensure that running jobs and their actions are monitored and progressed.

In an HA configuration, the servers either should be placed behind a load balancer or DNS round robin should be configured. Because each server can respond to any request, clients can interact with any Oozie server completely transparently. Session persistence is thus not required.

An Oozie HA setup is shown in Figure 12-10. In the diagram, users interact with Oozie via a load balancer making self-contained requests using the REST API. Oozie servers, keeping their state in an HA database, kick off workflows via launcher jobs (MapReduce jobs) running in YARN. When complete, these jobs make a request to a callback URL, also via the load balancer. Each Oozie server constantly monitors the outcome of launcher jobs and can process their completion.

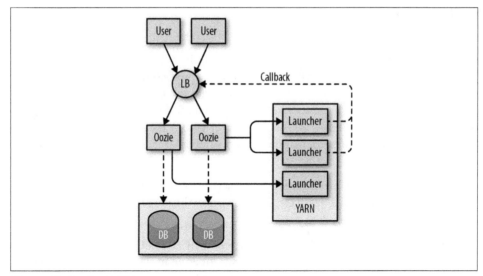

Figure 12-10. Oozie HA

Deployment considerations

Oozie HA is easy to configure, and there are relatively few considerations for the enterprise architect to note:

Use master nodes
  Although not a heavy resource user, Oozie suffers if you place it on extremely busy nodes. For this reason, you can place Oozie servers on master nodes, utility nodes, or edge nodes in the cluster but not on worker nodes.

Use an HA database
  Oozie servers store most of their state in a database, which should itself be highly available.

Configure security for HA
  Each Oozie server's Kerberos keytab should contain entries for both the load balancer DNS name and the actual hostname of the server. Similarly, if using SSL, the certificates should contain both the DNS name and actual hostname as subject alternative names.

Hue

Hue has long been the de facto web-based UI for Hadoop (although, more recently, UI components have also been provided via Ambari Views). Hue allows users to interact with HDFS, issue queries to Impala and Hive, construct Oozie workflows, and build dashboards over Solr indexes, and provides a host of other functionality.

Hue is a web application, and therefore, the normal methods for scaling and providing HA for such applications apply, with a couple of caveats. Hue stores most of its runtime state in an underlying database, including user and group definitions, access permissions, and running operations. This means the underlying database should be shared between all instances of Hue, which in turn means the database should support concurrent connections and should be configured for HA.

Currently Impala and Hive query sessions are tied to the Hue instance on which they were created, so it is important that clients of Hue always interact with the same server when running queries. This requirement means that we *must* apply session persistence when using a load balancer with multiple Hue servers. Load-balancer sessions can be HTTP-aware if the load balancer supports it.

> Currently, session persistence is required for both the Hue load balancer and any load balancers for Hive and Impala that Hue uses.

There is no concept of a master Hue server, so no failover needs to occur when a Hue server crashes or becomes unavailable. Instead, a user can simply navigate to another Hue server in the set, or the load balancer can automatically redirect traffic to a live server. As long as the secret key used to generate session cookies is shared across servers, a large amount of functionality continues undisturbed when a user moves between servers—with the exception of Hive and Impala SQL queries.

If the deployment best practices are followed, each Hue server can support up to 100 concurrent users.[4] If more users are expected, additional Hue servers are required to support the load. For any multiuser scenario, use of an external database, such as MySQL or PostgreSQL, is mandatory rather than the single-user SQLite database that Hue uses by default.

Deployment options

The general recommendations for Hue HA are as follows:

Use an independent load balancer
> This is the simplest configuration for Hue HA. A hardware or software load-balancer configuration is set up with source IP or HTTP session persistence across all Hue nodes. This has the drawback of requiring extra hardware or software configurations and limits the flexibility for dynamically adding or moving Hue servers.

---

4 See "Hue Performance Tuning Guide," (*http://gethue.com/performance-tuning/*) Hue, June 13, 2017.

Use Hue's built-in load balancer tool

Hue also comes with a built-in load-balancing daemon.[5] Although purely a software implementation, it has the nice feature of automatically integrating with Cloudera Manager's API to dynamically reconfigure HAProxy when Hue servers are added or removed. This mode can also automatically be deployed via Cloudera Manager. The drawback here is that the load balancer is hosted on a single node and, therefore, becomes another SPOF. However, multiple load balancers can be deployed in parallel on different nodes but with separate hostnames. One nice feature of the native load balancer is its ability to serve static content such as images, stylesheets, and JavaScript. This can markedly improve the performance of Hue.

Use a hybrid

These two preceding options both have their respective advantages and disadvantages. An optimal configuration might seek to combine both approaches to take advantage of the strengths of each. An independent load balancer provides a single hostname for the Hue HA deployment and directs traffic to multiple Hue native load-balancer instances, which provide content caching and serving. It is important to note that the independent load balancer still requires session persistence, as do the built-in load-balancer instances. Because the persistence can be applied at the HTTP session level (Layer 7) rather than at the TCP session level (Layer 4), the built-in balancers should still spread the load relatively equally across all Hue servers.

Some additional guidance for deploying Hue HA follows:

Configure security properly

It is important to be aware of all the possible hostnames through which a given Hue server might be accessed. If using TLS encryption with Hue, each server certificate needs all of the possible load-balancer hostnames, in addition to the hostname on which the Hue server is running, as subject alternative names. Similarly, if using the SPNEGO authentication method, each server's Kerberos keytab requires HTTP principals for its own fully qualified hostname and for each of the load-balancer hostnames.

Set up multitenancy

A common pattern is to provide different Hue instances for different tenants on the cluster, to allow separate administration and usage. In this case, each tenant needs its own separate Hue HA deployment. If the administration aspects can be overcome, we recommend using a shared infrastructure with more Hue servers.

---

5 See "Automatic High Availability with Hue and Cloudera Manager" (*http://bit.ly/2A6WXOs*) and "Automatic High Availability and Load Balancing of Hue in Cloudera Manager with Monitoring," (*http://bit.ly/2Q6hnl1*) Hue, December 8, 2015.

Configure apps for HA

Hue has a number of applications that interact with HA services, and these should each be configured to use the HA mode. Cluster management tools such as Cloudera Manager will configure most, if not all, of these properties for you.

For the file browser, we recommend configuring Hue to point to an HttpFS role, because it otherwise needs to be configured to point directly at one of the NameNodes. Of course, for maximum availability, that HttpFS role is ideally behind a load balancer.

The Oozie application automatically configures some properties when creating and submitting Oozie jobs. One of these refers to the active YARN Resource-Manager, and this should be configured to refer to the logical name of the YARN ResourceManager HA setup (usually, `yarnRM`).

If using HA for HiveServer2, the Hive SQL editor application should be configured accordingly and should be pointed toward the HS2 load balancer.

Similarly, for Impala, ensure that Impala SQL editor application refers to the load balancer, if one has been deployed.

Other Services

We cannot cover every service in the ecosystem, but other important services mentioned elsewhere in this book can be deployed in HA configurations. For details, see the following resources:

- Sentry (*http://bit.ly/2qWQNwl*)
- Ranger (*http://bit.ly/2Bo9JKz*)

Autoconfiguration

Cluster managers, such as Cloudera Manager and Ambari, often provide built-in wizards for those services that require explicit configuration to enable HA. These can also often be automated via APIs by configuration management software like Ansible.

We highly recommended using these capabilities, since the configuration of HA for some services can be intricate. For illustration, Cloudera Manager supplies auto-configuration wizards for HDFS, YARN, Oozie, and Sentry.

For other services, such as Hive, Hue, and KMS, the addition of extra roles is enough in itself to enable HA and to prompt the cluster manager to distribute the correct client configuration.

Summary

Architecting and configuring cluster services for HA can be a challenge, but the information in this chapter should equip you for the task. A fully HA cluster requires much thought and preparation at all layers of the stack. At the lowest level, as outlined in "Rack Awareness and Rack Failures" on page 165, the cluster architect needs to deploy the physical or virtual hardware with care to separate failure domains. At the next layer up, we need to provide HA or to configure our machines to use HA for supporting services such as Kerberos and LDAP.

A key supporting piece to many components is a relational database that can operate in an HA or fast-failover fashion—we cannot recommend highly enough making this an early part of deployment planning, because it is very difficult to add after the fact.

Similarly, many services can make use of load balancers as part of their HA strategy. Investigating the options in your enterprise early will pay dividends. After you have decided which load-balancer implementation to use, you should employ it for all the services that require one, noting that some require session persistence, whereas some can work without it.

With the physical infrastructure and supporting services in place, you can begin configuring cluster services for HA.

One thing we haven't really touched upon in this chapter is the cost of providing HA for all services. Providing full HA can potentially mean additional hardware and expense, which you might not be able to justify for nonproduction clusters. You should, therefore, establish how much downtime your cluster can tolerate outside of maintenance windows. It might be that rapid reestablishment of services on failure is sufficient and that a full-blown HA architecture is not warranted. Usually, though, it makes sense to make your production clusters as available as possible, and that means implementing the principles you find in this chapter.

## CHAPTER 13

Backup and Disaster Recovery

This chapter outlines the concerns around building a sound strategy for keeping data within a Hadoop-based system safe and available such that, in case of data loss through a user error (erroneously deleted data) or a disaster (such as loss of the entire cluster), a restore can be initiated and completed. This restore leaves the cluster users with some kind of reliable state so they can proceed with their business tasks.

Note that this is necessary, even with high availability (see Chapter 12) enabled, because restoring data also applies to problems that do not arise from maintaining a responsive service. Quite the contrary. Even with redundant components on every level of the stack, losing metadata or data may cause a disruption that can only be mitigated with the proper backup or disaster recovery strategy in place beforehand.

Context

Before we can look into the particular approaches, we first need to establish a context.

Many Distributed Systems

Hadoop is a complex system, comprising many open source projects that work in conjunction to build a unique data processing platform. It is the foundation for many large-scale installations across numerous industry verticals, storing and processing from hundreds of terabytes to multiple petabytes of data. At any scale, there is the need to keep the data safe, and the customary approach is to invest in some kind of backup technology. The difficulties with this approach are manifold.

First, data at scale becomes inherently difficult to move, which should be abundantly clear from the previous chapters. The inertia of data requires new approaches that either do not move data at all or keep movement to a minimum.

Second, traditional backup systems are tailored to specific, single-target systems, usually with standardized access protocols, such as JDBC or network shares. Hadoop, in many areas, does not conform to that.

A Hadoop cluster can include more than a dozen separate systems, with many storing their state in some kind of persistency layer—usually a database or the operating system's filesystems (see Chapters 3 and 7 for details.) Some of these subsystems have rudimentary support to also store their data on out-of-bounds services, such as NFS mounts. This does not address backup or recovery properly, though it could be employed as part of the overall backup architecture.

An additional complication is that even if a database is used by a particular system, that database is usually pluggable, such that there are many different variants from which to chose. Often, there is also an option to employ an embedded database, such as Derby or SQLite, enabling some kind of quick-start mode. It should be noted that this is never a good choice in a production system because these embedded databases also are usually single-user systems that do not allow concurrent users. This violates one of the core ideas of Hadoop. Further, they are not part of the overall monitoring and are difficult to back up while in use.

Finally, there are systems used in combination with Hadoop that are not considered part of the core stack (which varies with the distribution you choose) or of the actual user applications running within the cluster. All of these make onboarding users or applications for specific use cases a difficult process, unless a company-wide policy is in place to define where data needs to be stored by every single user and application, service, or other writing process.[1]

Policies and Objectives

The various components within the Hadoop ecosystem and bundled into the various distributions all deal in some way with stored and processed data. Yet not all persist data the same way, or with the same scope and retention policies. It is vital to dissect the entire stack to identify what needs to be addressed during a backup and what can be guaranteed, in terms of SLAs, with regard to scope, retention, and mean time to recovery (MTTR). Usually, these are expressed as a *recovery point objective* (RPO) or *recovery time objective* (RTO), often defined by the business continuity (BC) team:

- The RTO defines the maximum amount of time that a service may be unavailable without a significant impact on the business operations.
- The RPO defines the maximum amount of time for which data may be lost (for example, all transactions from the last two days). It does not directly define the

---

[1] This should be covered by an organization's information architecture (IA).

amount of data that can be lost but rather the impact that the data loss has on the business.

What About Active-Active?

A frequent topic when discussing backup and disaster recovery is the concept of *"active/active"*. It means that by some mechanism all data in multiple systems is exactly the same at any given time. The goal, among others (refer to Chapter 2), may be disaster tolerance, i.e. zero RTO and zero RPO. Fundamentally, an active/active system must replicate any data mutation consistently across all systems before returning success to clients.

In practice, most systems struggle to achieve this during extreme peaks in request rates or when network partitions occur and allow for eventual consistency amongst the participating systems. The frequency and size of mutations in the big data realm compound these problems to a point of impracticality, which we discussed in "Cluster Spanning" on page 173.

In addition, consider that replicating data before or after ingestion is not going to protect you from user mistakes such as deleting data.

Setting certain RTO and RPO limits is the main driver in the choice of backup strategies (discussed in detail in the following sections); for example, requiring an RPO of not more than one hour would preclude a backup once per day. On the other hand, asking for a low RTO often precludes the construction of a new cluster from scratch and instead requires an available warm or even hot standby cluster. This means that the RPO and RTO often define the entire cluster architecture, since without the proper assumptions, there is literally no way of automating a viable backup solution.

Failure Scenarios

The previous chapters have sufficiently introduced and discussed what a full-blown (or partial) Hadoop system looks like. What we need to understand now are the implications of failures to a cluster. Different scenarios have varying impact on the availability of the system and on the data it provides.

Note that Chapter 12 discusses how to mitigate the possibility of failures, from an operational point of view. With proper monitoring and alerting, many of the scenarios here can be avoided, yet certain types of failures can still occur.

Here is an overview of the more common sets of problems observed when operating a Hadoop cluster:

Detrimental node degradation

This is a special kind of partial failure of a node, which leaves it operational but with severe limitations. Hadoop users jokingly refer to it as the "John Wayne syndrome": in a Western-style movie, the protagonist is shot many times but refuses to go down. This scenario can create such a bottleneck within the overall cluster that its impact is observed globally.

Examples are corrupt disks, faulty network interface cards (NICs), or software bugs in Hadoop or in the underlying OS and its hardware drivers. The server performs its duties, but with many internal retries and error corrections, so that it appears, from the outside, to be very slow.

For simple, nondisruptive degradation of a node (see the next failure scenario), the various core components of Hadoop are well suited to detect the problem and to treat the server with care, eventually excluding it from the cluster (placing it on the ignore list), if the problem persists. But with detrimental node degradation, the detection may be delayed or altogether fooled, resulting in cluster performance at the level of the lowest denominator, which is the slowest server.

Partial node failure

A common issue, especially at scale, when operating Hadoop clusters is a partial node failure, in which, for example, a single disk fails or a (hopefully) redundant network card stops working. Ideally, these failures are tolerated (can be configured) and only lead to the partial degradation of the node's performance. As described earlier, the core systems in Hadoop (the resource scheduler and filesystem) are reasonably well equipped to handle such scenarios and to take the necessary actions—up to the mentioned ignore-listing of the node. Hadoop also allows for a graceful recovery of the node, while adding it back to the cluster with no interruption to service. Cluster management tools allow for the creation of alarms and SNMP traps that can be sent to the operations team for timely action.

Node failure

Should an entire node fail, and assuming the cluster is designed and implemented with all aspects of HA in mind (see Chapter 12), all systems will keep on working, though possibly with reduced capacity. Again, this failure scenario is built into the Hadoop core frameworks (that is, YARN and HDFS) and is properly handled.

Network partitioning

Here we experience issues in which parts of the cluster are separated by network problems, such that the parts cannot further communicate with the others. This scenario can lead to the previously mentioned *split-brain* problem, in which any now separate and isolated part of the cluster has to make a decision about what its state is. Can it still operate and serve user requests, or should it stop operating and wait (or shut itself down), while not serving any more requests? This is further complicated by the fact that the split has to be detected and recognized in the first place. There are situations in which servers continue to serve clients and are not at all aware their state is now questionable. This is especially true of requests that are in flight during the split, which might yield different outcomes than expected by the client.

In Hadoop, usually all of the HA implementations (for HDFS, YARN, Oozie, and HBase) are either based on stateless servers or backed by a cluster-central authority, namely a ZooKeeper quorum. They commonly comprise three or five servers that form a majority, using a distributed consensus protocol (refer to "Zoo-Keeper" on page 347). With this approach, the cluster components can determine their state because every client call has to eventually fall back to a majority of servers. In a network split, one part (or more) has no majority of nodes, leaving one part as the active one. This is only part of handling the problem, though. What about clients trying to send requests to servers? And what happens when the split is healed?

Clients usually have a list of the ZooKeeper quorum entries and ask directly for authoritative servers. Should the client have access to the surviving part, it can still operate. But what if all clients switch to the remaining active part, which might now be heavily degraded in performance? Could a production workload (including, for example, SLA batch workloads and interactive queries) still operate? This *must* be designed into the cluster architecture, or the outcome will be unpredictable.

Datacenter failure

The final failure scenario is for entire clusters to fail, usually during a datacenter outage. Here, only having mirrors or backups in remote locations provides for any reasonable continuity. Replicating data is discussed in detail in "Replication" on page 383 and "Data Replication" on page 388. Some tools, like HBase, have built-in replication support (see "HBase" on page 356). Others need to have devised an architecture covering the replication of data to other locations.

User failure

There is one more major type of failure to consider—user failure. There are two reasons why humans might affect a Hadoop cluster: either accidentally or maliciously. Be it the new admin who is not aware what a certain command does— and whether it is undoable—or the disgruntled employee with a red Swingline stapler, they both can wreak havoc. Their actions might leave services incapacitated or might reduce the amount of data to zero.

This type of failure is more unpredictable than the others, in terms of its effects. With enough intent a malicious user or administrator can do serious harm. The risks posed by the former can be somewhat mitigated with the right security measures (see Chapter 9), but a rogue administrator is a much more difficult problem. You need to consider having separate administrators for main and auxiliary clusters so that already-backed-up data in another physical location is safe.

Table 13-1 summarizes the support of each scenario mapped to the more important subsystems in a Hadoop cluster.

Table 13-1. Supported failure scenarios

Failure	HDFS	YARN	HBase	Oozie
Node degradation	Partial	Partial	Partial	Partial
Partial node failure	Yes	Yes	Yes	Yes
Node failure	Yes	Yes	Yes	Yes
Network partition	Partial	Partial	Partial	?
Datacenter failure	Optional	Optional	Optional	Optional
User failure	Partial	Partial	Partial	Partial

Where appropriate, we refer to the failure scenarios throughout this chapter.

Suitable Data Sources

Some parts of the Hadoop stack do not fall at all into the usual category of a data storage system. For example, Flume is used for message delivery purposes, building a topology of agents that pass messages as an event flow from node to node. Like in a message queue (MQ) system, the storage per node is limited and only meant to buffer data as long as it takes to be sent along and acknowledged by the next agent. Flume has a pluggable *channel* architecture, which comes with many implementations out of the box. A common choice is the durable file channel, storing uncommitted data local to the Flume agent until delivery is complete. In the event of a catastrophic node failure, the data that was stored locally is likely to be lost.

One might be tempted to opt for the database-backed Flume channel implementation instead, so that a highly available relational database management system (RDBMS) can be used to maintain access to the data from a replacement node. This raises the general question of how to best design a highly available system based on Hadoop, because the topology and persistency method choices will most likely have an impact on RTO and RPO. We address this in the following section.

Part of the onboarding procedure of users and applications is to identify which parts of the Hadoop stack are in use and what they are each expected to deliver, in terms of RTO and RPO. It might be acceptable to have a simplified—which might also imply better-performing—cluster architecture, if the RPO allows for the loss of short-term data. Each use case should be individually decided, and this requires very careful planning and agreement between the various stakeholders because the wrong choices could be detrimental. Appendix A offers a sample onboarding checklist that you can use as a starting point to define a more customized list, based on local specifications.

Strategies

There are also multiple ways to keep data safe, including replication, snapshots, and backups. There are fundamental differences between these approaches, making their use either prohibitive or, conversely, necessary to achieve a given RPO/RTO.

Replication

For low RPO/RTO requirements, or the fastest recovery option, a common approach is to keep multiple copies of the data in a warm or hot standby system. This allows applications to fail over quickly and to use the standby system to run additional processing jobs, which alleviates the pressure on the main system. Depending on the Hadoop subsystem considered, there are vastly different replication implementations —if they are supported out of the box at all.

In general, though, *replication* means sending all mutations from an originating system (leader) to one or more replica systems (followers). This also includes delete operations, and in the case of erroneous data deletion, there is a likely scenario in which permanent data loss is incurred.

On a file-based level, this can be compared with using the venerable rsync command-line tool, which allows synchronization of directories with their contained files, including across computer boundaries. The user faces a difficult decision— either also synchronize file removals, or retain the deleted files in the backup location. The former makes using the copy easy because it reflects the state of the last tool execution. But if you notice a removal *after* the tool is executed again, you have also removed the file in the copy. If you choose to retain the deleted files, you end up with a growing number of files, some of which are eventually outdated. This makes failover to the copy difficult, unless some sort of maintenance or cleanup process is in place to restore the last known consistent state (which also meets the RPO).

Snapshots

Another technique for securing copies of data is to use *snapshots*. Several Hadoop services, including HDFS and HBase, implement their own snapshot mechanisms. HDFS snapshots allow for taking a quick metadata-only stock of all files contained in a snapshot-enabled directory. It uses a *copy-on-write* approach in which all subsequent modifications cause behind-the-scenes archiving of files contained in an active snapshot. Access to the snapshot is provided by a special directory notation that exposes the snapshot by name as a subdirectory of the original directory.

Internally, all files either point to the unchanged live files or to archived files for any modified or deleted file. In HDFS, the client can only append to existing files, with a single writer process, at any point in time. This makes snapshotting more predictable because files cannot be freely mutated. When a snapshot is performed, all blocks that are complete are part of the snapshot. In other words, for a file that is still being written (for example, a web server log file), you are not able to snapshot the data in the currently uncommitted last block. This amounts to whatever the HDFS block size is set to, usually defaulting to 128 MB. See "Consistency" on page 386 for a discussion of what this means for applications.

HBase works in a very similar way, taking a snapshot of a table as a metadata operation and tagging all files belonging to the table on which the command operates. Should files be deleted, for example due to a compaction, the same mechanism of archiving and reference counting the underlying files takes place. A new snapshot does not occupy any additional storage, but does accrue more storage space as changes happen and additional files need to be retained. HBase snapshots do not use HDFS snapshots, but their own internal feature implementation. This means that HBase snapshots cannot be accessed directly through HDFS but need a special tool that is provided by HBase. Also, HBase snapshots need to trigger a flush operation to persist any pending mutations because they do not include the write-ahead logs. You need to consider this carefully because it might negatively affect the cluster performance.

In more general terms, snapshots allow for the freezing of some moment in time for the data they operate on. They provide a versioning mechanism, and, with the appropriate access tool, a consistent copy can be made. Snapshots are local to the storage system and do not help with disaster recovery, which means a proper backup architecture would include a copy of the snapshot to another system or cluster. Finally, not all tools have support for built-in snapshots, so this only applies where available.

Backups

A *backup* is essentially a point in time–based copy of data, which is then copied to another set of disks or servers as a safety measure. As mentioned, this could be used in the event of erroneous deletion (or modification) of data, or a server failure.

 For certain storage subsystems, such as HDFS, you can and should apply the appropriate access control mechanisms. You do so by using access control lists or employing tools like Apache Ranger or Apache Sentry, which avoid the deletion of data in the first place. For example, shared files in an HDFS directory named *public* would be set to read-only for all users.

For the former, it would be beneficial to have a short-circuit partial or full restore mechanism, depending on the location of the copy. For true disaster recovery, though, the copy should be versioned, retained as a configurable amount of copies, and stored in one or multiple locations so that the data can always be restored, even if the RTO is negatively affected.

Due to the complexity of Hadoop, there is no single solution that can provide a consistent backup across all the subsystems in the stack. A backup implementation can span many systems and use many techniques, including replication and snapshots. Based on the necessary RTO and RPO, the setup can vary a lot, so planning ahead of time is crucial to guaranteeing SLAs later on.

Virtualization Tools

Snapshotting is also available on setups where the storage layer is not just a direct connection to, for example, hard drives. Especially in virtualized environments, such as cloud infrastructures, the storage layer is often more elaborate and contains abilities to snapshot the current data.

In practice, this may seem like an option to solve the backup problem, but the opposite is true: storage-level snapshots are only as good as their integration with the higher-level tools. Using such snapshots is known to not work with HDFS data, which is very likely to create corrupt snapshots as far as HDFS is concerned.

The same is true for databases that are not integrated so that they flush out in-memory state before the snapshot takes place. In our experience, using low-level storage tools to facilitate backups is not a viable option.

Rack awareness and high availability

Hadoop—and specifically HDFS—has another feature, named *rack awareness* (see "Rack Awareness and Rack Failures" on page 165), provided to set up cluster topologies that allow for another frequently requested requirement for production-grade systems—HA.

It is certainly vital to design a cluster topology with rack awareness in mind to increase the availability of the data it is providing. It does not, though, replace an end-to-end replication or backup strategy, because it only deals with a subset of possible failure scenarios (see "Failure Scenarios" on page 379). More specifically, rack awareness allows for some failure scenarios not to affect cluster operations. It does not cover loss of data through user errors, such as accidental file deletion in HDFS, dropping managed tables in Hive, or deleting tables in HBase. It also does not handle more widespread outages, such as datacenter failures. Even network partitions/splits pose a hazard because you might end up with an operational part of the cluster (majority vote succeeds) but might not be able to access all the data.

Data Types

The next question to ask is, what do you need to back up from a Hadoop-based cluster to avoid data loss (apart from the mentioned RPO)? There are databases holding details such as state and schema, OS filesystems holding raw data, and operational systems storing temporal data. The rest of this chapter addresses those sources, per Hadoop subsystem, but it is worth first discussing what a backup should include. There are distinct sets of data types that warrant deeper consideration to determine their treatment:

Data
> This is the user data persisted in the configured storage systems. Hadoop ecosystem projects usually store their user and generated data inside HDFS, which means that it needs to be backed up somehow. With HDFS, a backup strategy could pin the entry point to specific, named directories.

Metadata
> There are parts of the processing system that need additional metadata, which applies structure to the usually unstructured (as in, unknown schema) raw data. One example is the shared Hive Metastore. It persist the user-defined schemas in a database that holds the mapping of tables and columns to data files, giving SQL-based access to the data itself.
>
> Something else to consider is HBase table information, imposing a similar schema to custom storage files underneath the HBase namespace or Cloudera Manager and Apache Ambari data, such as cluster setup details and user accounts.

Transient data
> Finally, there is the aforementioned transient data, such as temporary job files or Flume agent local data, like uncommitted records waiting for the upstream systems to acknowledge reception. Often, the RPO allows for omitting this kind of data from the backup. Designing the ingest system with downstream retention and a replay mechanism can alleviate the problem, but this, too, requires careful planning ahead of time.

Consistency

The last dimension to consider with regard to backup and disaster recovery within a Hadoop-based system is the consistency of the data inside a backup. Even when using HDFS snapshots to copy all raw files in a point-in-time version or when using transactional locking provided by the underlying databases for other parts of the system, what is actually part of the backup is still questionable. When you have many concurrent updates, like adding files to different directories in HDFS or data to different

---

HBase tables, you cannot ensure a truly consistent view as far as the user or the application is concerned.

The solution to this is up to the client application, which should store transactional information that allows for recovery from inconsistent application data. For example, in the case of disaster recovery, it may happen that the restored data contains some information from the latest pre-disaster modifications, but it is still partial (that is, incomplete) concerning the application. The developer needs to somehow guard against this and to ignore incomplete data, either by using provided mechanisms or by devising a data schema that ensures safe operations.

HBase could use a master table that is updated atomically, storing the last committed transaction, possibly with all of the included changes. Google Metastore and Percolator projects reference a transactional layer that enables optimistic, roll-forward transactions using tools such as schema design. Changes are staged and applied by the current writer—or any subsequent writer—before applying its modifications, in the case of the current writer being considered failed. Another possibility is a central transaction state server, which keeps a timestamp that is used to flag all correlated edits.

No matter how it is implemented, the reading application needs to support this mechanism in order to smoothly restart on partial data. The other option is to manually clean up partial updates before restarting the applications, most likely substantially increasing the MTTR.

Validation

After a backup or restore has been completed, it is prudent to validate the result. This is a complicated process within Hadoop due to the diverse nature of the systems involved. The easiest is HDFS, where a cyclic redundancy check (CRC) (checksum) operation compares the data in the source and target locations. An optimized version could use hashing algorithms, like Merkle trees, to speed up comparisons on incremental copies. Other parts of the stack are more involved and have no native support at all.

Another approach would be to provide validation rules that allow for automated checks after a backup or restore. For databases, this could include a restore of the SQL dump to a temporary database in the backup location and then specific SQL queries to validate the content. For example, if the database has updates every minute, the validation rule could check that the backup has updates up to a minute before the copy was made. Or, if there is an expected growth in raw data size or number of records, either the size of the SQL export file could be compared to the previous one or the temporary database could be used to perform a count, subsequently assessing the observed figures with respect to some user-defined thresholds.

For a restore, the original application code should include validation tests to confirm the integrity of the restored data, or another set of user-supplied rules should be used to verify the data. No matter which approach you choose, both the backup and the restore should include a verification step immediately after each is completed.

Summary

Summarizing the previous sections, we can postulate the following:

- Backups involve a combination of available techniques, or custom implementations for systems that lack built-in support.
- Snapshots only provide local versioning, and their consistency guarantees are not clear.
- Replication is not suitable as a backup, but it can help with business continuity.
- Consistency requirements must be handled on the client side.
- The RTO and RPO drive the cluster design and should be considered from the very beginning.
- There is no complete backup solution, which means a custom implementation is needed.

If you are interested in a commercial offering (such as WANdisco) we highly recommend that you conduct a comprehensive due diligence check based on the previously discussed topics.

Data Replication

Because replication helps in setting up a warm or hot standby copy, it is useful to understand more of the architectural implications of providing such support. There are two fundamental approaches to replication:

- Outside of the cluster, using techniques to split up traffic and to reliably deliver any modification to all configured locations
- Within the cluster, using built-in or custom jobs to replicate data between separate cluster instances or physically distributed clusters

Only a few systems (for example, HBase) have built-in support for replication. Some other areas are covered by Cloudera Backup and Disaster Recovery (BDR) or Hortonworks Data Lifecycle Manager (DLM), which allow the synchronization of data (HDFS) and metadata (Hive/Impala Metastore) across clusters using scheduled tasks.

For purely external traffic distribution, there are many more choices, starting with instrumenting the generating systems to tee off the data. Another, more hybrid approach is to use managed services, such as Apache Kafka or Apache Flume, to create a data bus that is then listened to and consumed by multiple target clusters. We discuss these separately next.

HBase

The built-in replication feature of HBase allows for fast shipping of all modifications of a configured column family to a different cluster. With proper network design and traffic shaping, this can be (and has been) done for years. The source and target can be in different datacenters and of completely different configurations. It is vital, of course, to have enough bandwidth between them to ensure a timely delivery. Should the bandwidth not match the average write throughput, the replication can obviously never catch up.

HBase also allows for complex replication scenarios, including master-follower and master-master, with circular dependencies if required. Every edit has the unique cluster ID attached to it so that replication across more than two clusters can be detected and properly handled.

Of course, since HBase is a low-latency system, its replication tries to be as timely as possible, shipping mutations across the interconnect while applying them to the peer systems. This means that HBase replication is good for syncing one or more hot standby clusters for fast failover. It does not replace the need to back up data (see "HBase" on page 396), however, because user failures, such as accidentally deleting data, are also replicated.

Cluster Management Tools

Commercial options to cover HDFS data and the Hive Metastore are available as Cloudera BDR and Hortonworks DLM, which support scheduled synchronization tasks to keep current copies. This usually is not for low-latency use cases but for a more coarse-grained schedule; for example, every hour.

For BDR and HDFS files, you also have the option to enable HDFS snapshots on the synchronized directories, which triggers a short-term snapshot while the sync is in progress. For DLM, this is a fixed requirement that cannot be changed. Using this feature ensures that all current files are frozen inside the snapshot and can be copied asynchronously without any impact on ongoing changes to the data in the source directory.

BDR also has the option to schedule regular snapshots within HDFS and to retain a configurable amount of them. It does not yet have the option to copy the snapshots to a remote location, making a true backup architecture more difficult. Additionally, BDR only operates in pull mode, meaning that the jobs run on the BDR server that has the tasks scheduled.

A restore is an ad hoc task on the cluster that needs it, essentially synchronizing the data from the dedicated backup cluster (it could even be a shared one) back to the cluster that needs the copy.

Kafka

A more recent hybrid idea is to use a managed service, namely Apache Kafka, to act as a replication system, multiplexing data into one or more Hadoop clusters. Figure 13-1 shows this with a single cluster, but the same can be done with more than one Hadoop cluster as final consumers.

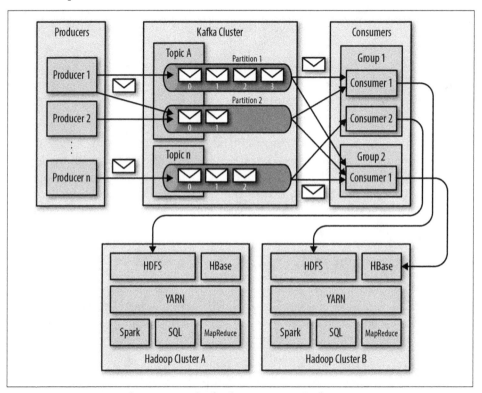

Figure 13-1. Ingesting data into multiple clusters using Kafka

The idea is to harmonize the data before it reaches Hadoop and then to send the messages reliably to each storage backend. Every Hadoop cluster can ingest the data at its own pace and can even recover from periods of unavailability (for example, for maintenance). This is facilitated by the Kafka consumer architecture, storing independent offsets into the buffered messages. This approach works particularly well for streaming use cases, in which data arrives in small units, usually referred to as *messages*, *events*, or *records*. This can be extended to include other auxiliary systems, such as

Flume, to route the events from loosely coupled systems to Kafka for datacenter-local staging (harmonizing).

Non-Event-Related Use Cases

Other use cases—for example, those including raw HDFS data, such as log files being delivered to an ingest layer—could still use Kafka to queue metadata about the ingested files and to initiate a subsequent asynchronous copy process. Currently, there is no native implementation of such a replication mechanism supplied with Hadoop. It would require a bespoke solution. "Case Study: Automating Backups with Oozie" on page 398 discusses an example implementation using Oozie.

A word of caution: using cluster-external replication is not without its challenges. Because each incoming data point is processed by each cluster separately, there may be side effects that can result in different cluster states. For example, assuming that data is merged from multiple sources (like insurance claims that are cross-checked with weather data), it could be that the dependent data arrives at varying times, yielding different results from the processing jobs.

Summary

We can summarize the previous sections as follows:

- Replication is necessary for low-latency use cases and fast recovery.
- It is only one part of the overall backup and disaster recovery strategy, because it does not handle versioning of data for point-in-time recovery.
- Only a few Hadoop systems have a replication feature, and they are significantly different from one another.
- Some tools exist to cover replication for certain systems in Hadoop, including Cloudera BDR and Hortonworks DLM (covering HDFS and the Hive Metastore).
- There are architectural choices that can help reliably deliver streaming data to one or more Hadoop systems.

Hadoop Cluster Backups

For every part of the Hadoop stack, there are decisions to be made about what is backed up, at what times, and what the SLAs (RTO and RPO) are, among other issues. The overall cluster architecture plays a vital role in what is and is not possible. A few more general prerequisites are:

- Full read access to all used RDBMSs is available (that is, database credentials).

- A technical user account is created that has access to all data in HDFS (files and directories) and HBase (namespaces and tables) that are to be included in the backup.

- HDFS snapshots are enabled for all directories that need to be backed up.

The caveats, as discussed throughout this chapter, include:

- Enabling snapshots takes care of file-level consistency, but may not sufficiently address the application-layer consistency.

- Using replication allows for faster failover in the case of a disaster, but does not replace a regular backup, allowing access to point-in-time versions of the cluster state and its stored data.

Now let's discuss the various subsystems of a common Hadoop cluster setup, starting with the backing databases used to retain the metadata and state.

Heterogeneous Systems

Replicating data from one cluster to another poses two major challenges:

Versioning
It is likely that replication or copying of data for backups is happening between clusters running different software versions. There are strategies in place for both HDFS and HBase that allow for reading or writing data across heterogeneous clusters.

For copying data between instances of HDFS, the HFTP filesystem implementation provides read-only access using HTTP, as opposed to the default binary API access. For example, copying from an older cluster and saving it into a new version, an administrator could run the following command on the newer cluster:

```
$ hadoop distcp -i hftp://sourceFS:50070/src \
    hdfs://destFS:50070/dest
```

The -i tells the command to ignore failures during the copy, so that the entire copy process does not fail due to, for example, intermittent connectivity issues.

For HBase, you need to ensure that the client version is supported by the servers. For replication, be sure that the used ZooKeeper clients can communicate with the remote servers.

Security
Another critical issue is how each cluster is secured. It is common for Hadoop clusters to use Kerberos (see Chapter 9) as their authentication mechanism. For two or more clusters to exchange data requires that they can talk to each other.

For Kerberos, it is also common to have remote clusters running in separate realms, which means that some form of cross-realm trust needs to be established. This has been solved, in practice, but is not an easy task and may require considerable time and resources to get right.

Additionally, after authentication comes authorization, trusted user accounts that can be used to ingest or divulge the data. This might necessitate technical user accounts with a broader set of privileges, and they need to be handled with care.

The bottom line is that it is possible to replicate or copy data across clusters running different versions, given the right circumstances and with enough effort. Should both versions be incompatible due to, for instance, a breaking protocol change between major versions, you are required to bring both (or all) of them into the same version range to make communication possible.

Databases

As an example, the Cloudera CDH online documentation has detailed information about which database to consider for a backup. Table 13-2 provides a summary.

Table 13-2. Overview of service databases and their expected sizes

Service name	DB name	Size
Cloudera Manager	cms	Small (< 100 MB)
Activity Monitor (MRv1)	amon	Large
Report Manager	rman	Medium
Hue	hue	Small
Hive Metastore (Beeswax)	metastore	Small
Sentry	sentry	Small
Oozie	oozie	Large
Cloudera Navigator Audit	nav	Large
Cloudera Navigator Metadata	navms	Small

There are two types of databases: those required by the common Hadoop components, and those required by the cluster management tools. Other distributions vary, especially in the latter.

Obviously, these databases are only present if the accompanying Hadoop subsystem is installed. For example, you only have access to the Oozie database if Oozie is installed on the source cluster. The mentioned documentation also explains the possible choices for backing up the databases, depending on the chosen RDBMS. For MySQL, for example, you can use the supplied mysqldump command-line tool to export the entire database into a text file, enabling the restoration of the database by executing the contained SQL statements (DDL and DML).

Only a proper production-ready database system (such as Oracle, MySQL, or PostgreSQL) can be relied upon to support consistent backups; the default embedded database systems are for testing only and may not support this functionality.

Subsystems

The following sections itemize, for every Hadoop subsystem, what to consider with regard to the backup process.

Cloudera Manager

Both Cloudera Manager and Navigator store details in various databases. These need to be backed up to retain the cluster configuration, as well as statistics, metrics, and metadata.

There are supported database system options, with a managed PostgreSQL instance being the suggested choice during installation. You can also use existing and self-managed systems, such as Oracle and MySQL. The choice should not cause differences in the overall size of the data they will contain but will influence the tools used to back up the data. The online documentation (*http://bit.ly/2Tu2qYR*) includes information on how to back up the supported databases.

In addition to the main Cloudera Manager database just discussed, there is also an option to extract the cluster setup using the REST-based Cloudera Manager API. The API returns a JSON-based cluster descriptor, which also contains most of the necessary cluster details, including users, hosts, clusters, services, and more. It is an additional measure to also back up the JSON descriptor, since it can be used to reconstruct the cluster by importing it into a new set of machines. A simple script using curl is sufficient to extract the descriptor and then save it to the backup HDFS cluster by way of a dedicated target directory. The JSON file should include the API version used to extract the descriptor—it is important to use the same API version when importing it again.

Apache Ambari

Similar to Cloudera Manager but available as open source, Apache Ambari is a cluster-management tool that enables administrators to perform various tasks in a graphical user interface (GUI). Ambari uses a single database to store all its settings and supports a number of common database systems.

The steps to back up the database are the same as discussed in the previous section.

HDFS

The raw data files in HDFS can be copied to a backup location and possibly stored with different properties, such as access mode, owner, compression type, and block replication count. Any professional, production-grade cluster architecture implies the existence of an information architecture that prescribes the layout of files within HDFS. With the use of the access control provided by HDFS and/or Sentry or Ranger, the layout defines how data is ingested, processed, and provided to consumers as part of data pipelines. The backup process should align with the IA and back up the selected data files in such a way that they can be restored without much manual intervention. The append-only, single-writer nature of HDFS simplifies the process, but to ensure consistency across many files, HDFS snapshots should be used to temporarily freeze the content of a directory. The backup process then reads the snapshot instead of the live directory and copies the data to a safe place. This is often implemented using the Hadoop-supplied DistCp (short for *distributed copy*) tool, or a variation thereof.

In addition to the data, HDFS also has metadata stored by the NameNodes, including the so-called *fsimage* file, along with any pending edits (see "HDFS" on page 348). There is an API call and a matching command-line wrapper that allows for the downloading of the image file from the active NameNode. It does not include the recent edit logs, however, which means that up to one hour's worth—which is the default setting for HDFS—of changes will be missing. It is therefore questionable whether to store this file at all, although in the case of a catastrophic failure and with all other forms of backup also failing, it is a viable option to keep some state of the cluster backed up for recovery, even if it is outdated.

Hive Metastore

Both Hive and Impala, which are vendor-provided SQL engines, share the same metadata backend—the Hive Metastore. It is backed by a relational database, with support for the common RDBMSs. The metadata includes the mapping of raw data stored in HDFS, HBase, and other pluggable storage backends into a relational model. It adds a schema to unstructured data, mapping values into columns with associated data types.

Backing up the metadata database requires the same approach used for the service databases discussed previously, including using the matching tools to extract a consistent copy of the entire database content. In addition, data could be replicated using an HA setup, as explained in "Hive" on page 359, or mirrored by an external tool, such as Cloudera BDR or Hortonworks DLM.

HBase

Although all data behind HBase is stored in HDFS, it is not possible to use HDFS snapshots to freeze its state, copy the data files, and subsequently restore it. There are so many files and in-memory data structures in HBase that, under heavy load, it is possible to snapshot an inconsistent state as far as HBase is concerned. Instead, a proper backup solution must use the supplied HBase snapshot tools, which have shipped with HBase since version 0.96/0.98. Snapshots allow freezing a consistent state with regard to tables and HBase metadata, and should be applied during an active backup process. The supplied tools enable snapshotting a table, exporting the contained files, and copying them to a safe location. After the copy operation succeeds, the snapshot can be deleted (or kept, if it is part of a more local recovery policy).

In addition, HBase ships with a replication feature that can be used to keep all mutations synchronized (though with latencies) across multiple clusters—including outside the boundaries of a datacenter. As previously discussed, replication is an additional measure that can (and should) be added to guarantee low RPO and RTO because a near real-time copy of the data is available on a standby cluster.

HBase also ships with the `Export` and `Import` tools, although both are less production-grade and heavily depend on proper use. The former exports a table into a file, but might do so while the table is being written to. This can cause inconsistencies in the backup, but it might work for idempotent updates, depending (again) on the use case. In other words, neither approach is truly consistent if the application is writing to more than one region, including multiple tables. A snapshot or export might happen between related mutations, with partial updates being included in the backup. The application must be able to handle this upon restoring data and resuming operations.

A final note: because HBase is frequently used in low-latency use cases, it may be prudent to perform backups in off-peak times, when the additional I/O to read the data is not as crucial or may have no impact at all.

YARN

All the job execution state is persisted in the *state store*, which comes with various implementations. It is either memory-, file-, or ZooKeeper-based, with the latter being used in HA setups (see "YARN" on page 353). Since job execution and its state are transient, storing the current information as part of a backup is usually nontrivial or even not wanted. Instead, during cluster recovery, it is important to have some means to restart the data pipelines on another system. This is done either using some authoritative messaging system, such as an MQ system, or using a replicated event log with Kafka. This is out of scope for our current discussion and is not addressed.

Oozie

Just like the Hive Metastore, Oozie has a relational database state store, backed by the common RDBMS choices seen earlier. The same rules apply: back up the database for recovery, and/or replicate for low RTO using a standby system (see "Oozie" on page 371). But contrary to the HMS, Oozie's state store also contains transient information, which includes where workflows are currently situated with regard to their actions. Additionally, the store holds the workflow definitions and all the higher-level information, such as coordinator and bundle details. It must be backed up to restore the data pipelines created in Oozie, unless some other deployment process is in place (for example, Chef, Ansible, or Puppet) to programmatically re-create the workflow setup.

Oozie also needs HDFS files, which represent the actual workflow, coordinator, and bundle definitions, any additional data and required library files, and more. You need to back these up using the HDFS approach (DistCp), as described in "HDFS" on page 395.

Apache Sentry

CDH comes with a central *role-based access control* (RBAC) feature, provided by Sentry, which establishes a single point of reference for all user activities. Its database-backed store holds all the defined roles and rules that apply to many client operations, across almost all Hadoop ecosystem tools. Like others, this database needs to be backed up regularly for recovery, and it requires the common tools just discussed.

Apache Ranger

Similar to Sentry, Ranger provides a central access control feature for Hadoop clusters. It uses an *attribute-based access control* (ABAC) approach to define policies. Ranger uses one of the common database systems to store its data. You need to ensure that its database is backed up on a regular basis, using the tools provided by the chosen database system.

Hue

Some Hadoop distributions include Hue as a graphical user interface for Hadoop, providing access for end users to HDFS, HBase, Oozie, and others. Its database stores users and their credentials as well as user data, such as saved queries. All the earlier remarks apply equally here—that is, the database is backed by a choice of RDBMSs, and extracting the data is dependent on the supplied tools. An optional mirroring of the database for HA is orthogonal to the backup efforts (see "Hue" on page 372).

Case Study: Automating Backups with Oozie

In this section, we put the concepts from the preceding sections to practice and present a framework in Oozie that performs the necessary backup and restore operations.

Introduction

One approach in Hadoop to automate the entire backup process is to create Oozie workflows—one for backup and one for restore. Each backup source is represented by a generic workflow that can back up, for example, a database, and all parameters, such as the URI, username, and password, are handed in at runtime. Figure 13-2 shows this in a simplified form (omitting all possible sources and the optional validation steps).

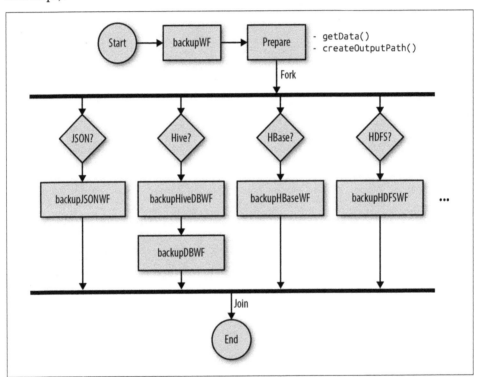

Figure 13-2. Backup workflow using Oozie

The validation steps are part of the subworkflows and are triggered if a flag is set. All generic workflows are combined into larger ones, with the configuration passed into the subflows. The main workflows are then instrumented using coordinators to run the backup (and restore, if needed) at fixed intervals. You can optionally configure subflows be configured to execute only at specific invocations of the workflow. This allows for different backup schedules for each source.

Overall, triggering the backup process is possible based on time or larger workflow events. Oozie supports multiple notions of scheduling workflows based on time, including a Linux Cron-style syntax. This can be used to run the backup once per hour or day. Alternatively, you could connect a backup run to the availability of certain files in HDFS. Oozie provides file-based triggers that can monitor a directory and start a workflow when a specific condition is met.

We first look at the various subflows and then combine them into the main backup workflow.

Subflow: HDFS

This flow is able to copy a dataset from a source to a target location, similar to rsync, though the capability here is more suitably provided by the distcp tool. It has options to retain deleted files or to synchronize between the source and target locations. Usually, the flow is invoked with a new, empty target directory, which makes the synchronization option often negligible:

```xml
<?xml version="1.0" encoding="UTF-8"?>

<!--
  Note: Using approach described in
    http://www.helmutzechmann.com/2015/04/23/oozie-loops/
-->
<workflow-app xmlns="uri:oozie:workflow:0.5"
name="backupHDFSWF">
  <parameters>
    <property>
      <name>counter</name>
      <value>1</value>
    </property>
  </parameters>
  <global>
    <job-tracker>${jobTracker}</job-tracker>
    <name-node>${nameNode}</name-node>
    <configuration>
      <property>
        <name>mapred.job.queue.name</name>
        <value>${queueName}</value>
      </property>
      <property>
        <name>oozie.launcher.mapred.job.queue.name</name>
        <value>${queueNameLauncher}</value>
      </property>
    </configuration>
  </global>
  <start to="checkIfDone" />
```

```
<decision name="checkIfDone">  ❶
  <switch>
    <case to="distCp">
      ${not empty wf:conf(concat("inclDirsHDFS_", counter))}
    </case>
    <default to="end" />
  </switch>
</decision>
<action name="distCp">  ❷
  <distcp xmlns="uri:oozie:distcp-action:0.2">
    <prepare>
      <mkdir path="${outputPath}/hdfs_${counter}"/>
    </prepare>
    <arg>-m</arg>
    <arg>10</arg>
    <arg>${wf:conf(concat("inclDirsHDFS_", counter))}
    /*</arg>
    <arg>${outputPath}/hdfs_${counter}</arg>
  </distcp>
  <ok to="loop" />
  <error to="failed" />
</action>
<action name="loop">  ❸
  <sub-workflow>
    <app-path>${wf:appPath()}</app-path>
    <propagate-configuration/>
    <configuration>
      <property>
        <name>counter</name>
        <value>${counter + 1}</value>
      </property>
    </configuration>
  </sub-workflow>
  <ok to="end" />
  <error to="failed" />
</action>
<kill name="failed">
  <message>HDFS backup script failed [error:
  ${wf:errorMessage(wf:lastErrorNode())}]
  </message>
</kill>
<end name="end" />
</workflow-app>
```

❶ The workflow loops over a list of directories. The first action is to check whether the loop is complete.

❷ The actual distcp action copies one directory.

❸ The loop action increments a counter that is used to enumerate over the list of directories.

Not deleting files can have a detrimental effect on the tools that use them. For example, not deleting files in a Hive warehouse directory can potentially corrupt the table it represents.

Subflow: HBase

As with HDFS, it is best for HBase tables to first apply a snapshot (the HBase native variant, not the HDFS snapshot feature) and to then export the included files. At the end, the snapshot can be dropped or it can be retained as part of an application-driven recovery architecture. As explained in "HBase" on page 396, HBase does not support cross-region (especially cross-table) consistent snapshots. Each table needs to be treated separately and copied to a location in the backup directory. The HBase backup workflow iterates over the given namespaces and/or tables (wildcards are allowed), applies the snapshot, exports the files directly to the backup location, and then removes the snapshot:

```xml
<?xml version="1.0" encoding="UTF-8"?>

<workflow-app xmlns="uri:oozie:workflow:0.5"
name="backupHBaseWF">
  <global>
    ...
  </global>
  <start to="runScript"/>
  <action name="runScript"> ❶
    <shell xmlns="uri:oozie:shell-action:0.3">
      <prepare>
        <mkdir path="${outputPath}"/>
      </prepare>
      <exec>hbaseBackup.sh</exec> ❷
      <argument>host=${host}</argument>
      <argument>port=${port}</argument>
      <argument>user=${user}</argument>
      <argument>password=${password}</argument>
      <argument>outputPath=${outputPath}</argument>
      <env-var>HADOOP_USER_NAME=${wf:user()}</env-var>
      <file>bin/helper.sh#helper.sh</file>
      <file>bin/hbaseBackup.sh#hbaseBackup.sh</file>
    </shell>
    <ok to="end"/>
    <error to="failed"/>
  </action>
  <kill name="failed">
    <message>HBase backup script failed
    [error: ${wf:errorMessage(wf:lastErrorNode())}]</message>
  </kill>
  <end name="end"/>
</workflow-app>
```

❶ The main workflow action is wrapped into an external script.

❷ The HBase backup script does all the work in taking a snapshot and then exporting it.

Subflow: Database

The database backup workflow has a simple decision node branching the execution
into subflows per database system. One implementation is the MySQL backup workflow, which uses the MySQL tool `mysqldump` to extract a copy of the entire named
database in the form of SQL DDL and DML commands. This file is then piped into a
location in HDFS.

First, the generic database backup workflow:

```
<?xml version="1.0" encoding="UTF-8"?>

<workflow-app xmlns="uri:oozie:workflow:0.5" name="backupDBWF">
  <start to="selectDBWF"/>
  <decision name="selectDBWF">
    <switch> ❶
      <case to="backupMySQLWF">${dbType eq "mysql"}</case>
      <!-- Enable future support for other database systems here
      <case to="backupPostgresWF">${jobType eq "postgres"}
      </case>
      <case to="backupOracleWF">${jobType eq "mysql"}</case>
        -->
      <default to="end"/>
    </switch>
  </decision>
  <action name="backupMySQLWF"> ❷
    <sub-workflow>
      <app-path>backupWF/backupDBWF/backupMySQLWF</app-path>
      <propagate-configuration/>
    </sub-workflow>
    <ok to="end"/>
    <error to="failed"/>
  </action>
  <kill name="failed">
    <message>Database backup failed
    [error: ${wf:errorMessage(wf:lastErrorNode())}]</message>
  </kill>
  <end name="end"/>
</workflow-app>
```

❶ The switch routes the flow based on the configuration settings.

❷ For MySQL, a special action is available that handles the backup specifics.

The workflow configuration is mostly set by defaults so that an administrator has to override only the necessary values (here, the database hostname):

```
#dbTypeHiveDB=mysql
dbHostHiveDB=muysql.foobar.com
#dbPortHiveDB=3306
#dbNameHiveDB=metastore
#dbUserHiveDB=hive
dbPasswordHiveDB=hivepw
```

And here's the MySQL-specific workflow:

```
<?xml version="1.0" encoding="UTF-8"?>

<workflow-app xmlns="uri:oozie:workflow:0.5"
name="backupMySQLWF-${dbName}">
  <global>
    ...
  </global>
  <start to="runScript"/>
  <action name="runScript">
    <shell xmlns="uri:oozie:shell-action:0.2">
      <prepare>
        <mkdir path="${outputPath}"/>
      </prepare>
      <exec>mysqlBackup.sh</exec> ❶
      <argument>dbHost=${dbHost}</argument>
      <argument>dbPort=${dbPort}</argument>
      <argument>dbName=${dbName}</argument>
      <argument>dbUser=${dbUser}</argument>
      <argument>dbPassword=${dbPassword}</argument>
      <argument>outputPath=${outputPath}</argument>
      <env-var>HADOOP_USER_NAME=${wf:user()}</env-var>
      <file>bin/helper.sh#helper.sh</file>
      <file>bin/mysqlBackup.sh#mysqlBackup.sh</file>
    </shell>
    <ok to="end"/>
    <error to="failed"/>
  </action>
  <kill name="failed">
    <message>MySQL backup script failed
    [error: ${wf:errorMessage(wf:lastErrorNode())}]</message>
  </kill>
  <end name="end"/>
</workflow-app>
```

❶ Invoke the shell script that does the actual backup, while passing in all parameters.

The shell script exports the SQL into HDFS:

```
#!/bin/bash
source ./helper.sh
```

```
dbHost=$(getOptionVal dbHost "$*")
dbPort=$(getOptionVal dbPort "$*")
dbName=$(getOptionVal dbName "$*")
dbUser=$(getOptionVal dbUser "$*")
dbPass=$(getOptionVal dbPassword "$*")
bkpRoot=$(getOptionVal outputPath "$*")

output=${bkpRoot}/${dbName}
srvArgs="--host=${dbHost} --port=${dbPort}"
dbmArgs=" --user=${dbUser} --password=${dbPass}"

mysqldump ${srvArgs} ${dbmArgs} ${dbName} | \
hdfs dfs -put - ${output}
```

Backup workflow

The mentioned main backup workflow ties all of the preceding elements together. It uses an XML-based properties file, named *config-default.xml*, which initializes the various settings with sensible defaults (shown abbreviated):

```
<configuration>
  <!-- General Settings -->
  <property>
    <name>outputPath</name>
    <value>${backupPath}</value>
    <description>The default output location for the backup</description>
  </property>
  ...
  <!-- Hive Metastore Settings -->
  <property>
    <name>backupHiveDB</name>
    <value>true</value>
    <description>Backup Hive Metastore database</description>
  </property>
  <property>
    <name>dbTypeHiveDB</name>
    <value>mysql</value>
    <description>Default database type is MySQL</description>
  </property>
  <property>
    <name>dbPortHiveDB</name>
    <value>3306</value>
    <description>Default MySQL port</description>
  </property>
  <property>
    <name>dbNameHiveDB</name>
    <value>metastore</value>
    <description>Default database name for the schema database</description>
  </property>
  <property>
    <name>dbUserHiveDB</name>
```

```
      <value>hive</value>
      <description>Default user owning the database</description>
  </property>
  <property>
      <name>dbPasswordHiveDB</name>
      <value>hive</value>
      <description>Default (weak) password for database user</description>
  </property>
  ...
  <!-- HDFS Data Settings -->
  <property>
      <name>backupHDFS</name>
      <value>true</value>
      <description>Back up HDFS data</description>
  </property>

  <!-- HBase Data Settings -->
  <property>
      <name>backupHBase</name>
      <value>true</value>
      <description>Back up HBase data</description>
  </property>
</configuration>
```

This includes Boolean flags defining what is included in a backup. Each of these flags may trigger a database, HDFS, or HBase backup set up with the default values, while overriding any of them with runtime settings. For example, a concrete properties file overrides all node settings with those pertaining to an actual Hadoop cluster.

After the workflow starts, it simply branches out in many parallel actions, implemented as subworkflows. These handle the aforementioned subworkflow implementations, specialized with, for example, database-specific settings. All the backup data is stored in one timestamped HDFS directory on the backup cluster executing the workflow. Each type of subflow further has its own subdirectory, storing its data in the form that is native to the task. For databases, this means that a database dump file containing SQL statements is stored, whereas for HDFS, the raw files are copied. Should any of the processing fail, the workflow aborts and reports the error. In the event that all subflows succeed, the main workflow also succeeds and exits with a positive return code.

Restore

A backup is only as good and useful as its use in the recovery of an unhealthy cluster. As with the failure scenarios, restoring metadata and raw data is a matter of the objective, and that can vary a lot. For example, if some data is lost due to user error, even the HDFS trash feature might be sufficient to recover it. But for more widespread problems, such as a total cluster failure, a restoration of the entire state at one point in time is needed. Based on the RTO, there are different scenarios possible:

Full rebuild

This scenario requires the cluster to be rebuilt, although the RTO may vary if the hardware and software configuration is already in cold or warm standby. If the entire cluster needs hardware and software provisioning, the RTO will be days, if not weeks. If there is hardware but it needs to be configured, using an automated deployment process should restore services, including the backed-up data, within days, if not hours.

One option to avoid the cost of having a cold standby cluster sitting around is the use of a public cloud offering such as Amazon Web Services (AWS). This allows for quick provisioning of a cluster of likely shared machines, which are then configured similarly to the lost local cluster. Obviously, the real difficulty here is to move the data during a recovery process, but this can be avoided by, for example, using Amazon S3 for backup data or having the cloud provider offer a high-bandwidth interconnect that allows you to copy the backup data when needed.

Partial rebuild

A partial rebuild is not about the failure of nodes, which is covered as part of the normal Hadoop cluster operations. Instead, it means that some data needs to be restored from backups. This can occur in hours, if not minutes, depending on the size of the data to be restored and how automated the process is.

Failover

In the case of RTOs of less than an hour or that border on real time, only a mirrored, replicated hot standby is viable. This requires one or more clusters of the same size (in terms of storage and processing resources) to be available at all times, with all data being replicated across in near real time.

All of the discussed caveats apply, including the observation that a true active-active setup with strict consistency guarantees is very difficult to achieve (and often is impossible to implement due to the cost of such an architecture).

The exercise of building an Oozie workflow that restores the data based on a set of configuration parameters is left to you. You can follow the same idea as presented in the previous section—that is, have one main workflow that is initialized with default values, and a separate subworkflow for each type of source that handles the specifics of the implementation.

Summary

This chapter raised a lot of questions and was able to give you only a limited set of tools with which to work to implement your own backup and disaster recovery strategy. Whatever you do, it will be bespoke as a whole, with possibly some help from specific scripts or software packages to make your journey easier. We would have loved to present you with a list of available backup solutions and to score them on some neutral scale so that you can pick what you need. Alas, there is no such one-size-fits-all solution because Hadoop is a diverse ecosystem that, depending on the chosen distribution, varies in its requirements with regard to data and metadata.

You are left with the task of carefully assessing your risk and then choosing the best approach to keep you safe from losing data. Define your RTO and RPO, and then use the presented ideas, such as building an Oozie-based workflow, to back up your important data on a regular basis. Also ensure that you include validation in your design, or you may still lose more data than expected in the case of a problem, if the backed-up data cannot be restored.

Finally, educate users to build their applications and pipelines with some level of resilience to failures. All users should know what could happen when the infrastructure experiences an unexpected hiccup. As long as everyone agrees, you can set expectations and ensure that fingers will not be unnecessarily pointed—especially not in your direction.

## PART III

Taking Hadoop to the Cloud

In the previous chapters, we studied how to build Hadoop clusters that meet enterprise requirements; we now turn our attention to achieving the same in the cloud. Cloud technology enables the entire stack of information technology to be consumed as fully programmable and automated services. For example, storage, networking, and servers become *infrastructure as a service* (IaaS), and platform-level software such as database deployments or access management software becomes *platform as a service* (PaaS). The high degree of programmability and automation allows almost complete self-service for the customer to control and customize each layer, from IaaS to PaaS.

Before large-scale public cloud computing became part of the mainstream in IT, virtualization for Hadoop was mostly considered an antipattern. This was in large part due to Hadoop's distributed nature and its extensive reliance on local disks on each server for efficient operation. Running Hadoop on clouds thus often boils down to one question: can I store all my data in the cloud and process it efficiently? The answer is yes.

Public cloud providers operate at such scale (often called *hyperscale*), that Hadoop environments and their high demand for I/O throughput can be accommodated at reasonable prices. In the meantime, Hadoop distributors have also acted on the significant opportunity of Hadoop in the cloud: they have massively invested in easing deployment (increasing performance and efficiency) as well as flexible cluster life cycle models (which support starting, growing, shrinking, and stopping on demand, without affecting the availability of data).

This provides compelling motivation for enterprises to move Hadoop clusters to cloud environments based on operational efficiency, and it has thus become a certainty that the cloud does not stop at Hadoop.

And so, to enable a solid understanding of the technologies that clouds are built on and the caveats when pairing them with distributed systems like Hadoop, we cover the following content in the remainder of the book:

- Chapter 14 introduces the technological building blocks that make up clouds, and fosters an understanding of how they are leveraged to address Hadoop specifics.

- In Chapters 15 and 16, we provide an overview of how to build big data clusters in private cloud environments and with public cloud providers.

- We provide detail around automation of big data clusters in the cloud as well as how to run them securely in Chapters 17 and 18, respectively.

Basics of Virtualization for Hadoop

In this chapter, we assess virtualization technologies on a basic level. Although virtualized IT infrastructure scales well when stacking individual small to medium-sized applications, scaling virtual compute clusters and distributed systems requires special attention.

We begin with compute virtualization, which means running virtual machines (VMs) in a *hypervisor*, such as KVM or VMware. This is the most basic and well-defined building block in virtualized infrastructure. (In addition to virtualization on hypervisors, *containerization* is an emerging and relevant technology for enterprises; we cover it in Chapter 15.)

Even more important to our discussion of Hadoop in the cloud is the subject of storage virtualization, which we look at next. This means abstracting storage devices into containers that are centrally hosted in remote storage arrays based on storage area network (SAN) or object storage technology.

The third layer of virtualization to consider is network virtualization, also referred to as *Software Defined Networks* (SDN). As we will see, your choice of virtualization mechanisms will drive the lifecycle model of your clusters in the cloud.

We will cover all of these subjects in this chapter.

Why Start So Basic?

Maybe you are wondering right now why you have to worry about this. After all, it's the cloud!

To be sure, the cloud makes running many applications much simpler, but architecting and running Hadoop requires extra thought and consideration. Hadoop, as a distributed system with its own resilience features, is not always a natural fit with virtualization technology. To bring it there, you need to understand how cloud infrastructure affects your cluster's performance, availability, and even the durability of your data.

If you want to build a private cloud to be able to support Hadoop, you simply have to know these things in order to even build a stable service.

When you run Hadoop in the public cloud, the very same technological concepts and their imperfections are at work under the hood, but the provider's hyperscale infrastructure allows you to make yourself less exposed to them.

If you are completely familiar with the underlying concepts and would prefer to jump straight to solutions, you can skip ahead to Chapters 15 and 16. Otherwise, it is well worth your time to take a step back and look at the actual problems that emerge when virtualizing Hadoop.

Compute Virtualization

CPU and RAM are basically resources that virtualize well, with minimal performance overhead when compared to bare metal, so we don't have to give particular consideration to them as a resource, per se. What we do need to consider, though, is the amount of each that we need to allocate to VMs for Hadoop and in what configurations.

Suppose we're in a greenfield situation in which we have to build the cloud, so to speak. The simple goal we have is to run Hadoop on a set of VMs, which in turn run on physical hosts.

> In clouds, a VM is typically referred to as an *instance*. In the remainder of the book, we use these terms interchangeably.

As with any virtual compute environment, we have to consider the following basic questions:

- How many VMs will be colocated on a physical host?
- How will the VMs holding the cluster nodes be distributed across physical hosts?

The answer to the first of these questions depends on the intended use case. Although Hadoop tolerates very small node configurations, the amount of RAM and CPU allocated to an instance ultimately defines which use cases can be implemented on the virtual cluster. Consider the high-end 2U worker node from "Server Form Factors" on page 91. If we wish to host three equally sized VMs on it, a hypervisor will allot less than 80 GB to a worker node. If, for example, our users intend to perform efficient joins between large tables, they may struggle to do so with smaller memory allocations. Often, however, the performance requirements for virtual Hadoop environments are more relaxed than on bare-metal infrastructure. At the other extreme, we have come across environments in which the complete hypervisor is dedicated to a single instance.

Virtual Machine Distribution

The second question about the distribution of VMs for a Hadoop environment is more involved. The provisioning mechanism of your virtualization software may colocate several master roles or worker roles from the same cluster on the same physical host in such a way that the failure of that host may disrupt the operation of the whole cluster!

Consider the scenario outlined in Figure 14-1, on the left. In this example, two virtual Hadoop clusters (dark gray, light gray) are deployed across five physical hosts. Here's what would happen in the event of a failure of one of these:

- If physical host 1 were to fail, the entire cluster1 would be without a NameNode and thus would stop functioning.

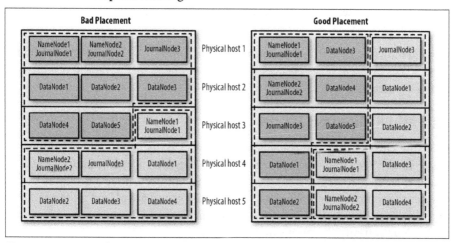

Figure 14-1. VM placement

- If physical host 4 were to fail, cluster2 would lose its HDFS quorum majority and would not allow any writes.

- If physical host 2 were to fail, some blocks on that host might be missing until it was fully recovered. This is because there is a high likelihood that there are some blocks in HFDS with all three replicas on DataNodes1–3. From the NameNode's point of view, this is perfectly legitimate, since it is not aware of the VM topology. The same applies to physical host 5 for cluster2.

- The only host in this example whose failure would not cause the failure of an entire virtual cluster is physical host 3.

Virtualization experts often claim that the loss of a physical host can be easily tolerated because the failed VMs can be automatically respawned on another hypervisor, but this is not guaranteed to work in the case of Hadoop. There are a few reasons for this:

- If you use local storage, you cannot migrate, because the to-be-migrated storage is not available due to the loss of the physical host.

- Migrating three Hadoop nodes might mean the need to provision a large amount of RAM. In the previous example, the equivalent of one physical host would have to be kept spare to tolerate the failure of another, which is not very economical.

 The problem of bad placement can sometimes be exacerbated by features of your cloud solution. For example, AWS provides optional placement groups which attempt to collocate VMs as closely as possible, to optimize network bandwidth.

Consider alternatively the setup on the right in Figure 14-1, where the distribution of VMs across physical hosts ensures that a failure of any one node will not bring down any of the virtual clusters.

Anti-Affinity Groups

For large clusters on a big collection of physical hosts, it can be a daunting task to juggle many VMs and their placement, which is why virtualization software often contains features to define rules for mutual anti-affinity among a group of VMs. This ensures that no two VMs of a given anti-affinity group are placed on the same physical host. The correct placement of VMs from Figure 14-1 could have been achieved via the four anti-affinity groups in Table 14-1.

Table 14-1. Example anti-affinity group definitions for two virtual clusters

Anti-affinity group	Members
Cluster1 master roles	NameNode1+JournalNode1, NameNode2+JournalNode2, JournalNode3
Cluster1 worker roles	DataNode1, DataNode2, DataNode3, DataNode4, DataNode5
Cluster2 master roles	NameNode1+JournalNode1, NameNode2+JournalNode2, JournalNode3
Cluster2 worker roles	DataNode1, DataNode2, DataNode3, DataNode4

For example, VMware supports the creation of anti-affinity groups as part of its Distributed Resource Scheduler (DRS) (*http://bit.ly/2OTe0sZ*). OpenStack, which we discuss in detail in "OpenStack" on page 435, features the Sahara plug-in (*http://bit.ly/2qZb04x*), which automates anti-affinity rules as part of cluster role definitions.

Alternatively, in contrast to providing anti-affinity purely at a host level, VMware offers an approach in which HDFS becomes aware of the hypervisor topology and can provide anti-affinity at the HDFS level. We cover this in "VMware and Pivotal Cloud Foundry" on page 442.

Achieving strong anti-affinity is often not possible. As we see in Chapter 16, there is limited support for this with public cloud providers. But the hyperscale characteristics in public clouds typically offer acceptable durability characteristics and give us ways to work around this, via backups.

If you are implementing a private cloud, it is basically up to you to find a solution to this problem. We show you what is possible today in Chapter 15.

Storage Virtualization

Similar to the storage stack in a bare-metal Hadoop cluster, virtual storage for Hadoop is typically more complex to deal with than virtual compute. Virtualization of storage may be performed by the hypervisor on locally attached disks, but it also frequently relates to remotely attached storage.

As we did earlier, let us imagine what we would have to consider if we were to build a storage solution for virtual Hadoop clusters ourselves.

The paradigm of remotely attached storage has been prevalent and heavily invested in by companies for nearly two decades. As Chapter 4 showed, many state-of-the-art datacenter networks are designed for north-south traffic, and oversubscription of ports is common. In that case, the same design naturally applies to the storage network.

Although the data path in Hadoop clusters can often deal with higher latencies, it suffers in overall performance if parallel storage throughput is not high. Hadoop may put such a strain on remotely attached storage and its network that it literally brings other workloads in the virtualization platform to a halt.

For virtual Hadoop clusters, we therefore have two feasible options:

- Local storage, which is attached to a server via SAS or SATA and directly virtualized by the hypervisor
- Highly scalable remotely attached storage, such as a SAN or object storage, with high parallel throughput

Let's look at each of these two options in turn.

Virtualizing Local Storage

When building virtual Hadoop clusters with local storage, we can safely assume that new hardware will be used because preexisting virtualization infrastructure typically does not contain enough local storage devices to implement HDFS in a useful manner.

With that assumption in mind, let's pick a 2U server with 24 disks, such as the one we introduced in "Server Form Factors" on page 91.

One way to virtualize its local disks is to merge them entirely into a storage pool, as shown in Figure 14-2 on the left. From this storage pool, logical volumes are exported. These are then presented as disks to the VMs. In practice, merging the disks into a storage pool means some form of Redundant Array of Independent Disks, which brings back all the disadvantages we discussed in "RAID?" on page 82.

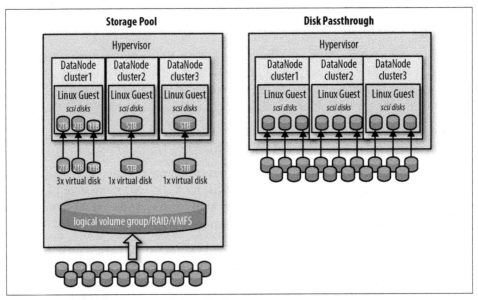

Figure 14-2. Options for virtualizing local storage

With some hypervisors, it's possible to export whole disks directly to the hypervisor, as shown in Figure 14-2 on the right. This might seem clumsy because it means that after a tenant uses these disks, their spare capacity is not available for other tenants. But even in the alternative case of using a logical volume in between, you ultimately need to rigidly assign the size of logical volumes to VMs. Any new tenant significantly reduces the capacity and available bandwidth for other tenants, whereas the previous approach arbitrates both via the hypervisor's storage pool.

> ## RAID and Storage Pools
>
> As we covered in "RAID?" on page 82, RAID on Hadoop can lead you down a slippery slope.
>
> On the other hand, in virtual environments, RAID can allow a single tenant to take advantage of the full bandwidth of all disks. In the storage pool example in Figure 14-2, for instance, the DataNode on cluster1 would benefit greatly in terms of storage throughput if cluster2 were currently idle and cluster3 not yet provisioned. By contrast, in the disk passthrough example, cluster1 will always be limited to a throughput of three disks, regardless of the state of the other clusters.
>
> An additional incentive could be to reduce the replication in Hadoop storage systems because of the increased durability of RAID. But who understands the exact ramifications of interspersing RAID 10/RAID 6/RAID 5 with two replicas? How is the collaboration between the Hadoop team and the server team? Also, losing a RAID array means completely losing a full replica for all virtual clusters at once.

In many on-premises scenarios, virtualized local storage may be the only option to virtualize Hadoop. But it makes storage for your tenants more complex and also stationary, or *sticky*, as we discuss in "Cluster Life Cycle Models" on page 425.

SANs

Another way to provide your clusters with disk devices is to use SANs. In simple terms, SANs send Small Computer Systems Interface (SCSI) disk blocks over a network between a client and a central storage array. The client is presented a disk, which *appears* to be local.

> SAN solutions can more generally be referred to as *remote block storage*; however, the definition of SAN comprises a specific set of storage protocols, and hence not all remote block storage solutions are automatically SANs.

SANs are most commonly implemented with *Fibre Channel* or *iSCSI*. You can see how both technologies differ in Figure 14-3.

Fibre Channel is the most common network technology used in the enterprise context to implement SANs. It uses the Fibre Channel Protocol (FCP) to transport SCSI storage commands and data blocks. Fibre Channel networks are mostly implemented on optical fiber technology. Multiple topologies are supported, but the most common by far is a fabric in which the plurality of all Fibre Channel switches act like a single big switch, providing a global namespace of ports.

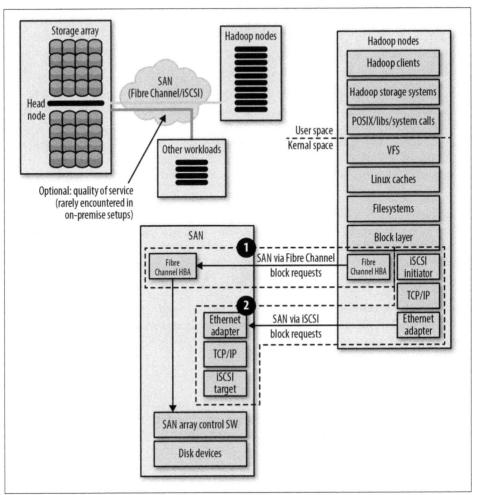

Figure 14-3. Two alternative SAN technologies: Fibre Channel and iSCSI

Servers that use Fibre Channel interface with the fabric via a *host bus adapter* (HBA). As far as Linux is concerned, an HBA is a storage controller that implements SCSI disks. The target at the other end of the fabric is likely a logical disk in a RAID array on a large enterprise storage system, as shown in Figure 14-3, which attaches a large number of disk enclosures to a few *head nodes*. Any such logical disk is addressable within the fabric via a worldwide port number (WWPN).

The fabric can be set up in a highly available fashion, such that the same WWPN can be reached via two completely redundant paths. Any such logical connection or set of these connections can be completely isolated in the fabric via a concept called *zoning*. The target storage system is responsible for isolating the logical storage volumes from each other, and it provides them as WWPNs in their corresponding zones.

iSCSI encapsulates SCSI command data blocks over IP networks. It uses TCP as the transport layer. The client system implements an *initiator*, which accesses remote *targets*. These targets hold the data and typically are a RAID array in an enterprise storage system.

In Linux, as shown in Figure 14-3, the iSCSI initiator is implemented as a set of kernel modules. The iSCSI target can also be operated on a remote Linux system, but in the enterprise context it's usually implemented on an enterprise storage system. Because TCP/IP is used, the actual route that SCSI traffic takes to travel from initiator to target is determined by the specifics of the given IP network.

As with Fibre Channel fabrics, it is possible to attach iSCSI targets in a highly available fashion by configuring redundant network access paths on the client. In Linux, for example, this is achieved by the *multipath daemon* (*http://bit.ly/2R6axJz*).

For performance, we strongly discourage implementing iSCSI networks over multi-hop routes as well as running any non-iSCSI traffic on them.

In the enterprise IT context, Fibre Channel is the dominant technology for SANs. Compared to iSCSI, however, Fibre Channel equipment is expensive, and because its application domain is specific to enterprise storage, it has so far not been subject to massive commoditization and it is not reusable beyond the storage realm.

So how do SANs apply to Hadoop?

Purists exclaim that SANs don't apply to Hadoop at all, but a growing group of experts argue that part of Hadoop's journey into enterprise computing is to make it fit in with the world of virtual storage.

As we will see in Chapter 16, public cloud providers excel at massively scaling remote block storage and they provide proper isolation and quality-of-service (QoS) policies and mechanisms. The economies of scale in public clouds have simply made SANs for Hadoop a reality.

Hadoop on SANs in on-premises environments, on the other hand, is not easy. The economical and technological strain it produces is often not at all justified, especially for large clusters. If you're thinking about it, plan on 5 to 30 worker nodes, unless you have built a dedicated high-parallel-throughput SAN infrastructure. Consider the following:

- In on-premises enterprise IT departments, iSCSI or Fibre Channel implementations often heavily oversubscribe the transport-level bandwidth, both on the network level and on the target enterprise storage system.

  This is due to the fact that only a fraction of the attached systems are reading and writing at any given instant. Oversubscribed SANs work well to provide high input/output operations per second and low latency because each of the many systems either accesses only relatively small amounts of storage at a given moment or serves client systems on the other end of the LAN, WAN, or World Wide Web.

- In Hadoop, all nodes regularly access large regions of storage sequentially in parallel. But they also talk to each other over the network (often the same network used for iSCSI) to shuffle join partitions, replicate data blocks, exchange results, heartbeat their health status, and more.

The difference becomes evident in Figure 14-3, in which many systems access a large SAN array. The total storage bandwidth is limited by the combined theoretical throughput of the head nodes that directly connect to the SAN fabric, while it distributes internally to storage enclosures that hold the physical disks.

As illustrated, this bandwidth is also shared with a potentially unknown and, more importantly, heterogeneous and therefore unpredictable set of workloads. Conversely, consider a rack with Hadoop nodes that use local storage, where a set of 12 disks are certainly more likely to be able to provide a sustained 1 GB/s of sequential storage throughput.

All that being said, Hadoop vendors nowadays provide guidance to safely deploy on remote block storage. For example, Cloudera has recently published a document[1] that provides detailed information about how to determine whether your SAN storage can sustain the planned workload.

Another fundamental aspect to consider is that, by default, SAN implementations apply error correction codes or other redundancy mechanisms, whereas HDFS uses its own replication mechanism for redundancy. We frequently witness a desire to drive down the cost of the expensive SAN technology by trading HDFS replicas for SAN-bound redundancy schemes. But in practice, the ramifications of mixing the durability mechanisms of HDFS and the underlying SAN infrastructure are not well understood.

It is critical to remember that a DataNode not only provides block storage, but also offers the only mechanism through which that block can be accessed. Say, for example, that, since you have SAN-level data redundancy, you wish to reduce the number of block replicas in HDFS from three to one. As a result, you reduce the available access paths to these blocks to just one node—the single DataNode that is configured to access the corresponding SAN volume. If the VM running said DataNode becomes unavailable, the NameNode reports its blocks as missing and no process can read the data, even though it is redundantly stored in the SAN.

---

1 "Cloudera Enterprise Storage Device Acceptance Criteria Guide" (*http://bit.ly/2zmJPWd*), Cloudera Inc., June 11, 2018.

To summarize, remote block storage services are becoming a reality for Hadoop, especially in public clouds, as we'll see in Chapter 16. SANs can be used to implement suspendable clusters, as described in "Cluster Life Cycle Models" on page 425. However, with on-premises installations, the cost/performance trade-off makes a SAN uneconomical for Hadoop in general, and it is often only viable for small clusters, such as development environments. In addition, the side effects of running on SANs are often not considered properly, even when small-scale implementations are pursued.

Object Storage and Network-Attached Storage

Object storage is an umbrella term that, in the context of the cloud, is often used to describe all scalable storage offerings that are not block-based. For Hadoop in the cloud, object storage can serve not only as a backup storage layer but also as the source of truth for all data, as we will see in the coming chapters. Some object storage systems offer connectors that map their own APIs into Hadoop-compatible filesystems, making it possible to use them directly via processing services such as Spark, Hive, or Impala.

Network-attached storage (NAS), a storage solution from the pre-cloud era, is closely related to object storage.

Network-attached storage

Similar to a SAN, NAS is attached to servers via some kind of network transport, most likely TCP/IP networking. In contrast to a SAN, NAS does not export a block device to clients, but instead exports a mountable filesystem interface such as Server Message Block (SMB) or Network File System (NFS).

> In layman's terms, NAS is a mounted network share and a SAN is a disk. The OS interacts with a SAN disk at the SCSI/ATA block layer, giving it full control over partitioning, the filesystem, and more. In contrast, a NAS solution requires a given network filesystem to be used for access.

To be entirely clear, a shared filesystem on NFS or SMB should never be used as an HDFS DataNode directory. Even though both of these filesystems terminate at the POSIX layer, as illustrated in Figure 14-4, it is not safe to run Hadoop storage systems such as HDFS, Kafka, or Kudu on NAS. All Hadoop storage systems expect a genuine block device to be able to guarantee the semantics of consistency operations when committing data to the storage layer.

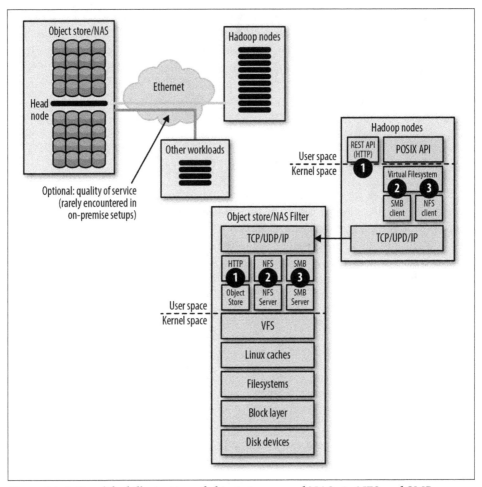

Figure 14-4. Simplified illustration of object storage and NAS via NFS and SMB protocols

An equally important and basic problem is that a state-of-the-art NAS filer would be completely overwhelmed by the amount of throughput that even a medium-sized Hadoop cluster generates, as mentioned in the previous section and shown in Figure 14-3.

NAS does have value, however, when used as a backup storage or ingest layer for Hadoop. This is common in on-premises environments and in public clouds. For example, Amazon offers NFS mounts via its Elastic File System (*https://aws.amazon.com/efs/*), and Microsoft provides SMB storage via Azure Files (*http://bit.ly/2DOB7nf*).

Object storage

Object storage, rather than being one single technology, is instead a concept that has many implementations. These range from products such as Ceph distributed by independent software vendors, as we'll see in Chapter 15, to large-scale public cloud services such as Amazon S3 (*https://aws.amazon.com/s3/*) and Microsoft Azure Data Lake Storage (*http://bit.ly/2zgzlYc*), which we cover in Chapter 16.

Object storage APIs are generally simpler than the traditional filesystem APIs offered by NAS and SAN technologies. Typically they use HTTP as their transport mechanism, as illustrated in Figure 14-4. Although object storage APIs can be viewed as less expressive than the POSIX standard, they have the distinct advantage that any user-space application can access them directly, even via internet connections, without the support of any filesystem drivers on the client side.

Thus, object storage implementations can provide massively scalable, reliable, and highly performant storage for Hadoop clusters, and a range of them are supported directly in Hadoop, as we'll see in Chapters 15 and 16. This is achieved via the provision of a Hadoop-compatible filesystem, which lets Hadoop services such as Spark, Hive, and others use the object storage layer in a distributed fashion, just like HDFS.

However, object storage systems differ significantly from one another in their APIs, both syntactically and semantically. For example, as we cover in "Cloud Providers" on page 457, some of them are strongly consistent whereas others are eventually consistent.

Network Virtualization

Network virtualization is also commonly referred to as *software-defined networking* (SDN). In this section, we provide basic information on SDN when using it in a virtualized Hadoop platform. Conceptually, and for the purpose of our discussion, network virtualization is the same as compute and storage virtualization: virtual networks are run on top of a physical network and, as far as the tenants are concerned, act exactly like physical networks.

SDN gives us two important benefits:

- Automatic configuration and provisioning of networks from a central software entity, known as the *control plane*
- Isolation of tenant network traffic throughout virtual and physical network devices on the *data plane*, which transports the actual network payload

SDN can be implemented entirely in software or via integration of compatible physical hardware:

Software-only

This approach uses network tunnels that *overlay* the existing and often heterogeneous hardware infrastructure with virtual switches and routers that use tunneling protocols such as VXLAN or Generic Routing Encapsulation (GRE). Consequently, these networks are also called *software overlay networks*. Interfacing with physical network equipment occurs on Open Systems Interconnection (OSI) layers 3 to 7 and is typically performed by a virtual bridge device.

Mixed

This approach combines the use of software and compatible hardware to implement virtual networks. The control plane, used for the creation and configuration of virtual networks, remains in software, whereas the data plane spans a mix of virtual and physical switches and routers. The participating hardware devices understand configuration protocols such as OpenFlow or VXLAN, on the control plane and implement the virtual networks on the physical layer accordingly. In contrast to software overlay networks, these hardware devices also provide physical isolation of traffic. As an example, consider an SDN-capable switch that receives configuration and data via OpenFlow and internally translates the virtual flows into VLAN IDs.

Why Is SDN Important?

Having a basic grasp on SDN for Hadoop is important for three reasons:

- If you are building a Hadoop service on a private cloud, that cloud may use SDN already as a means to strongly isolate tenants. If you run Hadoop on on-premises SDN, such as on an existing private cloud solution, you should carefully scrutinize it in terms of overall available bandwidth and scalability.

- SDN can slow down your cluster's performance. Virtual networks can impose an overhead and a performance penalty, especially at the endpoints, where they transition back into regular networks.

  A typical example of such an endpoint might be a storage appliance that does not directly support your choice of SDN technology and thus requires routing or bridging from the SDN layer into physical networks. Often, the appropriate network equipment that can bridge between virtualized networks and the storage network may be a significant cost factor and is thus too sparsely allocated to support Hadoop traffic.

- Implementing SDN is not easy. Its presence is a good indicator of how well a cloud solution is automated. If your underlying private cloud infrastructure does not leverage SDN, tenants might not be isolated on the network level, or manual configuration might still be required to provision tenants in such a way.

- Although completely transparent, SDN is omnipresent in the public cloud. Bearing this in mind help us to understand what is going on when the discussion turns to general aspects of service isolation and security in the cloud provider's backbone.

Although hyperscale public clouds depend on SDN through and through, and its benefits are obvious and enticing for on-premises environments as well, current implementations often prove to be too complex for enterprises to justify transitioning all network operations to SDN. For both software-only and mixed SDN, a range of open and proprietary implementation options exist. These need to be chosen from and integrated into overall operations in IT organizations. Often, the move to private cloud technology marks the initial adoption of some form of SDN in enterprises.

If you are reading this chapter because you need to bring Hadoop to an existing private cloud, requirements about network isolation and automation surely already exist. If tenants require strict isolation (say, if you were hosting Pepsi Cola and Coca Cola), you can achieve this via manual definitions of VLANs, but this is not sustainable when tenants come and go and expect self-service automation.

The marketplace and technology space of SDN as a whole is not easy to grasp and exceeds what we are able to cover in this book.

Hadoop itself makes no SDN-specific demands other than what we learned in Chapter 4, which is essentially lots of east-west traffic across many ports. But ideally, you would be able to leverage the quality-of-service (QoS) features that many of the SDN standards offer to shield other traffic from being affected by Hadoop.

There is also some academic work around leveraging bandwidth control capability for task scheduling in Hadoop or Hadoop-like systems.[2]

Cluster Life Cycle Models

At this point, we are well aware of the capabilities of virtual infrastructure. Compared to bare-metal clusters, we can use virtual infrastructure to leverage different *life cycle models* for Hadoop clusters.

An equally important term in this context is the *source of truth* for your data. In classic on-premises Hadoop installations, the storage systems, such as HDFS, Kafka, or Kudu, run on local disks and implement the source of truth for an organization. This conforms to a regular *long-lived life cycle* of a Hadoop deployment.

---

2 Peng Qin et al., "Bandwidth-Aware Scheduling with SDN in Hadoop: A New Trend for Big Data" (*https://arxiv.org/pdf/1403.2800.pdf*), March 2014.

In the cloud, and especially in public clouds, it is equally common that organizations choose object storage as the source of truth and Hadoop systems merely work on copies of this data or enrich the object storage layer with their analytic results. This enables purely project- or campaign-driven clusters, which are suitable for *short-lived*, or *transient life cycle* models.

The duration of a cluster (i.e., transient versus long-lived clusters) is only one way to look at cluster life cycles, and notions of what is transient and what time span qualifies as long-lived vastly differ from one organization to the next. But if we stick to how the source of truth for a cluster is implemented, we get a more concise picture of a cluster's life cycle, as shown in Figure 14-5.

That leads us to the following models, all of which are relevant for both public and private clouds:

Suspendable clusters

These use remote block storage and can be stopped and restarted later, as shown on the left in Figure 14-5. When a suspendable cluster is bootstrapped, remote disks are provisioned that remain available throughout the cluster's life cycle (1).

When it is suspended or stopped, the underlying remote data disks and the disk holding the OS are kept in the remote storage system. When it is restarted (1), the remote disks are reattached. Finally, when the cluster is terminated (4), the remote disks are deleted.

Optionally, suspendable clusters can be connected to an object storage layer, as discussed in "Object storage" on page 423. A suspendable cluster can function as transient or as long-lived. The source of truth may be implemented on the remote block storage layer or on the object storage layer.

Sticky clusters

In some cases, it is necessary to use local disks as the source of truth in your virtual cluster. The data itself thus sticks to the resulting cluster, which is considered a *sticky cluster*. As shown in the center of Figure 14-5, a sticky cluster is started (1) and runs perpetually (2). When the cluster is terminated (3), the data becomes permanently unavailable.

The most common reason for sticky clusters is that they are the only choice when Hadoop is virtualized on-premises. We have often seen that object storage or other secondary storage layers may still be available for those clusters as a source of ingest and a target for partial export of results, but they cannot function as the source of truth due to insufficient capacity or performance.

If the cluster uses storage pools, as discussed in "Virtualizing Local Storage" on page 416, it is theoretically possible to suspend the VMs of a sticky cluster. However, the storage that a suspended cluster consumes on the local disks puts a tight practical limit on this approach. Also, resuming a suspended cluster may not be possible if all compute slots are occupied by other tenants, so you would merely be able to offer to "park" a cluster's data with a undefined path for tenants to regain access to it.

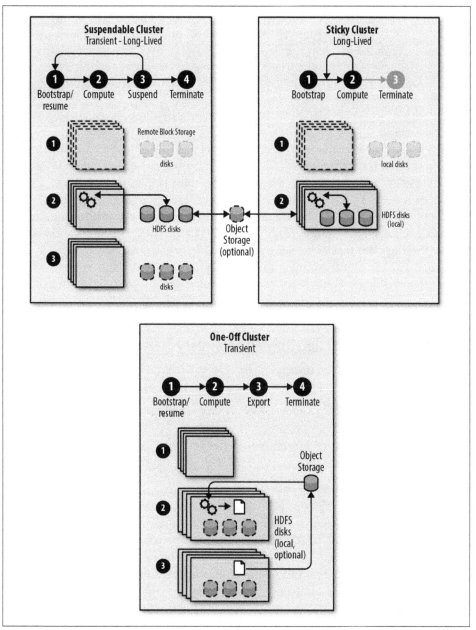

Figure 14-5. Cluster life cycle models

When you run a sticky cluster in a public cloud service, you should do backups to object storage. As we see in "High Availability" on page 488, you do not have control over storage anti-affinity in public clouds.

When you run sticky clusters on-premises, you have more control over durability, but only if you can guarantee strong anti-affinity among data nodes and highly available master roles, as we introduced in "Anti-Affinity Groups" on page 414. You should also think about ways to back up the most important parts of your data or at least have a documented pipeline for reconstructing them from source systems.

One-off clusters

These can take advantage of local storage as well, but in contrast to sticky clusters, they do not depend on it. The source of truth with one-off clusters resides in an object storage system. As shown on the right in Figure 14-5, these clusters typically are created (1) for a specific purpose and either import all the required data from object storage before they commence their compute phase (2), or execute that compute phase directly on object storage, while using local disks only for intermediate results between job stages. Before they are terminated (4), they export (3) all results—sometimes small, sometimes significant amounts—to the secondary storage layer. If you take this concept to its boundaries, the cluster's life cycle is the same as one job, hence the name *one-off*.

Can I Run Only on Secondary Storage?

For most workloads, a local instance of HDFS is still required. You should check with your distributor about which object storage solutions are supported in the public or private cloud, respectively.

Let's now turn to the aspect of *duration* in cluster life cycles. Clusters can be either transient or long-lived:

Transient clusters

These have a short lifespan, but what does this mean, exactly? In a very agile organization, short could mean anywhere between six hours and six days, whereas in a large corporation it probably means somewhere between six weeks and six months. Generally, a transient cluster can be categorized as campaign- or initiative-driven. Examples of this include creating a 360-degree customer view backing a marketing campaign or preparing a report for quarterly business results. Many organizations, especially in the public cloud today, even start clusters on a per-job basis, rather than on a per-project basis. This is facilitated by

SaaS offerings such as Cloudera Altus, Amazon Elastic MapReduce (EMR), or Azure HDInsight, all of which we introduce in Chapter 16.

No matter what the notion of time is, running transient clusters always requires an object storage layer to maintain the source of truth outside of the cluster. The source of truth also includes metadata; for example, table definitions in Hive or access control lists for HDFS. Many vendors provide solutions to manage this metadata outside of the life cycle of a cluster; for example, Cloudera SDX (*http://bit.ly/2OSrvZS*) or AWS Glue Data Catalog (*https://amzn.to/2z82ox9*).

Netflix (*http://bit.ly/2qWwLls*) is a good example of a large organization using object storage as the source of truth.

Long-lived clusters

Similar to the question of how long transient is, there is no universal notion of a long life for big data environments. But there are certainly environments that always have to be there, such as a reporting platform or the data layer of a web service. Many such clusters today are built in a cloud context, and their numbers are growing. They should be always on, and you do not want to reprovision such a service in another one-off cluster.

Figure 14-6 takes a detailed look at how data life cycle and cluster duration are related.

Suspendable clusters can be long-lived if they can be left running, or temporarily suspended. They can also be transient, when combined with a secondary storage layer. This model sounds intriguing in comparison, but remote block storage is typically the most costly option.

As indicated in the illustration, sticky clusters occupy assigned disk drives permanently, making it impractical to suspend them. They are thus long-running, to sustain the source of truth for the data. However, as also shown in Figure 14-6, this can be alleviated by combining them with an object storage layer or another form of secondary storage, even if only for data ingest and export.

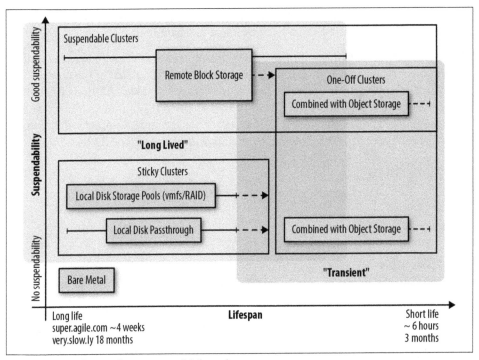

Figure 14-6. Cluster duration and life cycle

One-off clusters are the obvious candidate for transient clusters, but there is nothing that keeps you from running such clusters for longer periods of time.

Moving Further on Cluster Life Cycle

The previous discussion focuses on which basic life cycle model your cluster supports. There are further life cycle operations that you should consider, namely growing and shrinking the cluster at runtime. These advanced life cycle operations heavily depend on your overall ability to automate Hadoop, which is, in turn, defined by the Hadoop distribution and cloud infrastructure you choose and the management tools you can use.

We go into more detail on automating the deployment and configuration of virtual clusters in Chapter 17.

Summary

In this chapter, we covered the basics of virtual infrastructure and the challenges that can arise when using it to build Hadoop clusters.

We began by looking at compute virtualization and learned how VM distribution can affect service availability and data durability in virtual Hadoop clusters.

We then examined how virtual storage can be used in Hadoop, considering locally virtualized disks, remote block storage (aka SANs), and the various flavors of NAS and object storage. We briefly covered how remote storage systems can pose challenges with scalability and consistency when used for Hadoop. As we'll see in more detail in the next two chapters, this often requires enterprises to compromise between cost and performance.

These compromises are reflected in the three possible data retention (or rather, cluster life cycle) models we introduced here—suspendable clusters, sticky clusters, and one-off clusters—which define the way that users and applications can interact with your big data platform.

CHAPTER 15
Solutions for Private Clouds

This most important thing you need to know about private clouds is that no two private clouds are the same.

If you build a private cloud in an enterprise IT context, you need to choose a combination of the following:

- A provisioning software framework, such as OpenStack, OpenShift, or Cloud Foundry
- A hypervisor, such as VMware ESX, Xen, or KVM
- A block storage solution (depending on your environment, local disks or possibly a scalable SAN infrastructure from one of the well-known enterprise storage manufacturers)
- Optionally, an object storage implementation
- Optionally, a software-defined networking (SDN) solution

Because the landscape of private clouds is so diverse, the number of possible implementations is very large, and most of the components just discussed are typically delivered by third-party vendors.

Designing your cloud to be able to run Hadoop makes everything a little bit more interesting. Your storage system should support very high throughput rates, your network should be very fast, and your provisioning logic should be smart enough to distribute all cluster roles correctly on the right hosts.

This chapter provides a rundown of the key success factors of Hadoop on private clouds, rather than offering extensive coverage of each available technology asset. For this, we assume the vantage point of the cloud architect. If you are, instead, a user of private clouds—for example, a developer of big data applications—this chapter can equally have merit for you in terms of defining what you can expect from private clouds and Hadoop.

A private cloud is meant to consolidate, commoditize, and automate IT, and therefore, Hadoop is most likely just one workload among many. You ought to be mindful of existing requirements for the cloud platform, which typically define your latitude to implement a Hadoop solution on top.

Throughout the rest of this chapter, we use the three following key criteria to assess how a private cloud solution supports running Hadoop clusters:

Automation and integration
There is a large spectrum of automation in cloud services. For example, if network provisioning is largely managed by humans, it is debatable whether a platform fully qualifies as a cloud. For Hadoop, however, it is common practice that, at least initially, humans fill in the gap of dealing with cluster specifics when provisioning cloud infrastructure.

On the other hand, if your platform is completely self-serviced, you need to extend its automation capabilities to Hadoop and provide an appropriate multi-tenant user interface. Most enterprises do not develop this logic in-house; rather, they rely on third-party solutions. Both the user interface and the actual provisioning logic need to be aware of the specifics of Hadoop—that is, they need to understand the different services and their roles in the cluster, in terms of failure characteristics, different node layouts for master and worker roles, performance, scalability, and more, as we learned in Chapter 3.

Depending on your life cycle model, your implementation also might need to provide a solution for anti-affinity, as discussed in "Virtual Machine Distribution" on page 413 and "Anti-Affinity Groups" on page 414.

Finally, a crucial component in this approach is your choice of Hadoop distribution and how your cloud automation layer integrates with it. If you are used to managing your clusters with a tool such as Cloudera Manager or Apache Ambari, you need to ensure that your automation layer installs the infrastructure as well as the distribution's management tool. You should also be sure that it is then instructed to deploy the Hadoop software components by driving the corresponding vendor APIs in these management tools. We cover this in detail in Chapter 17.

Life cycle and storage
You need to decide which life cycle and storage model your cloud technology can support. Clouds with a remote storage layer require sufficient bandwidth, and an existing cloud platform may not have had Hadoop's bandwidth requirements in mind. If you intend to run jobs directly on remote storage (for example, HDFS on a third-party appliance, block devices on SAN, or Amazon S3–compatible

object storage), this will create strain on network infrastructure and you will almost certainly have to rely on some form of quality-of-service mechanism as tenants scale.

Sticky clusters with local storage, on the other hand, rely on the provisioning framework to provide strong anti-affinity.

Isolation
As we explored in Chapter 14, isolation of compute resources is possible via state-of-the-art virtualization software, which can also provide strong isolation for local storage resources. Remote storage solutions such as SANs and object storage—if they are available to your private cloud solution at scale—equally provide strong isolation between tenants, which also includes networks. If your private cloud supports internal parties only, you might not require network-level isolation, but it will be expected if you externalize your cloud solutions to third parties. If you pair network isolation with automation, you require a software-defined networking solution, which still poses a challenge to many enterprise IT organizations.

If you come to find that there is no easy way to run Hadoop on your preexisting cloud platform, you might need to consider complementing it with different hardware, possibly a different storage layer or servers with local storage.

The following sections cover some of the most popular private cloud solutions used in enterprises. We focus on how they cater to the points just itemized and the other things they bring to the table to support Hadoop.

OpenStack

OpenStack might best be described as a modular cloud operating layer. You can use it to build fully fledged clouds. Similar to an operating system, all components—especially for compute, storage, and network virtualization—use a pluggable driver model. Many third-party vendors contribute drivers for their own hardware or software solutions to become OpenStack-compatible; for example, SAN storage arrays, SDN control planes and switches, and hypervisors. OpenStack is fully open source. Commercial support, as with Linux and Hadoop, is provided by vendors such as Red Hat or Mirantis. Some other vendors have created purely commercial forks of Open-Stack, where it functions as the foundation of integrated proprietary private cloud offerings. Finally, there are a number of public cloud providers, such as RackSpace and Deutsche Telekom, that implement their public cloud offerings (*https:// www.openstack.org/marketplace/public-clouds/*) with OpenStack.

Let's assess OpenStack's support of Hadoop clusters by means of our three aforementioned key criteria.

Automation and Integration

OpenStack includes the Sahara plug-in (*http://bit.ly/2qZb04x*), which is intended to automate the provisioning of Hadoop clusters. Sahara is fully integrated into the OpenStack Horizon UI (*http://bit.ly/2qUb85w*), which is a self-service portal for OpenStack users. If you're interested, the Cloudera Engineering Blog provides an introduction to how a Sahara-based deployment process (*http://bit.ly/2QJ5rCz*) looks and feels.

Sahara allows the definition of anti-affinity rules for Hadoop cluster roles during the creation of clusters. It provides several provisioning plug-ins (*http://bit.ly/2ziAE8T*), including all for major Hadoop distributions. If you choose a commercial distribution, the distribution's management and deployment tools, such as Ambari or Cloudera Manager, are used for the installation of the cluster services.

Sahara also provides an Elastic Data Processing (EDP) facility (*http://bit.ly/2S3W3K4*) to create Hadoop jobs from the Sahara Horizon UI or a REST API. Similar to Amazon Elastic MapReduce (EMR), which we cover in "Amazon Elastic MapReduce" on page 462, EDP requires a data source, a job source, and a location output. EDP supports multiple job sources, such as Hive scripts or plain JAR files. A variety of job input and output data sources, such as HDFS, OpenStack Swift—which we introduce in the next section—and OpenStack's file share service, Manila (*http://bit.ly/2BoCOFH*), are supported. EDP can spontaneously launch clusters to run a job.

Life Cycle and Storage

As we just noted, OpenStack Sahara actively embraces the concept of transient clusters via EDP—but it also supports provisioning on long-lived bare-metal servers (*http://bit.ly/2DHiUIm*) via the Ironic component (*http://bit.ly/2BolT6f*), which can leverage raw local disks.

Apart from Ironic, OpenStack takes a twofold approach to persistent storage, similar to most public cloud offerings. On one hand, the Cinder component (*http://bit.ly/2OVhWcL*) provides a block storage service to instances, whereas on the other hand, the Swift component (*http://bit.ly/2BoD7Al*) implements an object storage service.

Cinder supports the use of persistent local disks as well as SAN volumes and many more technologies. Many third-party vendors are supported in Cinder (*http://bit.ly/MRuyB5*) and contribute drivers (*http://bit.ly/2QMaaU0*) correspondingly.

Swift is OpenStack's object storage implementation; it's built to leverage disks in a collection of commodity servers, although a few commercial storage appliances, such as EMC ECS (*http://bit.ly/2zV44JL*), are available as a drop-in replacement. Swift can be accessed from Hadoop by the Swift Hadoop client, which is an implementation of a Hadoop-compatible filesystem (*http://bit.ly/2A5vH3d*).

OpenStack's variety of storage options, in theory, support all of the life cycle models, but in practice, you need to tread carefully:

- Cinder can use local disks in commodity servers, but by default makes no guarantees about their location in a set of servers. In the commodity server case, Cinder manages a set of volumes created by Linux's Local Volume Manager(LVM) (*http://bit.ly/2R475PD*) and corresponding iSCSI or Fibre Channel targets on all participating hosts.

- The hypervisor on a host, such as KVM, is then assigned such volumes (*http://bit.ly/2Q0ZHHl*) according to user requests to Cinder. The volumes can reside on its local host or on distant hosts.

- You can instruct the affinity scheduler (*http://bit.ly/2zd0bR8*) to place a Cinder volume local to the instance, and Sahara can take advantage of this policy (*http://bit.ly/2DKeiBc*). You should ensure, however, that your distribution of OpenStack includes these features and that you indeed use them.

- It is also possible to provision Cinder on NFS (*http://bit.ly/2K9bHks*), which we do not consider feasible if you intend to offer HDFS as a durable storage solution, as we mentioned in "Network-attached storage" on page 421.

- The Swift filesystem implementation in Hadoop (*http://bit.ly/2DU46Gm*) is a backend for Sahara, but it might not be officially be supported by distributors.

This results in the following options for life cycle models on OpenStack:

One-off clusters
These are generally possible in OpenStack via both Cinder volumes and Swift storage (*http://bit.ly/2QKRd4l*). If you rely on Hadoop distributor support, though, we recommend that you scrutinize coverage of these storage backends. Alternatives, such as integrating Amazon S3–compliant storage into Sahara (see Chapter 16) are under development at the time of this writing.

Suspendable clusters
Suspendable clusters are feasible in OpenStack via a remote block storage layer, but all caveats about bandwidth limitations and supportability by Hadoop distributors apply. You need to present fully POSIX-compliant block storage devices to your instances; this will typically imply some form of remote block storage, such as SAN or Ceph, which we cover further later in this chapter.

Sticky clusters
These are difficult to implement with the currently available functions in OpenStack. The required instance-level anti-affinity is possible in OpenStack but is not fully integrated into Sahara. Instance-to-volume affinity is required as well, because by default Cinder does not make any guarantees that a volume is located

on the same host. As we covered, host-local disks/volumes are passed to instances via iSCSI, which may simply not be supported by distributors.

If Sahara is used, the model can effectively be chosen at cluster creation time by selecting from the supported data sources (*http://bit.ly/2BnsPjU*).

Isolation

OpenStack supports a variety of hypervisors (*http://bit.ly/P5x1tL*) via an abstraction layer in its Nova (*https://docs.openstack.org/nova/latest/*) component. Hypervisors are treated like drivers and, although most OpenStack development is historically done on KVM, commercial hypervisors such as Microsoft Hyper-V and VMware ESXi are seeing increasing support in the OpenStack community. Because all of the supported hypervisors are considered state of the art, the level of isolation on the compute portion of OpenStack-based clouds is deemed very strong.

As just mentioned, OpenStack provides pluggable support for a variety of storage implementations. These range from local storage to state-of-the-art block storage on SAN to object storage implementations like Ceph, which we briefly introduce in "Object Storage for Private Clouds" on page 448.

Similarly, network virtualization in OpenStack is also pluggable, and multiple options exist (*https://red.ht/2PIHfnC*).

On a management level, OpenStack separates tenants by projects. Identities are managed and mapped to those projects in the Keystone service (*http://bit.ly/2DByR1V*), similar to Identity and Access Management (IAM) in AWS, which we cover in detail in Chapter 18.

Summary

It is beyond the scope of this book to discuss OpenStack in full depth. In summary, it can be said that OpenStack provides the most flexible and holistic approach to build clouds via an extensive range of third-party hardware and software components.

Its modularity also brings an enormous amount of complexity, though, which can overwhelm many enterprise IT departments and which makes it very difficult to directly compare given OpenStack implementations. One step to successfully wield the complexity of OpenStack in the enterprise is to use an OpenStack distributor such as Red Hat. Integration with enterprise Hadoop distributions and their automation tools is continuously improving, as can be seen, for example, by the joint reference architecture (*http://bit.ly/2DPXQ2f*) developed by Cloudera and Red Hat.

OpenShift

OpenShift is a container-based platform for accelerated application development and deployment. It is available as open source software and is also commercially distributed by Red Hat, Pivotal, and others. It combines Docker as an OS-level technology to create *containers* and Kubernetes for automated deployment, scaling, and management of those containers.

In OpenShift, Docker leverages the resource isolation and abstraction features of the Linux kernel to provide Linux containers. To applications, a Docker container looks and feels like its own separate instance of Linux, although it is not a fully fledged virtual machine. Docker containers are created from a base image and a stack of functionality can be added on top via new layers without the need to change the underlying images.

Different containerized applications can then be conveniently scheduled onto the same Linux instance without the need to start VMs. Kubernetes further takes advantage of these features by bundling containers into application *pods*. Pods are guaranteed to run on the same Linux host, and they provide a means to group several microservices into a single colocated service unit. Kubernetes allows you to easily deploy and manage many pods as large-scale distributed applications across multiple physical servers, which it refers to as *nodes*. The plurality of all nodes and pods form a Kubernetes *cluster*.

OpenShift can significantly simplify the process of building applications and platform-as-a-service environments. For many enterprises, OpenShift and Kubernetes pave the way toward scalable microservices. They are actually used to build public clouds as well, like Deutsche Telekom's AppAgile service (*http://bit.ly/2FAWsCy*).

Let's apply our three assessment criteria to see how OpenShift can support Hadoop environments.

Automation

We are unaware of any specific OpenShift-provided user interface that would guide you through Hadoop deployments, other than some community-based templates that deploy the Apache distribution of Hadoop. We are also not aware of any efforts to integrate with distributor automation tools. As you'll see in the following sections, OpenShift includes the ingredients to support and automate all of our life cycle models. But there is no cohesive effort that we know of in the OpenShift or Kubernetes universe that's comparable to OpenStack Sahara and would interact with distributor management tools to facilitate a deployment or to use anti-affinity rules according to Hadoop cluster roles.

Life Cycle and Storage

OpenShift has a straightforward way of representing storage to pods as *volumes* (*http://bit.ly/2q7tOk5*) and supports a range of storage backends via volume plug-ins. Compared to standard ephemeral container storage in OpenShift, volumes provide the advantage that their content survives container crashes. But the life cycle of a standard volume is bound to the life cycle of a pod; as soon as the pod ceases to exist, the volume vanishes.

Persistent volumes (*http://bit.ly/2xRpKpj*), on the other hand, allow volumes to have a life cycle entirely independent of pods and are conceptually the closest to remote block storage in OpenShift.

Depending on the volume plug-in, persistent volumes can be shared across pods (*http://bit.ly/2TbmQp8*).

Unlike in OpenStack, there is no framework-level integration of object storage solutions in OpenShift. And of the set of supported storage backends (*https://red.ht/2DFwZ91*) for PersistentVolumes, only the NFS backend is a candidate for a shared secondary storage layer for Hadoop. The remaining storage plug-ins mostly qualify as block storage implementations, some of which can also be shared among pods.

OpenShift also supports fine-grained anti-affinity policies (*https://red.ht/2qN0kGj*) and features a local volumes (*http://bit.ly/2DlljHw*) storage type that automatically optimizes the physical node placement of a given pod to reside on the same host as the local volume for that node.

 Anti-affinity rules in OpenShift can be either *required* or *preferred*. Hadoop depends on strong anti-affinity to deliver on its durability characteristics for storage. We therefore strongly recommend only using required pod affinity rules for Hadoop deployments, since preferred rules do not guarantee enforcement.

This renders the following life cycle options for OpenShift:

Sticky clusters
These are, in theory, possible via the aforementioned local volumes. There does not seem to be widespread adoption of this approach in the industry at the moment, however, and it has likely not seen extensive testing coverage.

Suspendable clusters
These should be possible when using persistent volumes, as long as the backing storage is able to provide sufficient durability and performance. For most corporations, this would likely be an enterprise-grade SAN solution, which, under the assumption of sufficient bandwidth, would use the iSCSI or Fibre Channel volume backends.

One-off clusters

One-off clusters are difficult to achieve due to the lack of support for object storage connectivity, which leaves us with limited abilities for the source of truth. You can certainly ingest and export data via the supported NFS backend for persistent volumes, but Hadoop tools do not recognize such a volume as an implementation of a Hadoop-compatible filesystem. This means that services such as Spark or Impala are unable to read or write to it in parallel fashion.

Isolation

For many organizations, VMs provided by commercial hypervisor software are the accepted standard for isolating virtual environments. OpenShift deliberately opts for lightweight virtualization via containers (*https://red.ht/2A9YF1G*). It uses a mandatory combination of Linux namespaces (*http://bit.ly/2PIEfaS*), Security-Enhanced Linux (SELinux) (*http://bit.ly/2zllZtP*), and cgroups (*http://bit.ly/2PGvYE4*) to achieve isolation on its compute layer. Red Hat offers detailed information (*https://red.ht/2FxbyZH*) on how these mechanisms work together and how containers compare to VMs.

Kubernetes employs a holistic security concept (*https://red.ht/2BoEFKF*) that allows fine-grained authorization via role-based access control (RBAC) (*http://bit.ly/2OHTb3y*) for users and *security context constraints* (SCCs) (*http://bit.ly/2Pue1sy*) that constrain the actions that a given pod is allowed to perform on the host OS.

A fundamental resource that is subject to authorization in Kubernetes is a namespace (*http://bit.ly/2TvgHEs*), which groups resources in a cluster and provides isolation of these resources. OpenShift extends the namespace concept to projects (*http://bit.ly/2OMbBQw*) to provide fully fledged group-based multitenancy, which can also be integrated with multiple options for authentication (*http://bit.ly/2RQXE5J*).

The Kubernetes security concept also includes support of SDN (*https://red.ht/2QMPQlp*). By default, SDN is used in Kubernetes to provide a scalable virtual network infrastructure to each pod. Via the `ovs-multitenant` (*https://red.ht/2DHgwBo*) plug-in, this concept can be enhanced to enforce separation of traffic on the project level.

It entirely depends on your organization as to whether the Linux kernel mechanisms used by Docker are deemed sufficient to provide strong isolation guarantees.

Summary

The ease of containerized application pods combined with horizontal scalability makes OpenShift intriguing for rapid development/deployment cycles and DevOps-driven environments. The current focus of OpenShift is to excel in scalability and provide orchestration for microservices. Hadoop is typically not a good fit for microservices, but that being said, OpenShift comprises all the required mechanisms to cloudify Hadoop.

What is essentially missing is a cohesive component that automates Hadoop deployments and uses the existing affinity/anti-affinity mechanisms for Hadoop compute and storage.

In addition, Hadoop distributor support for running frameworks such as Spark on Docker and Kubernetes has not materialized yet, though it is likely to emerge soon. It is likely that big data resource scheduling frameworks and Kubernetes will converge in the future, but as of this writing, this is mere speculation.

VMware and Pivotal Cloud Foundry

Like OpenShift, Cloud Foundry is a PaaS offering. But in contrast to the container approach chosen by OpenShift, Pivotal Cloud Foundry is based on VMware. Cloud Foundry connects and combines many offerings from the EMC/Dell universe to build private cloud IaaS and PaaS stacks.

Even though we regularly see VMware hypervisors in virtualized on-premises Hadoop environments, we are not aware of an end-to-end automation offering. There is a plug-in available for Cloudera Director (*http://bit.ly/2BoQNeM*) that automates the provisioning of VMware-based infrastructure as a service, but the plug-in does not use the VMware Distributed Resource Scheduler (DRS) to achieve anti-affinity.

VMware has also been the driving force behind the contributions around Hadoop Virtual Extensions (HVE) (*http://bit.ly/2z9nOKg*), which introduce hypervisor awareness in HDFS's block placement hierarchy. However, HVE in its approach is strictly limited to HDFS and requires an external mechanism to reflect the topology of hypervisors in the virtual cluster to the NameNodes.

Do It Yourself?

By now, it should be clear that setting up a complete private cloud system is a daunting effort. In some cases that we have witnessed, even large enterprise IT organizations that cater to hundreds of thousands of users fail to implement these platforms in a sustainable way. When the goal is to cloudify Hadoop, the private cloud platforms we covered in the previous sections can really start paying off by offering self-service capabilities for a large amount of unmanaged clusters—for the sake of argument, let's say more than 30.

Not every organization needs this, though. For many, it might well be sufficient to offer capabilities that can spawn between 5 and 15 virtual Hadoop clusters within a reasonable amount of time.

We all know that engineers (and we don't exclude ourselves from that group) have a desire to build their own great and elegant solutions. As we will see, the large hyper-scale clouds by Amazon, Microsoft, and Google are elegant in many respects, but much of their greatness is achieved simply by economies of scale. Instead of trying to handcraft a cloud, one option might be to lower the bar, in terms of automation, and come up with a Hadoop Cloud–Lite.

Figure 15-1 shows an example of such a simplified solution. There are six physical hosts (hosts 1–6) that accommodate three virtual Hadoop clusters (clusters A–C). Each of the six hosts runs a state-of-the-art hypervisor, such as VMware, providing three VMs on each host. In the example, we use SAN storage for master nodes (hosts 1 and 2) and local disks in the worker nodes (hosts 3–6). Other implementations might use local disks for the master nodes as well, and in yet another configuration you might use a SAN for the worker nodes, if your bandwidth is sufficient.

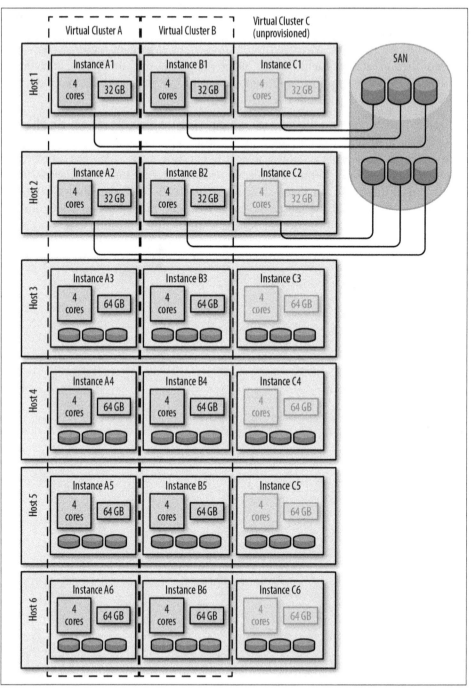

Figure 15-1. Simplified private cloud environment via preprovisioning

To simplify the provisioning of Hadoop, all instances (A1–A6, B1–B6, C1–C6) are preprovisioned when their physical environment is set up, giving us the following advantages during Hadoop deployment:

- Most important, anti-affinity is manually taken care of.
- Networks and VLANs for each virtual cluster already exist.
- Each instance has an IP and hostname in DNS.
- Each instance has the required storage backends connected and ready for use.
- Access credentials are prepared.

In Figure 15-1, virtual cluster A and virtual cluster B are already provisioned and running with Hadoop, whereas the VMs for cluster C are preprovisioned and dormant, while cluster C itself is not yet provisioned. The VMs can be preinstalled with Linux, but are suspended.

A deployment of Hadoop for a tenant would entail the following steps:

1. A vacant preprovisioned virtual cluster is chosen.
2. The instances belonging to the cluster are started.
3. The cluster's basic specification, comprising IPs, hostnames, and credentials, is passed to a Hadoop-level automation layer that begins to install Hadoop services (for example, Cloudera Director).
4. The requesting tenant receives the cluster's basic specifications and login credentials.

Automation

Although we essentially shortcut a lot of the difficult work on automated infrastructure provisioning, the challenge is obviously still the automation of the Hadoop services themselves. The following options exist:

- Script the entire deployment of Hadoop yourself. Given the increasing complexity of the Hadoop stack, you might want to constrain the number of services that are included in the deployment.
- Use management tools from a Hadoop distribution, such as Cloudera Manager or Ambari, to automate the deployment. As a prerequisite, you must automate the installation of the management tool itself. You would likely drive the tool via any of the many supported APIs, such as Python for Cloudera Manager (*https:// cloudera.github.io/cm_api/docs/python-client/*). As an input it suffices to supply the hostnames of the instances.

- Use a cloud orchestration tool such as Cloudera Director or Hortonworks Cloudbreak. This option is theoretically feasible because these tools can generally deploy on a bare-metal infrastructure or preprovisioned VMs via a specific bring your own node (*http://bit.ly/2Bq4Kcb*) plug-in. But these configurations are not officially tested by either provider and might not have the ability to persistently keep track of the state of a particular cluster.

A drawback with regard to automation when using preprovisioning is that it is difficult to programmatically scale the virtual Hadoop clusters. On the infrastructure level, you can preprovision additional IPs and keep extra headroom in the size of your VLAN. Obviously, scalability becomes less of a challenge when you can use remote storage.

As a final note, if you need to sustain a self-service UI, it must select from the list of available clusters and should feed all information about the virtual environment (such as hostnames, IPs, and credentials) into the aforementioned automation workflow.

Isolation

When you predeploy infrastructure and keep it dormant until usage, you can take advantage of existing isolation mechanisms such as VLANs for the network or storage pool reservations on remote block storage systems or secondary storage layers, which may be hard to automate in your organization. You can also predefine credentials and user identities—this is one of the trickiest parts of building a private cloud.

Life Cycle Model

All of the aforementioned life cycle models can theoretically be implemented when preprovisioning virtual clusters:

One-off clusters
  Implementing a transient cluster model in our example, like with any other solution, requires a secondary storage layer. The rest is as simple as terminating the VMs in the preprovisioned VLAN environment, while the VLAN, IPs, and hostnames can be reused. If local storage is used, it is good practice to deliberately wipe the local disk devices (*http://bit.ly/2DRj7J1*) to ensure that data from prior tenants is no longer readable. The secondary storage layer could be as simple as an NFS mount shared by all instances in a cluster, or an implementation of supported Hadoop object storage connectors. Bear in mind the constraints on object storage we covered in "Cluster Life Cycle Models" on page 425. Whichever solution you choose, the shared storage space needs to be preprovisioned on the backing storage system and the credentials need to be preconfigured in the instances.

Suspendable clusters

In our example solution, suspendability would necessitate that the worker nodes are also attached to a SAN. While this is theoretically possible, we have often seen on-premises SAN infrastructures that could not sustain Hadoop traffic. It is more feasible to implement the master roles on SAN storage, as they do not require a bandwidth-heavy workload profile. In any environment that involves SANs, especially in a production context, you need to carefully measure latencies for master roles and throughput characteristics for worker roles. If you run Hadoop with a distributor, which most enterprises do, it is also wise to seek clarification on supported configurations.

Sticky clusters

These can be easily set up in this environment by either dedicating the local disks in the cluster directly via the hypervisor or predefining storage pools in the hypervisor, as we introduced in "Virtualizing Local Storage" on page 416.

Summary

Some organizations are extremely agile and may finish a campaign based on Hadoop and big data technology in just a few days. In the majority of enterprises, however, it would be uncommon to see Hadoop tenants come and go with this frequency, as project team assembly and dataset migration require internal communication and approvals. In the latter case, we typically measure the lifetime of the Hadoop cluster in months as opposed to days. Long-lived virtual clusters on local disks (which our example shows), although the least cloud-like option, are an obvious match for this kind of scenario, for several reasons:

- A project that needs Hadoop for a few months can have its own environment at significantly improved turnaround times, compared to the setup of physical hardware.

- The fiscal depreciation cycle for hardware in enterprises is typically between 36 and 48 months. Virtualizing the hardware opens this investment up to multiple parties and helps to deal with concerns around budget.

- The possibility of setting up smaller, lightweight clusters encourages teams to follow the best practices of complementing their larger production clusters with development and staging environments that can be accommodated by the proposed platform.

The notion of preprovisioning infrastructure works against the grain of cloud computing, but it can certainly also serve IT organizations by addressing pressing concerns around provisioning time of lightweight Hadoop environments. Preprovision of infrastructure can help to establish a shorter project life cycle and to increase the reusability of hardware.

Object Storage for Private Clouds

So far we have focused on private cloud frameworks and their native support for storage options. This section offers brief information about options for providing object storage or other types of additional storage to your virtual clusters.

EMC Isilon

Isilon is an enterprise storage solution by EMC. It provides a full implementation of HDFS, which can be conveniently used as a remote HDFS instance. It is also possible to use the Isilon HDFS implementation as a drop-in replacement for a local HDFS instance by simply configuring the default Hadoop filesystem to point to the Isilon instances.

As depicted in Figure 15-2, unlike most remote storage appliances, Isilon is built as a distributed system of many storage nodes. These nodes communicate and distribute storage blocks via a high-speed backend network.

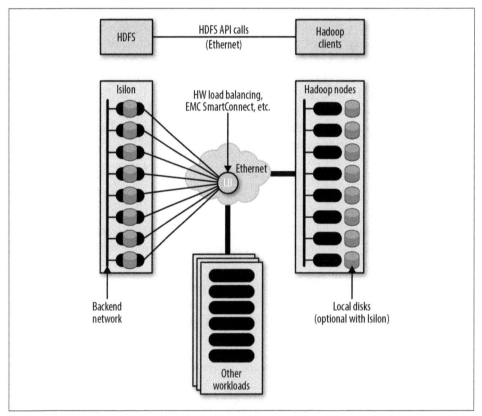

Figure 15-2. Using Isilon with Hadoop

Isilon supports multiple data protection methods—most importantly, various flavors of erasure coding that provide improved storage efficiency. To the outside world, each of the storage nodes is connected via a standard Ethernet frontend network and provides several storage interfaces, such as NFS and HDFS.

In the HDFS case, the Hadoop services communicate with Isilon directly via the HDFS client protocol. All Isilon nodes can be contacted by clients because they all implement the API of both the HDFS NameNode and the DataNode.

To provide clients with a single NameNode in their configuration, while at the same time distributing the load of client requests, it is standard practice to load-balance the client connections. EMC provides this load-balancing service as a built-in part of the Isilon offering.

You can use Isilon's HDFS interface as a remote HDFS instance, which works for YARN applications or Hive or Impala queries. You can also configure it as your cluster's `fs.defaultFS`, so that all services access it transparently and by default.

Regardless of the access mode, when using Isilon data, locality is lost and you are limited by the bandwidth and your proportional share of the overall network.

With Isilon, there is no use of the Linux page cache in your HDFS data path, which in turn means that short-circuit and zero-copy reads are not available. This might be perfectly sufficient for a range of use cases, such as background batch processing, hot archives, or virtualized Hadoop environments, but it can be limiting for a range of database queries that rely heavily on locality and on the benefits of caching hot datasets.

You should also be mindful of the following additional limitations:

- HDFS encryption does not work.
- HDFS access control lists do not work on Isilon, because it implements its own ACLs. ACLs are an important feature that enables many organizations to implement an information architecture on their datasets.

However, it is an increasingly common pattern for Hadoop clusters in the cloud to trade locality and performance for storage efficiency and modularity of compute and storage. This is also reflected in the emergence of HDFS erasure coding, as introduced in "Erasure Coding Versus Replication" on page 71. As you might expect, we'll see more examples of this pattern in Chapter 16.

The main criterion to consider when using Hadoop with Isilon is the interconnecting network. Although we have seen successful cases that connect medium-sized Hadoop clusters with a large Isilon array via a completely nonblocking network architecture, we have also seen Hadoop projects on Isilon that entirely fail to meet performance expectations due to network oversubscription.

With these caveats in mind, Isilon can offer a practical solution for private cloud Hadoop storage.

Ceph

Ceph is an open source distributed storage system that, over the years, has continuously gained in popularity for private cloud use cases. It provides remote block storage, a distributed filesystem called the Ceph Filesystem (CephFS), and Swift- and Amazon S3–compatible object storage.

At its core, Ceph is implemented as a distributed object store. It is typically implemented as a cluster of commodity servers. The majority of nodes offer local disks and run the Ceph *object storage daemon* (OSD). An type of cluster node runs *monitors*, which provide critically important cluster state and coordination for the OSD nodes. *Manager* nodes provide further monitoring capabilities and interfaces to external monitoring systems.

The most direct way to use Ceph is to communicate with the OSDs via the Reliable Autonomic Distributed Object Store (RADOS) protocol. Ceph encapsulates the protocol logic in the librados library, which is available in C, Python, and Java. As shown in Figure 15-3, librados is used throughout the Ceph storage stack in several intermediate layers that implement standard storage interfaces.

As shown in Figure 15-3, starting from the top, the following options exist to connect Hadoop clients to Ceph:

- Object storage, via the Ceph RADOS Gateway
- A distributed filesystem interface called CephFS
- Remote block storage

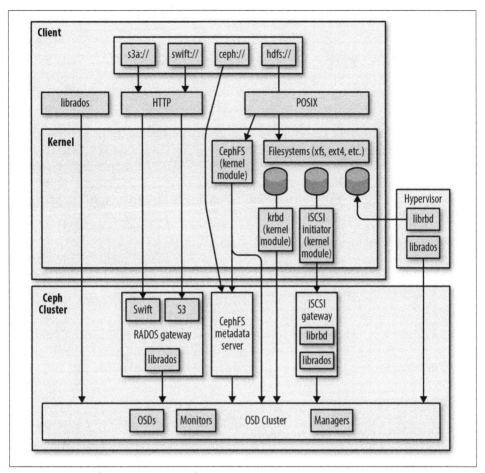

Figure 15-3. Hadoop access to Ceph

Object storage

Hadoop can use the S3A client, which we discuss in more detail in "AWS storage options" on page 459, as well as the Swift client, which we introduced in "Life Cycle and Storage" on page 436. The clients connect to Ceph's RADOS Gateway, which runs on a set of separate nodes in the Ceph cluster and maps the Amazon S3 and Swift protocols to `librados` calls. Authentication (*http://bit.ly/2zkEsqy*) works the same as with Amazon S3 (access key ID + secret; see "Amazon Simple Storage Service" on page 524). However, it is worth checking whether your Hadoop distributor supports accessing a Ceph-based Amazon S3 backend or a Ceph-based Swift implementation.

CephFS

Ceph provides CephFS, a distributed network filesystem. It extends the cluster by a set of *metadata servers* that maintain the shared filesystem's directory structure and all corresponding metainformation. CephFS clients use the `cephfs` Linux kernel module to mount content from Ceph in a POSIX-compliant way, similar to NFS, which we covered in "Network-attached storage" on page 421.

As we previously covered, however, we strongly advise against using a network filesystem as the backing store for HDFS data volumes. Instead, there is a CephFS plug-in (*http://bit.ly/2BnHQ5k*) that maps the HDFS API to Ceph and facilitates connections to the metadata servers as well as the OSDs on the storage nodes. The plug-in is provided directly by Ceph, after an initial effort (*http://bit.ly/2BqMT53*) to include it in the Hadoop codebase itself.

Hadoop clients need to enter the appropriate configuration data about the Ceph cluster in their *core-site.xml* and can then access Ceph via a special `ceph://` URI scheme. This configuration includes a shared secret to authenticate with the Ceph cluster, which is similar, for example, to how authentication is achieved in Amazon S3, as we'll see in Chapter 18.

To summarize, the CephFS plug-in is structured very similarly to Amazon S3 and the OpenStack Swift plug-in. Unlike those plug-ins, however, the CephFS plug-in is not part of the mainline Hadoop project, and it has not yet seen widespread use.

Remote block storage

Ceph supports multiple techniques to export block devices to clients. Like disks in a SAN, Hadoop can use these block devices for building an in-cluster HDFS instance.

Ceph remote block storage, which is officially called *RADOS Block Device* (RBD), however, does not directly use any of the SAN protocols we covered in "SANs" on page 417; rather, it uses `librados` as its transport layer.

There are three ways in which Ceph can expose block devices:

`librbd`

This is a user space library that is typically used in hypervisors to export Ceph RBDs to virtual machines. As displayed in Figure 15-3, `librbd` uses `librados` underneath to communicate directly with OSDs in the Ceph cluster and assembles objects onto disk which then are passed to the VMs in the format particular to the hypervisor. `librbd` is integrated with OpenStack (*http://bit.ly/2QWRYaA*) and can provide VMs as well as standard block device volumes, which can, in turn, be used for worker nodes.

`krbd`

    Alternatively, it is possible to mount RBDs directly in client systems via a kernel module called `krbd` that encapsulates the logic to build block devices from OSD objects as well as the `librados` communication. `krbd` is typically used for Ceph RDBs on bare-metal servers or in container-based environments such as Kubernetes.

iSCSI gateway

    Finally, the Ceph cluster can act as an iSCSI target by running a set of *iSCSI gateways*, as shown in Figure 15-3. The client system simply uses the existing iSCSI subsystem to provide SCSI disks locally and to act as an initiator toward the Ceph gateways.

Summary

Ceph is a genuine option for providing a remote storage layer for Hadoop in private clouds. Ceph also supports erasure coding, which can improve the storage efficiency of your big data solution. It is increasingly being recognized by Hadoop distributors as an asset to support private cloud scenarios. For example, Cloudera publishes a reference architecture (*http://bit.ly/2DocvRe*) on using its distribution on OpenStack with Ceph remote block storage.

Summary

The intent of this chapter was to make a little more sense of the subject of Hadoop in private clouds, but we understand that it is not an easy feat. Although a number of successful implementations exist here and there, the path to private clouds with Hadoop is far from being fully paved.

Because most enterprises rely on a mix of technologies, such as commercial Hadoop distributors, a private cloud software framework, and storage and compute virtualization technology, there is no single-source solution for Hadoop in the private cloud.

As a result, our overview of three approaches for cloudifying Hadoop via OpenStack, OpenShift, and a lightweight, do-it-yourself variant of on-premises virtualization called out shortcomings and peculiarities at the corresponding places. In our experience the options presented here are, at the time of this writing, the most suitable from a technological perspective, although we are fully aware of the multitude of alternative solutions.

## CHAPTER 16

Solutions in the Public Cloud

Our discussion of public clouds is different from that of private clouds. In contrast to private cloud Hadoop services, there are thousands of examples in which large organizations and enterprises are successfully running Hadoop in the public cloud.

In the coming chapters, we focus our discussion on the three largest public cloud providers in the market:

- Amazon Web Services (AWS)
- Microsoft Azure
- Google Cloud Project (GCP)

This chapter looks at the portfolios of our three cloud providers through the lens of Hadoop. We cover the key categories for each: instances, storage, and possible life cycle models. Next, we offer advice on how to use the provider portfolios to implement clusters and big data use cases.

Key Things to Know

Part of the value proposition for the cloud is that IT services become a black box that you do not have to worry about. This also means that you do not know what is going on inside the black box. For our intent of running Hadoop in a public cloud, this is mostly good news (and some bad news at the same time). Here are some key things to keep in mind:

Life cycle models
"Cluster Life Cycle Models" on page 425 explains that storage choices define the life cycle options of virtual Hadoop clusters. In the public cloud, much attention shifts toward transient life cycle models because they are much easier to

implement. You should take care when implementing sticky clusters in the public cloud, since the instances that host local disks may be colocated on the same physical host. We cover why this is the case in "Storage and Life Cycle Models" on page 478.

Storage

As we have seen throughout the book, choosing the right storage infrastructure often requires the most thought in your big data strategy. This remains true when deploying in a public cloud, although the calculus is now slightly different, for two key reasons:

- Economies of scale in public clouds actually open up the possibility of using remote block storage—for example, storage area networks—as the backing storage layer for HDFS at a reasonable (albeit still higher, compared to local disks) cost.

- Object storage solutions in the public cloud allow for the decoupling of storage from compute resource in your clusters, enabling use case–specific and transient cluster life cycles while maintaining a single, unified source of truth across all clusters. For details on this subject, refer to "Sharing Metadata Services" on page 511.

Storage offerings, in particular, are among the features where public cloud providers differ significantly. A thorough introduction to each public cloud vendor's storage portfolio is provided in "AWS storage options" on page 459, "Azure storage options" on page 465, and "Storage options" on page 471.

High availability (HA)

It is tempting to believe that public cloud services themselves automatically take care of HA; but in the case of Hadoop and big data deployments, it is key to understand the individual providers' concepts of HA in detail to make informed choices.

Another key thing to know in this context is that, for the most part, you have limited control over where your virtual machines are started. As we saw in "Virtual Machine Distribution" on page 413, placement of VMs and anti-affinity can be crucial to ensure HA and durability, especially if you rely on local disks in your instances. Remote block storage decreases the aforementioned concern around VM placement and multiple HDFS DataNodes being placed on the same physical host, but you can still lose access to blocks if three DataNodes happen to run on a single physical host. This is even more crucial for highly available master roles.

Public clouds also allow for a novel paradigm around HA: use object stores to provide availability and durability of data and expect your computational clusters to be short-lived and to fail. We cover the HA implications of running Hadoop in a public cloud environment in "High Availability" on page 488.

Automation

This may come as a bit of a shock to some classic enterprise IT organizations, but public clouds allow you to treat all infrastructure as code. Deploying a purpose-built cluster for your end-of-quarter reporting can become a fully scripted, automated, and repeatable process. Chapter 17 gives a more thorough introduction to the subject of automation of Hadoop in the cloud.

Security

In many organizations, the discussion around moving big data use cases to the cloud is dominated by security concerns. Secure Hadoop services in public clouds, even conforming to strict requirements, are perfectly possible. We discuss this important subject in much more detail in Chapter 18, covering, for example, how cloud identity and access management systems integrate with classic on-premises identity management solutions, how to implement perimeter security in public clouds, and what options you have around data encryption.

Cloud Providers

In this section, we take a look at the three biggest public cloud providers. Our focus here is mainly on the compute and storage aspects required to appropriately size Hadoop clusters. As we go through each cloud provider, we explore:

- Compute capabilities, with a look at each provider's various instance types and their features
- The structure and function of a provider's storage portfolio
- Built-in Hadoop services

Service offerings around networking and DNS, however, also play an important role when building clusters in public clouds. We cover them at a high level in "Network Architecture" on page 484.

AWS

AWS, which is seen as the inventor of the public cloud business model, provides a plethora of IaaS, PaaS, and SaaS offerings.

The AWS IaaS offering for compute virtualization is called Amazon Elastic Compute Cloud (Amazon EC2). Within EC2, AWS provides remote block storage via Amazon Elastic Block Store (EBS). AWS also offers object storage solutions, which we discuss. Although a few instance types in EC2 provide locally attached disks, some of them exclusively implement block devices via EBS. As we explain, the compute and storage offerings of AWS support nearly all of the life cycle models we have discussed.

AWS is currently available in 19 geographic locations, called *regions*. Each region is further divided into *availability zones*, which provide a high-bandwidth/low-latency subdivision of a region into distinct datacenters to offer improved failover characteristics for applications. AWS also provides a dedicated, isolated service for United States government agencies, called AWS GovCloud (US). The services we discuss in the following sections are available in all AWS regions.

AWS instance types

AWS offers a large number of instance types, grouped by five use case domains:

General-purpose instances (https://amzn.to/2PW6Icz)
> As the name implies, these instances serve the widest range of applications via a balanced relationship of compute and memory. In the past, general-purpose instances also featured local disks, but today they are available only with remotely attached block storage; that is, EBS (which we discuss in the next section). The M4 and M5 instance types from this group are very popular for implementing worker nodes for suspendable clusters.

Compute-optimized instances (https://amzn.to/2zd0dIs)
> This group comprises the C4 and C5 instance types and emphasizes cores over memory. C4 and C5 instances are popular for implementing compute-heavy worker nodes, as shown in "Implementing Clusters" on page 473. Like the general-purpose instances, they are now only available with EBS storage.

Storage-optimized instances (https://amzn.to/2PZsOLe)
> This group of instances uses local block devices, such as SCSI hard drives, solid-state drives (SSDs), or NVM Express (NVMe) drives, to achieve better performance or, alternatively, better price characteristics for storage. It is possible to attach up to 48 TB of local, transient, or *ephemeral* storage. These instances are often used to implement sticky clusters or one-off clusters that need the speed of local disks. As we describe in more detail in Table 16-6, the contents of those disks are lost during a crash or following certain life cycle actions, such as terminate or stop.

Memory-optimized instances (https://amzn.to/2QM3F3K)
> For Hadoop, these instances can be relevant for implementing memory-intensive use cases. We consider mostly the R4 series of instances in the following discussion. Although some instance types in this group also feature SSDs, their count is too small to consider them for worker nodes in sticky cluster implementations. This group also features the X1e instances that offer up to nearly 4 TB of

memory. Although single instances in this group can have up to 128 vCPUs, their count is small relative to the strong emphasis on RAM.

Accelerated-computing instances (https://amzn.to/2Kaozae)
This group features instances that offer graphics processing units (GPUs) as accelerators. For big data, this addresses the fast-growing realm of use cases around machine learning and deep learning.

All the instance classes, such as the M5 series, C5 series, and others in the aforementioned groups, themselves contain multiple instance types of increasing capabilities. Within each class, the nomenclature for the increase is typically *large, xlarge, 2xlarge … 16xlarge …,* and so on.

AWS storage options

AWS offers a sophisticated portfolio for storing data at large or small scale. As shown in Figure 16-1, the offering is organized by storage technologies.

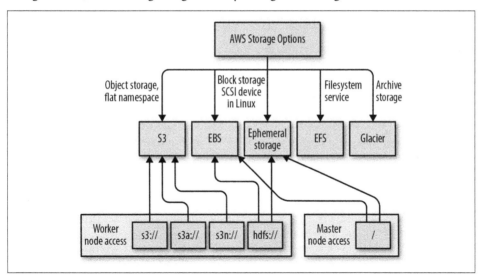

Figure 16-1. AWS storage options

The available storage options are:

Elastic Block Storage
EBS is the AWS solution for remote block storage. In practical terms, you can think of EBS as a gigantic SAN implementation. EBS provides raw block devices, referred to as *EBS volumes*. Although an EBS volume is not a physically dedicated SCSI disk, their performance characteristics make them suitable as the underlying storage for HDFS, when selected and configured in the correct way. AWS

offers different volume types, as shown in Table 16-1, to address different requirement profiles for latency and throughput.

Table 16-1. EBS volume types

EBS volume type	Implementation	Max. throughput	Max. IOPS
sc1	HDD	250 MB/s	250
st1	HDD	500 MB/s	500
gp2	SSD	160 MB/s	10,000
io1	SSD	500 MB/s	32,000

gp2 and io1 are SSD volumes. gp2 volumes provide a general-purpose mix of high input/output operations per second and fair bandwidth, while also striking a balance between price and performance. io1 provides the highest throughput and IOPS in the EBS portfolio. st1 and sc1 are hard disk drive (HDD) volumes. st1 volumes are throughput-optimized, whereas sc1 volumes yield only half of their performance and are considered cold storage.

EBS allows bursting throughput beyond the volume's limit, based on a bucket of burst credits. AWS provides detailed numbers on availability and fail rates for EBS storage, which we summarize in Table 16-8.

When using EBS for Hadoop, we strongly recommend that you use at least gp2 volumes for master roles, such as HDFS JournalNodes or ZooKeeper, and at least st1 volumes for worker roles, such as HDFS DataNodes or Kudu tablet servers. A common mistake when building a Hadoop cluster on EBS is that the sum of your mounted EBS volumes exceeds the total EBS bandwidth of the instance types in your cluster.

Further on, we recommend using EBS-optimized instances (*https://amzn.to/ 2LVmP8W*), which offer dedicated network capacity for EBS; nonoptimized instances share their network bandwidth for all services. In addition, for master roles, we strongly recommend using either EBS-optimized instances or instances that feature at least 10 Gb/s network bandwidth. The rationale for the latter is that although under normal conditions bandwidth and latency are independent, high bandwidth helps to sustain lower latencies in times of congestion, which is of key importance for said master roles.

EBS storage offers the ability to scale HDFS storage independently from compute, by adding more volumes to existing nodes. However, if you are after true elasticity, you might want to consider other, more natural cloud-native patterns, such as dynamically scaling your cluster by adding and removing compute instances and using object storage as the principal storage location.

In addition, EBS allows for snapshots (*https://amzn.to/2QaNwHP*) of the S3 object storage, as a more durable persistence layer. This can be a useful failsafe for master node disks. For HDFS DataNode disks, bear in mind that such a backup would contain content that is not usable by systems other than Hadoop, and it may be better to perform your backup via an Amazon S3 target.

Simple Storage Service

Amazon S3 is a massively scalable object storage service that defines its own protocol and API for storing data. All entities of data in S3 are called *objects*, and all objects are stored in *buckets*. Buckets provide a single flat namespace to organize data and to provide isolation between tenants. S3 uses HTTP as the transport protocol via RESTful PUT and GET methods and a SOAP interface.

Some operations in the S3 API are *eventually consistent* (*https://amzn.to/2KoiBTi*). This means some clients may still see old data after other clients have overwritten or deleted it. This could occur during a read operation or when listing a directory's contents. When talking about this, you will often hear the terms *read-after-write consistency* and *listing consistency* for directory listings. While other object store implementations provide both, S3 does not provide either. However, the operations are still atomic, meaning that either the old or new data will be fetched, as appropriate, but clients do not see corrupt data.

Hadoop offers the hadoop-aws module (*http://bit.ly/2Q57XpC*) to access S3. There are multiple clients available in the module, but the preferred one is the S3A client (*http://bit.ly/2A0j8ps*). As listed in the Hadoop documentation (*http://bit.ly/2PHKcVx*), other client libraries exist but are either unmaintained or already deprecated.

Certain problems in Hadoop processing arise around S3 consistency in practice. Consider, for example, when an automated process checks for the success of a Spark job by checking for its output. It might fail to see a successful run, due to eventual consistency. The best solution to this at the moment is S3Guard (*http://bit.ly/2DHTkCY*), which tracks metadata changes via an additional database and manages to fix most of the known problems.

Due to the nature of the S3 API, some calls remain unimplemented; for example, the append method of S3AFileSystem (*http://bit.ly/2OPhjRQ*).

Unlike EBS volumes, which appear simply as SCSI disks to your instance, S3 is accessed remotely by the Hadoop services using the S3 API with a set of configurable credentials. We cover this aspect in detail in Chapter 18.

For many organizations, S3 is a good choice for maintaining a single version of truth for their data since it has the best durability of all AWS storage systems. AWS provides a number of optimizations (*https://amzn.to/2Q3Bbp4*) to achieve maximum efficiency and performance on S3. In our experience, the effective limit on throughput to S3 is in the clients; that is, the number of instances in your cluster as well as the network bandwidth and the number of requesting threads on those instances.

Instance (ephemeral) storage

EC2 also offers a set of instances that feature local disks, which AWS refers to as *instance stores* (*https://amzn.to/2DHpRZQ*) or *ephemeral storage*. Table 16-2 shows examples of instances with ephemeral disks that can be useful configurations for worker nodes.

Table 16-2. Examples of configuration for instance storage in AWS

Instance	vCPU	Memory	Storage
d2.4xlarge	16	122	12 x 2 TB HDD
i3.8xlarge	32	244	4 x 1.9 TB NVMe SSD

Many newer-generation instance types have shifted to exclusively using EBS storage, although they offered local storage in previous generations. A good example of this is the M instance line. Although up to generation M3 these instance types used to have one or two local disks, M4 was only EBS. Compared to EBS, local disks provide a cost incentive, but they do not offer the ability to scale storage independently from compute.

 The content on ephemeral disks can be lost in its entirety when instances are stopped or when they crash. Although ephemeral disks can yield advantages in performance and provide an economic incentive, they have implications on your cluster's life cycle that you should fully understand prior to running HDFS on them. See "Storage and Life Cycle Models" on page 478 for a detailed discussion on this.

Amazon Elastic MapReduce

Amazon Elastic MapReduce (EMR) is a PaaS offering that is essentially a Hadoop distribution on AWS. As an AWS customer, it lets you deploy Hadoop clusters, including the underlying infrastructure for Hadoop as well as Hadoop services themselves.

Among other services, EMR includes:

- MapReduce/YARN
- Hive, Tez
- HBase
- Presto
- Spark

You can select from a set of preconfigured services or individually select the services you require on the cluster.

You can use HDFS on instances with local disks as the storage layer, but EMR also features the EMR File System (EMRFS), which is an implementation of the HDFS API on top of S3. EMRFS offers functionality to provide read-after-write consistency, called *consistent view*, which works similarly to S3Guard.

A common challenge that arises when working with transient life cycle models is that of retaining the metadata that defines the structure of your actual datasets; for example, the content of your Hive Metastore or authorization information about your datasets. EMR addresses this challenge via the AWS Glue Data Catalog (*https:// amzn.to/2z82ox9*), which can persist metadata information for data stored in S3 beyond the EMR cluster lifetime.

Although the ecosystem of big data software assets in classic Hadoop distributions such as Cloudera and Hortonworks is being expanded with, for example, Kafka and Kudu, EMR might already offer an adequate portfolio for some orgs. It also provides additional convenience as well as full integration into AWS. It is, however, by design bound to the AWS context and does not permit sourcing of multiple cloud vendors.

Finally, you need to consider that when AWS incorporates fixes into EMR, they are shipped to you in the form of a new virtual machine image, called an Amazon Machine Image (AMI). To apply the new AMI, you need to terminate and relaunch your cluster instances with the new AMI, which makes it difficult to maintain a long-running sticky cluster.

Caveats and service limits

When you initially set up your AWS account, certain default per-region limits apply to the majority of AWS services (*https://amzn.to/2K8Kkak*). Although public clouds are built for economies of (hyper)scale, even AWS needs to plan for large resource requests. The service limits also protect your organization from inadvertent infrastructure requests that could consume your quarterly IT budget in a five-hour straw fire (this actually happens). The limits are:

- 20 reserved instances per availability zone on EC2
- 300 TB of throughput-optimized HDDs (st1) on EBS per region
- 100 buckets per account for S3 object storage
- 5 virtual private clouds (VPCs) per region

In order to build anything beyond a small Hadoop deployment, you need to submit a corresponding request to extend the default boundaries of your account. It is worth having at least a rough estimate of your initial resource requirements and keeping tabs on your current and expected usage in order to get limit increase requests in before they become a project bottleneck.

Microsoft Azure

Microsoft, which is at the center of many on-premises enterprise IT stacks, is now the market challenger for public cloud services, with Microsoft Azure. Azure offers an extensive product portfolio by leveraging many of Microsoft's preexisting enterprise software offerings for office collaboration and identity management, while complementing them with innovations in large-scale distributed web services. This makes Azure attractive for big data use cases in the cloud.

Azure is currently available in 42 regions. Similar to the AWS GovCloud offering, Azure is distinguished in the European market with an isolated German region, which runs its own networking and is operated solely by German staff (referred to as the data trustee), in order to abide by EU data protection regulations. Like AWS, Azure regions are further subdivided into availability zones but additionally offer fault domains and availability sets (*http://bit.ly/2FnRYPv*), which we cover in more detail in "High Availability" on page 488. Although Azure features a great number of regions, it should be noted that certain instance types or products that are relevant to Hadoop, such as Azure Data Lake Storage, are not available in some of them.

Azure instance types

Similar to AWS, Azure offers several classes of instance types:

General-purpose VMs (http://bit.ly/2BbaIxn)
> Azure offers this group of instances to address the majority of use cases. There are as many as 10 different instance types within this group, some of which are simply predecessors of the latest generation. For Hadoop, you should mainly consider the DSv3-series and the Dv3-series because they provide adequate vertical scalability for, for example, worker nodes.

Compute-optimized VMs (http://bit.ly/2zch4v8)

This group comprises the F-series instances and newer generations thereof. These instances allow for building compute-heavy worker nodes, as shown in "Implementing Clusters" on page 473. You should use only the Fsv2-series, because it permits vertical scalability beyond 32 GB of memory, which is likely to be required in a medium-sized cluster.

Memory-optimized VMs (http://bit.ly/2DtaW4q)

Azure lists nine instance types in this group, including instances from the D-series, which are also listed under the general-purpose category. The D-, DS-, Dv2-, and DSv2-series instances are basically split into two groups.

The first group has a memory-to-vCPU ratio of 3.5 and is listed as general-purpose, whereas the second group has a memory-to-vCPU ratio of 7 and is listed as memory-optimized. The focus for memory-intensive big data use cases should be on the Ev3- and Esv3-series as well as the G- and GS-series, which provide superior vertical scalability and a memory-to-vCPU ratio of 7 and 14, respectively. The G-series also features up to 6 TB of local temporary SSD storage and is one of the few instances in the Azure portfolio that would allow for implementing sticky clusters.

Finally, there is the M-series, which is a potential but unlikely candidate for Hadoop: the smallest instance starts out with 1 TB of RAM, which is typically overkill for Hadoop worker nodes.

Storage-optimized VMs (http://bit.ly/2zgEJdT)

Azure offers the Ls-series for I/O-intensive workloads. It comes with a memory-to-compute ratio of 8, features up to 5.6 TB of local temporary SSD storage, and significantly improves local storage throughput compared to, for example, the G-series instances.

GPU-optimized VMs (http://bit.ly/2QLydT3)

Azure also offers as many as five different instance types that feature various types of NVIDIA GPU accelerators. Depending on the instance, one to four GPUs are attached.

Azure storage options

Azure has a comprehensive range of storage options, which are shown in Figure 16-2. Several key Azure storage technologies are organized under an umbrella service called *Blob storage*, which supports storage of binary data of all kinds.

In Azure, you can select from different storage accounts (*http://bit.ly/2Q2whIT*), such as GPv2, GPv1, or Blob only. These determine the options of actual storage products that you have. GPv2 is the successor of GPv1 and provides all of the latest storage types and features for Hadoop. In most cases, we recommended upgrading all GPv1 accounts to GPv2. In addition, it is possible to have a Blob-only storage account, which limits your account to block blobs, which we introduce in the following section.

Blob storage, or *Windows Azure Storage Blobs* (WASB), is used to provide several types of object storage services as well as remote block storage (that is, SANs) used for the SCSI disks in Azure VMs. Finally, and more recently, Azure has launched a special kind of large-scale storage platform that specifically supports big data use cases, called Azure Data Lake.

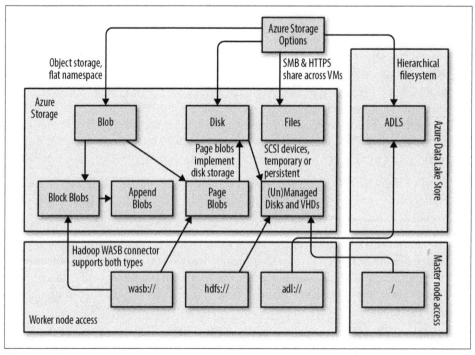

Figure 16-2. Azure storage options

Let's take a closer look at the Azure storage options:

Local temp storage

In Azure, every instance that is started in addition to the OS boot disk comes with a temporary disk, simply called the *temp drive*. The device typically grows in size and performance with larger instance types.

Because you get only a single device per instance, however, the function of a DataNode would be severely affected if the drive were unavailable. It is, therefore, normally not advisable to use the temp drive as backing storage for HDFS.

Like ephemeral disks in AWS, Azure temp drives are volatile. See Table 16-6 for a detailed look at this.

Azure Blob storage

Blob storage is one of the fundamental types of storage offered in Azure. As shown in Figure 16-2, three different blob types exist. To make sense of them, it may help to purely consider them as three different access patterns.

Block blobs provide a simple API to upload and commit objects (*blocks*) into the blob. The API provides a flat namespace that stores blobs in *containers*, which are equivalent to buckets in S3. Blocks can be inserted, overwritten, or deleted in their entirety, each of which requires a dedicated atomic commit operation. Block blobs are accessible from Hadoop as part of the WASB client.

Unlike block blobs, *append blobs* support appends, but they do not expose their internal block IDs and do not support updates or deletes. They are currently not used in any part of the Hadoop ecosystem.

Page blobs are small blobs organized into 512-byte pages. They are optimized for random I/O, and writes are immediately committed to storage. WASB's strong consistency (*http://bit.ly/2DHO0zn*) guarantees allow page blobs to be used to implement virtual block devices such as disks in Azure. As we show in Table 16-8, WASB achieves very high availability and data durability.

Blobs in Azure can be accessed via an object storage API, which is used in the `hadoop-azure` (*http://bit.ly/2DR2bSO*) storage module. Like the `hadoop-aws` module, `hadoop-azure` provides an implementation of the Hadoop abstract `File System` class, called `NativeAzureFileSystem` (*http://bit.ly/2K9TyTD*), which maps Hadoop filesystem API calls to Azure Blob API calls and is available under the `wasb://` URI scheme.

`NativeAzureFileSystem` uses block blobs and page blobs internally. Block blobs are used for the majority of accesses; for example, from Spark jobs or Hive queries. However, block blobs only support a maximum of 50,000 append operations. This is a problem for HBase, which frequently appends to its write-ahead log. To circumvent this problem, the WASB client also supports writing to page blobs. Like S3, WASB is an external service that requires client credentials in your configuration.

Disk storage

As depicted in Figure 16-2, disk storage is one of the principal storage types in Azure and provides remote block storage. All the disk types are based on *virtual hard disks* (VHDs), which are, in turn, saved as page blobs.

Unmanaged disks are VHDs that you provision separately from any compute resource in your storage account. You can connect unmanaged disks to your VMs, but they remain different entities with their own life cycles.

Managed disks are created in the background when you create VMs. They are subdivided into volumes backed by HDDs, called *standard disks*, and volumes backed by SSDs, called *premium disks*. Azure transparently manages the life cycle of the disks and aligns their fault domains with the VMs they are connected to. Microsoft publishes performance and scalability targets (*http://bit.ly/2TjfzE0*), which we summarize in Table 16-3.

We show only the largest possible volume sizes, to demonstrate maximum limits. Standard disks are sufficient, albeit not ideal, for worker node workloads, from a throughput perspective. When implementing master roles, make sure not to colocate multiple latency-sensitive services such as a ZooKeeper server and JournalNodes on a single standard disk, but provision multiple devices to ensure sufficient IOPS.

It is possible to back up managed disks via the Azure Backup service (*http://bit.ly/2zcbg4U*), which is Azure's equivalent of EBS snapshots and can be very handy, for example, to back up your NameNode's metadata.

Table 16-3. Azure managed disk types

Disk type	Implementation	Max. throughput	Max. IOPS
Premium disk (P50)	SSD	250 MB/s	7,500
Standard disk (S50)	HDD	60 MB/s	500

Azure Data Lake Storage

Microsoft Azure Data Lake Store (ADLS) is an additional storage offering in Azure that can be connected to Hadoop. ADLS is managed as a completely separate service and is optimized for analytics workloads with large concurrent access and high throughput.

The ADLS API resembles the HDFS API much more than the other object storage interfaces we have discussed. For example, it provides a file and directory structure and POSIX ACLs. ADLS offers read-after-write consistency. It is accessible for users by the `adl://` URL scheme, based on an implementation of the Hadoop `FileSystem` class, called `AdlFileSystem` (*http://bit.ly/2Q5jiWI*) in the Hadoop sources. It also implements the full WebHDFS REST API via HTTPS.

We cover aspects of security when using ADLS in "Microsoft Azure" on page 531.

ADLS shows performance characteristics (*http://bit.ly/2QOx90I*) similar to those of HDFS with managed disks, and publicly available data shows that the typical limit is client bandwidth rather than ADLS bandwidth. ADLS is supported as a persistent object storage layer with most Hadoop distributions, such as Cloudera (*http://bit.ly/2DGojPL*).

 ADLS, which launched in 2016, is now strongly recommended for Hadoop workloads over WASB. A good overview of the differences between the two services is contained in the documentation (*http://bit.ly/2QPiS3R*).

HDInsight

Similar to AWS EMR, Microsoft Azure offers HDInsight, which packages several big data open source projects into a managed service. Unlike AWS EMR, Azure does not distribute the components itself but bases its offering on the Hortonworks Data Platform (HDP) distribution of Hadoop. The services offered are:

- Hadoop (MapReduce)
- Spark
- Kafka
- Interactive Query (Hive LLAP)
- HBase or Storm

HDInsight currently allows the selection of only one of the aforementioned cluster types (*http://bit.ly/2QUpyxC*) and does not support the combination of different services within a single cluster. It can use either HDFS with instance VHDs or ADLS as the primary storage mechanism.

Like EMR, HDInsight provides cloud-native ease of use when creating Hadoop clusters but binds you to the service offering and cloud provider itself.

Caveats and service limits

One thing to bear in mind is that Azure currently does not support reverse DNS for the internal IP addresses of VMs (not to be confused with a VM's external IP address, for which reverse DNS is available in Azure). Because your cluster's components use the internal IPs to communicate internally, you are required to manually set up a DNS server, as shown in various examples (*http://bit.ly/2PIM3Jy*) on the web.

New Azure subscriptions are set up with relatively modest default limits (*http://bit.ly/2PvPseP*) (as low as, for example, 20 cores per region), so you need to plan to increase the limits on the various resources for your cluster deployments.

Google Cloud Platform

After Amazon and Microsoft, Google is the third-largest provider in the public cloud market. Google Cloud Platform (GCP) offers an extensive suite of cloud services, currently in 18 regions. Regions in GCP have between two and four zones, which are in isolated datacenter locations, much like with AWS and Azure.

Instance types

Google's main offering for IaaS computing services is called Google Compute Engine (GCE). GCE instances are categorized very simply by RAM and CPU. Different regions may run different generations of processors to implement the various instance types. GCP is differentiated in that it grants a *sustained use discount*, meaning that the hourly price for an instance decreases when it is continuously used. The instance types are categorized as follows:

High-CPU machine types (http://bit.ly/2RUMKfx)
As the name implies, these machines simply have a high ratio of vCPUs to memory—the highest when compared to the AWS and Azure portfolios. The maximum number of cores is 96, which is more than sufficient for most use cases we have encountered.

Standard machine types (http://bit.ly/2FpDH4P)
These are balanced instances that have a memory-to-vCPU ratio of 3.75 GB/core, which is a good match for worker nodes.

High-memory machine types (http://bit.ly/2QSBNet)
Google's high-mem instances feature a 2x higher memory-to-vCPU ratio than its balanced instances. While they do not provide as strong a focus on memory as some AWS or Azure instances, the high-mem instance class still should suffice for memory-intensive Hadoop use cases.

GCP also offers custom machine types (*http://bit.ly/2QNUNuz*), with which you define your own ratio of compute and CPU, within defined limits.

GCP's instance portfolio is at the same time very simple but very flexible, because it allows you to attach disks and GPUs (*http://bit.ly/2ONAivU*) to all instance types. This has big advantages for implementation of cluster life cycle models: you can turn any cluster into a suspendable cluster via persistent disks or local SSDs. Similarly, you can augment existing worker nodes to support deep learning use cases by attaching a GPU.

In Figure 16-4, we show examples of how GCP instances map to various Hadoop use cases.

Storage options

Google offers a straightforward portfolio for storage in the cloud, as shown in Figure 16-3. It consists of:

- Remote block storage, called *persistent disks*
- Options for high-performance local SSDs that can be requested for most instance types
- An object store service, called Google Cloud Storage (GCS)

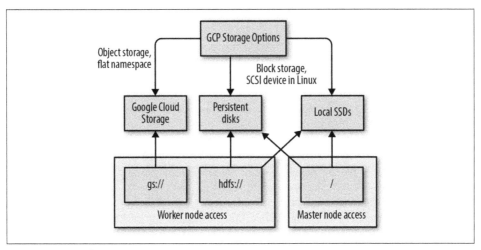

Figure 16-3. GCP storage options

Let's take a closer look at the options:

Persistent disks
   Google's solution for remote block storage is persistent disks, which are organized into *standard persistent disks* and *SSD persistent disks*. GCE can create persistent disks during instance creation, and you can create and connect disks to existing instances later. Persistent disks be provisioned up to a total amount of 64 TB per instance. Google specifies (*https://cloud.google.com/compute/docs/disks/*) IOPS per disk to scale linearly with the disk size, but the practical limits are defined per instance rather than per device, as shown in Table 16-4. Persistent disks also support snapshots (*http://bit.ly/2TkwyG2*).

Table 16-4. GCE disk types

Disk type	Implementation	Max. throughput (MB/s)	Max. IOPS
Standard persistent disks	HDD	180 read, 120 write (per instance)	3,000 read, 15,000 write (per instance)

Disk type	Implementation	Max. throughput (MB/s)	Max. IOPS
SSD persistent disks	SSD	800 read, 400 write (per instance, if more than 32 vCPUs)	40,000 read, 30,000 write (per instance, if more than 32 vCPUs)

Local SSDs

Google permits provisioning up to eight local SSD drives in any given instance, except for the very small *shared-core instances* (which have no relevance for Hadoop). Like instance storage in EC2, local SSDs are volatile and do not persist data beyond the life cycle of the instance. Local SSDs have a fixed size of 375 GB, and they are much faster than their remotely attached counterparts. They can be attached via SCSI or NVMe, the latter of which increases IOPS and throughput by a further 70% for reads and 30% for writes. Being able to attach these extra devices to any instance type greatly increases flexibility. They allow you to tend to requirements for very fast local I/O, but they also come at an increased cost compared to HDDs. Hence, local SSDs may not be the right option if you try to achieve better pricing by building a sticky cluster with local disks.

Google Cloud Storage

Google also features a massively scalable object storage implementation called GCS, which organizes all data into a flat namespace consisting of buckets and objects within them. It offers XML and JSON for API messages and uses HTTP(S) as the transport protocol. As summarized in Table 16-8, GCS offers very high durability and high availability of data, by storing data in multiple regions. It provides atomic read-after-write consistency. Like the other cloud storage implementations we've introduced, GCS is accessible by Hadoop via an implementation of the abstract `FileSystem` class (`GoogleHadoopFS`) and using the `gs://` URL scheme in filesystem paths. The source code is freely available under the Apache license, but GCS is currently not part of the Hadoop codebase and is distributed by Google itself.

Cloud Dataproc

Cloud Dataproc (*http://bit.ly/2DBN4Mj*) is GCP's PaaS offering for Hadoop and big data processing and includes the following software components:

- Spark
- Hadoop
- Pig
- Hive

In addition, it contains connectors for Google BigQuery (*http://bit.ly/2DFiscX*) and GCS, which is fully supported as a primary storage layer in Dataproc. The selection of components in Dataproc is somewhat limited and does not include any with streaming capabilities, such as Flume or Kafka. For streaming use cases, Google alternatively offers Dataflow (*http://bit.ly/2OepYSd*).

Caveats and service limits

Just like with the other public cloud providers, quotas apply to your account on GCP. However, Google does not specify default quotas. The quota mechanisms are instead described separately and more generically for compute (*http://bit.ly/2sqo0RO*) and storage (*http://bit.ly/2OVuSiP*).

Implementing Clusters

This section looks at examples of problems or use cases you might need to address in Hadoop and points you to solutions in the portfolios of all three public cloud providers we have covered here. These pointers are by no means exhaustive; sometimes an alternative instance or a different storage implementation might suit you better.

Instances

You must now be asking, which instances should I choose? This is not an exact science and heavily depends on your use case.

The initial consideration is the ratio of memory to compute capabilities. You can choose between *compute-heavy*, *memory-heavy*, and *balanced* instance classes, and the cloud gives you the ability to bring up purpose-specific clusters per use case, which over time yields a better total cost of ownership.

The second consideration is the size of the instances themselves. After you choose an instance class, you select an instance size, which gives you control over *vertical scalability* (scale-up). As with on-premises servers, vertical scalability is a complementary option to Hadoop's true strength, which is *horizontal scalability* (scale-out). If your workflow allows for transient clusters, you can change the instance size for new incarnations of the same workload as well as the number of instances, depending on data size and SLAs.

It is hard to come up with general rules on when to scale vertically rather than horizontally, but Figure 16-4 addresses both, to a fair degree. The chart categorizes common big data use cases by plotting typical per-instance compute and memory requirements for a production environment in the dark-coloured boxes (note that these do not mark minimum requirements). Each arrow represents the relationship between memory in gigabytes and the number of vCPUs. For example, for Impala as a standalone use case, 8 GB of memory per CPU core (represented as 8x) is a reasonable recommendation. As another example, we consider 4x a balanced configuration.

The chart also shows instance types (for worker nodes only) from the three cloud providers discussed here that provide a good match for the use cases in the illustration. You may notice a resemblance to a similar illustration in "Workload Profiles" on page 96, focused on on-premises deployments, where we plotted CPU and RAM on one axis against I/O capabilities on the other. In this illustration, we plot CPU against RAM.

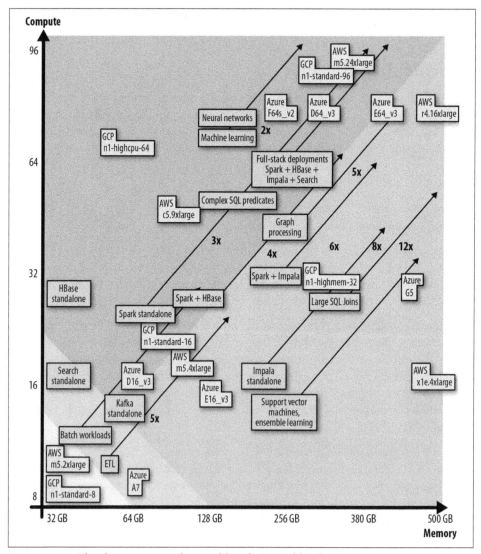

Figure 16-4. Cloud instances and typical big data workloads

The rationale for on-premises scenarios is to aim for a balance between compute and RAM because it is difficult to foresee all the application scenarios that might occur during the depreciation period of your hardware. In contrast, as a cloud user, you do not need to concern yourself with rigid hardware configuration and its depreciation, since you can adapt your requirements on a per–use case—or even per-job—level, and as we have seen, storage and storage bandwidth exist as decoupled resources.

Your experience might vary greatly, and the best way to select your instances is to analyze whether you are CPU- or memory-bound via tools like Cloudera Manager or Apache Ambari.

Let's look briefly at the workload classes listed in Figure 16-4:

2–3 GB/vCPU
Certain machine learning workloads, such as classification and clustering algorithms and neural networks, are computationally intensive even for relatively small datasets and would justify applying an instance in this range. Those workloads are, however, also excellent candidates for running on GPU-enriched instances. If you run an unspecified Spark workload, but your cluster is a standalone environment, the general recommendation is to configure slightly compute-intensive or balanced instances. After a dataset in a Spark job is in memory, the workload is generally CPU-bound. Generally, in this group, you would not consider instances below 24 cores.

 Classifying machine learning tasks, in general, is difficult because there is typically a data preparation and possibly a model training (build) phase involved prior to running the actual algorithm.

4–5 GB/vCPU
General batch workloads, ETL work, and Kafka generally fit into the balanced workload trajectory. If you mix slightly compute-intensive services, such as Spark, with a slightly memory-intensive service, such as HBase, in a single cluster, you should also deploy balanced instances. This category should be used for clusters that can be implemented on small instances, and balanced instances are also your best bet if you implement a one-size-fits-all cluster that combines many resource-hungry services, such as Spark, HBase, Impala, and Search.

6–8 GB/vCPU
SQL engines such as Impala heavily rely on materialized aggregates or partitioned join operations in memory. Any SQL query can also be computationally intensive, which is why nowadays we recommend at least 16 cores. What you should avoid at all costs is a join operation spilling to disk.

If you use HBase for scans, it can quickly become CPU-bound; the recommendation in this case would be to use Impala or Hive for scan-heavy workloads.

10–12 GB/vCPU

Although relatively uncommon, certain workloads require even more focus on memory. Sometimes—and despite a general paradigm to denormalize datasets in Hive or Impala—you need to run very large distributed joins. In this case, addressing the problem with even more RAM might be necessary. Also, certain machine learning algorithms, such as ensemble learning and support vector machines, often train and run best with a disproportionate amount of memory.

Each of the major providers offers an instance portfolio that allows us to address these big data use cases. While not an exhaustive list, Table 16-5 provides examples of high-CPU, high-memory, and balanced instance classes for each provider. For each instance class, we show the maximum amount of memory and number of CPU cores in separate columns. We also list how many instance sizes are available in the given class and what the ratio of memory to vCPUs is, just like we did earlier for the work-load classification.

Table 16-5. Cloud instance comparison

Instance class type	Provider	Instance class name	Number of instances in class	Max. instance memory	Max. instance CPUs	Memory/CPU ratio
High-CPU	AWS	C5 series	6	144 GB	72	2 GB/vCPU
	Azure	Fsv2-series	7	144 GB	72	2 GB/vCPU
	GCP	n1-highcpu	7	86.4 GB	96	0.9 GB/vCPU
Balanced	AWS	M5 series	6	384 GB	96	4 GB/vCPU
	Azure	Dv3-series	6	256 GB	64	4 GB/vCPU
	GCP	n1-standard	8	360 GB	96	3.75 GB/vCPU
High-mem	AWS	R4 series	6	488 GB	64	7.625 GB/vCPU
	Azure	G-series/GS-series	5	448 GB	32	14 GB/vCPU
		Ev3-series	6	432 GB	64	6.75–8 GB/vCPU
	GCP	n1-highmem	7	624 GB	96	6.5 GB/vCPU

The table shows some very impressive maximum values for memory and vCPUs. Large instance sizes are good but generally more expensive, and because Hadoop is a scale-out platform, your goal should be to strike a sensible balance between scale-up and scale-out. Our general recommendation is to initially establish the must-have requirement for the dominant resource (that is, memory or CPU) for a single instance and to then optimize your instance choice by the ratio of memory to CPU, which we show in the last column.

 In general, consider that all of the mentioned cloud vendors regularly refresh their instances to include latest-generation technology and that any discussion around instances is short-lived and exemplary. The AWS EC2 M4 series was recently superseded by the M5 series, the Azure DSv2–series has been superseded by DSv3, and so on. You should expect that every few months new instance types will be introduced, typically with slightly changed specifications.

When it comes to comparing compute power between cloud vendors, you should at minimum keep in mind the specifications of the underlying CPUs, such as core frequency and cache sizes, as well as the general time frames that the vendor uses. Sometimes, new chips introduce new core features that the cloud vendor can take advantage of in a newer generation of instances. An example of this is the adoption of Intel's SR-IOV capabilities (*https://amzn.to/2ONFmjU*), which significantly speed up throughput of external I/O in virtualized systems, which is also what we look at in the paragraphs that follow Table 16-5.

Monster Instances

Our evaluation in Table 16-5 actually does not include the high-end instances of AWS and Azure. AWS offers very large instances with its X1e line that top out at 3.9 TB of memory with 128 cores per instance. Similarly, Azure provides up to 3.8 TB and 128 cores with its M-series instances. GCP has a single instance called n1-megamem-96 that has over 1.4 TB of memory. Although they can technically be used to build Hadoop clusters, their specs exceed the requirements of most use cases, given Hadoop's ability to scale horizontally. Also, their ratio of memory to CPU is larger than 30, which will not provide any value-add in most use cases.

In most practical decisions, however, it comes down to cores and memory.

CPU-heavy instances

Although AWS and Azure offer instances that provide a huge number of vCPUs, as mentioned in "Monster Instances" on page 477, GCP scales to the highest vCPU count (96) within the CPU-heavy class. The very high vCPU-to-memory ratio of the *n1-highcpu* instance class is not a perfect match to the majority of Hadoop use cases, though, as depicted in Figure 16-4.

Balanced instances

This group of instance classes supplies the workhorses of most cloud-based Hadoop clusters. If you're in doubt about how your use cases will perform or if you don't know whether your cluster is memory- or CPU-bound, choose a balanced instance type. We can see in Table 16-5 that each vendor has an instance series that exactly fits our definition of balanced, which is roughly 4 GB/vCPU. On AWS, you can stick to the M5 or M4 instances. On Azure, it is mostly the Dv3-series that fits the balanced class. On GCP, choose n1-standard instances.

Memory-heavy instances

Azure provides two options in this category: the G-series that come with 14 GB/vCPU and the Ev3-series with 6.75–8 GB/vCPU. The G-series (not to be confused with GS-series) instances, however, feature local disks,so they might not be relevant to the chosen life cycle model for your architecture.

In AWS, the most relevant instance type for high-memory Hadoop use cases is likely the R4 series, with a memory/compute ratio of slightly higher than 7. AWS also has the X1 series, with a memory/compute ratio of about 15 GB/vCPU, but its smallest instance has more than 900 GB of memory, which is more than is necessary for a single instance given Hadoop's scalable nature. Finally, there is the X1e series, which starts with smaller instance sizes but has an even higher memory/compute ratio—more than 30—rendering it unsuitable for most Hadoop use cases.

GCP can scale its n1-highmem instances up to a portfolio-wide maximum of 624 GB, which addresses all but the most extreme high-memory use cases.

Instances summary

As we have seen, cloud providers take different approaches in the structure of their instance portfolios, but each of them provides solutions to address typical big data use cases. All providers permit significant vertical scalability, which some situations might require. Also consider existing reference architectures for the individual cloud providers from Hadoop distributors such as Cloudera (*http://bit.ly/2PBcReD*).

Storage and Life Cycle Models

Building on the concepts we introduced in "Cluster Life Cycle Models" on page 425, let us see how we can use the storage offerings of the three cloud providers we have just covered to implement various life cycle models for Hadoop clusters.

Suspendable clusters

At the time of this writing, in our experience, the majority of Hadoop clusters deployed in public clouds are built as *suspendable clusters*: EBS, Azure VHDs or managed disks, or Google persistent disks are used to implement the cluster's HDFS instance. For enterprises beginning to explore Hadoop-based data platforms in the cloud, remote block storage provides the most hassle-free and reliable path to success, even if it means sacrificing potential economic efficiencies. Most organizations augment suspendable clusters with an object storage layer such as ADLS, S3, or GCS, which we also highly recommend, especially to increase durability of data via regular backups.

 If you attach more remote disks to an instance, bear in mind that typically there is a per-instance limit of total available bandwidth for remote block storage and network traffic. Make sure that your network bandwidth does not become a bottleneck for HDFS block traffic, replication, or node-to-node communication.

For clusters without SLAs, such as development clusters, it is common practice to actually stop the clusters at the end of the workday (or an extended usage period) to reduce cost. In that context, we also see clusters with remote block storage effectively used as one-off clusters that go as soon as a job completes.

One-off clusters

In general, it is easier on public clouds to implement transient clusters as one-off clusters. As we covered in "Cluster Life Cycle Models" on page 425, a pure one-off cluster is entirely transient and gets its source of truth from an object storage layer.

It is an emerging model to use object storage to share data between many clusters that are spontaneously booted. For this model to work properly, metadata (such as the Hive Metastore and search collections) and authorization data (such as rules stored in Apache Sentry) can no longer be bound to any specific cluster and its life cycle but must also be saved in object storage or a tertiary layer, such as a database. An example of a product that focuses on just that is Cloudera SDX, which we cover in "Sharing Metadata Services" on page 511.

Here's a breakdown of how the individual cloud providers handle this type of cluster:

AWS

AWS is well suited for one-off clusters with S3, but you need to work around the consistency issues we covered earlier in this chapter when implementing multistage data pipelines that persist stages on S3 via tools like S3Guard. A good public example of this is S3mper (*http://bit.ly/2FqjDz7*), which Netflix created for this purpose. Also, increasingly often, use case–specific one-off clusters complement the larger perpetual clusters; for example, in development or staging environments.

Azure

> VHD-backed instances can be used for one-off models for which ADLS functions as the source of truth.

GCP

> When using GCS as the secondary storage layer, you need to include it into your Hadoop cluster by yourself. Because it is not part of Apache Hadoop, this code is currently not supported by any of the Hadoop distributors.

Sticky clusters

As we covered in "Cluster Life Cycle Models" on page 425, a sticky cluster uses local disks to implement an HDFS instance that is the source of truth for your data. And, as we saw in the previous sections, all three of the major cloud providers use local disks in some form. The physical hosts of your instances, in that case, have local disks that they export to your instances, as shown in Figure 14-2.

It is important that you regard these local storage volumes as *volatile* or *ephemeral*. When an instance is stopped and restarted, it is very likely to reboot on a different physical host. The cloud provider, in this case, has no practical way to migrate the local disks with your instance. For Hadoop, this means that you rely on HDFS to re-replicate the data that was previously on the instance's ephemeral disks.

Events leading to a restart can be triggered by users, scheduled by the cloud provider (e.g., scheduled events (*https://amzn.to/2DLloFq*) on AWS), or simply due to software or hardware failure.

Table 16-6 shows a range of possible events that may occur and how cloud providers deal with locally attached disks in each case. As we saw in "Key Things to Know" on page 455 and as we discuss in "Instance availability" on page 491, VM placement cannot be fully controlled, and therefore all HDFS replicas or highly available master service roles might appear on the same physical host. Because instances can be irrecoverably lost at any time, there is a certain risk that a local HDFS instance will suffer a catastrophic loss of DataNode disks.

Table 16-6. Ramifications of instance-level events on local storage

Provider	Host restart	Permanent host failure	Instance migration	Instance terminate	Instance stop/ shutdown	Instance restart	Disk failure
AWS	Data preserved	Data lost	Data lost	Data lost	Data lost	Data preserved	Data lost
Azure	Data lost	Data lost	Data lost	Data lost	Data lost	Data lost	Data lost
GCP	Preservation attempted	Preservation attempted	Preservation attempted	Data lost	Data lost	Data preserved	Data lost

In our experience, enterprises that are new to the cloud typically do not consider ephemeral disks as the basis for their initial deployments , and instead initially use remote block storage. That being said, some organizations have enough experience to implement long-running, sticky Hadoop clusters in public clouds and to use them as the source of truth for their data on those clusters.

If you consider using local storage in your public cloud Hadoop cluster, we highly recommend that you read "Instance availability" on page 491, in which we describe several ways to deal with these issues and to achieve higher availability and durability for sticky clusters.

Let's finish this section with a quick analysis of how individual cloud providers stack up with regard to sticky clusters:

AWS

AWS provides the most options around local storage capabilities. Clusters from instances with ephemeral disks thus might provide an incentive from a cost perspective because they do not require additional EBS volumes. Instance types in question are the D2 line: for example, the d2.4xlarge instance type with 16 vCPUs, 122 GB memory, and 24 TB raw storage in 12 hard drives. Alternatively, you can consider the H1 line, with less storage; for example, 8 TB raw storage across 4 HDDs with 32 vCPUs and 128 GB memory in the h1.8xlarge.

Azure

The maximum capacity of local storage in an instance is 6 TB, when using the G5 instance. This instance, however, boasts 448 GB of memory and 32 cores, which is typically too much to tend to just 6 TB of raw disk space in a Hadoop cluster. In addition, local disk capability and throughput are limited to a single temporary drive in Azure, and data is lost even just due to a reboot, as we have shown. Hence, sticky clusters are theoretically possible in Azure but not typically built in practice.

GCP

As we have covered, GCP can attach up to 8 SSDs to any instance type, for up to a total of 3 TB per instance. This is a fairly modest amount of storage for an HDFS DataNode, but since you can control the instance sizes, you may potentially be able to strike a good balance with modest instances as well. If you require large instances for your use case, however, 3 TB might not be enough local storage per instance to proceed with the approach. There is also no option to use HDDs, which might provide a better price point for bandwidth-oriented workloads.

Storage compatibility

The features and functionality of the cloud storage systems we've discussed are important, but for most enterprises, it is equally important how they interoperate with their Hadoop distribution of choice. Table 16-7 provides an overview of which storage systems can be used—and how—in a given distribution.

Table 16-7. Hadoop distribution interoperability with cloud storage solutions

	Cloudera CDH	Hortonworks HDP	Amazon EMR	HDInsight	GCP Dataproc
AWS S3	Yes	Yes	Yes, but take care in the choice of client libraries	N/A	N/A
AWS EBS	Yes	Yes, standard Cloudbreak image (miniviable-aws) for AWS uses EBS	Yes, but ephemeral	N/A	N/A
Azure managed disks (VHD)	Yes	Yes	N/A	Only for Apache Kafka, otherwise WASB	N/A
Azure ADLS	Supported for Spark, Hive, MapReduce 2, and HBase; not supported as a default filesystem	Yes, but blob-based default filesystem HDFS also required	N/A	Yes	N/A
WASB	Only for backup	Yes	N/A	Only with general-purpose storage account and standard storage tier	N/A
Google persistent disks	Yes	Yes	N/A	N/A	Yes
Google Cloud Storage	Recommended as backup layer, but the connector code is not supported	Yes	N/A	N/A	Yes

Storage and life cycle summary

At the end of this section, we recapitulate what we have learned about the storage offerings of each provider and we propose an initial approach to life cycle models that you might pursue:

AWS
> Provides a holistic storage portfolio with remote block storage (EBS) and several options for local disks, but Hadoop use cases need to circumvent the issues on eventual consistency with S3.

Azure

Provides even more storage options, but is slightly more complex, with Blob storage and virtual hard disks on the one hand and ADLS on the other. However, it does not use local disks much in its instance portfolio.

GCP

Offers the most flexibility because of its ability to combine a configurable amount of local disks with remote block storage (persistent disks).

Table 16-8 lists all the offerings, including availability and durability values as specified by the cloud providers. It also summarizes available storage classes and API capabilities.

Table 16-8. Summary of cloud storage solutions

Solution	Availability	Durability	Storage classes	API consistency
Amazon S3	99.5–99.9% (depends on storage class)	99.999999999% (11N)	Standard-Infrequent Access (IA), One Zone-IA, Glacier	Eventually consistent (can be improved with S3Guard or EMRFS)
Amazon EBS	99.999%	0.1–0.2% annual fail rate per volume	sc1, st1, gp2, io1	Fully consistent (POSIX/SCSI)
Azure Blob storage	99–99.99%	11N–16N	Hot, cool, archive	Strongly consistent
Azure Data Lake Storage	99.9%	ADLS is implemented as locally redundant storage (LRS, 11N)	Single	Strongly consistent
Azure managed disks	99.999%	LRS (11N)	Standard/Premium	Fully consistent (POSIX/SCSI)
Google persistent disks	No data	Three replicas	HDD/SSD	Fully consistent (POSIX/SCSI)
Google Cloud Storage	99.99–99.9%	11N	multi_regional, regional, nearline, coldline	Strongly consistent

In summary, all three providers offer options for storage that support the life cycle models we have discussed, in either a long-running or transient context.

The availability of economical remote block storage, in our experience, enables a safe default to get started with Hadoop in public clouds. However, you should fundamentally decide whether you want your source of truth to be on object storage or on other media.

If you begin with only remote or local block storage, you can introduce a backing object store at any point. Implementing the source of truth on object storage enables you to run a mix of one-off and long-running clusters, independent of whether the clusters themselves use local disks or remote block storage. As you can see in Table 16-8, object stores also generally have higher durability.

Building transient, use case–specific, or even one-off clusters backed by a shared object storage layer is a quickly emerging pattern for big data environments in the cloud and a typical progression from long-running clusters.

Network Architecture

Now that you know the relevant instance types and storage solutions for your cluster, we cover how to embed it into your provider's larger network and security infrastructure. Because there is a lot of commonality across the cloud providers we have covered, we provide the information in the form of a unified deployment blueprint, while calling out provider specifics where appropriate. Our blueprint is shown in Figure 16-5.

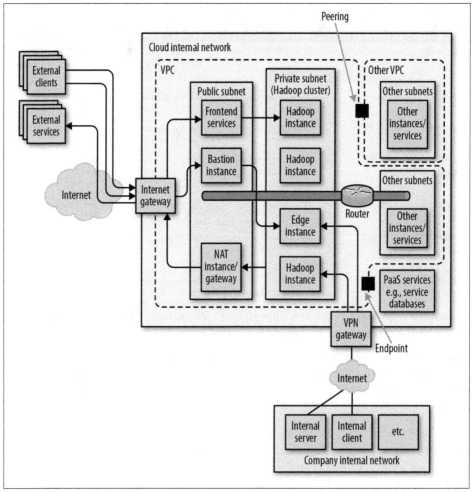

Figure 16-5. Typical deployment pattern for Hadoop

A fundamental concept is the VPC instance in which your cluster will reside. A VPC is the technical construct used by all cloud providers in which you build a cloud service. They fundamentally isolate your cloud services from other tenants. Although virtual private clouds go by this name in AWS and GCP, they are called *virtual networks* or VNets in Microsoft Azure. GCP permits spanning a VPC across multiple geographical regions, whereas in AWS and Azure they are limited to a single region. AWS and Azure do, however, allow VPCs to span availability zones.

A VPC can be segmented into different networks, or *subnets*. You can use subnets to create public and private segments of your VPC. For example, it is usually recommended to place a Hadoop cluster in a private subnet and use an additional public subnet to facilitate inbound and outbound traffic to your Hadoop services.

A subnet is considered private when it does not have any routes to an *internet gateway*, whereas a subnet is public when it has such a route. The internet gateway is a separate infrastructure service that bridges connections from the internet to the public subnet and vice versa. Depending on the cloud provider, it may have to be explicitly set up and configured.

Like with physical infrastructure, traffic between subnets is controlled via routes. Cloud providers try to offer convenience by automating routing as much as possible when you create instances and connect them to other cloud services. All the providers we've discussed allow you to change routes, add routes, and add new route tables via VPC-specific router instances. For example, at the center of the illustration, we can see our Hadoop cluster placed in a private subnet, which shields the cluster from direct internet connections, whereas necessary connections from the public are set up via explicit routes.

All traffic between subnets is also subject to firewalls in public clouds. This is yet another service that you need to explicitly configure. We provide a detailed discussion of cloud firewalls and perimeter controls in "Perimeter Controls and Firewalling" on page 551.

If you intend to offer frontend services, such as web applications that rely on data stored in Hadoop, we recommend placing them in a separate public subnet, which is shown to the left of the public subnet in Figure 16-5. Optionally, you can create other public or private subnets, as required, to segment additional components of your overall solution.

Although all frontend services most likely require direct access to certain hosts in the cluster via corresponding routes, direct users, such as developers or analysts, should access the cluster via dedicated edge hosts. This is a best practice for on-premises deployments, as well (see "Edge Nodes" on page 101).

If instances in the private subnet require the ability to access external services (for example, for software updates), this can be securely achieved by a dedicated Network

Address Translation gateway, allowing services in a private subnet to connect to the internet. (Services on the internet cannot initiate connections over the NAT gateway.) In our blueprint, the NAT gateway is placed in the public subnet. It is either an integrated services offering or has to be implemented explicitly on a dedicated instance.

Some organizations, however, do not expose their cloud-based Hadoop cluster externally and only access it internally. In both cases, you typically connect your internal company network to the cloud solution via a VPN gateway. Inbound traffic from the company network could originate from internal frontend services or directly from clients. For more details about the use of VPNs when integrating your cloud-based cluster into your corporate network, refer to "Perimeter Controls and Firewalling" on page 551.

If you need to bridge two VPCs—for example, two projects, each with its own cluster —that intend to share services and data, this can typically be done via *peering*, which connects multiple VPCs with each other without setting up routing or gateways. The peered VPCs appear as one and are automatically and internally routed via the cloud provider's backbone connections. The peering concept is called *VPC peering* on AWS and GCP, whereas on Azure it is referred to as virtual network peering.

Some solutions make use of other cloud offerings, such as managed relational databases. These can be connected without explicit routing if the cloud provider supports endpoints at the VPC boundary, which allows a simple connection to other services of the cloud provider. This feature is called VPC endpoints in GCP and AWS virtual network service endpoints in Azure.

Additionally, if you need to connect from clients outside of your internal company network, or if you do not yet have VPN connectivity to your cloud provider, it is possible to securely facilitate external access to cluster hosts via a *bastion instance* in the public subnet. Bastion hosts add a server as a level of indirection when accessing internal servers from a public network. The bastion instance can be used to transparently and securely forward outside connections to a configurable set of internal services without exposing the internal service endpoints. This is useful, for example, in combination with SSH agent forwarding (*https://amzn.to/2KsHJZa*) to access your Hadoop instances via SSH from the internet.

An architecture like this guarantees good modularization and perimeter security without sacrificing functionality or compromising usability. It is achievable with the cloud providers that we cover here, although, by necessity, we simplify the details to provide a high-level overview. We give a more detailed account and concrete examples of how to configure your perimeter controls in "Perimeter Controls and Firewalling" on page 551.

In general, we highly recommend familiarizing yourself with the essentials of cloud security, which we cover Chapter 18.

Beyond building a good perimeter architecture, you should turn your attention to network throughput. Unlike in on-premises scenarios, you only need to consider the specifications of the instance's network capabilities, since the overall implementation of the cluster network is conveniently hidden.

Maximum throughput is not only important to ensure that the network is not a bottleneck on individual instances for I/O when scaling them vertically, but also is significant for replication speed as you scale your cluster horizontally. The information that the providers specify around this subject is vague in some places, but we summarize what you should know in Table 16-9.

Table 16-9. Network performance specifications by cloud provider

Provider	Scalability	Maximum	Specifications	Dedicated bandwidth for remote block storage?
AWS	Throughput scales with instance; details depend on instance type	25 Gbps	Priority (for example, high or moderate) or concrete Gpbs	Yes (default or optional, depending on instance)
Azure	Throughput scales with instance; details depend on instance type	Up to 30 Gbps for egress; ingress not limited directly	Concrete Gbps	Yes (with premium disks)
GCP	Throughput scales equally with all instances	Capped at 16 Gbps	Concrete Gbps via formula: 2 Gbps/vCPU	No

In more detail:

AWS

AWS provides information about network throughput per instance type in its online documentation (*https://amzn.to/2Twf7lP*). Latest-generation instances (for example, M5 or C5) specify exact throughput numbers. For older instance generations (for example, M4 or C4), lower-end instances are often flagged simply as *moderate* (e.g., m4.large) or *high* throughput, whereas the larger instances (e.g., m4.16xlarge) are typically specified with concrete throughput numbers as well.

Key to network performance on AWS is the Elastic Network Adapter (*https://amzn.to/2Bq8avw*), which takes advantage of hardware optimizations in the host and is enabled in most latest-generation instances. It can also be enabled for some older-generation instances.

Azure

Like AWS, Azure structures information on network throughput per instance type (*http://bit.ly/2xkzKaa*). Exact throughput numbers are listed for all instance types. One thing to be mindful of is that Azure does not provide reverse DNS for internal IPs, which is required for Hadoop. Microsoft provides information on how you can achieve this manually (*http://bit.ly/2qWjmKs*).

GCP

In GCP, egress bandwidth is specified equally for all instances via a simple rule of 2 Gbps per vCPU. This bandwidth is capped, however, at 16 Gbps for any instance, and the available bandwidth includes write operations to persistent disks. On large instances that also need to perform lots of shuffle operations in big data use cases and disk I/O simultaneously, this could lead to a bottleneck. Unlike egress, there is no specified limit for ingress traffic.

We have not nearly covered all topics regarding networking in the cloud in this section. All cloud providers offer an enormous amount of control over VPC environments that will most likely enable you to implement and integrate any Hadoop use case. The physical implementation of public cloud networks remains, to a large degree, a black box to us, and most users want to keep it that way.

If you require further information about the configuration of networking with different cloud providers, we recommend studying the guides and how-tos offered by the public cloud providers:

- Amazon VPC User Guide (*https://amzn.to/2PKkP5o*) for AWS
- VNet Plan and Design Guide (*http://bit.ly/2QcbO4m*) for Microsoft Azure
- Virtual Private Cloud documentation (*http://bit.ly/2S8L9mt*) for GCP

High Availability

Cloud environments offer huge flexibility in the way resources can be provisioned and deployed. Many managed services, such as Amazon Relational Database Service (Amazon RDS), are highly available out of the box, but when it comes to deploying Hadoop clusters in the cloud we still need to think carefully about how to build robust architectures. For long-lived clusters, many of the concerns that hold for on-premises datacenter deployments are equally applicable in a cloud context. We have already covered some aspects of HA in the preceding sections and chapters, but in this section, we focus on and reiterate some of these concerns. We begin with the availability of the VMs themselves, followed by data, network, and service availability. Before all that, though, we discuss further why we actually need to consider availability at all.

The requirement for HA

You may be asking yourself, why do I need to consider HA at all? Isn't the cloud meant to take care of all this stuff for me? The answer to these questions is, as always, it depends. As we have seen, cloud vendors do offer managed Hadoop-like offerings: Amazon has EMR, Google has Dataflow, and Cloudera has Altus. For these environments, we largely need to focus only on deploying and running our applications, be they batch analytics in Spark or streaming processes in Apache Flink. But for sticky clusters, we are building fully fledged, long-lived clusters where availability must be provided.

There is another aspect to this, as well. As we have already discussed in "Cluster Life Cycle Models" on page 425, some clusters will be one-offs, spun up for some transient processing and then destroyed. In these scenarios, providing a fully fledged HA deployment is probably not worth the effort.

Some automated deployment solutions, such as Cloudera Director, provide all the necessary API hooks to automatically set up most aspects of Hadoop HA so that the incremental effort may not be too onerous. The implied focus in this section is on sticky, long-lived clusters, where such considerations are more important.

Compute availability

Most cloud providers do not talk in detail about how they build and operate their clouds. We can make inferences about the possible use of software-defined networking, massive storage arrays, live VM migration, and more, but the actual tools and techniques provide competitive advantage and are thus closely guarded secrets. The safest source of information when considering availability is the public documentation of each of the "big three" providers, but what do we need to consider about the availability guarantees of VMs that we provision?

Resource Locations

In general, in the cloud, each resource (disk, storage bucket, network interface, and compute instance, among other things) is defined with a given locality. It is important to know which locality a given resource you are using has—only then can you understand the implications for availability. There are basically four localities to consider:

Instance

> Some resources are only visible (and durable) within the scope of a single instance. An example of this is ephemeral instance storage.

Zone

> Although each cloud provider has a slightly different nomenclature, they each define the notion of a zone, which roughly equates to a datacenter in on-

---

premises terminology. Each zone has, for example, low-latency and high-bandwidth network connections. Zones are an important concept in availability terms because they often define a unit of resources that might all fail together (similar to a datacenter outage). Resources such as VPCs or networked block storage are often zone-local.

Regions

Groups of zones with geographic proximity (and thus low-latency network links between them) are grouped into regions. Usually, zones within a region are set up such that they cannot fail together. In the context of Hadoop, this means that for disaster recovery for long-lived clusters, you need to consider deploying distinct clusters in different zones—or even in different regions.

Global

The highest level of resource locality is global. These resources exist across all regions and zones and can be treated as permanently available. An example of these kinds of resources is user accounts. Note that some resources are regional in scope but might be accessible globally; for example, an S3 bucket.

Cluster availability. As discussed in "Resource Locations" on page 489, instances are deployed in zones, and in general, the only availability guarantees are *between* zones. That is, the provider makes guarantees that a failure in one zone will not affect other zones in the same region but usually does not guarantee the availability of instances within a zone. The general advice for architecting highly available applications in the cloud is to run instances in two or more zones. Although this is sound advice for a typical service-oriented architecture, for Hadoop clusters the picture is more complicated.

You might be tempted to conclude that the natural solution to all this is simply to span a single cluster across two or more availability zones, but this comes with additional considerations (see "Quorum spanning with three datacenters" on page 179 for a general discussion from a datacenter perspective). The first consideration is the volume of network traffic: as part of normal operation and computation, large amounts of data are routinely transferred between nodes. Although a region might comprise multiple zones connected by low-latency links, the links are probably not able to provide the same bandwidth that is available between nodes within the same zone, and certainly not within a placement group, which could lead to performance degradation. Some of that can be mitigated using hierarchical rack locations, but the options are rather limited here. For the most network-intensive use cases, deploying clusters this way might not be viable, but you should perform rigorous testing to determine what is viable for your use case.

The second challenge is that of maintaining availability of master services. Simply having nodes spread across two zones is not enough for a cluster to remain operational with HA; as we saw in "Cluster Spanning" on page 173, we have to maintain a quorum for master processes, such as ZooKeeper and HDFS JournalNodes. Since, by definition, a quorum requires an odd number of nodes to maintain consistency, with two zones we have a 50% chance of the cluster staying up in the event of a zone failure. To have the best chance of maintaining quorum, master services must be deployed across three zones. If you choose to do this, ensure that the chosen zones support the low latency required for master services, and rigorously test your workloads.

Spanning over three zones might not always be possible, as some regions might not have three zones to choose from.

Spanning a cluster over three zones is a valid deployment pattern for some well-chosen and well-tested use cases, but it still remains far more common to deploy clusters within a single zone.

In the latter case, you can employ the traditional on-premises approach to providing cross-region availability by simply deploying multiple clusters in more than one region and backing up or synchronizing data between them. You can, of course, use the same methods that are available in on-premises deployments (as covered in Chapter 13), but public clouds offer an even better way to share data: object storage layers can ensure that data is globally available and cloud services typically manage the mechanics of replication for you, providing an eventually consistent backup.

Ensuring that your ingest paths and consumer services can use cross-region clusters is up to you to architect, just as it is in on-premises deployments. These considerations are directly tied to the use case and are usually the domain of application architects—it's rare for a platform architect to be able to provide a generic solution that supports the active-active or active-passive georesilient requirements of all applications, even in the cloud.

Instance availability. We touched upon this aspect already, in "Sticky clusters" on page 480. When deploying into a virtualized environment, we need to consider the possibility of the failure of a physical server affecting multiple instances at the same time. To prevent issues emerging from concurrent failure, we want to avoid instances running certain roles on the same physical host. Although the probability of two instances being colocated might be considered slight at cloud scales, it cannot be discounted. If you are taking advantage of features such as AWS placement groups for high-performance networking, the probability of colocation may increase.

Placement Groups

Some public clouds offer additional control over where instances are deployed. For example, AWS provides placement groups (*https://amzn.to/2KqHJsk*), which can either spread instances across physical hardware and zones, or group them together into a cluster for high-performance networking between instances.

You need to consider what your requirements are when using placement groups. In the spread grouping case, instances could end up in different availability zones, which is probably not what you want for Hadoop. In the cluster grouping case, the cluster grouping will increase the probability of instances ending up on the same host, which means you need to give additional thought to data availability.

Each cloud provider provides a different mechanism to address this issue, and we look at some of the options next. Before we do, though, we should remind ourselves of the two primary reasons why we want to avoid colocation wherever possible:

Data colocation

It is theoretically possible (although unlikely) that all three copies of an HDFS block end up on the same physical host. Since we are often not given information about the physical location of nodes, we cannot use rack locality to address this issue: we do not know where the racks are or what instances are in them. In this case—when using local instance storage—if we lose the physical host, we lose the data (see Table 16-6).

> In addition to data disks, ensure that OS disks are placed on persistent storage, such as EBS on AWS or persistent disks on GCP, to allow rapid restarting of instances in the event of physical host failure.

Master colocation

It is also possible that two or more instances that are part of a quorum for a master process are physically colocated such that the failure of a node destroys the quorum. Unexpected failures of instances are rare, but they do happen.

> AWS spot instances, although economical, can be retired without warning. Do not use spot instances for master instances.

So, what can be done to address the colocation issues? There are a number of options, for better or worse:

Use large instance types

The largest instance types are highly ikely to map to different physical hots, simply because it is not possible to fit two such instances on the same host. This gives us an indirect, but rather blunt (and by no means guaranteed) mechanism of achieving physical isolation of master roles. The use of the larger types often allows us to take advantage of other features, too, like enhanced networking. Confirm with the provider the instance-to-host mapping before relying on this approach.

Use different instances types for the same role

Although this is perhaps inelegant, it is probable—but not guaranteed—that different instance types will be provisioned on different physical hosts.

Use dedicated hosts

AWS supports a purchase model based on dedicated hosts (*https://amzn.to/2DzZy76*). When using this option, you have much more control over which instances are deployed on which physical hosts.

Use failure domains

Azure is unique in providing *availability sets*, which define both failure and update domains for instances. The idea is that instances deployed in the same availability set are not subject to the same failures of physical hardware or updates and restarts of hypervisors. By default, three failure domains and five update domains are provided, which should be enough to maintain a quorum of master roles (*http://bit.ly/2S6ldHT*) in the event of a hardware failure. As such, use of availability sets should be regarded as a best practice for instances with master roles in Azure.

Planning for Maintenance

For long-running clusters, it is important to consider what action to take in the event of upcoming instance maintenance. For example, AWS notifies users of upcoming instance downtime through its events console. It is therefore important to have a migration plan in place, should one of these events affect three or more worker nodes (if using local instance storage for HDFS with threefold replication) or a majority of master nodes.

Azure users should take advantage of availability sets to avoid such correlated downtime events.

At the time of this writing, GCP does not appear to offer any controls over instance placement or to give notice of instance downtime, but it does make use of *live migration* to ensure that instances do not go down during maintenance.

Data availability

This aspect of availability was covered in detail earlier in this chapter, and we refer you to Table 16-8 for a summary of how cloud storage choices have a bearing on data availability.

The instance type defines how likely it is that replicas of an HDFS block end up on the same physical host. When using instance-local storage and to ensure full data availability in the face of physical host failure, architects can use the same tactics to effect anti-affinity that we saw earlier. In addition, the more DataNode instances you deploy, the smaller the overall chance of block colocation is—but this should not be relied upon for guaranteeing availability. For mission-critical datasets, consider increasing the replication factor if using instance-local storage.

Alternatively, data loss can be guarded against by using network-attached storage (such as EBS volumes) as instance disks or by using object storage as the source of truth or the backup location—or both.

Network availability

The last resource to consider is the network. This is actually the resource we need to worry about least. Since we are in a fully virtualized environment, we can defer much of the concern about redundant NICs, switches, and network topologies to the cloud provider. To be sure, there are optimizations we can arrange for, such as using placement groups to place instances together and using virtualization extensions to get the best performance from our virtual NICs, but in general we do not need to concern ourselves further. Part of the big attraction of cloud computing is that you get an excellent network.

Service availability

Finally, since we are concerning ourselves primarily with long-lived clusters, it is worth spending some time talking about how a cloud setting changes the way we set up a Hadoop cluster for HA.

The short answer to this is that almost all of the considerations for Hadoop service HA still apply: we still require the standard setup for HA described in Chapter 12 for HDFS, YARN, and other services. We still need database HA too, and should consider exposing client-facing services through load balancers.

Databases.   For services that use relational databases, such as the Hive Metastore, you need to ensure that the database is highly available. One approach is to run MySQL or Oracle on multiple instances and to configure them for HA just like you would in an on-premises environment.

Another approach, and one well worth considering, is to use a managed service offering from the cloud provider. Although it comes at an additional cost, a managed service like Amazon RDS or Google's Cloud SQL has significant advantages. Typically, such services do the hard work of providing HA, regular backups, security, and performance monitoring for you.

Ultimately, the choice depends on a number of factors, such as available budget and how comfortable your organization is configuring and running highly available databases.

Load balancers. Services that make use of load balancing have some slightly different options when running in the cloud. You can still use software load balancers (and DNS round robin), much as we did for on-premises deployments (see "Load Balancing" on page 334). Instead of hardware load balancers, however, most cloud vendors offer load-balancing services. For example, AWS has Elastic Load Balancing (ELB) (*https://aws.amazon.com/elasticloadbalancing/*) for routing traffic to different instances and, when combined with its DNS service Route 53, automatic redirection between different load balancers.

One advantage of these services is that they have HA and scaling built in, so you don't need to deploy multiple instances yourself. However, they often do not have the full capabilities of hardware load balancers. For example, unlike Google's Network Load Balancing (*http://bit.ly/2J87EUx*), as of the time of this writing, AWS ELB does not offer session affinity based on TCP flows, which rules it out for a number of use cases in Hadoop clusters. It is important to understand the limitations and capabilities of load-balancing services.

If you have advanced requirements, a third option to consider is virtualized load balancers, such as F5 Virtual Edition. These will probably provide the highest level of configurability and functionality but obviously come at an additional software cost.

Summary

There are differences among the providers, but not to the degree that it would impact the planning of any use case we have come across. The main message is that there are lots of choices on the infrastructure level, which is a good thing.

After scrutinizing and comparing instance portfolios with a focus on Hadoop, you now know a fair amount about how to build the core of your big data environment; that is, the cluster itself.

You saw some integration points on a very high level in "Network Architecture" on page 484, but you need more to come full circle on enterprise requirements in the cloud. In the next chapters, we consider security and automation. Note that these chapters do not cover any more ground on private clouds.

## CHAPTER 17

Automated Provisioning

One of the main attractions of using an IaaS platform is the prospect of fast, fully automated and repeatable cluster provisioning, entirely driven by configuration—an approach often referred to as *infrastructure as code*. In this chapter, we look at what we need to do to automate the process of deploying clusters, both long-lived and transient, and at some of the special considerations to take into account when operating in the cloud, such as integrating with security, shared metadata services, and growing and shrinking clusters.

Long-Lived Clusters

For the purposes of this discussion, *long-lived cluster deployments* are those with a life cycle that is governed outside of a specific workload or transient use case (see also "Cluster Life Cycle Models" on page 425). They may be used for multiple workloads, tenants, and use cases. Although their tenure can vary, typically such clusters have lifetimes measured in weeks to months rather than days. Standing up a cluster like this normally entails a few phases, as shown in Figure 17-1.

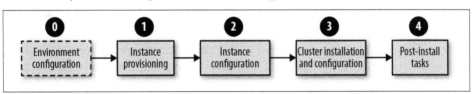

Figure 17-1. The five provisioning phases for long-lived clusters

Before examining each of the phases, we first cover the configuration and templating that should drive any automation solution.

Although this chapter focuses on cloud deployments, the general automation principles can—and should—also be used for on-premises deployments.

Configuration and Templating

Ideally, the input configuration files should completely describe the cluster and its requirements in a declarative format. The configuration should include details such as how many instances to provision and of what type; how to lay out the Hadoop daemons across these instances, how to configure them for this specific cluster, and in what order they should be deployed; how the cluster integrates with the wider environment; and more.

As we'll see in the following section, the separate phases need to be driven by different forms of input configuration or scripts. The key to making the definition of these many configurations tractable—and to making deploying clusters repeatable—is to abstract out all the complex configuration inputs into templates with placeholders for deployment-specific values. This concept should be familiar to anyone who has used a configuration management service, such as Puppet, Ansible, or Chef.

To illustrate the concept, consider Figure 17-2. The operator who is running the automated install defines everything unique to the particular cluster in a single configuration file. For example, the configuration file might specify the following:

- The cluster name
- The number of instances and instance types
- How many volumes the instances should have
- Which authentication identities and authorization groups to enable
- The hostname of an Active Directory server
- The software components to deploy
- The network security groups to apply

After the input configuration is defined, the automation process applies it to all of the templates. In turn, these interpolated templates are applied to the provisioning phases. The end result—if all has gone to plan—is a fully deployed and configured cluster, ready for use.

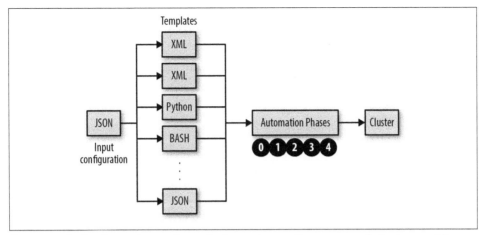

Figure 17-2. Configuration and templating as inputs for automated cluster provisioning

 A good way of creating the templates is to fully deploy and configure, by hand, a cluster that can act as a reference for the type that you want to deploy. The configuration and script templates can be extracted from this cluster and the cluster-specific elements (like hostnames and passwords) replaced by template variables.

In the following section, we assume that the input configuration for the cluster has been defined. The interpolation of templates is implicit in the description of what needs to happen in each phase. With that in mind, let's look at each of the phases in turn.

Deployment Phases

This section explores the five deployment phases outlined in Figure 17-1 in more detail, from environment configuration to post-install tasks.

Environment configuration

Some cluster configurations require certain prerequisites to be in place before they can be deployed. This is not a fixed list and depends on what is actually being deployed, but they include things like:

- MIT Kerberos KDC/Active Directory Server
- Bind server (if using custom DNS)
- IAM identities, roles, and policies
- Network security groups and firewall rules

- TLS certificate generation
- LDAP organizational unit creation
- One-time temporary passwords for joining a server to a domain
- Cloud storage resources
- Load balancer provisioning
- Database server provisioning and schema creation

These prerequisites are sometimes one-off requirements that can be reused across cluster deployments (hence the zero-numbering for this phase and dotted outline in Figure 17-1).

Instance provisioning

Assuming we have all prerequisites in place, the first phase is to obtain the instances on which the cluster will run. Typically, in this phase, the input configuration would define the following:

- Required instance type and number of instances for each of the machine classes (master, worker, edge, utility, and others)
- Instance image(s)—off-the-shelf or custom
- Disk configuration for each machine class—ephemeral versus network
- Network configuration—whether the instances have public IPs

Although we don't cover it here, this phase can easily be implemented using tools like Terraform (*https://www.terraform.io*) and Packer (*https://www.packer.io*) or by modules in Ansible and Puppet, among others.

Instance configuration

After an instance becomes available, there is usually some customization and extra configuration that needs to be performed. In this phase, all OS-level configuration and best practices should be ensured. For example, if using a cloud-supplied image, it is likely we will need to do some or all of the following:

- Linux kernel parameter tuning
- Linux file configuration; for example, */etc/krb5.conf, /etc/sysconfig/networking*
- Local user and group provisioning
- Access control setup; for example, SSH-authorized key definitions
- Disk formatting, filesystem creation
- Setup of required directory structures and permissions

- Software installation
- Joining to a centralized directory; for example, via SSSD or Centrify
- TLS certificate generation and/or retrieval and installation

 There is often an overlap between Phases 1 and 2, and some tasks could be baked into a predefined custom OS image with all customization and prerequisite software installed. Using custom images speeds up provisioning but comes at the cost of more upfront work to build the images. If the desire is to be able to deploy clusters in as short a time as possible, then this extra effort may be worthwhile. Take a look at technologies like Packer (*https://www.packer.io*) to automate the process of image creation.

Instances provisioned in Phase 1 can typically move straight into Phase 2 without waiting for other instances to be ready, since there are usually no dependencies between instances at this stage. The only caveat might be where some utility instances (e.g., databases and NTP, KDC, and LDAP services) that need to be in place before running some of the instance configuration scripts are being deployed as part of the pipeline. Often, these dependencies are deployed as part of Phase 0.

Cluster installation and configuration

By this stage of the pipeline, we should have all instances provisioned, configured, and ready for Hadoop installation. Some of the supporting software for managing Hadoop clusters may already be installed (for example, Cloudera Manager or Ambari). During this phase, the cluster software is installed and the various services and roles are provisioned—for example:

- Cloudera Manager/Apache Ambari (if not installed)
- Core Hadoop (HDFS, YARN)
- Spark
- HBase

As well as installing the software, this phase should configure services for things like authentication, authorization, high availability, and resource management. The result should be a fully functioning Hadoop cluster with all services configured to the relevant best practices.

The preferred approach to deploying cluster services is to use the API of one of the cluster managers. For example, Cloudera Manager deploys, configures, and starts a full cluster using a supplied template, and Ambari has a similar functionality based on blueprints.

This is usually the most expensive stage, and using custom images for each of the node types with software preinstalled can make a big difference. For example, Cloudera Manager supports the placement of parcels in a well-known location ahead of time, which can significantly reduce the provisioning time because cluster software does not need to be distributed to remote hosts.

Post-install tasks

The final phase is to perform any required last tasks on the cluster. These will depend largely on the intended use cases but could include such things as:

- Applying final network security rules and/or security groups
- Bootstrapping HDFS directories
- Creating Hive databases and tables (if not using shared metadata services)
- Creating Sentry roles
- Configuring YARN or Impala dynamic resource pools
- Smoke testing

The feature that most of these tasks will have in common is the requirement for a fully operational cluster. The output of this final phase should be a cluster that is ready to be used by the intended consumers.

After the cluster is ready, one last task might be to register it as a resource with a service discovery directory, for example Consul (*https://www.consul.io/*) or Eureka (*http://bit.ly/15Co2I7*), so that it can start to be used by users or processes.

Vendor Solutions

Some Hadoop vendors provide tools for streamlining deployments on public cloud services. It would be impossible to cover each of the vendors' offerings in detail, so we look at just one tool here: Cloudera Director. The general architecture, deployment, and integration process for this tool applies to all similar software.

Full disclosure: the author of this section is a Cloudera employee and is writing about the software with which he is most familiar. Although we focus on Cloudera Director here, we strongly encourage you to look at the similar offerings from other vendors, such as Hortonworks Cloudbreak (*http://bit.ly/2S6vy6W*) or MapR Orbit (*http://bit.ly/2OWIqKH*), and to evaluate which is most appropriate for your use case.

Cloudera Director

As of late 2017, Cloudera Director (*http://bit.ly/2S6wcRU*) can be used to provision clusters running Cloudera Distribution, including Apache Hadoop (Cloudera Distribution Hadoop [CDH]), on each of the three major public clouds (Amazon Web Services, Google Cloud Platform, and Microsoft Azure). Director advertises the following key features relevant to our discussion on automated provisioning:

- Automated provisioning of Cloudera Manager and CDH clusters and supporting databases
- Deployment of secure, Kerberos-enabled clusters (with a preexisting KDC)
- Deployment of highly available services
- Scaling clusters: expansion and contraction of clusters by adding and removing worker nodes
- Ongoing management: master instance migration

Cloudera Director has two components: a command-line client and a server, as shown in Figure 17-3. The server provides a UI interface as well as an API, and is backed by a database. The command-line client can do simple installations directly against the cloud APIs or, for more complex deployments, the command-line interface can be used to interact with the server via its API.

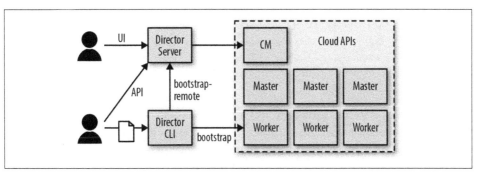

Figure 17-3. Architecture of Cloudera Director

 Deployments requiring anything more than the basic CDH configuration should use the server API directly via the provided API libraries in Python and Java or via the CLI with a configuration file describing the deployment.

With respect to the generic deployment phases outlined in Figure 17-1, Cloudera Director covers all of Phases 1–3 and many of the tasks in Phase 4. Some of the relevant sections from a configuration file are highlighted in Figure 17-4.

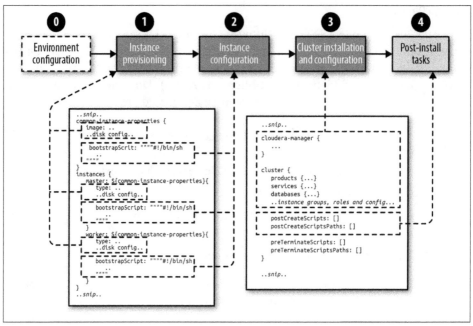

Figure 17-4. How software like Cloudera Director fits into the provisioning phases

Consult the documentation (*http://bit.ly/2S6wcRU*), samples (*http://bit.ly/2DUcCVQ*), and SDK (*http://bit.ly/2OWItpR*) for Cloudera Director installations for specifics about the configuration file syntax and the API.

Although many of the tasks that you may want to automate as post-install tasks can be done via post-creation scripts or recipes, some tasks are best executed outside of the vendor tool. As an example, consider the configuration of cloud network security rules for the cluster instances. If this is managed in a tool like Puppet, is much easier to modify and reapply the rules without the task being tied to the provisioning process. A similar argument applies to the one-off prerequisite tasks. Both of these types of tasks are more suited to an external configuration management tool.

Ongoing management

If you choose to use a vendor tool, you should be aware of the available functionality for ongoing management of long-lived clusters. Some operations might be supported directly by the tool, whereas others might require custom automation.

For example, adding and removing instances and migrating roles can be done within Cloudera Director, but other operations, such as major version cluster upgrades, must be done outside of Director. You can find a list of management responsibilities in the documentation (*http://bit.ly/2KrWZWg*).

One-Click Deployments

Each cloud provider maintains a marketplace of products where users can deploy or purchase images preconfigured for software stacks. Cluster deployments of the popular Hadoop distributions are available in some or all of the marketplaces, such as Cloudera on Azure (*http://bit.ly/2OYr1BD*) or MapR Converged Community Edition (*https://amzn.to/2KoNBm7*).

Although convenient for exploration purposes or proof-of-concept clusters, these products are generally not suitable for production deployments because they offer limited scope for customization beforehand. Instead, they should be considered as reference implementations.

One option is to use the marketplaces to get started with supporting services and then use them to deploy fully configured and integrated clusters. For example, in the Azure Marketplace, the Cloudera Director (*http://bit.ly/2TDdHWO*) product deploys the Director Server, a MySQL database, and a DNS server to provide forward and reverse IP lookups for instances in your Azure Virtual Network.

Homegrown Automation

Naturally, you are not compelled to use any of the vendor offerings to do automated deployments to the cloud. Each cloud vendor has a rich set of APIs for provisioning nodes and services. In the same way, the Hadoop vendors also maintain APIs to their cluster managers that enable provisioning and configuration of clusters, and you can use these via tasks in an automation system such as Puppet or Chef. As we'll see in the following sections, for full automation, some degree of integration with these tools is required.

However, use caution if you're going down the fully customized deployment route. Vendors spend a lot of engineering time and effort developing and testing their solutions against the major cloud providers—almost certainly more time and effort than an individual enterprise can devote to the same task. You should make an objective assessment as to how much effort it is worth spending to reinvent the wheel here. What's more, vendors offer support for their solutions.

Hooking Into a Provisioning Life Cycle

As we have just shown, vendor solutions can automate a lot of the process, but there are certain tasks at either end that can only be automated with the aid of either custom scripts or a configuration management system (CMS).

Typically, the vendor solutions have APIs which can be called from those tools. In this model, the CMS runs everything in Phase 0 and then creates a configuration using its templating capabilities with which it can kick off the vendor tool deployment. This is treated as a black-box task and covers Phases 1–3 or 1–4 of the process. Finally, the CMS resumes control. This is illustrated in Figure 17-5, with a summary of the kinds of tasks that can be done in each phase.

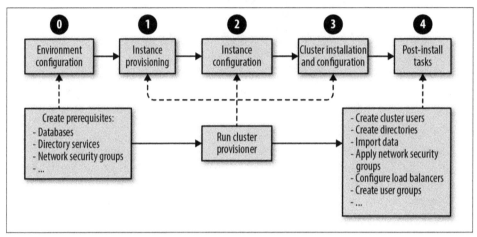

Figure 17-5. Combining a CMS and a vendor tool to perform end-to-end automation

If you're using a CMS to run the entire process, it makes sense to move some of the post-install tasks out of the scripts or recipes used by the vendor tool and into distinct CMS tasks. The configuration and repeatable execution of these tasks are probably better managed in the CMS, especially if they are being used for ongoing maintenance of the cluster. Abstract actions, like HDFS directory creation or Hive database creation, can be composed into useful utilities for onboarding new applications or new use cases to the cluster. A CMS allows for this using a declarative configuration describing the prerequisites of the application.

Scaling Up and Down

One thing you want from any automation solution is the ability to expand and contract clusters as demand varies. This doesn't necessarily mean a full migration to the transient cluster model. Sometimes, it is desirable to have a core set of nodes around all the time to service "normal" workloads and to have the ability to surge the number of compute-only nodes in times of peak demand. These extra workers often don't need the full suite of roles. For example, they might only need YARN NodeManagers in order to run Spark containers.

If scaling clusters up and down is something you plan to do often, you should consider automating the process or using a solution that has scaling capabilities, such as

Cloudera Director. Automation helps reduce the burden and avoid human error. The phases to automate when scaling a cluster up could include:

1. Provision and customize new instances, including such tasks as:
   a. OS configuration
   b. Cluster manager software installation
   c. Kerberos integration
   d. TLS deployment
   e. Adding to network security groups (if not part of provisioning process)
2. Add new hosts to the cluster manager (if using one).
3. Deploy and configure service roles to the new instances, and refresh master roles if required.
4. Perform any data balancing required (for example, if the new nodes have HDFS DataNodes).

Think carefully about whether to deploy HDFS DataNodes to the new instances, especially if the expansion is going to be a short-lived compute burst. The pain of remote reads is probably outweighed by the greater pain of the potentially slow process of graceful decommissioning on contraction (see "Shrinking HDFS" on page 508). If you're using object storage for most data, it's almost certainly not required to deploy DataNodes, and a decent general principle is simply to only expand HDFS and never shrink it.

If you find you need to shrink the cluster, the required stages look something like this:

1. Back up critical data to object storage.
2. Decommission instances in batches (remove roles from master list, replicate data, and more).
3. Delete hosts from cluster manager.
4. Delete instances.
5. Restore any data from object storage as required.
6. Perform any final service and data rebalancing.

Just as we saw for deploying new clusters, end-to-end automation here needs a combination of a CMS, custom scripts, and vendor tools.

Shrinking HDFS

Take extra care when deploying short-lived HDFS DataNodes to grow and shrink the cluster. As a best practice, use rack locality hints to ensure that at least one copy of the data on these nodes is stored on the core set of cluster nodes.

If you're removing HDFS DataNodes, be sure to do so in sensibly sized batches to prevent replication storms (and potential data loss, if rack locality has not been correctly configured). An alternative strategy is to simply either use object storage exclusively or to back up and restore any data from object storage before and after shrinking the cluster.

All of these steps can be automated via cloud and cluster manager APIs. If you are using a vendor solution to provision clusters and it supports growing and shrinking, you do not need to automate many of them, because they are handled for you. Be sure to check what functionality the vendor tool supports.

Our general advice is simply to avoid having to shrink HDFS altogether.

Deploying with Security

Special consideration needs to be given to automating a secure cluster installation. There is typically a raft of supporting services and potentially complex events to do it correctly.

Integrating with a Kerberos KDC

As discussed in Chapter 9, the backbone of any secure Hadoop cluster deployment is Kerberos, so if you need to provision a secure cluster, you need a KDC. You must either tell all of your instances to talk to an existing KDC, or deploy and configure your own. We talked about the trade-offs in "Kerberos Integration" on page 296.

Remember that, in a secure Hadoop cluster, one requirement is that every cluster user can be resolved by the OS. Therefore, as part of your flow, you need to automate some sort of integration with an identity service, like Active Directory or OpenLDAP. We explore these options in "Identity Provider Options for Hadoop" on page 517.

If you decide you need to deploy a new KDC server for the cluster, this falls under Phase 1 (see Figure 17-1) and is best performed by your CMS. For example, you could use Ansible to spin up an instance in AWS, install MIT KDC and OpenLDAP servers, and configure SSSD on every instance to resolve users and groups via LDAP. The configuration of each host happens in Phases 2–4. If you prefer an integrated identity service, you can deploy FreeIPA (*http://bit.ly/2Bo52Ad*) or Active Directory and automatically have your instances join a domain using something like realmd (*http://bit.ly/2DBLsCf*) or Centrify (*http://bit.ly/2PIIuCZ*).

With the right combination of scripts and configuration, it is perfectly possible to fully automate provisioning a Kerberos-secured cluster. It is also worth mentioning that there is often direct support for configuring Hadoop to use security in provisioning tools like Cloudera Director.

TLS

If you have a requirement for wire encryption on your cluster, you need to configure TLS for your services and to deploy server certificates to all your nodes. Automating TLS can be a challenge because it requires a bit of back and forth between servers. Essentially, there are three options for deploying TLS certificates:

Signed by a root or intermediate certificate authority (CA)
> If you want to have your server certificates signed by a trusted CA, you have to generate certificate signing requests from your server certificates and submit them to the CA. After the CA has processed the CSRs, the signed public certificates need to be deployed back to the servers.

Self-sign your certificates using your own CA
> The sequence of steps is the same as those in the previous option, but in this case you have full control of the CA and can automate the CSR signing and distribution process.

Use server certificates
> The final option is to not sign any of your certificates but to collect all of the individual public certificates for each instance into a single trust file and spread it around the cluster.

Obviously, one of the first two options is preferable. In the ideal case, a private certificate never leaves the system for which it was generated. Instead, the CSR is sent to the signing authority and the signed certificate is returned. Some enterprises provide an automatic signed certificate generation service with a one-time download of the private certificate. Usually, though, in a cloud context, the second option (self-signing) is more common.

> If you're shipping private keys around, be sure to protect them with restrictive file permissions, strong network security rules, secure transport, and a strong passphrase.

Again, it might be possible to use a vendor solution to automate much of this.

Transient Clusters

For a transient workload, it rarely makes sense to create a long-running cluster with all the integration hooks an enterprise supports. Developers and business teams often want the flexibility to run their jobs without requiring enterprise IT to build them a cluster. To service this demand, the likes of Amazon, Google, and Microsoft—in addition to cloud-neutral vendors like Cloudera or Qubole—have developed job-oriented frameworks which abstract away the business of spinning up and configuring clusters.

Instead of thinking about the cluster, users submit a workload, such as a sequence of Hive queries or Spark jobs, and the framework automatically provisions a cluster and runs the job. Naturally, for this all to work, the input and output data to and from these jobs needs to be sourced from a location independent of the cluster that runs the job. Luckily, cloud object storage offerings such as Amazon S3 and Microsoft ADLS provide the perfect location for such data.

Cloud-provider networks are specially architected and optimized to make the access to data in object or cloud storage efficient and resilient. This makes the separation of compute and storage viable for analytical workloads. Reproducing this in a private cloud setting is an undertaking not to be taken lightly, but tools like OpenStack, with its Swift object storage component (*http://bit.ly/2DADWaB*), are opening this up as a possibility.

The typical flow of a transient workload is shown in Figure 17-6 and proceeds as follows: (1) a user submits a workload to the API of the workload automation tool; (2) the framework uses the cloud APIs to spin up an entire cluster for the workload; (3) after the cluster is up and running, the tool submits the jobs in the workload; (4) each job accesses remote cloud storage for its input and output; and (5) finally, the automation tool tears down the cluster.

This is relevant to the chapter because these services offer automation of cluster provisioning out of the box and expose APIs to allow job submission automation. You need to assess whether deploying long-lived clusters or running transient clusters is the right choice for your customers.

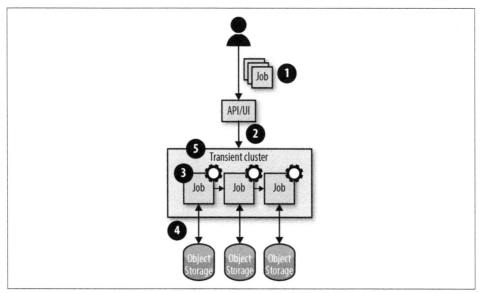

Figure 17-6. Submitting a workload to a transient workload automation tool

Unfortunately, covering each of the services in detail is beyond the remit of this chapter, but here are some starting links for further information:

- Amazon Elastic MapReduce (*https://aws.amazon.com/emr/*)
- Google Cloud Dataproc (*https://cloud.google.com/dataproc/*)
- Microsoft Azure Batch (*https://azure.microsoft.com/en-us/services/batch/*)
- Cloudera Altus (*https://www.cloudera.com/products/altus.html*)
- Qubole Data Service (*https://www.qubole.com/products/qubole-data-service/*)

Sharing Metadata Services

In on-premises deployments it is common for different clusters to make use of shared supporting infrastructure services, such as Active Directory, DNS, NTP, and others. By contrast, metadata services such as the Hive Metastore or Sentry are rarely shared and are deployed separately for each cluster. Typically, the data that the services relate to is contained within the cluster itself. But with the growing trend toward the separation of compute and storage comes an increased desire to share metadata about data stored in remote object storage between different compute clusters.

The use of shared services like Hive Metastore is a relatively new development but is quickly gaining traction and is an essential requirement when using a shared storage layer. Without a centralized metadata service, there is a real risk of competing and overlapping operations from different clusters (such as table partition additions and deletions or INSERT OVERWRITE queries) rendering the data inconsistent, corrupted, or both. To be clear, this is still an unsolved problem even within a single cluster, in which processes running in Hive, Spark, and Impala can all manipulate and modify the same data without regard to one another—but the problem is potentially exacerbated in the cloud, where the potential for overlap is extended to multiple clusters.

 Projects such as Netflix's Iceberg (*http://bit.ly/2DyUHDb*) are attempting to address the issue of inconsistency that results from simultaneous and competing modification of tabular data.

As of this writing, users of Amazon EMR can use the Glue Data Catalog (*https://amzn.to/2zjnkkY*), Hortonworks has published its plans for shared service with the DataPlane Service (*http://bit.ly/2DRghE2*), and Cloudera users can deploy shared Hive Metastore and Sentry services via the Shared Data Experience (*http://bit.ly/2S0ENVW*) functionality.

From an automation point of view, whether using long-lived or transient clusters, this simply means that it is best to automatically configure clusters to point at these shared services rather than deploying new versions of these same tools for each cluster.

Summary

In this chapter, we looked at the major considerations when automating cluster deployments in the cloud with respect to persistent and transient workloads. The cloud offers the exciting prospect of managing, operating, and evolving your Hadoop infrastructure entirely through code.

We presented a model for thinking about the general stages of deployment and configuration automation, and we encourage you to adapt this to your own requirements. The recommended approach involves a mixture of CMS and vendor-supplied automation tools, like Cloudera Director, but if you can reduce your deployment specifications to a handful of declarative configuration files, you can track these through source control and can be truly flexible in the way you manage your cloud infrastructure. We also explored the automation of transient workloads, in which the cluster and infrastructure are entirely abstracted away from the user.

Given the right tooling and approach, deploying fully configured and secured clusters in the cloud is well within your grasp.

## CHAPTER 18

Security in the Cloud

At this point, the path to securing an on-premises cluster is well-trodden. As covered in Chapter 9, vendor distributions of Hadoop contain a full suite of products and features providing authentication, authorization, auditing, and encryption. In this chapter, we explore how operating in a public cloud should change your approach to security. It is impossible to cover all aspects of cloud security in a single chapter, but we aim to provide you with enough information to feel comfortable about architecting Hadoop-based solutions. We begin by briefly outlining the risks and threat model for running in the cloud. Following that, we dive into the specifics for Hadoop security, including identity management, securing object storage, encryption, and network security.

To keep our discussion focused, we mostly deal with unmanaged clusters using the sticky or suspendable deployment patterns (see "Cluster Life Cycle Models" on page 425), rather than managed PaaS offerings such as Amazon Elastic MapReduce (Amazon EMR) or Google Dataproc. For additional information, review the documentation of the providers themselves. As a general reference, we also highly recommend *Moving Hadoop to the Cloud* (O'Reilly) by Bill Havanki.

Assessing the Risk

As an enterprise architect, you might be asking yourself what security you need in the cloud. There are a few ways to answer this question, depending on the level of risk your enterprise is willing to adopt. The right questions to ask are really about what the risks are and how you mitigate those risks. No system is perfectly secure (including your own datacenters), and the public cloud is no different. But there are reasonable steps you can take when designing a cloud deployment that reduce the risks to levels equivalent to, or even lower than, those in your own on-premises environments. Finally, there are many aspects to security, and your risk profile or cloud usage patterns might require the configuration of some aspects of security but not others.

Many organizations are wary of storing and processing their data on public clouds. For some this may be for legal or policy reasons—for example, the European Union's General Data Protection Regulation (GDPR) legislation has strict regulations—while for others it might be that they are simply not confident they can guarantee their data is safe from exposure through accident, misconfiguration, or deliberate hacking. Not knowing the physical location of your data can be disconcerting, as can be the thought of processes from a different user account running on the same physical host, even from a separate virtual machine. Of course, public cloud vendors point out that many of these concerns are unfounded. Cloud providers take great pains to ensure a secure operating environment for their tenants, and when correctly configured for security, these venues should certainly be regarded as safe and secure places to store and process your data.

From a physical point of view, public cloud datacenters are probably more secure than most enterprise datacenters (see, for example, Google's approach (*http://bit.ly/2R30ODu*)). In hardware and software, hypervisor implementations are, by this stage, very mature and the risk of exposure through exploits of security bugs (through so-called *VM escapes*) is, thankfully, extremely low. When such exploits are detected,[1] the providers move fast to address them. For example, they were very quick to address the recent Meltdown and Spectre attacks (*https://www.meltdownattack.com*). In fact, a Google employee was among the first to discover and report the vulnerabilities. The cloud vendors put a lot of effort into making sure their offerings are as secure as they can be.

Security and isolation between tenants is at the very heart of how cloud compute offerings are designed. As we saw in "Network Architecture" on page 484, at the network level, each tenant is placed inside a completely isolated software-defined virtual network, which is accessible to only its own instances (hence the *private* in virtual private cloud). As we demonstrate in the following sections, by default, the access to these networks is strictly locked down and you must explicitly allow certain inbound and outbound traffic, according to your requirements. Likewise, instance and remote block storage are completely isolated to your instances.

By default, the cloud-provided instance images are set up with remote login access limited to a user-defined set of SSH key pairs unique to your project. Access to cloud services and APIs, such as object storage or managed databases, is mediated through users in a sophisticated Identity and Access Management (IAM) process, and

---

1 See, for example, the Venom (*http://venom.crowdstrike.com/*) vulnerability and CVE advisories for Xen (*https://xenbits.xen.org/xsa/*), QEMU (*http://bit.ly/2BplSPi*), and KVM (*https://lwn.net/Articles/619332/*).

programmatic access is provided using access tokens that can be time-bound (more on this later in the chapter).

Ultimately, though, it is up to an enterprise's risk team to make the assessment of the risk of storing data and running processes in the public cloud. As with any good security architecture, we should begin by building a *risk model*, which outlines the possible risks and their mitigations.

Risk Model

In this section we look at some of the security risks that may exist when deploying in the public cloud. It is assumed that a common mitigation for each of the risks is configuring the Hadoop software with strong authentication, authorization, and auditing. In addition, some datasets will require at-rest and in-flight encryption.

Every deployment has its own risk profile, and just as you do when deploying on-premises clusters on your own infrastructure, you should compile a comprehensive threat model of your own for your intended usage before building out a security architecture.

Environmental Risks

Environmental risks are those associated with physical access to datacenters, servers, and hardware. Some of these risks include:

Malicious administrators

Just as in on-premises datacenters, certain personnel in cloud datacenters have direct physical access to machines and hardware and often have privileged access to servers. Although it is unlikely, it is possible that these personnel might be motivated to hostile actions, either through their own malicious intent, for financial gain, or because they are susceptible to criminal or outside pressure. These admins might have:

- Root access to servers or hypervisors

- Access to the physical network to tap and monitor traffic

- Access to physical storage media, such as locally attached disks, used disks, or storage arrays

Malicious tenants

Fellow users of the cloud service might also be a threat. Hackers looking for ways to effect a VM escape might seek to take advantage of known or unknown bugs in the virtualization software. (Typically, such attacks target the virtualized device drivers. See, for example, the Venom attack.) Such exploits seek to access the hypervisor software and, therefore, any other VM running on the same physical machine. It also gives them some degree of general access to the network as (at least subnet-local) traffic can be promiscuously sniffed by the NICs on the server.

Criminal access

Another possibility is that criminals might have effected access to the cloud infrastructure—servers, network, and other hardware—either physically or virtually. Alternatively, such actors might be monitoring the network links from the datacenter to the wider internet.

Platform vulnerabilities

No human-made system is without flaws, and there might be bugs or security flaws in the cloud architecture, software, and user interfaces used to administer cloud service deployments. Because clouds introduce more software complexity, the chances of such bugs are theoretically higher, although as already mentioned, it should be noted that cloud providers are extremely vigilant in hunting out such vulnerabilities and patching them as soon as they are discovered.

Mitigation

The common risk to all of these is exposure of data through unauthorized access to the cloud substrate or services. By definition, exploits of environmental risks would be nonspecific and opportunistic in nature, with attackers casting a wide net rather than looking for a specific tenant or dataset.

Some of this risk is naturally mitigated by the tight isolation provided by a VPC, but a common additional mitigation is to employ both at-rest and in-flight encryption to protect your data. There are many options to consider when employing encryption, and we cover this in detail later in the chapter.

Deployment Risks

Deployment risks include the following:

Human error

Either through accidental misconfiguration or incomplete understanding of the security settings for a cloud service, access might be opened to systems by an enterprise's own administrators or users. Such accesses include:

Network access

VPC settings, VPNs, internet gateways, firewalls, security groups

Data access

Security settings on local or object storage

System access

Ability to log in to the boxes via SSH or web-based console via accidentally exposed credentials or lax controls

A typical case could be criminals using compromised credentials to use computational resources for their own purposes, such as bitcoin mining.

Application design

Often, real-world cloud deployments include some sort of application or intermediary API layer that accesses cluster services and data. To prevent accidental exposure to data and systems, these applications and APIs need to be carefully designed such that their authentication and authorization controls are at least as strong than those on the cluster. It is no good to effectively secure your cluster only to leave doors open elsewhere.

Mitigation

The first mitigation for much of this is to provide adequate training for the system administrators who are responsible for the deployments. The next is to define solid procedures. For example, you might specify that, for production deployments, service configurations should be validated by at least two people before rollout. In addition, application designs can and should be reviewed by your internal security teams and, at least for the most secure applications, penetration tested.

You can also minimize deployment risk in general by adopting a principle of least exposure for your systems—for example, by preferring to deploy clusters within private subnets and by employing solid perimeter controls.

The impact of credential compromise can be limited through the use of multifactor authentication and a regular policy of rotating API access tokens for cloud services. In addition, for sticky and suspendable clusters, you need to configure most or all of the same authentication and authorization controls for the Hadoop cluster services that we covered in Chapter 9.

In the following sections, we cover the extra considerations for configuring secure Hadoop clusters in cloud deployments, including identity management for authentication and authorization, object storage security, encryption, and network security.

Identity Provider Options for Hadoop

When considering authentication and authorization, we limit our discussion to two particular identity domains: identities for running and using Hadoop cluster services and identities for using cloud storage.

Remember, we are not considering Hadoop PaaS offerings such as Amazon EMR or Google Dataproc in this chapter.

As we saw in Chapter 9, for the majority of services in a Hadoop cluster, user authentication is provided through Kerberos—and by and large, this remains the case when deploying in a public cloud. As we saw in Chapter 10, the principals used to identify users and services in a Hadoop cluster need to be both defined in the Kerberos KDC and resolvable as users capable of running Linux processes on each node in the cluster.

You need to consider the following questions (and their follow-ups):

- Where should I run my ID service?
- Should it be on-premises and connected to cloud clusters by VPN, or should it be run in the cloud?
- Can I use one of the managed services provided by AWS, Microsoft, or Google?
- Which identities (users and groups) should I use? Should I use the same identities as in my on-premises infrastructure or a completely new set of identities for the cloud?

Unfortunately, there is no one correct answer to all of these questions, because each enterprise has its own standards and circumstances, but we discuss some possible approaches here. Although we highlight three options, there are also numerous valid combinations and hybrid approaches.

As with on-premises clusters, using a unified identity management service such as Active Directory (AD) or Red Hat Identity Management (IdM) offers the easiest route to satisfying authentication and authorization controls. Integrating the OS into AD or IdM can be made part of the automated provisioning of VMs.

All major providers also offer secure ways to effectively extend your corporate network to cloud instances using VPNs. As previously noted, the security measures that providers put in place are at least as rigorous as those in most on-premises datacenters. With that in mind, it is a reasonable option to reuse existing on-premises user accounts and authorization groups with Hadoop clusters running on cloud instances. This comes with the advantages of centralized account administration and convenience for end users, who do not need to use new account IDs and passwords. (Of course, this kind of decision needs a proper risk assessment and sign-off from an enterprise's internal technical risk team.) Clearly, however, when no connectivity to the enterprise network is possible, creating new users and groups in the cloud is unavoidable. Let's consider the options in more detail.

Option A: Cloud-Only Self-Contained ID Services

The first option to consider is to treat each cluster as a self-contained authentication environment, as shown in Figure 18-1. Each cluster has its own ID service for all technical and user accounts and groups. Although we show each cluster running in a separate subnet within the same VPC, this model could equally employ separate VPCs per cluster.

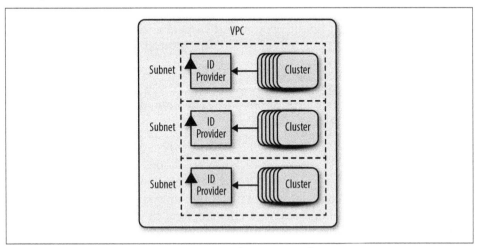

Figure 18-1. Self-contained authentication for separate clusters

This option has the principal advantages of both simplicity and security isolation. It is simple because, when deploying each cluster, an authentication service is deployed on a VM in the same group of nodes. The ID service is dedicated to the cluster and can share the same downtime and availability requirements as the cluster it is supporting. This also makes it simpler from an operational point of view. Any outages affect only the cluster to which it is dedicated.

From a security isolation point of view, this approach means that any security compromises are potentially limited to a single cluster and that breaches can be very easily locked down (although see the following discussion of cross-realm trusts). In addition, because it is isolated, it is likely that administration rights to create, modify, and delete identities in the ID service can be delegated to the group running the cluster rather than being centrally controlled. For all intents and purposes, identities are unique to the cloud and are managed separately in each cluster.

The major drawback of this option is that there is no reuse of identities, which makes it problematic when you deploy more than one sticky or suspendable cluster. Users who want to access cluster services need to be onboarded to each and every cluster they use, with different management of passwords and group memberships. Managing many clusters in isolation like this could quickly become tedious and error-prone, especially when group memberships must be added or revoked for authorization.

A further drawback is the requirement for cross-realm trusts between KDCs in different clusters, which is necessary when users or services from one cluster need to interact with services in another cluster. Putting trusts in place is not an issue—a one-way trust is sufficient in many cases—but it is an additional administration burden and reduces the isolation between clusters.

Finally, this option might not be applicable if corporate standards dictate a single, centrally managed identity for users when accessing production systems.

In practice, this option is not generally recommended, except for clusters with the most stringent security requirements. It can be useful, however, for one-off clusters that bootstrap their own security setup automatically from scratch.

Option B: Cloud-Only Shared ID Services

Instead of deploying an ID service for each cluster, another approach is to share an ID service between all of the deployed cloud clusters, as shown in Figure 18-2. This is similar to the setup that most enterprises have on-premises, where clusters and services belong to a domain and, if required, different domains are clustered into forests (to borrow AD terminology). In this model, though, identities and groups remain unique to the cloud.

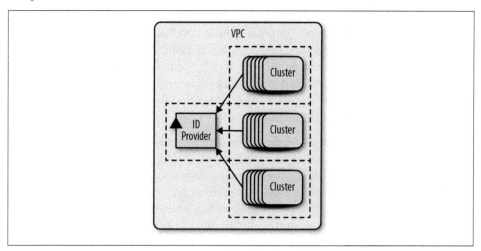

Figure 18-2. Shared ID services

The main advantage of such an approach is that it makes managing authentication, authorization, and interoperability for multiple clusters much easier. All identities and groups can be centrally managed, while maintaining security isolation from on-premises identities. Moreover, managing and maintaining highly available identity services should be cheaper since the same instances can be used by multiple clusters.

Some degree of isolation is lost when compared to Option A, such that a compromised identity could potentially be used on a number of clusters. However, this risk can possibly be mitigated through other measures, such as perimeter controls, firewalls, and Hadoop policies. We also lose some of the autonomy of each cluster for maintenance, administration, and downtime.

Cloud-Managed ID Services

Cloud service providers also offer managed services for identity management, such as hosted AD instances. These can be attractive since they take away the pain and bother of setting up instances, installing and configuring, and generally worrying about concepts like availability.

Integrating these managed services with your clusters usually looks much like Option B, although you could run a separate service for each cluster in the manner of Option A. The same advantages and disadvantages apply. The major additional advantage of using a managed identity provider is that it removes the need to do it yourself. One disadvantage is that, as part of the convenience, you lose the ability to customize the configuration of the identity service—which may or may not be a problem, depending on what functionalities your Hadoop distribution requires.

Managed services can be an attractive option, but they might not provide all the features you need for security integration. For example, do they provide secure communication via LDAPS? Can you integrate with them at the OS level? Find out which requirements exist for your Hadoop distribution, and test run the integration in a development environment.

Option C: On-Premises ID Services

As we mentioned, cloud networks can be made to be secure extensions of on-premises networks through the use of VPN gateways. This opens up the possibility of integrating cloud deployments with existing on-premises infrastructure and services, such as AD. Almost all enterprises have centralized IT to manage these services, and this again takes such concerns off the plate of the cloud cluster system administrators. A key advantage is the ability to use existing identities on cloud clusters and to easily extend current policies and trust relationships around authentication and authorization to the cloud.

There are a couple of disadvantages to this option, though. First, it requires that the system administrators responsible for AD (or similar) agree to the approach. It usually takes some convincing and demonstration of cloud security controls before they are willing to increase the potential attack surface of corporate infrastructure. Additional security controls on cloud-deployed infrastructure might be requested as a result, which could lead to loss of configuration agility for those administering the cloud clusters.

Second, a large concern with this option is request latency for authentication and authorization operations. Even with the use of dedicated direct connections to cloud providers from corporate infrastructure, the latency of requests is dramatically increased when compared to requests within the cloud network, and this usually results in very poor performance.

To counter this last point, a best-practice architecture is to host a local mirror instance of a directory (or relevant subset of it) within the cloud, as shown in Figure 18-3. Identities and groups can be manually (or automatically) synced to the cloud instance from the on-premises providers.

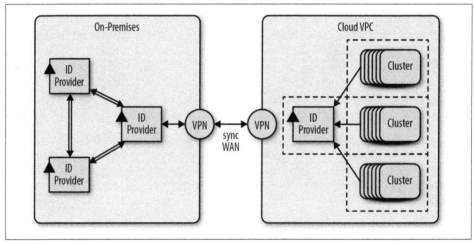

Figure 18-3. Mirrored on-premises ID services

The architecture addresses the two major concerns of security and performance. A directory mirror (potentially managed by centralized IT) prevents direct access to on-premises services from cluster nodes. Access to the on-premises directory can be firewalled off to one or two fixed cloud IPs and limited to specific sync-based functionality. On-premises services are implicitly protected from network risks such as denial-of-service attacks. Furthermore, directory administrators retain full control over the directory contents. Finally, the performance concerns are addressed by keeping all identity requests local to the cloud network and limiting VPN-based connections to periodic batch synchronizations where latency is not a major concern.

This final approach is recommended for most enterprises because it provides the smoothest integration experience for users of clusters, whether they are in the cloud or on-premises.

Object Storage Security and Hadoop

So far, our cloud deployment discussion has not introduced anything vastly different from the security principles we apply for on-premises architectures. In the following few sections, we briefly cover some unique authentication and authorization concepts that come up when using services available only in the cloud.

There are many services offered by cloud vendors, ranging from processing engines to key-value stores to file and block storage. A complete overview is well beyond the scope of this chapter, so instead we focus purely on the security options around the object storage services of the three cloud vendors. This section introduces some key concepts. Encryption of object storage is covered in "Encryption for Data at Rest" on page 535.

Identity and Access Management

Each vendor offers an IAM framework to enable fine-grained access control to the various cloud resources and services. A top-level account within a cloud service can create a number of subusers via IAM, to which different roles and permissions can be applied. The top-level account, the *root account*, has full access to all data and services that it is paying for, but access for IAM users can be more restricted.

In Linux systems administration, it is considered bad practice to perform operations directly as the root user. Instead, it is best to work with regular users with group memberships and sudo rights to run privileged tasks without the need to reveal the root password. The same principle applies in a cloud context: permissions for cloud-native services and resources (e.g., object storage, VM instances, networks, and more) can be granted to IAM users and groups and access to the root account can be restricted. Resource usage can be audited and easily restricted or revoked, without the need to compromise the root account credentials.

When granting permissions with IAM, we can use two approaches:

Role-based access control (RBAC)
> *Roles* are granted to an IAM user or group of IAM users, and a set of *permissions* (which can often also be grouped into *policies*) is applied to each role, specifying what the users can and cannot do with the account's resources at different *scopes*. For example, an account-wide privilege might be added to allow a role to read any data in cloud storage. Role access can also be applied at the resource level scope, perhaps to allow write access to a particular storage bucket. Roles can also be applied to nonuser objects such as VM instances or applications.

User-based access control

In contrast to RBAC, we can also apply permissions on resources directly to particular IAM users and groups—for example, using access control lists (ACLs) on buckets and objects.

Both approaches can be used in combination, but, in general, user-based access control is considered a less flexible approach than the RBAC approach because it requires administrators and data owners to keep close track of which specific resources have defined accesses for individual IAM users or groups. In contrast, roles can easily have their permissions changed or be added to or removed from users in a single command. A common best practice is to use roles and permissions at both the account and the resource level. For example, read access might be granted to a role for all data in cloud storage while write access is controlled at a bucket level.

You can find out more about the IAM functionalities of the major cloud providers in their respective documentation.

Amazon Simple Storage Service

Amazon S3, introduced in "AWS storage options" on page 459, is a popular way of storing large amounts of arbitrary data at low cost. As we discussed in "Identity and Access Management" on page 523, users can authenticate to S3 using the top-level AWS account credentials or—much preferred—IAM user credentials. The specific details of the different account and credentials types are covered in the AWS documentation (*https://amzn.to/2QcfgvQ*). Access to S3 is managed via secured REST API interactions using *access keys*, which consist of an *ID* (think username) and a *secret key*.

In terms of authorization, buckets and objects are locked down to the creating user by default. Additional access to data can be defined via both resource and user policies:

Resource policies

These are policies or ACLs on the resources themselves (buckets and objects):

- *Bucket policies* are specified using JSON syntax. These define who can do what to the bucket itself or objects in the bucket: for example GET, PUT, DELETE, and LIST. You can find out more, and see a full list of permissions in the Amazon S3 documentation (*https://amzn.to/2Afrx90*). These policies can be very expressive and can be applied to IAM users, groups, and roles. Because roles can be applied to nonuser objects, such as instances or applications, this means that policies can control access by end users, programmatic users and instances.

- ACLs can be applied to buckets and objects to define PUT/GET permissions for specific AWS accounts and groups.

User policies
This is a JSON policy defining an IAM user's access to S3 buckets and objects.

Hadoop integration

Apache Hadoop has built-in integration (*http://bit.ly/2OVsBnK*) for accessing data from S3, which is presented as a Hadoop-compatible filesystem (with a few caveats about its adherence to POSIX semantics and behavior). Buckets and objects are resolved using a URL syntax with the form *s3a://<bucket>/<dir>/<object>* (the integration has gone through a number of iterations, and previous *s3://* and *s3n://* schemes are now deprecated). There are a number of methods of authenticating to the AWS API, as implemented by a number of pluggable authentication providers, which we describe below.

Temporary security credentials. These are obtained from the AWS Security Token Service using a persistent identity (either an AWS root account or an IAM user). Temporary credentials can be valid for periods from 15 minutes to a maximum of 36 hours (or 1 hour, if issued by an AWS root account) and consist of an access key ID, a secret access key, and a session token. Here is an example of obtaining a token using the AWS command-line tool (response edited for clarity and shortened with ellipses):

```
$ aws sts get-session-token
{
  "Credentials": {
    "SecretAccessKey": "irjQmOQPW/tY3BGbJ...BTm2XI+Pm9dPxCK",
    "SessionToken": "FQoDYXdzEDoaDChdP8rP...Wa4ohLvszQU=",
    "Expiration": "2017-09-15T12:23:32Z",
    "AccessKeyId": "ASIAJXSCLG742QXSQNKQ"
  }
}
```

Such credentials can be supplied directly in Hadoop configuration variables or placed in a Hadoop credentials provider file on HDFS and used by the org.apache.hadoop .fs.s3a.TemporaryAWSCredentialsProvider authentication provider. Temporary credentials are analogous to HDFS delegation tokens. Due to their expiration, they are not suitable for long-lived applications, such as Spark Streaming jobs, or for long-running services such as Impala or HBase.

Hadoop Credentials Provider Files

Hadoop has a useful general-purpose mechanism for protecting sensitive credentials in a file on HDFS. This mechanism is supported by a number of specific credentials providers, such as those for S3 and ADLS. The Credentials Provider API (*http://bit.ly/2zkssFg*) provides a command-line tool to write sensitive configuration values into a file with restrictive permissions. For example:

```
$ hadoop credentials create fs.s3a.access.key \
  -value "ADKJFJXSCFG832QXSQNKQ" \
  -provider -provider \
  jceks://hdfs@nameservice1/user/ian/s3.jceks
$ hadoop credentials create fs.s3a.secret.key \
  -value "fskQmOQPW/tY3BGbJC/kEosJJBTm2XI+Pk5pPxCK" \
  -provider -provider \
  jceks://hdfs@nameservice1/user/ian/s3.jceks
$ CREDPROP=hadoop.security.credential.provider.path
$ JCEKS=jceks://hdfs@nameservice1/user/ian/s3.jceks
$ hdfs dfs -D ${CREDPROP}=${JCEKS} -ls s3a://bucket/and/path
```

You can reference this file via the `hadoop.security.credential.provider.path` property and use it in jobs and applications. With the right permissions, sensitive credentials do not need to be exposed in configuration files, although anyone with read access to the file can read the values. Just as Kerberos keytab files need to be jealously protected with file permissions, credentials files also need to be readable by only the users whose credentials they contain. This approach is a best practice to protect individual credentials but is less useful when using a single set of credentials to grant access to a wide user base.

Persistent credentials. Either an AWS root user or an IAM user can provide an access key and secret key in the *core-site.xml* Hadoop configuration file or in a Hadoop credentials provider file on HDFS. This method is used by the `org.apache.hadoop.fs.s3a.SimpleAWSCredentialsProvider`. Needless to say, this option should be used with care because *core-site.xml* files may be widely readable.

Environment variables. The `com.amazonaws.auth.EnvironmentVariableCredentials Provider` gives access through some standard environment variables (`AWS_ACCESS_KEY_ID`, `AWS_SECRET_ACCESS_KEY`, and, optionally, `AWS_SESSION_TOKEN` if using temporary credentials). These environment variables need to be set for every process accessing S3, including "worker" processes such as Spark executors or Map-Reduce mappers and reducers.

Instance roles. Amazon EC2 instances can be assigned an IAM role, conferring them rights to S3 buckets. If using the `com.amazonaws.auth.InstanceProfileCredential` `sProvider`, the credentials are dynamically obtained using the Instance Metadata Service, which is accessible only from the instance itself.

Anonymous access. Finally, read-only access can be granted to anonymous users using the `org.apache.hadoop.fs.s3a.AnonymousAWSCredentialsProvider`.

Multiple credential provider implementations can be used simultaneously by specifying a comma-separated list of class names in the `fs.s3a.aws.credentials.provider` configuration property. These are evaluated in order. A credentials file can be used to avoid placing credentials directly in configuration files, but for shared credentials this is less advantageous. Some vendors provide additional mechanisms, such as the Cloudera S3 Connector Service (*http://bit.ly/2KpiS8q*), to hide sensitive credentials from end users.

Further information

The source documentation is the most authoritative source for more information. Useful pages include "Managing Access Permissions to Your Amazon S3 Resources" (*https://amzn.to/2FzaHHP*), "Overview of Managing Access" (*https://amzn.to/2DAvPuW*), and "Guidelines for Using the Available Access Policy Options" (*https://amzn.to/2DMUtcx*).

GCP Cloud Storage

Google provides object storage via its Cloud Storage (*https://cloud.google.com/storage/*) service. Just like in S3, data is organized into top-level containers, called buckets, with subdirectories and files.

Google also has an IAM story similar to that of AWS, in which a root account can create users, groups, and service accounts. In GCP, these IAM identities are referred to as *members*, which can be assigned roles, and roles can be assigned permissions. Sets of permissions can be combined into *policies*. By default, the Cloud Storage APIs and tools use OAuth 2.0 for authentication, with two means of access: *user accounts* and *service accounts* (see the documentation (*http://bit.ly/2QZciYE*)). Google Cloud Storage also supports HMAC-based authentication with *developer keys*, akin to Amazon S3 credentials.

Service accounts have a private key, which is used to make a direct request to authentication services for an access token. When operating in a user account authentication flow, the end user must allow the application to access the data before an appropriate access token is passed to the application. This access token is then used to authenticate subsequent interactions with the Cloud Storage APIs. Tokens are requested with specific OAuth scopes, which define the level of authorization access, subject to the actual permissions set on resources or roles granted to members (as defined by IAM policies or ACLs). There are five defined scopes (*http://bit.ly/2TBaU0n*) relevant to Cloud Storage scenarios:

`read-only`
> Read user objects/list buckets

`read-write`
> Read/write user objects

`full-control`
> Read/write user objects and set user IAM policies

`cloud-platform.read-only`
> Read all user data across GCP services for this account

`cloud-platform`
> Full privileges to GCP services for the user

Authorization for members can be administered on resources using IAM policies and ACLs, which can be used independently or in combination:

IAM policies
> Policies allow roles to be assigned one or more sets of permissions, such as `storage.buckets.create`, `storage.buckets.delete`, and `storage.object.get`. There are built-in roles that can be applied via policies at the project level or at the bucket level. Permissions granted through policies apply to all objects within the bucket.

ACLs
> When fine-grained access control on objects within buckets is required, users can employ bucket or object ACLs, which specify permissions for a given scope (where, in this case, the scope indicates who has been granted the permission). Scopes can refer to member identities, such as a user or group, and to wider contexts, such as projects, domains, and even all Google account holders. Valid permissions (and the OAuth 2.0 scopes) are `READER` (same as `read-only`), `WRITER` (`read-write`), and `OWNER` (`full-control`).

Depending on the interaction mechanism (code, command-line utility, etc.) and the access location (GCP instances or outside GCP), there are different ways to specify the private key or developer keys to use for the authentication flow, including instance service accounts, environment variables, configuration files, and supplied client libraries. We cover only the Hadoop-specific authentication scenarios here.

Hadoop integration

Hadoop integration is provided by the `bigdata-interop` (*http://bit.ly/2QaXx7X*) project maintained by Google. As yet, it is not part of the Apache Hadoop distribution. A prebuilt JAR can be placed on the classpath of a Java process (including distributed processes running in YARN containers), and authentication configuration is defined dynamically in the Hadoop configuration or placed in *core-site.xml*. Google Cloud Storage is presented as a Hadoop-compatible filesystem with URLs like *gs://<bucketname>/path/to/data*.

As already mentioned, there are two mechanisms for authenticating to GCP, service accounts and user accounts, and we cover how to use both of these approaches in Hadoop. In both cases, the GCP project ID must be specified in the Hadoop configuration; for example, via the *core-site.xml* file:

```
<property>
  <name>fs.gs.project.id</name>
  <value>ian-acme</value>
</property>
```

Service account. Service accounts can be created within a GCP project using the IAM interface. Credentials for a service account are either obtained implicitly from the instance (if the instance was assigned the service account when it was created) or explicitly by specifying the service account ID and credentials file in the Hadoop configuration. Upon creation of a service account, credentials can be downloaded for the account in either JSON or PKCS12 (P12) format. To use a service account in Hadoop, the P12 format is required. New credentials can also be issued to an existing service account, if you need both JSON and P12 formats. Note that, when explicitly setting the service account, you cannot place the credentials directly in the configuration files. Instead, a file location on the local disk must be specified.

Service account authentication is selected by setting the `google.cloud.auth.ser vice.account.enable` property to `true`. Because this property defaults to `true`, it is enough to simply read from a *gs://* URL to use an implicit instance service account. When using nondefault or noninstance credentials, two more properties must be specified:

```
<property>
  <name>google.cloud.auth.service.account.email</name>
  <value>svc-test@ian-acme.iam.gserviceaccount.com</value>
</property>
<property>
  <name>google.cloud.auth.service.account.keyfile</name>
  <value>creds/ian-acme-35acea0addbe.p12</value>
</property>
```

Note that the keyfile resides on a local disk, so it should be either placed on each node or (preferred) shipped with a job using MapReduce or Spark distributed cache mechanisms. As with all files that contain passwords (keytabs, SSH private key files, and credentials files), the file contents should be protected with strict file permissions.

The service account (which is just another IAM member) can be granted access permissions to buckets and objects using policies or ACLs.

User account.   When accessing user data (which might not be in the same GCP account), a user account and credentials have to be specified via three configuration parameters. This involves a two-phase authorization process—the OAuth 2.0 installed application authentication flow (*http://bit.ly/2OWwWXM*). In the first phase, a logged-in user creates an OAuth client ID using the Google API console. The resultant client ID and secret are placed into the Hadoop configuration, as shown here (IDs shortened with ellipses):

```
<property>
  <!-- Set to false to turn on client auth flow -->
  <name>google.cloud.auth.service.account.enable</name>
  <value>false</value>
</property>
<property>
  <name>google.cloud.auth.client.id</name>
  <value>17022934910...nfp.apps.googleusercontent.com</value>
</property>
<property>
  <name>google.cloud.auth.client.secret</name>
  <value>34Q_J86ZhkjhsgTRYDco2wR8XNz</value>
</property>
```

As part of the installed application workflow, the user has to issue a one-time authorization to allow the application to access data on its behalf. In this case, with the previous configuration in place, run (output edited for clarity):

```
$ hdfs dfs -ls gs://ian-testing/test-noaa/
17/09/25 15:20:24 INFO gcs.GoogleHadoopFileSystemBase:
  GHFS version: 1.6.0-hadoop2
Please open the following address in your browser:
  https://accounts.google.com/o/oauth2/auth?
  client_id=170229349103-fg7d9...p.apps.googleusercontent.com&
  redirect_uri=urn:ietf:wg:oauth:2.0:oob&response_type=code&
  scope=https://www.googleapis.com/auth/devstorage.full_control
Please enter code:
```

The user can open the URL (note the OAuth scope of full_control here), obtain the code, and supply it to the command-line tool, which writes a JSON credentials file to

~/.credentials/storage.json. This file can be copied (taking care with permissions) and referenced via the following property:[2]

```
<property>
  <name>fs.gs.auth.client.file</name>
  <value>/home/ibuss/storage.json</value>
</property>
```

The obtained credentials file has an expiration lifetime, but it also has a refresh token that the application can use to obtain a new access token.

Further information. Much more detail can be found in the official documentation. Some useful starting points include:

- Hadoop integration (*http://bit.ly/2S5aKfN*)
- OAuth 2.0 flows (*http://bit.ly/2zi4gmO*)
- IAM for cloud storage (*http://bit.ly/2A6VQOU*)
- Authentication mechanisms (*http://bit.ly/2QZciYE*)

Microsoft Azure

As we introduced in "Azure storage options" on page 465, Azure offers virtual hard disks (VHDs) for VM disk storage as well as the Azure Blob storage client (*http://bit.ly/2OWNrmv*) and ADLS (*http://bit.ly/2PMOR8J*) as secondary storage layers.

Unlike Google and Amazon, Microsoft had the advantage of an existing mature identity management service in AD, and Azure makes extensive use of this. Azure Storage uses a cloud-based version of AD, which can also be integrated with existing on-premises AD installations.

Authorization is managed through AD RBAC for storage account administration, like creation of storage accounts and generation of keys (so-called *management plane authorization*). Access control for data (*data plane authorization*) is handled slightly differently in each storage offering, as discussed in the next few sections.

Disk storage

You can use Azure RBAC to assign three different roles on the management plane to several users on a managed disk. Users can be *owners*, who manage everything including access, *contributors*, who manage everything except access itself, or *readers*, who can view anything but cannot make changes. Operations on the management

---

2 Note that, at the time of this writing, the documentation in the project incorrectly lists this property as `google.cloud.auth.client.file`.

plane include being able to copy the contents of the disk to another storage account. Permissions on the data plane obviously depend simply on what the disk is attached to.

Blob storage

An Azure Blob storage account has permanent access credentials, referred to as access keys, which can be used for programmatic access to data stored in Blob storage. These access keys should be carefully protected because they grant full access to your container and its contents.

In addition to permanent access keys, temporary access credentials can be issued in the form of *shared access signatures* (SASs). These are URI parameters that include an authentication token and that define which level of access has been granted on given resources (such as storage accounts, containers, or blobs) and for how long. For example:

```
?sv=2017-04-17
&ss=b&srt=sco&sp=rwdlac
&se=2017-09-26T00:12:14Z
&st=2017-09-25T16:12:14Z
&spr=https
&sig=FSvKMt62%2F23xo7od2VbLtm24AunhRPEs6gmJ3Du5%2FWc%3D
```

The SAS is signed by an access key, and the Blob storage service is able to validate a SAS with a supplied signature and parameters using the same underlying key. If you generate SASs with a similar template multiple times, you can save these as *stored access policies*.

ADLS

ADLS uses Azure AD for authentication and authorization of account-level functions and POSIX ACLs for data access control:

- RBAC roles can be assigned to users and groups in Azure AD and largely define which management functions a user or group can perform, such as assigning users to roles or creating roles. From a data access perspective, only the *Owner* role has full unfettered access to all data within the Data Lake Store. All other RBAC-defined roles are subject to POSIX ACLs.

- POSIX ACLs can be applied to resources in ADLS (root folder, subfolders, and files). These ACLs should be extremely familiar to HDFS or Linux system administrators as they follow the POSIX approach of *owner*, *group*, and *other* being granted read, write, and/or execute access. Up to nine additional custom ACLs can be added, and the documentation recommends making use of AD groups when defining access on resources.

ADLS makes use of OAuth 2.0 access tokens in a similar way to Google Cloud Storage and provides for both service account and user account access:

Service account access
> To enable service account access, Azure allows an administrator to create applications in Azure AD and to assign these applications to the ADLS storage account. Each application has a unique ID and can have one or more access keys generated for it. In addition, an Azure account has a URL endpoint from which OAuth 2.0 access tokens can be obtained using the application ID (referred to as the client ID in the Hadoop integration) and the access key.

User account access
> A user who wants to access data must log in and obtain a refresh token, which can be used by an application to obtain OAuth 2.0 access tokens on behalf of the user. The aforementioned URL token endpoint can be used to obtain refresh tokens. The process is a standard OAuth 2.0 authorization flow (*http://bit.ly/2r0zWc2*).

Hadoop integration

Integration with Azure Blob storage and ADLS is built in as modules in Apache Hadoop.

Azure Blob storage. Although using ADLS is advised for Hadoop workloads, objects stored in Blob storage can also be read via the `hadoop-azure` module (*http://bit.ly/2OW9zxs*).[3]

Blobs are referenced using URLs of the form *wasb[s]://<container>@<storageaccount>.blob.core.windows.net/path/within/container*. Although insecure access over HTTP is possible, the TLS-secured *wasbs://* scheme should be used.

Authenticated access to Blob storage is configured by providing one of the two access keys for the storage account in the following property in *core-site.xml* (example values formatted to fit on page):

```
<property>
  <name>
    fs.azure.account.key.mystorageact.blob.core.windows.net
  </name>
  <value>ZWNkODAyODk0OTE5...kUQ1oiUkFDstp3C2v4u9ELQ==</value>
</property>
```

---

3 Note that we tested the integration using Hadoop 3.

This parameter can be placed in a credentials provider file to keep the shared secret out of configuration files. (Note that this does not mean that only the right people can read the value. Filesystem permissions need to be in place for that.)

There is also a mechanism for making use of SASs by creating a REST service that issues such tokens on demand. For further details, see the Hadoop documentation (*http://bit.ly/2AckYnp*).

ADLS. ADLS support is provided by the `hadoop-azure-datalake` module (*http://bit.ly/2A8DahS*). Configuration properties are added to the *core-site.xml* file to define the authentication credentials. For service accounts, we simply supply the following parameters (example values again formatted to fit the page):

```
<property>
  <name>fs.adl.oauth2.access.token.provider.type</name>
  <value>ClientCredential</value>
</property>
<property>
  <name>fs.adl.oauth2.refresh.url</name>
  <value>https://login.microsoftonline.com/...</value>
</property>
<property>
  <name>fs.adl.oauth2.client.id</name>
  <value>c18781a0-286f-431c-a28f-c378db1cd444</value>
</property>
<property>
  <name>fs.adl.oauth2.credential</name>
  <value>ZDQwN...jOS/0/TNjLTgyYmMtYzEwNzU1NjE=</value>
</property>
```

For user accounts, a refresh token must first be obtained, as noted earlier. Armed with this, we can configure *core-site.xml* as follows:

```
<property>
  <name>fs.adl.oauth2.access.token.provider.type</name>
  <value>ClientCredential</value>
</property>
<property>
  <name>fs.adl.oauth2.client.id</name>
  <value>c18781a0-286f-431c-a28f-c378db1cd444</value>
</property>
<property>
  <name>fs.adl.oauth2.refresh.token</name>
  <value>fdb8fdbecf1d03ce5e6125c067733c0d51de209c</value>
</property>
```

Again, Hadoop credentials files can be used to protect these parameters.

Further information

You can find additional reading and more information at the following links:

- Overview of security in ADLS (*http://bit.ly/2S1MSd3*)
- AD authentication in ADLS (*http://bit.ly/2S6F6yP*)
- Sample REST calls for OAuth 2.0 authentication flows (*http://bit.ly/2S6NZbD*)
- Azure Storage security guide (*http://bit.ly/2OThdbV*)
- Apache Hadoop Azure Blob Storage Support (*http://bit.ly/2OW9zxs*)
- Apache Hadoop Azure Data Lake Support (*http://bit.ly/2A8DahS*)

Auditing

There are two aspects to auditing Hadoop clusters when running in the cloud. For sticky and suspendable clusters, there is the traditional auditing functionality of the frameworks and services running within the cluster—HDFS access, Hive and Impala queries, HBase queries, and more.

Unlike in a typical on-premises cluster, in the cloud, users and applications on one-off and sticky clusters often source their data from services running elsewhere in the cloud. The most obvious and prevalent example is accessing data in object storage (Amazon S3 and Google Cloud Storage, among others), but others include services like Amazon AWS DynamoDB. For on-demand processing, such as that provided by Cloudera Altus or EMR, there is auditing around the creation of on-demand clusters and the running of workloads. Documenting the full audit capabilities of the cloud providers is beyond the scope of this book, but here are some useful links to get you started:

- Cloud Audit Logging (*http://bit.ly/2S3uqRn*)
- Cloud Audit Logging with Google Cloud Storage (*http://bit.ly/2qY04V4*)
- AWS CloudTrail (*https://amzn.to/2S9PtC3*)
- Amazon S3 Server Access Logging (*https://amzn.to/2PC593U*)
- Azure logging and auditing (*http://bit.ly/2PF0Bd3*)

Encryption for Data at Rest

Encryption is a key criterion for many organizations to move to the cloud. On the one hand, there are obvious attack vectors that encryption protects against, which we decribe in "Environmental Risks" on page 515. However, many requirements for encryption in the cloud stem from legal obligations.

Consider, for example, the following scenario. Under EU data protection law, individuals may revoke consent to process their data at any time and may also demand the physical deletion of the data. A regular delete operation often just unlinks data from its metadata, with no deliberate action to overwrite or physically destroy the data in question. Encryption provides an easy proof that data is indeed inaccessible, even if unauthorized users were to gain access to the physical media. Depending on the granularity of encryption operations, it is also possible to destroy the key and thereby ensure that the data is permanently inaccessible. This is an important consideration because the question of who is liable for ensuring deletion of user data often cannot be answered in an easy way and is deemed a subject for future case law.

This is only one example of why establishing an encryption strategy may be among the most important tasks in order to achieve clearance to run enterprise workloads in the cloud, depending on your specific location and legal requirements.

Increasingly, as more mission-critical workloads are moved to the cloud, it is also important to understand the amount of lock-in to a given platform such a choice entails.

Requirements for Key Material

Typically, enterprises have very high standards for key material creation and persistence. On-premises encryption is typically taken care of by the local security team, which simply has a trusted source of cryptographically strong key material. In the cloud, the discussion is about whether the cloud provider can be trusted to achieve the same standards, or it would assist you in proving the standards had been met when liability is unclear.

Typical requirements for key material in encryption use cases include:

Confidentiality
> The most obvious requirement is to guarantee that gaining access to the key material is impossible. For example, HDFS Transparent Data Encryption (TDE), which we covered in Chapter 9, uses a Java KeyStore (JKS) to persist keys by default, which is simply based on a file. A plain file in the filesystem alongside the main cluster provides too much of an attack vector for many organizations, which is why Hadoop distributors supply alternative key stores, as already covered.

High availability
> The keys must never be inaccessible or even lost, because all of the encrypted data would be inaccessible or even lost along with them.

High quality
> The strength of cryptographic material depends, for example, on a true source of random data to provide for sufficient entropy when keys are created.

Such requirements are regulated in much more detail by quality standards such as the Federal Information Processing Standard (FIPS) or Payment Card Industry (PCI) standard, among others. Meeting these standards often is a legal obligation for organizations, which are required to achieve certification of their products and services.

Options for Encryption in the Cloud

Let's begin with a high-level overview of the feasible options for encrypting your data in the cloud. We will look at the options in more detail in the following sections of this chapter.

Figure 18-4 illustrates three available options. Note that all the options use a hierarchy of keys, in which lower-level keys are encrypted with higher-level keys and, ultimately, with a master key, as we introduced in "HDFS Transparent Data Encryption" on page 274.

In all of the options, some of the low-level keys materialize in plain text in the memory of the cloud provider's compute infrastructure for a limited amount of time.

Briefly, these options can be summarized as follows:

Option 1: On-premises key persistence

This option allows you to maintain your master keys in your own datacenter within a key persistence layer such as Cloudera Key Trustee. The master keys are kept only transiently in the HDFS Key Management Server (KMS) service. Although it is the most rigid form of key management in the cloud, it is also by far the most complex option. The encryption is conducted by HDFS client programs on the HDFS block level, which also means that this method works only for HDFS content and not for data in object storage implementations such as Amazon S3 or ADLS. We consider the feasibility of this method in more detail in "On-Premises Key Persistence" on page 539.

Option 2: In-cloud key persistence

In this option, the cloud provider creates and maintains all key material, including master keys, in a special key management solution, typically backed by a hardware security module on the cloud provider's premises. The encryption is conducted at or below the storage volume level, depending on the cloud provider's implementation. The mechanics of this option are largely transparent to Hadoop. This option is generally very convenient and not complex, but it strongly depends on the individual cloud provider's service, which we look at in detail in "Encryption via the Cloud Provider" on page 539.

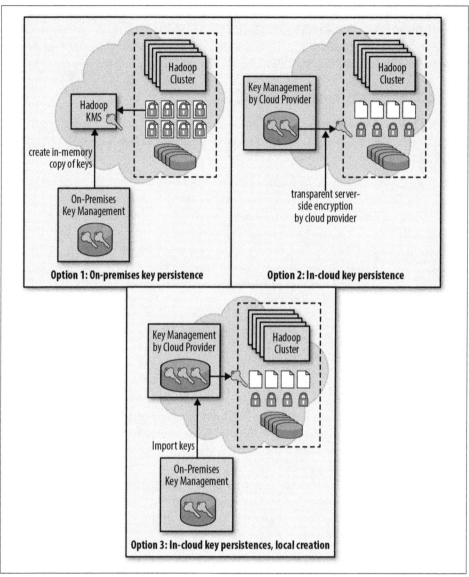

Figure 18-4. High-level options for encryption in the cloud

Option 3: In-cloud key persistence with local key creation (BYOK)

This option is the same as Option 2, except that the master keys are created locally and then imported into the cloud provider's key management solution via a secure channel. This concept is also commonly referred to as *bring your own key* (BYOK), and we cover it in more detail in "BYOK" on page 542. As with Option 2, this option will place your master keys on the cloud provider's hardware security module (HSM), but they originate from your own key management solution.

In our experience, these are the main possibilities. Theoretically, other approaches could be pursued, but we do not feel that they would add value compared to what we outline here. We can further summarize the options as follows:

Option 1
Keep master keys on your premises only, resulting in a complex split into a cloud and an on-premises portion

Options 2 + 3
Take advantage of the cloud providers' integrated key management solutions.

The following sections cover them in more depth, with a focus on the latter options.

On-Premises Key Persistence

When implementing on-premises key persistence, data is directly encrypted in Hadoop via HDFS TDE, as described in Chapter 9. If you are already familiar with HDFS TDE, you will understand Option 1.

However, you should carefully consider whether the number of deposit requests to your key persistence layer might have a performance impact for your use cases, given that the communication takes place over a VPN connection. The number of encryption and decryption operations depends on the query system that accesses the underlying HDFS infrastructure as well as user behavior and, most importantly, the number of users and the size of your cluster.

Encryption via the Cloud Provider

In this section, we look at the details of in-cloud key persistence and how cloud service providers implement their solutions around this.

A central piece in this discussion is the concept of a key management service (KMS). We introduce KMSs conceptually, as well as BYOK and server-side encryption. After this, we look at the options you have with each of our three cloud providers.

Later, in "Encryption Feature and Interoperability Summary" on page 547, we provide side-by-side comparisons of key management solutions combined with Hadoop products.

Are My Keys Secure?

For many organizations, this is the *Gretchenfrage* (*http://bit.ly/2S6Oz9j*) of moving critical data to the cloud.

Local law may be at odds with the legislation of the country in which the cloud provider is incorporated. For services rendered in the EU, this complexity is compounded by the recently introduced GDPR legislation, which regulates that service providers in their relationship with end users are liable for certain operations on data performed by subcontractors. These service providers, in turn, would be cloud providers, in our discussion.

Because the services live by economies of scale, you should assume that your provider will attempt to accommodate multiple tenants on the overall solution. Just like with your own infrastructure, it would not be economical to purchase a separate HSM fleet per use case. Therefore, the cloud provider requires administrative access to backing HSMs in order to properly maintain the service.

AWS and Azure offer HSMs to persist the key material. Some designs, like Azure Key Vault, partner with a third-party HSM provider, whereas AWS has moved over to provide its own implementation of HSMs. All vendors state that key deposits cannot be exported.

Requests by law enforcement to cloud providers to surrender certain data are common and documented by both AWS (*http://bit.ly/2TxcqR1*) and Azure, the latter of which lists regular law enforcement requests (*http://bit.ly/2Q4O42b*) separately from US national security orders (*http://bit.ly/2Ttd7e7*). To our knowledge, there is no precedent for what would happen if the surrender of key material was demanded and it's not clear whether the underlying KMSs would succeed at technologically preventing this.

Cloud Key Management Services

A key management service is conceptually similar to the KMS component in HDFS TDE, but it manages encryption keys for all conceivable uses cases in the cloud.

A KMS persists *master keys* (MKs), which are used for envelope encryption, as we introduced in "At-Rest Encryption" on page 270. Client applications can then request, via an API, the encryption of lower-level keys with the MK. In the example shown in Figure 18-5, the client application is a storage system that provides a storage volume, and the lower-level key is a *volume key* (VK).

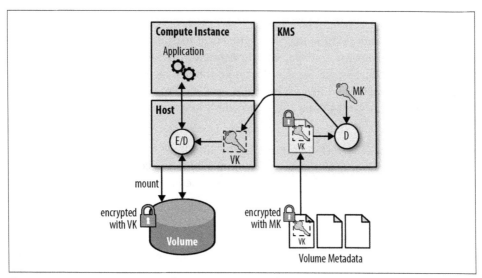

Figure 18-5. Transparent envelope encryption with a KMS

When the compute instance on the host requests data from the volume, the host transparently retrieves the encrypted form of the VK from the volume itself and sends it to the KMS for decryption. The host then transparently performs encryption and decryption operations for the compute instance.

A KMS client can really be anything. It could also be software running in the compute instance, a user wanting to directly store a secret for an application, or, as in the example, another cloud service that requires key management. AWS, for example, uses AWS KMS to provide transparent encryption in the case of Amazon Elastic Block Store (EBS) volume encryption. In this case, the service itself transparently encrypts the data and automatically manages key creation and usage, and you still have the option of explicitly controlling which keys are used.

When evaluating a KMS solution you should look for the following:

- Is it fully programmable via APIs? Which languages are supported?
- Does it fully integrate with the corresponding identity and authorization solutions of the cloud provider?
- Does it support a way to import keys? (We cover this in "BYOK" on page 542.)
- Can you rotate and revoke keys, and is data maybe even automatically reencrypted after a rotate?

Server-side and client-side encryption

Server-side encryption (SSE) is mainly a syntactical marker, meaning that encryption and key management are transparently integrated into a storage service. In Azure, SSE is shorthand for Storage Service Encryption, but it signifies the exact same concept. *Client-side encryption* means, basically, you encrypt data yourself, and you can typically still take advantage of a cloud provider's key management infrastructure for it.

In our description of at-rest encryption in the cloud, we focus on SSE. But you can think of Hadoop transparent data encryption, which we covered in "On-Premises Key Persistence" on page 539, as an example of client-side encryption that does its own key management.

BYOK

Let us consider the following scenario: an organization requests a cloud provider to prove the strength of cryptographic material that the provider creates. To do so for a specific customer key, the cloud provider must examine it, which is typically not desired by the customer. To get around this particular problem, the customer can create the key itself and import it into the cloud provider's key management solution.

This scenario is commonly also referred to as "bring your own key" and is supported by both Azure and AWS. This was the third option (in-cloud key persistence with local key creation) that we introduced in "Options for Encryption in the Cloud" on page 537. In addition to the ability to prove the strength of the key, common drivers for BYOK include the ability to retain an offline copy for disaster recovery purposes and the ability to share key material between cloud and on-premises applications.

The import is typically constrained to master keys, which then can be used to create (and encrypt) further application-specific keys. BYOK might require you to manually reencrypt your data when you roll a master key. Some providers also explicitly support control of imported key expiration and guarantee that your imported keys are automatically deleted after expiration.

Encryption in AWS

You can achieve at-rest encryption in multiple ways on AWS. With the exception of ephemeral instance storage, all storage services in AWS support built-in encryption, where encryption keys are transparently managed by AWS. As introduced in "AWS storage options" on page 459 for Hadoop, AWS EBS, S3, and ephemeral instance storage are relevant storage options for direct use with Hadoop. With the exception of instance storage, it is possible to provide data encryption without any Hadoop involvement. In addition, Amazon offers a dedicated key management service, AWS KMS, to go beyond the features of the built-in encryption alternatives. Let's take a closer look at the options.

AWS KMS

This is the KMS service within AWS. It consolidates key management operations for customers and integrates key management seamlessly with a variety of other services. It is used internally by other AWS services, such as EBS. KMS comprises user-facing hosts that implement the KMS API as well as a layer of hardened hosts in the backend to which the KMS hosts delegate the actual cryptographic operations, such as key generation, encryption, and decryption.

The hosts in the backend are a combination of hardware security appliances (HSAs) and hardware security modules (HSMs). In previous versions of KMS, AWS relied on SafeNet Luna appliances to implement the HSM layer, but it has transitioned to a custom HSM design (*http://bit.ly/2DFoRov*) owned by AWS itself. Encryption and decryption in AWS KMS only occur on HSAs and HSMs, which process key material in volatile memory. The HSAs return their results via secured transport to the KMS hosts in encrypted form. The KMS service automatically scales and is highly available.

KMS refers to MKs as *customer master keys* (CMKs), which are at the top of the key hierarchy. Authorized users can create *customer data keys* underneath a CMK. When saved, CMKs are encrypted with a *domain key*. The domain key is rotated daily. Accordingly, existing CMKs are reencrypted on a daily basis. Applications can use the securely transferred plain-text version of the key to encrypt, before disposing of it. The KMS-encrypted version of the key is stored in the application's metadata. The encrypted key can only be decrypted by invoking the KMS service.

AWS KMS provides rich authentication and access control of customer requests, including integration with AWS IAM. It also offers the ability to import master keys via its API to implement BYOK patterns. An imported key can be locally created and is then encrypted with a public key, which has been made available by a preceding KMS API call. Imported master keys can be configured to expire at a given point in time.

AWS KMS allows automatic rotation of master keys and can automatically re-encrypt data in the background, if the corresponding master keys are created in KMS. Imported master keys cannot be automatically rotated. A manual key rotation may require manual reencryption of your data; AWS provides a whitepaper (*http://bit.ly/2A724hD*) that contains further details.

Instance storage

As covered in "AWS storage options" on page 459, some instance types in AWS EC2 have local disks outside of the EBS world, called *instance storage*. On those instances, it necessary to fall back to client-side encryption, as outlined in the AWS Security Blog (*https://amzn.to/2qWMWiG*), for example.

EBS

EBS provides built-in encryption capabilities (*https://amzn.to/2BkO5GS*), for which it uses KMS to encrypt/decrypt a VK and performs the encryption transparently in the hypervisor, as shown in Figure 18-5. As implied by the name, the VK is specific to the EBS volume which is encrypted. KMS is the only entity that can decrypt the VK using a CMK. You can explicitly configure which CMK to use, including imported keys. By default, when you do not configure a key, EBS uses an automatically created key.

S3

S3 supports both client-side encryption and server-side encryption. SSE is requested as part of the S3 REST API (*https://amzn.to/2KmL6kl*); for example, during a put request, SSE is available in three modes (*https://amzn.to/2zkmdBo*):

- Keys managed directly by S3 (SSE-S3)

- Keys managed by AWS KMS, including BYOK (SSE-KMS)

- Keys supplied by the application (SSE-C); the key must be supplied via HTTPs for each operation

Encryption in Microsoft Azure

Just like AWS, Microsoft Azure offers multiple ways to encrypt data at rest. As we covered in "Azure storage options" on page 465, all storage offerings in Azure that are relevant to Hadoop are either based on Blob storage or ADLS. Both of these offerings come with built-in, transparent encryption support and provide full integration with Azure's dedicated key management service, Azure Key Vault. The options are:

Key Vault

Similar to AWS KMS, Azure Key Vault is a KMS that can persist and supply encryption keys to other services in Azure. Many of those services use it internally and transparently to manage their encryption keys. Microsoft itself depends on Key Vault and specifies high fault tolerance and corresponding availability SLAs (*http://bit.ly/2PGKr31*). Keys in Key Vault are not part of any hierarchy. They also cannot be exported or modified after they have been provisioned.

Microsoft does not expose exact details of the hardware components in its documentation (*http://bit.ly/2Fve2HU*). However, it optionally offers an HSM-based persistence layer (*http://bit.ly/2DO65vH*) in its perimeter, similar to AWS KMS. For this, Key Vault uses third-party HSMs by Thales.

Key Vault is most commonly used to transparently supply encryption keys for Azure Blob storage SSE (*http://bit.ly/2ziBbIi*), but it also supports BYOK. It relies on a process designed for the safe transport and import of customer key material, as described in the Azure documentation (*http://bit.ly/2Fv7d9a*). With a sup-

---

ported Thales HSM appliance, it is possible to create a key on-premises, which can then be securely imported by encrypting it with a key encryption key (KEK) from Key Vault. The KEK is asymmetric, and the private portion only exists on the Thales HSM in Key Vault. Thales attests that neither the private portion of the KEK nor the imported key will leave the HSM.

You can use multiple programming languages when accessing Key Vault, among them Java, Node.js, and a REST API.

Key Vault also supports access control and integration with AD for identity management. If vault-wide configuration actions are performed, RBAC from Azure Portal or its REST API is used. For actual key operations, so-called *key vault access policies* (*http://bit.ly/2DQmVdE*), which map privileges on keys to roles, are used.

In addition, Key Vault can automatically rotate keys and collect audit logs.

Azure Blob storage
Encryption on Azure Blob storage is simply called Storage Service Encryption (SSE), and transparently uses Azure Key Vault. Keys in Key Vault are transparently created after the customer enables encryption on the storage account level in the Azure UI. Azure recently started to support an option for bringing your own key when enabling SSE.

Managed disks and VHDs
Managed disks and VHDs can be encrypted by simply enabling SSE, as just described, on the storage account level. Alternatively, it is possible to use *Azure Disk Encryption* (ADE) (*http://bit.ly/2OSMOKQ*) to encrypt individual disks. ADE and SSE exist as side-by-side alternatives.

Although SSE is performed within the storage service, ADE takes place in the VM. Cryptographic operations are performed via *dm-crypt* in Linux VMs and via BitLocker in Windows VMs. When enabled via the Azure UI or PowerShell commands, Azure can directly encrypt the underlying VHD and can configure the use of those services accordingly in the operating system's storage subsystem.

ADE is directly integrated with Key Vault. However, a given key vault needs to be explicitly enabled for disk encryption, after which keys can be created for ADE. Additionally, a key vault access policy and Azure AD permissions for ADE need to be established. In summary, ADE can be thought of as client-side encryption integrated at the operating system level. A full example of the necessary steps can be studied in Microsoft's documentation (*http://bit.ly/2qZ8SK7*).

ADLS

ADLS supports fully transparent encryption (*http://bit.ly/2Q7PatL*). As opposed to Key Vault, ADLS uses a hierarchy of keys to encrypt data via envelope encryption. Encryption in ADLS is configured on the ADLS account level. A *master encryption key* (MEK) in Azure Key Vault encrypts a *data encryption key* (DEK).

The MEK is only persisted on Key Vault and never leaves its perimeter. The DEK is stored in ADLS, but only in encrypted form. The DEK can only be decrypted in Azure Key Vault. The DEK exists in decrypted form only in memory (in the cache). The MEK can be either an imported (customer-managed) key or an Azure-managed key.

This choice of an imported key versus an Azure-managed key has to be made when encryption for an ADLS account is enabled and cannot be changed later on. An MEK can only be explicitly be revoked when it is a customer-managed key.

The blocks themselves are encrypted by a *block enryption key* (BEK), which is specifically generated for each block from the DEK and the block's data itself. The BEK is not saved, is only generated on demand, and is discarded after an encryption or decryption operation.

Encryption in GCP

Google also offers a variety of ways to encrypt data at rest. Persistent disks in Google Compute Engine and in Google Cloud Storage (GCS) are encrypted by default, and Google transparently manages encryption keys. In addition, Google provides a KMS called Cloud KMS that lets you control the process of creating and managing encryption keys. The options are:

Cloud KMS

With Google Cloud KMS, you can generate encryption keys that protect your data on persistent disks and GCS, and you can centrally manage those keys. The keys in Cloud KMS are master keys (KEKs). They are used to encrypt the actual DEKs on the storage services, as we introduced in Figure 18-5.

You can also centrally rotate and revoke keys. When you rotate a key, Cloud KMS automatically knows whether to use an older version or the new version, but it does not reencrypt data in the background. BYOK is not possible with Cloud KMS, because it does not provide a way to import your own keys. However, as we you'll see later in this list, persistent disks and GCS allow you to specify your own key when creating disks or objects.

Google does not provide many details around exactly how keys in Cloud KMS are persisted, but it specifies that Cloud KMS does not use HSMs.

Local SSDs

Local SSDs are always transparently encrypted with an ephemeral key generated by Google. The key is only materialized within the context of the VM and is bound to the life cycle of the disk. Local SSDs, however, cannot be encrypted with customer-supplied keys and do not support integration with Cloud KMS.

Persistent disks

As mentioned earlier, persistent disks are encrypted by default. Google transparently creates the required encryption keys when you create the disks for a VM and automatically recovers them when resuming after a prior suspend operation. Google also permits use of keys created in Cloud KMS (*http://bit.ly/2OQmTTT*) to wrap the disk encryption keys, which gives you a way to centrally manage disk encryption and helps you to better separate duties.

When you create a persistent disk, you can also import your own key material (*http://bit.ly/2A6MpiE*), which Google then uses to wrap its own key material that is used for actual disk encryption. To protect your key during import, you can also wrap it with an RSA public key that Google provides.

However, this happens outside of Cloud KMS and Google does not persist the imported keys. This means that, when you use imported keys on a persistent disk and you resume instances with such disks, you must provide the key as part of the restart operation.

GCS

Similar to persistent disks, GCS always encrypts (*http://bit.ly/2Fx3E2i*) data on the server side before it gets written to physical disks. Google transparently uses envelope encryption with regularly rotated master keys.

In addition, GCS allows you to configure keys stored in Cloud KMS to be used as master keys for GCS buckets or objects. This method of key management is referred to as customer-managed keys (*http://bit.ly/2DORpMS*).

Alternatively, and similarly to importing keys for persistent disks, you can also supply your own key material for GCS, but such customer-supplied keys (*http://bit.ly/2PBPfXg*) can neither be imported into Cloud KMS nor are they persisted in any way. This means that you must supply the key for each GCS API operation.

Encryption Feature and Interoperability Summary

We have established by now that encryption in the cloud for Hadoop leaves us with a daunting number of configurations and ramifications to consider. In this section, we recapitulate the facts with side-by-side listings of the technologies used in this chapter's solutions.

Table 18-1 shows how the various storage solutions of cloud providers integrate with their key management solutions.

Table 18-1. Cloud storage solution integration with key management

Feature	Integrated key management by provider?	Integrated with provider's KMS solution?	BYOK via provider's KMS solution?	BYOK standalone?
AWS EBS	Yes, automatic KMS interaction	Yes	Yes	No, EBS uses AWS KMS internally
AWS S3	Yes, standalone key management by S3	Yes	Yes	Yes, key is provided for each operation
Azure managed disks	Yes, SSE by default	Yes	Yes	No
Azure ADLS	Yes	Yes	Yes, Key Vault + customer managed keys	Yes, Key Vault + service managed keys
Azure Blob storage	Yes	Yes	Yes	Yes
Google persistent disks	Yes	No	Yes	Yes, key must be provided whenever instance is started
GCS	Yes	Yes	No	Yes, key is provided for each operation

Table 18-2 provides key facts on the BYOK solutions we studied in this chapter.

Table 18-2. Considerations for BYOK

Feature	Confidential user key import?	Colocation of keys with other tenants?	Protection against export of imported master keys via API?
AWS KMS	Yes, AWS	Yes	Yes (HSM is managed by AWS)
SSE-S3	No import, but key is provided via HTTPS for each operation	Yes	Yes, only stores customer key's HMAC for verification
Azure Key Vault	Yes, Azure provides public key to wrap secret	Yes	Yes (HSM is managed by Azure)
Google Cloud KMS	No	Yes	Yes
Cloudera Navigator KMS	N/A	No	Yes
Hortonworks Ranger KMS	N/A	No	Yes

Table 18-3 shows a more detailed comparison between various key management solutions.

Table 18-3. Enterprise integration features for key management solutions

Feature	Hardware implementation	Scalability	Manual management overhead	Need to manually ensure HA	Key access control
AWS KMS	AWS custom design	Automatic, 1,000 master keys per account and region]	Very low	No (11 9s durability)	Integrated (AWS IAM)
SSE-S3	Unknown	Automatic	Very low	No, integrated into S3 base functionality	Integrated via regular S3 access control
Azure Key Vault	Thales nShield HSM family	Automatic, transactions/s limits apply	Very low	No	Yes, integrated with Azure AD
Google Cloud KMS	No usage of HSMs	Automatic, account-specific quotas apply	Very low	No, SLAs apply	Integrated with Google Cloud IAM
Cloudera Navigator KMS	Software database, Thales HSMs or SafeNet (Gemalto) Luna/KeySecure HSMs	Manual	HSM and Hadoop distribution specific	Yes	Hadoop KMS ACLs
Hortonworks Ranger KMS	Software database or SafeNet Luna	Manual	HSM and Hadoop distribution specific	Yes	Hadoop KMS ACLs

Recommendations and Summary for Cloud Encryption

We have covered a lot of ground in this section. When you move big data applications to the cloud and you have a hard requirement for encryption, you should initially understand the options we've presented and your own requirements for key persistence:

On-premises key persistence

Although a price has to be paid in operational complexity, on-premises key persistence for Hadoop deployments in the cloud can fulfill the standards of confidentiality, high availability, and high quality of key material.

This is, to our knowledge, the only option that provides a practical way to avoid persistence of key material off-premises, but you should seriously consider whether you can maintain the complexity.

However, if you have an approved standard, fully educated security ops teams, and key administrators for Hadoop based on KTS/KMS on-premises and if you have the required approval and sign-offs by your security board, this might actually be simpler than getting approvals for encrypting mission-critical data in the cloud by an untested, internally unapproved methodology.

This option is not practical if you intend to support a large number of transient Hadoop clusters for spontaneous use cases in your organization.

In-cloud key persistence

If your requirements allow for persisting key material in the cloud, both Microsoft Azure and AWS offer a rich and easy-to-use feature set around encrypting data in all of their services. Google's Cloud KMS currently does not provide a way to bring your own key and does not provide HSMs.

But all in all, providers help to significantly ease the burden on your team of dealing with a rather complex technology stack around encrypting data in distributed systems. Also consider that you might not need full control over your key material for each and every use case. Plus, it is always good practice to encrypt, even if the data is not mission-critical.

In-cloud key persistence with local key creation

If you have specific requirements around key backups and the key creation process itself, those can easily be addressed by both providers we have covered that implement BYOK. When there are mere cautions and no legal requirements around in-cloud key persistence, BYOK can also help to reach middle ground by working with the key expiration features that are offered by some of the providers that we have discussed.

Encryption and safeguarding data for many use cases is one of the final pieces of the puzzle required for pervasive enterprise adoption of data-intensive cloud use cases. Although a detailed analysis of your requirements is most likely necessary, encrypting big data in Hadoop is already possible today.

Encrypting Data in Flight in the Cloud

We covered encryption in flight for Hadoop and other services from the big data realm in "In-Flight Encryption" on page 237. Unlike encryption at rest, encrypting data for Hadoop in flight is not any different in the cloud than in an on-premises scenario. Still, you should review a few basic points when considering in-flight encryption for Hadoop:

How does the cloud provider protect data in flight?

You must fundamentally decide whether the isolation mechanisms that the cloud providers give you are enough or whether you must encrypt network communication on top. All of the providers we've discussed give you a guarantee that traffic is completely isolated within the VPC boundaries via mechanisms like SDN and strict perimeter security. Google, for example, gives a thorough explanation of how perimeter security and automatic encryption in flight (*https:// cloud.google.com/security/encryption-in-transit/*) is used in GCP.

Which cluster services should use encryption in flight?

As we covered in "How Services Use a Network" on page 107 and "In-Flight Encryption" on page 237, there are many network communication flows within big data clusters, but a fair amount of those—for example, shuffle traffic during a Spark job—by design, never leave the local network. It may be sufficient in your organization to protect only certain web UIs, such as the Spark History Server web UI.

How can I manage certificates for services in the cloud?

If you do decide to implement encryption in flight for all or some services on your big data clusters, the hard work boils down to certificate management, as with any other application that you move to the cloud. Where the certificates are created and how the chain of trust works heavily depends on your organization and exceeds the scope of this book. To get started, you should try to determine which of the following scenarios applies in your case:

- Your cluster's certificates are issued by a single on-premises root CA.

- Your root CA could be based in the cloud. Examples include AWS Certificate Manager (*https://amzn.to/2Qcjaou*) or Azure AD (*http://bit.ly/2FMz3OH*).

- You are running an intermediate CA in the cloud that issues certificates for your cluster which are signed by your on-premises root CA.

Perimeter Controls and Firewalling

As we saw in "Network Architecture" on page 484, all cloud providers offer network virtualization and isolation between tenants, and instances are deployed into these virtual networks. By default, access to the instances via the virtual networks is locked down from outside access, and often nodes are not allocated a public IP at all. Access to the instances is controlled by virtual network firewalls, internet gateways, and security groups. Virtual networks can also be made to be extensions of an on-premises network via VPN gateways without having to assign cloud instances external IP addresses.

> The security around VPNs is beyond the scope of this book. For more on this topic, see *Network Security Assessment*, 3rd Edition, by Chris McNab (O'Reilly).

Understanding the various options is essential to any architect wishing to put together secure Hadoop clusters in the cloud. Because each provider manages these aspects slightly differently, in the following sections we provide a brief overview of the perimeter controls for virtual networks and instances as they relate to Hadoop.

But before diving into the details for each provider, let's recap some of the recommended essentials of Hadoop cluster network security and enlighten our discussion with an example. One of the recommended deployment setups (whether on-premises or in the cloud) has network firewalls controlling outside access to all cluster nodes (see Chapter 11). In general, the worker nodes should not be accessible from outside of the perimeter—access by users should be mediated via edge services operating on well-known ports, which can be exposed by a firewall to a range of source IPs. Ideally, edge service nodes host services, such as HttpFS, HiveServer2, Hue, Impala load balancers, the HBase REST server, and more, that obviate the requirement for users to talk directly to worker nodes.

In some cases, though, applications running outside the cluster may need access to worker nodes—for example, if they are using HBase or Kudu directly—but the list of ports exposed to external clients should be limited. Between the cluster nodes, however, we strongly recommend that all network communication be allowed to avoid having to maintain a long (and potentially mutable) list of host-port rules.

 There are valid reasons for deviating from this model, but we use it as a base for the following discussion.

We use a common example setup for all three providers, as shown in Figure 18-6. In the example, all cluster and application instances are deployed in the cloud inside a virtual network, called *bigdata*, which is connected to an enterprise on-premises network via a VPN. The cluster master, worker, and edge nodes are placed in a dedicated subnet, *futura*.

Within the cloud, applications running on instances in the *garamond* subnet need to use HBase and so need access to ports 2181 (ZooKeeper) and 60000 (HBase Master) on the master nodes, and port 60020 (HBase RegionServer) on the workers.

From the enterprise network, we have developers who want to review the progress and logs of YARN jobs (port 8080 on the masters and 8042 on the workers) and business users who want to use Hue (8889), submit Hive queries (10000) and Impala queries (21050), and run Oozie jobs (11443).

Note that these are just some of the possible ports that may need to be exposed. In a real deployment you would likely need to configure more rules to allow job submission, SSH access, and more, but this is enough for our example.

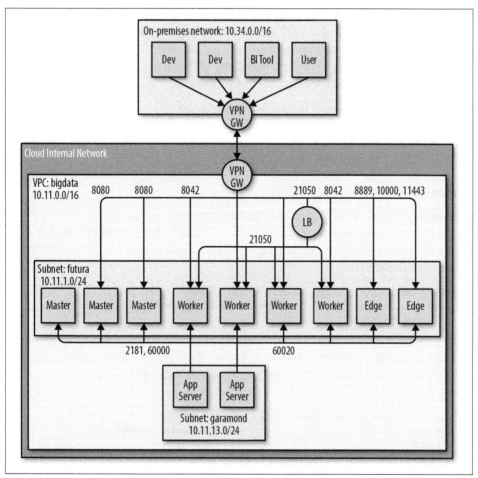

Figure 18-6. Example scenario for configuring perimeter controls

There will inevitably be aspects of network security that we do not cover in this section, but treat it as a primer for your use case and refer to the official documentation for definitive configuration specifics. For recommended network topologies and security, a good additional reference is Chapters 4 and 14 of *Moving Hadoop to the Cloud* (*http://bit.ly/2S1PBDl*) by Bill Havanki.

GCP

In GCP, VPCs are global resources with regional subnets, which can span availability zones. Network access control to instances is governed by firewall rules. All VPCs have base rules disallowing any ingress and allowing any egress traffic to and from any instance. The default VPC also comes with a set of default rules allowing all internal traffic, all external ICMP (such as *ping*), and all incoming SSH traffic.

Custom VPCs, which we assume we are using here, have no additional rules. Instances get a private IP within the VPC subnet for the region and can also have an external IP configured, although in general it is recommended that clusters not have public IPs assigned unless absolutely necessary. Unless using a VPN, any traffic from outside the VPC must use the external IP of an instance.

Firewall rules can be defined for particular protocols, source and destination ports, and source and destination IPs. In addition, sources and destinations can be specified using *network tags*. This is a very useful feature that we employ in our sample use case.

Example implementation

First, we want to allow all internal traffic between the cluster nodes, so all the instances need to be tagged with a common cluster identifier. In our example, we tag all of the cluster instances with a network tag of `futura` and create a firewall rule with the following parameters:

```
name=>futura-all-internal, network=>bigdata, priority=>16384,
    direction=>ingress, action=>allow, targets=>tag=futura,
    source=>tag=futura, protocols=all
```

Next, we want to allow general access to Hue, Oozie, and HiveServer2 running on the edge instances from any other instances within the VPC and from on-premises IPs via the VPN gateway. We tag the edge instances with `futura-edge` and define the following rule:

```
name=>futura-edge, network=>bigdata, priority=>8192,
    direction=>ingress, action=>allow, targets=>tag=futura-edge,
    source=>ip-ranges:10.34.0.0/16,
    secondary-source=>tag=bigdata,
    protocols=>tcp:8889;tcp:10000;tcp:11443
```

In addition, we want to allow developers to check the status and progress of their YARN jobs running on the cluster for which access to both the YARN ResourceManager and NodeManager UIs is required. In this example, we know that developers require access from on-premises machines running on the VPN.

 In general, it is preferable to set up a SOCKS proxy to allow web UI access rather than to rely on firewall rules.

Let's tag the worker machines with `futura-worker` and the master machines with `futura-master` and define the following firewall rules:

```
name=>futura-worker-dev, network=>bigdata, priority=>8192,
    direction=>ingress, action=>allow, targets=>tag=futura-worker,
    source=>ip-ranges:10.34.0.0/16, protocols=>tcp:8042

name=>futura-master-dev, network=>bigdata, priority=>8192,
    direction=>ingress, action=>allow, targets=>tag=futura-master,
    source=>ip-ranges:10.34.0.0/16, protocols=>tcp:8080
```

Finally, as in the example diagram (Figure 18-6), we want to allow an application running in the same VPC to access HBase. For efficiency, the application needs access to directly talk to the HBase RegionServers. The application server instances are running with a known service account, *garamond-app@bigdata-proj.iam.gserviceaccount.com* (an example of authorization based on instance credentials). Therefore, we create the following rules:

```
name=>futura-garamond-app-master, network=>bigdata,
    priority=>8192, direction=>ingress, action=>allow,
    source=>service-account=garamond-app@bigdata-...ceaccount.com,
    protocols=>tcp:2181,tcp:60000

name=>futura-garamond-app-worker, network=>bigdata,
    priority=>8192, direction=>ingress, action=>allow,
    source=>service-account=garamond-app@bigdata-...ceaccount.com,
    protocols=>tcp:60020
```

AWS

In AWS, VPCs are isolated networks and the basic building blocks of network security. A VPC can span an entire region and contain multiple subnets, each of which is located in a single availability zone. VPCs have a completely isolated IP address space, and subnets within the same VPC are composed of nonoverlapping slices of that space. Provided they have nonoverlapping IP spaces, VPCs can also be peered together. Like in GCP and Azure, instances in VPCs and subnets can route to the internet via internet gateways and can optionally be assigned publicly accessible IPs, in addition to the private IPs they are assigned by default.

From a network security standpoint, there are two features to consider. At a subnet level there are *network access control lists* (*https://amzn.to/2PBSduS*) that allow firewall rules to be defined. At a finer-grained level, instances are assigned to *security groups* (*https://amzn.to/2PG9JhP*), which apply more firewall rules at an instance level. Network ACLs are an optional feature, but instances must belong to a security group. If none is assigned, the default security group is used.

Network ACLs are fairly straightforward and control inbound and outbound IP flows to subnets. Inbound and outbound connections can be filtered based on the source or destination IP Classless Inter-Domain Routing (CIDR) range and destination port or port range.

Security groups are applied at the instance level, and up to five can be applied at one time. Security group rules define allowed inbound and outbound connections from IP ranges or other security groups to ports or port ranges. Unlike network ACLs, security groups do not have deny rules. Because the rules are allow-based, there is an implicit rule that denies any traffic not permitted by any of the active security groups.

Example implementation

The default security group for instances launched within a VPC allows all traffic between instances that group and allows all outbound connections. However, to insulate from changes to the default security group, it is preferable to create a new security group—futura-all, which in this example has the ID sg-61366512—for all instances in the cluster. The following rule in the group allows all traffic between cluster instances (you may also want to add SSH traffic from outside the VPC, if not using a jump server):

```
Type=>All traffic, Protocol=>All, Port Range=>All,
    Source=>sg-61366512
```

After instance provisioning, additional security groups can be created and attached to the instances. For the edge nodes, we want to allow access to ports 8889, 10000, and 11443 from anywhere in the same VPC and from the on-premises network attached via a VPN gateway. Here, the VPC IP range is 10.11.0.0/16, so we define a security group called futura-edge with the following rules:

```
Type=>Custom TCP Rule, Protocol=>TCP, Port=>11000,
    Source=>10.11.0.0/16
Type=>Custom TCP Rule, Protocol=>TCP, Port=>10000,
    Source=>10.11.0.0/16
Type=>Custom TCP Rule, Protocol=>TCP, Port=>8889,
    Source=>10.11.0.0/16
Type=>Custom TCP Rule, Protocol=>TCP, Port=>11000,
    Source=>10.34.0.0/16
Type=>Custom TCP Rule, Protocol=>TCP, Port=>10000,
    Source=>10.34.0.0/16
Type=>Custom TCP Rule, Protocol=>TCP, Port=>8889,
    Source=>10.34.0.0/16
```

In the AWS console (or via the API), you can attach additional security groups to an instance, so each edge instance should be assigned both futura-all and futura-edge. The rules are combined together into a single effective rules list.

For the master nodes, we need to allow access to ZooKeeper and the HBase Master for the Garamond app, instances of which run in a different security group with the ID sg-34624663. Also, on-premises developers need access to the YARN Resource-Manager web UI. The following rules for the new security group futura-master define that behavior:

```
Type=>Custom TCP Rule, Protocol=>TCP, Port=>2181,
   Source=>sg-34624663, Description=>ZK access for Garamond
Type=>Custom TCP Rule, Protocol=>TCP, Port=>60000,
   Source=>sg-34624663, Description=>HBase Master for Garamond
Type=>Custom TCP Rule, Protocol=>TCP, Port=>8080,
   Source=>10.34.0.0/16, Description=>YARN RM access
```

Finally, on the workers, we require access to the HBase RegionServers for the Garamond app and access to the YARN NodeManager UIs for the developers on the on-premises network. A `futura-worker` security group might look like the following:

```
Type=>Custom TCP Rule, Protocol=>TCP, Port=>60020,
   Source=>sg-34624663, Description=>HBase RS for Garamond
Type=>Custom TCP Rule, Protocol=>TCP, Port=>8042,
   Source=>10.34.0.0/16, Description=>YARN NM access
```

Azure

In Azure, a VPC is called a *VNet* and is tied to a particular Azure region. Each VNet has a private, isolated IP range, and one or more subnets can be created that divide the VNet IP range into nonoverlapping segments. Azure has the concept of *network security groups* (NSGs) (*http://bit.ly/2KiMnZy*), which consist of a set of firewall-like rules governing inbound and outbound traffic to resources. An NSG can be applied to NICs attached to VMs or subnets and, like a VNet, is tied to a specific region.

 If no NSG is applied to a resource, implicitly all inbound and outbound traffic is allowed—including from the internet. Mandatory NSGs should be a best practice, as outlined in the Azure Network Security Best Practices (*http://bit.ly/2zgtfqQ*) in the official documentation.

NSGs can filter traffic based on the standard 5-tuple of source and destination IP, source and destination port, and protocol. In this sense, Azure is slightly less flexible than AWS and GCP. To maintain some flexibility, increased usage of subnets may be necessary to logically group instances for access control purposes. However, it is possible to apply NSGs at the NIC level and at the subnet level. The rules are combined into an effective set of rules with the subnet rules applied first and then the NIC rules. In addition, sources for rules can be based on *service tags*, which represent Azure services like Virtual Network or Storage.[4]

The default rules for an NSG are as follows. For ingress:

---

4 As of late 2017, more advanced tagging functionality is in the works in the form of *application security groups* (*http://bit.ly/2R1VWyq*).

AllowVnetInBound
>   Allow all traffic from the same VNet.

AllowAzureLoadBalancerInBound
>   Allow all traffic from Azure load balancers.

DenyAllInBound
>   Deny all other traffic.

And for egress:

AllowVnetOutBound
>   Allow all outgoing traffic to the same VNet.

AllowInternetOutBound
>   Allow all outgoing traffic to the internet.

DenyAllOutBound
>   Deny all other traffic.

Use case implementation

The main principle behind our example (again to stress that it is just an example of a fairly well-locked-down cluster) is to deny all inbound access, allow all internal traffic, and allow traffic from external nodes to specific ports, depending on machine type. The easiest way to achieve this is to have the cluster nodes (master, utility, edge, and worker) in a dedicated and exclusive subnet and then to apply NSGs, at the NIC level, to the various machine types.

Therefore, the following base rules should apply to each NSG we create (you'll probably also want to add a rule for SSH traffic to administer the boxes):

```
sourceip=>*, destinationip=>*, sourceport=>*,
  destport=>*, protocol=>any, action=>deny, priority=>4096
sourceip=>10.11.1.0/24, destinationip=>*, sourceport=>*,
  destport=>*, protocol=>any, action=>allow, priority=>4095
```

In our example, we have three classes of machine in our cluster—master, worker, and edge—so we create three NSGs to control access to the machines. The choice here is to not use a subnet-level NSG, because rules would need to be created in both NIC- and subnet-level NSGs.

For our working example, we create a `future-worker-nsg` security group for the worker machines and add the following rules (in addition to the common base rules) for the various worker accesses:

```
sourceip=>10.34.0.0/16, destinationip=>*, sourceport=>*,
  destport=>8042, protocol=>tcp, action=>allow, priority=>4000
```

```
sourceip=>10.11.13.0/24, destinationip=>*, sourceport=>*,
    destport=>60020, protocol=>tcp, action=>allow, priority=>3999
```

This grants developer access to YARN NodeManager UIs running on port 8042 (the on-premises developer machines are in the 10.34.0.0/16 subnet) and application access to HBase RegionServers running on port 60020 (where the application servers are running in the 10.11.13.0/24 subnet).

For the master nodes, a `future-master-nsg` group would have the following rules:

```
sourceip=>10.34.0.0/16, destinationip=>*, sourceport=>*,
    destport=>8080, protocol=>tcp, action=>allow, priority=>4000
sourceip=>10.11.13.0/24, destinationip=>*, sourceport=>*,
    destport=>60000, protocol=>tcp, action=>allow, priority=>3999
sourceip=>10.11.13.0/24, destinationip=>*, sourceport=>*,
    destport=>2181, protocol=>tcp, action=>allow, priority=>3998
```

Finally, the edge nodes would have the following `future-edge-nsg` rules:

```
sourceip=>10.34.0.0/16, destinationip=>*, sourceport=>*,
    destport=>8889,10000,11443, protocol=>tcp,
    action=>allow, priority=>4000
servicetag=>VirtualNetwork, destinationip=>*, sourceport=>*,
    destport=>8889,10000,11443, protocol=>tcp,
    action=>allow, priority=>3999
```

Summary

We have covered a lot of ground in this chapter, touching on the essentials of authentication, authorization, auditing, and encryption when running Hadoop in the cloud. Getting the correct security architecture can be hard, but with an understanding of how the different components operate, it is perfectly possible to deploy clusters with comprehensive security. We highly recommend using a peer-reviewed automation process to ensure that security settings are properly applied and to minimize the chance of human error.

As with any deployment, you should take time to assess which security features are actually necessary to mitigate the assessed risk.

Backup Onboarding Checklist

The following is an example of a checklist that can be used to onboard new backup users (see Chapter 13). It focuses on the inherent needs of the user, but also the possible options around the chosen data sources. It does not ask for replication at all, which is a separate task.

The overall size of a backup is computed based on the size for each source × the number of copies to keep (not taking delta backups into account for now).

Backup Onboarding Checklist

Name of Cluster:

_____

Owner:

_____

Backup

Overall Quota:

_____ (e.g., 5 TB)

Schedule:

☐ Hourly ☐ Daily ☐ Weekly ☐ Monthly
☐ Custom: _____

Retention:

_____ (e.g., 5 backups, or 3 years)

Location:

_____ (storage details)

Target RTO:

_____ (e.g., 1 day)

Target RPO:

_____ (e.g., 2 hours)

Services

Cloudera Manager

Backup CM database:
  ☐ Yes ☐ No
Database Type:
  ☐ MySQL ☐ PostgreSQL ☐ Oracle
  ☐ Other: _____
Database Credentials:
  Provided? ☐ Yes ☐ No
  ☐ Other: _____
Schedule:
  ☐ Hourly ☐ Daily ☐ Weekly ☐ Monthly
  ☐ Custom: _____
Retention:

_____

Quota:

_____ (e.g., 300 MB)

Target RTO:

_____ (e.g., 1 day)

Target RPO:

_____ (e.g., 2 hours)

Backup of database storing all Cloudera Manager information, such as CM clusters, users, hosts, services, and management services. The CDH online documentation has more detailed information.

Backup CM API:
  ☐ Yes ☐ No
Host Name (with Port):

_____

REST Endpoint:

_____ (optional)

TLS: ☐ Yes ☐ No
Credentials:
  Provided? ☐ Yes ☐ No
  ☐ Other: _____

Schedule:
☐ Hourly ☐ Daily ☐ Weekly ☐ Monthly
☐ Custom: _____
Retention:

_____

Quota:

_____ (e.g., 100 MB)

Calls CM REST API (default /cm/deployment) and saves returned JSON structure, containing the current cluster configuration, including clusters, users, host, services, etc.

HDFS

Backup HDFS Data:
☐ Yes ☐ No
Host Name (with Port):

_____

Secure:
☐ Yes ☐ No
Realm:

_____ (optional)

Principal/Username:

_____

Credentials:
Provided? ☐ Yes ☐ No
Other: _____
Schedule:
☐ Hourly ☐ Daily ☐ Weekly ☐ Monthly
☐ Custom: _____
Retention:

_____

Quota:

_____ (e.g., 50 TB)

Target RTO:

_____ (e.g., 1 day)

Target RPO:

_____ (e.g., 2 hours)

Directories included in backup:

Path:

[1] _____

    Freq: _____   Ret: _____   Qta: _____   Snap: _____

[2] _____

    Freq: _____   Ret: _____   Qta: _____   Snap: _____

[3] _____

    Freq: _____   Ret: _____   Qta: _____   Snap: _____

Legend:

- Path: Path to HDFS directory to be included in backup
- Frequency (Freq): The schedule when to backup up directory (e.g., 4 hrs)
- Retention (Ret): How long is the data retained (e.g., 5 copies, or 1 year)
- Quota (Qta): Maximum quota for backup storage needed (e.g., 1 TB)
- Snapshot (Snap): HDFS snapshots are enabled for location (e.g., Yes)

 Each directory is backed up into the versioned target directory. If snapshots are enabled—which is the recommendation—then one is performed around the copy operation.

Save NameNode Metadata: ☐ Yes ☐ No

 HDFS API (either the HDFS DFSAdmin with the `-fetchImage` option, or the `/getimage` endpoint of the active NameNode) to save the latest filesystem image (named *fsimage*; does not include the recent edits). It is recommended to also configure a shared filesystem (NFS mount, for example) to retain both image and edit files in an out-of-band (outside the cluster, or failure group) location for faster recovery.

HBase

Backup HBase Data:

☐ Yes ☐ No

ZK Quorum (with Port):

    1. _____

    2. _____

    3. _____

Secure:
  ☐ Yes ☐ No
Realm:

_____ (optional)
Principal/Username:

_____

Credentials:
  Provided? ☐ Yes ☐ No
  Other: _____
Schedule:
  ☐ Hourly ☐ Daily ☐ Weekly ☐ Monthly
  ☐ Custom: _____
Retention:

_____

Quota:

_____ (e.g., 50 TB)
Target RTO:

_____ (e.g., 1 day)
Target RPO:

_____ (e.g., 2 hours)

Tables (namespaces) included in backup:

Table:
  [1] _____
      Freq: _____ Ret: _____ Qta: _____ Snap: _____
  [2] _____
      Freq: _____ Ret: _____ Qta: _____ Snap: _____
  [3] _____
      Freq: _____ Ret: _____ Qta: _____ Snap: _____

Each table is backed up into the versioned target directory. If snap-shots are enabled—which is the recommendation—then one is per-formed around the copy operation.

Hive/Impala

Backup Schema Data:
  ☐ Yes ☐ No
Backup HDFS Data:
  ☐ Yes ☐ No

Database Type:
  ☐ MySQL ☐ PostgreSQL ☐ Oracle
  ☐ Derby [NOT SUPPORTED]
  ☐ Other: _____
Database Credentials:
  Provided? ☐ Yes ☐ No
  Other: _____
Secure:
  ☐ Yes ☐ No
Realm:
  _____ (optional)
Principal/Username:

  _____
Credentials:
  Provided? ☐ Yes ☐ No
  Other: _____
Schedule:
  ☐ Hourly ☐ Daily ☐ Weekly ☐ Monthly
  ☐ Custom: _____
Retention:

  _____
Quota:
  _____ (e.g., 50 TB)

Warehouse directories included in backup:

Path:
  [1] _____
      Freq: _____ Ret: _____ Qta: _____ Snap: _____
  [2] _____
      Freq: _____ Ret: _____ Qta: _____ Snap: _____
  [3] _____
      Freq: _____ Ret: _____ Qta: _____ Snap: _____

Hive has both metadata, and raw HDFS data. The latter can be included here, or alternatively it can be covered in the earlier HDFS section.

Sqoop

Backup Sqoop database:
  ☐ Yes ☐ No

Database Type:
   ☐ PostgreSQL ☐ Derby [NOT SUPPORTED]
   ☐ Other: _____
Database Credentials:
  Provided? ☐ Yes ☐ No
  Other: _____
Schedule:
   ☐ Hourly ☐ Daily ☐ Weekly ☐ Monthly
   ☐ Custom: _____
Retention:

_____

Quota:
   _____ (e.g., 300 MB)
Target RTO:
   _____ (e.g., 1 day)
Target RPO:
   _____ (e.g., 2 hours)

Oozie

Backup Oozie database:
   ☐ Yes ☐ No
Database Type:
   ☐ MySQL ☐ PostgreSQL ☐ Oracle
   ☐ Derby [NOT SUPPORTED]
   ☐ Other: _____
Database Credentials:
  Provided? ☐ Yes ☐ No
  Other: _____
Schedule:
   ☐ Hourly ☐ Daily ☐ Weekly ☐ Monthly
   ☐ Custom: _____
Retention:

_____

Quota:
   _____ (e.g., 500 MB)
Target RTO:
   _____ (e.g., 1 day)
Target RPO:
   _____ (e.g., 2 hours)

Hue

Backup Hue database:
☐ Yes ☐ No
Database Type:
☐ MySQL ☐ SQLite [NOT SUPPORTED]
☐ Other: _____
Database Credentials:
Provided? ☐ Yes ☐ No
Other: _____
Schedule:
☐ Hourly ☐ Daily ☐ Weekly ☐ Monthly
☐ Custom: _____
Retention:

_____

Quota:
_____ (e.g., 500 MB)
Target RTO:
_____ (e.g., 1 day)
Target RPO:
_____ (e.g., 2 hours)

Contains the Hue user details (name, role, etc.).

Sentry

Backup Sentry database:
☐ Yes ☐ No
Database Type:
☐ MySQL ☐ PostgreSQL ☐ Oracle
☐ MariaDB
☐ Other: _____
Database Credentials:
Provided? ☐ Yes ☐ No
Other: _____
Schedule:
☐ Hourly ☐ Daily ☐ Weekly ☐ Monthly
☐ Custom: _____
Retention:

_____

Quota:

_____ (e.g., 500 MB)

Target RTO:

_____ (e.g., 1 day)

Target RPO:

_____ (e.g., 2 hours)

Index

full rebuild, 406

R

R language, 144, 150
rack awareness
    and high availability, 385
    eliminating with cluster spanning, 174
racking servers
    in Layer 1, 133
    space and racking constraints in datacenters, 169
racks
    failure of, 75
    inter-rack throughput, 226
    intra-rack throughput, 225
    placing far apart, 173
    rack awareness and rack failures, 165
    rack locality, 5
    rack unit (U), 91
    rack-mount form factors, 91
        standard, comparison of, 94
RADOS Block Device (RBD), 452
Raft consensus algorithm, 333
RAID, 60, 416
    and storage pools in virtual environments, 417
    configuration for master disks, 346
    Hadoop and, 82
    RAID 10 for broker data disks in Kafka, 370
    RAID-0 arrays, 84
    RAID1 for HDFS metadata, 353
    SCSI SYNCHRONIZE CACHE command, not passed to disks, 90
raised-floor cooling, 162
RAM (random access memory), 47
    in computer architecture for Hadoop, 55
range partitioning, 20
Ranger, 197, 375
    backing up Apache Ranger, 397
    centralized authorization control for Kafka, 270
    centralized authorization with, 258
    centralized management of YARN queue access controls, 262
    HDFS ACLs, controlling, 261
    Key Management Server, 275, 278
    Key Management Server (KMS), 272
    using in HBase, 265
RDBMS (relational database management systems), 194, 201
read system call, 61, 64

read-ahead caching, 83
reads
    effects of disk and storage controller caches on throughput, 89
    HDFS client local to DataNode process or remote client, 64
    measuring speed of distributed reads in HDFS, 228
    measuring speed of single reads in HDFS, 228
    performance, erasure coding vs. replication, 78
    short-circuit and zero-copy reads, 65
realmd library, 293, 508
realms (Kerberos), 242
    superuser privileges shared across clusters in, 253
rebuilds
    full, 406
    partial, 406
records, 390
recovery, 377
    (see also backups and disaster recovery)
    erasure coding vs. replication, 78
recovery point objective (RPO), 181, 378
recovery time objective (RTO), 181, 201, 378
Red Hat
    information on OpenShift container security, 441
    installing and starting NTP service daemon, 191
    Kickstart, 186
    OpenShift distribution, 439
    OpenStack distribution, 435, 438
    package management, 208
    Red Hat Enterprise Linux (RHEL), 187
        eCryptfs support removed in RHEL 7, 273
        obtaining sysbench, 215
    Satellite, 186
    systemd-based Linux, installing and starting caching daemon, 192
Red Hat Identity Management (IdM), 285
    providing KDC and user/group lookup via LDAP, 286
reduce stage (MapReduce), 11
Redundant Array of Independent Disks (see RAID)
refresh tokens, 533

---

workload isolation, multiple clusters for, 33
   in HBase, 33
   in Kafka, 34
   independent storage and compute, 35
   sizing of multiple clusters, 34
workloads
   cluster life cycle events and, 36
   sizing clusters by, 41
   workload isolation and data replication, 43
   workload profiles and ramifications on
      hardware selection, 96
world scheme (ZooKeeper), 262
write system call, 61
write-ahead logging, 33
write-back caching, 83
writes
   effects of disk and storage controller caches
      on throughput, 89
   measuring speed of distributed writes in
      HDFS, 228
   on-disk cache and, 88
   performance, erasure coding vs. replication,
      77
   single writes, measuring speed for HDFS,
      228

X
X.509, 240, 307
x86 architecture
   commodity servers based on, 46
   role of, 48
XFS filesystem, 69

Y
Yahoo! Cloud Serving Benchmark (YCSB), 234
YARN, 2
   authorization in, 261
   backing up, 396
   edge node interactions with, 319

effect on distributed writes in HDFS, 229
high availability, 353-356
   automatic failover, 355
   deployment recommendations, 356
   manual failover, 355
NUMA optimizations for, 54
overview, 7
ResourceManager, web UI, 312
service level authorization settings for clients, 257
short-circuit reads, 68
yum package manager, 208

Z
Zab consensus algorithm, 333
Zeppelin, 313, 325
zero-copy reads (HDFS), 66
   benefits of, 67
ZKRMStateStore, 356
zones, 490
zoning, 418
ZooKeeper, 8
   authorization in, 262
   dependencies, 9
   high availability, 347-348
      deployment considerations, 348
      ephemeral nodes, 347
      failover, 348
   quorum-based consensus system, 114
   quorums, 333
   sensitivity to network latency, 109
   transactional qualities for random-access
      clients, 195
   use for metadata and coordination by Solr,
      368
   use for persistent state storage for YARN,
      354
ZooKeeper Failover Controller (ZKFC), 351
   roles and interactions, 352

About the Authors

Jan Kunigk has worked on enterprise Hadoop solutions since 2010. Before he joined Cloudera in 2014, Jan built optimized systems architectures for Hadoop at IBM and implemented a Hadoop-as-a-Service offering at T-Systems. In his current role as a solutions architect he makes Hadoop projects at Cloudera's enterprise customers successful, covering a wide spectrum of architectural decisions regarding the implementation of big data applications across all industry sectors on a day-to-day basis.

Ian Buss began his journey into distributed computing with parallel computational electromagnetics whilst studying for a PhD in photonics at the University of Bristol. After simulating LEDs on supercomputers, he made the move from big compute in academia to big data in the public sector, first encountering Hadoop in 2012. Having had lots of fun building, deploying, managing, and using Hadoop clusters, Ian joined Cloudera as a solutions architect in 2014. His day job now involves integrating Hadoop into enterprises and making stuff work in the real world.

Paul Wilkinson has been wrestling with big data in the public sector since before Hadoop existed and was very glad when it arrived in his life in 2009. He became a Cloudera consultant in 2012, advising customers on all things Hadoop: application design, information architecture, cluster management, and infrastructure planning. After a torrent of professional services work across financial services, cybersecurity, adtech, gaming, and government, he's seen it all, warts and all. Or at least, he hopes he has.

Lars George has been involved with Hadoop and HBase since 2007, and became a full HBase committer in 2009. He has spoken at many Hadoop User Group meetings, and at conferences such as Hadoop World and Hadoop Summit, ApacheCon, FOSDEM, and QCon. He also started the Munich OpenHUG meetings. Lars worked for Cloudera for over five years as the EMEA chief architect, acting as a liaison between the Cloudera professional services team and customers and working with partners in and around Europe, building the next data-driven solutions. In 2016 he started his own Hadoop advisory firm, drawing on what he had learned and seen in the field for more than 8 years. He is also the author of *HBase: The Definitive Guide* (O'Reilly).

Colophon

The animal on the cover of *Architecting Modern Data Platforms* is a yellow-billed oxpecker (*Buphagus africanus*), a bird that lives in the savannahs of sub-Saharan Africa. They are called "oxpeckers" because they perch on large mammals (both wild and domestic) to feed on ticks and other insects. Beyond removing parasites from the larger animals, oxpeckers also eat blood, using their beaks to make existing sores and wounds on their host bleed. However, most mammals seem to tolerate this in exchange for the removal of pests and the birds' ability to act as an early warning system for danger nearby.

These birds gain benefits from mammals in other ways as well: they collect their hair in order to construct nests within tree holes, roost on them at night (out of breeding season), and hitch rides on them during the day. Oxpeckers live in flocks; females lay 2-3 eggs, and chicks are fed by both their parents and other adults until they fledge in about 25 days.

The yellow-billed oxpecker is about 8 inches long, and has a brown body, tan underbelly, and a distinct yellow beak with a red tip. There is a related species called the red-billed oxpecker, which is submissive to its yellow-billed cousins wherever their ranges overlap.

Many of the animals on O'Reilly covers are endangered; all of them are important to the world. To learn more about how you can help, go to *animals.oreilly.com*.

The cover image is from Lydekker's *Royal Natural History*. The cover fonts are URW Typewriter and Guardian Sans. The text font is Adobe Minion Pro; the heading font is Adobe Myriad Condensed; and the code font is Dalton Maag's Ubuntu Mono.

Learn from experts.
Find the answers you need.

Sign up for a **10-day free trial** to get **unlimited access** to all of the content on Safari, including Learning Paths, interactive tutorials, and curated playlists that draw from thousands of ebooks and training videos on a wide range of topics, including data, design, DevOps, management, business—and much more.

Start your free trial at:
oreilly.com/safari

(No credit card required.)

CPSIA information can be obtained
at www.ICGtesting.com
Printed in the USA
BVHW062324121218
535388BV00011B/117